ENVIRONMENT IN THE COURTROOM II

UNIVERSITY OF CALGARY
Press

ENVIRONMENT
IN THE COURTROOM II

edited by
Alastair R. Lucas &
Allan E. Ingelson

University of Calgary Press
2500 University Drive NW
Calgary, Alberta
Canada T2N 1N4
press.ucalgary.ca

LIBRARY AND ARCHIVES CANADA CATALOGUING IN PUBLICATION

Title: Environment in the courtroom II / edited by Alastair R. Lucas & Allan E. Ingelson.
Names: Lucas, Alastair R., editor. | Ingelson, Allan, 1958- editor.
Description: Includes bibliographical references and index.
Identifiers: Canadiana (print) 20220248753 | Canadiana (ebook) 20220248788 | ISBN 9781773853789 (hardcover) | ISBN 9781773853796 (softcover) | ISBN 9781773853802 (Open Access PDF) | ISBN 9781773853819 (PDF) | ISBN 9781773853826 (EPUB)
Subjects: LCSH: Environmental law—Canada.
Classification: LCC KE3619 .E55 2022 | LCC KF3775.ZA2 E55 2022 kfmod | DDC 344.7104/6—dc23

The University of Calgary Press acknowledges the support of the Government of Alberta through the Alberta Media Fund for our publications. We acknowledge the financial support of the Government of Canada. We acknowledge the financial support of the Canada Council for the Arts for our publishing program.

Alberta Government   Canada   Canada Council for the Arts   Conseil des Arts du Canada

Copyediting by Tania Therien
Cover image: Colourbox 8525371 and 17535021
Cover design, page design, and typesetting by Melina Cusano

Table of Contents

Preface

Enforcement of Canadian environmental law is a dynamic and exciting area that is playing an increasingly important role in furthering the sustainable development policies adopted by federal, provincial, and territorial governments. During the last three years, with financial support from Environment and Climate Change Canada and the Alberta Law Foundation, the Canadian Institute of Resources Law (CIRL), a federal not-for-profit organization created by the Faculty of Law at the University of Calgary in 1979, and its partners at the Université Laval and Dalhousie University, have organized national annual environmental law symposiums in Halifax, Calgary, and Quebec City as part of the "Environment in the Courtroom" national continuing legal education series. Lawyers in private practice; Crown counsel; corporate counsel; administrative lawyers; legal scholars, including those teaching environmental law at universities and colleges; lawyers employed by NGOs and industry organizations; law students; and environmental consultants in Canada and other countries reported that the invited presentations, discussion, and associated papers provided practical and valuable information on current and important environmental issues. The collection of papers in this book provides insights on the environmental law experience, leading judicial decisions, and the important procedural and theoretical aspects of environmental litigation in a variety of Canadian provinces and territories, as well as in the United States, a nation with a shared common law and civil law heritage.

The second volume of *Environment in the Courtroom* is divided into three parts that examine the following important topics in environmental law:

- protection of the marine environment
- enforcement issues in Canadian wildlife protection
- enforcement of Canadian greenhouse gas (GHG) emissions laws

Environment in the Courtroom discusses significant issues and challenges in Canadian environmental law today and is intended to be a source of relevant, current, and useful information for both Canadian and international audiences, as well as lawyers and non-lawyers. The volume contains a variety of perspectives and insights from experienced and prominent Canadian legal practitioners and scholars, but also reviews experiences in other legal systems with similar issues. Because we have had legal professionals from outside of Canada participate in the symposiums, individuals in other nations interested in comparative legal studies will also find this book a useful reference on current Canadian environmental legal issues.

It is a pleasure to thank and acknowledge the numerous contributors to the volume who have shared their knowledge and experience. In particular, we would like to thank the following individuals for their extraordinary contributions: J. Owen Saunders, Jamie Benidickson, Phillip Saunders, Paule Halley. We would like to thank the law students: Akinbobola Olugbemi, Vanessa Morton, Akindele Tawoju, Joshua Hobbs, Kathryn Owad, Ramanjeet Sohal, Adewale Ajayi, Oluwabukola Agbede, Paul Reid, Laura Hall, Temitope Onifade, Christopher Phillips, Hong Feng, David Hillier, Francco De Luca, Logan Lazurko, Alexander Crisp, Tyler Anthony, Alex Ikejiani, and the CIRL Post-Doctoral Research Fellows: Chilenye Nwapi and Ifeoma (Laura) Owosuyi for their research assistance. Finally, we would like to acknowledge the administrative assistance of Nancy Money and Jane Rowe, who have contributed to the success of the second volume of *Environment in the Courtroom*.

Introduction

The Context

This book examines the application and enforcement of Canadian environmental law. It is not about environmental law generally. It focuses on the idea of enforcement and enforcement techniques including administration of environmental statutes and enforcement of specific decisions and orders. There are two enforcement aspects. One is decisions and decision processes concerning approvals and related decisions for projects and activities involving, for the purposes of this book, marine waters, wildlife, and energy and other greenhouse gas emitting actions. This establishes the baselines for enforcement. The second is explicit actions by authorized public officials (ministers and their authorized representatives—such as the federal ministers of fisheries and oceans and transport) and tribunals (such as the Canada Energy Regulator and the Alberta Energy Regulator) to enforce the legal duties that these decisions create. This includes powers of public officials or tribunals to issue orders requiring cessation of defined activities and imposing conditions.

This second enforcement aspect includes techniques that involve enforcement proceedings before tribunals and courts. These are the "courtrooms" that are central to the book's perspective. The nature of the proceedings depends on the relevant statutory powers and processes. It is usually at the discretion of authorized public officials to develop and implement policies to guide the choice of enforcement tools in particular cases.

There are also a set of statutory offence provisions that proscribe specified conduct. These offences can be prosecuted in the courts, and guilty defendants can be penalized by fines, prescribed conduct (such as soil or water remediation), and even imprisoned.

Such offences are not pure criminal offences that require proof of intent. Rather, they are regulatory offences that require only proof of proscribed conduct and normally include a "due diligence" defence—proof that an accused took reasonable care to prevent the damage in question.

Environmental statutes also include rights of appeal. Decisions and orders by officials can be challenged in appeals to specialized appeal tribunals (such as environmental appeals boards) or directly to courts. Appeal tribunal decisions may be subject to judicial review by courts concerning procedural fairness and reasonableness of decisions.

It is in this sense that this book is about "environment in the courtroom." Decisions about environmental approvals, as well as decisions about enforcing environmental requirements, are adjudicated in tribunal proceedings that the public sees only through scattered media reports and commentary. This book is intended to provide a broader legal perspective of environmental law enforcement. Because each subject area—marine environment, wildlife protection, and GHG emissions reduction—has its own legal enforcement regime, it is helpful to consider each within broader legal enforcement principles and techniques. It is also necessary to consider unique subject based trends and emergent issues. Chapter authors bring the expertise to review and assess these enforcement regimes and offer conclusions as well as prospects for reform.

This book's three focus areas are not the only environmental law fields in which enforcement issues can be identified, but they are active areas that present challenging problems. In environmental justice terms, they are matters of restorative (or reparation) justice, concerning the fair and equitable exercise of statutory approval and enforcement powers, and participatory justice, concerning citizens' rights to participate effectively in decisions that affect them.

Content and Structure of the Book

SECTION 1: MARINE ENVIRONMENT PROTECTION

These chapters assess significant international legal regimes and the Canadian legislation that implements them. They identify apparent gaps between international obligations and Canadian legal regimes (**Lalonde**). International law, as **Lavallée** notes in Section 3, is voluntary, leaving broad implementation scope for country governments. As ocean science and technology develops (**Wallace**), this gap theme emerges in relation to ship source pollution (**Cullen**), offshore structure decommissioning (**Watt**), liquefied natural gas (LNG) powered Arctic ships (**Pamel and Wilkins**), Arctic electricity generation and transmission (**Muir**), and tidal power (**LeBlanc and Stewart**).

Domestically, as **Moreira** shows, the federal *Fisheries Act* has been the pillar for fish and fish habitat protection. This Act has a long-established enforcement regime that has accommodated emerging Indigenous rights, though only to a minor degree. Yet, potential remains for "braiding" Canadian and international law together for fisheries management (**Nowlan, Kirby, Lloyd-Smith, and Neasloss**). **Dogra**'s chapter offers insights into the operation of the Canada-Nova Scotia Offshore Petroleum Board from a regulator's perspective.

SECTION 2: ENFORCEMENT ISSUES IN CANADIAN WILDLIFE PROTECTION

The international–domestic law gap also emerges in relation to wild animal and plant protection under the international *Convention on International Trade in Endangered Species of Wild Fauna and Flora* (*CITES*) and Canada's *Wild Animal and Plant Protection Regulation of International and Interprovincial Trade Act* (**Bankes**). The author also identifies interpretive uncertainties in the latter's enforcement regime, exacerbated by the lack of case law guidance. **Saunders**'s discussion of the Atlantic Bluefin Tuna Management regime also reveals the international–domestic law gap.

First Nations reconciliation in relation to wildlife is a work in progress, with government and Indigenous wildlife paradigms not in alignment (**Donihee**). But actions such as buffalo reintroduction to Banff National Park show recognition of Indigenous law and tradition (**Hamilton**). **Jaremko** shows complexity resulting from multiple jurisdictions—federal, provincial, Indigenous, and municipal—in her assessment of Alberta wildlife law.

An emerging theme is the development of new non-regulatory enforcement approaches in wildlife protection law. These include market-based conservation under Alberta's *Land Stewardship Act* (**Poulton**). **Van Nes** reviews administrative monetary penalties (AMPs), which provide an efficient alternative to regulatory prosecutions. Another tack, discussed by **Kwasniak**, is private common law supported conservation arrangements such as easements and restrictive covenants.

Citizen litigation to prod governments to action has played a wildlife protection role. A good example are the lawsuits by environmental NGOs to require species listing and habitat protection under the federal *Species at Risk Act*. This is assessed by **Tuytel and Venton** in relation to West Coast killer whale protection. They show that these legal actions are in response to statute interpretation uncertainty that enabled poor government enforcement responses.

SECTION 3: ENFORCEMENT OF CANADIAN GREENHOUSE GAS EMISSIONS LAWS

GHG law enforcement presents legal issues that will continue as governments pivot toward net-zero emission goals. Again, broad voluntary international "commitments" opened the way for both international and domestic disputes (**Lavallée**). **L'Esperance** pinpoints the necessity of this kind of country commitment to address broad scope problems like GHG emissions from international shipping. **Lavallée** shows that an important strand has been federal–provincial constitutional litigation culminating in the Supreme Court of Canada's endorsement of exclusive federal jurisdiction to legislate carbon price stringency. A major underlying factor is the significant GHG contribution from the Alberta oil sands sector (**Lucas and Almeida**). The result is federal–provincial carbon pricing agreements under the framework of the federal *Greenhouse Gas Pollution Pricing Act* (**Stewart and Carrière**), as well as federal (**Ingelson**) and provincial methane emission reduction regulations. There is also room for municipal action as **Kwasniak** points out. These issues are not relevant only to energy as **Benidickson** shows in his chapter on reducing GHG emissions from agriculture.

Trudeau assesses the Quebec cap-and-trade approach that has been recognized as equivalent under the federal price stringency scheme, along with Alberta's legislation that includes carbon-pricing and methane-reduction schemes that apply to the oil sands. **Wright**'s analysis of the Quebec–California cap-and-trade linkage agreement identifies the fragility of subnational agreements because of too easy withdrawal, as shown by Ontario's exit from the agreement.

SECTION 1

Protection of the Marine Environment

1

Ship Source Pollution Regimes (Canada)—A Primer

Peter J. Cullen[1]

Introduction

This chapter serves as an introduction to a subject that has occupied ship owners, operators, directors, investors, lenders, insurers, shippers/charterers, trade groups, environmentalists, legislators, and lawyers for some time. Much as the *Exxon Valdez* grounding in Alaskan waters in 1989 gave rise to the *Brander-Smith Report*,[2] which focused on Canada's ability to handle major oil spills (and the need for more oversight into tanker operations in Canadian waters) and led to changes in Canada's pollution laws, similar major foreign incidents have laid the groundwork for international cooperation in advancing structured pollution regimes for shipping.

Such cooperation has resulted in a body of international conventions developed through the International Maritime Organization (IMO)[3]—assisted, amongst other interested parties, by the Comité Maritime International (CMI)[4] and many national maritime law associations.[5] A number of these conventions will be discussed in greater detail below. At the same time, trade associations have developed platforms to drive policy issues and garner support for "green" initiatives in Canadian waters and bilateral arrangements.[6]

Ship source pollution is not limited to oil pollution. It may encompass a series of events, mishaps, circumstances, and substances in respect of fossil fuels (oil and related petroleum products), hazardous and noxious substances, and ballast water, not to mention recycling practices and wreck removal. One may go further and include air particles (emissions and bulk cargo residues) and waste (sewage, garbage, etc.). While oil remains the principal source of concern due to its persistent and particularly harmful environmental characteristics (in terms of substance, duration, impact, and cleanup cost), air pollution has increasingly become the focus of recent marine environmental efforts.

Background

Canada is a confederation whose jurisdictions and powers are limited by the *Constitution Act, 1867*.[7] Also limited by this Act are the powers of the federal authority, which has sole jurisdiction over navigation and shipping throughout the country's navigable waters, both internal and external.

Canada's authority over its external waters is limited to its territorial sea (12 NM from Canada's jurisdictional coastline) and the adjoining exclusive economic zone, which stretches 200 NM beyond the jurisdictional coastline.[8] Such waters may be further extended depending on the nature of the underlying continental shelf.

Generally speaking, Canada's pollution laws apply to contamination of navigable waters, be they on freshwater or seawater (whether ice-covered or not). Provincial and territorial pollution laws apply to non-navigable waters and provincial/territorial shorelines. On occasion, such jurisdictions may overlap depending on the nature and effect of the contamination. Thus, charges under both the federal and provincial/territorial pollution statutes may be laid in connection with marine contamination. In Canada's Arctic regions, this would include the province of Quebec's (and to a lesser degree the province of Newfoundland & Labrador's) northern non-navigable waters and shorelines, and the non-navigable waters and shorelines of the three territories—Nunavut, the Northwest Territories, and the Yukon Territory—in addition to Canada's large expanse of arctic waters.

In 1985, Canada enacted the *Arctic Waters Pollution Prevention Act* (*AWPP*),[9] an Act that has since been made subject to Canada's principal oil pollution liability statute—the *Marine Liability Act* (*MLA*).[10] The *AWPP* prohibits the deposit of waste in arctic waters. The term "arctic waters" is defined[11] as "the internal waters of Canada and the waters of the territorial sea of Canada and its exclusive economic zone, within the area enclosed by the 60th parallel of north latitude, the 141st meridian of west longitude and the outer limit of the exclusive economic zone; however, where the international boundary between Canada and Greenland is less than 200 nautical miles from the baselines of the territorial sea of Canada, the international boundary shall be substituted for that outer limit," and this essentially covers the Arctic Archipelago. As the international boundary between Canada and Greenland is less than 200 nautical miles from the baselines of Canada's territorial sea, the outer limit in that area is replaced by the international boundary. The term "waste" is broadly defined to cover any substance that, if added to water, would degrade or alter the quality of such water to an extent detrimental to their use by man or by any animal, fish, or plant that is useful to man.[12] This definition parallels the definition of "pollutant" under the *MLA*.[13]

Internationally, Canada is a signatory to the IMO's *International Convention for the Prevention of Pollution from Ships, 1973*, and its *Protocols of 1978 and 1997* (*MARPOL*), the main international convention for preventing ship source pollution by oil (Annex I), sewage (Annex IV), garbage (Annex V), airborne substances (Annex VI), and other noxious goods shipped by water (Annexes II and III). In 2014, the IMO completed its initial work on the Polar Code (*The International Code for Ships Operating in Polar Waters*)[14] by way of certain safety related requirements adopted by its Maritime Safety Committee. In 2015, several environmental provisions were adopted by the IMO's Marine Environment Protection Committee in Part II of the Polar Code and implemented through amendments to certain *MARPOL* provisions. The Polar Code entered into force on January 1, 2017, becoming mandatory for all ships under construction or not yet built, with a transition period until January 1, 2018, for vessels launched before the entry into force date. Provisions of the Polar Code were incorporated into domestic legislation on December 19, 2017, with the repeal and replacement of the regulations under the *AWPP*—essentially updating the regulations in accordance with the safety and environmental provisions of the Polar Code.[15]

Oil Pollution

Canada is a signatory to several international conventions relating to oil pollution, including *MARPOL Annex I, the International Convention on Oil Pollution Preparedness Response and Cooperation, 1990*, and the *International Convention on Civil Liability for Bunker Oil Pollution Damage, 2001* (the *Bunker Convention*). These conventions have been incorporated into federal legislation in whole or in part under the *Canada Shipping Act* (*CSA*) and the *MLA*[16]—occasionally with some modifications (some of which are described below)—and apply to Canada's navigable waters. In essence, they establish the principle that the ship (and its interests), as the polluter, sits on the front line of liability.

An important modification in the *MLA* concerns the liability rules of the *International Convention on Civil Liability for Oil Pollution Damage, 1992* (the *Civil Liability Convention*) that applies to all ships that cause oil pollution, with special rules in Division 1 of the *MLA* in respect of "convention ships"—tankers carrying persistent oil in bulk as cargo. The liability of non-convention ships is found in Division 2 of the *MLA*, where "oil" is defined in broader terms as meaning oil of any kind or in any form (including petroleum, fuel oil, sludge, oil refuse, and oil mixed with wastes—but not dredged spoil).[17] Also, a "ship" is defined as any vessel or craft designed, used, or capable of being used—either solely or partly—for navigation, without regard to its method of propulsion or lack of propulsion and includes stranded, sunk, or wrecked vessels.[18] The difference between Division 1 and 2 vessels is also relevant in terms of access to the 1992 International Oil Pollution Compensation Fund (IOPC Fund) (limited to spills involving convention vessels under Division 1).

Pollution under the *MLA* (Division 1 or 2) essentially gives rise to strict liability (not dependent on proof of fault or negligence) for oil pollution damage, including any damage as a result of impairment to the environment and the costs of reasonable measures of reinstatement, as well as the costs and expenses incurred by the federal minister of fisheries and oceans, an authorized response organization under the *CSA*,[19] or others in respect of measures taken to prevent, repair, remedy, or minimize oil pollution damage. This includes the minister's reasonable costs of monitoring a spill and cleanup efforts. As the Canadian Coast Guard (and its fleet of icebreakers, tenders, and patrol vessels) and Fisheries and Oceans Canada (and its fleet of patrol and inspection vessels) report to the minister, it is these entities who are generally engaged in such matters.

The *CSA* sets forth the framework for pollution prevention and response measures and enforcement.[20] In respect of oil, ships are required to have an arrangement in place with a recognized (certified) response organization that will adequately deal with the total quantity of oil (both as cargo and fuel) carried on board, and in respect of the waters navigated, in the event of a pollution incident. The ship is also required to carry a declaration in a due form that identifies the name and address of the ship's insurers for liability pollution insurance coverage and confirms that the response arrangement (and identifies the persons authorized to implement the arrangement) is in place. The *CSA* requires oil handling facilities (operators) to have similar arrangements/declarations in place.

The authority and practice of pollution response officers are also set forth in the *CSA*.[21] Where the officer reasonably believes that a ship might discharge or might have discharged a pollutant, the officer may direct the ship to moor or anchor. Also, the officer may board and take samples, declare an emergency zone, direct any person to provide reasonable assistance or information (logbooks, etc.), or use any computer system or data processing system to examine data, etc. The officer may also detain a ship.

The *CSA* empowers the minister of fisheries and oceans, on a reasonable belief that a ship has discharged, is discharging, or is likely to discharge a pollutant, to take measures to repair, remedy, minimize, or prevent pollution damage. The minister may monitor measures taken by the ship's interests in respect of any pollution, actual or anticipated, and may direct such interests to take any needed measures. The minister may also step in and take over the cleanup.

Canada has also enacted portions of the IOPC Fund, the *1992 Civil Liability Convention*, and the *2003 Supplementary Fund Protocol*[22] through the *MLA*. Under Part 6 of the *MLA*, shipping interests are entitled to limit their liability for pollution damage, including preventive and remedial measures in certain instances. Thus, where claims exceed such limitation amounts, which ordinarily are funded by the ship's interests, including its liability insurers, recourse may be made to the IOPC Fund. However, in certain instances, recourse may be made to Canada's Ship-source Oil Pollution Fund (SOPF)[23] which is administered by a federally appointed administrator. These funds collect contributions from shippers to ensure that at the end of the day there is a fund of last recourse.

Canada's Admiralty Court, the Federal Court, has *in rem* jurisdiction in respect of navigation and shipping matters. It is a national admiralty court that sits across the country, and it is the same Admiralty Court[24] referred to in the *MLA* in respect of limitation proceedings and related claims for pollution matters under the Fund regimes.

Additional relevant pollution statutes that have occasionally been applied where there are overlapping federal departments or overlapping jurisdiction with provincial/territorial non-navigable waters or shorelines include (by way of example) the federal *Migratory Birds Convention Act, 1994*,[25] the *Canadian Environmental Protection Act, 1999*,[26] Newfoundland and Labrador's

Environmental Protection Act,[27] and Nova Scotia's *Environment Act*.[28] These statutes generally provide that oil pollution constitutes a strict liability offence (without proof of fault or negligence) and, like the *MLA*, generally target the owner, custodian, or person who had the charge, management, or control of the polluting substance (such as the shipowner or bareboat charterer). Some reach further and hold that the directors or officers of a company that commits an offence may be presumed to have participated in the offence unless they can establish that they exercised due diligence and took all necessary precautions to prevent such offence.

Hazardous and Noxious Substances

To cover those products not subject to the "oil conventions," the IMO has developed a similar strict liability resume for noxious or dangerous substances. These include liquefied gases, liquid substances with certain flashpoints, harmful products carried in containers, and bulk solid materials possessing chemical hazards. Recent studies have demonstrated increased traffic in the number of container ships carrying packaged hazardous and noxious substances (HNS) as well as growth in the number of chemical tankers and liquefied natural gas (LNG) and liquefied petroleum gas (LPG) tankers. The IMO reports that some 2,000 different "types of HNS" are regularly transported by sea and some 200 million tonnes of chemicals are traded annually.[29]

Typically known as the "*HNS Convention*,"[30] this regime provides a structure to compensate parties damaged through the international or domestic carriage by sea of qualifying substances not covered by the *Civil Liability Convention* or the *Bunker Convention*. Once the *HNS Convention* comes into force (only five countries have acceded to or ratified the convention to date—twelve are required), receivers of "contributing cargo" will be required to contribute to the HNS Fund. As with the oil conventions, the *HNS Convention* upholds the principle that the "polluter pays."

The *HNS Convention* sets out a prevention, preparedness, and response regime via the *CSA*, and a framework for liability and compensation via the *MLA*. The ship's interests are the first to pay under a similar strict liability regime up to a maximum limit, supported by compulsory insurance, with a compensation fund sitting atop, financed through contributions paid by receivers of HNS.

While the *HNS Convention* has yet to come into force (Canada ratified the *HNS Convention* on April 23, 2018), the *MLA* currently obliges receivers of certain HNS cargoes to report to the minister of transport and the SOPF administrator. Transport Canada published new reporting requirements in December 2016 following a consultation with stakeholders. Also, an online HNS and Oil Electronic Reporting System were introduced to facilitate HNS disclosure.[31]

Ballast Water

In 2004, the IMO adopted the *International Convention for the Control and Management of Ships' Ballast Water and Sediments* (the *BWM Convention*).[32] Canada ratified the *BWM Convention* in 2010, and it entered into force on September 8, 2017. The convention has been ratified by eighty-three states, representing over 81 percent of world shipping tonnage.

The *BWM Convention* is designed to control the spread of invasive aquatic species picked up in ballasting operations in foreign waters and subsequently transferred to domestic waters. In Canada, this has led to a conflagration of "zebra mussels" and other invasive species, particularly in the Great Lakes. With few known predators, such species, if left unchecked, can interfere, and at times destroy, elements of such waters' ecosystems.

Canada currently has a strong Water Ballast Program,[33] and the implementation of the *BWM Convention* places Canadian shipping interests in a delicate position. The United States has not signed the *BWM Convention*, and its several border states and ports on the Great Lakes have adopted different criteria to handle such ballast water issues. A further challenge has risen on the technical side. The freshwater and cold temperatures of the Great Lakes may not permit the tested technology used in other parts of the marine world to properly function. Thus, Canadian shipping interests face the prospect of reporting to several masters with uncertain requirements or solutions.

International shipping's major concerns with this convention have aptly led their leaders to urge uniformity and for governments to act on the "ballast water chaos."[34] While the Canadian government proposed new *Ballast Water Regulations*[35] in June 2019 to better implement the *BWM Convention*'s goals, Canadian shipping has expressed concern that the proposal does not reflect the state of available technology, and that it clashes with the US framework.[36]

Ship Recycling and Wreck Removal

To ensure a secure (from a safety perspective) and environmentally sound regime to recycle ships at the end of their operational lives, the IMO adopted the *Hong Kong International Convention for the Safe and Environmentally Sound Recycling of Ships* (the *Hong Kong Convention*) in 2009.[37] The goal was to reduce unnecessary risk to human health, safety, and the environment in the scrapping of vessels, including oil rigs and related oil platforms. Typically, older ships contain quantities of environmentally hazardous substances, including asbestos, heavy metals, hydrocarbons, ozone-depleting chemicals, and related toxins. The *Hong Kong Convention* provides guidelines to inventory hazardous materials, develop suitable ship recycling plans and recycling facilities to mitigate health and pollution hazards, and document recycling steps and adherence to best environmental practices. In addition, parallel guidelines have been established for the inspection, survey, and certification of ships to disclose and record hazardous materials.

The *Hong Kong Convention* requires adoption by fifteen states, representing 40 percent of the world merchant shipping tonnage, before it enters into force (Canada signed the convention in 2009 but has not ratified it). While the convention has yet to come into force, its guidelines have increasingly been adopted by shipowners, and compliant recycling facilities are developing.

Although not strictly part of such "recycling" efforts, the IMO has also turned its sights onto "wreck removal" issues. The *Nairobi International Convention on the Removal of Wrecks, 2007*[38] (the *Nairobi Convention*) provides a structure for the prompt and effective removal of shipwrecks and cargoes located beyond territorial seas that may otherwise adversely impact marine and coastal environments.

The *Nairobi Convention* has been in force since April 2015 and has been ratified by forty-nine states, representing over 73 percent of world shipping tonnage. Canada acceded to the *Nairobi Convention* on April 30, 2019 and has incorporated certain provisions of the convention in the *Wrecked, Abandoned or Hazardous Vessels Act*[39] (the *WAHV Act*), which came into force on July 30, 2019.

The *WAHV Act* establishes wreck reporting requirements, criteria for determining hazards to the environment and navigation, measures to facilitate the removal of ships and cargo, and liability provisions and insurance requirements for damages and compensation. This is essentially strict liability, with certain exceptions on the part of the ship's interests for the cost of locating, marking, and removing wrecks and for remedial efforts. Ships that do not comply with the *WAHV Act* may be refused access to Canadian waters, fined, or detained.[40]

Air Pollution

On July 1, 2010, IMO's revised *MARPOL Annex VI, Regulations for the Prevention of Air Pollution from Ships*[41] (the *Air Pollution Regulations*) came into force to tackle the increasingly prominent environmental issue of air pollution. The amendments, adopted by the IMO in 2008, introduced stricter emissions caps and emission control areas (ECAs), essentially sensitive sea zones with increased emissions standards. In 2012, Canada enacted the *Vessel Pollution and Dangerous Chemicals Regulations*[42] (the *VPDC Regulations*) under the *CSA*, incorporating provisions of the *Air Pollution Regulations*, with Canada's Atlantic and Pacific coasts being included in the *Air Pollution Regulations*' North American ECAs.

The *Air Pollution Regulations* and *VPDC Regulations* address various forms of ship source air pollution, including most importantly nitrogen oxides (NO_x), sulphur oxides (SO_x), and particulate matter (PM) produced by marine diesel engines. Although shipping by water remains the most energy-efficient method of transporting goods, it contributes 15 percent of the world's NO_x emissions and 13 percent of its SO_x emissions.[43] NO_x are gases that are harmful to human health and lead to acid rain and the accumulation of ground-level ozone.[44] NO_x emission levels depend on engine efficiency and design. SO_x cause similar health and environmental effects to NO_x but depend on sulphur content in bunker fuel.[45] For its part, PM consists of residual fuel combustion particles that, when emitted close to shore, contribute to smog and form "black carbon," a significant factor in climate change.[46]

The *VPDC Regulations* limit PM emissions within one mile from shore through a visual smoke density chart used to quantify the approximate density of ships' exhaust.[47] NO_x are controlled by emission limits that vary depending on the age of the vessel, the size and output of the engine, and the rated engine speed in crankshaft revolutions per minute.[48] The regulations also contain energy efficiency requirements for marine engines, which target CO_2 emissions, although ships are a relatively insignificant contributor of CO_2 emissions, as compared to SO_x, NO_x, and PM emissions.[49] Foreign ships in Canadian waters, and Canadian ships worldwide, are also required to keep either a Canadian Air Pollution Prevention Certificate or its international equivalent onboard as proof of compliance.[50] Furthermore, both the *Air Pollution Regulations* and *VPDC Regulations* have imposed gradual restrictions on the maximum percentage of sulphur allowed in bunker fuel. On January 1, 2015, the sulphur limit in ECAs, including Canada's Atlantic and Pacific coasts, was reduced from 1.00 percent to 0.10 percent. More recently, the worldwide limit outside of ECAs, including Canada's Arctic coast, dropped from 3.50 percent to 0.50 percent on January 1, 2020. It is anticipated that the 2020 measures will have an important environmental and health impact, reducing SO_x emissions by 77 percent or 8.5 million metric tons.[51] However, this will not be without a profound economic impact on the marine shipping and fuel industries. In 2016, the OECD projected that the 2020 measures could potentially cost the shipping industry up to $30 billion annually in additional costs.[52]

The shipping industry has been preparing for the new fuel regulations, increasingly relying on environmental technologies such as exhaust gas cleaning systems, also known as "scrubbers"—which are provided for in the *VPDC Regulations*, allowing ships to use fuel with a higher sulphur content than the prescribed limit[53]—and phasing in cleaner, higher-quality fuels with less sulphur.

Conclusion

Global trade increasingly requires the carriage of hazardous commodities and materials by sea over long distances, potentially putting the marine venture, human health, and the environment at risk. Diligence, new technology, and adherence to better practices are mitigating factors, but without uniform standards and coordinated enforcement, they will only go so far.

Industry leaders, stakeholders, and governments, through the IMO and other supporting institutions, must continue to advance broad uniformity, compliance, and enforcement efforts. They must continue to seek an elevated standard of pollution prevention and environmental safety, in balance with trade necessities, on a priority basis. While enormous advancements have been made, the "greening" of the shipping industry to achieve and maintain best environmental practices and common standards at large remains ongoing.

NOTES

1 Partner, Stikeman Elliott LLP (Montréal). This paper is based in part of the author's contribution to the *Report on the Legal Framework for Civil Liability for Vessel Source Oil Spills in Polar Regions*, edited by LR Overby (CMI Yearbook, New York I, 2015, for section on Canadian law. See <comitemaritime.org/wp-content/uploads/2018/06/CMI_Yearbook_2015-FINAL.pdf> at 376. The author also wishes to recognize the assistance of his colleagues Arad Mojtahedi (with its initial preparation) and Simon Ledsham (for the 2020 review and update).

2 Public Review Panel on Tanker Safety and Marine Spills Response Capability, *Final Report: Protecting Our Waters* (Ottawa: Minister of Supply and Services Canada, 1990).

3 The IMO is a United Nations specialized agency tasked with the responsibility to improve the safety and security of shipping, including the mitigation of pollution risks.

4 Comité Maritime International <comitemaritime.org>.

5 See e.g., the Canadian Maritime Law Association <www.cmla.org>.

6 See Green Marine, <www.green-marine.org> (an organization based in Québec City, QC and Seattle, WA, composed of leading Canadian and US associations that represent more than five hundred companies in the maritime sector. It promotes a voluntary environmental certification program for sectors of the North American marine industry). See also Highway H2O, <www.hwyh2O.com> (an initiative supported by the St. Lawrence Seaway Management Corporation (Cornwall, ON) and the Saint Lawrence Seaway Development Corporation (Washington, DC) in their drive to encourage shipping as a viable alternative to road and rail traffic for the transport of bulk cargoes, including liquid bulk).

7 *Constitution Act, 1867*, 30 & 31 Vict, c 3, ss 91 and ff.

8 *Oceans Act*, SC 1996, c 31. (NM refers to nautical miles.)

9 *Arctic Waters Pollution Prevention Act*, RSC 1985, c A-12 [*AWPP*].

10 *Marine Liability Act*, SC 2001, c 6 [*MLA*].

11 *AWPP, supra* note 9, s 2.

12 *Ibid.*

13 *MLA, supra* note 10, s 47.

14 International Maritime Organization, *International Code for Ships Operating in Polar Waters* (Polar Code), [2015] MEPC 68/21 at 3.

15 See *Arctic Shipping Safety and Pollution Prevention Regulations*, SOR/2017-286.

16 *Canada Shipping Act*, SC 2001, C 26 [*CSA*]; *MLA, supra* note 10, Schedules 5, 6, 7 and 8.

17 *MLA, supra* note 10, s 75.

18 *Ibid.*

19 *CSA, supra* note 16.

20 *Ibid*, Part 8.

21 *Ibid*, Part 9.

22 The International Oil Pollution Compensation Funds, <www.iopcfunds.org/about-us/legal-framework/>. See also the *MLA, supra* note 10, Parts 6 and 7 and Schedules 5, 6, 7 and 8.

23 Ship-source Oil Pollution Fund, <www.ssopfund.ca/>.

24 *MLA, supra* note 10, s 2.

25 *Migratory Birds Convention Act*, SC 1994, c 22.

26 *Canadian Environmental Protection Act, 1999*, SC 1999, c 33.

27 *Environmental Protection Act*, SNL2002, c E-14.2.

28 *Environment Act*, NS 1994-95, C 1.

29 The International Oil Pollution Compensation Funds, "The HNS Convention Why It Is Needed: Compensation for Damage Caused by Hazardous and Noxious Substances Transported by Sea" (last visited 10 June 2020) at 1–6, online (pdf): *International Maritime Organization* <wwwcdn.imo.org/localresources/en/MediaCentre/HotTopics/Documents/HNS%20ConventionWebE.pdf> [perma.cc/YTT2-J8YL].

30 International Maritime Organization, *International Convention on Liability and Compensation for Damage in Connection with the Carriage of Hazardous and Noxious Substances by Sea 1996*, [2010] online: *International Maritime Organization* <www.hnsconvention.org/> [*HNS Convention*].

31 See *Marine Liability and Information Return Regulations*, SOR/2016-307. See also "The HNS and Oil Electronic Reporting System. Le système de déclaration électronique pour les SNPD et les hydrocarbures" (last visited 10 June 2020), online: *Transport Canada* <stats.tc.gc.ca/HNS/Login.aspx> [perma.cc/P8MY-DS67].

32 International Maritime Organization, *International Convention for the Control and Management of Ships' Ballast Water and Sediments*, [2004] BWM/CONF/36 [*BWM Convention*].

33 Transport Canada, *Discussion Paper: Canadian Implementation of the Ballast Water Convention* (Ottawa: Transport Canada, 2012). See also the *Ballast Water Control Management Regulations*, SOR/2011-237 (under the *CSA*).

34 See International Chamber of Shipping "Urgent Need for Governments to Act on Ballast Water Chaos" (8 September 2016), online: *International Chamber of Shipping* <www.ics-shipping.org/press-release/urgent-need-for-governments-to-act-on-ballast-water-chaos/> [perma.cc/Q4W8-4EZ4].

35 *Ballast Water Regulations*, SOR/2021-120.

36 See Canadian Shipper "Chamber of Marine Commerce Releases Its 2020 Government Wish List" (15 January 2020), online: *Canadian Shipper* <www.marinedelivers.com/policy-priorities/> [perma.cc/7URR-LCRS].

37 International Maritime Organization, *The Hong Kong International Convention for the Safe and Environmentally Sound Recycling of Ships*, [2009] SR/CONF/45 [*Hong Kong Convention*].

38 International Maritime Organization, *Nairobi International Convention on the Removal of Wrecks*, 18 May, 2007 (entered into force: 14 April 2015) [Nairobi Convention].

39 *Wrecked, Abandoned or Hazardous Vessels Act* SC 2019, c 1.

40 *Ibid*, ss 74, 82, 90, 110.

41 Annex VI was introduced through the *1997 Protocol to MARPOL*, which came into force in 2005, and which was ratified by Canada in March 2010.

42 *Vessel Pollution and Dangerous Chemicals Regulations*, SOR/2012-69 [*VPDC Regulations*].

43 See ClearSeas "Air Pollution and Marine Shipping" (2019), online: *ClearSeas* <clearseas.org/en/air-pollution/> [perma.cc/7H5N-RM3K] [Marine Shipping]. See also Council of Canadian Academies, "The Value of Commercial Marine Shipping to Canada: The Expert Panel on the Social and Economic Value of Marine Shipping to Canada" (2017) at 38, 70, online (pdf): *ClearSeas* <clearseas.org/wp-content/uploads/2017/05/ValueMarineShipping_fullreport_EN.pdf> [perma.cc/RXT7-3K6D].

44 See Marine Shipping, *supra* note 43.

45 *Ibid.*

46 *Ibid.*

47 See *VPDC Regulations*, *supra* note 42, ss 117–119.

48 *Ibid*, ss 110–110.6.

49 *Ibid*, s 116.2; Marine Shipping, *supra* note 43 (ships contributed 2.2 percent of global CO_2 emissions in 2012).

50 See *VPDC Regulations*, *supra* note 42, s 122.

51 See "Sulphur 2020—Cutting Sulphur Oxide Emissions" (last visited 10 June 2020), online: *International Maritime Organization* <www.imo.org/en/MediaCentre/HotTopics/Pages/Sulphur-2020.aspx> [perma.cc/9XSN-FT56].

52 See Organization for Economic Cooperation and Development, "Reducing Sulphur Emissions from Ships: The Impact of International Regulation" (9 May 2016) at 10–42, online (pdf): *International Transport Forum* <www.itf-oecd.org/sites/default/files/docs/sulphur-emissions-shipping.pdf> [perma.cc/XJE9-ZS9T]. See also Dan Healing, "New Shipping Rules Expected to Impact Canadian Oilsands Industry in 2020," Global News (28 December 2019), online: *Global News* <globalnews.ca/news/6343041/marine-fuel-imo-2020-oilsands-canada/> [perma.cc/8FXR-826P].

53 See *VPDC Regulations*, *supra* note 42, s 111(4).

2

Environmental Protection and Offshore Petroleum Activities: A Regulator's Perspective

Shanti Dogra[1]

Introduction

The Canada-Nova Scotia Offshore Petroleum Board (Board or CNSOPB) regulates the oil and gas industry operating off the coast of Nova Scotia. Under the *Canada-Nova Scotia Offshore Petroleum Resources Implementation* Acts of 1987 and 1988 (*Accord Acts*),[2] one of the core responsibilities of the board is the protection of the environment during all phases of offshore petroleum activities. Broadly, the board's goal is to ensure that these activities are conducted in a manner in which environmental hazards are properly identified and associated risks are assessed, mitigated, and managed.

Offshore petroleum activities range from geotechnical work, seismic surveys, and exploratory drilling to development and production projects. These produce environmental effects consisting of noise, air, and liquid emissions to the marine and atmospheric environments. Some of them include operational discharges in the form of drilling fluid, cuttings, liquid wastes, and fugitive emissions. Although the probability of large petroleum spills is very low, they also must be assessed and responses planned for.

Since there are a variety of tools to promote environmental protection that the board uses, this chapter will briefly touch upon some of the more significant aspects of its regulatory program. These include environmental assessment, environmental protection plans, environmental effects monitoring, compliance/enforcement, regulatory coordination, and stakeholder engagement.

Environmental Assessment

One of the most essential tools in protecting the environment and the first step in the regulatory process is an environmental assessment (EA).[3] Offshore petroleum activities cannot proceed without board authorization, and, as part of the authorization process, operators are required to conduct project EAs.[4]

The EA generally must identify potential adverse environmental effects, propose measures to mitigate those effects, and consider residual effects, which essentially predict the significant adverse environmental effects of projects after mitigation measures are implemented, including a follow-up program to verify the accuracy of the EA and the effectiveness of those mitigation measures. It is imperative to examine residual effects to determine the likelihood, severity and significance of a proposed project's environmental impacts.[5] A focus on assessing environmental impacts respecting valued components (VCs) lies at the heart of the EA exercise.

VCs are notable features of the natural and human environment that have the potential to be impacted by the proposed activities. Within the temporal and spatial boundaries regarding the footprint of the proposed activity, the board requires that the VCs evaluated include fish and fish habitat, marine mammals and sea turtles, marine benthos, migratory birds, species at risk and their critical habitat, special areas, and other ocean users such as commercial fisheries, Aboriginal fisheries, and marine shipping.

Depending on the VC, the board will require detailed information to ascertain how a given activity may result in residual environmental impacts after mitigation is taken into account. Seismic surveys, for example, must assess species of special status in a study area and the assessment of the potential for disturbance to or displacement of these species due to noise, vessel presence, and the possibility of ship strike.[6] Included in the assessment is the means by which potential adverse effects are mitigated through operational procedures and how proposed strategies and action plans are demonstrated to be consistent with other laws such as the *Species at Risk Act* and the *Migratory Birds Convention Act, 1994*.[7]

In addition to identifying and assessing VCs, EAs must address other possible effects. The most significant of these often pertain to accidents and malfunctions that may occur in connection with the activity. For a drilling project, for example, this entails identifying worst-case accident scenarios from spills of fuel, drilling fluid/mud, and spills from a blowout.[8] In describing its spill probability analysis and other modelling, the proponent will outline its spill prevention and response safeguards, incorporate these within an overall project plan, and design mitigation measures to prevent or reduce adverse effects. These include standard mitigation measures, industry best management practices, and compliance with requirements under the *Accord Acts* legislation.[9] To this end, the board must be satisfied with the proponent's approach to risk management, and that it will take all reasonable measures to minimize the probability of malfunctions and accidents, and if they occur, it will mitigate the impacts by implementing appropriate emergency response and contingency plans.

Another key EA component is assessing potential cumulative effects whereby the proponent's activity could result in environmental effects acting in combination with the residual effects of other projects and activities that have been or will be carried out. By looking at other ocean users and assessing any overlaps that impact applicable VCs, design and operational procedures can be implemented to mitigate or minimize adverse effects resulting from these cumulative effects.

Environmental Protection Plan

An environmental protection plan (EPP) can be considered the proponent/operator's primary document detailing its mitigation requirements. Whereas the EA presents a project conceptually, the EPP sets out in practice the who, what, when, and how an operator will protect the environment while conducting its activity. By regulation, the EPP must set out the procedures, practices, resources, and monitoring necessary to manage hazards and protect the environment.[10] The operator's EPP must be submitted in support of its application for authorization since the board must be satisfied that the operator's equipment and installations are fit for the purposes for which they are to be used, that the operating procedures relating to them are appropriate for those uses, and that the personnel, employed in connection with them, are qualified and competent.[11]

Another requirement of the EPP is that it must be a component of an operator's management system and an operator's plan to implement its environmental protection measures effectively.[12] The system must include co-ordinating arrangements between the operator and its contractors and set out the contractors' activities within the scope of the operator's EPP. The system should also be linked to the operator's environmental policy, which should form part of the core values of the system, and the policy should include a policy statement that establishes the basic environmental principles applicable to the planned activity. The statement sets the tone for environmental responsibility and performance.

Additionally, the EPP must refer to specific plans, procedures, work instructions, operating manuals, and other documents intended to direct the work of personnel at the installation. These documents must be written to demonstrate how the activity is to be conducted in a manner that conforms to the environmental policy, which ensures that the EA environmental mitigation commitments are met, limits for discharges are not exceeded, and that the operator's objectives and commitments are met.

As to in-depth planning, since each exploration, development, and production work or activity is unique, the management system should enable an operator to determine environmental hazards associated with all aspects of the planned work or activity. Also, an operator should be allowed to evaluate the risk potential of such hazards and to identify and implement appropriate mitigation strategies. Consequently, the EPP will contain a summary of studies undertaken to identify hazards, evaluate risks, and the results of those studies, as well as a summary of the means to avoid, prevent, reduce, or manage risks to the natural environment.

The EPP also must describe any planned discharges, the limit on these discharges, and, for waste discharges, the equipment and procedures for treatment, handling, and disposal of waste materials. Since emissions and discharges associated with offshore drilling and production are well known, the board has co-published guidance[13] that discusses the board's expectations of the discharge limits for a variety of waste streams.

Environmental Effects Monitoring

Environmental effects monitoring (EEM) is a science-based performance measurement tool used to verify environmental effects predicted during an EA and to evaluate the efficacy of mitigation measures. In the offshore context, it involves scientific monitoring of the effects of petroleum activities on specific components of the surrounding environment. Producing operators are required to conduct EEM programs throughout each year, and the program design may change yearly. EEM is required for all development projects, and at times for certain exploration activities depending on the commitments made in an EA.

In 2005, the board, the Canadian Environmental Assessment Agency (CEA Agency), Fisheries and Oceans Canada (DFO), and Environment and Climate Change Canada (Environment Canada) developed an EEM process framework. The purpose of the framework was to strengthen cooperation and coordination between the government, regulators, and industries when designing, implementing, and reviewing EEM programs. As part of the framework, a periodic synopsis report is prepared by the board as a public-facing document that summarizes the EEM reports that have been submitted to the board over the years.[14]

The EEM reports have verified the predictions of environmental effects on a variety of VCs through experimentation, including

- monitoring of produced water effects on marine life (taint, chemical body burden, and fish health);
- water column monitoring through scraping shellfish (mussel) samples directly from platform legs or moored cages and in-lab testing;
- sediment/benthic habitat and chemistry monitoring, involving retrieving sediment samples. The same samples are used to determine possible toxicity in sediments;
- seabird monitoring consisting of relatively continuous and opportunistic observations from platforms and project vessels using trained observers;
- oiled beached-bird surveys on Sable Island; and
- marine mammal monitoring to gauge the extent of possible sound-related effects.

Monitoring parameters may change from year to year as the EEM programs adapt to better understand findings from past surveys. Over a decade of monitoring, results have shown that:

- much more benthic habitat was created from production platforms and subsequent creation of a "reef effect" than was originally lost;

- programs to date have not found evidence of tainting effects in mussel samples;
- oiling of beached birds has not been attributed to the petroleum industry but rather to shipping and other vessel traffic;
- a predicted plume of drilling waste was only detected once and appeared lighter and shorter-lived than modelled; and
- some species of marine mammals have shown no avoidance behaviour related to underwater noise from seismic programs (dolphins in particular).

Success in some areas of effects monitoring may naturally lead to improving the methods and processes used to evaluate the relationship between offshore petroleum activities and the receiving environment. Once knowledge concerning a particular interaction is developed, the remaining unknowns become the new questions that guide and drive future monitoring.

Compliance and Enforcement

The board has in place a regulatory compliance monitoring program to evaluate operator compliance with environmental regulatory requirements while conducting authorized petroleum activities. Operators are required to submit reports detailing the status of their work programs on an ongoing basis along with other documentation to demonstrate compliance with regulatory requirements. Operational status reports are provided daily for drilling and production activities and weekly for other activities. Reports filed with the board are reviewed by staff to identify environmental compliance issues, which are addressed accordingly.

Board conservation officers regularly conduct environmental audits and inspections at offshore worksites and operator offices to verify compliance. Specifically, the officers have the authority to enter and inspect a place used for a work or activity. They have powers to do various things, including pose questions, conduct tests, take samples, remove anything for examination, take photographs or measurements, use a computer system, have a document produced or prepared, use copying equipment, be accompanied by any individual, and meet in private with any individual with consent.[15]

For the purposes of conducting formal investigations, a justice of the peace may issue a warrant, on an *ex parte* application, which authorizes an officer to enter a place and search for and seize anything, if there are reasonable grounds to believe the place contains evidence of the commission of an offence.[16] In urgent circumstances, however, it is not necessary for the officer to first obtain a warrant.

The board has an established compliance and enforcement policy to address situations of regulatory non-compliance where operator action is insufficient. Enforcement actions may include facilitated or directed compliance; issuance of orders, directives, or notices; suspension or revocation of approvals and authorizations; issuance of administrative monetary penalties; and prosecution in the court system.

Regulatory Coordination

In February of 2013, the federal auditor general's commissioner of the environment and sustainable development (CESD) tabled an audit report[17] on the performance of the board's environmental regulatory program. This report came after a rigorous review of the board's management of environmental risks and impacts associated with offshore oil and gas activities. While the report concluded on balance that the board exercised due diligence when assessing and approving projects and activities, it did identify areas for improvement. After the report was tabled, the board released a statement outlining its response and action plan.[18]

One of the main findings of the CESD audit was that the board should have in place up to date and effective agreements with other federal organizations that may be involved in, or support, the board's regulatory mandate respecting spill preparedness, prevention, and response.

Memoranda of Understanding

In response, memoranda of understanding (MOUs) have since been created or updated with a number of departments and bodies, including Transport Canada Marine Safety and Security, the Canadian Coast Guard, Environment Canada, DFO, the Canada Energy Regulator, and the Canada-Newfoundland and Labrador Offshore Petroleum Board.

To summarize these recent MOUs:[19]

MOU between the CNSOPB and the Canadian Coast Guard

The CNSOPB signed a new MOU with the Canadian Coast Guard to coordinate activities related to safety and environment response (including spill response), to cooperate and share information, and to promote safety and environmental protection through effective spill preparedness and response, as well as training and exercises.

MOU between the CNSOPB and Transport Canada Marine Safety and Security

The CNSOPB updated its MOU with Transport Canada Marine Safety and Security to facilitate coordination of offshore oil and gas activities where possible and to avoid duplication of work in relation to marine safety, occupational safety and health, and environmental protection. Also, the MOU provides clarification on the use of the National Aerial Surveillance Program in monitoring spill incidents.

MOU between the CNSOPB and the Canada-Newfoundland and Labrador Offshore Petroleum Board and the Canada Energy Regulator

The CNSOPB entered into this MOU with these respective Boards to enhance the cooperation and coordination of activities between the participants related to safety, security, the environment, and resource conservation, including activities respecting regulatory matters, the sharing of resources, and emergency management.

MOU between the CNSOPB and Environment Canada

The CNSOPB updated its MOU with Environment Canada to facilitate and promote the protection of the environment, preparedness and response to oil spills, and conservation of migratory birds and species at risk during offshore oil and gas activities. Furthermore, this MOU details how the Integrated Satellite Tracking of Pollution program may be used to track oil and gas environmental incidents.

MOU between the CNSOPB and Fisheries and Oceans Canada

The CNSOPB updated its MOU with DFO to facilitate and promote effective coordination between both organizations. This MOU details how the CNSOPB and DFO will collaborate on the development and implementation of integrated management plans for marine and coastal waters in respect of the offshore area, including associated actions pertaining to the management of Canada's commercial, recreational, and Aboriginal fisheries, at-risk aquatic species and their critical habitat. The board is also involved in initiatives led by DFO related to marine protected areas and integrated management planning under the *Oceans Act*.[20]

Concerning the board's relationship to DFO and Environment Canada, it is worth noting that the three agencies work closely, particularly on the review of EAs whether they are conducted under the *Accord Acts* or *Impact Assessment Act* (*IAA*).[21] For *Accord Acts* EAs, the board relies on DFO for scientific expert advice respecting fish, marine mammals, and fisheries. It relies on Environment Canada respecting species at risk, marine birds, and spill response. Conversely, the board, as a federal authority under *IAA*, provides advice on environmental impacts and mitigation from its perspective through in-house expertise (geologists, drilling engineers, facilities engineers, and others) to the Impact Assessment Agency and other federal authorities.

Stakeholder Engagement

Complementing the above-noted tools, the board maintains an open working relationship with various stakeholders with interest in offshore petroleum activities. The following are three of the main approaches the board uses to ensure open and transparent relationships with stakeholders.

Minimizing Impacts to Fisheries

The board requires operators to conduct offshore activities in a manner that minimizes the impact on fisheries, marine fish resources, and fish habitat. The presence of vessels associated with offshore petroleum exploration and development activities may require the use of space that may also be occupied by commercial fisheries.

Standard marine protocols to communicate and avoid collision with other vessels, including a notice to mariners, are required for all offshore activities under the board's jurisdiction. There is a requirement for a 500 m safety zone[22] around drilling and production installations, where non-project vessels are restricted from entering. Outside of this zone, petroleum operators are required to work with commercial fishing vessels to minimize interactions.

In addition to the above protocols, the board requires a fisheries liaison officer to be present on all seismic vessels using air-gun arrays and to minimize navigational interactions with active fisheries in the area. Knowledgeable fisheries liaison officers help ensure effective communication between petroleum operators and fishers. The board also evaluates other offshore activities during the EA process to determine if there is a need for a fisheries liaison officer. As a secondary role, the fisheries liaison officer may also monitor and record marine mammal and seabird observations.

Fisheries Advisory Committee

The board's Fisheries Advisory Committee (FAC) includes representatives from various fishing groups, DFO, the Nova Scotia Department of Agriculture and Fisheries, Natural Resources Canada, and the Nova Scotia Department of Energy. FAC members provide advice and suggestions to the board for consideration in work authorization applications, regulations, and guidelines. Meetings are held quarterly, and briefings are sent out to inform and engage members in a discussion of upcoming projects and other petroleum-related activities. Committee members are provided with notice of all EAs and invited to submit comments to the board for consideration during the review processes.

International Offshore Petroleum Environment Regulators

The board is a founding member of the International Offshore Petroleum Environment Regulators (IOPER). The IOPER is a collaborative group of national regulators whose members are dedicated to raising environmental performance standards within the offshore petroleum exploration and production industry. This includes standards applicable to the industry's regular operations, as well as environmental emergency prevention, preparedness, and response.

Conclusion

From the board's perspective, decisions on EAs must be based on sound science and the appropriate information about the natural environment and how proposed activities may impact it. While activities are underway, the application of practical plans and mitigation measures will ideally result in minimal residual effects. Monitoring and studying environmental effects to verify assessment predictions and to evaluate mitigation leads to a greater understanding of what is happening to the natural environment. Regulatory coordination and information sharing provide a framework for government bodies, industry, and other stakeholders to ensure environmental protection continues to evolve and improve for existing and future projects.

NOTES

1 General Counsel—Canada-Nova Scotia Offshore Petroleum Board, Halifax. Disclaimer: The views presented in this paper and accompanying presentation are the author's own and are not intended to represent the Canada-Nova Scotia Offshore Petroleum Board.

2 *Canada-Nova Scotia Offshore Petroleum Resources Implementation Act*, SC 1988, c 28; *Canada-Nova Scotia Offshore Petroleum Resources Implementation (Nova Scotia) Act*, SNS 1987, c 3. Citations will be to the federal version of the legislation. [Collectively, the *Accord Acts*.]

3 The board conducts or participates in three kinds of EAs: strategic EAs for a regional area subject to a call for bids and the potential issuance of exploration licences; project-specific EAs under the *Accord Acts* for geophysical and geotechnical activities; and project-specific EAs under the *Canadian Environmental Assessment Act, 2012* (*CEAA 2012*, as of 2019 now the *Impact Assessment Act* [*IAA*]) for exploratory drilling, development, and decommissioning/abandonment activities.

4 *Accord Acts*, *supra* note 2, ss 140, 142.

5 Government of Canada "Determining Whether a Designated Project is Likely to Cause Significant Adverse Environmental Effects under the Canadian Environmental Assessment Act, 2012" (18 November 2019) online: *Government of Canada* <www.canada.ca/en/impact-assessment-agency/services/policy-guidance/determining-project-cause-significant-environmental-effects-ceaa2012.html>.

6 See e.g., the board's *Scoping Document for Environmental Assessment BP Exploration (Canada) Ltd: Tangier 3D Seismic Survey Exploration Licences 2431, 2432, 2433, and 2434* (Halifax: Canada-Nova Scotia Offshore Petroleum Board, August 2013). EA documents are available on the board's website: <www.cnsopb.ns.ca/>.

7 *Species at Risk Act*, SC 2002, c 29 and *Migratory Birds Convention Act*, SC 1994, c 22.

8 See "Shelburne Basin Venture Exploration Drilling Project—Environmental Assessment Report" (2015) at 58–88, online (pdf): *Impact Assessment Agency of Canada* <iaac-aeic.gc.ca/050/documents/p80058/101799E.pdf> [perma.cc/8V4J-5HC2].

9 See especially the *Nova Scotia Offshore Drilling and Production Regulations*, SOR/2009-317; the *Nova Scotia Offshore Installation Regulations*, SOR/95-191.

10 The *Nova Scotia Offshore Drilling and Production Regulations*, *supra* note 9, s 9.

11 The *Accord Acts*, *supra* note 2, s 143.1.

12 See the *Environmental Protection Plan Guidelines* (issued March 2011 jointly by the CNSOPB, the Canada-Newfoundland and Labrador Offshore Petroleum Board, and the National Energy Board).

13 See *Offshore Waste Treatment Guidelines 2010*; *Offshore Chemical Selection Guidelines for Drilling & Production Activities on Frontier Lands 2009* respectively (issued jointly by the CNSOPB, the Canada-Newfoundland and Labrador Offshore Petroleum Board, and the National Energy Board).

14 See Nova Scotia Legislature "A Synopsis of Nova Scotia's Offshore Oil and Gas Environmental Effects Monitoring Programs: Summary Report" (2011) at 1–17, online (pdf): *Nova Scotia Legislature* <o-nsleg-edeposit.gov.ns.ca.legcat.gov.ns.ca/deposit/b10643766x.pdf>.

15 The *Accord Acts*, *supra* note 2, s 194.

16 *Ibid*, s 197.1.

17 Office of the Auditor General of Canada "2012 Fall Report of the Commissioner of the Environment and Sustainable Development" (2012), online: *Office of the Auditor General of Canada* <www1.oag-bvg.gc.ca/internet/English/parl_cesd_201212_e_37708.html> [perma.cc/Q846-7DKX].

18 Canada-Nova Scotia Offshore Petroleum Board (CNSOPB), "Regarding the Federal Auditor General's Commissioner of the Environment and Sustainable Development's (CESD) Report—Chapter 1: Atlantic Offshore Oil & Gas Activities" (5 February 2013), online: *Canada-Nova Scotia Offshore Petroleum Board* <www.cnsopb.ns.ca/sites/default/files/resource/cesd_news_statement_feb_5.pdf> [perma.cc/ZEC5-2M4S].

19 Link to the MOUs: <www.cnsopb.ns.ca/environment/cesd-audit>.

20 *Oceans Act*, SC 1996, c 31.

21 CNSOPB, "Environmental Protection," online: CNSOPB <www.cnsopb.ns.ca/what-we-do/environmental-protection>; Memorandum of Understanding between CNSOPB and Fisheries and Oceans Canada (DFO), s 6.2; Memorandum of Understanding between CNSOPB and Environment Canada, s 5.2.

22 *Nova Scotia Offshore Area Petroleum Drilling and Production Regulations* (NS Reg 336/2009) s 72.

3

Protection of the Marine Environment: The International Legal Context

Suzanne Lalonde[1]

> The protection of the marine environment is an area where the jurisdictional rules of the law of the sea and the objectives, principles and approaches of international environmental law meet and influence each other to form the "international environmental law of the sea."[2]

Schiffman characterizes the increasing concern for the status of the marine environment[3] in the latter half of the twentieth century as one of "the most remarkable developments in the field of international law."[4] This new consciousness has led to a proliferation of legal rules and arrangements to address key threats to ocean health: overfishing, vessel and land-based pollution, the introduction of invasive species, the destruction of habitats, and the loss of biodiversity among other significant challenges. However, the legal regime for the protection of the marine environment, as Frank explains, has a distinct character compared to the one governing the protection of the terrestrial environment. At sea, states are not as free to impose protective measures as they are on land; they must respect the jurisdictional rules of the law of the sea.[5] "These rules place certain constraints on the capacity of coastal States to unilaterally control the environmental impact of sea-based activities."[6]

This chapter begins by identifying some of the most important soft law and conventional law instruments aimed at the protection and preservation of the marine environment. The chapter then considers the prescriptive and enforcement powers that exist to ensure compliance with those rules.

The Environmental Law of the Sea

The international regime for the protection of the marine environment is based on two separate but interdependent bodies of law that interact and complement each other to create a dynamic and effective system.[7] They include (A) an umbrella framework that sets out general principles and rules of global application, and (B) a regulatory regime composed of tailored instruments with technical standards to implement the general principles or rules.

AN UMBRELLA FRAMEWORK

The output of some highly influential international conferences and organizations, together with the *1982 Convention on the Law of the Sea* (*UNCLOS*), form the foundation upon which rests the environmental law of the sea.

The *1972 United Nations Conference on the Human Environment* (*UNCHE*) (Stockholm, Sweden)

Described as the "conceptual cornerstone of modern international environmental law,"[8] the *1972 United Nations Conference on the Human Environment* (*UNCHE*) and one of its key declarations, the *Declaration of the United Nations Conference on the Human Environment* (*Stockholm Declaration*),[9] enunciated principles and recommendations of direct relevance for the marine environment. Principle 7 of the declaration provided that "States shall take all possible steps to prevent pollution of the seas by substances that are liable to create hazards to human health, to harm living resources and marine life, to damage amenities or to interfere with other legitimate uses of the sea."

Of perhaps even greater significance, principle 21 recognized "the sovereign right of States to exploit their own resources pursuant to their own environmental policies," while imposing upon them the correlative responsibility "to ensure that activities within their jurisdiction or control do not cause damage to the environment of other States, or of areas beyond the limits of national jurisdiction."[10]

Though not legally binding, the *Stockholm Declaration* nevertheless exerted considerable influence on the subsequent development of new global and regional instruments addressing specific sources of marine pollution.[11] The *UNCHE* and its declaration of principles also provided a decisive impulse to the Third United Nations Conference on the Law of the Sea launched in 1973.

The *1982 United Nations Convention on the Law of the Sea (UNCLOS)*

In 1982, after nearly ten years of negotiations, the *UNCLOS* was adopted to establish "a legal order for the seas and oceans" that would promote "the equitable and efficient utilization of their resources, the conservation of their living resources, and the study, protection and preservation of the marine environment."[12] Birnie and Boyle wrote that at the time of its adoption, the *UNCLOS* was considered the "strongest comprehensive environmental treaty in existence or likely to emerge for quite some time."[13] Most legal authors and governments, including non-parties such as the United States, recognize that since they entered into force on 16 November 1994, the environmental provisions established by the convention have gained nearly universal acceptance and thus reflect customary law.[14]

Due to the intersectoral nature of marine issues, the *UNCLOS* addresses the environment in several different sections (e.g. Parts V and VII on the conservation and management of living resources in the exclusive economic zone (EEZ) and high seas or Part XIII on marine scientific research).[15] However, Part XII of the *UNCLOS* is specifically dedicated to the protection and preservation of the marine environment and establishes an overall framework of governing principles and general obligations.[16]

Article 192 of the *UNCLOS* illustrates the comprehensive nature of this regime by placing a general and unqualified obligation on states "to protect and preserve the marine environment." Franckx emphasizes that Article 192 represents the first time such a strong and broad obligation has been included in a general international treaty.[17] Echoing principle 21 of the *Stockholm Declaration*, Article 193 of the *UNCLOS* confirms that states "have the sovereign right to exploit their natural resources pursuant to their environmental policies and in accordance with their duty to protect and preserve the marine environment." However, Roberts argues that by giving priority to the preservation of the environment over the sovereign right of states to exploit their natural resources, Article 192 is more strongly expressed than principle 21.[18]

The content of this general duty is clarified in Article 194. States are required to take all necessary measures to prevent, reduce, and control marine pollution[19] using the best practical means at their disposal and according to their capabilities.[20] They must also take all necessary measures to protect and preserve "rare and fragile ecosystems as well as the habitat of depleted, threatened or endangered species and other forms of marine life" (Article 194, para 5). Six main sources of pollution are identified and addressed in further detail in subsequent articles: pollution from land-based and coastal activities (Article 207), seabed activities within national jurisdiction (Article 208), activities in the area (Article 209), ocean dumping (Article 210), vessels (Article 211), and or through the atmosphere (Article 212).

Finally, states are subject to a series of procedural obligations: the notification of imminent or actual damage (Article 198), the development of pollution contingency plans (Article 199), cooperation through scientific research (Articles 200–201) and technical assistance (Article 202), the monitoring of the risks or effects of pollution (Article 204), and the publication of the results of those monitoring activities (Article 205). In addition, Article 206 requires states "as far as practicable" to conduct environmental impact assessments (EIAs) of activities under their jurisdiction or control with the potential to cause substantial pollution or significant harm to the marine environment. Finally, Article 235 imposes a general duty to compensate for pollution damage and to cooperate in the development of international law relating to responsibility and liability.[21]

Release in 1987 of "Our Common Future"

In 1987, the World Commission on Environment and Development (WCED), which had been set up in 1983, published a report entitled "Our Common Future."[22] The document came to be known as the *Brundtland Report* after the WCED's Norwegian chairwoman, Gro Harlem Brundtland. Tasked with preparing an environmental perspective to the year 2000 and beyond, the *Brundtland Report* called for a global strategy that united economic and social development with the environment: "The 'environment' is where we live; and 'development' is what we all do in attempting to improve our lot within that abode. The two are inseparable."[23]

Choy explains that in an attempt to mitigate the destructive environmental consequences of economic growth, "the report introduced a new growth model 'that is forceful and, at the same time, socially and environmentally sustainable', placing great emphasis on the need to manage and use natural resources wisely so as to uphold the principle of intergenerational equity."[24] The *Brundtland Report* thus emphasized the need to observe the biological constraints on or the physical foundation of economic activity.[25]

> The first [foundational principle] referred to the need to live within nature's limits. Development was sustainable, we said, if, at a minimum, it did not endanger the natural systems that support life on earth—the atmosphere, the waters, the soils and the living beings.[26]

The WCED also concluded that poverty was a significant cause and effect of global environmental problems and that "there was little hope of solving those problems unless and until members of the international community developed the will and the means to resolve problems of human development."[27]

To solve the interrelated problems of environmental degradation and economic/social development—while promoting equity, growth, and environmental stewardship—the *Brundtland Report* recommended a radical transformation of nations' goals and policies to support "sustainable development." Sustainable development is defined as "development that meets the needs of the present without compromising the ability of future generations to meet their own needs."[28]

> One of the major purposes of the concept of sustainable development is to coordinate the relationship between resource uses and environmental protection. Under this concept, they are not contradictory, much less conflict, but can interplay mutually. Environmental protection is necessary to achieve the goal of resource uses which are sustainable, and economic benefits deriving from resources can provide the conditions in which environmental protection can best be achieved.[29]

The WCED's urgent call to global action was the impetus for the 1992 Earth Summit in Rio, which produced important and influential documents including the *Rio Declaration on Environment and Development* (the *Rio Declaration*), *Agenda 21*, and the legally binding *Convention on Biological Diversity* (*CBD*).[30] Choy writes that "Our Common Future" was "further cemented with an appreciable dose of authority with the adoption of the *Johannesburg Declaration* at the 2002 World Summit on Sustainable Development."[31]

The *1992 United Nations Conference on Environment and Development (UNCED)* also known as the Earth Summit (Rio de Janeiro, Brazil)

Sands has suggested that, in its significance, the Rio meeting is comparable to major multilateral peace conferences such as the 1919 Versailles Conference, given the significance placed on the "security of the planet" and the "risk to humans and other species."[32] One of the key objectives of *UNCED* was a comprehensive program to guide states in pursuing sustainable development. The major agreements reached at the Earth Summit include two binding instruments, the *CBD* and the *United Nations Framework Convention on Climate Change* (*UNFCCC*),[33] as well as three non-binding instruments including the *Rio Declaration*[34] and *Agenda 21*.[35]

The general principles embodied in the *Rio Declaration* are operationalized through detailed provisions, specific recommendations and guidelines in the forty chapters of *Agenda 21*, and *UNCED*'s plan of action. Chapter 17 on "Protection of the Ocean and All Kinds of Seas, including Enclosed or Semi-enclosed Seas, and Coastal Areas and the Protection, Rational Use and Development of their Living Resources" serves as a blueprint for the future development of the international environmental law of the sea. While the *UNCLOS* is referenced as providing the "international basis" for the protection and sustainable use of the marine environment, *Agenda 21* calls for a new approach to marine issues. The introduction to Chapter 17 asserts that this approach must be "integrated in content" and "precautionary and anticipatory in ambit."[36] In addition to promoting a precautionary approach to ocean preservation (17.22, para a), Chapter 17 urges states to conduct environmental assessments of all potentially hazardous activities (17.22, para b), to apply clean technologies, and to commit to the polluter-pays principle (17.22, para d).

States are also recommended to take measures to address marine degradation (not only pollution) from land-based activities (17.24–29) and to assess the need for additional measures to control sea-based activities such as shipping, dumping, offshore oil and gas platforms, and ports (17.30–35). Furthermore, Chapter 17 places a strong emphasis on monitoring, reporting, and financial and technical assistance (17.35–37, 17.41–42).

As Frank emphasizes, "[d]espite its legally non-binding nature, Chapter 17 had a decisive influence on the further development of the marine environmental regime and its principles and recommendations have worked as guidelines for states and international organizations in the implementation of their commitments under the *LOSC* [*UNCLOS*]."[37] Birnie and Boyle stress that the "focus is no longer principally on the control of sources of marine pollution, but more broadly on the prevention of environmental 'degradation' and the protection of ecosystems."[38] According to the authors, the interplay between *Agenda 21* and the *UNCLOS* has effected substantive changes to the law of the sea and has led, for instance, to the rewriting of regional seas-agreements on the Mediterranean, the Baltic, and the Northeast Atlantic; revision of the *London Convention*; extension of treaty schemes on liability for pollution damage; and the adoption at Washington in 1995 of a declaration and Global Programme of Action for the Protection of the Marine Environment from Land-based Activities.[39] In addition,

> [a] precautionary approach to the protection of marine ecosystems and biological diversity is now addressed in many of these treaties and in various other ways, in particular through the Conventions on Biological Diversity and Climate Change, the 1995 Agreement on Straddling and Highly Migratory Fish Stocks (UN Fish Stocks Agreement), the 2004 Ballast Water Convention, and the creation of specially protected areas by IMO [International Maritime Organization] and under regional seas agreements.[40]

The 2002 World Summit on Sustainable Development (WSSD) (Johannesburg, South Africa)

Ten years after the Earth Summit, the World Summit on Sustainable Development (WSSD) was held to review the progress made in the implementation of *Agenda 21* but dedicated only marginal attention to the world's oceans and seas. Indeed, the Plan of Implementation (WSSD Plan) only deals with the marine environment in paragraphs 29–34 of section IV on "Protecting and Managing the Natural Resource Base of Economic and Social Development" and most of the relevant provisions relate to fisheries.[41] Nevertheless, Frank insists that the contribution of the WSSD Plan to the preservation of the marine environment should not be underestimated.[42] The WSSD Plan reaffirms the commitments made under Chapter 17 (e.g. an integrated approach to ocean management), and, in regard to certain key obligations, it attaches clear targets and timetables (e.g. the application of an ecosystem approach by 2010 and the establishment of a network of representative marine protected areas by 2012).[43] The WSSD Plan reaffirms in five separate paragraphs, the need to conduct EIA to achieve the goal of sustainable development[44] and attaches great importance to the transfer of marine science and technology.[45] In addition, the WSSD Plan urges the wide ratification and effective implementation of existing legal agreements and programs of action for the effective conservation and management of the oceans.

The Tenth Meeting of the Conference of the Parties to the Convention on Biological Diversity and the Aichi Biodiversity Targets[46]

In 2010, a "Strategic Plan for Biodiversity 2011–2020" was adopted by the Conference of the Parties to the *CBD* (194 state parties), with the vision that "by 2050, biodiversity is valued, conserved, restored and wisely used, maintaining ecosystem services, sustaining a healthy planet and delivering benefits essential for all people."[47] The strategic plan includes twenty ambitious conservation targets, known as the Aichi Biodiversity Targets. Together, they set out the global framework for priority actions on biodiversity conservation.[48]

Strategic Goal C aims "to improve the status of biodiversity by safeguarding ecosystems, species and genetic diversity" and in terms of the marine environment, includes Target 11:

> By 2020, at least 17 per cent of terrestrial and inland water, and 10 per cent of coastal and marine areas, especially areas of particular importance for biodiversity and ecosystem services, are conserved through effectively and equitably managed, ecologically representative and well connected systems of protected areas and other effective area-based conservation measures, and integrated into the wider landscapes and seascapes.[49]

The state parties agreed to translate this overarching framework into revised and updated national biodiversity strategies and action plans and also committed to periodically report on their progress.

2030 Agenda for Sustainable Development

In September 2015, at a historic United Nations Summit, 193 world leaders adopted the 2030 Agenda for Sustainable Development,[50] which embraces the three dimensions of sustainability defined in the *Brundtland Report*: economic, social, and environmental. Described in the introduction to the declaration as "a set of universal and transformative Goals and Targets," they aim to achieve "a more sustainable, equitable, prosperous and peaceful planet."[51]

> The 2030 Agenda for Sustainable Development, adopted by all United Nations Member States in 2015, provides a shared blueprint for peace and prosperity for people and the planet, now and into the future. At its heart are the 17 Sustainable Development Goals (SDGs), which are an urgent call for action by all countries—developed and developing—in a global partnership.[52]

A "Technical Note" drafted by the Secretariat of the *CBD* emphasizes that the 2030 Agenda is entirely consistent with other international commitments including the "Strategic Plan for Biodiversity" adopted at the Tenth Conference of the Parties in 2010. "The SDGs and the Strategic Plan are mutually supportive and reinforcing, and therefore the implementation of one contributes to the achievement of the other."[53]

SDG 14, captioned "Life Below the Water," represents the first time that the oceans and seas have been the subject of an SDG in United Nations discussions.[54] Defined as the need to "[c]onserve and sustainably use the oceans, seas and marine resources," SDG 14 identifies "careful management of this global resource as a key feature of a sustainable future." To promote ocean health, the 2030 Agenda advocates more effectively managed and better-resourced marine protected areas together with the adoption of regulations to reduce overfishing, marine pollution, and ocean acidification.

SDG 14 is broken down into distinct targets with specific "indicators" to assist states in measuring their progress.[55] They include Target 14.1: "By 2025, prevent and significantly reduce marine pollution of all kinds, in particular from land-based activities, including marine debris and nutrient pollution." The corresponding indicator (14.1.1), or statistical data to be gathered in support, is an "[i]ndex of coastal eutrophication and floating plastic debris density." Target 14.4 requires that by 2020, states "effectively regulate harvesting and end overfishing, illegal, unreported and unregulated fishing and destructive fishing practices and implement science-based management plans." Indicator 14.4.1 recommends that data be gathered on the "[p]roportion of fish stocks within biologically sustainable levels." Echoing Strategic Goal C (Target 11) from 2010, Target 14.5 exhorts states to "conserve at least

10 percent of coastal and marine areas, consistent with national and international law." Indicator 14.5.1 encourages states to report on the "[c]overage of protected areas in relation to marine areas."

In June 2017, the member states of the United Nations gathered at the first-ever global Ocean Conference[56] and committed to a set of ambitious measures to support the implementation of SDG 14. The outcome declaration, *Our Ocean, Our Future: Call for Action*, underlined the need to integrate SDG 14 and its interrelated targets "into national development plans and strategies, to promote national ownership and to ensure success in its implementation by involving all relevant stakeholders, including national and local authorities, members of parliament, local communities, indigenous people, women and youth, as well as the academic and scientific communities, business and industry."[57] It also affirms in paragraph 11, the "need to enhance the conservation and sustainable use of oceans and their resources by implementing international law as reflected in the United Nations Convention on the Law of the Sea."[58]

A REGULATORY REGIME

The Third Law of the Sea Conference (1973–1982) was not considered the appropriate forum to devise operational provisions that, by their very nature, are normally highly technical and require significant expertise. In addition, several international regulatory instruments with specialised standards were already in place. In light of these considerations, the participating delegations agreed to establish a broad jurisdictional framework and to rely, by means of rules of reference, on the various operational standards adopted by relevant organizations. As a result, various articles of the *UNCLOS* require that contracting parties give effect to the generally "accepted" or generally "applicable" international rules and standards defined by the "competent international organizations."[59]

These "competent international organizations" are not specifically identified in the *UNCLOS*. However, Article 2(2) of Annex VIII of the convention, which provides that the lists of experts composing the special arbitral tribunal must be established by the "competent organization" in specified fields, provides some guidance: in the field of fisheries, by the Food and Agriculture Organization (FAO) of the United Nations; in the field of protection and preservation of the marine environment, by the United Nations Environment Programme (UNEP); in the field of marine scientific research, by the Intergovernmental Oceanographic Commission; and in the field of navigation, including pollution from vessels and by dumping, by the IMO. Generally accepted international rules and standards, however, can also be adopted by organizations other than those referred to in Article 2(2) of Annex VIII. Frank refers to the International Atomic Energy Agency (IAEA), for instance, as the competent international organization for the adoption of global standards for the safe transport of nuclear materials.[60] These and other international organizations and agencies have developed technical guidelines and legal measures to give effect to general conservation commitments. The following list is *not* exhaustive but is merely indicative of the varied sources that operationalize the "international environmental law of the sea."

- *International Convention for the Regulation of Whaling*, 1946 (International Whaling Commission [IWC])
- *International Convention Relating to Intervention on the High Seas in Cases of Oil Pollution Casualties*, 1969 (IMO)
- *Convention on the International Regulations for Preventing Collisions at Sea* (COLREG), 1972 (IMO)
- *Convention on the Prevention of Marine Pollution by Dumping of Wastes and other Matter*, 1972 (and the *1996 Protocol*) (IMO)
- *International Convention for the Prevention of Pollution from Ships (MARPOL)*, 1973 (as modified by the *Protocol of 1978* and by the *Protocol of 1997*) with its six technical annexes (I: Regulations for the Prevention of Pollution by Oil; II: Regulations for the Control of Pollution by Noxious Liquid Substances in Bulk; III: Prevention of Pollution by Harmful Substances Carried by Sea in Packaged Form; IV: Prevention of Pollution by Sewage from Ships; V: Prevention of Pollution by Garbage from Ships; and VI: Prevention of Air Pollution from Ships) (IMO)
- *International Convention on Standards of Training, Certification and Watchkeeping for Seafarers (STCW)*, 1978 (IMO)
- *International Convention on Oil Pollution Preparedness, Response, and Cooperation*, 1990 (IMO)
- *Code of Conduct for Responsible Fisheries*, 1995 (FAO)

- *Agreement to Promote Compliance with International Conservation and Management Measures by Fishing Vessels on the High Seas*, 1995 (FAO)
- *Joint Convention on the Safety of Spent Fuel Management and on the Safety of Radioactive Waste Management*, 1997 (IAEA)
- *Strategy for the Implementation of the Code of Conduct for Responsible Fisheries*, 1999 (FAO)
- *Protocol on Preparedness, Response and Co-operation to Pollution Incidents by Hazardous and Noxious Substances*, 2000 (IMO)
- *International Convention on the Control of Harmful Anti-fouling Systems on Ships*, 2001 (IMO)
- *International Convention for the Control and Management of Ships' Ballast Water and Sediments*, 2004 (IMO)
- *The Hong Kong International Convention for the Safe and Environmentally Sound Recycling of Ships*, 2009 (IMO)
- *Agreement on Port State Measures to Prevent, Deter and Eliminate Illegal, Unreported and Unregulated Fishing*, 2010 (FAO)
- *Regulations for the Safe Transport of Radioactive Material*, 2012 (IAEA)
- *International Code for Ships Operating in Polar Waters (Polar Code)*, 2017 (IMO)
- *Guidelines for Conducting Integrated Environmental Assessments*, 2019 (UNEP)
- *Guidelines for the Monitoring and Assessment of Plastic Litter and Microplastics in the Ocean*, 2019 (UNEP)

In the field of the protection and preservation of the marine environment, UNEP's Regional Seas Programme, launched in the wake of the 1972 *UNCHE*, has been one of its most significant achievements. Both the *UNCLOS* and Chapter 17 of *Agenda 21* place a strong emphasis on regional cooperation,[61] considered in many cases to be a more efficient response to specific geographic, oceanographic, and ecological challenges. Frank also points out that regional agreements between states sharing similar interests "result in a lower level of compromise, stronger commitments and higher environmental standards compared to global instruments."[62] As a result, in nearly all major regional seas, from the Caribbean to the South Pacific Ocean, the ocean framework regime has been implemented by means of regional conventions adopted under the auspices of UNEP.[63]

The development of marine environmental rules and technical standards has also taken place within the framework of several multilateral environmental agreements that extend their scope to oceans and seas: for example, the *Convention on Wetlands of International Importance* (*Ramsar Convention*), 1971; the *Convention Concerning the Protection of the World Cultural and Natural Heritage* (*World Heritage Convention*), 1972; the *Convention on the Conservation of Migratory Species of Wild Animals* (*Bonn Convention*), 1979; the *Basel Convention on the Control of Transboundary Movements of Hazardous Wastes and their Disposal*, 1989; and the aforementioned *CBD*, 1992.

As for the regulation of fishing activities, the fundamental obligation in the *UNCLOS* that states should cooperate to ensure the conservation and optimal utilization of fisheries, both within and beyond the EEZ,[64] has been operationalized through the adoption of the 1995 Fish Stocks Agreement[65] and the establishment of regional fisheries management organizations or arrangements (RFMO/As). Now established in the majority of high seas areas that have major deep-sea fisheries,[66] RFMO/As are usually tasked with collecting fisheries statistics, assessing resources, making stock management decisions, and monitoring activities. As emphasized by the FAO, they play "a pivotal role in facilitating intergovernmental cooperation in fisheries management"[67] and are increasingly guided by the ecosystem approach to fisheries.

On December 24, 2017, following a two-year preparatory committee process, the United Nations General Assembly (UNGA) adopted Resolution 72/249 to convene an intergovernmental conference (IGC) to develop an international legally binding instrument on marine biodiversity in areas beyond national jurisdiction (ABNJ).[68] The first three sessions of the IGC took place in New York from September 4 to 17, 2018, March 25 to April 5, 2019, and August 19 to 30, 2019. Unfortunately, by Resolution 74/543 of March 11, 2020, and due to the COVID pandemic, the UNGA decided to postpone the fourth session and consideration of the revised draft of the agreement to a later date.[69]

Nearly two-thirds of the ocean lies in ABNJ.[70] While several instruments and institutions already promote the conservation and sustainable use of marine biodiversity in ABNJ,[71] Tladi argues that they "bear no real relationship to one another and operate independent of each other without an overarching framework to ensure structure, consistency and coherence."[72] This fragmentation, according to experts at IDDRI,[73] has left gaps in the framework: "not all human activities in ABNJ are adequately regulated; not all regions are covered; and some organizations exercise their mandate with limited reference to modern governance principles, such as the ecosystem approach, the precautionary principle, or the need for transparent and open decision-making processes."[74]

The new treaty will be an "implementing" agreement under the *UNCLOS* to adapt the convention's general provisions on the protection of the marine environment to the specific threats to, and use of, marine biodiversity in ABNJ.[75] The negotiations have thus far focused on four thematic areas: marine genetic resources (MGRs), area-based management tools including marine protected areas, EIAs, capacity-building, and the transfer of marine technology. Questions to be resolved include whether access to MGRs in ABNJ should be regulated (and if so, how) and whether benefits derived from their use or commercialization should be shared (and if so, with whom and how).[76] Negotiations will also touch upon the respective roles of global and regional bodies in EIA processes and whether rules or guidance should be developed on when activities in ABNJ trigger the need for an EIA, the type and amount of information to be included in EIAs, and whether the new treaty should cover strategic environmental assessments. Other key issues and responsibilities, many of them highly contentious, remain to be negotiated and finalized.[77]

The Jurisdictional Regime

In customary international law of the sea, the flag state alone was responsible for ensuring that ships complied with internationally accepted standards in respect of safety at sea and the protection of the marine environment. Article 91 of the *UNCLOS* recognizes the sovereignty a state exercises over its vessels, and Article 94 identifies several obligations that flow from this attribution of nationality. Every flag state must effectively exercise its jurisdiction and control in administrative, technical, and social matters over ships flying its flag. In particular, the flag state must take all necessary measures to ensure that all of its ships are seaworthy (Article 94, para 3a), are regularly inspected by a qualified surveyor (Article 94, para 4a) and are manned by a qualified crew fully conversant with the applicable international regulations concerning the safety of life at sea; the prevention of collisions; and the prevention, reduction, and control of marine pollution (Article 94, para 4c). In taking the measures called for in paragraphs 3 and 4, the flag state is required to "conform to generally accepted international regulations, procedures and practices and to take any steps which may be necessary to secure their observance" (Article 94, para 5, and Article 217).

Unfortunately, as König reports, several flag states do not fulfil their obligations under the *UNCLOS*, a problem "aggravated by—but by no means confined to—so-called 'flags of convenience' where less scrupulous operators register their ships under the flags of states which they know will not require full compliance with international standards."[78] To fill the gap, port states and coastal states have been entrusted by the convention with additional prescriptive authority (the capacity of states to adopt legislation, including environmental rules) and enforcement powers (the capacity of states to bring about compliance with those rules and punish violations).

Port states have the right to impose national standards as a condition of entry of foreign vessels into their ports, internal waters, and offshore terminals (Article 211(3) of the *UNCLOS*). Since these areas are part of the port state's sovereign territory, where the right of innocent passage does not exist, its prescriptive jurisdiction is not restricted. As a result, the coastal state can even impose construction, design, equipment, and manning standards (CDEM standards) that are stricter and more costly for shipowners than the recognized international standards.[79] As for their enforcement powers, Article 220(1) provides that port states have the right to enforce their national rules and standards against foreign vessels that are voluntarily within their ports or offshore terminals when an illegal discharge has occurred in their internal waters, territorial sea, or EEZ.[80]

To strengthen the protection of the marine environment in other states' maritime zones and on the high seas, König explains that port states have been entrusted by Article 218(1) with the additional right to enforce "applicable international rules and standards," that is, *MARPOL* standards, against a foreign vessel in case of any illegal operational discharge. "If the discharge violation occurs in a third state's maritime zones, the port state may not institute proceedings unless requested by that state (Article 218, para. 2). That coastal state may step in and take over the investigation and proceedings at any time (Article 218, para. 4)."[81] When instituting proceedings against a foreign vessel and its crew for a discharge violation that occurred on the high seas, the port state must have due regard to procedural safeguards such as the right of the flag state to take over the proceedings at any time and the obligation to release the vessel and crew upon the posting of a reasonable bond.

In addition, port states can enforce "applicable international rules and standards relating to the seaworthiness of vessels" (CDEM standards) to prevent severe damage to the marine environment by substandard ships. To this end, Article 219 allows the port state to take administrative measures to prevent such a vessel from sailing or order it to proceed to the nearest repair yard.[82] Thus, as König emphasizes,[83] the *UNCLOS* empowers port states to utilize their enforcement powers not only in their interest but also in the international community's interest, a development Wolfrum described as a "profound modification of international law."[84] However, several important reasons have hampered the effective exercise of port states' jurisdictional authority. States are not always willing to act and invest precious financial and personnel resources when their interests are not directly affected. In addition, port states that undertake strict controls are afraid of putting themselves at a competitive disadvantage compared to neighbouring countries. To address these and other challenges and wield their enforcement powers more efficiently, port states in various parts of the world have established *regional* port state control (PSC) regimes.[85]

For their part, coastal states must respect the limits imposed by the *UNCLOS* on their capacity to control the activities of foreign vessels in waters under their sovereignty and jurisdiction. The level of control exercised by a coastal state varies according to the kind of activity involved and the maritime zone concerned.[86] It also, generally, decreases as the distance from the shoreline increases.

Internal waters (i.e. all waters on the landward side of the baselines[87] including ports) are treated just like land territory and are under the full sovereignty of the coastal state.[88] Recognized as an integral part of a state's national territory, international law thus provides that internal waters are subjected to the full force of the coastal state's legislative, administrative, judicial, and enforcement powers. As such, the coastal state is free to apply national laws and determine conditions of entry for foreign vessels. It is in the exercise of this sovereign authority that the United States, following the *Exxon Valdez* tragedy, banned all single-hull oil tankers from entering its ports (1990) without seeking prior approval from the IMO, and that the European Union introduced a similar ban following the sinking of the *Prestige* (2002). However, Birnie et al noted that in the interests of comity and freedom of navigation, most states have shown restraint in the unilateral regulation of foreign ships within their internal waters.[89]

As Article 2 of the *UNCLOS* declares, the sovereignty of a coastal state extends to its territorial sea up to 12 nautical miles from its baselines. The *UNCLOS* and other international treaties recognize the coastal state's right to ensure the environmental protection of its territorial waters. According to Birnie and his colleagues, this right includes three important powers: "the designation of environmentally protected or particularly sensitive sea areas, the designation and control of navigation routes for safety and environmental purposes, and the prohibition of pollution discharges."[90]

In the exercise of each of these powers, the coastal state enjoys a substantial measure of freedom; it can, for example, impose stricter pollution discharge standards than the international standards defined by the *MARPOL* convention. However, Article 21(2) of the *UNCLOS* excludes from the coastal state's jurisdiction the right to adopt laws or regulations in regard to the design, construction, manning, or equipment of foreign vessels unless such rules give effect to international standards (essentially the standards set by the *MARPOL* and the *International Convention for the Safety of Life at Sea* [*SOLAS*]). Article 21(4) also refers to "generally accepted international regulations" in regard to national legislation for the prevention of collisions at sea. Paragraphs 2 and 4 reflect the important limitation that is placed upon the control exerted by a coastal state in its territorial sea: the right of innocent passage that by virtue of Article 17, is conferred upon the ships of all nations, both civilian and military. To protect freedom of navigation, Article 24 of the *UNCLOS*, together with other provisions, commands that "[t]he coastal state shall not hamper the innocent passage of ships through the territorial sea except in accordance with this Convention."

What then, asked Birnie et al, can a coastal state "legitimately do when a foreign vessel is found violating international pollution regulations in the territorial sea, or when it poses a risk of accidental pollution or environmental harm?"[91] What enforcement powers does a coastal state wield in its territorial waters? Without doubt, a coastal state is not authorized to deny or suspend the right of innocent passage of a ship merely because it is carrying dangerous or environmentally risky cargo. In such circumstances, the international legal regime merely confers upon the coastal state the right to take certain precautionary measures to minimize the environmental threat. It may, for example, require ships carrying nuclear or other inherently dangerous or noxious substances to carry specific documents and observe special precautionary measures approved by the IMO and the IAEA or established by international agreements such as *MARPOL*.[92] Article 22(2) of the *UNCLOS* also allows coastal states to confine the passage of "tankers, nuclear-powered ships and ships carrying nuclear or other inherently dangerous or noxious substances" to specific sea lanes in the interests of "safety, the efficiency of traffic and the protection of the environment."[93]

State practice, together with special areas protocols[94] and the designation of particularly sensitive sea areas [PSSAs] by the IMO, also recognize the right of coastal states to regulate the passage of ships through designated environmentally sensitive areas to minimize the risk of adverse impacts or serious pollution. Mandatory ship reporting is a common element of such schemes, but additional measures may also be imposed with IMO's approval. For example, under the *1972 Marine Protection, Research and Sanctuaries Act* and as approved by the IMO, the United States designated the Florida Keys as an "area to be avoided" and prohibited the operation of tankers in those waters. However, as Birnie et al emphasized, though ships may be required to avoid certain areas, "the right of innocent passage is not lost."[95]

The mere violation of a coastal state's laws and regulations will not necessarily deprive a foreign vessel of its right of innocent passage. As Article 19(2) specifies, the passage of a foreign ship is only considered to be prejudicial to the peace, good order, or security of the coastal state (and therefore not innocent) if it engages in "(h) any act of wilful and serious pollution contrary to this Convention." This provision, therefore, necessarily excludes any right of intervention in cases of accidental pollution and even if operational pollution is often deliberate, it is seldom "serious" and may be justified by weather or distress. Thus, the strong wording of Article 19(2)(h) ensures that ships causing operational pollution will rarely cease to be exercising innocent passage. Nor will a violation of construction standards be considered, in and of itself, a threat to the peace, good order, or security of the coastal state, depriving a ship of its right of innocent passage. And yet, as Birnie et al confirmed, "[o]nly when they lose this right can their entry into territorial waters be denied, or their right of passage terminated by eviction or arrest."[96] In most cases, enforcement by port states will be the preferable and more efficient solution.[97]

In the EEZ, which extends up to 200 nautical miles from the baselines, coastal states have sovereign rights over living and mineral resources and jurisdiction over the protection and preservation of the marine environment.[98] This zone does not exist automatically but must be claimed, and in the case of pollution jurisdiction, Birnie et al stated that legislation will usually be necessary for the coastal state to acquire the required competence.[99]

Regarding the conservation of living resources, coastal states are required under Article 61 of the *UNCLOS* to determine the allowable catch of the living resources in their EEZs, and, through "proper conservation and management measures," ensure their maintenance and avoid their over-exploitation. Paragraph 3 of Article 61 further provides that conservation measures "shall also be designated to maintain or restore populations of harvested species at levels which can produce the maximum sustainable yield." Article 73(1) provides for the enforcement of such laws and measures: "[t]he coastal State may . . . take such measures, including boarding, inspection, arrest and judicial proceedings, as may be necessary, to ensure compliance." Procedural safeguards are however provided in the other paragraphs of Article 73: arrested vessels and their crews must be promptly released upon the posting of a reasonable bond or other security (para 2); coastal state penalties for violations of fisheries laws and regulations may not include imprisonment, in the absence of specific agreements, nor any other form of corporal punishment (para 3); and in cases of arrest or detention of foreign vessels, the coastal state must promptly notify the flag state (para 4).

Within the EEZ, coastal states are granted the power to regulate pollution from seabed activities under their jurisdiction (Article 208), dumping (Article 210), and vessel source pollution (Article 211, para 5). In regard to seabed activities and dumping, the *UNCLOS* provides that coastal state laws and regulations "should be no less effective than international rules, standards and recommended practices or procedures."[100] However, both Articles 208 and 210 encourage states, acting through competent international organizations or diplomatic conferences, to harmonize their policies and devise "global and regional rules, standards and recommended practices and procedures." As for the prevention, reduction, and control of pollution from vessels, a coastal state's regulatory jurisdiction is limited to the application of "generally accepted international rules and standards" established by the competent international organization (Article 211, para 5).

In this context *MARPOL* regulations and other international standards adopted by the IMO thus represent the normal limit of coastal state competence and act as a necessary restraint where there is evident potential for excessive interference with shipping.[101]

Mandatory reporting or routeing schemes require IMO's approval if they extend to the EEZ and must be supported by scientific and technical evidence.[102] The designation of special areas or PSSAs by the IMO under Article 211(6) does not confer any power on coastal states to set national construction or equipment standards for ships entering their EEZs. However, it does allow them to apply national standards relating to pollution discharges or navigational practices in those special areas. The only other exception to the *UNCLOS*'s marked preference for international standards and regulations within the EEZ is found in Article 234. This article, the outcome of strong diplomatic pressure from Canada and Russia, applies to ice-covered waters within the limits of the EEZ. It allows coastal states a broad discretion to adopt national standards for pollution control, provided that such measures have "due regard to navigation" and are non-discriminatory.

Coastal states are not given full jurisdiction to enforce international pollution regulations against ships passing through their EEZ. As we have seen, they can do so if the vessel voluntarily enters their ports or offshore terminals, but as Birnie et al explained, in other cases their powers are graduated according to the likely harm.[103] The constraints placed on the coastal state's enforcement powers are summarised by König:

> They range from asking a vessel to disclose information on its identity, itinerary and other relevant information in order to establish whether a violation has occurred (article 220, para. 3, LOSC), to undertaking physical inspection in the case of a substantial discharge causing significant pollution if the vessel has refused to give information at all, or if this information is manifestly wrong (article 220, para. 5, LOSC). Only if the illegal discharge is causing or threatening to cause major damage to the coastline or to any resources of the coastal State's territorial sea or EEZ, may that State institute proceedings, including the detention of the vessel.[104]

In situations where a foreign vessel has been detained, Articles 223 to 233 of the *UNCLOS* impose certain procedural safeguards, including the obligation to release the ship and its crew as soon as a reasonable bond has been posted (Article 226, para 1(b)). König also highlights the power conferred upon coastal states by Article 221 of the *UNCLOS* to take and enforce measures to prevent actual or threatened damage to their coastline—"or related interests, including fishing"—as a result of a maritime casualty.[105]

On the continental shelf, which extends up to 200 nautical miles from the baselines and in certain cases, even beyond that limit,[106] coastal states have sovereign rights for the purpose of exploring and exploiting its natural resources. According to Molenaar, these sovereign rights seem to include prescriptive and enforcement powers to manage and conserve the living resources on the continental shelf (sedentary species).[107] Coastal states can also take "reasonable measures" for the prevention, reduction, and control of pollution from pipelines, but cannot impede the laying or maintenance of cables or pipelines by other states.[108] As noted above, Articles 208 and 210 grant coastal states pollution jurisdiction as far as sea-bed activities and dumping are concerned but encourage the development of "global and regional rules" through competent international organizations and conferences. As for the enforcement of such rules, the location of the offending ship, within the EEZ (as described above) or on the high seas (port state and flag state enforcement), will dictate the extent of the coastal state's powers.

As Frank emphasizes, the *UNCLOS*'s jurisdictional provisions were drafted to achieve a balance between coastal states' extended environmental interests and the rights of other states to exercise their traditional freedoms,[109] especially the freedom of navigation. As a matter of compromise, the *UNCLOS* gives precedence to multilateral cooperation either among states directly, through the adoption of tailored legal instruments and arrangements, or within competent international organizations or general diplomatic conferences.

NOTES

1 PhD (Cantab), Faculty of Law, Université de Montréal.

2 V Frank, *The European Community and Marine Environmental Protection in the International Law of the Sea* (Leiden: Martinus Nijhoff Publishers, 2007) at 11 [Frank].

3 *Ibid* (according to Frank, "it is commonly agreed that the term 'marine environment' refers to the ocean space taken as a whole i.e., the surface of the sea; the water column;

the subsoil; the seabed and the atmosphere above them and everything comprised in that space, both physical and chemical components, including marine life" at 13).

4 HS Schiffman, "International Law and the Protection of the Marine Environment" in A Schwabach & AJ Cockfield, eds, *International Law and Institutions* (Oxford: EOLSS Publishers Co. Ltd., 2009) 213 at 213.

5 Frank, *supra* note 2 at 11.

6 *Ibid.*

7 *Ibid.*

8 J Roberts, *Marine Environment Protection and Biodiversity Conservation—The Application and Future Development of the IMO's Particularly Sensitive Sea Area Concept* (Berlin: Springer, 2007) at 17 [Roberts].

9 *Declaration of the United Nations Conference on the Human Environment* [*Stockholm Declaration*], 16 June 1972, 11 ILM 1416. For a comprehensive overview of the outcomes of the Conference and a detailed analysis of the Declaration, see LB Sohn, "The Stockholm Declaration" 14 Harv In'l LJ (1973) 423.

10 Roberts, *supra* note 8 at 19.

11 *Ibid* at 20 (according to Roberts, it was in response to the recommendations of the Stockholm Conference that an intergovernmental conference was convened in London and adopted the *Convention on the Prevention of Marine Pollution by Dumping of Waste and Other Matter*, 29 December 1972, in force 30 August 1975, 11 ILM (1972) 1294) at n 37.

12 *United Nations Convention on the Law of the Sea*, adopted 10 December 1982, in force 16 November 1994, 1833 UNTS 3, preamble.

13 PW Birnie & A Boyle, *International Law and the Environment*, 2nd ed (Oxford: University Press, 2002) at 348 [Birnie & Boyle].

14 See Frank, *supra* note 2 at 16, n 33.

15 *Ibid* at 17.

16 Roberts, *supra* note 8 at 21–22.

17 E Franckx, "Regional Marine Environmental Protection Regimes in the Context of UNCLOS" 13 Int'l J Mar & Coast L (1998) 307 at 310–311.

18 Roberts, *supra* note 8 at 23. See also Birnie & Boyle, *supra* note 13 at 350.

19 This positive duty involves protecting the marine environment from harm in areas under coastal states' jurisdiction (Article 194 paragraph 1) but also in areas beyond their jurisdiction or control (paragraph 2) as well as in regards to other states and their environment (paragraph 2).

20 However, Article 194(1) of the *UNCLOS* encourages states to harmonize their national policies.

21 Frank, *supra* note 2 at 20.

22 World Commission on Environment and Development, *Our Common Future*, 4 August 1987, transmitted to the General Assembly as an Annex to Document A/42/427, online (pdf): <sswm.info/sites/default/files/reference_attachments/UN%20WCED%201987%20Brundtland%20Report.pdf> [perma.cc/6HRL-DX4H] [*Brundtland Report*].

23 *Ibid* at 14.

24 YK Choy, "28 Years into 'Our Common Future': Sustainable Development in the Post-Brundtland World" 2 *Sustainable Development* (2015) 1197, at 1197–98, quoting the *Brundtland Report*, *supra* note 22 at 14 [Choy].

25 *Ibid* at 1198.

26 Quote from Jim MacNeill, the lead author of the *Brundtland Report*, reflecting on the state of the world twenty-five years after its publication, quoting the report, *supra* note 22, at 55, para 9. J MacNeill, "Brundtland Revisited," 4 February 2013, available on the OpenCanada.org website at <www.opencanada.org/features/brundtland-revisited/>.

27 J Lemons, "Sustainable Development and Environmental Protection: A Perspective on Current Trends and Future Options for Universities" 19:2 Environmental Management (1995) 157 at 157.

28 *Brundtland Report*, *supra* note 22 at 24, para 27.

29 K Zou, "Introduction" in K Zou, ed, *Sustainable Development and the Law of the Sea* (Leiden: Brill/Nijhoff, 2017) 1 at 2.

30 *Convention on Biological Diversity*, adopted 22 May 1992, in force 29 December 1993, 1760 *UNTS* 143.

31 Choy, *supra* note 24 at 1198.

32 PH Sands, "UNCED and the Development of International Environmental Law" 3 YB Int'l Env L (1992) 3.

33 *United Nations Framework Convention on Climate Change*, adopted 9 May 1992, in force 21 March 1994, 1771 *UNTS* 107.

34 *Rio Declaration*, adopted 14 June 1992, UN Doc. A/Conf.151/5/REV.1, 31 *ILM* (1992) 874.

35 *Agenda 21*, adopted 14 June 1992, UN Doc. A/Conf.151/26 (1992). The other non-binding instrument was the *Authoritative Statement of Principles for a Global Consensus on the Management, Conservation and Sustainable Development of All Types of Forests.*

36 See paragraph 17.1, Chapter 17, *Agenda 21*, online: <www.un.org/Depts/los/consultative_process/documents/A21-Ch17.htm> [perma.cc/B5D6-XB2A].

37 Frank, *supra* note 2 at 23–24.

38 Birnie & Boyle, *supra* note 13 at 384.

39 *Ibid.*

40 *Ibid* at 384–385.

41 The Plan of Implementation is available, online (pdf): <www.un.org/esa/sustdev/documents/WSSD_POI_PD/English/WSSD_PlanImpl.pdf> [WSSD Plan].

42 Frank, *supra* note 2 at 23.

43 WSSD Plan, *supra* note 41, paras 30(b) and (d) and 32(c).

44 WSSD Plan, *supra* note 41, paras 19(e), 36(c), 62(h), 97(d) and 135.

45 WSSD Plan, *supra* note 41, paras 36(a).

46 The Tenth Meeting of the Conference of the Parties to the Convention on Biological Diversity was held from 18–29 October 2010 in Nagoya, Aichi Prefecture in Japan.

47 Decision X/2 adopted 29 October 2010 by the 194 State Parties, UNEP/CBD/COP/DEC/X/2 (29 October 2010), online (pdf): <www.cbd.int/doc/decisions/cop-10/full/cop-10-dec-en.pdf> [perma.cc/7TSF-JLSW].

48 Convention on Biological Diversity, "Biodiversity and the 2030 Agenda for Sustainable Development—Technical Note" (last visited 22 June 2021) at 1–25, online (pdf): *Convention on Biological Diversity* <www.cbd.int/development/doc/biodiversity-2030-agenda-technical-note-en.pdf> [perma.cc/9PC3-T7FL] [Biodiversity and the 2030 Agenda].

49 Convention on Biological Diversity, "Aichi Biodiversity Targets" (2010), online: *Convention on Biological Diversity* <www.cbd.int/sp/targets/> [perma.cc/SN5Y-HY6J].

50 General Assembly Resolution 70/1, *Transforming Our World: The 2030 Agenda for Sustainable Development*, A/RES/70/1 (2015).

51 Fondation Tara Océan "The Sustainable Development Goals: A To Do List for the Planet" (last visited 17 June 2020), online: *Fondation Tara Océan* <oceans.taraexpeditions.org/en/m/environment/les-objectifs-de-developpement-durable-odd/> [perma.cc/2VYB-BKQD] [Fondation Tara Océan].

52 "Sustainable Development Goals" (last visited 17 June 2020), online: *Sustainable Development Goals Knowledge Platform* <sustainabledevelopment.un.org/sdgs> [perma.cc/CT83-59X2].

53 "Biodiversity and the 2030 Agenda," *supra* note 48.

54 Fondation Tara Océan, *supra* note 51.

55 The global indicator framework was developed by the Inter-Agency and Expert Group on SDG Indicators and agreed to, as a practical starting point, at the 47th session of the UN Statistical Commission held in March 2016. See the Sustainable Development Goal Indicator website at <unstats.un.org/sdgs/> [perma.cc/44D3-7YJX].

56 United Nations "Our oceans, our future: partnering for the implementation of Sustainable Development Goal 14" (last visited 8 December 2021), online: *United Nations* <oceanconference.un.org/about> [perma.cc/PCV5-SH98].

57 United Nations, *Our Ocean, Our Future: Call for Action*, 30 June 2017, UNGA, 71st Sess, 2016–2017, A/71/L.74, online: <digitallibrary.un.org/record/1290893?ln=en> at para 9 [perma.cc/FDC9-Y5JJ].

58 *Ibid.*

59 See e.g., *UNCLOS*, arts 210(4) "Pollution by dumping" and 210(1) "Pollution from vessels."

60 Frank, *supra* note 2 at 25.

61 The *UNCLOS* calls for regional harmonization, for example, with regard to land-based pollution in art 207(3) and marine pollution from seabed activities within national jurisdiction under art 208(4).

62 Frank, *supra* note 2 at 29.

63 See e.g., the *Convention on the Protection of the Marine Environment of the Baltic Sea Area [Helsinki Convention]*, 1992; the *Barcelona Convention for the Protection of the Mediterranean against Pollution*, 1976 (and related Protocols as amended); and the *Convention for the Protection of the Marine Environment of the North-East Atlantic* [OSPAR], 1992.

64 See e.g., *UNCLOS*, arts 63 and 118.

65 *The United Nations Agreement for the Implementation of the Provisions of the United Nations Convention on the Law of the Sea of 10 December 1982 relating to the Conservation and Management of Straddling Fish Stocks and Highly Migratory Fish Stocks*, adopted 4 August 1995, entered into force 11 December 2001, 2167 UNTS 3.

66 RFMO/As include Northwest Atlantic Fisheries Organization (NAFO), North-East Atlantic Fisheries Commission (NEAFC), South East Atlantic Fisheries Organisation (SEAFO), Commission for the Conservation of Antarctic Marine Living Resources (CCAMLR), South Pacific Regional Management Organisation (SPRFMO), North Pacific Fisheries Commission (NPFC), Southern Indian Ocean Fisheries Agreement (SIOFA) and the General Fisheries Commission for the Mediterranean (GFCM). See "Regional Fisheries Management Organizations and Deep-sea Fisheries" (2020),

online: *Food and Agriculture Organization of the United Nations* <www.fao.org/fishery/topic/166304/en> [perma.cc/WMH9-YPS6].

67 *Ibid.*

68 For a brief account of the process leading up to the intergovernmental conference, see V De Lucia, "The BBNJ Negotiations and Ecosystem Governance in the Arctic" (2019) 103756 Marine Policy 1.

69 See 23 March–3 April 2020, UNGA, 4th Sess, 2020, A/CONF.232/2020/3, online: <undocs.org/en/a/conf.232/2020/3> [perma.cc/F5YL-AL5J].

70 These areas include the high seas (the water column beyond the EEZs of coastal states) and the area (the seabed and ocean floor, and subsoil thereof beyond their continental shelves).

71 See the general obligations identified in our discussion of the environmental provisions of the *UNCLOS*, including Articles 194(2) and 209. For a general overview, see Section 3 "Existing Framework for Conservation and Sustainable Use of Marine Biodiversity in ABNJ" in G Wright et al, "The Long and Winding Road: Negotiating a Treaty for the Conservation and Sustainable Use of Marine Biodiversity in Areas beyond National Jurisdiction" (2018) 8/18 IDDRI Studies at 23 [IDDRI Report].

72 D Tladi, "Ocean Governance: A Fragmented Regulatory Framework" in P Jacquet et al, eds, *Oceans: The New Frontier—A Planet for Life* (Delhi: TERI Press, 2011) 99 at 101.

73 Institut du développement durable et des relations internationales.

74 IDDRI Report, *supra* note 71 at 31.

75 The *UNCLOS* already has two other implementing agreements on mining in the deep seabed and on straddling and highly migratory fish stocks.

76 "Marine Biodiversity beyond National Jurisdiction" (last visited 17 June 2020), online: *New Zealand Foreign Affairs & Trade* <www.mfat.govt.nz/en/environment/oceans/marine-biodiversity-beyond-national-jurisdiction/> [perma.cc/2NQV-7GJW].

77 For a comprehensive discussion of the principal issues to be negotiated, see the IDDRI Report, *supra* note 71.

78 D König, "The Enforcement of the International Law of the Sea by Coastal and Port States" 62 ZaöRV (2002) 1 at 4 [König].

79 *Ibid* at 5.

80 *Ibid.*

81 *Ibid* at 6.

82 *Ibid.*

83 *Ibid.*

84 R Wolfrum, "Means of Ensuring Compliance with and Enforcement of International Law" 272 Rec des Cours (1988) 1 at 154.

85 Since 1994, Canada is a member of the Paris PSC regime created in 1982 by the Paris Memorandum of Understanding, which has now been accepted by 27 states.

86 Frank, *supra* note 2 at 17.

87 *UNCLOS*, art 8(1).

88 *UNCLOS*, art 2. See also *Military and Paramilitary Activities in and against Nicaragua (Nicaragua v United States of America)*, Merits, Judgment, ICJ Rep 1986, 14 at 111 ("[t]he basic legal concept of State sovereignty in customary international law, expressed in, *inter alia*, Article 2, paragraph 1 of the United Nations Charter, extends to the internal waters . . . of every State and to the air space above its territory" at para 212).

89 P Birnie, A Boyle & C Redgwell, *International Law & the Environment*, 3rd ed (Oxford: Oxford University Press, 2009) at 414. See also RR Churchill & AV Lowe, *The Law of the Sea*, 3rd ed (Manchester: Manchester University Press, 1999), ch 3 [Birnie, Boyle & Redgwell].

90 Birnie, Boyle & Redgwell, *supra* note 89 at 414. The authors refer to, for example, chapter V of the *International Convention for the Safety of Life at Sea (SOLAS)* in terms of the right to devise "mandatory vessel traffic management" schemes in the territorial sea and Article 21(1)(f) of the *UNCLOS*, Article 4(3) of the 1972 *London Convention* and Article 4(2) of the 1973 *MARPOL* as sources of the coastal state's authority to prohibit pollution discharges in its territorial sea.

91 Birnie, Boyle & Redgwell, *supra* note 89 at 415.

92 *UNCLOS*, art 25.

93 Birnie, Boyle & Redgwell, *supra* note 89 at 415.

94 See e.g., the 1990 Kingston Protocol for Specially Protected Areas and Wildlife [SPAW] in the Wider Caribbean Region.

95 Birnie, Boyle & Redgwell, *supra* note 89 at 416.

96 *Ibid* at 417.

97 *Ibid.*

98 *UNCLOS*, arts 56 and 57 .

99 Birnie, Boyle & Redgwell, *supra* note 89 at 418.

100 Article 208(3) and 210(6).

101 Birnie, Boyle & Redgwell, *supra* note 89 at 419. See also König, *supra* note 78 at 4.

102 *SOLAS Convention, Regulation V/8 and V/8-1.* See J Roberts, "Protecting Sensitive Marine Environments: The Role and Application of Ships' Routing Measures" (2005) 20 Int'l J Mar & Coast L 135.

103 Birnie, Boyle & Redgwell, *supra* note 89 at 420.

104 König, *supra* note 78 at 5.

105 *Ibid.* Paragraph 2 of Article 221 defines "maritime casualty" as a "collision of vessels, stranding or other incident of navigation, or other occurrence on board a vessel or external to it resulting in material damage or imminent threat of material damage to a vessel or cargo." The exercise of these powers is however regulated by the 1969 *International Convention Relating to Intervention on the High Seas in Cases of Oil Pollution Casualties.*

106 *UNCLOS*, art 76(1).

107 EJ Molenaar, "Addressing Regulatory Gaps in High Seas Fisheries" 20 IJMCL (2005) 533 at 558.

108 *UNCLOS*, art 79(2).

109 Frank, *supra* note 2 at 19.

4

The *Fisheries Act* as an Environmental Protection Statute

A. William Moreira[1]

Introduction

Protection of the marine (in the sense of oceanic) environment in Canadian law primarily relies on the application of federal legislation; however, constitutional limitations on the scope of federal jurisdiction somewhat constrain to specific subject matters, the valid enactment and application of federal statutes.[2] One such statute is the *Fisheries Act*,[3] which predominantly deals with the regulation of the fishing industry and of the activity of fishing in waters to which it applies. Also, a portion of it (generally ss 34 to 41 inclusive) deals with the protection of fish habitat and related prohibitions against pollution.

The habitat protection provisions of the *Fisheries Act* have a long history. Language corresponding to the present s 36(1) that prohibits the "throwing overboard" of "prejudicial or deleterious substances" in "any water where fishing is carried on," which was introduced by the 1927 statutory revision,[4] but which is said to have been enacted in 1914.[5] Section 36(3) was enacted in 1970 in substantially its present form[6] while section 35(1), which was enacted in 1977, was amended in 2013.[7] This chapter provides an update regarding the long-standing use of these two sections as the primary environmental protection provisions of the *Fisheries Act* throughout the years of 2002 to 2016. For additional information regarding how the subject law has evolved since 2016, see the addendum attached to this chapter.

It must be stated at the outset that although they apply to all waters under Canadian jurisdiction, these provisions of the Fisheries Act are more frequently engaged in the context of pollution of inland (as opposed to oceanic) waters principally because oceanic pollution tends to be ship-sourced, and resulting legal proceedings are generally more efficiently conducted under other more subject-specific federal statutes that apply to shipping.

Federal Constitutional Powers

Despite the possibility of debate on whether the results would be the same under contemporary theories of cooperative federalism in Canada, the scope of federal jurisdiction to include environmental protection provisions in the *Fisheries Act* was considered. Also, for all practical purposes, this situation was considered settled in two 1980 decisions of the Supreme Court, *Fowler v. R* and *Northwest Falling Contractors v. R.*

In *Fowler v. R*[8] the accused had been prosecuted under the then section 33(3) of the *Fisheries Act*, which prohibited persons engaged in "logging, lumbering, land clearing or other operations" from putting "slash, stumps or other debris into any water frequented by fish." Briefly summarized, the unanimous court held this section *ultra vires* Parliament as a "blanket prohibition of certain types of activities, subject to provincial jurisdiction, which does not delimit the elements of the offence so as to link the prohibition to any likely harm to fisheries."[9]

With a contrary result, *Northwest Falling Contractors v. R*[10] upheld the validity of the then section 33(2), which essentially functioned the same as the present section 36(3) by prohibiting the release of a deleterious substance into water frequented by fish. A fuel pipe on a wharf had broken, spilling diesel fuel into tidal waters in a bay. The same unanimous court as in *Fowler* found the section valid as legislation in relation to "sea coast and inland fisheries" for purposes of s 91(12) of the *British North America Act*[11] (as it was then named). It stated that the power to regulate the fisheries includes the protection of the creatures that are part of them[12] and that the challenged section intended to protect fisheries by preventing substances deleterious to fish from entering waters frequented by fish. Thus, the section addresses a "proper concern of legislation under the heading Sea Coast and Inland Fisheries."[13]

In *R v. MacMillan-Bloedel Limited,*[14] the accused logging firm was charged under the then s 31 (later but no longer s 35(1)) with harmful alteration, disruption, or destruction (HADD) of fish habitat resulting from its operations on an unnamed creek inhabited by a unique species of small fish. The fish were isolated by impassable waterfalls from other watercourses, and there was, in fact, no sport or commercial fishery in the waters where the operations were conducted. The majority of the British Columbia Court of Appeal (BCCA) held that constitutionally, the *Fisheries Act* could validly apply only where a "fishery" existed, and because the alleged offence did not occur in such a place, the accused was entitled to an acquittal.

This BCCA decision was generally neither widely considered nor followed, perhaps because of its very unusual facts, and it remained uncriticized for many years. Finally, in *R v. BHP Diamonds Inc.*[15] criticism was offered by the Supreme Court of the Northwest Territories. The accused developer of a mine built a diversion channel between certain lakes and was charged with three counts under the *Fisheries Act*: two counts under s 36(3) (deleterious substance, resulting from downstream sedimentation) and one count under s 35(1) (harmful alteration of habitat, as it then was, resulting from the channel itself). The accused developer then sought to rely on *MacMillan-Bloedel* by arguing that there was no "fishery" in any of the affected lakes. The Court rejected this argument, saying that

> [53] It is this *obiter* comment [in *Northwest*] which appears to have encouraged the majority in *MacMillan Bloedel* (1984). The majority took the view that Martland J. contemplated the existence of waters with fish in them that did not constitute fisheries. I disagree that this is a reasonable interpretation of the language used by Martland J. in the judgment as a whole.
>
> ...
>
> [57] For these reasons and with respect, I am in disagreement with the narrow approach taken by the majority in *MacMillan Bloedel* (1984). In my view, the fish and fish habitat of Kodiak Lake, Little Lake and Moose Lake are afforded the protection of the federal *Fisheries Act* for the reason that they are part of the fisheries resource, a natural resource and a public resource of this country. To protect fish and fish habitat is to protect the resource (fishery).[16]

These criticisms may, however, be themselves *obiter dicta* because the court found evidence of the existence of a fishery in the watershed of which the named lakes form a part. Therefore, the "watershed is distinguishable from the small isolated stream in *MacMillan Bloedel*."[17] Furthermore, the court ultimately acquitted *BHP Diamonds* because of appropriate permitting of the works and the accused's establishing a due diligence defence.[18]

Note that in a later consideration of *BHP Diamonds*, the British Columbia Provincial Court considered itself still bound by *MacMillan-Bloedel*.[19] Both *BHP Diamonds* and *MacMillan-Bloedel* were referred to by the Ontario Superior Court in *R v. Zuber*.[20] Here, the court, without expressing any preference between the two authorities, held that the *Fisheries Act* habitat protection provisions validly apply to waters in which there are either commercial or recreational fisheries.

SECTION 35(1)—HARMFUL ALTERATION, DISRUPTION, OR DESTRUCTION OF HABITAT

From its enactment in 1977, until a significant amendment came into force in 2013, the substantive prohibition in s 35(1) read:

> 35(1) No person shall carry on any work or undertaking that results in the harmful alteration, disruption or destruction of fish habitat.

> Under the first of the so-called omnibus bills[21] that arose out of the winter 2012 federal budget, this was replaced by sections 35(1) and 2(2) as follows:

> 35(1) No person shall carry on any work, undertaking or activity that results in serious harm to fish that are part of a commercial, recreational or Aboriginal fishery, or to fish that support such a fishery.

> 2(2) For the purposes of this Act, serious harm to fish is the death of fish or any permanent alteration to, or destruction of, fish habitat.

From their enactment in 2013, these amendments persisted until these sections were once again amended in 2019.

On the face of the 2013 amendments, one might have thought that the addition of "activity" to "work or undertaking" would enlarge the scope of operations to which the section applies. Conversely, the requirement of proof that the affected fish indeed support a "commercial, recreational or Aboriginal fishery" may restrict the section's scope of application consistently with the constitutional theory in *MacMillan-Bloedel*. The requirement in the now repealed section 2(2) that there be either death of fish, or "permanent alteration" or "destruction" of habitat, might have been thought to clarify significant prior controversy in the jurisprudence over what words are qualified by the former "harmful" and in any case what degree of "harm" was required to be proved. One might reasonably have expected to await initiation of, and decisions in prosecutions under, these new provisions in order to understand their impact as environmental protection measures.

During its six-year lifespan, there were only two reported judicial decisions of prosecutions under the 2013 amended section 35(1),[22] with there being one other notation of a conviction on the federal website.[23] Perhaps, it can be speculated based on the sparse number of reported enforcement proceedings in the nearly six years since the amendment came into force that officials were in fact declining to prosecute under this section, either for policy reasons or because of perceived proof problems associated with the amended statutory language.

There are, however, published references to these amendments in contexts other than prosecutions.

Courtoreille v. Canada[24] involved an application by the Chief of Mikisew Cree First Nation for judicial review of the decision to introduce into Parliament the omnibus bill by which section 35(1) was amended, on grounds (among others) that there had not been sufficient prior consultations with affected Aboriginal peoples. Although mostly the decision involves lengthy and fascinating discussion of the distinctions between political processes and justiciable issues, the Federal Court said with specific reference to the 2013-amended section 35(1):

> [91] Hence the amendments to the *Fisheries Act* removed the protection to fish habitat from section 35(1) of that *Act*. The Applicant submitted that this amendment shifted the focus from fish habitat protection to fisheries protection which offers substantially less protection to fish habitat and the term "serious harm" permits the disruption and non-permanent alteration of habitat.
>
> . . .
>
> [93] I agree that no actual harm has been shown, but that is not the point. As the Supreme Court of Canada in *Haida Nation* at paragraph

> 5 has said, the "potential existence" of harm (in that case, the potential right as title to land, here to fishing and trapping) is sufficient to trigger the duty. I find that, on the evidence, a sufficient potential risk to the fishing and trapping rights has been shown so as to trigger the duty to consult.
>
> . . .
>
> [101] . . . In addition, for the reasons the Applicant expressed above, the amendment to s. 35(1) of the *Fisheries Act* clearly increases the risk of harm to fish. These are matters in respect of which notice should have been given to the Mikisew together with a reasonable opportunity to make submissions.

In the result, the court issued a declaratory judgment that the government should have consulted on the introduction of the bill, but in view of the enactment of the resulting legislation ordered no other remedy.[25]

Under section 35(2), which was also amended by the 2012 omnibus bill, considerable provision is made in respect of regulatory permissions for and/or ministerial permitting of works, undertakings, or activities, which when available, exclude contravention of the 2013-amended section 35(1). Substantial and very detailed guidance is provided on the website of the Department of Fisheries and Oceans[26] as to the kinds of works or activities that may be performed without the need to seek ministerial permit. As examples only, cottage docks and boathouses below a maximum size, dredging below specified maximum areas for recreational and commercial purposes, and installation of new or replacement moorings, all of which on occasion previously gave rise to prosecutions, are said not to require departmental review.

In summary, given the passage of time since the coming into force of these amendments, it may be submitted based on the lack of reported convictions and substantial reductions in scope of application, that the former HADD prohibition, once a very vigorous environmental protection element of the *Fisheries Act*, has indeed lost much of its historic effectiveness.

UPDATE ON SECTION 36(3)—DEPOSIT OF DELETERIOUS SUBSTANCES

Section 36(3), the long-standing prohibition against the deposit of deleterious substances into waters frequented by fish, was not the subject of amendment in the 2012 omnibus bill and has fully retained its utility and its frequent use in environmental protection prosecutions. Recurring case-specific issues continue to arise and be the subject of judicial decisions. For example, whether proof has been made of the deleterious quality of the particular substance or whether the accused has made out the "due diligence" defence—retain all their vigour and utility for the defence side in *Fisheries Act* prosecutions.

By way of a very brief substantive update, the following decisions are noted.

There had been some earlier inconsistent jurisprudence regarding whether it is sufficient to prove the deleterious quality of the substance itself, or whether the deleterious impact on receiving waters must be proved. It now appears to have been settled by the Ontario Court of Appeal in *R v. City of Kingston*[27] that the proof must relate to the substance alone, and not its effect in waters into which it is discharged.

In *R v. Williams Operating Corporation*,[28] a case in which the discharged substance was deemed deleterious by regulation, the court made the somewhat sweeping statement that *de minimus not curat lex* does not apply to public welfare offences or strict liability offences,[29] including environmental offences.

In *R v. MacMillan Bloedel Limited*,[30] replacement of a buried pipe was recommended because of its age but the replacement was assigned low priority by the accused because an inspection described the pipe as being in "mint condition." The pipe failed, and a deleterious substance was discharged from it not because of age but because of "microbiological corrosion." Finding unforeseeability of the actual failure mechanism, the majority of the BCCA acquitted on the basis of the first branch of the "due diligence" defence—the accused's honest and reasonable but mistaken belief in the soundness of the pipe.[31]

In *Canada (Fisheries and Oceans) v. Ontario (Ministry of Transportation)*[32] a provincial highway washout, believed to be caused by a blocked culvert, deposited debris into a nearby stream and lake. The province was prosecuted and convicted under both section 35(1) (pre-2013 amendment language) and 36(3). On appeal, it was argued that the two convictions represented double jeopardy contrary to the so-called *Kienapple*[33] principle. The court upheld both convictions, noting that section 35(1) protected habitat and section 36(3) protected water quality, and, although subtle, these differences were sufficient to exclude the argument of double jeopardy.[34]

Newfoundland Recycling Limited v. The Queen[35] is noteworthy both because it is an actual case of discharge of a deleterious substance into tidal waters and, more broadly, because it involves the increasingly serious environmental (and economic) problem of derelict ships. The accused had been engaged in 1994 to scrap an out-of-service ship and arranged for the ship to be berthed at a private wharf in Long Harbour, Newfoundland. Deconstruction of the ship proceeded sporadically but was never completed, and the remains of the ship sank at the berth in 1999 causing the discharge of oil. Ownership of the ship at all these times was unclear, but it was not alleged that the accused was the owner. The accused argued that they were under no contractual duty to care for the ship. The court considered that the principal issue was whether the appellant had sufficient "control" of the ship to have "permitted" the discharge of oil contrary to section 36(3). The Newfoundland and Labrador Supreme Court upheld the trial court's conviction based on a conclusion that the accused "had the ability to exercise control" over the ship and its "failure to make certain" that the [ship] was safe and secure at the time of the sinking "permitted the deposit" of the deleterious substance.[36]

A selective update is also offered of noteworthy sentences imposed on convictions under section 36(3), which can be found in full detail on the federal government's website.[37] Of note is the extent to which penalty amounts are directed to be paid into the federal Environmental Damages Fund.

Panther Industries Limited, the nature of whose business is not given, was ordered by the Alberta Provincial Court on July 28, 2015, to pay in total $370,000 into the Environmental Damages Fund plus a $5,000 fine resulting from a single spill of 150,000 litres of hydrochloric acid. Of this total amount payable to the Environmental Damages Fund, $170,000 was ordered on conviction under section 36(3) of the *Fisheries Act*, $150,000 on conviction of failure to respond to an environmental emergency, and $50,000 on conviction of failure to have an adequate emergency plan, the last two matters being violations of, respectively, *CEPA 1999*[38] and the *Environmental Emergency Regulations*[39] made under that Act. The note on the website asserts that this is the first conviction under the *Environmental Emergency Regulations*.

In a case of industrial pollution of tidal waters, Catalyst Paper of Powell River, British Columbia, on December 18, 2015, was directed to pay $200,000 ($15,000 in fines plus $185,000 payable to the Environmental Damages Fund) on conviction of three counts under section 36(3) of releasing untreated pulp and paper effluent on two occasions—3.5 million litres on September 4, 2012, and 100,000 litres on September 18, 2012.

Involving the same industry and somewhat similar facts, Northern Pulp Nova Scotia Corporation was, on May 13, 2016, ordered to pay $225,000 apparently related to a single count under section 36(3) arising from release from a pipeline break of 47 million litres of untreated pulp and paper effluent. The whole amount of these funds was directed to be paid to the Environmental Damages Fund for distribution (whether under court order or not is not clear) of $75,000 to each of the Mi'kmaw Conservation Group, the Pictou County Rivers Association, and Pictou Landing First Nation.

Teck Metals Ltd. was on March 4, 2016, ordered to pay $3 million in penalties on conviction of three counts under section 36(3) involving the release of 125 million litres of effluent into the Columbia River between November 28, 2013 and February 5, 2015. It appears that the whole of this amount is payable to the Environmental Damages Fund.

Demonstrating that Her Majesty prosecutes Herself, the Nova Scotia Provincial Court, on April 20, 2016, ordered the Department of National Defence to pay $100,000 for violation of section 36(3) arising from the spill of 9,000 litres of diesel oil from the naval vessel HMCS *St. John's* at Halifax Harbour on May 8, 2013. Of this amount, $98,000 was directed to the Environmental Damages Fund.

Addendum: April 2020 Update Notes

There are two substantial points on which the subject law has evolved since 2016.

SECTION 35(1)—HARMFUL ALTERATION, DISRUPTION, OR DESTRUCTION OF HABITAT

This concerns the repeal of the long-standing prohibition against HADD of fish habitat contained in section 35(1) of the *Fisheries Act* made effective November 25, 2013, and its replacement in that same section with a prohibition against work, undertaking, or activity that "results in serious harm to fish." Both of these are now changed by amendments enacted by SC 2019 c 14, in force effective August 28, 2019.

First, the former prohibition against HADD has been re-enacted as s 35(1):

> 35(1) No person shall carry on any work, undertaking or activity that results in the harmful alteration, disruption or destruction of fish habitat.

Second, the 2013 prohibition against serious harm to fish was amended though substantially re-enacted as what is now s 34.4(1):

> 34.4(1) No person shall carry on any work, undertaking or activity, other than fishing, that results in the death of fish.

Finally, by way of update on these points, there has been one reported prosecution under section 35(1) as it was between November 2013 and August 2019, in which organizers of an off-road all-terrain vehicle competition were convicted for causing the course to include an unbridged watercourse crossing.[40] Additionally, there was another prosecution under the 2013-amended section 35(1) that, despite having taken place after August 2019, regarded events that occurred while section 35(1) was still in its 2013 iteration.[41] Here, the defendants had obtained an authorization under section 35(2)(b) of the *Fisheries Act* prior to causing serious harm to fish. The issue in this case focused on whether the defendants failed to comply with the various conditions imposed by the authorization.

SECTION 36(3)—DEPOSIT OF DELETERIOUS SUBSTANCES

Prosecutions since 2016 have seen significant increases in the severity of penalty amounts. By way of supplement to the list of sentences imposed upon conviction under section 36(3) included in this chapter, the following are noted. All amounts mentioned below are totals that typically include fines plus ordered contributions to the federal Environmental Damages Fund, the latter of which are usually the larger portion. These four cases are understood to have been the judicial acceptance of joint recommendations made pursuant to "settlement" agreements between the Crown and the accused corporations.

- *R v. Canadian National Railway*,[42] Alberta Provincial Court 2017, unreported. Penalties totalled $2 million. In addition to the summary information to be found on the website of Environment and Climate Change Canada (as it is now known) there is reference to this decision in *R v. Kirby Offshore*, mentioned below.
- *R v. Montreal, Maine and Atlantic Railway*,[43] Quebec Provincial Court 2018, unreported. This was the environmental prosecution that arose from the Lac Megantic rail casualties of July 2015. The railway was fined $1 million under *Fisheries Act* section 36(3).
- *R v. Husky Oil*,[44] Saskatchewan Provincial Court, 2019, unreported. Noteworthy because convictions were entered under both the *Fisheries Act* s 36(3) and the *Migratory Birds Convention Act 1994* section 5.1(1). Total penalties were $2.5 million. This also is referred to in the *Kirby Offshore* decision.
- *R v. Kirby Offshore*.[45] Noteworthy because convictions were entered under both the *Fisheries Act* s 36(3) and the *Migratory Birds Convention Act 1994* section 5.1(1), and because prosecution for ship-source pollution was brought under these Acts and not under the *Canada Shipping Act 2001*, which prescribes lower maximum fine amounts. Total penalties were $2.9 million.

NOTES

1 A William Moreira, QC, FCIArb, Partner, Stewart McKelvey, Halifax.

2 Other federal statutes generally accepted to impose penal consequences for marine pollution include the *Canada Shipping Act, 2001*, SC 2001 c 26; the *Migratory Birds Convention Act, 1994*, SC 1994 c 22; and, in respect of the specific maritime subjects to which it applies, the *Canadian Environmental Protection Act, 1999*, SC 1999 c 33 [*CEPA 1999*].

3 *Fisheries Act*, RSC 1985 c F-14.

4 *Fisheries Act*, RSC 1927 c 73, s 44.

5 *Fisheries Act*, 1914 c 8, s 44 (according to the legislative history notation).

6 *Fisheries Act*, RSC 1970 1st Supp c 17, s 3.

7 *Fisheries Act* SC 1976-77 c 35, s 5.

8 *Fowler v R* [1980] 2 SCR 213 [Fowler]

9 *Ibid*, per Martland J at 226.

10 *Northwest Falling Contractors v R* [1980] 2 SCR 292 [*Northwest*].

11 *British North America Act*, 30&31 Vict. c 3 (UK), now named *Constitution Act, 1867.*

12 *Northwest, supra* note 10, per Martland J at 300.

13 *Ibid* at 301.

14 *R v MacMillan-Bloedel Limited*, [1984] 2 WWR 699 (BCCA) [*MacMillan-Bloedel*].

15 *R v BHP Diamonds Inc*, 2002 NWTSC 74 [*BHP Diamonds*].

16 *Ibid* at paras 53, 57.

17 *Ibid* at para 58.

18 *Ibid* at para 205.

19 *R v Sapp*, 2004 BCPC 442 [*Sapp*].

20 *R v Zuber*, 2004 CanLII 2459 (ONSC) [*Zuber*].

21 SC 2012, c 19, ss 133(4), 142(2); amendments in force November 25, 2013.

22 See *R v DP World Prince Rupert Inc*, 2019 BCPC 302 and *R v French*, 2018 ABPC 296.

23 Government of Canada, "Company Sentenced to Pay $3,500,000 for Obed Mountain Mine Spill" (12 June 2017), online: *Government of Canada* <www.canada.ca/en/environment-climate-change/services/environmental-enforcement/notifications/company-sentenced-obed-mountain-spill.html>.

24 *Courtoreille v Canada*, 2014 FC 1244.

25 *Ibid* at para 109.

26 See generally Government of Canada online: *Government of Canada* <www.dfo-mpo.gc.ca/pnw-ppe/index-eng.html> [perma.cc/UV9C-N9CC].

27 *R v City of Kingston*, 2004 CanLII 39042 (ONCA).

28 R v Williams Operating Corporation, 2008 CanLII 48148 (ONSC).

29 *Ibid* at para 86.

30 *R v MacMillan Bloedel Limited*, 2002 BCCA 510.

31 *Ibid* at para 51.

32 *Canada (Fisheries and Oceans) v Ontario (Ministry of Transportation)* 2014 ONSC 7071.

33 *Kienapple v R* [1975] 1 SCR 729 [Kienapple].

34 2014 ONSC 7071 at paras 44, 45. Note also in respect of what seems to be double jeopardy the brief notes on the "Enforcement Notifications" page of Environment and Climate Change Canada's website, *supra* note 23 to effect that Wesdome Gold Mines Limited was on 25 February 2016 separately convicted and fined in respect of violations of both the *Fisheries Act* and unspecified "provincial offences."

35 *Newfoundland Recycling Limited v The Queen* 2008 NLTD 38, leave to appeal refused 2009 NLCA 29.

36 *Ibid* at paras 34, 35.

37 *Zuber, supra* note 20.

38 *CEPA, supra* note 2.

39 *Environmental Emergency Regulations* SOR/2003-307.

40 *R v French*, 2018 ABPC 296.

41 *R v DP World Prince Rupert Inc*, 2019 BCPC 302.

42 *R v Canadian National Railway* (15 June 2017), (AB PC); Environment Canada, "Canadian National Railway Company to pay over $2.5 million in penalties for environmental offences" (16 June 2017) online: *Environment Canada* <www.ec.gc.ca/alef-ewe/default.asp?lang=En&n=BB89523C-1>.

43 *R v Montreal, Maine and Atlantic Railway* (5 February 2018), (QC PC); Government of Canada, "Company Found Guilty of Fisheries Act Violation in Lac-Mégantic Derailment Case" (9 February 2018) online: *Government of Canada* <www.canada.ca/en/environment-climate-change/services/environmental-enforcement/notifications/company-guilty-fisheries-act-violation-lac-megantic-derailment.html>.

44 *R v Husky Oil* (12 June 2019), (SK PC); Environment Canada, "Husky Oil Operations Limited Fined $2.7 Million for Federal Offences Related to the Pipeline Release of Oil into the North Saskatchewan River" (12 June 2019), online: *Government of Canada* <www.canada.ca/en/environment-climate-change/services/environmental-enforcement/notifications/husky-oil-operations-limited-fined-for-federal-offences.html>.

45 *R v Kirby Offshore*, 2019 BCPC 296.

5

Offshore Arctic Electricity Generation and Transmission Structures

Magdalena AK Muir[1]

Introduction

Offshore and coastal electricity generation and transmission infrastructures have a unique role and importance in northern Canada and the Arctic. This chapter considers electricity generation and transmission and grid infrastructure in coastal and marine zones in northern Canada and the Canadian and European Arctic, including Russia. There is a consideration of the impact of generation and transmission on northern and Arctic environments and climate adaptation and mitigation, including the potential role of the courtroom. Lastly, the chapter concludes with recommendations for strengthening and providing for more adaptive and resilience of electricity generation and transmission infrastructure in these regions.

Arctic and Northern Canadian Context

The geography, weather, development, and small populations in northern and Arctic Canada encourage decentralized energy use and generation. There is limited transmission and grid infrastructure, small urban settlements, and a few industrial mining and hydrocarbon projects with high energy requirements. Climate and other global environmental changes are making significant impacts throughout the region, with major implications for electricity generation, transmission, and infrastructure in coastal and marine regions.[2]

Industrial energy demand in these regions varies significantly with the opening and closing of remote mining and hydrocarbon operations. This industrial load has been historically satisfied by imported hydrocarbons and electricity generated by diesel. However, more efficient diesel generation, renewable energy, and alternative hydrocarbons such as natural gas, liquefied natural gas, and propane are increasingly being used or considered within industrial developments.

Other developing industries and sectors such as fisheries, foods, port and marine transport, and coastal and marine tourism require electricity generation and transmission infrastructure, and will evolve in the context of climate, global pandemics such as COVID-19, and other environmental and social changes.[3] The climate, topography, industrial development, and the small population of northern and Arctic Canada encourage a decentralized pattern of energy use with major electricity development focusing on industrial projects with overall high energy requirements and their adjacent communities. This industrial demand varies significantly with the opening and closing of remote hydrocarbon and mining operations that will be affected in the future by climatic and other environmental changes.[4]

Though the industrial load has traditionally been met by imported hydrocarbons and electricity generated by diesel, the high cost for imported hydrocarbons, the environmental implications for northern communities, and carbon emissions encourage the consideration of other options to generate electricity, with hydroelectric generation and solar energy being the preferred options.[5]

In 2014, the Standing Senate Committee on Energy, the Environment, and Natural Resources initiated a study of energy use and supply in Canada's territories. This resulted in the 2015 report entitled *Powering Canada's Territories*.[6] The report examined existing territorial energy systems and identified obstacles and opportunities facing each territory in making energy affordable, reliable, and sustainable for its residents and businesses, focusing on electricity generation and transmission.

The Standing Senate Committee on Energy, the Environment, and Natural Resources found northern electricity systems to be aging, underperforming, or functioning at capacity; that territorial communities were highly dependent on diesel generation; and that there was a lack of financial capacity by utilities and northern governments to advance major electricity generation and transmission projects due to small local rate and tax base, and territorial and local limits for borrowing.

Small remote communities predominantly rely on diesel generation. Electricity options are constrained for coastal and island communities, as these Arctic communities are far from southern electricity and natural gas grids.

A 2015 report noted that all three territories have developed energy strategies to promote and support renewable energy, increase energy efficiency, and reduce dependency on carbon-intensive fuels. In the Yukon and Northwest Territories (NWT), new opportunities for natural gas generation and biomass heating were diversifying the territorial energy mix. While coastal and island communities in the Nunavut Territory are solely reliant on diesel generation, this marine territory has some of the most abundant ocean current and tidal energy resources in the world.

Significant economic and technical challenges for Canada's northern communities include small, isolated land bases, the cost of transmission connections, and difficult environments for installation, maintenance, and repair. Finally, the 2015 report noted that all the territories have studied projects that would connect them to southern transmission systems but did not construct long-distance transmission lines as the costs were too high. For example, the Nunavut Territory explored hydroelectric projects but could not afford the costs of dams to supply Iqaluit and the Kivalliq coast. As a result, within that 2015 report, the Standing Senate Committee on Energy, the Environment, and Natural Resources suggested innovative financing, such as loan guarantees, to help the territories build these generation and transmission projects.[7]

Mining in northern Canada may actually be underdeveloped largely because of the high costs of electricity generation and transmission infrastructure. This has been referred to as Canada's largest infrastructure deficit and adds significant costs, resulting in exploration costs that may be up to six times higher than in southern Canada. Mine capital costs may be up to two and a half times more, and mine operating costs thirty to sixty percent higher. Combined, these large infrastructure costs hinder northern growth and affect competitiveness.

All mines have electrical generation and transmission challenges. For example, all six mines in the NWT and Nunavut are off-grid and require diesel power. In some cases, wind generation provides part of the energy. Due to remote locations, the costs and logistics for fuel are high in this region. There may also be carbon tax implications despite the lack of viable alternatives.[8]

Historic mines have also contributed to legacy infrastructure. Examples include Arctic communities such as Yellowknife in the NWT and Rankin Inlet in Nunavut; highways connected to mines near Yellowknife, Pine Point, and Fort Resolution in the NWT; the railway to Hay River and Pine Point; all three hydroelectric facilities in the NWT; the building and expansion of coastal and marine shipping and ports, airports and railways, microwave and internet communications.

The high cost for imported hydrocarbons and related environmental implications in northern and Arctic locations encourages the consideration of other options to generate electricity with hydroelectric, solar, or wind renewable energy being preferred options.[9]

Innovative infrastructure and renewable energy generation will continue to develop. For example, the proposed Kivalliq Hydro-Fibre Link, being developed by the Kivalliq Inuit Association and Anbaric Development Partners, is a 230KV electric system from northern Manitoba to the Kivalliq region of Nunavut that will delivery renewable energy and internet service to Nunavut communities and mines.[10]

Sustainability in northern and Arctic Canada is affected by transportation infrastructure, the reliability of the northern electrical system, alternative electricity generation, economic development, environmental protection, and adaption to climate change. Many of the challenges of northern transportation and related infrastructure will increase due to environment and climate change.

Longer-term impacts of climate change will be significant and have major impacts on operation and maintenance costs, as well as on the design and planning of capital projects with long-term infrastructure requirements.[11] These impacts and infrastructure needs have not all been determined or documented yet.

With climate change, shorter and warmer winters are accelerating permafrost degradation, which in turn affects the structural integrity of roads and increases maintenance and repair costs. Changing weather patterns also result in more freeze-and-thaw cycles, which increase damage to road and highway surfaces and maintenance and repair costs. Increased precipitation and permafrost degradation can also lead to an increase in erosion and subsidence on northern highways.[12]

Increasing navigability of Arctic marine waters is a significant issue leading to opportunities and potential challenges. For example, diminishing sea ice may allow for greater navigability, but more water traffic presents risks to coastal communities from oil and chemical spills, accidents and emergencies. There are also few docks and small ship harbours, which add to the costs of shipping, since materials and supplies must be transferred to barges or boats, moved to the beach, and off-loaded again.[13] The development of commercial fisheries in Canada's northern territories will require new and expanded ports and coastal infrastructure.[14]

Standards have a crucial role to play in addressing challenges in the electrical systems of the Canadian Arctic, which are subject to the Canadian Electrical Code.[15] The code covers a wide array of electrical systems and processes: the safety of electrical installations, the evaluation of electrical equipment or installations, power distribution and transmission circuits, industrial or institutional installations, and the inspection of electrical installation in residential buildings.

To illustrate, power quality and voltage fluctuations are more common in northern and Arctic Canada due to adverse weather conditions and wildlife interfering with transmission lines. Similarly, electrical equipment, designed and tested to operate in less extreme conditions, can be affected by deep and prolonged cold, and may perform or fail differently in extreme cold. In some cases, there may be challenges with grounding electrical systems. Safe distribution of electricity can be a challenge when overhead wiring is not feasible. Cold weather electrical applications may require specific standards, with one example being plumbing vent stacks that are heated to prevent vent freezing.

Alternative energy may assist in alleviating economic and environmental challenges resulting from heavy reliance on hydrocarbons. The reliance and use of hydrocarbons has led to a number of key economic and environmental challenges. Since almost all hydrocarbons are imported, they are costly and subject to delivery disruptions, and northern communities can face energy security challenges, as recently illustrated by Covid-19 disruption of supply chains. This reliance on hydrocarbons also has significant environmental effects, contributing to climate change and pollution, as well as adversely affecting the health of local communities and peoples.[16]

There are strong benefits in advancing the use of alternative energy sources, particularly low-impact renewable energy such as wind and solar photovoltaic technologies, since this offers energy security and diminishes adverse environmental impacts. Renewable energy options have been limited due to high installation costs, design issues, and lack of energy storage.

However, the potential for renewable energy is supported by decentralized electrical systems.

Another factor supporting other forms of renewable energy is the lack of financing among utilities and territorial governments for major hydroelectric projects. These factors make smaller scale and less capital-intensive renewable energy options more viable. Scientific research to develop smart energy systems, including combined heat and energy, and the integration of renewable generation and energy storage could be beneficial for advancing the uptake and application of renewable energy.

Biofuel and even modular nuclear reactors are being considered in Canada and elsewhere. For example, wood pellets have emerged as an alternative heating source in the NWT due to government strategies to advance biomass use. Standards have a crucial role in addressing such challenges. As will be discussed below, Russia is developing floating nuclear power plants (FNPP).

ELECTRICITY GENERATION INFRASTRUCTURE

With very limited exceptions, electricity generation along Canada's Arctic coasts and throughout Nunavut occurs through diesel facilities that may be nearing the end of their life cycle and operating at capacity. All of Canada's northern territories and Arctic coasts and islands are engaged in ongoing examination and review of electricity generation options.

For example, NT Energy's twenty-year vision for electricity supply in the NWT[17] notes a more diversified electricity generation portfolio that includes different renewable energy sources and greater grid interconnection for the Mackenzie Delta and Beaufort Sea. This is a region that already has great supply diversification in a solar installation in Fort MacPherson and in the use of natural gas, and now propane, in Inuvik. Natural gas and propane "burn more cleanly than diesel fuel and they cause less contamination and produce fewer toxic pollutants and greenhouse gas emissions that impact on the environment and climate change."[18]

The Fort Simpson Solar Energy Project is the largest solar photovoltaic array, displacing diesel generation and reducing carbon emissions. The Northwest Territories Power Corporation (NTPC) owns and operates the system, which was built by SkyFireEnergy. The $1.07 million project cost was funded by the NWT government (the departments of Environment and Natural Resources and Industry, Tourism and Investment) with the balance of the project funded by NTPC, all through the territorial government's Energy Priorities Framework. On bright days, the project generates up to 100 kilowatts, supplementing the community's use of diesel, and reducing the generation of greenhouse gases (GHG) by approximately 76 tonnes annually.[19] In contrast, Nunavut's electricity, heating, and transportation needs are currently met primarily by diesel.

Natural gas exists on Arctic islands, but is neither produced nor located close to communities. The Qulliq Energy Corporation (QEC), formerly the Nunavut Power Corporation, relies on older diesel plants to generate electricity for communities. Diesel prices vary and must be shipped thousands of kilometres by marine transport, resulting in Canada's most expensive electricity.

QEC has considered developing hydroelectricity near Iqaluit. As a result of the natural lake and the high head, a small dam at Jaynes Inlet (Qikiqgijaarvik) could create water storage. Run-of-the-river hydro projects could then be used with the dam to supply Iqaluit with year-round electricity. QEC has considered using a public-private partnership to raise the money to build the plant, and there have been suggestions to use companies with experience building dams in Greenland in order to lower construction costs. However, costs, credit, and finance access for QEC and the Nunavut territorial government remain barriers to implementation.

Nunavut has wind resources, but it has not been cost effective to extensively develop them. Windmill projects in Kugluktuk, Cambridge Bay, and Rankin Inlet produced little energy and were expensive to develop. The technology is sensitive to cold weather, requires frequent maintenance, and onsite technicians are not always available. As a result, there are high costs to maintain and repair the windmills, and power bills have not been reduced. QEC has also considered using wind power to supply heat; a project in Cape Dorset may use wind turbines to heat water and provide heat for buildings.[20]

The Canadian High Arctic Research Station, based in Cambridge Bay, uses an innovative mix of renewable energy and energy efficiency measures. One of the objectives of the station is to focus on sustainable energy research for all the northern territories.[21]

Because of the small coastal and island populations in northern Canada, there have been consistent attempts to link industrial development, particularly mining and hydrocarbons, with electricity generation facilities so that an industrial consumer could support the development of generation. Successful examples of linking industrial development and electricity generation have occurred in the Yukon and NWT mining sector but are yet to happen in Arctic coastal regions, in part due to limited offshore hydrocarbon activity and the distance between remote mining sites and Arctic communities.

COASTAL TIDAL, WIND, AND SOLAR OPPORTUNITIES IN NORTHERN AND ARCTIC CANADA

Tidal energy resources have been studied in northern Canada since 2006. Among the places identified as having the fastest tidal flows—and good potential for power generation—are the Hudson Strait in Nunavut and Ungava Bay in northern Quebec.

Quebec's theoretical potential for hydrokinetic energy has been estimated at 4,288 MW (38 terawatt-hours/year), only a portion (10 percent–15 percent) of which would be technically feasible. Over 97 percent of this Quebec resource is located near the Ungava Bay coast, a region far removed from Hydro-Québec's transmission system and major load centres in the province. There have been discussions of developing tidal power in Ungava Bay, but this is made difficult by costs, the remote location, and the fact that the bay is ice-free for only a small part of the year (approximately sixty days).[22]

SCANDINAVIAN AND RUSSIAN RENEWABLE ENERGY GENERATION

Greenland has the most similar climate, environment, and population to Nunavut, but demonstrates a more sustainable approach to energy. Greenland is switching from diesel to hydroelectricity, with funding for dams from Nordic Investment Bank, and significantly lower hydroelectric construction costs than in northern and Arctic Canada.

Alternative energy technologies are also being explored. For example, a pilot plant in Nuuk uses hydroelectricity to electrolyze water into hydrogen and oxygen. Hydrogen is then stored for conversion into electricity, and on-demand heat, in a fuel cell. Excess heat from hydrogen production and fuel cells heats Nuuk as electricity is used by buildings or enters the local transmission system.[23] Research and financing are two of the reasons for this more sustainable energy approach.

Long-term European, regional, and national funding are available for the research and implementation of sustainable energy projects in Greenland and the Scandinavian Arctic, which in turn encourages the development and implementation of pilot and full-scale projects. The Nordic Investment Bank's mandate includes sustainable energy and climate. As a result, the bank has invested extensively in sustainable energy projects in the region including offshore wind development, hydroelectric projects that substitute for diesel generation, projects to increase energy efficiency, and combined power, heat, and water projects. This funding has led to successful implementation and operation of projects, which in turn encourages investments in other projects.

Within the Russian Arctic, switching to wind- and solar-diesel-hybrid energy, instead of relying primarily on diesel sources, is being considered. Extreme climate change and unpredictable weather conditions in the Russian Arctic complicate access to remote locations. Off-grid transmission mitigates concerns about energy security risks related to long transmission lines, such as disruption. Off-grid sources supply energy to about two-thirds of Russia's territory and to more than 80 percent of the Russian Arctic.[24]

Different problems with renewable energy sources across the Russian Arctic regions must be addressed and overcome with innovative local approaches. Wind energy in the largest wind potential areas (such as Tiksi or Anadyr) must use equipment designed specifically for these regions. In places with a milder climate, wind/diesel or wind/solar-diesel units produced positive results. The only large solar energy sector in Russia so far is in the Yakutia region.[25]

Nuclear power is another option: Russia and China have agreements to build nuclear power reactors in China and are working together to develop both nuclear and wind power projects for the Arctic regions.[26] The first industrial scale wind park above the Arctic Circle will be near Murmansk, and COVID-19 has not delayed the progress of construction. RusHydro has launched a wind power plant (900-kilowatt) in the Russian Arctic (Tiksi in the Yakutia region), which is designed to become part of an integrated energy complex that includes a diesel power plant.[27]

By far the most interesting development is the Akademik Lomonosov FNPP, commissioned on May 22, 2020 for the Pevek, Chukotka region in the Russian Far East. It is the first operational FNPP to deliver electricity and heat in the Russian Arctic. It was designed by Rosatom, the Russian state-owned nuclear energy corporation, which plans to mass-produce the power plant in shipbuilding facilities and then tow them to ports near locations requiring electricity, with the objective of providing energy to remote areas in an efficient and environmentally friendly way.[28]

The FNPP, at 144 metres long and 30 metres wide with a displacement of 21,000 tonnes, consists of a reactor vessel and a floating power unit (FPU). The FPU is equipped with two KLT-40S reactor systems, similar to those used on icebreakers, each with a 35 MW capacity. Refuelling of the reactor is required every three years, and spent nuclear fuel is stored onboard. The nuclear FPU is expected to last forty years, with the potential for the life cycle to be extended an additional fifty years before decommissioning. At that point, the FPU will be towed to a special deconstruction and recycling facility, leaving no spent nuclear fuel or radioactive waste behind in the Arctic.[29]

The facility is expected to be a steady source of energy for the port city of Pevek and the entire Chukotka Autonomous Okrug, Russia. Electricity generated by the FNPP is transmitted to coastal infrastructure situated at Pevek, with the onshore system being composed of a three-phase alternating current generator, main switchgear, and standby diesel generators. The plant cannot be removed from mooring, and there is a backup system that can keep the reactor cooling for twenty-four hours without an electricity supply.

The facility has already started to produce electricity in the isolated Chaun-Bilibino network, providing energy for 100,000 people and power for oil platforms. Rosatom head Alexei Likhachev stated: "It is perhaps a small step towards sustainable development in the Arctic—but it's a giant step towards decarbonization of remote, off-grid zones and a turning point in the global development of small modular nuclear plants. Floating nuclear power plants could help supply energy to remote areas without long-term commitments and without the need for large investments into conventional power stations on mostly uninhabitable land."[30]

In 2020, the Moscow Institute of Physics and Technology announced that construction had commenced on an international Arctic research station with the purpose of exploring environmentally friendly technologies aimed at supporting and maintaining remote settlements and facilities in the Arctic region. The station will have a modular structure and rely on renewable energy and hydrogen fuel, with energy autonomy provided by solar, wind, and hydrogen energy.[31]

ELECTRICITY TRANSMISSION INFRASTRUCTURE

Currently there is no extensive electricity grid infrastructure, other than small community-based transmission systems, across any of the Canadian Arctic coasts and islands. Linking industrial development to transmission infrastructure has been considered but not realized for the NWT or Nunavut, particularly in the coastal and island regions. More expansive development of northern transmission infrastructure may occur in the near future, including linkages to northern mining development. For example, the NWT twenty-year vision for electricity supply projects the expansion and interconnection of transmission infrastructure for the Mackenzie Delta Beaufort Sea region.[32]

The Kivalliq Hydro-Fibre Link is being developed by the Kivalliq Inuit Association and Anbaric Development Partners and is a 230 kV electric system from northern Manitoba in the Kivalliq region of Nunavut that will deliver reliable renewable energy and internet service to Nunavut communities and mines. Regarding this link, Natan Obed, president of Inuit Tapiriit Kanatami has stated: "The federal government's ongoing work on the Arctic Policy Framework should include investment in telecommunications and renewable energy infrastructure to address these challenges and support infrastructure projects initiated by Inuit . . . The Manitoba-Nunavut hydroelectric power line transmission and fibre optics project would . . . create prosperity for Inuit in Nunavut that in turn benefits all Canadians."[33]

There is also the possible expansion of Hydro-Québec transmission infrastructure to Ungava Bay and the Hopes Advance iron mine project near Ungava Bay. The Hopes Advance iron mine would initially self-generate electricity using diesel from 2018 to 2025. After 2025, the mine is scheduled to be connected to the Hydro-Québec transmission system, as transmission expands to that region.[34]

A Greenlandic study[35] released in November 2015 suggests Greenland could generate enough hydroelectricity to supply its own needs and export excess power to Nunavut through an eight-hundred-kilometre submarine transmission line.[36] This study is part of a larger North Atlantic Energy Network (NAEN) proposed to link Iceland, the Shetland Islands of Scotland, Greenland, and Canada.

Greenland now supplies hydroelectricity to six of its towns, including the capital Nuuk, from five hydroelectric plants.[37] Greenland has studied hydroelectric generation potential since 1976 and, although potentially viable, NAEN suggests that more detailed studies are needed to determine if developing more hydro power might be economically feasible in the future.[38] Greenland still hopes to attain up to 90 percent of its electricity from hydroelectric dams by 2030.[39]

OTHER CIRCUM-ARCTIC RENEWABLE ENERGY GENERATION AND TRANSMISSION

The Longyearbyen coal-fired power plant is Norway's only coal-fired plant, consuming 22,000 tons of locally produced coal, and producing approximately 50,000 tons of greenhouse gas emissions annually. To replace the existing coal-based electricity generation, transmission lines linking Svalbard Island with the coast of northern Norway are being contemplated.

A transmission line could provide wholly renewable energy and integrated wind supply, and support other innovations such as electric cars and boats. Svalbard already has the necessary expertise because of an existing submarine fibre optic cable linking the island to the mainland. However, the costs for the long-distance submarine transmission line are estimated to be between 323 to 539 million euros.[40]

Further submarine transmission lines have been proposed by NAEN between Greenland, Iceland, the Faroe Islands (Denmark), and Norway.[41]

Arctic Fibre is a three-phase submarine cable project, planned to connect Asia, Canada, and Europe through the Arctic Ocean. Phase 1–Alaska is a 2,250 km submarine fiber optic cable main trunk line between Nome and Prudhoe Bay. Phase 2–Asia plans to extend the backbone cable from the Nome branching unit west to Asia, with options for additional branches into Alaska. Phase 2 will thus create an option for a diverse path out of the United States to Asia. Phase 3–Canada-United Kingdom is intended to extend the subsea system east of Prudhoe Bay, the Alaska branching unit, along the lower Northwest Passage to Canada and continuing to the United Kingdom. Phase 3 will connect to northern Canadian communities and will provide a secure low transmission route from Europe to Asia, and a diverse route option out of North America to Europe.[42]

The Phase 1–Alaska was launched for service in early December 2017.[43] Quintillion Subsea Holdings LLC (Quintillion) acquired the assets of Arctic Fibre in May 2016.[44] Arctic Fibre was the third private sector company trying to bring fibre optic to Nunavut. However, the development of fibre optic broadband projects in the Arctic may require government help, as vast geography and small markets make it challenging for private sector initiatives.

More global and far-reaching transmission systems have also been proposed. For example, in 2015, the Chinese State Grid Corp. introduced the proposed Global Energy Interconnection (GEI), which envisions the Arctic as a source of renewable energy and proposes a global transmission infrastructure that includes the Canadian Arctic.[45] The *Wall Street Journal* has also profiled this initiative, which is breathtaking in its scope.[46]

The Global Energy Interconnection Development and Cooperation Organization (GEIDCO) is an international organization set up and tasked to promote the establishment of the GEI system, to meet the global demand for electricity in a clean and green way, to implement the United Nations "Sustainable Energy for All" and climate change initiatives, and to serve the sustainable development of humanity.[47]

An interconnecting subsea cable between Iceland and neighboring European countries has been discussed for decades. However, it is only recently that advancements in technology have made it a realistic option to connect Iceland with other European countries with such a cable. In 2010 the Icelandic electricity company Landsvirkjun started a new study to evaluate the feasibility of a high voltage direct current (HVDC) cable between Iceland and Europe, which would be the world's longest submarine HVDC power cable. The study addresses issues like potential business models, markets, and congestion management. The cable would be at least 1,000 km in length, which is almost double the length of the longest existing subsea HVDC cable today: the NorNed interconnector between Norway and the Netherlands. If the cable extended from Iceland all the way to the European continent (instead of only to Scotland) its length would be around 1,900 km. The maximum depth under the ocean would be about 1,000 m and the transmission capacity would probably be between 600 and 1,000 MW.[48]

The HVDC cable that will provide for the transmission of hydroelectricity from Norway and offshore wind energy from the United Kingdom between the two countries is proceeding.[49]

The Russia-Japan Energy Bridge was expected to start in 2020 but has not yet begun.[50] With a value of approximately 6 billion US dollars, the power plant, in the central part of Sakhalin, will have a capacity of up to 1050 MW generated by coal, and may be joined by a hydropower plant and direct current power line to La Perouse Strait, followed by a submarine power line to Japan.[51]

Similarly, construction on the Russia-North Korea Power Bridge (Primorye-Rosan), a project valued at approximately 3 billion US dollars, was expected to start in 2022. Although few details are known, the bridge would supply electricity from Primorye (Russia) to Rason (North Korea), and connect where the borders of North Korea, China, and Russia intersect.[52]

Interestingly, Emrod, a New Zealand company, has proposed to use wireless systems to transmit power between any two points that can be joined with line-of-sight relays (potentially thousands of kilometres apart). The system uses a transmitting antenna, a series of relays, and a receiving rectenna—the beams use the non-ionizing industrial, scientific and medical band of the radio spectrum (including frequencies used on Wi-Fi and Bluetooth). This ensures higher safety, and works in any atmospheric conditions, including rain, fog, and in the presence of dust. A prototype has been built by Powerco, New Zealand's second largest electricity distribution company, which will be the first to pilot this Emrod technology.[53]

Northern Infrastructure Standardization Initiative

Standards are important for the future development of electricity generation and transmission infrastructure in northern and Arctic Canada.[54] The Northern Infrastructure Standardization Initiative (NISI) is designed to build a "climate-resilient" future with northern standards. Northern and Arctic Canada is highly vulnerable to climate change and is impacted by changing temperatures and precipitation patterns, permafrost degradation, and coastal erosion. Since 2011, the Standards Council of Canada (SCC) has been working with communities, standards development organizations, and experts to develop standards that consider climate change impacts on northern infrastructure design, planning, and management. NISI standards will help building owners and operators, and public and community infrastructure operators to build and maintain infrastructure in a changing climate. Some aspects of CSA standards addressing permafrost, extreme weather, and climate changes are discussed below.[55]

CSA S500:14 (R2019): Thermosyphon Foundations for Buildings in Permafrost Regions

This standard "provides requirements for all life-cycle phases of thermosyphon foundations for new buildings on permafrost," (i.e. site characterization, design, installation, commissioning phases, and monitoring and maintenance phases). The objective is "to ensure the long-term performance of thermosyphon-supported foundation systems under changing environmental conditions."[56]

CSA S501:14 (R2019): Moderating the Effects of Permafrost Degradation on Existing Building Foundations

Since permafrost degradation can cause damage to buildings or structures constructed on permafrost, this standard lays out the steps that should be undertaken to moderate the effects of permafrost degradation on existing buildings or structures including ports, roads, infrastructure, and coastal facilities.[57]

CSA Plus 4011:19: Technical Guide: Infrastructure in Permafrost: A Guideline for Climate Change Adaptation and CSA Plus 4011.1:19: Technical Guide: Design and Construction Considerations for Foundations in Permafrost Regions

The standards are intended for individuals who have a role in planning, purchasing, developing, or operating community infrastructure in permafrost regions; and are intended to inform decision makers of the impacts of climate change on permafrost when considering new community infrastructure.[58]

CSA W205:19: Erosion and Sedimentation Management for Northern Community Infrastructure

This "applies to the management of erosion and sedimentation risks, including the evaluation, planning, design, implementation, monitoring, and maintenance of erosion and sedimentation risk management strategies and mitigation measures" for infrastructure.[59]

CSA S505:20: Techniques for Considering High Winds and Snow Drifting and their Impact on Northern Infrastructure

This particular standard "addresses risks to northern infrastructure due to wind, snow, and snow drifting."[60]

CSA 2501–500: Geotechnical Site Investigations for Building Foundations in Permafrost Zones

Finally, this standard addresses the design of building foundations with consideration to the prevailing conditions at building sites.[61]

Environmental Considerations Including the Role of the Courtroom

As electricity generation in the Canadian Arctic coasts and islands is still predominantly diesel, there are many adverse existing environmental aspects, including pollution, particulate matter, and GHG emissions. Any transition to less carbon-intensive hydrocarbons, such as natural gas and natural gas liquids, or hybrid diesel renewable energy systems, is likely to be environmentally and socially beneficial. Therefore, there is a positive environmental benefit for this transition and change.

In contrast, the expansion of the existing limited community-based transmission systems to more extensive transmission systems, high voltage long distance transmission systems, or submarine transmission systems, could potentially have adverse environmental implications. Some of these environmental implications are consistent with terrestrial and submarine transmission systems elsewhere,[62] while other environmental implications are specific to Arctic coasts and islands.

There are northern and Arctic-specific environmental implications for transmission lines, whether coastal or submarine, such as impacts on permafrost, ground stability, coastal erosion and ice scour, and the need to modify more southern construction techniques.

For example, like pipelines, these transmission lines and related structures might need to be insulated or cooled to avoid melting permafrost. For facilities located on river channels or coasts, such as in the Mackenzie Delta Beaufort Sea region, additional factors such as river ice break-up, ice jam flooding, coastal erosion, and sea-level rise would need to be considered.

For transmission lines and structures, changes in the ground thermal regime, drainage and terrain stability, all of which may result from a warming climate over the lifetime of such a transmission, must be considered.

There is also the need to closely monitor the performance of the transmission line and right-of-way to maintain line integrity and minimize environmental impact, which in the context of northern and Arctic communities may have to occur remotely, or by satellite-based monitoring.

The use of ice roads and all-season roads needs to be considered in relation to the construction, maintenance, and monitoring of transmission systems. Reductions in ice thickness associated with climate warming reduce the maximum loads that can be safely transported. Initially, modifications in ice-road construction could function as an effective adaptation. Over time, as ice roads become impractical, there will be a need to provide alternative transportation. If there is a navigable river, increased use of barge transport might be possible. Construction of all-weather roads may be an option, but these are more costly to build and maintain compared to winter roads and have greater environmental impacts and implications.

There are unique legal structures and processes, including co-management regimes under Canada's northern and Arctic comprehensive land claims agreements, which incorporate environmental measures and mitigation and which include the participation of local communities within their mandates, processes, and structures.[63]

Though the courtroom is not entirely excluded, many of the environmental and social issues in relation to electricity generation and transmission may initially and primarily be considered under these legal structures and processes.

As the electricity generation and transmission lines expand, or are linked to significant hydrocarbon or mining developments, fisheries, tourism, or settlements, there may be greater potential for communication, engagement, and dispute resolution to reach an agreement or address gaps or inadequacies for these structures and processes.[64]

Conclusion

The chapter has discussed existing and proposed electricity generation and transmission for Canada's northern and Arctic coasts and islands. It has also briefly explored near-future and distant-future opportunities and innovations that may affect this region and the European and Russian Arctic. This entire circum-Arctic region is promising for climate adaptation and mitigation, future investment, policy development, and public-private partnerships for electricity generation and transmission projects.

NOTES

1 Magdalena AK Muir, BA, JD, LLM is a researcher affiliated with the Energy Management Program of the Haskayne School of Business at the University of Calgary and Research Associate of the Arctic Institute of North America since 1991. She has been a researcher and professor at Aarhus University, Aarhus, Denmark; Columbia University, New York City; John Hopkins University, Washington, DC; the University of Delaware, Wilmington, Delaware, and the University of London. She collaborates with the United Nations Department of Economics and Social Affairs at the United Nations Headquarters in New York City on implementation of the United Nations Sustainable Development Goals. She conducts research on Arctic infrastructure; carbon sequestration and trading; climate impacts, scenarios, and adaptation; renewable energy; sustainable energy, heat and water applications; and sustainable fisheries, wildlife, tourism, and natural resource uses. Further information at <arctic.ucalgary.ca/research-associate-magdalena-muir> and <www.researchgate.net/profile/Magdalena_Muir>.

2 Canada, Natural Resources Canada, *Canada's Marine Coasts in a Changing Climate* (Ottawa: Natural Resources Canada, 2016), online: *Government of Canada* <www.nrcan.gc.ca/climate-change/impacts-adaptations/what-adaptation/canadas-marine-coasts-changing-climate/18388>.

3 Magdalena AK Muir, "Future Scenarios for the Arctic Ocean and Implications for Arctic High Seas Regulation, Ecosystems and IUU Fishing" (Paper delivered at the 10th International Forum on Illegal, Unreported and Unregulated Fishing, London, UK, 16–17 March 2017) [unpublished]; Arctic Monitoring and Assessment Programme, *Adaptation Actions for a Changing Arctic: Perspectives from the Bering-Chukchi-Beaufort Region* (Oslo: Arctic Monitoring and Assessment Programme [AMAP], 2017); Magdalena AK Muir & Sami Areikat, "Utilizing Global Sustainable Tourism Council Criteria and Green Destinations Standards to Achieve Sustainable Development for Caribbean and Pacific Islands during COVID-19" (Paper delivered at the International Conference on Sustainable Development 2020, New York City, NY, 21–22 September 2020); Magdalena AK Muir, "Role of Energy and Water Systems, and Renewable Energy and Aquifer Management for Food Security" (Paper delivered at the International Institute of Sustainable Development's Water Innovation Centre and Global Water System Project Conference on Water–Energy–Food Security Conference in Winnipeg, 1–4 May 2012) [unpublished]; Magdalena AK Muir, "Illegal, Unreported and Unregulated Fishing in the Circumpolar Arctic" (2010) 63:3 Arctic 373; Magdalena AK Muir, "Inuit Rights, Traditional Knowledge, Northern Land Claims and Implications for Offshore Development and Air and Marine Transport in Canadian Arctic" (Paper delivered at the International Arctic Offshore Conference, Arctic Research Centre, Aarhus University, Denmark, 27–28 November 2014) [unpublished]; Sima Zerehi, "10 Nations Gather in Iqaluit for Arctic Fisheries Negotiations", *CBC News* (6 June 2016), online:<www.cbc.ca/news/canada/north/%20arctic-fisheries-international-meeting-iqaluit-1.3666217> [perma.cc/N2CC-ZX5B]; Sima Zerehi, "Nunavut Fisheries Casting a Net for Federal Infrastructure Money", *CBC News* (25 March 2016), online: <www.cbc.ca/news/canada/north/%20nunavut-fisheries-federal-budget-1.3506668> [perma.cc/Q52C-3JBL].

4 Tristan Pearce et al, "Climate Change and Mining in Canada: Mitigation and Adaptation Strategies for Global Change" (2011) 16:3 Mitigation and Adaptation Strategies for Global Change, online: <www.researchgate.net/publication/229032096_Climate_change_and_mining_in_Canada>.

5 Magdalena AK Muir, "Integrating Renewable Energy, Heat, and Water Quality and Quantity in Sustainable Energy and Water Projects for the Circum-Arctic and Northern and Remote Regions of Canada" (Paper delivered at QUEST International Conference, Arctic Institute of North America, Winnipeg, November 2012), online (pdf): <arctic.ucalgary.ca/sites/default/files/Nov-2012-MAKMuir-QUESTInternationalConference-Paper.pdf> [perma.cc/H7TH-6QE6] [Muir, "Integrating Renewable Energy"]; Canadian Polar Commission, "Energy in the Canadian North: Recent Advances and Remaining Knowledge Gaps and Research Opportunities" (31 March 2014), online: *Canadian Polar Commission* <www.polarcom.gc.ca/sites/default/files/energy_summary.pdf> [perma.cc/5NBQ-XZZR] [Canadian Polar Commission]; Canadian Northern Economic Development Agency, *Northern Economic Index* (Ottawa: Canadian Northern Economic Development Agency, 2016), online: *Government of Canada* <www.cannor.gc.ca/eng/1387900596709/1387900617810> [perma.cc/WB68-9PL9]; National Research Council & the Canadian Chamber of

Commerce, *Developing the Economic Potential of Canada's Territories* (Ottawa: the Canadian Chamber of Commerce, 2012).

6 Standing Senate Committee on Energy, the Environment, and Natural Resources, *Powering Canada's Territories* (2015), online: <sencanada.ca/Content/SEN/Committee/412/enev/rep/rep14jun15-e.pdf> [perma.cc/2NGG-KXLA]; Canadian Polar Commission, *supra* note 5.

7 *Ibid.*

8 NWT & Nunavut Chamber of Mines (2019), online: *NWT & Nunavut Chamber of Mines* <www.miningnorth.com/>; NWT & Nunavut *Chamber of Mines Levelling the Playing Field: Supporting Mineral Exploration and Mining in Remote and Northern Canada* (April 2015), online (pdf): *NWT & Nunavut Chamber of Mines* <www.miningnorth.com/_rsc/site-content/library/publications/Levelling_the_Playing_Field_-_Final.pdf> [perma.cc/8PNG-2ZAR].

9 Muir, "Integrating Renewable Energy," *supra* note 5; see Yereth Rosen, "Across Arctic North America, Solar Energy Is Gaining a Foothold", *Arctic Today* (4 September 2020), online: <www.arctictoday.com/across-arctic-north-america-solar-energy-is-gaining-a-foothold/>; Kevin McGwin, "Arctic Europe Shows that Remoteness Doesn't Have to Hinder Renewable Energy Growth", *Arctic Today* (8 September 2020), online: <www.arctictoday.com/arctic-europe-shows-that-remoteness-doesnt-have-to-hinder-renewable-energy-growth/>; Yereth Rosen, "A Simmering Aleutian Volcano Could Provide the Breakthrough Geothermal Energy Project Alaska Has Been Waiting for", *Arctic Today* (9 September 2020), online: <www.arctictoday.com/a-simmering-aleutian-volcano-could-provide-the-breakthrough-geothermal-energy-project-alaska-has-been-waiting-for/>; Yereth Rosen, "Alaska's Experience Shows Benefits—and Challenges—of Wind Energy in the Arctic", *Arctic Today* (16 September 2020), online: <www.arctictoday.com/alaskas-experience-shows-benefits-and-challenges-of-wind-energy-in-the-arctic/>; Kevin McGwin, "Wind Energy Conflicts Show How Arctic Renewable Energy Projects Can Founder", *Arctic Today* (23 September 2020), online: <www.arctictoday.com/wind-energy-conflicts-show-how-arctic-renewable-energy-projects-can-founder/>; Melody Schreiber, "How Energy Storage Can Be the Key to Developing Renewable Energy in Remote Arctic Communities", *Arctic Today* (30 September 2020), online: <www.arctictoday.com/how-energy-storage-can-be-the-key-to-developing-renewable-energy-in-remote-arctic-communities/>.

10 Kivalliq Hydro-Fibre Link, "An Empowering Plan for Canada's North", online: *Kivalliq Hydro-Fibre Link* <www.kivalliqlink.ca/about> [perma.cc/R3AB-FTPC] ["An Empowering Plan"].

11 Government of Northwest Territories, "7.3 Trends in Shipping in the Northwest Passage and the Beaufort Sea" *NWT State of the Environment Report* (Yellowknife: Environment & Natural Resources, 29 May 2015), online: www.enr.gov.nt.ca/en/state-environment/73-trends-shipping-northwest-passage-and-beaufort-sea [perma.cc/LT3R-XG25]; "Arctic Response Technology—Oil Spill Preparedness Joint Industry Programme" (2018), online: *International Association of Oil and Gas Producers* <www.arcticresponsetechnology.org> [perma.cc/9XWT-65N8]; Council of Canadian Academies, "Commercial Marine Shipping Accidents: Understanding the Risks in Canada, Workshop Report" (Ottawa: Council of Canadian Academies, 28 April 2016), online: *Council of Canadian Academies*, <cca-reports.ca/reports/commercial-marine-shipping-accidents-understanding-the-risks-in-canada/> [perma.cc/CG8X-ZAZU]; Kayle Hatt, "Isolated Communities and Inadequate Airstrips: The Challenges

of Airport Infrastructure in Northern Canada" (2016) 3:2, online: *Northern Public Affairs* <www.northernpublicaffairs.ca/index/volume-3-issue-2-building-new-partnerships/isolated-communities-and-inadequate-airstrips-the-challenges-of-airport-infrastructure-in-northern-canada/> [perma.cc/W555-7WEY]; Sima Sahar Zerehi, "Wind, Solar Energy Real Options for Canada's Remote Arctic Communities" *CBC News* (17 September 2016), online: <www.cbc.ca/news/ canada/north/wind-solar-energy-arctic-1.3766381> [perma.cc/H48F-544K]; Chris Windeyer, "The Slow Fight for Renewable Energy in Canada's North" *Open Canada* (4 January 2016), online: *OpenCanada* <www.opencanada.org/features/slow-fight-renewable-energy-canadas-north/> [perma.cc/JB5W-GZCJ]; Standing Senate Committee on Energy, the Environment, and Natural Resources, *supra* note 6; C Waters & R Didsbury, "Small Modular Reactors—A Solution for Canada's North?" (2012) 1:2 AECL Nuclear Review 3, online: <pubs.cnl.ca/doi/pdf/10.12943/ANR.2012.00012>.

12 Canadian Standards Association Group, "Canada's North—Discovering How Standards Can Contribute to Safety, Sustainability & Economic Growth" (Toronto: Canadian Standards Association Group, September 2017) at 46, online (pdf): *Canadian Standards Association Group* <www.csagroup.org/wp-content/uploads/CSA_Group_Canada_North_Research_Paper_EN.pdf> [perma.cc/L57H-9777] [Canadian Standards Association Group].

13 *Ibid.*

14 Territory of Nunavut, Government of Nunavut, Department of Environment, *Nunavut Fisheries Strategy 2016 to 2020* (Iqaluit: Department of Environment, Fisheries and Sealing Division, 2016).

15 *Canadian Electrical Code*, CSA C22.1-98.

16 Canadian Standards Association Group, *supra* note 12.

17 NT Energy, *A Vision for the NWT Power System Plan* (Hay River, NT: NT Energy, December 2013), online: <www.ntpc.com/docs/default-source/default-document-library/psp-december-10_2013.pdf?sfvrsn=0> [perma.cc/22HH-SWK7] [NT Energy Report].

18 Natural Resources Canada "Natural Gas for Transportation" (19 December 2018) online: *Government of Canada* <www.nrcan.gc.ca/energy-efficiency/transportation-alternative-fuels/alternative-fuels/natural-gas-for-transportation/3525>; Natural Resources Canada "Propane" (19 December 2018) online: *Government of Canada* <www.nrcan.gc.ca/energy-efficiency/transportation-alternative-fuels/alternative-fuels/propane/21611>.

19 "Fort Simpson Solar Energy Project," online: *NTPC* <www.ntpc.com/energy-alternatives/current-alternative-energy-projects/fort-simpson-solar-energy-project> [perma.cc/3RL6-MXUR]; Muir, "Integrating Renewable Energy," *supra* note 5.

20 "QEC Energy Framework: The Cost of Generating Electricity in Nunavut" (March 21, 2018), online (pdf): *Qulliq Energy Corporation* and <www.qec.nu.ca/sites/default/files/qec_energy_framework_-_generation_-_april_18_eng.pdf> [perma.cc/X79C-3HLT]; Qulliq Energy Corporation "Renewable Energy," online: *Qulliq Energy Corporation* <www.qec.nu.ca/power-nunavut/renewable-energy> [perma.cc/AW8D-DLUY].

21 Government of Canada, "Welcome to the Canadian High Arctic Research Station Campus" (2019), online: *Government of Canada* <www.canada.ca/en/polar-knowledge/CHARScampus.html> [perma.cc/WH2F-Y52X].

22 Hydro-Québec, *A Renewable Energy Option: Hydrokinetic Power* (Montreal: Hydro-Québec, 2015), online (pdf): <www.hydroquebec.com/data/developpement-durable/pdf/file-hydrokinetic.pdf> [perma.cc/WV63-QKB4].

23 Climate Greenland, "Hydropower" (last visited 5 December 2021), online: *Climate Greenland* <climategreenland.gl/en/municipality/efforts-to-reduce/hydropower/>.

24 Anatole Boute, "Off-Grid Renewable Energy in Remote Arctic Areas: An Analysis of the Russian Far East" (2016) 59 Renewable and Sustainable Energy Reviews 1029, online: <www.sciencedirect.com/science/article/abs/pii/S1364032116000642>.

25 VKh Berdin et al, "Renewable Energy in Off-grid Settlements in the Russian Arctic" (2017), online (pdf): *World Wildlife Fund* <eic-ano.ru/en/publications/articles/_download/renewable_russian_arctic.pdf> [perma.cc/VG6N-RHM9]; Dmitry Solovyev, Maria Morgunova & Alexander Solovyev, "Creating a Synergy: Renewable Energy to Develop the Russian Arctic" in Valeriy Kharchenko & Pandian Vasant, eds, *Renewable Energy and Power Supply Challenges for Rural Regions* (United States: IGI Global, 2019) at 138; The Northern Forum, "Alternative Energy in Yakutia" (10 October 2017) online: *The Northern Forum* <www.northernforum.org/en/news/303-alternative-energy-in-yakutia>.

26 Tsvetana Paraskova, "China Interested in Arctic Nuclear, Wind Cooperation with Russia" (7 October 2019), online: *Oilprice* <oilprice.com/Latest-Energy-News/World-News/China-Interested-In-Arctic-Nuclear-Wind-Cooperation-With-Russia.html> [perma.cc/T9TT-KZ57].

27 Deutsche Welle, "Russian Wind Power Blows Hot and Cold", *Deutsche Welle* (25 April 2019), online: <amp.dw.com/en/russian-wind-power-blows-hot-and-cold/a-48452677> [perma.cc/TF9Z-P49B]; Charles Digges, "Coronavirus Hasn't Slowed Construction Progress at Russia's Arctic Wind Farm", *Bellona* (11 June 2020), online: <bellona.org/news/arctic/2020-06-coronavirus-hasnt-slowed-construction-progress-russias-arctic-wind-farm> [perma.cc/2CJZ-QACV].

28 Thomas Nilsen, "The Reactors Aboard a Power Plant Bound for Russia's Arctic Have Been Tested to Full Capacity", *Arctic Today* (26 April 2019), online: <www.arctictoday.com/the-reactors-aboard-a-power-plant-bound-for-russias-arctic-have-been-tested-to-full-capacity/> [perma.cc/QGX3-D8SE].

29 Akademik Lomonosov, floating nuclear power plant website at <www.fnpp.info/>.

30 NS Energy, "Akademik Lomonosov Floating Nuclear Power Plant," online: *NS Energy* <www.nsenergybusiness.com/projects/akademik-lomonosov-floating-npp/> [perma.cc/D9VM-SNQK]; Anmar Frangoul, "A Floating Nuclear Power Plant Has Started to Produce Electricity in a Remote Region of Russia", *CNBC* (20 December 2019), online: <www.cnbc.com/2019/12/20/floating-nuclear-plant-produces-electricity-in-remote-russian-region.html> [perma.cc/NL79-MLHK]; Agence France-Presse, "Russia's Floating Nuclear Power Plant Completes Arctic Transfer, Reaches Pevek Port" *Tech2* (16 September 2019), online: *Firstpost* <www.firstpost.com/tech/science/russias-floating-nuclear-power-plant-completes-arctic-transfer-reaches-pevek-port-7346551.html> [perma.cc/KN3L-2TT7]; Mary Ilyushina, "Russia Plans to Tow a Nuclear Power Station to the Arctic: Critics Dub It a 'Floating Chernobyl'", *CNN* (30 June 2019), online: <www.cnn.com/2019/06/28/europe/russia-arctic-floating-nuclear-power-station-intl/index.html> [perma.cc/48MY-G7SU].

31 Philip Gordon, "Russia Announces New Renewables-Powered Arctic Research Station" (20 February 2020), online: *Smart Energy International* <www.smart-energy.com/renewable-energy/russia-announces-new-renewables-powered-arctic-research-

station/>[perma.cc/XD4F-UAAM]; Atle Staalesen, "In Swaggering Move on Remote Arctic Tundra, Russia Intends to Show Off a Life without Oil", *The Barents Observer* (30 January 2020), online: <thebarentsobserver.com/en/arctic/2020/01/swaggering-move-remote-arctic-tundra-russia-intends-show-life-without-oil> [perma.cc/SLL4-T3AF].

32 NT Energy Report, *supra* note 17 at 31, 59–65.

33 "An Empowering Plan," *supra* note 10; "Memorandum: Government of Canada Support for Electric Transmission and Fibreoptic Development in Nunavut's Kivalliq Region to Standing Committee on Finance of the Government of Canada" (Kivalliq Inuit Association & Anbaric Development Partners, 3 August 2018), online (pdf): <www.ourcommons.ca/Content/Committee/421/FINA/Brief/BR10006859/br-external/KivalliqInuitAssociation-e.pdf> [perma.cc/W3LW-3LSE].

34 Oceanic Iron Ore Corp, Investor Presentation (April 2020), online (pdf): *Oceanic Iron Ore Corp* <oceanicironore.com/_resources/presentations/Corporate-Presentation.pdf> [perma.cc/R6LH-PEMR].

35 Arne Villumsen, "North Atlantic Energy Network Greenland" (Greenland Innovation Centre, November 2015), online: <www.scribd.com/document/295501482/NAEN-Greenland-2016#download&from_embed> [perma.cc/WRS2-9FC5].

36 Brian Pehora, "Greenland to Nunavut Electricity Exports? It Just Might Be Possible: Study Finds Undersea Transmission Cable Could Supply Hydro-electricity to Iqaluit", *Nunatsiaq News* (14 January 2016), online: <nunatsiaq.com/stories/article/65674greenland_to_nunavut_hydro_exports_it_just_might_be_possible/> [perma.cc/R7YG-CLLB].

37 Government of Greenland, "Existing Hydroelectric Power Plants in Greenland," online: *Government of Greenland* <www.businessingreenland.gl/en/Erhverv/Vandkraft/Eksisterende-vandkraftvaerker> [perma.cc/X8Z4-LJLK].

38 Arne Villumsen, "Appendix B North Atlantic Energy Network Greenland" (November 2015), online: *Greenland Innovation Centre* <www.scribd.com/document/295501482/NAEN-Greenland-2016> at 3, 32–33; Brian Pehora, "Greenland to Nunavut Electricity Exports? It Just Might Be Possible", *Nunatsiaq News* (14 January 2016), online: <nunatsiaq.com/stories/article/65674greenland_to_nunavut_hydro_exports_it_just_might_be_possible/>.

39 See Kevin McGwin, "As Greenland Seeks to Diversify its Economy, Water Is Shaping Up as a Key Element", *Nunatsiaq News* (27 January 2020), online: <nunatsiaq.com/stories/article/as-greenland-seeks-to-diversify-its-economy-water-is-shaping-up-as-a-key-element/> [perma.cc/X4W4-JUMH]; World Wildlife Fund, "Renewable Energy across the Arctic: Greenland Report" (July 2017), online (pdf): <awsassets.wwfdk.panda.org/downloads/Greenland_RenewableEnergyAcrossTheArctic_July_2017.pdf> [perma.cc/E9BB-GWJL].

40 Thomas Nilsen, "Svalbard Could Turn from Dirty Coal to Zero Emission Power Supply", *The Barents Observer* (23 August 2016), online: <thebarentsobserver.com/en/arctic/2016/08/svalbard-could-turn-dirty-coal-zero-emission-power-supply#:~:text=Photo%3A%20Thomas%20Nilsen-,Svalbard%20could%20turn%20from%20dirty%20coal%20to%20zero%20emission%20power,Russian%20settlements%20on%20the%20archipelago> [perma.cc/Y86B-UW2G].

41 Engerati, "Steps towards a North Atlantic Energy Network" (19 July 2016), online: *Engerati* <www.engerati.com/article/steps-towards-north-atlantic-energy-network> [perma.cc/X7PA-MD7W].

42 Submarine Cable Networks, "Arctic Fiber", online: *Submarine Cable Networks* <www.submarinenetworks.com/en/systems/asia-europe-africa/arctic-fiber>.

43 Winston Qiu, "Quintillion Activated Arctic Subsea Cable" (13 December 2017), online: *Submarine Cable Networks* <www.submarinenetworks.com/en/systems/asia-europe-africa/arctic-fiber/quintillion-activates-arctic-subsea-cable>.

44 Winston Qiu, "Arctic Fibre Acquired by Quintillion Networks" (22 May 2016), online: *Submarine Cable Networks* <www.submarinenetworks.com/en/systems/asia-europe-africa/arctic-fiber/arctic-fibre-acquired-by-quintillion-networks>.

45 State Grid Corporation of China, "2016 International Conference on Global Energy Interconnection Opens in Beijing" (30 March 2016), online: <m.geidco.org/pcarticle/1475>.

46 Brian Spegele, "China's State Grid Envisions Global Wind-and-Sun Power Network", *Wall Street Journal* (30 March 2016), online: <www.wsj.com/articles/chinas-state-grid-envisions-global-wind-and-sun-power-network1459348941> [perma.cc/ALR2-DUVY].

47 "Connectivity Initiatives around the World: Global Energy Interconnection," online: *Global Infrastructure Connectivity Alliance* <www.gica.global/initiative/global-energy-interconnection-development-and-cooperation-organization-geidco> [perma.cc/5Z6E-RGQM].

48 "HVDC Subsea Link," online: *ASKJA Energy: The Independent Icelandic and Northern Energy Portal* <askjaenergy.com/transmission/hvdc-subsea-link/> [perma.cc/NWW3-RVEL].

49 "Full Power Ahead for UK to Norway Under-sea Power Cable", *BBC News* (3 October 2021) online: <www.bbc.com/news/uk-england-tyne-58772572>.

50 James Crompton, "10 Major Transmission & Distribution Projects in 2019 and Beyond" (26 June 2019), online: *Fircroft* <www.fircroft.com/blogs/10-major-transmission-and-distribution-projects-in-2019-and-beyond-91772616236> [perma.cc/4HB8-UYVB] [Crompton].

51 "Skoltech Starts Preliminary Feasibility Study of Russia-Japan Energy Bridge" (26 July 2016), online: *Skoltech, Center for Energy Science and Technology* <crei.skoltech.ru/cest/2016/07/26/skoltech-starts-preliminary-feasibility-study-of-russia-japan-energy-bridge/>.

52 Crompton, *supra* note 50.

53 Loz Blain, "NZ to Trial World-First Commercial Long-Range, Wireless Power Transmission" (3 August 2020), online: *New Atlas* <newatlas.com/energy/long-range-wireless-power-transmission-new-zealand-emrod/> [perma.cc/38RD-F7AV]; Off Grid Energy Independence, "NZ Launches World-First Long Range Wireless Power Transmission" (11 August 2020), online: *Off Grid Energy Independence* <www.offgridenergyindependence.com/articles/21390/nz-launches-world-first-long-range-wireless-power-transmission> [perma.cc/5LXP-ZL8V].

54 Joanne Warren & Joseph Haimowitz, *Economic Value of Standards* (Ottawa: The Conference Board of Canada, 2007), online: <www.iso.org/sites/materials/benefits-of-standards/benefits-detailf767.html?emid=8>; International Organization for Standards, "Economic Benefits of Standards Volume 1" (2011), online (pdf): <www.iso.org/files/live/sites/isoorg/files/archive/pdf/en/pub100288.pdf>.

55 Standards Council of Canada, "Northern Infrastructure Standardization Initiative" (2019), online: *Standards Council of Canada* <www.scc.ca/en/nisi>; National Round Table on the Environment and Economy, "True North: Adapting Infrastructure to Climate Change in Northern Canada" (26 November 2009), online (pdf): <nrt-trn.ca/

wp-content/uploads/2011/08/true-north-eng.pdf>; National Research Council, The Canadian Chamber of Commerce, *National Building Code of Canada* (Ottawa: The Canadian Chamber of Commerce, 2015), online: *Government of Canada* <nrc.canada.ca/en/certifications-evaluations-standards/codes-canada/codes-canada-publications/national-building-code-canada-2015>; Heather Auld et al, "The Changing Climate and National Building Codes and Standards" (Paper delivered at the Ninth Symposium on the Urban Environment, Keystone, CO, 1–6 August 2010), online: <ams.confex.com/ams/19Ag19BLT9Urban/webprogram/9URBAN.html>; Canada Mortgage and Housing Corporation, "Design and Construction of the Northern Sustainable House—Inuvik, Northwest Territories" (2018), online: *Canada Mortgage and Housing Corporation* <www.cmhc-schl.gc.ca/en/data-and-research/publications-and-reports/design-and-construction-of-the-northern-sustainable-house-inuvik-northwest-territories>.

56 Standards Council of Canada, *CSA S500:14 (R2019): Thermosyphon Foundations for Buildings in Permafrost Regions* (Toronto: CSA Group, 2014), online: <store.csagroup.org/ccrz__ProductDetails?viewState=DetailView&cartID=&portalUser=&store=&cclcl=en_US&sku=CAN%2FCSA-S500-14>.

57 Standards Council of Canada, *CSA S501:14 (R2019): Moderating the Effects of Permafrost Degradation on Existing Building Foundations* (Toronto: CSA Group, 2014), online: <store.csagroup.org/ccrz__ProductDetails?viewState=DetailView&cartID=&portalUser=&store=&cclcl=en_US&sku=CAN%2FCSA-S501-14>.

58 Standards Council of Canada, *CSA Plus 4011:19: Technical Guide: Infrastructure in Permafrost: A Guideline for Climate Change Adaptation* (Toronto: CSA Group, 2019), online: <store.csagroup.org/ccrz__ProductDetails?viewState=DetailView&cartID=&portalUser=&store=&cclcl=en_US&sku=2703076> and Standards Council of Canada, *CSA Plus 4011.1:19: Technical Guide: Design and Construction Considerations for Foundations in Permafrost Regions* (Toronto: CSA Group, 2019), online: <store.csagroup.org/ccrz__ProductDetails?viewState=DetailView&cartID=&portalUser=&store=&cclcl=en_US&sku=CSA%20PLUS%204011.1%3A19>.

59 Standards Council of Canada, *CSA W205:19: Erosion and Sedimentation Management for Northern Community Infrastructure* (Toronto: CSA Group, 2019), online: <store.csagroup.org/ccrz__ProductDetails?viewState=DetailView&cartID=&portalUser=&store=&cclcl=en_US&sku=CSA%20W205%3A19>.

60 Standards Council of Canada, *CSA S505:20: Techniques for Considering High Winds and Snow Drifting and Their Impact on Northern Infrastructure* (Toronto: CSA Group, 2020), online: <store.csagroup.org/ccrz__ProductDetails?viewState=DetailView&cartID=&portalUser=&store=&cclcl=en_US&sku=CSA%20S505%3A20>.

61 Standards Council of Canada, *BNQ 2501-500: Geotechnical Site Investigations for Building Foundations in Permafrost Zones* (Toronto: CSA Group, 2017), online: <www.bnq.qc.ca/en/standardization/civil-engineering-and-urban-infrastructure/geotechnical-site-investigation-for-building-foundations-in-permafrost-zones.html> [perma.cc/FTQ7-N9FB].

62 Magdalena AK Muir, "Social Acceptance and Development of the North Sea Offshore Grid" (2013) 4:2 RELP 143.

63 Magdalena AK Muir, "First Nation/Government Resource Management Regimes: Emerging Models of Joint Management and Public Government for the Northwest Territories" *Environmental Law in the North American Context* (Montreal: Canadian Bar Association, 1996) 2; Magdalena AK Muir, *Comprehensive Land Claims Agreements for the Northwest Territories: Implications for Land and Water Management* (Calgary: Arctic Institute of North America and Canadian Institute of Resources Law, 1994); Magdalena AK Muir, "Impact of Existing and Proposed Aboriginal Claims Agreements on Environmental Review in the Northwest Territories" (1991) 1 J ELP 283.

64 Magdalena AK Muir, "Future Scenarios for the Arctic Ocean and Implications for Arctic High Seas Regulation, Ecosystems and IUU Fishing" (Paper delivered at the 10th International Forum on Illegal, Unreported and Unregulated Fishing, London, UK, 16–17 March 2017) [unpublished]; Arctic Monitoring and Assessment Programme, *Adaptation Actions for a Changing Arctic: Perspectives from the Bering-Chukchi-Beaufort Region* (Oslo: Arctic Monitoring and Assessment Programme [AMAP], 2017); Magdalena AK Muir & Sami Areikat, "Utilizing Global Sustainable Tourism Council Criteria and Green Destinations Standards to Achieve Sustainable Development for Arctic, Caribbean and Pacific Islands during COVID-19" (Paper delivered at the International Conference on Sustainable Development 2020, New York City, NY, 20–22 September 2020); Charles J Vörösmarty et al, *Motivating Research on the Science Communications Front: Conveying the Nature and Impacts of Rapid Change in Ice-Dominated Earth Systems to Decision Makers and the Public* (Washington: National Science Foundation & World Bank Workshop, 2014); Magdalena AK Muir, "Arctic Resource Development and Climate Impacts, Adaptation and Mitigation Project: Initial Summary of Climate Impacts and Adaptation for Energy, Mining and Infrastructure in Canada's North" (2012), online (pdf): *Arctic Institute of North America* <arctic.ucalgary.ca/sites/default/files/December-2012-MAKMuir-ArcticResourceDevelopment-ClimateImpactsAdaptation.pdf> [perma.cc/Q72Z-68JC].

6

Braiding Together Indigenous and Canadian Legal Traditions for Fisheries Management: Recent Pacific Coast Experience

Linda Nowlan,[1] *Alexander Kirby,*[2] *Georgia Lloyd-Smith,*[3] *and Doug Neasloss*[4]

Introduction

In the past two centuries, the Canadian state has attempted to take control of fisheries through the imposition of Canadian fisheries laws on Indigenous peoples. By depriving them of control over fisheries, Canadian fisheries law ignored Indigenous laws and imposed its own, in a system that has often put economic imperatives before fisheries conservation.

This chapter discusses how Indigenous and Canadian legal traditions might be braided together to uphold the inherent authority of Indigenous laws and achieve better conservation of fish and other marine species. It examines three recent cases in which Indigenous nations successfully implemented conservation decisions based on their legal traditions, across the Pacific north and central coast and Haida Gwaii. Emerging out of these cases, this chapter will posit three new legal principles, which together could constitute the possible foundations of a new and more equitable relationship between Canadian and Indigenous legal traditions: the "duty to conserve," the "right to conserve," and the "power to conserve."

Numerous statutory and policy responses lie ready at hand for willing state governments. Comprehensive legislation, mandating a new relationship between Canadian and Indigenous legal traditions, remains perhaps the fastest and most effective means of effecting change in this area. Additional Canadian statutory and policy responses include expansion of the direct authority to enforce Indigenous law under the *Fisheries Act*, the use of joint decision-making for fisheries, and recognition of the enforcement authority of Indigenous guardians.

The benefits of braiding together Indigenous, Canadian, and international law are manifold. Collaborating with Indigenous nations as equal partners in marine conservation is an important step in beginning to heal the linked political and ecological harms caused by centuries of colonialism.

The Context

Canadian law has regulated fisheries and protected fish habitats since the early days of Confederation. Indigenous peoples have governed their territories, including managing fisheries according to their laws, for millennia. Despite two centuries of repression and deliberate attempts to erase them, these long-standing Indigenous legal traditions continue to "survive under layers of state regulation."[5] Today, many Indigenous nations are engaged in revitalizing their distinct Indigenous legal traditions. The Canadian government has been slow to recognize Indigenous laws and to begin the process of reconciling its asserted jurisdiction over fisheries with existing Indigenous jurisdiction. With Canada's full support for the *United Nations Declaration on the Rights of Indigenous Peoples* (UNDRIP)[6] and the enactment of the *United Nations Declaration on the Rights of Indigenous Peoples Act* (the *UNDRIP Act*),[7] the need to give effect to Indigenous peoples' laws has gained momentum, particularly in Canadian adjudicative processes.[8]

The precarious health of the global oceans and fisheries, documented by numerous recent studies, is a strong warning about this approach to fisheries conservation.[9] British Columbia's experience with a broad range of declining fisheries echoes this warning.[10] The time is ripe for a new approach that upholds, instead of ignores, Indigenous legal traditions.

In thinking about the relationship between Indigenous and Canadian legal traditions, we take guidance from a recent report, "UNDRIP Implementation: Braiding International, Domestic and Indigenous Laws" from the Centre for International Governance Innovation.[11] The following excerpt is particularly instructive:

> A braid is a single object consisting of many fibres and separate strands; it does not gain its strength from any single fibre that runs its entire length, but from the many fibres woven together. Imagining a process of braiding together strands of constitutional, international and Indigenous law allows one to see the possibilities of reconciliation from different angles and perspectives, and thereby to begin to reimagine what a nation-to-nation relationship justly encompassing these different legal traditions might mean.[12]

The implementation of the UNDRIP and the Canadian constitution requires the reconciliation of legal traditions. At the same time, the braiding together of Indigenous and Canadian legal traditions has the potential to lead to better fisheries and fish habitats management, by grounding decisions at a more local level with those who know the resource best. As Canadian law increasingly fails to achieve even its modest conservation objectives, Indigenous legal traditions offer an ethic rooted in thousands of years of successful stewardship. In the cases examined in this chapter, the application of contemporary Indigenous laws led to better conservation outcomes.[13]

This chapter will explore possible means of upholding Indigenous fisheries laws without relying on the courts. Numerous statutory and policy responses lie ready at hand for willing state governments.

Comprehensive legislation, mandating a new relationship between Canadian and Indigenous legal traditions, remains perhaps the fastest and most effective means of effecting change in this area.[14] This chapter will focus on additional Canadian statutory and policy responses, including an expansion of the direct authority to enforce Indigenous law under the *Fisheries Act*, the use of joint decision-making for fisheries, and recognition of the enforcement authority of Indigenous guardians.

The legal authors of this paper are non-Indigenous, Canadian-trained lawyers without extensive training in the three Indigenous legal traditions discussed in this paper. For this reason, the case studies presented do not engage in a meaningful way with the substantive Indigenous legal principles and decision-making processes used to inform the fisheries management decisions. This chapter is unevenly weighted in its focus on possible legal responses in Canadian law to uphold Indigenous legal traditions. We acknowledge this as a limitation of our work. By focusing primarily on Canadian law in this analysis, we do not mean to undermine the legitimacy or importance of Indigenous legal traditions. It reflects our training and orientation, and we acknowledge our duty to learn as we continue to decolonize our practice.[15]

To be clear, the authority of Indigenous nations to protect and steward their traditional territories does not depend on recognition from the Crown for its existence and legitimacy. Indigenous nations will continue to uphold their laws, regardless of Canada's response. Increased recognition of Indigenous law and jurisdiction, however, would help unlock this wealth of willingness, knowledge, and ability. Recognition is not a liability for the Canadian state, but an opportunity—both to remake its relationship with Indigenous peoples and protect the oceans in a time of unprecedented environmental upheaval.

Background and Legal Framework

THE FOUNDATIONS OF FISHERIES LAW: INDIGENOUS LEGAL TRADITIONS AND THEIR MARGINALIZATION IN CANADIAN LAW

"There is no single Act in the whole of Canada that raises more problems between authorities and Indian people than the *Fisheries Act*."[16]

Before colonial settlers arrived, Indigenous nations were governing their territories, including their fisheries, according to their distinct legal traditions.[17] Conflicts over fisheries management and conservation involving Indigenous nations[18] began soon after colonial settlers arrived and persist today. For over a hundred and fifty years, Canadian laws have ignored Indigenous laws, restricted Indigenous nations' access to their fisheries, and limited fisheries rights to bare subsistence alone. The Canadian state forced Canadian fisheries laws upon Indigenous peoples. The state viewed these laws as the only law of Canada. Indigenous peoples who chose to abide by the Canadian law faced discrimination, as many were unable to obtain commercial fishing licences.[19]

Indigenous nations managed fisheries according to their legal traditions along the Pacific coast long before either the province of British Columbia or any Canadian fisheries laws came into being. Despite the stubborn refusal of the Canadian authorities to recognize Indigenous laws, the historical record documents numerous stories and examples of these laws.[20] Despite systemic attempts by the Crown to destroy them, many of these laws, including deciding who can catch fish, at what locations and in what quantity, continue to be practiced today.

The laws of the three nations discussed in this chapter continue to guide their fisheries management.[21] As Doug Neasloss, the current elected chief of Kitasoo/Xai'xais[22] explains, "The Kitasoo/Xai'xais and their neighbours have been making and enforcing fisheries management decisions for thousands of years."[23] The same can be said for the Haida and the Heiltsuk who continue to govern their territories under their distinct laws.

The imposition of Canadian law attempted to replace these localized systems of fisheries and fish habitats management with a centralized, authoritarian model, designed to benefit white settlers. While the centralized Canadian system uses licences and leases to allocate the fishery, local Indigenous law determines ownership through familial and clan ties, until ". . . the wealth of the fishery became apparent to non-Natives, [when] the state replaced the local with the central, the specific with the general, and reallocated the fisheries in the process."[24]

The federal *Fisheries Act*, the main law used to make these changes, came into effect in British Columbia on July 1, 1877. Through a series of regulatory changes, Canadian law restricted First Nations fisheries by imposing novel legal requirements: requiring permission for fishing of any kind, requiring a fishing licence for any non-food fish capture, specifying the types of gear that could be used, the places that could be fished, and the times when fishing could take place. By 1894, the Dominion had assumed control of the entire salmon fishery. The legal capture of the resource was complete.[25]

The Supreme Court of Canada summarized this history of the regulation of fisheries in British Columbia in *Jack v. The Queen*:

> The federal Regulations became increasingly strict in regard to the Indian fishery over time, as first the commercial fishery developed and then sport fishing became common. What we can see is an increasing subjection of the Indian fishery to regulatory control. First, the regulation of the use of drift nets, then the restriction of fishing to food purposes, then the requirement of permission from the Inspector and, ultimately, in 1917, the power to regulate even food fishing by means of conditions attached to the permit.[26]

Two stories from different parts of the province demonstrate the vastly different ways Indigenous peoples and colonial settlers perceived fisheries law. The imposition of licences and in particular licence fees, were contrary to many Indigenous peoples' ways of thinking about who was allowed to fish.

In 1888, Guardian McNab met with the Nisga'a attempting to enforce the newly enacted fisheries licence fee. In a telling meeting, a Nisga'a chief informed Guardian McNab that the Dominion of Canada was violating Nisga'a law as the Nisga'a owned the Nass River and the fish, and any fees collected should come to them:

> . . . [T]he chief very gravely informed me that I had done very wrong in collecting money for fishing on the Nass, without having asked permission from him, that the river belonged to him and his people, that it was right that the white men should buy licences, but that he and his people should receive the money, that they were entitled to it all; but that as I had been sent to collect it, they were willing that I should retain half for my trouble.[27]

Another story comes from Naxaxalhts'i, Albert (Sonny) McHalsie of the Stó:lō Nation:

> Ownership of fishing grounds is through family. But then you wonder, why do people look at ownership as individual then? What happened there? And then I started to understand, well, back in the late 1800s the Fisheries Act was created and all these different laws were made that didn't allow our people to sell fish any more. They said that only saltwater fish could be sold and that it is illegal to sell anything caught in freshwater. So, they took away our economy and, not only that, they wanted to start regulating our fishing. So, they imposed fishing permits on our people. What's on the fishing permit? It doesn't talk about the extended family or family ownership. The *Department of Fisheries and Oceans didn't take into consideration the fact that we had our own rules and our own regulations about who has access to fishing grounds and who fishes where. We have our own protocols and our own laws.* Instead, they imposed a fishing permit that had an individual's name on it. And it said that individual could fish from such and such place to such and such place. So, it's almost as though it is wide open: you can fish anywhere in there. So right away they ignored our own laws and protocols of where to fish. It took the

all-encompassing perspective of ownership of fishing grounds—our wide perspective of it—and narrowed it to an individual perspective. So that a lot of our fishers now, up in the canyon, look at their fishing spot as their own. I've heard some of them say, "It's mine and only mine." And "No one else can fish here, not my brothers, not my sister, not my mom or my dad. That is my spot." I couldn't believe it when I heard one of the fishers say that. That's how some of the fishers think. So, they have to change that again. [emphasis added][28]

These stories highlight how the imposition of Canadian law on these nations marginalized their legal traditions in a way that is difficult to justify on either legal or moral grounds.

THE FOUNDATIONS OF FISHERIES LAW: CONSERVATION AND THE "INDIAN" FISHERY

In the late nineteenth and early twentieth centuries, the Canadian state enforced a new system of "scientific" laws based on European understandings of the biological world that ignored Indigenous systems of knowledge and law.

It is in this context that the idea of "conservation" first emerged as the dominant principle of Canadian fisheries management, an idea that continues to govern its political and legal discourse to this day. Indeed, the "paramount regulatory objective" of the Department of Fisheries and Oceans (DFO) is conservation.[29]

In theory, Canadian and Indigenous laws may share a central concern for the "conservation" of marine animals, habitats, and ecosystems. The apparent simplicity and objectivity of this idea, however, belies a sharply contested meaning. What does it mean to practice effective conservation? What are the roles of individuals in stewarding the land and waters? What is an acceptable level of risk to marine species and ecosystems? How do we even know what kinds of risks certain activities will entail? How should economic interests be balanced against these risks? Canadian and Indigenous legal orders can and do answer these questions very differently. A key question is which laws will be applied and who gets to decide?

Indigenous peoples practiced effective conservation for thousands of years prior to the advent of the European settler state. By depriving them of control over fisheries, Canadian fisheries law ignored Indigenous conceptions of conservation and stewardship. Instead, it imposed its own based on biological science and capitalist imperatives of economic growth. For the previous one hundred and fifty years, the state assumed responsibility for what marine conservation means in Canada.

The fact remains, of course, that Indigenous peoples continue to rely on fisheries for sustenance. To reconcile the presence of Indigenous people to this new regime of Canadian science and law, the Canadian state turned to a new legal and political construct—the "Indian fishery." The Indian fishery was a policy designed to accommodate Indigenous interests in fish while transferring "all management of this crucial food and commercial resource . . . to the state."[30]

This new fishery worked by drawing a harsh and artificial line between fishing for food and fishing for commerce. Insofar as Indigenous people wished to continue fishing for their sustenance, it was their right to do so. Insofar as they wished to participate in trade, their activities would, however, be subject to the full regulatory apparatus of the state, which operated largely to marginalize and exclude them.

Professor Diane Newell identifies two major discontinuities to which this artificial division gave rise. First, it separated harvesting for food from harvesting for cultural, social, or economic purposes, a distinction unknown in most Indigenous societies; and second, it severed the connection between the control and the exploitation of marine resources.[31]

These two discontinuities were essential to the colonial project of subjugation and subordination. By limiting Indigenous claims to the fishery to subsistence alone, the "Indian fishery" ensured these claims would be self-limiting, predictable, and amenable to state control. In this way, Indigenous claims could be comfortably integrated within the new colonial model of state conservation and control. The sustenance requirements of Indigenous peoples would constitute yet another predictable variable among many to be considered in allocating the fishery. At the same time, by severing actual control of fisheries from the mere exploitation of them, the new "Indian fishery" ensured that power remained firmly in the hands of the state.

This model continues to structure the relationship between Indigenous nations and the Canadian state with regard to marine conservation. While Indigenous nations continue to practice their laws and exercise their inherent authority when it comes to fisheries management, the state continues to ignore them and forge ahead with its centralized system.

SPARROW, VAN DER PEET, AND THE CONSTITUTIONALIZATION OF ABORIGINAL RIGHTS

Aboriginal rights are the modern analogue of the "Indian fishery." These rights assumed their modern form in 1982, with the repatriation of the Canadian constitution. Section 35 of the new *Constitution Act* extended constitutional protection to "existing aboriginal and treaty rights of the aboriginal peoples in Canada."[32] In other words, recognition of Aboriginal rights became a foundational principle of the nation's constitutional order.

The expansion and growth of judicial interpretation of Aboriginal rights under Canada's new constitutional order must be understood against the persistence of the stubborn patterns of exclusion and subordination that characterized the invention of the "Indian fishery" in the previous century. The constitutionalization of Aboriginal rights has, so far, failed to transform the essential character of the "Indian fishery" as an instrument of colonial policy and subordination.

In *R v. Sparrow*, a ground-breaking fishing rights case from 1990, and the first interpretation of section 35 by Canada's highest court, the Supreme Court of Canada recognized a constitutionally protected Aboriginal right to fish for the first time for the Musqueam people. Even as it did so, *Sparrow* also outlined several circumstances that would constitute legitimate regulation of an Aboriginal constitutional right.[33] Foremost among these was "conservation."[34] A recognized Aboriginal right to fish would entitle Indigenous people to fish at certain times and in certain ways prohibited to other individuals. The ultimate message of *Sparrow* was clear, however: control of the resource itself would remain in the hands of the Canadian state.

Despite their constitutionalization, Aboriginal rights under *Sparrow* remained much the same colonial construct as they had prior. Section 35 of the constitution merely entrenched Aboriginal entitlement to a share in the fishery. It did not affect the state's ultimate control over these resources. Indeed, Aboriginal fishing rights only became relevant after the state had already decided how to conserve fisheries.

A subsequent trilogy of fishing cases elaborated on the nature and limitations of Aboriginal rights. In the British Columbia case of *Van der Peet* released in 1996, the court explored the origins of these rights. Aboriginal people enjoy constitutional protection; the court explained, "because of one simple fact: when Europeans arrived in North America, [A]boriginal peoples were already here, living in communities on the land, and participating in distinctive cultures, as they had done for centuries."[35] The purpose of the "special legal and constitutional status of [A]boriginal peoples" was to reconcile "pre-existing [A]boriginal rights with the assertion of Crown sovereignty."

As it gave with one hand, however, the *Van der Peet* decision took with the other. Despite its apparent embrace of Aboriginal rights, *Van der Peet* placed strict limitations on the recognition of these rights in Canadian courts. Not only did it preserve the old distinctions between food and commercial fisheries, *Van der Peet* also held that every Aboriginal right must be rooted in "a practice, custom or tradition integral to the distinctive culture of the [A]boriginal group claiming the right" at the time of first contact.[36]

Henceforth, the central question governing the recognition of contemporary Aboriginal rights would be whatever the court deemed "*was, once upon a time, of central significance to 'Indians.'*"[37] As John Borrows has observed, the *Van der Peet* test turned lawyers and judges into "amateur historians," embarking on elaborate inquiries into the "essence" of Indigenous cultures at the time of first contact.[38]

Unsurprisingly, the *Van der Peet* test has met with extensive criticism.[39] No one knows precisely what it means for a practice to be "integral," nor what it is that makes a culture truly "distinctive." In addition to the challenge of demonstrating this elusive cultural essence, the test imposes the historical and evidentiary burden of proving it on Indigenous nations hundreds of years after the fact.

Van der Peet and *Sparrow* remain leading authorities on Aboriginal rights in Canada. The present state of Aboriginal fishing rights is typical of both the limitations and the possibilities of Aboriginal rights under these decisions. On the one hand, Aboriginal fishing rights are among the most commonly proven Aboriginal rights in Canada. Indigenous nations have undoubtedly benefited from the improved access to fisheries such rights have facilitated over the past two decades as they may also include commercial fishing rights. On the other hand, under the *Van der Peet* test, these rights have been interpreted as narrowly as possible, mainly to continue to preclude the possibility of substantial Indigenous control over Canadian fisheries.

Professor Sarah Hamill proposes that the key to the 1996 *Van der Peet* trilogy "is not so much the question of what the law is, but who gets access to what resources and under what law."[40] These cases, in other words, are about control over the fisheries—a control the Canadian state is reluctant to relinquish, despite its constitutional obligations to Indigenous peoples.

Even as they purport to offer greater recognition to Indigenous peoples, these cases demonstrate the continuing refusal of the Canadian state to return substantial control to Indigenous peoples over their traditional territories. Arguably, Aboriginal rights remain instruments of colonial subjugation and control, even to this day.

Three Recent Pacific Fisheries Cases

As Canadian law continues to grapple with the question of Aboriginal rights, Indigenous legal traditions are undergoing a revitalization of their own. As Indigenous legal traditions achieve wider recognition, the artificial distinction between the use of marine resources and their management, allocation, and conservation is becoming increasingly untenable. The time is ripe for a new conception of Aboriginal rights in Canada—one which embraces the right not merely to a larger share of resources, but to substantial control over how these resources are managed, allocated, and conserved as defined under distinct Indigenous legal traditions.

Despite the reluctance of the courts to embrace the authority of Indigenous law, such recognition is arguably consistent with the principles of the common law. As Justice McLachlin (as she then was) wrote in her dissent in *R v. Van der Peet*:

> The history of the interface of Europeans and the common law with aboriginal peoples is a long one. As might be expected of such a long history, the principles by which the interface has been governed have not always been consistently applied. Yet running through this history, from its earliest beginnings to the present time is a golden thread—the recognition by the common law of the ancestral laws and customs of the aboriginal peoples who occupied the land prior to European settlement.[41]

Although the majority of the court declined to embrace this principle, there are signs of change in the air. The three cases discussed below illustrate three ways in which Indigenous peoples have successfully asserted and implemented their laws in recent years. The first two cases involve commercial herring openings in the Central Coast and Haida Gwaii over a three-year period, and the third concerns crab fishery closures on the central coast.

Three distinct legal principles emerge out of these examples, which together, we suggest, point the way to a new conception of the respective roles of Canadian and Indigenous law in marine conservation. These are:

1. The duty to conserve: a constitutional duty on the part of the Crown to manage marine resources sustainably;
2. The right to conserve: the right of Indigenous peoples to make decisions about how the resources of their traditional territory are managed, allocated, and conserved using their laws;
3. The power to conserve: the ability of Indigenous peoples to enforce their laws effectively.

Conservation must be understood through perspectives of both western laws and Indigenous laws. At present, these concepts of the duty, right, and power to conserve have received varying degrees of legal recognition under Canadian law. However, Indigenous peoples have already demonstrated their transformative potential by taking action both within and outside the legal system to put them into practice. A conception of "Aboriginal rights" recognized by Canadian courts, which encompasses these three principles, could transform such rights from instruments of colonial policy to an effective means of decolonizing marine conservation by braiding together Indigenous and Canadian legal traditions.

THE DUTY TO CONSERVE: HAIDA HERRING DECLARATION, INJUNCTION, AND CO-MANAGEMENT 2015

The first of these principles, the duty to conserve, is the closest to achieving outright recognition in the Canadian legal system. The duty to conserve refers to the emerging legal principle that the Crown has a constitutional responsibility to protect certain resources, including marine species. In practice, the existence of this duty provides a means for Indigenous nations to challenge and overturn government decisions about the management, allocation, and conservation of marine resources. This, in turn, can open a space for Indigenous law and knowledge to play a recognized role in marine conservation.

The assertion of Aboriginal fishing rights underlies the duty to conserve. This duty is a logical extension of such rights. An Aboriginal right to fish presupposes the existence of fish to harvest.[42] If the Crown makes decisions that threaten the long-term viability of species that are the subject of these rights, the Crown has effectively violated the rights themselves.

The first case study comes from Haida Gwaii. It exemplifies the potential of this novel duty as a means of challenging the authority of the Canadian state over fisheries management and conservation decisions.

In 2015, the Haida Nation sought and won an injunction prohibiting the DFO from opening the Haida Gwaii herring fishery, after many years of closure.[43] This case is one of several cases in recent years where Indigenous peoples have used Aboriginal rights to challenge DFO decision-making based on their assessment of necessary conservation measures.[44] Drawing on traditional knowledge, including oral accounts attesting to the decline of the herring fishery from its former abundance,[45] the Haida successfully overturned the DFO's decision to open the herring fishery in the face of clear evidence of the vulnerability of herring stocks.

Herring is central to Haida culture, traditions, and way of life. Yet herring stocks have declined precipitously over the last century. Traditional knowledge from Haida Gwaii demonstrates the true extent of the decline. One Haida elder spoke in an interview of "great big herring the size of humps," but it is very rare today to find herring as big as a 2–3 lb pink, or hump, salmon.[46] The accounts of other elders corroborate this picture, which describes the roaring of sea lions and the sound of the herring flipping at night. The decline in herring populations is also reflected in Haida place names, which highlight locations of formerly abundant herring, but where few herring are found today (e.g. Ch'axa'y or "Sizzling [with herring] Water").[47] This decline alarms the Haida and many other Indigenous nations who rely on this food. The last roe herring fishery in the Haida Gwaii stock area was in 2002. The last commercial spawn-on-kelp fishery in this area occurred in 2004.

The Haida challenge emerged from the decision of DFO in 2014 to open the Haida Gwaii herring fishery after more than a decade of sporadic closures.[48] When DFO again proposed reopening the Haida Gwaii herring fishery in 2015, the Council of the Haida Nation (CHN) alerted DFO of their intention to seek court action. When DFO did not respond, the CHN sought an injunction on the basis that the herring stock was too vulnerable to sustain an opening, that the DFO had failed to consult them adequately, and that there was no long-term plan to rebuild the herring population. In these circumstances, allowing the opening to proceed would cause irreparable harm, necessitating the intervention of the court.

The court sided with the Haida. The Federal Court confirmed the Nation's ability to challenge and overturn the Crown's decision to open a fishery. The judge found that the failure to consult meaningfully and the unilateral imposition of "a highly questionable opening" of the fishery constituted irreparable harm.[49] The court drew upon the "long-term co-management relationship between Canada and the Haida Nation in Gwaii Haanas" and concluded that there was "a heightened duty for DFO and the Minister to accommodate the Haida Nation in negotiating and determining the roe herring fishery in Haida Gwaii, given the existing Gwaii Haanas Agreement, the unique Haida Gwaii marine conservation area, the ecological concerns, and the duty to foster reconciliation with and protection of the constitutional rights of the Haida Nation."[50] The judge also cited the decline in herring population and the high level of uncertainty in the population forecast. He found that "Canada's unilateral implementation of the roe herring fishery in Haida Gwaii for 2015 compromises, rather than encourages, the mandated reconciliation process."[51] The president of the Haida Nation celebrated the court decision in a press release, which noted Haida law: "Our laws bid us to address issues with yahgudaang (respect for all things) and not just from an economic perspective. This win is another step to building herring stocks, and in doing so, contributes to an economy that will provide a reasonable living for our people, and the path of reconciliation with Canada."[52]

In December 2015, the DFO announced that there would be no 2016 commercial herring fishery in Haida Gwaii waters.

The Haida approached this challenge from a position of relative strength. The Supreme Court of Canada had found more than a decade prior to this judgment that the Haida have a strong case for Aboriginal title to both terrestrial and marine Haida territory.[53] Haida Gwaii's unique co-management bodies and pre-existing agreements with the Crown also strengthened their legal position regarding herring. Nevertheless, the Haida decision confirmed that the Crown has a legally enforceable responsibility to practice effective conservation.

This responsibility, in turn, points to a greater role for Indigenous law in making decisions about marine conservation. The judge in *Haida* specifically cited the "need for a better and independent science review of the herring stocks, the lack of inclusive decision-making . . . respect for local First Nations insights, and a willingness to build a collaborative understanding of the state of the herring in the shared ecosystem" without, however, referring specifically to Indigenous law.[54]

With legal precedents already established, recognition of a duty to conserve on the part of the Crown has already opened the possibility, if not the legal necessity, for greater Indigenous participation in decision-making regarding marine conservation. Holding the Crown to this duty will continue to enlarge the role of Indigenous perspectives, knowledge, and law in governing Canada's oceans.

THE RIGHT TO CONSERVE: HEILTSUK BLOCKADE OF FISHERIES AND OCEANS OFFICE TO PROTEST COMMERCIAL HERRING FISHERY, 2015

Recognition of a duty to conserve alone, however, is not enough to ensure the braiding together of Indigenous and Canadian laws. This is because the duty to conserve continues to take for granted the inherent authority of the Canadian state over marine conservation. Though such a duty may entail a greater role for Indigenous peoples in making conservation decisions, it fails to recognize the underlying authority of Indigenous peoples to decide for themselves how to manage, allocate, and conserve the resources of their traditional territories.

Important and effective though it may prove, the duty to conserve is perhaps best understood as an intermediary stage on the path towards a broader recognition of Indigenous law and sovereignty. The duty to conserve points to another more fundamental legal concept: the right to conserve—that is, the right of Indigenous peoples to manage the land in accordance with their perspectives, knowledge, and law. Applying Indigenous laws will not necessarily lead to improved conservation, though, in these cases, that was the result.

No Canadian court has yet recognized such a right. Recognition of a right to conserve would represent a significant, logical, and legally defensible extension of the constitutionally guaranteed Treaty and Aboriginal rights to hunt, fish, and trap.[55] Similarly, while alternative approaches, like the assertion of Aboriginal title, offer a different legal route to the recognition of similar rights of management and control, the difficulties of achieving judicial recognition of these rights are equally imposing.

The second case study demonstrates the strategies employed by Indigenous peoples to assert their right to conserve without direct recourse to the Canadian legal system. By taking strategic, direct action, Indigenous peoples have begun to assert their rights to conserve, while establishing a firm foundation for their recognition by the Canadian state in the future.

Like the Haida, the Heiltsuk, located on the Central Coast around the town of Bella Bella, have historically harvested herring products for millennia. Archaeologists estimate that the Heiltsuk have harvested herring for approximately 2,500 years.[56] They manage the herring fishery and spawn-on-kelp fishery by restricting access to harvest zones defined by kinship systems.[57]

In 2014, the DFO opened the Central Coast commercial herring fishery. The Heiltsuk, like the Haida, objected to the opening. After raising their concerns with the DFO, the Heiltsuk chose to adopt a strategy of direct enforcement of their laws. When the DFO opened a limited commercial seine-net fishery without Heiltsuk consent, members went out in their boats to try to stop the harvest. Though harvesters had caught seven hundred tonnes of herring by this point, the Heiltsuk convinced the commercial boats that were getting ready to harvest to leave the area, escorted by Heiltsuk patrols.[58]

In March 2015, after negotiations over a commercial herring gillnet fishery stalled, the Heiltsuk Nation again opposed the opening of a commercial herring fishery and used a variety of strategies, including a blockade of the local DFO office, to enforce their decision. Over a hundred members of the Heiltsuk Nation occupied the local DFO office, giving the DFO until noon the next day to close the waters to this fishery.[59] Ultimately, the DFO closed the fishery, and the commercial boats exited Heiltsuk waters escorted by Heiltsuk patrols.[60] The occupation was a response to the opening of the commercial herring fishery without the consent of the Heiltsuk. It also represents a deeper, long-standing dispute over the management of fisheries in Heiltsuk territorial waters.

The Heiltsuk maintain a right to manage the herring fishery grounded in both Heiltsuk and Canadian law.[61] Under Canadian law, the Heiltsuk's right to the herring fishery and to gather herring-roe has been judicially recognized.[62] Under Heiltsuk *gvi'ilas* (law), all members have a responsibility to care for the land and sea that predates the arrival of the Canadian state and legal system.[63] Heiltsuk *gvi'ilas* and authority authorized the occupation of the DFO office, a point reflected in the eviction notice tacked up to the DFO office, which read:

Due to Lack of Respect for Heiltsuk Gvilas ["laws"], You are Hereby Given a Notice of Eviction from the Heiltsuk Nation.

In 2016, to avoid another conflict, the DFO and the Heiltsuk attempted to reach an agreement on the terms of the herring season. When those meetings came to an impasse, the Heiltsuk worked directly with commercial fishers, culminating in the Herring Management Plan signed by DFO and Heiltsuk First Nation.[64] The terms of the plan include no-go zones designated by the Heiltsuk,[65] a significantly smaller catch (approximately 7 percent of the usual catch),[66] prohibition of the night fishery, and incorporation of Heiltsuk knowledge into the management plan. These measures put in place to address the Heiltsuk's conservation concerns also illustrate Heiltsuk *gvi'ilas* and traditional fisheries management practices.

Indigenous nations have used blockades on numerous occasions to stand up against unwanted development on their traditional territories, both on land and on the water.[67] The Heiltsuk occupation of DFO offices is an example of an action that resulted in at least a short-term successful resolution.[68]

These actions sometimes bring Indigenous peoples into conflict with the Canadian legal system. In no way are these actions "lawless." They are based on a firm foundation of Indigenous law. By asserting their *gvi'ilas*, regardless of their status in the eyes of Canadian law, the Heiltsuk successfully exercised control over one key conservation decision affecting their territory. Such actions form part of a wider history of Indigenous-led conservation that demonstrates "the social and environmental benefits that could result from returning a stake in the environment and its management to local resource users."[69] Recognition by the Canadian legal system of Indigenous legal authority in this area could enhance these benefits immeasurably.

THE POWER TO CONSERVE: CENTRAL COAST FIRST NATIONS CRAB FISHERY CLOSURES, 2014

The third and final case study exemplifies a necessary ancillary of any meaningful right to conserve. If the right to conserve refers to the right to make meaningful decisions about conservation, the power to conserve refers to the ability to enforce those decisions on the land and the water effectively.

"Enforcement" is the process of ensuring that societal norms, legal or otherwise, are obeyed. Effective enforcement can encompass a wide range of activities, from the simple discovery of violations to education to punishment and deterrence.

At present, Canadian law places severe limitations on the enforcement of Indigenous laws. On the one hand, Canadian law only permits certain individuals to wield the traditional law enforcement powers of search, seizure, and detainment. On the other hand, its failure to recognize Indigenous law means that even those who do possess these powers cannot use them to enforce Indigenous law.

In certain respects, the power to conserve is perhaps the most aspirational of the three principles outlined in this paper. Not only would this require recognition of Indigenous law itself, but it would also require recognition of the rights of Indigenous peoples to enforce that law against Indigenous and non-Indigenous Canadians alike.

In other respects, however, the power to conserve is the most accessible of these principles—the easiest, in other words, to implement, even amid the current legal landscape in Canada. Although Canadian law currently fails to recognize the authorized use of force by Indigenous Nations to enforce their legal norms, many effective enforcement strategies are available. The final case study in this paper demonstrates the potential of these "soft" enforcement strategies. The proven success of these soft strategies, in turn, can support the argument for granting more robust and effective powers.

Central Coast Nations have been formally expressing concerns to DFO about declining food, social, and ceremonial (FSC) catch rates for a variety of species, including Dungeness crab, since 2007. In 2014, the Kitasoo/Xai'xais and the three other member nations of the Central Coast Indigenous Resource Alliance (CCIRA)—Heiltsuk, Nuxalk, and Wuikinuxv—proposed a network of Dungeness crab closure areas to combat the decline in stocks and to meet conservation and community needs. The nations shared the notice of closures, declared under Indigenous law, with the DFO. At the time, the DFO denied the necessity for closure areas, citing a lack of evidence.

In response, the Kitasoo/Xai'xais along with the other CCIRA nations and collaborating scientists developed (and raised money to pay for) an experiment to examine fishery effects on crab populations. One key aspect of the experiment was the maintenance of ten scientific closure areas—the control groups that measured the effect of harvest pressure. The study compared these sites to ten open sites. The nations used traditional knowledge to select both open and closed sites. Community input received during the

Marine Plan Partnership (MaPP) marine spatial planning process identified the closed sites as particularly important for FSC fisheries.

The results from this study showed that the closures resulted in significant benefits for the crab population. Preliminary results over a ten-month period in 2014 showed that both the body size and the numbers of Dungeness crab increased at the closed sites. Meanwhile, at the open sites, the size and population of crabs decreased.[70] This suggests that where commercial fishing occurs, a decline in numbers and body size of Dungeness crab results.

The CCIRA nations attempted to negotiate with DFO to have the closures imposed under Canadian law. In 2014, however, though requested by the First Nations to do so, the DFO chose not to recognize or communicate these closures at the time.[71]

The nations then directly asked for compliance with the closures from commercial and recreational fishers, through contacts during patrols and the posting notices of the closures throughout the communities. Compliance with the closures was high, in part because the closures were reasonably sized and located. Members from the nations also conducted regular patrols as part of the Guardian Watchmen program, an Indigenous enforcement and monitoring program discussed in more detail below.

In 2016, one of the ten scientific crab closure areas in Mussel Inlet was the site of conflict arising from the actions of a commercial fisher and lack of action on the part of the DFO. During a routine patrol, Guardian Watchmen discovered a number of commercial crab traps set within the closure area and informed the DFO. A telephone conference followed, and the DFO agreed to contact the fisher and inform him of the closure. According to the DFO, contact was made, and the fisher said that he would remove his traps and return the crabs to the water. Approximately a week later when the fisher returned for his traps, the Guardian Watchmen questioned him, and he claimed that the DFO had not contacted him. Following the conversation with the Guardian Watchmen, the fisher did move the traps outside the area but failed to return approximately three hundred crabs caught inside, potentially impairing the experiment. A second teleconference ensued, and the DFO informed the Kitasoo/Xai'xais that they would not enforce the scientific closure.

If DFO had enforced the closure area by removing the traps, or by taking action against the fisher, or by allowing the Guardian Watchmen to remove the traps, the experimental integrity would not have been risked. As of March

2018, DFO has not taken action against the fisher for this violation of the scientific closure.

While some fishing continued in the closed area, the DFO further risked relations with the Kitasoo/Xai'xais by threatening to immediately report any Kitasoo/Xai'xais enforcement of the closure area to the local RCMP branch. Since Guardian Watchmen did not remove the crab traps from the closure area (in part because the DFO had allegedly notified the fisher), no report was made. However, the DFO did notify RCMP about the possibility of charges being laid against Guardian Watchmen, which resulted in local officers visiting the resource stewardship director of Kitasoo/Xai'xais at home to advise him of their mandate and responsibility. These tactics hindered the Guardian Watchmen's ability to enforce the scientific closure areas declared under Indigenous law.

The DFO finally recognized these closed areas in the 2018/2019 Integrated Fisheries Management Plan for Crab by Trap fishing.[72]

One conclusion from the study was the value of Indigenous management. The study results "provided evidence that fishery closures declared under Indigenous law—effectively social agreements between First Nations and the public without the benefit of federal legislation—could solve a marine conservation problem, albeit temporarily."[73] Indigenous laws and guidance from hereditary chiefs are foundational to the 2017 Kitasoo/Xai'xais Management Plan for Pacific Herring, which cites stories and principles from the nation's Indigenous law archives.[74]

The efficacy of such Indigenous management ultimately rests on the power to conserve wielded by Indigenous nations. Without the ability to enforce their conservation decisions in the real world, such decisions will remain merely symbolic or theoretical. The power to conserve need not come from the state. Indeed, this example demonstrates the potential of working outside the state, by practicing effective communication and building strong relationships, to secure meaningful compliance with Indigenous law. Communication and relationships alone, however, can only go so far. State recognition of a power to conserve would permit Indigenous guardians to wield a full range of robust enforcement powers, which would considerably enhance their ability to put Indigenous law into practice.

JUDICIAL RESPONSES AID THE BRAIDING TOGETHER OF INDIGENOUS AND CANADIAN FISHERIES CONSERVATION LAW

The recognition of each of the three legal principles discussed above presents unique challenges. Each has already received varying levels of recognition from the courts—from implicit recognition for the duty to conserve to continued intransigence in failing to acknowledge the authority of Indigenous people to make effective conservation decisions of their own and enforce them in the world.

Overall, the jurisprudence has been disappointing in this area. The case law has placed so many hurdles in the way of recognizing even the most basic of Aboriginal rights, that it may legitimately be asked whether the interpretation of section 35 rights has not subverted its acknowledged purpose of reconciliation.[75] Indeed, many cases explore the conditions needed for the government to justify infringing Aboriginal rights, rather than giving equal weight to Indigenous legal traditions. Numerous cases illustrate examples of legislation or regulations found to constitute a *prima facie* infringement of or interference with an Aboriginal right to fish, including fishing closures,[76] gear restrictions,[77] prohibitions against fishing in a traditional fishing territory, requirements to obtain a permit for a traditionally harvested species of spawn-on-kelp,[78] limits on the method, timing or extent of fishing,[79] imposing a user fee,[80] limiting the amount harvested through the exercise of a commercial right,[81] and a blanket prohibition on fishing without a licence.[82]

At the same time, each of the three principles discussed above can be derived from established doctrines already endorsed by the courts and enshrined within the constitution. There is no need for a judicial revolution to achieve substantial change—instead, what is needed is an appropriate and informed regard for the legitimacy of Indigenous law. It bears repeating that the authority of Indigenous nations to govern their territory is inherent and does not depend on recognition from the Canadian state.

Still, there is potential for immense change, even within the confines of the otherwise conservative legal system in Canada. At present, however, this potential has mostly gone unrealized.

Three Statutory and Policy Responses to Recognize Indigenous Authority to Fisheries in British Columbia

The urgent imperatives of reconciliation and conservation demand a swifter response. There is no need to rely on the slow progress of the common law to make space for Indigenous law in Canada. Indeed, there are a number of statutory and policy responses Canadian governments can take in the nearer term to recognize Indigenous law and authority over fisheries.

Three of these possible Canadian legal responses are touched upon here: formal recognition of Indigenous law and authority through the *Fisheries Act*; the use of joint fisheries management boards, which may apply both Indigenous and Canadian law; and enforcement of Canadian and Indigenous law by the Guardian Watchmen. On their own, these responses will not address the fundamental injustice of the Crown's unfounded assertion of sovereignty and authority over the lands and waters of Canada. There are, of course, many alternative responses.

Indigenous nations and the DFO are also exploring other responses, such as the negotiation of fisheries enforcement Memoranda of Understanding, protocols, and management plans that satisfy both Canadian and Indigenous law, which in many cases are not mutually exclusive.

Marine spatial planning conducted by the MaPP, which resulted in completed plans for the north and central British Columbia coasts based on both Canadian and Indigenous legal principles, is another promising response to the challenges of ocean management.[83]

Canada can draw on innovative models for recognizing Indigenous law and authority over fisheries in other countries. An example is the Hawai'ian government-designated community-based subsistence fishery areas (CBSFAs) to incorporate customary Indigenous laws related to fisheries into Hawai'ian state law.[84] In New Zealand, state law now allows *mataitai* reserves "to recognize and provide for Maori customary marine management practices, including food gathering."[85] Though not without criticisms, these examples provide possibilities for Indigenous nations and Canada to explore in the coming years.

In addition to strong moral imperatives, the three Canadian legal responses discussed below present possible short-term solutions in the face of broader systemic issues.

FISHERIES ACT RECOGNITION OF TREATY RIGHTS/INDIGENOUS LAW

There are several ways to amend the *Fisheries Act* to better recognize and uphold Indigenous authority and laws.

One example is recognizing the authority of more Indigenous nations to enact their own fisheries laws. Modern treaties may recognize the authority of a First Nation to enact certain laws in relation to fisheries. The federal *Fisheries Act* grants powers to enforce certain Indigenous fisheries laws as recognized in select final agreements. For example, a fishery officer or fishery guardian may enforce Nisga'a laws made under the Fisheries Chapter of the Nisga'a Final Agreement given effect by the *Nisga'a Final Agreement Act*. The power also extends to Tla'amin Laws, Tsawwassen Laws, and Maanulth Laws, as defined in their respective *Final Agreement Acts*.[86]

This section of the *Fisheries Act* could cover other nations' laws, outside of the Treaty process. Features of the Indigenous laws that could be legislated would be determined through nation-to-nation dialogue and might include the territorial scope and the importance of territoriality,[87] decision-making processes, and respect for non-human life.[88]

There are several ways to incorporate a broader recognition of Indigenous laws and authority into the *Fisheries Act*. The limited review of the Act completed in 2019 did not significantly address this issue.

Recently, the government announced a fisheries initiative with the National Indigenous Fisheries Institute, which could address this topic. Another venue could have been the federal "Review of Laws and Policies Related to Indigenous Peoples" initiative. A Working Group of Cabinet Ministers, chaired by the minister of justice seeks to "ensure that the Crown is meeting its constitutional obligations with respect to Aboriginal and treaty rights; adhering to international human rights standards, including the United Nations Declaration on the Rights of Indigenous Peoples; and supporting the implementation of the Truth and Reconciliation Commission's Calls to Action."[89] This initiative was cancelled in 2018 when the prime minister replaced the working group with the Cabinet Committee on Reconciliation.

One of the key calls to action from the Truth and Reconciliation Commission (TRC) is the adoption of the UNDRIP into Canadian law.[90] The federal government has pledged to fully implement the UNDRIP into Canadian law[91] and has fulfilled its pledge as the *UNDRIP Act* was passed and received royal assent on 22 June 2021.[92] Several articles of the UNDRIP support the argument for Indigenous decision-making power over fisheries and fisheries conservation, including

> Article 18: Indigenous peoples have the right to participate in decision-making in matters which would affect their rights, through representatives chosen by themselves in accordance with their own procedures, as well as to maintain and develop their own indigenous decision-making institutions.
>
> Article 29: Indigenous peoples have the right to the conservation and protection of the environment and the productive capacity of their lands or territories and resources. States shall establish and implement assistance programmes for indigenous peoples for such conservation and protection, without discrimination.
>
> Article 32: Indigenous peoples have the right to determine and develop priorities and strategies for the development or use of their lands or territories and other resources.[93]

Full implementation of the UNDRIP in Canadian law and statutory recognition of Indigenous law in the *Fisheries Act* are both ambitious and important undertakings that can change the course of fisheries conservation in British Columbia and all of Canada. Following the enactment of the *UNDRIP Act*, the next step is the preparation of the action plan required by Section 6 of the *UNDRIP Act*.[94] The *UNDRIP Act* contains two pivotal provisions. One, the Act mandates the federal government to ensure that the laws of Canada are consistent with the requirements set out in UNDRIP and two, the Act lays emphasis on the duty of the government to consult with Indigenous peoples and obtain the free, prior, and informed consent of Indigenous people in decision making. However, the effect of the Act on Indigenous peoples is heavily dependent on the action plan and all the other implementation measures employed by the government.[95]

Douglas Harris's work highlights the need for these initiatives when he speaks of the Heiltsuk's continuing conflict with the Crown over fisheries that centre over "competing territorialities and over the legitimacy of two different but increasingly intertwined legal traditions. The Canadian state struggles to erase internal boundaries and to absorb another legal regime:

Heiltsuks struggle to have their boundaries and their legal traditions recognized as such; and the SCC, a forum which they share . . . struggles to *reconcile* Aboriginal rights with the interest of non-Native Canadians."[96]

JOINT MANAGEMENT OF FISHERIES

Creating joint fisheries management bodies designed to implement both Canadian and Indigenous laws is another legal response that could help recognize Indigenous authority over fisheries and allow space for the two legal traditions.

A type of this body exists along the Pacific coast for fisheries that occur within the boundaries of a marine protected area designated under both Haida and federal law. The Archipelago Management Board (AMB) in Haida Gwaii governs management and operation of the Gwaii Haanas National Park Reserve, National Marine Conservation Area Reserve (NMCAR), and Haida Heritage Site.[97] The AMB will develop ecosystem objectives that are concentrated on fisheries.[98] The ecosystem objectives will be an important part of the Gwaii Haanas management plan and will be implemented through regulation. The *Canada National Marine Conservation Areas Act* gives the federal environment minister general powers to make regulations regarding NMCARs; where such regulations affect fisheries, however, they can be made only on the recommendation of the minister of fisheries and oceans.[99]

The AMB's role in fisheries has already been tested. In response to the dispute over reopening the commercial herring fishery that arose in Haida Gwaii, the AMB debated what action to take about the part of the herring fishery conducted in NMCAR waters. It recommended that the DFO minister keep the herring fishery closed, in accordance with the decision of the CHN. However, when the minister decided in favour of re-opening, the AMB's DFO representative had to support the minister's decision, triggering the first dispute resolution process in the AMB's history.[100] This dispute has yet to be resolved, but already the resolution process has been helpful to "better define the areas of disagreement between the CHN, DFO and Parks Canada."[101]

In the 2015 Haida herring injunction case, the court found there was "a heightened duty for DFO and the minister to accommodate the Haida Nation in negotiating and determining the roe herring fishery in Haida Gwaii, given the existing Gwaii Haanas Agreement, the unique Haida Gwaii marine conservation area, the ecological concerns, and the duty to foster reconciliation with and protection of the constitutional rights of the Haida Nation."[102]

Reflecting on the benefits of the AMB, Jones et al note that "local co-management agreements provide a foundation for place-based management and exercise of rights at a meaningful scale" and that "long-term efforts required to establish co-management agreements . . . can have important downstream effects on the assertion of First Nations rights."[103]

Joint bodies explicitly designed for managing fisheries may provide better models for the Pacific Coast. A joint body is one possible way to resolve the long-standing dispute between the Nuu-chah-nulth Nations and the Crown about commercial fishing rights, which is still not finally decided.[104] After reviewing the inadequacy of the jurisprudence on Aboriginal fishing rights with a focus on this dispute, Professor Joshua Nichols proposes that "[t]he most stable outcome would be to establish a territorial boundary in which the Nuu-chah-nulth Nations can laterally co-manage the fishery with the DFO under the shared and overriding limitation imposed by the need to ensure sustainability."[105]

The Fisheries Joint Management Committee (FJMC) composed of representatives appointed by the federal and Inuvialuit governments pursuant to the 1984 *Inuvialuit Final Agreement* (*IFA*) is one model to consider.[106] The legal requirements for the minister to implement, reject, or vary an FJMC recommendation and to provide written reasons for that response strengthens the committee's advisory role.[107]

A different fisheries regime is possible. The three case examples discussed in this chapter show the momentum for change. Numerous fisheries and oceans agreements between the Crown and First Nations in British Columbia also demonstrate momentum towards fisheries co-governance, such as the *Reconciliation Framework Agreement for Fisheries Resources*,[108] the joint Haida-federal decision to close SG̱aan Ḵinghlas–Bowie Seamount Marine Protected Area to all bottom-contact fishing,[109] and the *Reconciliation Framework for Bioregional Oceans Management and Protection*.[110] The transformation of terrestrial forest and protected area management in the Great Bear Rainforest (GBR), "one of the most robust examples of agreements that move toward reconciliation by promoting ecosystem protection in the GBR and fostering economic development and social well-being for First Nations and local communities in the region"[111] over the past two decades, is another potent example of the type of change that is needed.[112]

Canada can also learn from marine shared–decision-making models in other countries. For example, in New Zealand, in local fishery areas called *taiapure*, "Maori participate in the management, including in the formulation of regulations for management of the fish."[113]

To braid Indigenous and Canadian law together in a meaningful way, Indigenous nations and the Crown should co-create joint bodies using a process that is equally informed by Indigenous perspectives and laws.

ENFORCEMENT OF CANADIAN AND INDIGENOUS LAW BY THE GUARDIAN WATCHMEN

Indigenous guardians are people who work for their Indigenous nations to "monitor and protect the lands and waters on their territory to ensure a vibrant future for generations to come."[114] The number of guardian programs across the country is growing.[115] One such program is the "Coastal Guardian Watchmen," an identifier and brand created by an alliance of Indigenous nations currently administered by the Coastal First Nations—Great Bear Initiative (GBI). One of the main goals of the GBI is for nations to work together to rebuild and exercise their inherent authority over marine and terrestrial territories. Guardian Watchmen derive "authority and jurisdiction from [their] traditional laws to manage and safeguard the lands and waters of our territories for the health of future generations."[116]

Coastal Guardian Watchmen range in title from resource technicians and fisheries guardians to park rangers and community watchmen. The program has steadily grown since 2005 and now includes an extensive two-year First Nations Stewardship Technicians Training Program. The Coastal Guardian Watchmen program has been successful at getting eyes and ears on the territory every day. The Guardians on the ground and the water enforcement presence can augment the enforcement efforts of federal and provincial enforcement officers.

However, as explored in the example from Kitasoo/Xai'xais territory, there are situations when enforcement powers are required to ensure fishers comply with laws. With a few exceptions, the federal government has yet to formally recognize the authority of Guardian Watchmen to enforce Canadian and Indigenous laws. As such, questions about the extent of the authority of Guardian Watchmen to enforce Canadian and/or Indigenous law remain unresolved, resulting in ongoing conflicts.

Despite the federal government's mandate under the *Fisheries Act* to conserve fish, there are insufficient resources devoted to enforcement of fisheries laws. The lack of enforcement is notable in the absence of DFO patrols in

Kitasoo/Xai'xais territory and a resulting enforcement vacuum. To help fill the gap, Kitasoo/Xai'xais Guardian Watchmen carry out some of the duties of federal fisheries officers, particularly patrol and observation. The Guardian Watchmen, who have a substantial presence in the territory, provide direct and detailed evidence of *Fisheries Act* violations to the DFO. However, after the Guardian Watchmen report infractions, the DFO may decide not to enforce its regulations.

The Guardian Watchmen came face-to-face with this inability to enforce *Fisheries Act* violations in 2016 when they documented a commercial crab vessel violating the eighteen-day maximum soak time for crab traps. The Guardian Watchmen informed the DFO of the violation. Still, the DFO failed to remove the traps, informally indicated that it would not enforce over-soak violations, and indicated that the Guardian Watchmen could be charged under the *Fisheries Act* if they pulled the traps. This approach fostered distrust and doubt in the DFO's ability to protect the resource, but fortunately, it may be shifting. The DFO has now charged the captain of the vessel, who pleaded guilty when he learned that the Guardian Watchmen who initially provided the information about the infraction had been subpoenaed by government lawyers to testify. This outcome shows promise, but it does not address the immediate enforcement that was necessary to prevent the crabs in the over-soaked traps from dying.

Though the Guardian Watchmen currently have little recognized, formal authority to enforce Canadian law, the organization has the potential to undertake uniquely Indigenous enforcement, empowering these nations to steward their traditional marine territories according to their priorities and legal traditions. In New Zealand, Maori guardians can participate in fisheries management of their territory and have formal enforcement powers.[117] In Australia, the federal government has invested in the "Working on Country" program that trains and employs Indigenous rangers to patrol their territories.[118] In Canada, formal recognition of the enforcement authority of the Guardian Watchmen could be one way to improve conservation outcomes for fisheries.

Conclusion

This chapter highlighted recent conflicts between Indigenous and Canadian federal government management of fisheries on the north and central Pacific Coast and Haida Gwaii. The cases reflect underlying disputes over the authority to manage fisheries as well as competition between "two different but increasingly intertwined legal traditions."[119] These cases point the way to a new conception of the relationship between Indigenous and colonial systems of conservation. Three legal principles express this new relationship: the duty to conserve, the right to conserve, and the power to conserve.

Canadian fisheries law is entrenched in the colonial legal system. It was established, in part, to disenfranchise Indigenous people and consolidate fisheries management power in the Canadian state. Decolonization of this body of law is needed to reflect changes in the interpretation of Aboriginal rights in the Constitution and to uphold Canada's recent promise to ensure Canadian laws conform with the UNDRIP.

As Professor Gordon Christie describes:

> If one were to employ the metaphor of braiding laws together, the image would then be of separate parties—the Crown and numerous distinct Indigenous communities—each enjoying authority over some common territory, each coming to the exercise of braiding with their own strands of law, and together having to work out how state law and Indigenous law could be interwoven, with guidance from international law, to form a single, strong rope.[120]

There are many possible ways to braid together Indigenous and Canadian law for fisheries management. At the heart of all of these paths is recognition of the legitimacy of Indigenous law authority over fisheries in Canadian law. All of these responses require a shift from "consolidated access and regional-scale strategies to increasingly local-scale approaches that can better achieve conservation outcomes and benefits for First Nation communities."[121]

The benefits of braiding together Indigenous, Canadian, and international law, we argue, are manifold. Conservation is a political, as well as an ecological practice. Two centuries of state-controlled conservation efforts have caused untold damage both to Indigenous nations and to the ecological systems on which they depend. Their history is inextricably linked. So too, this chapter suggests, is their future. Collaborating with Indigenous nations as equal partners in marine conservation is an important step in beginning to heal the linked political and ecological harms caused by centuries of colonialism. Indigenous legal traditions can and should play a critical role in fisheries management and environmental governance more generally in Canada.[122]

As Chief Doug Neasloss of Kitasoo/Xai'xais notes, "the Kitasoo/Xai'xais and their neighbours have been making and enforcing fisheries management decisions for thousands of years. Canada should take advantage of the Kitasoo/Xai'xais' willingness, knowledge, and ability to steward fisheries resources, by working with it not against it."[123]

NOTES

1 Senior Director, University of British Columbia Sustainability Initiative, Vancouver, British Columbia.

2 Associate, Arvay Finlay LLP, Vancouver, British Columbia.

3 Staff lawyer, West Coast Environmental Law Association, Vancouver.

4 Chief Councillor, Kitasoo/Xai'xais First Nation.

5 Douglas Harris, "Territoriality, Aboriginal Rights, and the Heiltsuk Spawn-on-Kelp Fishery" (2000) 34:1 UBC L Rev 195 at 202 [Harris].

6 See Tim Fontaine, "Canada Officially Adopts UN Declaration on Rights of Indigenous Peoples", *CBC News* (10 May 2016), online: <www.cbc.ca/news/ indigenous/canada-adopting-implementing-un-rightsdeclaration-1.3575272> [perma.cc/97XM-F6U6].

7 Department of Justice, "Legislation to Implement the United Nations Declaration on the Rights of Indigenous Peoples Becomes law," online: *Department of Justice* <www.canada.ca/en/department-justice/news/2021/06/legislation-to-implement-the-united-nations-declaration-on-the-rights-of-indigenous-peoples-becomes-law.html> [perma.cc/KKV7-DWZF].

8 United Nations General Assembly, *United Nations Declaration on the Rights of Indigenous Peoples: Resolution / Adopted by the General Assembly*, A/RES/61/295 (13 September 2007) [UNDRIP]. Article 27 states that "States shall establish and implement, in conjunction with indigenous peoples concerned, a fair, independent, impartial, open and transparent process, giving due recognition to indigenous peoples' laws, traditions, customs and land tenure systems, to recognize and adjudicate the rights of indigenous peoples pertaining to their lands, territories and resources, including those which were traditionally owned or otherwise occupied or used. Indigenous peoples shall have the right to participate in this process."

9 Boris Worm et al, "Rebuilding Global Fisheries" (2009) 325:5940 Science 578; Daniel Pauly et al, "Fishing Down Marine Food Webs" (1998) 279:5352 Science 860; Douglas J McCauley et al, "Marine Defaunation: Animal Loss in the Global Ocean" (2015) 347:6219 Science 247; Benjamin S Halpern et al, "Spatial and Temporal Changes in Cumulative Human Impacts on the World's Ocean" (2015) 6 Nature Communications 1; Graham J Edgar et al, "Global Conservation Outcomes Depend on Marine Protected Areas with Five Key Features" (2014) 506:7487 Nature 216.

10 Statistics Canada, "Status of Major Fish Stocks" (10 May 2017), online: *Government of Canada* <www.canada.ca/en/environment-climate-change/services/environmental-indicators/status-major-fish-stocks.html> [perma.cc/WMG4-H4FS]; Randall M Peterman & Brigitte Dorner, "A Widespread Decrease in Productivity of Sockeye Salmon (*Oncorhynchus nerka*) Populations in Western North America" (2012) 69:8 Canadian Journal of Fisheries and Aquatic Sciences 1255.

11 Brenda L Gunn et al, "UNDRIP Implementation: Braiding International, Domestic and Indigenous Laws—Special Report" (31 May 2017), online (pdf): *Centre for International Governance Innovation* <www.cigionline.org/sites/default/files/documents/UNDRIP%20Implementation%20Special%20Report%20WEB.pdf> [perma.cc/34FZ-3G3J] at 3.

12 *Ibid.*

13 This is not to say that the application of all contemporary Indigenous laws will result in "conservation" outcomes in the Western sense. Indigenous laws, like all laws, address a range of topics, from governance to addressing human harms to resource management. These laws change with the needs of the time so following Indigenous legal procedures may result in different outcomes depending on the circumstances.

14 A comprehensive solution to the recognition of Indigenous law by the Canadian state would be the passage of an *Indigenous Law Reconciliation Act*. See John Borrows, "Indigenous Legal Traditions in Canada" (2005) 19 Wash UJL & Pol'y 167 at 215–220; John Borrows, *Freedom and Indigenous Constitutionalism* (Toronto: University of Toronto Press, 2016) at 179–80.

15 For more on the duty to learn, see former Chief Justice Lance Finch's article "The Duty to Learn: Taking Account of Indigenous Legal Orders in Practice" (Paper presented at the "Indigenous Legal Orders and the Common Law," British Columbia Continuing Legal Education Conference, Vancouver, November 2012). Paper available for order at the British Columbia Continuing Legal Education website, online: <www.cle.bc.ca/onlinestore/productdetails.aspx?cid=648>.

16 *R v Cooper*, [1979] 4 CNLR 81, Cunliffe Barnett J, quoted in Douglas Harris, *Fish, Law, and Colonialism: The Legal Capture of Salmon in British Columbia* (Toronto: University of Toronto Press, 2001) at 214.

17 For example, in Kitasoo territory, there is a place where the frame of a big house still stands. This big house was used as a court for mediating resource disputes within the Kitasoo, and with neighbouring nations to the north and south. Similar gathering places existed all along the coast.

18 The term Indigenous nation is the preferred term used in this paper as the term for the descendants of the original peoples of North America. The term Aboriginal is also used to refer to the Canadian legal context. Other terminology in quotes remains unchanged.

19 Harris, *supra* note 5 at 74.

20 *Ibid* at 61.

21 Russ Jones, Catherine Rigg & Evelyn Pinkerton, "Strategies for Assertion of Conservation and Local Management Rights: A Haida Gwaii Herring Story" (2017) 80 Marine Policy 154 [Jones, Rigg & Pinkerton]; Russ Jones & Terri-Lynn Williams-Davidson, "Applying Haida Ethics in Today's Fishery" in *Just Fish: Ethics and Canadian Marine Fisheries* (St. Johns: ISER, 2000) at 100; Alisha Gauvreau et al, "Everything Revolves around the Herring: The Heiltsuk–Herring Relationship through Time" (2017) 22:2 Ecology and Society; "Kitasoo/Xai'xais Management Plan for Pacific Herring" (2018) at 4–33, online (pdf): *Kitasoo/Xai'xais* <klemtu.com/wp-content/uploads/2018/05/KX-Herring-Mgmt-Plan-Jan-2018-final.pdf> [perma.cc/9BH3-J42R] [Kitasoo/Xai'xais].

22 The Kitasoo/Xai'xais First Nation is largely made up of members from three backgrounds: the Kitasoo, the Xai'xais, and the 'Qvúqvaỳáitx̌v.

23 Doug Neasloss, personal communication (13 January 2017) [Neasloss].

24 Harris, *supra* note 5 at 208.

25 *Ibid* at 14–78.

26 *Jack v The Queen* [1980] 1 SCR 294 at 310, 100 DLR (3d) 193.

27 Harris, *supra* note 5 at 63.

28 Naxaxalhts'i, Albert (Sonny) McHalsie, "We Have to Take Care of Everything That Belongs to Us" in Bruce G Miller, eds, *Be of Good Mind: Essays on the Coast Salish* (Vancouver: UBC Press, 2007) 82 at 97–98.

29 *R v Marshall*, [1999] 3 SCR 533 at para 40, 179 DLR (4th) 193: "[t]he paramount regulatory objective is the conservation of the resource. This responsibility is placed squarely on the Minister and not on the aboriginal or non-aboriginal users of the resource."

30 Dianne Newell, *Tangled Webs of History* (Toronto: University of Toronto Press, 1993) at 62.

31 *Ibid*. See also Harris, *supra* note 5 at 67.

32 *Constitution Act, 1982*, being Schedule B to the Canada Act 1982 (UK), 1982, c 11.

33 *R v Sparrow*, [1990] 1 SCR 1075 at 1113, 70 DLR (4th) 385 [*Sparrow*].

34 *Ibid*.

35 *R v Van der Peet*, [1996] 2 SCR 507 at para 30, 137 DLR (4th) 289 [*Van der Peet*].

36 *Ibid* at para 46.

37 John Borrows, "Challenging Historical Frameworks: Aboriginal Rights, The Trickster, and Originalism" (2017) 98:1 Canadian Historical Review 114 at 120.

38 *Ibid*.

39 *Van der Peet*, *supra* note 35, left the law of Aboriginal rights to fish in an "inchoate condition." See Rosanne Kyle, "Aboriginal Fishing Rights: The Supreme Court of Canada in the Post-Sparrow Era" (1997) 31:2 UBC L Rev 293; John Borrows, "Frozen Rights in Canada: Constitutional Interpretation and the Trickster" (1997) 22:1 Am Indian Rev 37 at 37–64; Russel Lawrence Barsh & James Youngblood Henderson, "The Supreme Court's Van der Peet Trilogy: Naive Imperialism and Ropes of Sand" (1996) 42:4 McGill L J 993 at 993.

40 Sarah Hamill, "The Public Right to Fish and the Triumph of Colonial and Dispossession in Ireland and Canada" (2017) 50:1 UBC L Rev 53 at 53.

41 *Van der Peet*, *supra* note 35 at para 263.

42 Tim Thielmann, "A Duty to Conserve: Articulating the Crown's Obligation to Protect Species of Significance to Aboriginal Peoples" (Paper delivered at the Insight's 6th Annual Western Canada Aboriginal Law Forum, Vancouver, 11 May 2010) at 4, online (pdf): *DGW* <www.dgwlaw.ca/web/wp-content/uploads/2014/12/Duty_to_Conserve.pdf> [perma.cc/9MKY-4YEZ].

43 *Haida Nation v Canada (Fisheries and Oceans)* 2015 FC 290, [2015] FCJ No 281 (QL) [*Haida*].

44 See *Ahousaht First Nation v Canada (Fisheries and Oceans)*, 2015 FC 253; *Ahousaht First Nation v Canada (Fisheries and Oceans)*, 2014 FC 197.

45 Russ Jones, "Application of Haida Oral History to Pacific Herring Management" in N Haggan, B Neiss, I Baird, eds, *Fishers' Knowledge in Fisheries Science and Management* (Paris: UNESCO, 2007) at 103.

46 *Ibid*.

47 Iain McKechnie et al, "Archaeological Data Provide Alternative Hypotheses on Pacific Herring (*Clupea pallasii*) Distribution, Abundance, and Variability" (2014) 111:9 Proceedings of the National Academy of Sciences E807-E816.

48 A chart illustrating the herring closures in the three herring management regions of Haida Gwaii, the Central Coast, and the West Coast Vancouver Island from 1990–2015 is included in Russ Jones, Catherine Rigg, and Evelyn Pinkerton, "Strategies for Assertion of Conservation and Local Management Rights: A Haida Gwaii Herring Story" (2017) 80 Marine Policy 154 at 159.

49 *Haida*, *supra* note 43.

50 *Ibid* at para 53.

51 *Ibid* at para 54.

52 Council of the Haida Nation, "Sustaining Herring Stocks: Injunction Granted" (6 March 2015) at 1–2, online (pdf): *Haida Nation* <www.haidanation.ca/wp-content/uploads/2017/03/Haida-Herring.pdf> [perma.cc/3MNY-ZDUC].

53 *Haida Nation v British Columbia (Minister of Forests)*, 2004 SCC 73, [2004] 3 SCR 511. No cases have yet established the existence of Aboriginal title to marine areas in Canada. The decision in *Tsilhqot'in Nation v British Columbia*, 2014 SCC 44, [2014] 2 SCR 257, lays a stronger foundation for such claims to occur.

54 *Haida*, *supra* note 43 at para 59.

55 Lynda M Collins & Meghan Murth, "Indigenous Environmental Rights in Canada: The Right to Conservation Implicit in Treaty and Aboriginal Rights to Hunt, Fish, and Trap" (2010) 47:4 Alta L Rev 959.

56 Miles Powell, "Divided Waters: Heiltsuk Spatial Management of Herring Fisheries and the Politics of Native Sovereignty" (December, 2012) 43:5 Western Historical Quarterly 463.

57 See Gauvreau et al, *supra* note 21 at 9. "Each family was given responsibility over specific lands and waters, and by following the laws of gvi'ilas and lhaxvai, implemented measures designed to ensure sustainable harvest of herring within those areas (HTC 2005)." Sustainability was key to ensuring a continued relationship with herring (Table 3, Topic 5).

58 Mark Hume, "Heiltsuk First Nation Claims Victory over Disputed Herring Fishery", *The Globe and Mail* (1 April 2015), online: <www.theglobeandmail.com/news/british-columbia/heiltsuk-first-nation-claims-victory-over-disputed-herring-fishery/article23757390/> [perma.cc/FLZ9-TZNN].

59 Justin McElroy, "Heiltsuk Nation Occupying Local DFO Office to Protest Commercial Fishery", *Global News* (29 March 2015), online: <globalnews.ca/news/1910658/heiltsuk-nation-occupying-local-dfo-office-to-protest-proposed-fishery/> [perma.cc/9BWS-ME8F].

60 Jenny Uechi, "Heiltsuk Celebrate as Fishing Boats Forced to Leave Traditional Waters", *Vancouver Observer* (2 April 2015), online: <www.vancouverobserver.com/news/breaking-heiltsuk-celebrate-fishing-boats-forced-leave-traditional-waters.html> [perma.cc/QM6W-S76G].

61 Harris, *supra* note 5 at 195.

62 *R v Gladstone*, [1996] 2 SCR 723, 137 DLR (4th) 648 [*Gladstone*].

63 Frank Brown & Y Kathy Brown, "Staying the Course, Staying Alive—Coastal First Nations Fundamental Truths: Biodiversity, Stewardship and Sustainability" (2009) at 1–82, online (pdf): *Biodiversity BC* <www.biodiversitybc.org/assets/Default/BBC_

Staying_the_Course_Web.pdf#search=%22staying%20the%20Course%20staying%20 alive%22> [perma.cc/5X4J-S6EY].

64 "Historic Joint Management Agreement Marred by Conflict" (27 March 2016), online: *Heiltsuk Nation* <www.heiltsuknation.ca/historic-joint-management-agreement-marred-by-conflict/> [perma.cc/TM4V-ZTRC].

65 "Exciting News for Heiltsuk Herring" (16 January 2016), online: *Heiltsuk Tribal Council* <heiltsuktribalcouncil.wordpress.com/2016/01/16/exciting-news-for-heiltsuk-herring/> [perma.cc/KVB4-JRLF].

66 "Bella Bella Herring Fishery to Re-Open with Much Smaller Catch", *CBC News* (19 January 2016), online: <www.cbc.ca/news/canada/british-columbia/heiltsuk-dfo-herring-agreement-1.3409704> [perma.cc/ZKC5-Z28S] [*CBC News*].

67 For more on the topic of Indigenous civil (dis)obedience, see: John Borrows, *Freedom and Indigenous Constitutionalism* (Toronto: University of Toronto Press, 2016).

68 *CBC News*, *supra* note 66.

69 Miles Powell, "Divided Waters: Heiltsuk Spatial Management of Herring Fisheries and the Politics of Native Sovereignty" (2012) 43:5 Western Historical Quarterly 463 at 484.

70 *Ibid* at 52.

71 Alejandro Frid, Madeleine McGreer & Angela Stevenson, "Rapid Recovery of Dungeness Crab within Spatial Fishery Closures Declared under Indigenous Law in British Columbia" (2016) 6 Global Ecology and Conservation 48 at 49.

72 "2018/2019 Integrated Fisheries Management Plan for Crab by Trap" (last visited 14 June 2020), online: <www.pac.dfo-mpo.gc.ca/fm-gp/mplans/2018/crab-crabe-sm-2018-eng.html>. Full plan available by request to: jennifer.gordon@dfo-mpo.gc.ca.

73 *Ibid* at 49.

74 "Kitasoo/Xai'xais," *supra* note 21.

75 Russel Lawrence Barsh & James Youngblood Henderson, "The Supreme Court's Van der Peet Trilogy: Naive Imperialism and Ropes of Sand" (1996) 42:4 McGill L J 993.

76 *R v Douglas et al*, 2007 BCCA 265, 278 DLR (4th) 653; *R v Marshall* [1999] 3 SCR 456, 1999 CanLII 665 (SCC) [Marshall]; *R v Robinson*, [1991] 4 CNLR 125 (BC Prov. Ct.).

77 *Sparrow*, *supra* note 33.

78 *R v Adams* [1990] BCJ No 3012; *R v Colin Richardson and Harold Wilson* File No. 1793C Masset Registry 20 Aug 1990.

79 *R v Badger* [1996] 1 SCR 771, 133 DLR (4th) 324; *Marshall*, *supra* note 76.

80 *R v Cote* [1996] 3 SCR 139, 138 DLR (4th) 385.

81 *Gladstone*, *supra* note 62.

82 *R v Nikal* [1996] 1 SCR 1013, 133 DLR (4th) 658.

83 See Linda Nowlan, "Brave New Wave: Marine Spatial Planning and Ocean Regulation on Canada's Pacific" (2016) 29 J Environmental Law and Practice 151.

84 Mehana Blaich Vaughan, Barton Thompson & Adam L Ayers, "Pāwehe Ke Kai a'o Hā'ena: Creating State Law Based on Customary Indigenous Norms of Coastal Management" (2017) 30:1 Society & Natural Resources 1.

85 Catherine J Iorns Magallanes, "Maori Cultural Rights in Aotearoa New Zealand: Protecting the Cosmology that Protects the Environment" 21:2 Widener L Rev 273 at 304 [Magallanes].

86 *Fisheries Act*, RSC 1985, c F-14, s 5(4). Amendments to the Act in 2019 did not affect this section.

87 Harris, *supra* note 5.

88 Russ Jones, Catherine Rigg & Lynn Lee, "Haida Marine Planning: First Nations as a Partner in Marine Conservation" (2010) 15:1 Ecology and Society 12; Susanna Quail, "Yah'guudang: The Principle of Respect in the Haida Legal Tradition" (2014) 47:2 UBC L Rev 673.

89 "Working Group of Ministers on the Review of Laws and Policies Related to Indigenous Peoples: About the Working Group of Ministers" (last visited 14 June 2020), online: *Government of Canada* <www.canada.ca/en/privy-council/services/review-laws-policies-indigenous.html> [perma.cc/6F2A-HHPF].

90 Truth and Reconciliation Commission of Canada, *Canada's Residential Schools: Reconciliation—The Final Report of the Truth and Reconciliation Commission of Canada*, vol 6 (Montreal-Kingston: McGill-Queen's University Press, 2015) at 28.

91 Indigenous and Northern Affairs Canada, "Canada Becomes a Full Supporter of the United Nations Declaration on the Rights of Indigenous Peoples" (10 May 2016), online: *Government of Canada* <www.canada.ca/en/indigenous-northern-affairs/news/2016/05/canada-becomes-a-full-supporter-of-the-united-nations-declaration-on-the-rights-of-indigenous-peoples.html> [perma.cc/8A6S-MYQZ].

92 Department of Justice, "Legislation to Implement the United Nations Declaration on the Rights of Indigenous Peoples Becomes Law" (last visited 25 June 2021), online: *Government of Canada* <www.canada.ca/en/department-justice/news/2021/06/legislation-to-implement-the-united-nations-declaration-on-the-rights-of-indigenous-peoples-becomes-law.html> [perma.cc/KKV7-DWZF].

93 *UNDRIP*, *supra* note 8.

94 Allan Gregg, "Reconciliation Will Require a Paradigm Shift—and an Indigenous Veto over New Development Could Usher in This Better Canada", *The Globe and Mail* (18 June 2021) online: <www.theglobeandmail.com/opinion/article-reconciliation-will-require-a-paradigm-shift-and-an-indigenous-veto/> [perma.cc/KPE6-A6KL].

95 *Ibid.*

96 Harris, *supra* note 5 at 199.

97 *Gwaii Haanas Agreement* (1993); *Gwaii Haanas Marine Agreement* (2010).

98 *Gwaii Haanas Marine Agreement* (2010), *supra* note 97, s 4.1(b).

99 *Canada National Marine Conservation Areas Act*, SC 2002, c 18, s 16 (2).

100 Jean Phillip Sargeant, *Assessing the Cooperative Management Regime in Gwaii Haanas National Park Reserve, National Marine Conservation Area Reserve and Haida Heritage Site* (Master of Resource Management Thesis, Isafjorður: University of Akureyi, 2015), online (pdf): <skemman.is/bitstream/1946/25473/1/Sargeant-Final%20Thesis.pdf> [perma.cc/QK2B-KFHJ].

101 Jones, Rigg & Pinkerton, *supra* note 21 at 164.

102 *Haida*, *supra* note 43 at para 53.

103 Jones, Rigg & Pinkerton, *supra* note 21 at 165.

104 The latest court decision was issued in April 2018: *Ahousaht Indian Band and Nation v Canada (Attorney General)*, 2018 BCSC 633. For a history of the case and comment on the latest decision see *Wallopadmin, Ahousaht Indian Band and Nation v Canada (Attorney General)*, 2018 BCSC 633—Case Summary (22 June 2018), online: *Mandell Pinder* <www.mandellpinder.com/ahousaht-indian-band-and-nation-v-canada-attorney-general-2018-bcsc-633-case-summary/> [perma.cc/ZK62-5RL7].

105 Joshua Nichols, "Of Spectrums and Foundations: An Investigation into the Limitations of Aboriginal Rights" in Robert Hamilton et al, eds, *Wise Practices: Exploring Indigenous Economic Justice and Self-Determination* (Toronto: University of Toronto Press, 2021) 115 at 142.

106 *Inuvialuit Final Agreement* (1984), s 14(61).

107 Burton Ayles, Louie Porta & Red McV Clarke, "Development of an Integrated Fisheries Bo-Management Framework for New and Emerging Commercial Fisheries in the Canadian Beaufort Sea" (2016) 72 Marine Policy 246.

108 Bessie Brown, "Canada and the Coastal First Nations Take a Step Forward in the Management of Fisheries Resources for the North and Central Coast of British Columbia" (11 October 2017), online: *Coastal First Nations Great Bear Initiative* <coastalfirstnations.ca/canada-coastal-first-nations-take-step-forward-management-fisheries-resources-north-central-coast-british-columbia/> [perma.cc/UM5M-6YMC].

109 "Haida Nation and Canada Increase Protection at the SG̱aan Ḵinghlas—Bowie Seamount Marine Protected Area" (19 January 2018), online: *Council of the Haida Nation* <www.haidanation.ca/?nooz_release=haida-nation-and-canada-increase-protection-at-the-sg%CC%B2aan-k%CC%B2inghlas-bowie-seamount-marine-protected-area> [perma.cc/H429-SUWE].

110 "Reconciliation Framework for Bioregional Oceans Management and Protection" (21 June 2018) online: *Government of Canada* <pm.gc.ca/eng/news/2018/06/21/prime-minister-and-pacific-north-and-central-coast-first-nations-welcome-agreement> [perma.cc/PTJ8-5W95].

111 Deborah Curran, "'Legalizing' the Great Bear Rainforest Agreements: Colonial Adaptations Toward Reconciliation and Conservation" (2017) 62:3 McGill L J 813 at 859.

112 *Ibid* at 833–834. Curran notes that in this set of agreements "[a]ll parties acknowledged that the existing landscape of colonial entitlements was no longer working and that jurisdiction over activities on the landscape needed to be restructured to include other authorities—namely, First Nations."

113 Magallanes, *supra* note 85 at 303.

114 Coastal Stewardship Network, "Guardian Watchmen Programs Overview", online: *Coastal First Nations Great Bear Initiative* <coastalfirstnations.ca/our-environment/programs/coastal-guardian-watchmen-support/> [perma.cc/W8HP-WDYE].

115 See the Indigenous Guardians Map, in the "Indigenous Guardians Toolkit" (2017), online: *Indigenous Guardians Toolkit* <www.indigenousguardianstoolkit.ca/> [perma.cc/727H-8EK3].

116 *Ibid.*

117 Magallanes, *supra* note 85 at 304.

118 The PEW Charitable Trusts, "Working for Our Country—A Review of the Economic and Social Benefits of Indigenous Land and Sea Management" (12 November 2015), online (pdf): *The PEW Charitable Trusts* <www.pewtrusts.org/-/media/post-launch images/2015/11/economicandsocialbenefitsindigenouslandwhitepaper.pdf> at 13.

119 Harris, *supra* note 5 at 199.

120 Gordon Christie, "Indigenous Legal Orders, Canadian Law and UNDRIP" in Centre for International Governance Innovation, ed, *UNDRIP Implementation: Braiding International, Domestic and Indigenous Laws—Special Report* (Waterloo, ON: Centre for International Governance Innovation, 2017), 48 at 48.

121 Jones, Rigg & Pinkerton, *supra* note 21 at 12.

122 Jessica Clogg et al, "Indigenous Legal Traditions and the Future of Environmental Governance in Canada" (2016) 29 J Environmental Law and Practice 227.

123 Neasloss, *supra* note 23.

7

LNG-Fuelled Vessels—Environmentally Friendly Ships for the Arctic

Peter Pamel[1] *and Robert C. Wilkins*[2]

Introduction

This chapter was written for the October 2016 Canadian Institute of Resources Law Symposium and reflected the perspective and context at that time. A postscript has been added to provide updates on the current state of affairs in relation to the use of liquefied natural gas (LNG) as fuel for vessels. It has been prepared following the same structure and using the same subheadings as the original paper for ease of reference. In addition, the information reflected in this postscript does not reflect the impact that the current global COVID-19 pandemic has had and will continue to have on the supply and pricing of LNG or the marine trade.

Background: What Is LNG and Why Are We Talking about It Now?

AIR POLLUTION RESTRICTIONS: INTERNATIONAL CONVENTION FOR THE PREVENTION OF POLLUTION FROM SHIPS, EMISSION CONTROL AREAS, AND THE EUROPEAN UNION

IMO 2020 (International Maritime Organization 2020) is the term used to describe the next step of the implementation of the regulations to Annex VI of the *International Convention for the Prevention of Pollution from Ships* (*MARPOL*), which, as of January 1, 2020, includes reducing the global sulphur content in fuel to 0.5 percent.[3]

To achieve this objective, ships will be required to use fuel oils with sulphur content of less than 0.5 percent mass by mass, compliant exhaust gas cleaning systems (EGCS or scrubbers),[4] or non-fuel oil alternatives such as LNG. Carriage of non-compliant fuel oil for combustion purposes for propulsion onboard a ship (unless fitted with scrubbers) is also prohibited.[5]

Since January 1, 2015, the sulphur limit for fuel oil used by ships operating in emission control areas (ECAs) designated by the IMO for the control of sulphur oxides has been 0.10 percent mass by mass. The IMO 2020 does not affect these ECAs.

There are now four designated ECAs in effect globally:

1. Baltic Sea area;
2. North Sea area;
3. the North American ECA running along the eastern and western coasts of Canada, the United States (including southeast Alaska and the main Hawaiian Islands), and France (for Saint-Pierre and Miquelon) and extends some 200 nautical miles from the coastline, but below 60 degrees north latitude;[6] and
4. the United States Caribbean Sea ECA, covering certain waters adjacent to the coasts of Puerto Rico and the US Virgin Islands.[7]

LNG INVESTMENT

Currently, a regasification terminal in Saint John, New Brunswick, operated by Canaport LNG, is the only such terminal in Canada;[8] however, several LNG export facilities have been proposed: thirteen in British Columbia, two in Quebec, and three in Nova Scotia, while long-term export licences have been issued to twenty-four LNG projects since 2011.[9]

Investment in LNG facilities has increased with demand. Total investment in LNG, according to the International Energy Agency (IEA), reached $50 billion in 2019, primarily in the United States and Canada.[10] Moreover, according to the predictions of McKinsey & Company, expansion in the gas and LNG markets will continue, with LNG demand expected to increase 3.6 percent per year to 2035.[11]

LEGAL FRAMEWORK

To ensure compliance with the new measures, the IMO's Marine Environment Protection Committee (MEPC) released the "2019 Guidelines for Consistent Implementation of the 0.5 percent Sulphur Limit under MARPOL Annex VI"[12] (Guidelines) to provide guidance to state parties, as the enforcement, compliance, and monitoring of the IMO 2020 sulphur limit is the responsibility of the state parties (including both flag states and port states) that have ratified *MARPOL* and acceded to Annex VI.

These Guidelines were adopted for port state control under *MARPOL* Annex VI, chapter 3, providing updated enforcement guidance for provisions including Regulation 13, "nitrogen oxides" and Regulation 14, "sulphur oxides and particulate matter." Port states should take appropriate measures to ensure compliance, such as conducting initial inspections based on documents and other possible materials, including remote sensing and portable devices. Given "clear grounds" to conduct a more detailed inspection, the port state may conduct sample analysis and other detailed inspections to verify compliance to the regulation, as appropriate. If the ship is non-compliant with the IMO 2020, the port state may prevent it from sailing until it takes measures to achieve compliance and should report a non-compliant ship to the flag state. In case of fuel oil non-availability, the ship must notify the port or flag state. This notification is commonly referred to as a Fuel Oil Non-Availability Report (FONAR).

In addition, on January 1, 2017, the IMO's *International Code for Ships Operating in Polar Waters* (Polar Code)[13] came into effect, which includes amendments to *MARPOL* to add stricter discharge requirements, including prohibitions on discharges of oil and noxious liquid substances in Arctic waters. The Polar Code prompted the adoption, in Canada, of the *Arctic Shipping Safety and Pollution Prevention Regulations*.[14] The Polar Code and Canada's new regulations include a variety of safety and pollution prevention measures, including those related to vessel design and equipment, vessel operations, and crew training. Drawing from decades of experience as an Arctic regulator, Canada played a key leadership role in developing the Polar Code at the IMO.[15]

Furthermore, the use and carriage of heavy fuel oil (HFO) is banned in Antarctic waters under *MARPOL*, and the IMO Polar Code recommends that states follow the same practice in the Arctic.[16] The IMO has agreed on a draft regulation that would phase out the use and carriage of HFO in the Arctic. The draft regulation, which moved forward for consideration by the MEPC in October 2020 (MEPC 76), allows for the continued use of HFO until July 1, 2024.[17]

Moreover, Transport Canada has issued a policy, "Requirements for Vessels Using Natural Gas as Fuel," which came into force on July 28, 2017, addressing the need to clarify and provide guidance on the requirements involved in designing and constructing natural gas-fuelled vessels, 24 m in length or longer, under the Canadian flag. This policy establishes how the *International Code of Safety for Ships Using Gases or Other Low Flashpoint Fuels*[18] (*IGF Code*), which is a sub-instrument of the *International Convention for the Safety of Life at Sea*[19] (*SOLAS*), will be applied to vessels under the Canadian flag.[20]

A permit from the Canada Energy Regulator (CER) is required to export LNG from Canada.[21] Bill C-69 replaced the National Energy Board (NEB) with the CER and implemented the new *Impact Assessment Act* (*IAA*),[22] replacing the *Canadian Environmental Assessment Act, 2012* (*CEAA 2012*). Regulations such as the *Designated Classes of Projects Order*[23] and the *Physical Activities Regulations*,[24] which identify projects that will require federal review under *IAA*, and the *Information and Management of Time Regulations*,[25] which identifies information to be submitted and criteria for setting, managing, and suspending time limits along, with Bill C-68 and Bill C-69, came into force on August 28, 2019.[26]

Advantages and Challenges for Using LNG as Vessel Fuel

There are varying reports on the advantages of using LNG as a marine fuel. Despite the clear advantages in most aspects, such use is not without its challenges.

The life cycle greenhouse gas (GHG) emissions of LNG are estimated to be 6 to 10 percent less than emissions from HFO, which is currently the most commonly used shipping fuel.[27] However, some environmentalists have raised concerns in relation to "methane slips," the release of natural gas (methane) inadvertently into the atmosphere through leaks, which has up to twenty-five times the climate warming effect of carbon dioxide. For example, the International Council on Clean Transportation reported that LNG use as fuel would emit between 70 and 82 percent more GHG emissions over the short-term compared to clean distillate fuels, mainly due to methane slips.[28]

Despite the challenges, there is an increasing availability of natural gas sources and a significant number of first-movers initiatives with a growing number of ships adopting LNG as fuel.[29] In addition, efficient engines, careful LNG transfer procedures, and proper education and training can significantly reduce the amount of methane slip that occurs during ship refuelling and operating, increasing the benefit of using LNG as a marine fuel.

SHIP DESIGN

LNG as a marine fuel is currently being used in certain vessels, usually in LNG carriers, which use natural boil-off of LNG to supply their engines. However, this approach has started to spread over other types of vessels, such as ferries, containerships, tankers, and offshore vessels, and the number of shipping companies ordering new buildings with LNG as a marine fuel is increasing.[30]

BUNKERING FACILITIES

In 2017, according to the company DNV, sixty locations in Singapore, the Middle East, Europe, and the Caribbean were capable of supplying LNG. As of 2019, according to the industry-coalition organization SEA-LNG, ninety-three ports were able to deliver LNG. An additional fifty-four ports were known to be in the process of preparing facilities to deliver LNG. LNG can also be transferred ship to ship; by February 2020, twelve bunkering vessels were available to deliver LNG, up from six in 2019, and an additional twenty-seven had either been ordered or commissioned.[31]

In Canada, while the ongoing operation of LNG terminals generally falls under provincial regulation, most LNG terminal proposals require both federal and provincial environmental assessments and permits. A permit is required from Canada's federal energy regulator to export LNG from Canada. In addition, LNG facilities are classified as industrial sites and must meet all federal, provincial, and municipal standards, codes, and safety regulations. The Canadian Standards Association (CSA) has a specific standard for LNG production, storage, and handling.[32] This standard establishes essential requirements for the design, installation, and safe operation of LNG facilities. Furthermore, the *Constitution Act, 1982* establishes several protections regarding the traditional rights of Aboriginal peoples part of which is anchored on the right to be consulted by government and participate in respect of any energy project that may potentially impact on their lives, environment, and resources.[33]

TRAINING OF CREW MEMBERS

Amendments to the Standards of Training, Certification, and Watchkeeping (STCW), which came into force in January 2017, introduced training for ships following the *IGF Code*. As such, flag states shall ensure that a certificate of proficiency is issued to seafarers who are qualified under the STCW. There is a provision of equivalency, especially for those who have been onboard LNG or gas carriers.[34]

LNG-Fuelled Vessels in Operation

The number of vessels fuelled by LNG has steadily increased. According to SEA-LNG, in June 2019, 163 ships were using LNG for fuel, while eight months later that number had grown to 175. The number of LNG-fuelled ships on order has also grown: in June 2019, 155 had been ordered, and by February 2020, that number had increased to 203.[35] According to Gibson Shipbrokers, between January and April 2021, twenty-seven LNG-fuelled vessels had been ordered.[36]

Here are a few new examples of LNG-fuelled vessels in operation:[37]

Containers

- The *Isla Bella*, owned by TOTE in partnership with General Dynamics NASSCO, is considered the world's first LNG-powered container ship, the first of two Marlin-class containerships, and the largest LNG-powered dry cargo ship.[38]
- According to SEA-LNG, "in February 2019, Hapag-Lloyd announced it would undertake the world's first conversion of a container ship to LNG. The retrofit of the *Sajir* was to take place in 2020 and presents the opportunity for its 16 LNG-ready sister ships to also undergo conversion."
- In September 2019, the *CMA CGM Jacques Saadé*, with a 23,000 twenty-foot equivalent unit capacity, became the largest LNG-fuelled container ship in the world. By 2022, CMA CGM, the container transportation and shipping company, plans to

have eight additional LNG-fuelled containerships of the same capacity, and an additional eleven with a lower capacity.[39]

- The largest LNG dual-fuel combination container/roll-on–roll-off ship ever built in the United States entered the fleet of shipping company Matson Inc. in December 2019.[40]

Pure Car and Truck Carriers

- The first, trans-Atlantic LNG-fuelled pure-car-and-truck carriers were the *Siem Confucius* and *Siem Aristotle*, operated by Siem Car Carriers, between Europe and China.[41]
- As of September 2019, the world's largest LNG-fuelled pure-car-and-truck carrier had been ordered by the company NYK and would be the first large LNG-fuelled pure-car-and-truck carrier to be built in Japan.[42]

Tankers

- In December 2019, the oil firm Petronas announced that its the shipping division planned to convert half of its oil tanker fleet (which included sixty vessels) to dual-fuel LNG by 2030.[43]
- The *Creole Spirit*, an LNG tanker built in 2016, with its two-stroke engine technology is termed the world's most efficient LNG ship with the lowest freight cost per unit. In addition to the engine, "the reduction in the number of cylinders requiring overhaul, the reduction in the size of the complex electrical systems and the introduction of a passive partial reliquefaction system contribute towards improving the overall efficiency and reducing cost."[44]

Cruise & Ferry

- The US cruise ship operator Carnival's 20-deck *Aidanova* became the world's first cruise ship fully fuelled by LNG. Propelled by four dual-fuel engines, it runs on LNG 98 percent of the time, even though it still carries marine gas oil for safety reasons.[45]

- BC Ferries, as of 2019, already had two ships running on LNG. As part of its fleet renewal, it plans to build an additional five LNG-fuelled ferries.[46]
- The first cruise ship based in North America to be fuelled by LNG, and also Carnival Cruise Line's largest, the *Mardi Gras*, was set to debut in 2020. At the time of writing, Carnival Cruise Lines planned to deliver a second LNG-fuelled cruise ship to the brand by 2022.[47]
- MSC Cruises' LNG-fuelled *Grandiosa* was launched on November 10, 2019. Capable of accommodating more than 6,000 passengers on its Mediterranean tours, the *Grandiosa* is one of example of a trend toward first-class ships powered by LNG.[48]
- The world's largest LNG-fuelled roll-on/roll-off ferry will be operated by the Australian company, SeaRoad, following completion of construction in Germany.[49]

Conclusion

Over the next thirty years, the Conference Board of Canada estimates that adding 30 million tons per year of LNG to the export market will also add approximately $7.4 billion to the national economy and create an average of 65,000 jobs annually.[50] The Norwegian company, DNV, predicts that LNG will dominate ship fuelling by 2050.[51] Beside the potential for economic development, the creation of afore-discussed initiatives and policy instruments, together with conscious practical implementation of the shift to use LNG for vessels, will also foster regulatory efforts for the protection of the Arctic environment.

NOTES

1 Justice Pamel was appointed to the Federal Court on May 2, 2019. He is no longer a partner with the Shipping Group at Borden Ladner Gervais. The authors would like to thank and acknowledge Nigah Awj, an associate lawyer with the Shipping Group of Borden Ladner Gervais in Montreal for her most valuable assistance in updating this paper with the preparation of this postscript.

2 Robert C Wilkins is a Retired Advocate and Honorary Life Member of the Canadian Maritime Law Association.

3 *MARPOL* Annex VI, *Regulations for the Prevention of Air Pollution from Ships*, Regulation 14 re sulphur oxide emissions, in force as of May 19, 2005, and Regulation

13 on nitrogen oxide emissions (or the associated NOx Technical Code 2008), which entered into force on 1 July 2010; see MEPC 176 (58), adopted in July 2005 and in force October 2008. See also "Prevention of Air Pollution from Ships" (accessed 14 June 2020), online: *International Maritime Organization* <www.imo.org/OurWork/Environment/PollutionPrevention/AirPollution/Pages/Air-Pollution.aspx> [perma.cc/8CSD-V8CR].

4 Ships that have been fitted with open-loop scrubbers need to be aware of the risk that they may not be permitted to operate these within the territorial waters of certain port states. Also for a comparative analysis between scrubber technology and LNG, see D Kolich & F Kurtovic, "LNG VS Scrubber Technology in Future Green Ships" (accessed 14 June 2020) at 1–12, online (pdf): *Croatian Scientific Bibliography CROSBI* <bib.irb.hr/datoteka/1032238.Kolich_Kurtovic-SMATECH_2019.pdf> [perma.cc/UEX4-H2AF].

5 "Sulfur 2020—Cutting Sulphur Oxide Emissions" (last visited 14 June 2020), online: *International Maritime Organization* <www.imo.org/en/MediaCentre/HotTopics/Pages/Sulphur-2020.aspx> [perma.cc/H7SY-Y4N2].

6 Amendments to *MARPOL* Annex VI to establish the North American ECA entered into force on 1 August 2011, with a twelve-month period before becoming effective. Coordinates for the North American ECA can be found in Resolution MEPC.190(60).

7 Designated under *MARPOL* amendments adopted in July 2011, with expected entry into force on 1 January 2013, and taking effect twelve months later on 1 January 2014; International Maritime Organization, "IMO 2020—Cutting Sulphur Oxide Emissions", online: *International Maritime Organization* <www.imo.org/en/MediaCentre/HotTopics/Pages/Sulphur-2020.aspx>.

8 See "Canadian LNG Projects" (31 December 2018), online: *Natural Resources Canada* <www.nrcan.gc.ca/energy/energy-sources-distribution/natural-gas/canadian-lng-projects/5683> [perma.cc/N5BC-ZXVP] [LNG Projects].

9 *Ibid.*

10 Owain Johnson, "As Natural Gas Production Increases, Here's How LNG Is Changing the Global Market" (7 November 2019), online: *Business Insider* <www.businessinsider.com/sc/new-development-in-natural-gas-production-can-change-the-market-2019-11> [perma.cc/8EXS-LGZK].

11 "Global Gas and LNG Outlook to 2035" (4 September 2019), online: *McKinsey & Company* <www.mckinsey.com/industries/oil-and-gas/our-insights/global-gas-and-lng-outlook-to-2035> [perma.cc/94KS-FRKX].

12 Resolution MEPC.320(74), (accessed 14 June 2020) at 1–19, online (pdf): *International Maritime Organization* <wwwcdn.imo.org/localresources/en/OurWork/Environment/Documents/Resolution%20MEPC.320%2874%29.pdf> [perma.cc/26WJ-3M55].

13 See IMO Resolutions MSC.385(94) and MEPC.264(68).

14 *Arctic Shipping Safety and Pollution Prevention Regulations*, SOR/2017-286.

15 See "Transport Canada Introduces New *Arctic Shipping Safety and Pollution Prevention Regulations*" (10 January 2018), online: *Government of Canada* <www.canada.ca/en/transport-canada/news/2018/01/transport_canadaintroducesnewarcticshippingsafetyandpollutionpre.html> [perma.cc/L2NW-CTDP].

16 See "International Maritime Organization Moves Ahead with Oceans and Climate Change Agenda—Briefing 17" (11 July 2017), online: *International Maritime Organization* <www.imo.org/en/MediaCentre/PressBriefings/Pages/17-MEPC-71.aspx> [perma.cc/DC2F-Q63F].

17 See Malte Humpert, "IMO Moves Forward with Ban of Arctic HFO But Exempts Some Vessels until 2029", *High North News* (24 February 2020), online: <www.highnorthnews.com/en/imo-moves-forward-ban-arctic-hfo-exempts-some-vessels-until-2029> [perma.cc/YNQ6-JZFR].

18 *International Code of Safety for Ships Using Gases or Other Low Flashpoint Fuels*, 11 June 2015, MSC. 391 (95) (entered into force on 1 January 2017).

19 *International Convention for the Safety of Life at Sea*, 1 November 1974, 1184 UNTS 3 (entered into force 25 May 1980).

20 See "Marine Safety Management System: Tier 1-Policy—Requirements for Vessels Using Natural Gas as Fuel" (last visited 14 June 2020) at 1–13, online (pdf): *Transport Canada* <www.tc.gc.ca/eng/marinesafety/requirements-vessels-using-natural-gas-fuel.html> [perma.cc/5XMW-TJJS].

21 Government of Canada, "Canadian LNG Projects", online: *Government of Canada* <www.nrcan.gc.ca/our-natural-resources/energy-sources-distribution/clean-fossil-fuels/natural-gas/canadian-lng-projects/5683>; Canada Energy Regulator, "Export and Import Licence Applications", online: *Canada Energy Regulator* <www.cer-rec.gc.ca/en/applications-hearings/view-applications-projects/lng-export-licence/index.html>.

22 *Impact Assessment Act*, SC 2019, c 28, s 1.

23 *Designated Classes of Projects Order*, SOR/2019-323.

24 *Physical Activities Regulations*, SOR/2019-285.

25 *Information and Management of Time Regulations*, SOR/2019-283.

26 See "Bill Amendments" (31 July 2018), online: *Government of Canada* <www.canada.ca/en/services/environment/conservation/assessments/environmental-reviews/bill-c-69.html> [perma.cc/49CM-3CYF].

27 "LNG & Marine Shipping" (accessed 14 June 2020), online: *ClearSeas* <clearseas.org/en/lng/> [perma.cc/Q8ZE-HV9Q].

28 Nikita Pavlenko et al, "The Climate Implications of Using LNG as Marine Fuel" (January 2020), online (pdf): *The International Council on Clean Transportation* <theicct.org/sites/default/files/publications/Climate_implications_LNG_marinefuel_01282020.pdf> [perma.cc/P5NH-CT9C].

29 European Maritime Safety Agency, "Guidance on LNG Bunkering to Port Authorities and Administrations" (31 January 2018), online (pdf): *Paris Mou* <www.parismou.org/sites/default/files/EMSA%20Guidance%20on%20LNG%20Bunkering.pdf> [perma.cc/YWM4-HCV5].

30 Llorenç Sastre Buades, *Implementation of LNG as Marine Fuel in Current Vessels: Perspectives and Improvements on Their Environmental Efficiency* (Master's Thesis, Facultat de Nàutica de Barcelona Universitat Politècnica de Catalunya, Barcelona, February 2017), online (pdf): *Up Commons* <upcommons.upc.edu/bitstream/handle/2117/106327/125548_Implementation%20of%20LNG%20as%20marine%20fuel%20in%20current%20vessels,%20perspectives%20and%20improvements%20on%20their%20environmental%20efficiency.pdf> [perma.cc/R7SH-MGDV].

31 See World Maritime News, "SEALNG: 175 LNG-Fueled Ships in Operation, 203 on Order" (18 February 2020), online: *Offshore Energy* <www.offshore-energy.biz/sealng-175-lng-fueled-ships-in-operation-203-on-order/> [perma.cc/U9L5-R2VQ]; see also "LNG Bunkering: Technical and Operational Advisory" (accessed 14 June 2020), online (pdf): *ABS* <ww2.eagle.org/content/dam/eagle/advisories-and-debriefs/ABS_LNG_Bunkering_Advisory.pdf> [perma.cc/S83L-3FVX].

32 *Canadian Standards Association Standard*, CAN/CSA Z276-01 (R2006).

33 Christina Hoicka, Katarina Savic & Alicia Campney "Reconciliation through Renewable Energy? A Survey of Indigenous Communities, Involvement, and Peoples in Canada" (2021) 74 *Energy Research & Social Science* at 3.

34 ABS Group, "LNG Fueled Vessel Crew Training and Competence" (20 February 2020) at 1–20, online (pdf): *Maritime College* <www.sunymaritime.edu/sites/default/files/2020-03/ABS%20Crew%20Training%20and%20Competence.pdf> [perma.cc/833F-7YQB].

35 See Sea-LNG Ltd, "LNG as a Marine Fuel–Our Zero Emissions Future Starts Now" (February 2020), online (pdf): SEA\LNG <sea-lng.org/wp-content/uploads/2020/02/200214_SEALNG2019reviewDIGITAL_compressed.pdf> [perma.cc/PU7V-X5K9] [LNG as a Marine Fuel].

36 Jasmina Ovcina, "Gibson: 27 LNG-Fuelled Ships Ordered So Far This Year" (12 April 2021), online: *Offshore Energy* <www.offshore-energy.biz/gibson-27-lng-fuelled-ships-ordered-so-far-this-year/> [perma.cc/5C52-WK9S].

37 LNG as a Marine Fuel, *supra* note 35.

38 MI News Network, "10 Noteworthy LNG-Powered Vessels" (13 December 2019), online: *Marine Insight* <www.marineinsight.com/tech/10-noteworthy-lng-fueled-vessels/> [perma.cc/SHL3-K38M] [MI News Network].

39 LNG as a Marine Fuel, *supra* note 35, at 6.

40 *Ibid* at 7.

41 *Ibid.*

42 *Ibid.*

43 *Ibid* at 9.

44 MI News Network, *supra* note 38.

45 See Karolin Schaps, "LNG-Fuelled Ship Order Book Bulges: More Vessels Are Under Construction than the Entire Existing Fleet as IMO 2020 Looms" (16 September 2019), online: *Petroleum Economist* <www.petroleum-economist.com/articles/midstream-downstream/lng/2019/lng-fuelled-ship-order-book-bulges> [perma.cc/DE93-JJSC]; Ship & Bunker, "World's First LNG Powered Cruise Ship to Trial Fuel Cells" (15 October 2019), online: *Ship & Bunker* <shipandbunker.com/news/world/391202-worlds-first-lng-powered-cruise-ship-to-trial-fuel-cells>.

46 LNG as a Marine Fuel, *supra* note 35, at 11.

47 See Carnival Corporation & Plc Sustainability "Pioneering Liquefied Natural Gas" (2018), online: *Carnival Corporation & Plc Sustainability* <carnivalsustainability.com/highlights/pioneering-liquefied-natural-gas/> [perma.cc/MM3T-E3RV].

48 Frances Marcellin, "Onboard MSC Grandiosa: A Glimpse into the Future of LNG" (18 February 2020), online: *Ship-Technology* <www.ship-technology.com/features/msc-grandiosa-review/>.

49 MI News Network, *supra* note 38.

50 LNG Projects, *supra* note 8.

51 Fathom World, "LNG to Dominate Fuel Mix in 2050 says DNV GL" (13 September 2019), online: *Fathom World* <fathom.world/lng-to-dominate-fuel-mix-in-2050-says-dnv-gl/> [perma.cc/YCF8-BMP7].

8

Going with the Flow: Tidal Regulation in Atlantic Canada

Catherine A. LeBlanc[1] *and Christopher J. Stewart*[2]

Increased demand for renewable energy has led to an interest in the immense potential for tidal energy development in Atlantic Canada. Unlike the sun or the wind, tides are predictable and easier to integrate into existing power distribution systems.[3] However, the powerful tides have not made it easy for baseline data collection or technology testing.[4] The many unknowns combined with a multitude of stakeholders and government jurisdictions have led to questions on how to adequately and effectively regulate tidal development. It has been said that "tide and time wait for none." Are regulators doing enough to keep up with the flow?

Tidal Power Generation

There are two main types of tidal power generation: tidal range and in-stream. A tidal range system generates power through the difference in the height of the water and can be in the form of a dam, barrage, or lagoon.[5] In contrast, in-stream tidal energy is generated by the open flow of water through turbines.[6] In-stream turbines can be installed one at a time and are easier to remove than tidal-range barrages.[7] The Fundy Ocean Research Centre for Energy (FORCE) has secured multiple berths located in the Minas Passage on Nova Scotia's Fundy Coast in which developers can test their in-stream turbines. These berths have created international interest in tidal energy development in Atlantic Canada.

Who's in Charge?

It may be surprising to learn that maritime boundaries in Atlantic Canada are not clearly defined. This includes federal-provincial as well as interprovincial boundaries.[8] Even within provincial waters, both federal and provincial governments have jurisdiction.[9] Municipal governments may also require certain permits and licences for tidal power generation. Within the multiple levels of government, certain environmental reviews seem to overlap. It is only in recognizing the perspective and expertise of each stakeholder, whether the various levels of government or other organizations, that tidal power regulation can be purposeful and effective.

FEDERAL REGULATION

Although provincial governments have jurisdiction over power-generation facilities, there are many aspects of tidal power that fall under federal authority. The legislation listed in Table 8.1 provides a general overview of the types of federal requirements that would apply to a tidal project. For example, any in-stream tidal project of 50 MW or more would trigger an environmental assessment under the *Impact Assessment Act* (*IAA*).[10] This environmental assessment may be completed under the auspices of a "Responsible Authority" such as the Canada Energy Regulator (formerly the National Energy Board).[11] Smaller tidal projects may also require environmental assessments under the *IAA* where there is significant public concern or environmental effects.[12] Additionally, tidal projects would require permits such as those required under the *Fisheries Act*[13] and the Canadian *Navigable Waters Act*.[14]

Under the *IAA*, consultation and cooperation between departments and with other levels of government is required as part of the environmental assessment.[15]

Table 8.1 Federal regulatory overview

IAA, 2019[1]	Environmental assessment if over 50 MW
Canadian Energy Regulator Act[2]	Approval for inter-provincial power lines
Canadian Navigable Waters Act[3]	Permit—watercourse alteration
Species at Risk Act[4]	Permit—interference with species at risk
Migratory Birds Convention Act[5]	Permit—interference with migratory birds
Fisheries Act[6]	Permit—interference with fish
Oceans Act[7]	Ocean management
Canada National Marine Conservation Areas Act[8]	Protection of designated conservation areas
Canada Shipping Act 2001[9]	Shipping requirements
Canadian Environmental Protection Act[10]	Permit—ocean disposal

1 *Supra* note 10.
2 *Canadian Energy Regulator Act*, SC 2019, c 28, pt 4.
3 *Supra* note 14.
4 *Species at Risk Act*, SC 2002, c 29.
5 *Migratory Birds Convention Act*, SC 1994, c 22, s 5.
6 *Supra* note 13.
7 *Oceans Act*, SC 1996, c 31.
8 *Canada National Marine Conservation Areas Act*, SC 2002, c 18.
9 *Canada Shipping Act, 2001*, SC 2001, c 26.
10 *Canadian Environmental Protection Act, 1999*, SC 1999, c 33.

PROVINCIAL REGULATION

In Atlantic Canada, each province has chosen a different approach to tidal power development and regulation. In 2012, the PEI Energy Commission determined that tidal development costs could be "prohibitively high" for the province, although it remained open to future reassessment.[16] Similar conclusions were reached in Newfoundland & Labrador.[17] In the meantime, the province was willing to share its knowledge and experience in dealing with hostile

Table 8.2 New Brunswick regulatory overview

Clean Environment Act[1]	Environmental assessment if power facility over 3 MW
Electricity Act[2]	Application for power facility
Crown Lands and Forests Act[3]	License/leases for Crown land
Heritage Conservation Act[4]	Protection of historic sites
Fish and Wildlife Act[5]	Protection of fish and wildlife
Species at Risk Act[6]	Permit—interference with species at risk
NB Policy[7]	Guideline—tidal regulation
Submerged Land Policy[8]	Guideline—underwater structure regulation
Coastal Areas Protection Policy[9]	Guideline—coastal protection

1 *Clean Environment Act*, RSNB 1973, c C-6.
2 *Electricity Act*, SNB 2013, c 7.
3 *Crown Lands and Forests Act*, SNB 1980, c C-38.1.
4 *Heritage Conservation Act*, SNB 2009, c H-4.05.
5 *Fish and Wildlife Act*, SNB 1980, c F-14.1.
6 *Species at Risk Act*, RSNB 2012, c 6.
7 Government of New Brunswick, "Natural Resources and Energy Development", online: *Government of New Brunswick* <www2.gnb.ca/content/dam/gnb/Departments/nr-rn/pdf/en/Publications/CLM0222009.pdf>.
8 Government of New Brunswick, "Natural Resources and Energy Development", online: *Government of New Brunswick* <www2.gnb.ca/content/dam/gnb/Departments/nr-rn/pdf/en/Publications/CLM0142004.pdf>.
9 Government of New Brunswick, "Natural Resources and Energy Development", online: *Government of New Brunswick* <www2.gnb.ca/content/dam/gnb/Departments/nr-rn/pdf/en/Publications/CoastalFacts.pdf>.

environments.[18] In New Brunswick and Nova Scotia, the powerful tides of the Bay of Fundy have led to a more active involvement in tidal power development.

New Brunswick

The province of New Brunswick has required that, by 2020, 40 percent of in-province electricity sales must be from renewable resources.[19] In support of tidal power development, the province created the *Allocation of Crown Lands for Tidal In-Stream Energy Conversion Projects* (NB Policy) in 2011 which replaced a prior interim policy.[20] Under the NB Policy, different regulation parameters would be applied to each stage of the project.[21] These projects

Table 8.3 Nova Scotia regulatory overview

Environment Act[1]	Environmental assessment if over 2 MW
MRA[2]	Tidal project permit
Electricity Act[3]	Tidal project approval
Crown Lands Act[4]	Leases/permits for Crown land
Special Places Protection Act[5]	Protection of historic sites
Wilderness Areas Protection Act[6]	Authorization of the minister required
Endangered Species Act[7]	Permit—interference with endangered species
Beaches Act[8]	Permit—structures located on the beach
Statement of Best Practices for In-Stream Tidal Energy[9]	Guideline—tidal regulation

1 *Environment Act*, SNS 1994-95, c 1 [*Environment Act*].
2 *MRA*, *supra* note 47.
3 *Electricity Act*, SNS 2004, c 25.
4 *Crown Lands Act*, RSNS 1989, c 114.
5 *Special Places Protection Act*, RS, c 438.
6 *Wilderness Areas Protection Act*, 1998, c 27.
7 *Endangered Species Act*, SNS 1998, c 11.
8 *Beaches Act*, RS, c 32.
9 Nova Scotia Department of Energy and Marine Renewables, "Statement of Best Practices for In-Stream Tidal Energy Development & Operation: Standards and Practices For In-Stream Tidal Energy" online: *Nova Scotia Department of Energy and Marine Renewables* <energy.novascotia.ca/sites/default/files/Statement%20of%20Best%20Practices%20Booklet.pdf>.

would also be subject to provincial legislation as shown in Table 8.2. Since the creation of the NB Policy in 2011, tidal power development in New Brunswick has remained stagnant over recent years. However, a recent summit held in Saint John may create a surge of interest in this type of energy generation.[22]

Nova Scotia

Similar to New Brunswick, the province of Nova Scotia has also set a goal of 40 percent of renewable energy by 2020.[23] However, contrary to its neighbouring province, Nova Scotia has forged ahead with tidal-specific regulation.[24] The regulations under the Nova Scotia *Environment Act* and the

Electricity Act set out environmental requirements based on the size of the tidal project.[25] The province has also established a guaranteed feed-in tariff (FIT) with the province-wide electrical utility for commercial development and community-owned projects (COMFIT),[26] although the latter has since been closed because of high costs.[27] Nova Scotia also recently introduced the *Marine Renewable-energy Act* (*MRA*).[28] The *MRA* has provided a legislative framework for a tidal project permit system. An overview of Nova Scotia legislation applicable to tidal projects is included at Table 8.3.

The first major in-stream tidal project in Atlantic Canada was the installation of the FORCE demonstration site in the Minas Passage. For the project's environmental assessment, both the federal and provincial governments agreed to collaborate through a "one-window" joint review.[29] The federal *Canadian Environmental Assessment Act, 2012* (*CEAA 2012*, now *IAA*) and Nova Scotia's *Environment Act* have specific provisions allowing collaboration between governments.[30] The one-window process allows for more certainty on behalf of the tidal developer that all applicable permits and licences have been requested, as well as reducing time and resources for the inter-governmental review where certain sections of review would have overlapped if done separately. The provision for a permanent tidal-specific one-window committee has since been added to Nova Scotia legislation.[31]

Marine Area Protection

Marine areas in Atlantic Canada are home to diverse inhabitants and activities. Certain areas are designated for protection through federal legislation, such as the *Oceans Act* or the *Species at Risk Act*, as well as provincial legislation. Protected areas may also be designated by organizations, for example, the UNESCO Fundy Biosphere Reserve. Aside from protected areas, a potential tidal project may come into conflict with fishing rights, navigation, aquaculture installations, recreational activities, or other energy projects.[32]

Different approaches have been brought forward to minimize any potential conflicts. Under the NB Policy, a developer must ensure that the proposed project does not encroach on other activities and is located at least 100 m away from any designated area. The NB Policy also limits tidal projects to a maximum output of 7.5 MW in the "Resource High Activity Area" located around Grand Manan Island. In contrast, the province of Nova Scotia has established a list of Marine Renewable Electricity Areas (MREA) that are the most suitable for tidal projects.[33] Any addition to the list must undergo a public consultation process and environmental assessment.[34] Additionally, all MREA's are to be reviewed within twenty years to minimize any impact on other marine activities.[35]

There have also been concerns expressed over the scope of environmental reviews in relation to protected areas. Existing environmental review classifications are based on the size of the tidal project.[36] However, this factor does not account for the size of the marine area or the proximity to protected areas.[37] Additionally, in-stream tidal projects can easily be expanded and it is important that any initial environmental review take this into consideration.[38] Further, multiple turbines or projects in one area could create cumulative effects over time.[39] Finally, there are also natural changes that occur in the marine environment.[40]

Risk Assessment and Management

In 2011, a series of models were created to study the environmental effects of offshore renewable energy that included in-stream tidal energy.[41] Although these models provided light on the types of environmental risks, there are still many unknowns related to risk assessment and management in tidal projects.

Many environmental legislative regimes specify a precautionary approach with regard to environmental risks.[42] However, there is certain knowledge that will only be gained when the technology is tested in real circumstances. This type of risk mitigation is known as an adaptive approach.[43]

In July 2016, the Fundy Inshore Fisherman's Association launched a judicial review of the Nova Scotia minister of the environment's decision to allow deployment of the Cape Spear Tidal Venture at the FORCE test site.[44] The judicial review application concerns, among others, the applicability of the precautionary and adaptive management approaches within the current regulatory system.[45] This case illustrates the difficulties with risk assessment in tidal projects and also the importance of consultation. Many stakeholders will be closely watching the outcome and implications of the judicial review application.[46]

Future Framework

It is generally agreed that tidal energy is more environmentally viable than traditional energy sources.[47] However, the many unknowns associated with new technology and its effects on the environment raise many questions and concerns. This is where effective regulation can bridge the gap between emerging technology and renewable energy goals. Regulation must ensure that important water resources are protected while also encouraging renewable energy initiatives.

Going forward, an effective regulatory framework will involve continued collaboration between all levels of government and other stakeholders. The province of Nova Scotia has already specifically provided for tidal development in its legislation, whereas the province of New Brunswick may be left behind when commercial tidal development becomes reality. Although it is important to establish a regulatory framework, it should be periodically assessed as technology advances. Atlantic Canada has the opportunity to set an example in tidal energy development and this includes providing a framework to ensure minimal environmental impact.

NOTES

1 Associate, Stewart McKelvey, Moncton, NB.

2 Office Partner, Stewart McKelvey, Moncton, NB.

3 Acadia Tidal Energy Institute, *Community and Business Toolkit for Tidal Energy Development* (2013) at 13 [Acadia Tidal Energy Institute].

4 *Ibid* at 82; "Failed Tidal Turbine Explained at Symposium", *CBC News* (July 8, 2011), online: <www.cbc.ca/news/canada/nova-scotia/failed-tidal-turbine-explained-at-symposium-1.1075510>.

5 Acadia Tidal Energy Institute, *supra* note 3 at 11–13.

6 *Ibid.*

7 Fundy Force, "Barrage vs In-stream," online: *Fundy Force* <fundyforce.ca>.

8 Meinhard Doelle et al, "The Regulation of Tidal Energy Development off Nova Scotia: Navigating Foggy Waters" (2006) 55 UNBLJ 27 at 34–41.

9 *Ibid* at 35.

10 *Impact Assessment Act*, SC 2019, c 28; *Regulations Designating Physical Activities*, SOR/2012-147 at 2–3.

11 *Canadian Environmental Assessment Act, 2012*, SC 2021, c 19, s 52 [*CEAA 2012*], s 9.

12 *Ibid*, s 9(2).

13 *Fisheries Act*, RSC 1985, c F-14, s 35.

14 *Canadian Navigable Waters Act*, RSC 1985, c N-22, s 5.

15 *Supra* note 14.

16 PEI Energy Commission, *Final Report: Charting Our Electricity Future* (Sept 2012) at 40, 60.

17 E4tech, *Newfoundland & Labrador Energy Innovation Roadmap: Priority Identification* (St. John's: Newfoundland & Labrador Department of Natural Resources, 2010), at 13.

18 *Ibid.*

19 *Electricity from Renewable Resources*, NB Reg 2015-60, s 3(1).

20 Government of New Brunswick, *Allocation of Crown Lands for Tidal In-stream Energy Conversion Projects* (2011).

21 *Ibid* at 28–30.

22 Government of New Brunswick, *Tidal Energy Opportunities Summit* (April 26, 2016) [*Tidal Energy Opportunities*].

23 *Renewable Electricity Regulations*, NS Reg 155/2010, s 6A [*Renewable Electricity*].

24 Robert O Fournier, *Marine Renewable Energy Legislation* (18 July 2011) at 16, online (pdf): *A Consultative Process* <oera.ca/sites/default/files/2019-05/Marine%20Renewable%20Energy%20Legislation%20%E2%80%93%20Report.pdf> [Fournier].

25 *Environmental Assessment Regulations*, NS Reg 26/95; *Tidal Energy Opportunities, supra* note 32.

26 Community Feed-In Tariff (COMFIT).

27 *Renewable Electricity, supra* note 42, s 19, 21; *Government of Nova Scotia, COMFIT*, online: <energy.novascotia.ca/renewables/programs-and-projects/comfit> [perma.cc/39JR-NQSP].

28 *Marine Renewable-energy Act*, SNS 2015, c 32 [*MRA*].

29 AECOM, *Fundy Tidal Energy Demonstration Project Volume I: Environmental Assessment* (2009) at 7 [AECOM, *Fundy Tidal Energy*].

30 SNS 1994-95, c.1.

31 *Renewable Electricity, supra* note 42, s 35.

32 AECOM, *Tidal Energy: Strategic Environmental Assessment (SEA) Update for the Bay of Fundy* (2014) at 125.

33 *MRA, supra* note 28, s 13–16.

34 *Ibid*, s 20.

35 *Ibid*, s 23.

36 *Regulations Designating Physical Activities, supra* note 10, s 2–3; *Environmental Assessment Regulations, supra* note 25; *Environmental Impact Assessment Regulation*, NB Reg 87-83.

37 Lisa Isaacman, Graham Daborn & Anna M Redden, *A Framework for Environmental Risk Assessment and Decision Making for Tidal Energy Development in Canada* (Wolfville, NS: Acadian Estuarine Center for Research [ACER], 2012) at 19–20 [Isaacman, Daborn & Redden].

38 *Ibid* at 18.

39 *Ibid*; AECOM, *Fundy Tidal Energy, supra* note 32 at 204–205; Fournier, *supra* note 24 at 61.

40 Isaacman, Daborn & Redden, *supra* note 37 at 8; Acadia Tidal Energy Institute, *supra* note 3 at 83.

41 Lisa Isaacman & Graham Daborn, *Pathways of Effects for Offshore Renewable Energy in Canada* (Wolfville, NS: ACER, December 2011).

42 *CEAA 2012, supra* note 11, s 6(2); *Environment Act, supra* note 30, s 2(b)(ii); Justin G Fisch, "Tidal Energy Law in Canada: Hindering an Untapped Potential for International Primacy" (2016) 21 Appeal 37 at 54 [Fisch].

43 Isaacman, Daborn & Redden, *supra* note 40 at 9–10; Fisch, *supra* note 42 at 54.

44 *Bay of Fundy Inshore Fisherman's Association v Nova Scotia Minister of the Environment* [No 453771], Amended Notice of Application for Judicial Review (July 25, 2016); Letter from the Minister of the Environment to FORCE (June 20, 2016).

45 *Ibid.*

46 The Supreme Court of Nova Scotia dismissed the application for judicial review in *Bay of Fundy Inshore Fisherman's Association v Nova Scotia (Environment)*, 2017 NSSC 96.

47 Fisch, *supra* note 42 at 55.

9

Pressures on the Ocean: Scientific Perspective

Douglas Wallace[1]

Introduction

A key aspect of the ocean is its fluid motion and connectivity, which means that cause and effect (e.g. sources/causes and damages/impacts) are usually separated geographically. The legal and courtroom implications and consequences of this connectivity have commonalities, conceptually, with those encountered in areas such as long-range air pollution, water resources, and groundwater use/contamination. Dealing with such issues can be complex and often slow, in part because of jurisdictional issues but also because of the scientific difficulty of attribution (i.e. linking cause with effect). Given that legal remedies to conflicts and damages associated with the marine environment are complex and slow to establish, it is worth peering into the future and looking back on the recent past to identify trends in order to anticipate issues that could impact future development, application, or interpretation of legislation. This type of trend analysis or projection is generally undertaken by the scientific community in isolation, sometimes with the subsequent production of "Summaries for Policymakers" or other guidance for non-scientists. In this paper, I follow this approach and present an overview of ongoing and future changes of the marine environment at large scales, which I believe are increasingly the causes or drivers ("forcings") for damage and conflicts at local and regional scales that end up being litigated in the courtroom.

Despite having taken the conventional, "isolated" approach for this paper, I believe it is becoming necessary to connect legal, enforcement, and scientific communities more effectively and regularly in a joint process of envisioning the ocean's future. Ideally, this would lead to policies and legal approaches better suited to altered situations of the future ocean. However, such cooperative visioning would also recognize that policy and regulation of human activities play an increasingly important role in determining the future state of the marine environment.

The Nature of Ocean Change

Pressures on the ocean environment are strongly mediated by two main classes of forcing: 1) "direct" human forcing linked to societal change and specific human actions, including technology development, population growth, and growing demands for living and non-living resources; and 2) "indirect" forcing associated with human activity, especially energy-use and agriculture, which with present technologies, impact climate and ecosystems on a global scale.

Direct Human Forcing: Human population is projected to rise to between 9.6 and 12.3 billion by the end of this century, with the bulk of the growth occurring in Africa.[2] The low elevation coastal zone (LECZ; elevation <10m) was home to 625 million people (c. 10 percent of the global population) in 2000 despite representing only 2.3 percent of global land area.[3] Projections under various scenarios suggest that the population of the LECZ will increase to between 1 and 1.4 billion by 2060, representing c. 12 percent of the global population. Whereas the bulk of the coastal population is located in Asia, the most dramatic growth will be in Africa, especially West Africa. In contrast, Canada's coastal population is projected to rise moderately from its 2000 value of 1.2 million to about 1.6 million in 2060.

A recent landmark review on "marine defaunation"[4] noted the widening range of direct human pressures on the marine environment. The authors suggested that the ocean is starting to experience human alteration of habitat analogous to the habitat degradation on land that was set in motion by the industrial revolution. Their list of recent developments includes the growth and expansion of coastal cities, land reclamation, advancements in seafloor mining, dredging, oil and gas extraction, tidal/wave energy generation, growth of marine transport, and the development of ocean farming, in addition to the growth of industrial fishing and bottom trawling that has been underway for some time.

Indirect Forcing: Energy use and resulting future emissions of CO_2 are the subject of representative concentration pathways (RCPs),[5] which are projections of future pathways of greenhouse gas concentrations and radiative forcing up to 2100 based on scenarios of socio-economic and technological change. The four RCPs (2.6, 4.5, 6, and 8.5) project atmospheric CO_2 levels of c. 400, 500, 600, and 950 ppm respectively by the end of this century. These are, in turn, associated with projected warming, sea-level rise, changes to ice-cover, and other phenomena (see below for more detail) that are projected using climate models.[6]

This indirect forcing is global in scope, so that regional and local changes, pressures and impacts on the marine environment and individual communities are, increasingly, the result of activities that are initiated and ongoing far away in both space and time. An obvious example of this is the rapidly changing transportation and hunting environment of Canada's northern peoples, which results from climate change and the reduction of Arctic sea ice extent. Similarly, property damage due to rising sea-levels cannot be attributed to specific individuals, organizations, or even countries: the cause is of global extent and involves the actions of most humankind.

Such climate-related changes to the ocean include physical changes such as ocean warming, sea-level rise, changes in sea-ice extent and iceberg distributions and, potentially, changes in the frequency and intensity of storms and their large-scale ocean circulation. These physical changes impact, in turn, the chemical and biological processes that alter marine ecosystems. However, in addition to such changes resulting ultimately from changes in radiative forcing, there is additional global-scale forcing associated with the changing chemical composition of the atmosphere. In particular, there is considerable concern that the ocean's uptake of anthropogenic CO_2, and the associated decrease in seawater pH, is adversely affecting certain marine species and/or life-stages of aquatic organisms. This process of "ocean acidification"[7] has potential implications for corals and other carbonate-shell forming organisms, including commercially valuable species such as oysters and related marine food chains. Global changes to the nitrogen cycle, especially the long-range transport of fixed, bio-available nitrogen from land to remote, nutrient-deficient ocean "deserts" via atmospheric transport, is now also recognized to have the potential to impact marine ecosystems on large scales[8] in addition to the more acute, local impacts of coastal eutrophication.

The Confluence of Simultaneous Change and Marine Risk

Both classes of forcing (direct and indirect) are operating simultaneously and globally so that the overall human relationship with the ocean and human exposure to marine-related risk, is impacted by both and their confluence.

On the one hand, technological developments and rapid population and economic growth in the coastal zone are altering the ways in which humans make use of and interact with the marine environment. These changing uses can be causes of conflict, especially where new uses are introduced in the vicinity of traditional or historical uses. Examples are numerous and varied and include the development of aquaculture, growth in the use of ocean spaces for tourism or renewable energy generation, the ever-deeper global development of offshore oil and gas resources, growth of coastal megacities, the development of larger ships and associated ports, etc. In addition to these new uses and developments, existing and longer established use patterns are also changing. For example, the over-exploitation of capture fisheries in waters adjacent to developed countries, together with technology development, has led to a massive global shift of fishing pressure towards waters surrounding less-developed nations, for example in Africa.[9] Whereas impacts and conflicts resulting from these changing human uses of the ocean are usually national, regional, or local, the trends and patterns of change have globalized. This implies a need for exchanging views on how to minimize conflicts or damage and manage the response to change on a global scale.

On the other hand, primarily as a consequence of fossil-energy use but also as a result of other global-scale industries such as agriculture, the planetary environment itself is changing, including increasingly rapid changes within and around the ocean. Here, the issue is frequently related to climate change and its knock-on consequences such as sea-level rise or the dramatic reductions of sea-ice cover in the Arctic. The changing human use of the ocean is taking place in the context of these rapid and large-scale environmental changes. Examples of these ongoing and projected changes are listed below, with most information referenced to the Intergovernmental Panel on Climate Change (IPCC).[10]

Warming: The globally averaged surface temperature has warmed by 0.85°C since 1850. This has not been spatially uniform, and a few oceanic regions (including the northwest Atlantic) experienced no significant long-term warming. The warming extends into the deep ocean (<2000m). By the end of this century, models project global surface temperatures to be at least 1.5°C higher relative to 1850 for all RCPs except RCP2.6, and >2°C for RCP6.0 and RCP8.5.

Sea-level rise: Over the past century, global sea level rose by 0.19 m, a faster rate than the previous 2000 years. Thermal expansion, melting of glacial ice, and large ice sheets have contributed roughly equally to this increase. Projections of future rise are dependent on the RCP and remain controversial. The rate and even sign of sea-level rise is non-uniform and is particularly variable around Canada due to differences in response to loss of land-ice since the last ice age. Global estimates of relative sea-level rise are 0.42 m and 0.85 m for RCP4.5 and RCP8.5 respectively,[11] with projections for the Canadian coastline ranging from <0 to 0.7 m (RCP4.5) depending on location.

Ice-cover changes: The annual mean Arctic sea ice extent decreased dramatically between 1979 and 2012 at a rate of 3.5 to 4.1 percent per decade. Summer extent decreased from 9.4 to 13.6 percent per decade. Projected summertime reductions by the end of this century range from 43 percent (RCP2.6) to 94 percent (RCP8.5) and from 8 percent to 34 percent for RCP8.5 in the winter season. Hence, an ice-free summertime Arctic Ocean is projected for only the most extreme climate-change scenario.

Ocean acidification: Projected changes in surface ocean pH by the end of this century depend strongly on the amount of CO_2 emitted and range from 0.06 (RCP2.6) to c. 0.31 for RCP8.5.

Ocean Value and Changing Marine Risk

The intersection or confluence of these two classes of forcing means that the nature and amplitude of marine-related risks are changing. These risks are to human life (including quality of life), marine ecosystems, and property and economic activity in and around the oceans.

Ocean-related activities, industries, and ecosystem services have considerable economic value. The global GDP of the "ocean economy" has been estimated at US$2.5 trillion per year, equivalent to that of the seventh largest national economy.[12] This figure does not include the GDP associated with offshore fossil-energy and other uses of the sub-seafloor.

In some cases, marine risk is altered by fundamentally new hazards that did not exist previously. The Fukushima radiological disaster[13] was the consequence of a hazard that did not exist several decades earlier. The Deepwater

Horizon disaster[14] is another such example. More commonly, it is the frequency or amplitude of long-existing hazards that is altered, such as sea-level rise or coastal flooding. Changing vulnerability to hazards, for example, due to changing use of the coastal zone, contributes significantly to altered risk.

This global phenomenon of ongoing major change is the context for legal disputes that arise in connection with ocean activities and associated risks and damages.

Emerging Issues Facing the Ocean

A number of fundamentally new emerging issues are worth mentioning specifically. Each issue has the potential to radically change the way in which we use the ocean.

Geoengineering: Intentional large-scale manipulation of planetary processes is discussed increasingly as a possible approach for mitigation of dangerous climate change. Two main approaches are considered:[15] (1) reducing levels of greenhouse gases in the atmosphere; and (2) altering radiative forcing. Schemes have been proposed for use on land, the atmosphere, space, and the ocean. The ocean-based schemes[16] are focused on CO_2 removal and include ocean fertilization: ocean alkalinity modification and deliberate manipulation of upwelling and downwelling circulation. Their effectiveness has been questioned[17] and even with optimistic estimates of carbon sequestration efficiency, the potential for CO_2 uptake via ocean fertilization is small relative to future emissions. Nevertheless, interest continues in the idea of adding small amounts of "limiting" nutrients (e.g. iron) in areas where other essential nutrients are in excess in order to initiate phytoplankton uptake of CO_2. Some of the interest likely lies with the closely associated potential for manipulating plankton blooms in order to increase fish stocks. For example, a controversial iron fertilization effort was conducted by the Haida Salmon Restoration Corporation 200 nautical miles west of Haida Gwaii in 2012, partly for CO_2 sequestration but mainly to investigate a hypothesis that linked "natural" iron deposition from volcanic ash and recruitment of Pacific salmon. The fertilization, with over 100 tonnes of iron sulphate and iron oxide, was conducted (without prior approval) and has been investigated by Environment Canada.

In addition to issues of legality and effectiveness, fertilization approaches have the potential for unintended consequences: for example, they can trigger the risk of toxic algae growth. The addition of a limiting nutrient in one location may prevent subsequent utilization of other, excess nutrients "downstream," thereby "robbing" downstream ecosystems.

Deep-sea mining: There has been a recent upsurge of interest in deep ocean mining, as indicated by the granting of twenty-seven contracts for deep ocean mineral exploration of ferromanganese nodules, crusts, and massive sulphide deposits by the International Seabed Authority.[18] Two national governments have granted mining licences for massive sulphides within their economic zones. On the other hand, shallow-water mining has been restricted as a result of environmental concerns. Nevertheless, the increased interest suggests that as technological barriers to deep ocean mining are overcome and if commodity prices become attractive, the potential exists for rapid growth of marine mining in the deep ocean.

Offshore Aquaculture: Aquatic systems (ocean and freshwater) presently supply c. 2 percent of the global food supply, despite biological productivity of the oceans and land being roughly equivalent.[19] On the other hand, aquatic systems already supply almost one-third of the animal meat consumed by humans and c. 12 percent of total animal protein. Aquaculture is already similar in magnitude to production from capture fisheries and there is a widespread view that feeding the Earth's future population will require massive expansion of ocean aquaculture.[20] This is likely to exacerbate conflicts with other ocean uses through competition for space and due to environmental impacts. The potential of moving aquaculture of plants, molluscs, and fish further offshore is viewed as a likely development due to space availability and the increased potential for diffusion of wastes.[21] Both technological and regulatory factors are limiting this expansion presently, and the potential of offshore aquaculture to contribute significantly to global food production is questioned. However, as technology improves, growth can be expected to develop rapidly.

Summary and Some Implications for the Future

At the turn of the century, the renowned marine ecologist Jeremy Jackson published a seminal article[22] that chronicled the history of human disturbance (i.e. pressures) on marine ecosystems. It is instructive to revisit this article c. fifteen years later. At that time, the history of disturbances was dominated by fishing, which was also the first major human pressure on the ocean dating back to the beginning of the Holocene. This has been followed, more or less sequentially, by pressures arising from coastal pollution, mechanical habitat destruction associated with coastal structures, invasive species introductions associated with marine transportation and, most recently, climate change. Based on the situation today, a number of emerging and potential threats can be added to Jackson's list including coastal aquaculture, deep-water resource extraction, faster and larger ships, ocean acidification, global changes in nutrient supply, the potential for offshore aquaculture, and even direct interventions into the planetary-scale processes in the form of geoengineering.

As discussed above, a key characteristic of our times is that these pressures on our oceans are multi-faceted (involving simultaneous societal and environmental change), changing rapidly (and accelerating), and global in scale. The nature of the change presents enormous challenges to scientists, policymakers, and those responsible for regulating use of the marine environment. Due to the rapidity and potential magnitude of the consequences of change, policy must increasingly be based on projections of how the oceans are likely to look and behave in the future.

These projections represent a major scientific challenge that must, ultimately, rely on models that take into account the complex and non-linear interactions, thresholds, and even tipping points that exist in the Earth System and the oceans. These interactions include those of humans and their technologies and policies. Hence, the models must represent changing processes and the behaviour of an entire planet and its human population (which, obviously, is not replicated), and include representations of processes that are operating on global scales and forces, often with no historical counterparts for comparison. Hence, the development of science-based projections of the future state of the ocean is a "grand challenge" to the scientific method. Duarte[23] has analyzed this grand challenge and discussed possible approaches to addressing it and, especially, "validating" or testing projections of the future ocean state. However, he also noted the importance of scientists, policymakers, and managers working closely together to develop the capacity to manage ocean problems adaptively "where uncertainties and unknowns are addressed through a learning-by-doing approach."[24]

NOTES

1 Canada Excellence Research Chair in Ocean Science and Technology, Department of Oceanography, Dalhousie University.

2 P Gerland et al, "World Population Stabilization Unlikely this Century" (2014) 346:6206 Science 234, DOI: <10.1126/science.1257469>.

3 B Neumann et al, "Future Coastal Population Growth and Exposure to Sea-Level Rise and Coastal Flooding—A Global Assessment" (2015) 10(3):e0118571 PLoS ONE, DOI: <10.1371/journal.pone.0118571>.

4 DJ McCauley et al, "Marine Defaunation: Animal Loss in the Global Ocean" (2015) 347:6219 Science 247, DOI: <10.1126/science.1255641>.

5 DP van Vuuren et al, "The Representative Concentration Pathways: An Overview" (2011) 109:5 *Climatic Change* at 21, DOI: <10.1007/s10584-011-0148-z>.

6 Intergovernmental Panel on Climate Change, online: <www.ipcc.ch/report/ar5/>.

7 International Geosphere-Biosphere Programme, Intergovernmental Oceanographic Commission, Scientific Committee on Oceanic Research, *Ocean Acidification Summary for Policymakers—Third Symposium on the Ocean in a High-CO2 World* (Stockholm: International Geosphere-Biosphere Programme, 2013).

8 I-N Kim et al, "Increasing Anthropogenic Nitrogen in the North Pacific Ocean" (2014) 346:6213 Science 1102, DOI: <10.1126/science.1258396>.

9 B Worm et al, "Rebuilding Global Fisheries" (2009) 325:5940 Science 578, DOI: <10.1126/science.1173146>.

10 "Summary for Policymakers" in TF Stocker et al, eds, *Climate Change 2013: The Physical Science Basis, Contribution of Working Group I to the Fifth Assessment Report of the Intergovernmental Panel on Climate Change* (Cambridge, UK & New York: Cambridge University Press), online (pdf): <www.ipcc.ch/site/assets/uploads/2018/03/WG1AR5_SummaryVolume_FINAL.pdf>.

11 M Carson et al, "Coastal Sea Level Changes: Observed and Projected during the 20th and 21st Century" (2016) 134 Climatic Change 269, DOI: <10.1007/s10584-015-1520-1>.

12 Ove Hoegh-Guldberg et al, *Reviving the Ocean Economy: The Case for Action—2015* (Gland & Geneva: World Wildlife Fund, 2015).

13 International Atomic Energy Agency, *The Fukushima Daiichi Accident*, 1st ed, STI/PUB/1710 (Vienna: International Atomic Energy Agency, 2015).

14 National Commission on the BP Deepwater Horizon Oil Spill and Offshore Drilling, *Deep Water: The Gulf Oil Disaster and the Future of Offshore Drilling—Report to the President* (Washington: US Government Printing Office, 2011).

15 JG Shepherd, "Geoengineering the Climate: An Overview and Update" (2012) 370:1974 Phil Trans R Soc A 4166, DOI: <10.1098/rsta.2012.0186>.

16 Z Zhang et al, "Review of Geoengineering Approaches to Mitigating Climate Change" (2015) 108 J Cleaner Production 893, DOI: <10.1016/j.jclepro.2014.09.076>.

17 DWR Wallace et al, *Ocean Fertilization: A Scientific Summary for Policy Makers*, IOC/BRO/2010/2 (Paris: IOC/UNESCO, 2010).

18 S Petersen, A Krätschell & MD Hannington, "The Current State of Global Activities Related to Deep-sea Mineral Exploration and Mining" (EAGE/DGG Workshop on Deep Mineral Exploration, 18 March 2016, Münster, Germany), DOI: <10.3997/2214-4609.201600033>.

19 Y Olsen, "How Can Mariculture Better Help Feed Humanity?" (2015) 2 Front Mar Sci 46, DOI: <10.3389/fmars.2015.00046>.

20 CM Duarte et al, "Will the Oceans Help Feed Humanity?" (2009) 59:11 BioScience 967, DOI: <10.1525/bio.2009.59.11.8>.

21 P Edwards, "Aquaculture Environment Interactions: Past, Present and Likely Future Trends" (2015) 447 Aquaculture 2, DOI: <10.1016/j.aquaculture.2015.02.001>.

22 JBC Jackson et al, "Historical Overfishing and the Recent Collapse of Coastal Ecosystems" (2001) 293:5530 Science 629, DOI: <10.1126/science.1059199>.

23 CM Duarte, "Global Change and the Future Ocean: A Grand Challenge for Marine Sciences" (2014) 1 Front Mar Sci 4015, DOI: <10.3389/fmars.2014.0006>.

24 *Ibid* at 13.

10

Anticipating and Avoiding Environmental Protection Disputes during Decommissioning of Oil and Gas Projects Offshore Canada

Daniel Watt[1]

Introduction

Decommissioning an offshore oil and gas project involves the risk of adverse effects on the marine environment and those who rely on marine resources. Concerns from stakeholders such as environmental groups, Indigenous peoples, and commercial fisheries are thus inevitable. Operators are therefore well-advised to anticipate and seek to minimize stakeholder concerns over environmental issues.

Canada's regulations on decommissioning, however, are relatively untested. Only one Canadian offshore project has been fully decommissioned: the Cohasset-Panuke Project (Cohasset) ceased production in 1999 and was fully decommissioned and abandoned in 2006.[2] Since then, the Atlantic regulatory regime[3] has been amended by the *Energy Safety and Security Act*,[4] while more recently, the *Canadian Environmental Assessment Act, 2012* (*CEAA 2012*)[5] was replaced with the *Impact Assessment Act* (*IAA*).[6] Indigenous law has also evolved considerably. Aside from significant spills, therefore, anticipating what environmental disputes may arise in decommissioning involves a degree of speculation.

The law, Cohasset experience, and current climate of project approvals suggest that the likeliest source of environmental disputes during decommissioning will be interest groups, Indigenous peoples, and other stakeholders opposing regulatory approval. For context, this paper outlines decommissioning methods and processes. Potential areas of dispute are then examined in light of the regulatory framework, the Cohasset experience, and other examples. The paper concludes with some suggestions for how to avoid or minimize disputes.

For ease of reference, the *Accord Act* is referred to throughout.

The Decommissioning Process

The optimal decommissioning method will depend on several factors, including environmental considerations. Three primary methods are as follows:

1. *Complete removal*—often asserted as the most environmentally sound strategy,[7] this requires deconstructing the installation and removing the pieces to onshore sites for disposal, reuse, or recycling. The work can be dangerous and intensive. Further, complete removal can, paradoxically, disrupt marine biotic communities.
2. *Partial removal*—involves removing certain components to shore for disposal, reuse, or recycling, while leaving others in place or relocating them to another marine location.
3. *Secondary uses*—platforms are re-purposed in place or at another location, for uses such as: renewable energy, port and harbour infrastructure, search and rescue bases, vessel navigation bases, meteorological stations, and aquaculture.

The work required will depend on the method and other considerations. The typical process will involve planning, cessation of production, well plugging and abandonment, removal of hazardous products and hydrocarbons, platform preparation (or "hook down"), topsides removal, substructure removal, subsea infrastructure removal, site remediation, topsides and substructure reuse and recycling, and monitoring for pollution of any components or material left *in situ*.[8]

The method and process proposed will invariably engage environmental considerations and the risk of opposition.

The Regulatory Framework

The regulation of decommissioning in Canada involves both international and domestic law.

INTERNATIONAL OBLIGATIONS

Canada is party to treaties that address offshore decommissioning. The genesis of the international framework was the 1958 *Geneva Convention on the Continental Shelf*, which confirmed coastal states' rights to construct installations on the continental shelf and to explore and exploit its natural resources.[9] It also required that abandoned installations be "entirely removed."[10]

The 1982 *United Nations Convention on the Law of the Sea* (*UNCLOS*) eclipsed the *Geneva Convention*, giving coastal states the exclusive right to construct, authorize, or regulate offshore installations within territorial seas and exclusive economic zones, or on the continental shelf.[11] *UNCLOS* also permits partial removal under certain conditions.[12]

The 1972 *Convention on the Prevention of Marine Pollution by Dumping of Wastes and Other Matters*[13] and the *1996 Protocol*[14] are also relevant. The *1996 Protocol* allows for disposal at sea of platforms or structures where the coastal state approves the dumping by issuing a special permit, the conditions and criteria for which are set out in the protocol.[15]

Key provisions of these instruments have been enacted in Canadian legislation.[16]

ACCORD ACT AND THE CANADA-NOVA SCOTIA OFFSHORE PETROLEUM BOARD

The primary regulatory legislation in the Nova Scotia offshore comprises the *Accord Act* and its provincial mirror legislation, which establish the Canada-Nova Scotia Offshore Petroleum Board (CNSOPB).[17] CNSOPB is responsible for administering the legislation and managing offshore resources.[18] Its responsibilities include environmental protection and licensing and offshore exploration and development, among other duties. The *Accord Act* provisions and other legislation applicable to approval processes are discussed below.

Disputes over Decommissioning Approvals

The proponent or operator must obtain approvals and authorizations for decommissioning during project development and before decommissioning operations commence. Environmental assessments (EAs) or impact assessments (IAs) and public input are required at both stages. Depending on the project, the public input may involve full hearings. It is at the specific authorization stage that the operator is most likely to encounter opposition. Such opposition may result in applications for injunctive or other relief. Even absent litigation, approvals may be delayed, denied, or issued with undesirable conditions. To minimize these risks, the approval process must be deftly managed.

APPROVAL AND AUTHORIZATION PROCESS

Two tiers of approval for decommissioning are required under the *Accord Act*:

- First, a "development plan" containing the basic terms of the proposed project must be submitted and approved.[19]
- Second, authorizations to carry out specific works or activities in the context of the project, called "work authorizations," must be applied for and issued.[20]

Approval stages are lightning rods for opposition. Decisions made by the operator at each stage can foment immediate environmental disputes or lay the groundwork for future opposition.

Development Plan

The development plan is the basic document governing reservoir development and is necessary for a production licence.[21] It must include provisions for decommissioning.[22] CNSOPB by policy also requires a "decommissioning and abandonment program" to be in the Development Plan.[23]

Development Plans, and their decommissioning programs, must satisfy, among regulatory components, an environmental impact statement (EIS), and a public review.[24] Both components engage public input into the proposed decommissioning.

Public Reviews

CNSOPB may "conduct a public review in relation to the exercise of any of its powers or the performance of any of its duties where the Board is of the opinion that it is in the public interest to do so."[25] Its policy is to require a public review for the approval of major development projects.[26] Depending on the scale of the proposed project and the degree of public interest it engages, CNSOPB may either request written public submissions or appoint a commission responsible for conducting a public hearing.

ENVIRONMENTAL IMPACT STATEMENTS, IMPACT ASSESSMENTS, AND ENVIRONMENTAL ASSESSMENTS

The development plan will also trigger either an IA under the *IAA* or an internal EA by the CNSOPB. The following applicable works trigger an IA under the *IAA*:[27]

> 34 The drilling, testing and abandonment, in an area set out in one or more exploration licences issued in accordance with the *Canada Petroleum Resources Act*, the *Canada–Newfoundland and Labrador Atlantic Accord Implementation Act* or the *Canada-Nova Scotia Offshore Petroleum Resources Accord Implementation Act*, of offshore exploratory wells in the first drilling program, as defined in subsection 1(1) of the *Canada Oil and Gas Drilling and Production Regulations*, SOR/2009-315.
>
> 35 The construction, installation and operation of a new offshore floating or fixed platform, vessel or artificial island used for the production of oil or gas.
>
> 36 The decommissioning and abandonment of an existing offshore floating or fixed platform, vessel or artificial island used for the production of oil or gas that is proposed to be disposed of or abandoned offshore or converted on site to another role.
>
> 40 The construction, operation, decommissioning and abandonment of a new offshore oil and gas pipeline, other than a flowline as defined in subsection 2(1) of the *Canada Oil and Gas Installations Regulations*.

Accordingly, development projects and certain required works, such as well abandonments or decommissioning activities, will trigger an IA under the new *IAA*.

It is clear that the *IAA* will not restore responsibility to conduct federal IAs to the CNSOPB.[28] However, it is not yet entirely clear whether IAs of designated offshore projects will be conducted by the new Impact Assessment Agency or whether the minister of environment and climate change must refer such projects to the more onerous review panel process.[29]

Regardless of who conducts IAs for the decommissioning of offshore projects, there will certainly be requirements for public consultation and input at both the planning and assessment phases. In the planning phase (following which the agency must determine whether a designated project will require an IA), the agency "must ensure that the public is provided with an opportunity to participate meaningfully . . . including by inviting the public to provide comments. . . ."[30] If the agency conducts a resulting IA, the agency must again ensure an opportunity for meaningful public participation in the IA[31] and must invite the public to comment on the draft IA report.[32] If the IA is referred to a review panel, the panel must "hold hearings in a manner that offers the public an opportunity to participate meaningfully" in the IA.[33] The hearings will generally be public.[34]

Projects that do not trigger the *IAA* will still be subject to a so-called "*Accord Act*" EA conducted by CNSOPB. The *Guidelines* specify that EAs for works that do not engage *IAA* will mirror the process prescribed by the 1992 *Canadian Environmental Assessment Act* (*CEAA 1992*).[35] The comprehensive study report required of proponents must consider, among other things, public comments.[36]

AUTHORIZATIONS FOR DECOMMISSIONING WORK

Authorization must also be obtained for the work the decommissioning plan entails.[37] An EA is required.[38] As noted above, an IA under the *IAA* will be triggered by certain activities. Further, depending on the level of public interest in the project, CNSOPB may exercise public review powers.

The EA/IA process and public review discussed above are equally applicable to work authorizations. Work authorizations thus also involve public input and a risk of opposition. The risk of opposition to the proposed operations exists at both approval stages. However, opposition to decommissioning is more likely to occur at the work authorization stage, when decommissioning stands alone under the regulatory spotlight. Conversely, if all goes as planned, development plans are approved decades before decommissioning commences. Opposition during project development is less likely to focus on the decommissioning plan.

The development plan remains relevant to avoiding environmental disputes. However, an approved development plan cannot be amended without CNSOPB approval.[39] If an amendment is sought during the decommissioning phase, there may be greater pressure on CNSOPB to conduct a public hearing or to seek more public input. This alone can cause delay and foment opposition. As discussed below, the Cohasset experience bears this out.

Moreover, the public perception of the plan's legitimacy may be undermined, particularly if the proposed method is partial removal or is less costly for the operator. The story will invariably be framed as the operator seeking to cut corners at the expense of the environment—even if the evidence suggests partial removal is optimal from an environmental perspective.

Sources of Disputes

Probable sources of dispute are suggested by the potential effects that will be assessed in the EA/IA process. For instance, the following non-exhaustive litany of factors must be considered under the *IAA*: changes to the environment or to health, social, or economic conditions and the positive and negative consequences of these changes that are likely to be caused by the carrying out of the designated project (including "cumulative effects"); any impact on Indigenous groups and any adverse impact on Indigenous or Treaty rights; the purpose of and need for the project; alternative means of carrying out the project that are technically and economically feasible, including through the use of best available technologies, and the effects of those means; alternatives to the project that are technically and economically feasible and directly related to the project; Indigenous knowledge provided with respect to the project; the extent to which the designated project contributes to sustainability; the extent to which the project's effects hinder or contribute to the government of Canada's ability to meet its environmental obligations and its commitments in respect of climate change; considerations related to Indigenous cultures; community knowledge provided with respect to the designated project; public comments; any assessment of the effects of the project conducted by or on behalf of an Indigenous governing body; and, the intersection of sex and gender with other identity factors.[40] This list provides fertile ground for potential opposition to any activity associated with an offshore petroleum project.

Aside from the obvious likelihood of challenges from environmental groups, the Cohasset experience suggests that decommissioning operations may also conflict with fish and fish habitat and, depending on the area, the current use of resources by Indigenous peoples.

Environmental Groups

Environmental groups are an obvious source of challenge to decommissioning. The European reaction to Shell's decommissioning of the *Brent Spar*, an oil storage facility, was extreme, but illustrative. The *Brent Spar* was redundant. In 1991, Shell commissioned independent studies and, after three years of consultations, endorsed deep water disposal in the remote North Atlantic. The method was deemed superior in the areas of safety, environmental impact, and cost. International, regional, and UK regulations then permitted the proposed dumping.

Despite its legality, the 1995 UK approval of Shell's proposal triggered an immediate, dramatic, and occasionally violent public backlash. Greenpeace activists occupied the *Brent Spar* as it was being towed to the disposal site. Protestors boycotted, vandalized, and shot at Shell service stations in Germany. Germany's chancellor and other heads of state argued against Shell's plan at the June 1995 G7 summit in Halifax.

Shell eventually abandoned the operation. It re-initiated consultation and engaged governments, consultants, scientists, and public input. Ten years and £60,000,000 later, Shell cut up the *Brent Spar*. Large parts of it were used to construct a ferry terminal in Stavanger, Norway.

The *Brent Spar* decommissioning illustrates the politically volatile character of offshore oil and gas operations. It also underlines the importance of operators looking beyond mere compliance with existing regulations when navigating the decommissioning process—and the potentially costly effects of failing to do so.[41] Shell had a regulatory green light, but an insufficient degree of stakeholder consensus regarding its plan ultimately doomed that plan.

Indigenous Peoples

The Crown has a constitutional duty to consult with, and, where appropriate, to accommodate, Indigenous peoples in relation to action that may adversely impact claimed or established Indigenous or Treaty rights.[42] Decommissioning activities may adversely affect Indigenous or Treaty rights, such as those relating to fishing. In such cases, the Crown will be subject to a duty to consult and, where necessary, to accommodate applicable Indigenous groups before giving regulatory approval for the activities.

The consultative process adds a layer of complexity to project approvals and increases the risk of dispute and litigation. Damages, injunctive relief, or orders to complete consultation prior to the activity taking place are some of the remedies available for breach of the duty to consult.[43]

Cohasset is again instructive. In 1990, nine years before decommissioning, the proponent's development plan stated:

> When the Cohasset and Panuke fields have been depleted, the production facilities will be removed. Wells will be abandoned in accordance with all regulations, and well jackets removed to a level below the seabed. Residual hydrocarbons in the flowlines will be flushed out to the Cohasset facility, and the flowlines recovered for possible future use . . .[44]

The proponent thus committed to complete removal. This reflected the requirements of the Geneva Convention, rather than *UNCLOS* and *London Convention* provisions, which permitted partial removal.

In 2003, the successor operator, EnCana, proposed to disconnect the subsea flow lines, cables, and manifold ends and leave them on the seabed. It applied to amend the development plan. This triggered an EA under *CEAA 1992* and a forty-five-day consultation involving written public comment. During this process, Indigenous groups expressed concern that the EA and consultation process failed to address impacts on Indigenous rights to access fisheries resources. The Native Council of Nova Scotia wrote that "the EA was devoid of information as to our . . . issues, concerns, interests and needs, and our current use of resources and future uses."[45] At the time, Mi'kmaq peoples participated in the commercial fishery as an incident of Treaty rights following *R v. Marshall*.[46] The council complained that there was a failure to discharge the duty to consult.

Although the plan ultimately received regulatory approval, the council's concerns exposed the project to possible delay, claims for damages, or injunctive relief. Since 2004, jurisprudence has only strengthened the duty to consult. Today, it seems likelier that litigation, rather than public complaint, would result.

An inquiry from an Indigenous association about EnCana's liability post-decommissioning[47] also resulted in CNSOPB requiring EnCana to submit an adequate plan addressing post-abandonment ongoing liability as a condition of its approval.[48]

The Crown cannot delegate its duty to project proponents, but it may require proponents to consult with Indigenous groups as a precondition to approval. Whether the Crown or operators bear the consultative work, the Cohasset experience confirms the value of incorporating Indigenous consultation into the approvals process.

Commercial Fisheries

The third potential source of discord is commercial fisheries. Indeed, commercial fishing interests articulated strong reservations about Encana's Cohasset proposal, citing potential harm to biomass (quahog), hazards to gear, and obstruction of fisheries.[49]

The EA was in favour of the proposal, noting the partial removal option would be less disruptive for the environment than complete removal,[50] and the board ultimately approved the plan. However, CNSOPB's approval was subject to the conditions that EnCana undertake mitigation and follow-up measures, remove the topsides of the subsea installation, and submit an adequate plan addressing post-abandonment ongoing liability.[51]

Conclusion

Risk of opposition to decommissioning over environmental issues exists at the approvals required during project development and during decommissioning operations. Even if litigation does not erupt, the costs of project delays—particularly if the installation is no longer earning its keep—are reason enough to try to anticipate, address, and minimize other stakeholders' concerns over environmental issues.

The examples examined above suggest that operators should consider the following when planning for and seeking approvals of decommissioning operations:

- EnCana's proposal for partial removal may have been opposed by commercial fisheries and Indigenous groups even though that plan was contained in the originally approved development plan. However, the amendment itself, and the public consultation it triggered, might have been avoided by more flexible drafting of the decommissioning program in the development plan. Moreover, had the possibility of partial removal been included in the original development plan, the proposal would perhaps have been subjected to less scrutiny.

- Operators should consult with, anticipate, and address the interests of other commercial and non-commercial stakeholders in proposed decommissioning operations. The *Brent Spar* incident suggests that this should include efforts to gauge and manage public perception of the proposed operations.
- Where decommissioning operations have the potential to impact Indigenous or Treaty rights, direct consultation with Indigenous groups by the operator may be an effective method of achieving consensus and Indigenous support for the selected operations. Operators might also foster the support of affected Indigenous groups with impact benefits agreements or provisions in statutorily required benefits plans.
- Where proposed operations may impact fishery interests, anticipating and addressing those impacts through the EA/IA process might help achieve consensus in selecting operations. Monitoring environmental changes, as well as changes in fishing technology, will enhance the extent to which the operations respond to the fishery's interests.
- The Cohasset experience suggests that where partial removal is contemplated, anticipating and establishing terms of continuing liability and financial responsibility early on may help achieve consensus with relevant stakeholders.

NOTES

1 Partner, McInnes Cooper LLP, Halifax. This paper draws on McInnes Cooper's *Offshore Oil and Gas Decommissioning Best Practices* (2016), which, of course, the author highly commends.

2 Since the writing of this paper, two additional gas projects offshore Nova Scotia have been decommissioned: Encana's Deep Panuke project and ExxonMobil's Sable Offshore Energy Project. The decommissioning of these projects will offer additional insights in the future.

3 *Canada–Nova Scotia Offshore Petroleum Resources Accord Implementation Act*, SC 1988, c 28 [the *Accord Act*]; *Canada-Nova Scotia Offshore Petroleum Resources Accord Implementation* (Nova Scotia) Act, SNS 1987, c 3; *Canada–Newfoundland and Labrador Atlantic Accord Implementation Act*, SC 1987, c 3; *Canada–Newfoundland and Labrador Atlantic Accord Implementation Newfoundland and Labrador Act*, RSNL 1990, c C-2.

4 *Energy Safety and Security Act* SC 2015, c 4 [*ESSA*].

5 *Canadian Environmental Assessment Act, 2012*, SC 2012, c 19, s 52 [*CEAA 2012*].

6 *Impact Assessment Act*, SC 2019, c 28, s 1 [*IAA*].

7 A Fowler et al, "A Multi-Criteria Decision Approach to Decommissioning of Offshore Oil and Gas Infrastructure" (2014) 87 Ocean and Coastal Management at 20.

8 "Decommissioning in the North Sea: Review of Decommissioning Capacity" (2014) at 1–99, online (pdf): *Decom North SeaArup* <decomnorthsea.com/uploads/pdfs/projects/Decommissioning-in-the-North-Sea-Demand-vs-Capacity_low-res.pdf> [perma.cc/7ERW-LPKD]; J Groot, "Engineering Aspects of Decommissioning" in M Hammerson, ed, *Oil and Gas Decommissioning: Law, Policy and Comparative Practice* (London: Globe Law and Business, 2013).

9 1958 *Geneva Convention on the Continental Shelf*, 29 April 1958, 450 UNTS 11 art 5 (entered into force 10 June 1964) [*Geneva Convention*].

10 *Ibid*, art 5(5).

11 *United Nations Convention on Laws of the Sea*, 10 December 1982, 1833 UNTS 3 arts 2, 60, 80 (entered into force 16 November 1994) [*UNCLOS*].

12 *Ibid*, arts 1(5), 60(3), 194, 210(5) and 216.

13 *Convention on the Prevention of Marine Pollution by Dumping of Wastes and other Matters*, 29 December 1972, 1046 UNTS 120 (entered into force 30 August 1975) [*London Convention*].

14 *1996 Protocol to the Convention on the Prevention of Marine Pollution by Dumping of Wastes and Other Matter*, 7 November 1997, 36 ILM 1, art 1(4.1) (entered into force 3 March 2006) [*1996 Protocol*].

15 *Ibid*, art 4, Annex I, Annex II, para 17.

16 The *Oceans Act*, SC 1996, c 31 (incorporates the provisions of *UNCLOS* that confirm Canada's sovereignty and sovereign rights in its respective maritime zones). See also the *Canadian Environmental Protection Act, 1999*, SC 1999, c 33 (*CEPA*) at Division 3; the *Regulations Respecting Applications for Permits for Disposal at Sea*, SOR/2001-275, which has been replaced with the *Disposal at Sea Application Permit Regulations*, SOR/2014/177 (incorporates the provisions of the *London Convention* and *1996 Protocol*).

17 *Accord Act*, *supra* note 3. Decommissioning may also require compliance with a number of other, primarily federal, statutes.

18 *Ibid*, ss 8, 18.

19 *Ibid*, s 143.

20 *Ibid*, ss 140, 142.

21 *Ibid*, s 143(1).

22 *Nova Scotia Offshore Petroleum Installations Regulations*, SOR/95-191, s 42 [*Installation Regulations*].

23 CNSOPB, *Guidelines on Plans and Authorizations Required for Development Projects* (16 August 1995) at para 5.8 [*Guidelines*].

24 *Ibid* at para 2.

25 *Accord Act, supra* note 3 at s 44(1).

26 *Ibid*, s 44(1); *Guidelines, supra* note 23 at para 2.4.

27 *Physical Activities Regulations*, SOR/2019-285, ss 34–36, 40.

28 Pursuant to s 87 of *ESSA* (adding ss 142.02 to the *Accord Act*), effective 26 February 2016, CNSOPB was given authority to hold public hearings, a precondition to qualify as a "responsible authority" under *CEAA 2012* for designated projects, which would enable CNSOPB to conduct EAs under that legislation: *CEAA 2012, supra* note 5, s 15(1). However, draft regulations identifying the projects for which CNSOPB would be responsible under *CEAA 2012* were never enacted, and with *CEAA 2012*'s repeal, the attempt at restoring CNSOPB responsibility for federal EAs/IAs appears stillborn.

29 Under the *IAA*, the default position is that IAs of most designated projects are conducted by the Impact Assessment Agency unless the minister of environment and climate change exercises her discretion to refer IAs of such projects to the more onerous review panel process if the minister considers that process to be in the public interest. See *IAA, supra* note 6, ss 36(1). However, the minister must refer projects under the jurisdiction of the other federal "life-cycle" regulators—the Canada Energy Regulator (CER) (formerly National Energy Board) and Canadian Nuclear Safety Commission (CNSC)—to review panels: *IAA, ibid*, ss 43. At present, projects under CNSOPB or Canada–Newfoundland & Labrador Offshore Petroleum Board (CNLOPB) jurisdiction are not subject to the same mandatory panel review. But Bill C-69, which enacted the *IAA*, includes amendments to the *IAA* make projects under CNSOPB/CNLOPB jurisdiction subject to the mandatory review panel and other unique requirements currently applied to the CER and CNSC: see Bill C-69, *An Act to Enact the Impact Assessment Act and the Canadian Energy Regulator Act, to Amend the Navigation Protection Act and to Make Consequential Amendments to Other Acts*, ss 2–8.1.

30 *IAA, supra* note 6 at s 11.

31 *Ibid*, s 27.

32 *Ibid*, s 28(1).

33 *Ibid*, s 51(c).

34 *Ibid*, s 53(3).

35 *Canadian Environmental Assessment Act*, SC 1992, c 37 [*CEAA 1992*]; *Guidelines, supra* note 23 at para 2.3.

36 *Guidelines, supra* note 23 at para 2.4.

37 *CEAA 1992, supra* note 35, ss 140, 142.

38 *Ibid*, s 142(4)(b).

39 *Accord Act, supra* note 3 at s 143(5).

40 *IAA, supra* note 6 at s 22(1).

41 "Brent Spar Dossier" (2008), online (pdf): *Shell UK* <www.shell.co.uk/sustainability/decommissioning/brent-spar-dossier/_jcr_content/par/textimage.stream/1426853000847/32a2d94fa77c57684b3cad7d06bf6c7b65473faa/brent-spar-dossier.pdf> [perma.cc/5NY5-2F2K] at 4–128.

42 *Haida Nation v British Columbia (Minister of Forests)*, 2004 SCC 73 [*Haida*].

43 *Ibid* at paras 13–14; *Rio Tinto Alcan Inc v Carrier Sekani Tribal Council*, 2010 SCC 43 at para 37.

44 LASMO, "Cohasset Panuke Development Plan" (7 March 1990) at 5.8.2.

45 Letter from the Native Council of Nova Scotia to CNSOPB (18 November 2004).

46 *R v Marshall* [1999] 3 SCR 456.

47 Letter to the CNSOPB by the Netukulimkewe'l Commission (21 July 2004).

48 CNSOPB, "Application to Amend the Cohasset Development Plan: Decision Report" at para 7.8 [Decision Report].

49 Letter to the CNSOPB by Clearwater Seafoods (22 June 2004); Letter to the CNSOPB by Seafood Producers Association of Nova Scotia (23 June 2004).

50 Jacques Whitford Environmental Limited, "CEAA Screening Level Environmental Assessment Cohasset Panuke Phase II Decommissioning," prepared for EnCana Corporation in April 2004.

51 Decision Report, *supra* note 48 at para 7.8.

SECTION 2

Enforcement Issues in Canadian Wildlife Protection

11

Enforcement of the Wild Animal and Plant Protection and Regulation of International and Interprovincial Trade Act

Nigel Bankes[1]

Introduction

The *Wild Animal and Plant Protection and Regulation of International and Interprovincial Trade Act*[2] (*WAPPRIITA* or the Act) is Canada's implementing legislation for the *Convention on International Trade in Endangered Species of Wild Fauna and Flora* (*CITES* or the Convention).[3] However, the Act and regulations[4] go beyond merely implementing *CITES* and, in practice (and in conjunction with relevant provincial and territorial law), also serve to regulate interprovincial trade in wildlife.[5] Thus, while one of the legislation's objectives is undoubtedly implementation of *CITES*, other objectives include controlling the spread of alien or exotic species and disease,[6] and assisting provinces in the enforcement of their wildlife statutes and regulations.

This chapter begins with a short introduction to the Convention and then examines *WAPPRIITA* and the regulations, drawing examples from the interpretive case law. This chapter does not deal with sentencing decisions or administrative monetary penalty decisions.[7]

The Scheme of the Convention

The Convention aims to restrict and regulate trade in threatened and endangered species. Appendix I to the Convention lists species threatened with extinction; Appendix II lists species not yet threatened with extinction but which "may become so unless trade in specimens of such species is subject to strict regulation in order to avoid utilization incompatible with their survival." Trade in Appendix I species is strictly controlled and is not permitted for commercial purposes. Trade requires both an export permit and an import permit. Trade in Appendix II species is less strictly controlled and only requires an export permit. An export permit may only be issued if the scientific authority of the state of export has made a "no-detriment finding," that is, a finding that "such export will not be detrimental to the survival of the species."[8] "Look alike" species may also be listed in Appendix II. The Conference of the Parties (which meets every three years) has elaborated on many of the requirements of the Convention, including the form of the permit.[9]

The Scheme of the Act

This part of the chapter examines the scheme of the Act. It begins with an examination of the scope of the Act through a consideration of the definitions of the Act (as supplemented by the regulations) and the main prohibitions established by the Act. The chapter then considers the case law dealing with some of the administrative powers under the Act, specifically the power to detain and inspect. The final section in this part deals with the offence and punishment provisions. Environment and Climate Change Canada (ECCC) oversees enforcement of the Act assisted by customs officials at ports of entry. ECCC "maintains enforcement agreements and memoranda of understanding with Manitoba, Saskatchewan, Alberta, British Columbia, the Northwest Territories and Nunavut. Under the agreements and memoranda of understanding, these four provinces and two territories are responsible for enforcing *WAPPRIITA* with respect to interprovincial wildlife trade, while the Department oversees the enforcement of *WAPPRIITA* for international trade."[10]

SCOPE, DEFINITIONS, AND PROHIBITIONS

The Act applies to "plants" and "animals," each of which is defined in terms of a species of flora or fauna listed in a *CITES* appendix.[11] However, the regulation-making power of the Act[12] allows the governor in council to amend the definitions of animal and plant for the purposes of individual sections of the Act, as noted below.

The main operative provisions of the Act consist of a set of prohibitions. Section 6(1) prohibits the *import* into Canada of "any animal or plant that was taken, or any animal or plant, or any part or derivative of an animal or plant, that was possessed, distributed or transported in contravention of any law of any foreign state." The key element of this prohibition is clearly taking in violation of the law of another state. While on its face, this only applies to Convention-listed species, the regulations redefine the terms animal and plant for the purposes of this prohibition to mean *any* animal or plant.[13]

Section 6(2) creates a second prohibition that applies to the import or export of Convention species (or any part or derivative of) except in accordance with a permit issued under section 10. In this case, the regulations redefine animals and plants with respect to the different activities of export and import. With respect to import, the definition of plant is unchanged while the definition of animal is expanded to include mongoose, raccoon dog, starlings, mynas, oxpeckers,[14] and any species of the order Caudata (salamander).[15]

With respect to export, the regulations expand the definition of animal and plant in each case, on a contingent basis, to include any species for which the transportation out of a province is regulated by the province.[16]

It is, of course, the Crown's responsibility, if it alleges that goods are being imported into Canada without the necessary permit under sections 6(2) and 10, to demonstrate that the goods do indeed need a permit, that is, that they are a "part or derivative of" a listed animal or plant.[17] In so doing, the Crown may take advantage of a presumption created by section 20 of the regulations:[18]

> Where a person imports into Canada or exports from Canada anything that is identified by a mark, label or accompanying document that indicates that the thing is an animal or plant, or a part or derivative of one, that is listed in Schedule I or II, that thing is, unless there is evidence that raises a reasonable doubt to the contrary, deemed to be the thing so identified.

Nevertheless, it will still be necessary for the Crown to establish that the label corresponds to a listed species. While that may be straightforward in many cases, *R v. Kwok Shing Enterprises Ltd*[19] illustrates that that may not be the case where the label is in a foreign language or uses a non-Roman script, or where a species has multiple names, or where there are many species of a particular plant type but only some of which are listed. In *Kwok Shing*, the accused was charged with importing a listed plant without the necessary permit. The goods imported consisted of individual packages of Lidan tablets. The exhibited package was described as:[20]

> . . . a small cardboard box containing a clear plastic bottle and a one-page brochure. . . . There is a list of ingredients. . . . The ingredients are listed in Chinese characters and Latin.
>
> . . . Each one lists the second ingredient as Radix Saussurea. It is the nature of this second ingredient, which is the central focus of this trial.

Appendix I of *CITES* lists the plant, *Saussurea costus*, as do the regulations.[21] The defence argued that the Crown had "failed to prove beyond a reasonable doubt that the words, *Radix Saussurea*, as they appear on parts of Exhibit 1, describe a plant referred to in Section 20 of the Regulations." The only evidence as to the meaning of the words and what they might describe came from two Crown witnesses, one of whom was described as having worked as a customs inspector for seven to eight years; the other was described as a conservation officer. Both claimed experience in using lists prepared by Environment Canada as well as reference works and claimed that, on this basis, they were able to satisfy themselves that the Chinese characters used on the labels were referencing *Radix Saussurea*. Neither witness was fluent in either written or oral Chinese: their only background was based on experience working with lists and textbooks and some instruction received from (the unnamed) "Scientific Authority of Canada."[22] While Judge Low seems to have been of the view that the expert evidence tendered by these witnesses was admissible, he concluded that it had serious shortcomings and was entitled to little weight. Accordingly, Judge Low was "not satisfied beyond a reasonable doubt that the words *Radix Saussurea* found with Exhibit 1 are to be interpreted to mean the species of plant *Saussurea Costus (=Lappa)*."[23] It may be useful for future guidance to list the shortcomings identified by Judge Low:[24]

> a) There is no evidence . . . whether any of the books read by these two officers are regarded as authorities on the subject;
>
> b) There is no evidence as to the names of any of these books;

c) There is no evidence that the lists of Chinese Characters relied on by Officers Graham or Cooper were accurate nor am I prepared to infer this simply from their use of the lists as there are other problems with the accuracy of the lists;

d) The list in Exhibit 4 states that it was compiled by Laura Merz, but there is no evidence of her capacity or role with Environment Canada;

e) Officer Cooper agreed in cross-examination that there was more than one list prepared by Environment Canada, they were not necessarily the same, and this might affect an individual list's reliability;

f) The problem with the accuracy of the lists was compounded by the fact that neither Officer Graham nor Cooper had any fluency in the Chinese language;

g) Officer Graham, although not qualified as an expert, was nonetheless a highly experienced officer. He testified that the Chinese Characters he observed on Exhibit 1 were for the words Radix Saussurea not Saussurea Lappa as testified to by Officer Cooper;

h) Officer Cooper relied, to some extent, upon the opinion of a person he called the Scientific Authority of Canada in forming his own opinion about the TCM pharmaceutical use of the words, Radix Saussurea. There is no evidence as to who this person is or their qualifications or background, other than Officer Cooper's assertion that the person was regarded as an authority on plants.

Other provisions of *WAPPRIITA* expand the regulatory scope of the Act to cover the *interprovincial* transportation of animals and plants. Section 6(3) prohibits interprovincial transport of an animal or plant (or any part or derivative of) without a permit issued under section 10 from one province to another,[25] while section 7(1) requires that any provincial rules with respect to permitting should be observed as part of interprovincial transport. Similarly, section 7(2) makes it an offence to transport an animal or plant (or any part or derivative of) from one province to another where that "animal or plant that was taken, or any animal or plant, or any part or derivative of an animal or plant, that was possessed, distributed or transported in contravention of any provincial Act or regulation."[26] Once again, the regulations expand the definitions of plant and animal on a contingent basis. Thus, in the case of section 6(3), the definition of plant or animal is expanded to include any plant or animal the "import" of which into the relevant province is regulated or prohibited.[27] Similarly, the regulations expand the definition of plant or animal for the purposes of section 7 to include any plant or animal, the "export" of which from the relevant province is regulated or prohibited.[28]

Section 8 of the Act also prohibits, "subject to the regulations," knowingly being in possession of a listed species (or any part or derivative thereof)[29] that has been imported or transported in contravention of the Act, or for the purpose of transporting between provinces or exporting in contravention of the Act, or for the purposes of distributing—but only if the species is listed in Appendix I of *CITES*. Section 8 is not further defined or expanded upon by the regulations.

Section 10 authorizes the minister to issue permits on such terms and conditions as the minister thinks fit for the import, export, or interprovincial transport of an animal or plant. Consistent with the Convention, section 6(1) of the regulations provides that a person importing a species listed in Appendix II of the Convention does not need a permit to import "where the person has obtained, before import, a permit certificate or written authorization that satisfies the requirements of the Convention and is granted by a competent authority in the country of export."

An important result of the expansion of the definitions of animals and plants is that an accused will frequently face liability under both provincial or territorial wildlife legislation and *WAPPRIITA*. For example, a person who harvests wildlife illegally in province A and transports that wildlife to province B will commit an offence under A's Wildlife Act, likely also under B's Wildlife Act, and also under *WAPPRIITA* (and in some cases other federal legislation such as the *Migratory Birds Convention Act*). In *R v. Ensor*, the accused was charged with multiple offences under Yukon's *Wildlife Act* and regulations and also under *WAPPRIITA*.[30] The charges under the *Wildlife Act* included two charges with respect to being in possession in the Yukon of wildlife killed contrary to the laws of another jurisdiction (British Columbia); in addition, the accused was charged under section 7(2) of *WAPPRIITA*. Ensor pleaded guilty to all of the offences.[31] In *R v. LaPrairie*, the Crown originally proceeded under both territorial legislation and *WAPPRIITA* but subsequently stayed the charges under the territorial legislation when the accused pleaded guilty to the charges under section 6(3) of *WAPPRIITA*.[32]

THE POWERS OF OFFICERS AND ANALYSTS: DETENTION AND INSPECTION

The Act is implemented by designated officers and analysts. Officers have the powers of a peace officer for the purposes of the Act.[33] Under section 13, an officer may detain "[a]nything that has been imported into or is about to be exported from Canada or has been transported, or is about to be transported, from a province to another province . . . until the officer is satisfied that the thing has been dealt with in accordance with this Act and the regulations."[34]

The Power to Detain

The scope of the power to detain goods was examined in *Druyan v. AG Canada*.[35] In that case, Druyan, a collector of Inuit art, purchased certain Inuit art items from an online auction in Denmark. The items consisted of ten tupilaks made from sperm whale ivory, two tupilaks made from caribou antler, and a kayak figurine made from wood, seal leather, and seal bone. The items were inspected and detained by an official of Environment Canada at the time of entry. Druyan did not have an import permit for the items, but the items were accompanied by a document in the Danish language issued by the Danish Nature Agency, Denmark's management authority for the Convention. Further inquiries of the Danish authorities by Environment Canada revealed that the document was not an export permit but instead certified that the objects were pre-Convention. The document was intended for use within the European Union. All of the objects, save the sperm whale ivory tupilaks, were subsequently returned to Druyan. Sperm whale is listed in Appendix I of *CITES*. Druyan commenced an application for judicial review of the decision to detain the tupilaks and an order setting aside that decision and authorizing importation.

Noting that there was no binding precedent with respect to the applicable standard of review of the power to detain under section 13, Justice O'Keefe applied the *Dunsmuir* factors[36] concluding that they indicated a deferential standard of review. Justice O'Keefe was not swayed in this by the indication from some cases that international conventions (and hence implementing legislation) should be interpreted consistently and thus on a correctness standard. That was not the case where, as here, "the convention in issue allows state parties to choose how to achieve the convention's objectives"[37] and where the officer was exercising powers conferred by the Act and regulations.[38] Here, Article XIV(1)(a) of the Convention expressly authorized states to take stricter domestic measures than those required by the Convention.[39] That was important in this case because *WAPPRIITA* did not expressly carry through the exemption contained in Article VII (2) for pre-Convention goods.[40] In sum, the standard of review was reasonableness, which meant that the court should not intervene in the officer's decision to detain the goods if the decision was "transparent, justifiable, intelligible and within the range of acceptable outcomes."[41] While this might ordinarily require examination of the reasons offered for the decision, where no reasons were given, and where there was no duty to provide reasons, it was appropriate for the court to identify possible reasons[42] and thus, "the officer's decision will be set aside only if the record does not disclose how the facts and applicable law could possibly support the officer's conclusion."[43]

Justice O'Keefe concluded that the original decision to detain the goods was reasonable. There was no import certificate, and the officer could not read the accompanying documentation. While the Danish certificate met the criteria of Article VI (3) of the Convention, it did not meet the criteria elaborated by Conference Resolution 12.3.[44] Furthermore, it was not even unreasonable to detain the non-sperm whale items (which were not made from listed species) since the Danish certificate did not specify the sources of the materials.[45]

Justice O'Keefe went on to examine whether the officer had reasonably concluded that Druyan was in breach of any of the prohibitions contained in the Act—presumably on the basis that the officer could not reasonably continue to detain the tupaliks if there was no breach. The counsel for the attorney general argued that the officer could have concluded that Druyan was in breach of both sections 6(1) and 6(2). Justice O'Keefe, however, decided that there was no indication that the officer relied on this section[46] and, furthermore, that there was no reasonable basis on which the officer could have concluded that there had been a contravention of the law of any foreign state.[47] In order for the officer to have been able to reasonably reach such a decision, there should "at least be some evidence before the decision-maker that Denmark's laws were violated."[48] That was not the case: "Here, the record discloses nothing. There is no evidence that the exporter was convicted or is being charged of some regulatory or criminal offence, nor is there any communication from an official in Denmark saying that an offence was committed. . . ."[49]

By contrast, Justice O'Keefe was of the view that an officer could reasonably have concluded that the importation was in breach of section 6(2) of the Act. Section 6(2) requires that an importer have a permit, and Druyan had no such permit. Furthermore, while section 6 of the Regulations creates some exemptions from the need to hold a permit, none of these exemptions applied to products created from sperm whale since it is an Appendix I species. In reaching this conclusion, Justice O'Keefe also rejected the argument that the regulations should have been read as containing an additional exemption for pre-Convention goods. While Justice O'Keefe was prepared to accept that the Danish certificate was adequate for the purpose of demonstrating that the goods were pre-Convention—notwithstanding some formal deficiencies,[50] it was reasonable for the officer not to have regard to the exemption contained in the Convention.[51] This was because "the officer was required to implement the Act, so any exemptions have to be found in the legislation, not the Convention. Further, article XIV(1)(a) of the Convention itself allows state parties to adopt stricter legislation than the Convention requires."[52] Furthermore, Justice O'Keefe was of the view that the failure to provide an exemption for pre-Convention goods was entirely consistent with the purpose of the Act. He reasoned that the decision not to create the exemption:[53]

> . . . closes the market for products from Appendix I species, thus removing any financial incentives for poachers to kill the animals anyway and fabricate their age. That is rationally connected to the purpose of protecting endangered species. An exemption for pre-Convention goods certainly does not advance the objectives of the *Act*, so it was reasonable for the officer to obey the plain meaning of the legislation and not read in the exemption that the applicant wants.

The Power to Inspect

Officers also have broad powers to enter premises and conduct inspections in any place "in which the officer believes, on reasonable grounds, there is anything to which this Act applies, or there are any documents relating to the administration of this Act or the regulations" and may do so without a warrant, except in the case of a dwelling place.[54] In exercising this section 14 power of inspection, an officer may:[55]

> **(a)** open or cause to be opened any container that the officer believes, on reasonable grounds, contains such a thing;
>
> **(b)** inspect any such thing and take samples free of charge;
>
> **(c)** require any person to produce for inspection or copying, in whole or in part, any document that the officer believes, on reasonable grounds, contains any information relevant to the administration of this Act or the regulations; and
>
> **(d)** seize anything by means of or in relation to which the officer believes, on reasonable grounds, this Act or the regulations have been contravened or that the officer believes, on reasonable grounds, will afford evidence of a contravention of this Act or the regulations.

The section 14 power of inspection was judicially considered in *R v. Leong*.[56] Leong was charged with six counts of importing live corals into Canada without a section 10 permit and, therefore, in breach of section 6(2) of the Act. Leong filed an application to exclude evidence, which led the court to examine, *inter alia*, whether an officer had obtained evidence in accordance with the section 14 power of inspection. Leong was expecting a shipment of goods through the Vancouver International Airport. On arrival, the goods were moved to a "sufferance warehouse" where they could be inspected before being released to the importer. A number of officials, including Buchart, were present at the warehouse to conduct an inspection of the goods and accompanying documents. Leong also showed up at the warehouse. He was carrying a number of plain manila folders, which Buchart asked to see. Leong initially declined but eventually handed them over for inspection after being told that the officers would not release the shipment until they had the opportunity to review the documents.

One of the questions that arose in the course of argument on a *voir dire* was whether or not Buchart was examining the documents based upon the power to inspect conferred by section 14(1). Judge Smith concluded that Buchart was not. Judge Smith observed that the purpose of conferring a power of inspection in section 14 and similar powers conferred by the *Fisheries Act*[57] was to permit an inspection without requiring a warrant.[58] Judge Smith went on to observe that the original encounter with Leong was in the public part of the warehouse; the officers did not need a warrant to be in that public area. Thus "the officers' attendance at the public area of the Warehouse was not an 'inspection' of the Warehouse within the meaning of s.14(1)"[59] and since there was no inspection Butchart[60]

> . . . had no statutory authority to compel the production to her of the documents in Mr. Leong's possession while he stood in the Warehouse.
>
> [153] That is to say, a section 14(1) inspection is a precondition to a s. 14(1)(c) compulsion power and, given that there was no section 14(1) inspection, the officer could not lawfully rely on subsection 14(1)(c) to justify the warrantless compelled production of the folders and documents enclosed therein, and Mr. Leong was under no correlative duty under s. 14.2 to give her the documents.

THE OFFENCE AND PUNISHMENT PROVISIONS

Any person who breaches any provisions of the Act or a provision of certain designated regulations[61] or a court order under the Act commits an offence.[62] The prohibitions contained in section 6 of the Act create strict liability offences;[63] section 8 applies to a person who knowingly possesses an animal or plant or derivative thereof and is thus a *mens rea* offence, which requires the Crown to prove intent.[64]

In *R v. Clemett*, the accused was charged under both section 6(1) and section 8 with respect to the importation of an Alaskan brown bear that the accused had shot and killed in Alaska.[65] The harvest was alleged to be illegal on the basis that the bear was taken in breach of an Alaskan law that prohibited the taking of big game with the use of bait or scent lures. In addition, there was also alleged to be a breach of a provision of the federal (US) *Lacey Act* for the export of wildlife taken in violation of a law or regulation of a state.

Judge Van de Veen concluded that the Crown had proven the elements of the offence under section 6, including the breach of Alaskan and federal law.[66] Judge Van de Veen then went on to consider the defence of due diligence, acknowledging that the accused was entitled to an acquittal if he could show that he had taken all reasonable steps to avoid the commission of the offence, or that he held a reasonable belief in a set of facts which, if true, would render the acts or omissions innocent.[67] The court rejected submissions to the effect that the accused was entitled to rely on the fact that he was hunting with a licenced guide (as he was required to do). The Alaskan regulations made it clear that the use of a guide did not relieve a hunter from responsibility for knowing the regulations and hunting in accordance with the regulations. Furthermore, the evidence showed that the accused had made no effort to acquaint himself with the regulations, notwithstanding that the accused and his friends had, in the past, been concerned about the standards employed by the guide. In sum, the accused failed to establish a due diligence defence to the section 6 offence.

The court concluded, however, that the Crown had not succeeded on the section 8 charge. To succeed on that charge, the Crown had to "prove beyond a reasonable doubt that the accused knew or was wilfully blind that he was violating the law by shooting his bear over bait."[68] Judge Van de Veen's assessment was that "the evidence falls just short of the reasonable doubt standard of proof in relation to the accused's knowledge or wilful blindness that his bear was lured by bait."[69] In so concluding, it is evident that Judge Van de Veen applied the "knowingly" requirement not just to the act of possession but also with respect to the knowledge that the bear had been taken in breach of Alaskan law.

Conclusions

WAPPRIITA is the implementing legislation that Canada relies on to fulfil its obligations under *CITES*. However, the Act and the regulations go beyond *CITES*. The Act and regulations cover additional species, and they extend some of the rules and prohibitions to cover interprovincial and international trade.

The limited case law on the Act and regulations draws attention to the following:

- The Act and regulations should be interpreted according to the ordinary rules of interpretation, and no great heed should be paid to the fact that *WAPPRIITA*, *inter alia*, implements *CITES*, given that the legislation also has other objectives: *Druyan v. AG Canada*.

- While the Crown may rely on the presumption created by section 20 as to the utility of marks, labels, and accompanying documents, it still has the responsibility in the case of *CITES*-listed species to show that the marks, labels etc. pertain to a listed species: *Kwok Shing*.
- A charge under section 6 requires evidence that the law of another state was breached: *Druyan v. AG Canada* and *R v. Clemett*.
- The power to detain under section 13 is an administrative act. The standard of review with respect to the (continued) exercise of the power to detain is reasonableness: *Druyan v. AG Canada*.[70]

The power to inspect under section 14(1) does not afford an officer an independent power to require a person to produce a document without a warrant. An officer can only exercise this power if the officer has entered a place for the purposes of ensuring compliance with the Act and where the officer believes on reasonable grounds that there are things or documents relating to the administration of the Act or regulations: *R v. Leong*.

NOTES

1 Professor of Law, University of Calgary, <ndbankes@ucalgary.ca>.

2 *Wild Animal and Plant Protection and Regulation of International and Interprovincial Trade Act*, SC 1992, c 52 [*WAPPRIITA*]. Prior to its adoption, Canada implemented its *Convention on International Trade in Endangered Species of Wild Fauna and Flora* (*CITES*) obligations through regulation under the *Export and Import Permits Act*, RSC 1985, c E-17. See also the former *Game Export Act*, RSC 1985, c G-1.

3 3 March 1973, 993 UNTS 243, Can TS 1975 No 32 [*CITES*], online: <cites.org/>.

4 *Wild Animal and Plant Trade Regulations*, SOR/96-263 [*WAPTR*]. For the Regulatory Impact Analysis Statement (RIAS) of the original version of the regulations, see Regulatory Impact Analysis Statement, (1996) C Gaz II, 1797 [RIAS]. The RIAS describes the Act as "framework legislation." Environment and Climate Change Canada (ECCC) issues an annual report on the implementation of the Act and the regulations. See ECCC, "Wild Animal and Plant Protection and Regulation of International and Interprovincial Trade Act: Report" (last modified 3 April 2013), online: *Government of Canada* <publications.gc.ca/site/eng/9.505775/publication.html>.

5 Section 4 of the Act provides that "[t]he purpose of this Act is to protect certain species of animals and plants, particularly by implementing the Convention and regulating international and interprovincial trade in animals and plants" (*WAPPRIITA*, *supra* note 2, s 4).

6 See RIAS, *supra* note 4 at 1797; *R v LaPrairie*, 2003 YKTC 24 at para 9 (a case dealing with the interprovincial transport of wood bison from Alberta to the Yukon). LaPrairie was charged with an offence under section 6(3) of *WAPPRIITA*. The court noted that "[a]lthough the specific concern in this case is the possibility of introducing disease to the wood bison already in the Territory, the danger of unregulated movement of plants and animals goes well beyond this. The world is replete with examples of situations in which the release of exotic species in new areas has had an unintended and devastating impact on the environment or on indigenous species." *Ibid* at para 16.

7 For sentencing decisions, see *R v Deslisle*, 2003 BCCA 196; *Marsland v The Queen*, 2012 SKCA 47; *R v LaPrairie*, 2003 YKTC 24; *R v Clemett*, 2016 ABPC 248; *R v Shmyr*, 2017 YKTC 53; *R v Ensor*, 2017 YKTC 2; *R v Luah*, 2006 ABCA 217. For administrative monetary penalty decisions, see *1952157 Ontario Inc v Canada (Environment and Climate Change)*, 2019 EPTC 5; *Bhaiyat v Canada (Environment and Climate Change)*, 2019 EPTC 1.

8 *CITES*, *supra* note 3, art IV. Environment Canada (now ECCC) is the designated management authority and scientific authority for *CITES*. Fisheries and Oceans Canada is responsible for *CITES*-listed aquatic species, including fish, marine plants, and marine mammals. Natural Resources Canada serves as an advisor with respect to timber species.

9 See especially "Conference Resolution 12.3, Permits and Certificates" (accessed 27 November 2021), online (pdf): *CITES* <cites.org/sites/default/files/document/E-Res-12-03-R18.pdf> [*CITES* Conference Resolution 12.3].

10 ECCC, "Wild Animal and Plant Protection and Regulation of International and Interprovincial Trade Act: Annual Report for 2015" (accessed 1 December 2021) at 2, online (pdf): *Government of Canada* <publications.gc.ca/collections/collection_2016/eccc/CW70-5-2015-eng.pdf>. These annual reports also contain discussion of enforcement activities and more detailed discussions of a number of examples.

11 *WAPPRIITA*, *supra* note 2, s 2.

12 *Ibid*, s 21(1)(c).

13 *WAPTR*, *supra* note 4, s 4.

14 *Ibid*, Schedule II.

15 *Ibid*, s 5.

16 *Ibid*, s 7.

17 See e.g., *WAPPRIITA*, *supra* note 2, s 6(1).

18 *WAPTR*, *supra* note 4, s 20 (under the heading entitled "labelling"). Note, however, that in *R v Kwok Shing Enterprises Ltd*, 2001 BCPC 305, counsel for the accused indicated that s\he intended to question the constitutionality of s 20. In the end, it was not necessary for the court to consider the argument.

19 *R v Kwok Shing Enterprises Ltd*, 2001 BCPC 305 [Kwok Shing].

20 *Ibid* at paras 5, 6.

21 *Ibid* at para 7; *WAPTR*, *supra* note 4 564, Schedule I, Part II, Item 1.12.0.

22 The Scientific Authority for Canada under *CITES* is either ECCC or the Department of Fisheries and Oceans.

23 *Kwok Shing*, *supra* note 19 at para 40.

24 *Ibid* at para 38.

25 But see *WAPTR*, *supra* note 4, s 11 (a section 10 permit is not required "where all required provincial permits have been obtained").

26 *Ibid*, s 7(2).

27 *Ibid*, s 10.

28 *Ibid*, s 12.

29 It follows from the use of "knowingly" that the section 8 offences require that the Crown demonstrate *mens rea*. See *Marsland v The Queen*, 2012 SKCA 47 at para 30.

30 *R v Ensor*, 2017 YKTC 1.

31 See also *R v Shnyr*, 2017 YKTC 53. The accused was charged and convicted under the Yukon *Wildlife Act* with providing false information and hunting when not permitted but was also charged under *WAPPRIITA* for transporting moose parts to Alberta, which were not legally possessed in the Yukon because the original hunt was illegal.

32 *R v LaPrairie*, 2003 YKTC 24 at para 7.

33 *WAPPRITTA*, *supra* note 2, s 12.

34 *Ibid*, s 13.

35 *Druyan v AG Canada*, 2015 FC 705 [*Druyan*].

36 See *Dunsmuir v New Brunswick*, 2008 SCC 9 [*Dunsmuir*]. The leading decision on standard of review is now *Canada (Minister of Citizenship and Immigration) v Vavilov*, 2019 SCC 65 [*Vavilov*].

37 *Druyan*, *supra* note 35 at para 38.

38 *Ibid.*

39 *Ibid.*

40 *Ibid* at para 57. Article VII(2) of *CITES* provides that "[w]here a Management Authority of the State of export or re-export is satisfied that a specimen was acquired before the provisions of the present Convention applied to that specimen, the provisions of Articles III, IV and V shall not apply to that specimen where the Management Authority issues a certificate to that effect." *CITES*, *supra* note 3, art VII(2). There is a partial exemption in s 13 of *WAPTR*, but this is only an exemption for the purposes of s 8(c) of the Act. See *WAPTR*, *supra* note 4, s 13; *WAPPRIITA*, *supra* note 2, s 8(c).

41 *Druyan*, *supra* note 35 at para 40; *Dunsmuir*, *supra* note 36 at para 47. For current requirements with respect to reasons, see *Vavilov*, *supra* note 36.

42 See *Druyan*, *supra* note 35 at para 40, citing *Alberta (Information and Privacy Commissioner) v Alberta Teachers' Association*, 2011 SCC 61 at para 54.

43 *Druyan*, *supra* note 35 at para 41, citing *Newfoundland and Labrador Nurses' Union v Newfoundland and Labrador* (Treasury Board), 2011 SCC 62 at para 16.

44 *Druyan*, *supra* note 35 at para 42, citing *CITES* Conference Resolution 12.3, *supra* note 9.

45 See *Druyan*, *supra* note 35 at para 45.

46 *Ibid* at para 52.

47 *Ibid* at para 51.

48 *Ibid.*

49 *Ibid* at para 52. See by contrast *R v Clemett*, *supra* note 7 where the evidence before the court included an agreed statement of facts as well as evidence from state enforcement officials and other parties and evidence as to Alaskan and federal law. There was ample

evidence on which to conclude that the bear in question had been taken in breach of both state and federal law.

50 See *Druyan*, *supra* note 35 at para 58.

51 See *ibid* at para 50. Or perhaps more accurately, an officer could not reasonably have concluded that the certificate was not adequate to demonstrate pre-Convention status.

52 *Ibid*. Justice O'Keefe also noted that section 13(1)(a) of the regulations create an exemption for possession of a pre-Convention good and that such express language could also "have been used had Canada wanted to create the same exemption for importing" (*Ibid* at para 60).

53 *Ibid* at para 61.

54 *WAPPRIITA*, *supra* note 2, s 14.

55 Ibid, s 14(1).

56 *R v Leong*, 2014 BCPC 99.

57 *Fisheries Act*, RSC 1985, c F-14, s 49.

58 *R v Leong*, *supra* note 56 at para 145.

59 *Ibid* at para 151.

60 *Ibid* at paras 152–153.

61 The designated regulations are regulations designated under paragraph 21(1)(g.1) of *WAPPRITTA*, which seems to allow any provision of the regulations to be so designated. No provisions are currently so designated.

62 *WAPPRITTA*, *supra* note 2, s 22.

63 *R v Clemett*, 2016 ABPC 137, at paras 12, 18.

64 *Ibid* at paras 12, 33.

65 *Ibid*.

66 *Ibid* at paras 15–17.

67 *Ibid* at para 19.

68 *Ibid* at para 33.

69 *Ibid*.

70 See *Vavilov*, *supra* note 36.

12

Reconciliation—Territorial Wildlife Regimes and the Future of the Northern Wildlife Resource

John Donihee[1]

Introduction

This chapter explores the role of land claims and co-management systems in restoring Aboriginal wildlife rights and harvesting practices. It will describe the effect of this northern system of rights and institutions on territorial wildlife laws and argue that this framework offers important lessons about reconciliation in relation to wildlife and habitat management and protection. It will also argue that these lessons are critical to the future of northern wildlife populations and to Canada's obligations to northern Indigenous peoples. Finally, it is argued that this approach to wildlife management is consistent with the courts' decisions on reconciliation and could be helpful in the provinces.

Conserving Wildlife: The State and Community Wildlife Management Paradigms

From time immemorial, the Indigenous peoples of Canada's northern territories[2] managed their use of wildlife on the basis of their spiritual, cultural, and community-based values.

First Nations and Metis, the Inuvialuit and Inuit, had their own systems of rules, customs, and wildlife management based on their traditions, cultures, and belief systems. This wildlife management paradigm was integral to the organization of these Indigenous societies. It was based on intimate knowledge of the land and animals and on traditional ecological knowledge.[3] It never entirely disappeared.

Euro-Canadian wildlife management rules emerged from a different tradition and belief system, and these Euro-Canadian values shaped the rules that were enshrined in statute and enforced by the courts.

Beginning during the period of Canada's western and northern expansion and until 1982, these Euro-Canadian rules were applied and expanded in the territories to the detriment of the Indigenous, community-based wildlife management systems. The clash of these wildlife management paradigms resulted in the erosion of Aboriginal[4] and Treaty rights to wildlife and wildlife harvesting, including the right to make local decisions about these activities.[5]

Over time, the community paradigm continually gave way to the state paradigm as law enforcement presence and wildlife management efforts intensified in the territories.[6] The tension between these paradigms continued to exist until land claim negotiations were completed[7] and section 35[8] jurisprudence[9] began to push back against the dominant state paradigm.

THE STATE PARADIGM

At the end of the nineteenth century, a similar ethical and conceptual framework for wildlife conservation and management emerged in Canada and the United States. This framework incorporated a rejection of the excesses of commercial or market hunting and of the English or European "privileged approach" to the allocation of wildlife resources. This framework incorporated the emerging body of wildlife science, management skills, and law capable of husbanding the resource in pursuit of the goal of "wise use."

In Canada, wildlife professionals share this broadly accepted framework of principles that underlies our wildlife law and facilitates the management of wildlife.[10] This wildlife law paradigm has evolved over the last one hundred and fifty years[11] and is a reflection of the values, principles, and legal traditions of the dominant, that is, Euro-Canadian culture.[12]

Under the state paradigm, the managers are separated from the users. Management and control of publicly owned wildlife require formal, centralized authority, established by Parliament or the legislature, assigned to a minister of the Crown and enforced by game management officials, the police, and the courts. Such a system is bureaucratic and hierarchically organized. The Euro-Canadian approach to wildlife management is also science-based and purportedly value-free.

The elimination or strict management of commercial hunting requires tight control on the transportation, storage, sale, barter, or trading of the products of the hunt. This is achieved by way of licensing systems, the creation of statutory offences prohibiting the sale of game, and the enforcement of these rules. Such a system permits the killing of wildlife only in situations where it is used for food, fur, or for the defence of persons or property. Although trophy hunting is allowed, the wasting of the game meat generated by trophy hunts is prohibited.

THE COMMUNITY-BASED PARADIGM

Systems of local or community-based control of wildlife harvesting activities developed in many Indigenous societies as a means of resource conservation and management. These systems often went hand in hand with a system of territorial use or land tenure, so that families, clans, or even individuals held and managed defined hunting or fishing territories. Indigenous community-based management systems[13] share a number of characteristics that can be used to describe the community-based wildlife paradigm.

Indigenous fishing, hunting, and gathering territories used for resource conservation were described in Labrador as early as 1915 by the American ethnologist Speck.[14] Most native peoples in North America had systems of land tenure that involved rules for resource allocation within the group and for control of access to those resources. In Inuit societies, wildlife harvesting required an organizational structuring for the integration of the personnel, equipment, and economic resources necessary for the hunt. This system required a social network with rules to direct interpersonal and intergenerational relations so as to form an efficient means of directing harvesting activities in a high-risk natural environment.[15]

In the community system, the users are also the managers.[16] In such societies, all members accumulate and share knowledge about the resource that is managed through harvesting activities. This "Indigenous system of management" is a core feature of all northern native cultures. "Community-based (but not family-based) territories were probably the primary practice for resource management at one time in North America."[17] The authorities indicate that these community-based self-management practices are highly resilient systems of wildlife use and management. They are local and consensual, communal in the use of territory and the sharing of the products of the hunt, and enforced through social and cultural controls. This paradigm does not need external or formal mechanisms to achieve management goals or the enforcement of rules. It is informal, flexible, and adaptable.

Effects of the Application of the State Paradigm to Aboriginal Harvesting

Even a very brief consideration of some of the restrictions imposed on Aboriginal harvesters shows how significantly the regulatory framework established as a result of the state wildlife paradigm affected the exercise of Aboriginal harvesting rights over the years. Despite the liberalization of the rules applied to the interpretation of treaties over this period, the jurisprudence indicates that, ultimately, the courts would see to the enforcement of the dominant wildlife paradigm in the territories.

Prior to 1982, Aboriginal rights to wildlife could be regulated, and if the intention was clear enough, extinguished by the enactment of federal or territorial legislation, without the need for justification.[18]

From 1917 until its amendment in 1994, the *Migratory Birds Convention Act*[19] (*MBCA*) and regulations prohibited spring hunting and hunting in bird sanctuaries, set bag and possession limits, and prohibited the sale and buying of birds and eggs. Exemptions for native persons from the requirement for a permit were, however, granted.

Territorial wildlife law after 1960,[20] specifically, game ordinances,[21] applied to Indians and Inuit automatically, unless a contrary intention appeared. Indigenous hunting for food on unoccupied Crown land was protected as long as the game was not declared to be in danger of becoming extinct. However, several key species including barren ground caribou, muskox, polar bear, and wood bison, were declared to be in such danger in the Northwest Territories (NWT) in the 1960s. The harvesting of muskox was prohibited for over fifty years and then, when subsequently permitted, was managed under strict quota. Polar bear and wood bison have also been managed since the 1960s on the basis of a strict quota system. Only barren ground caribou populations that rebounded in the 1980s escaped a quota system under the game ordinance.[22]

Over time, the Crown imposed progressively tighter restrictions on the barter, sale, or other exchange of wildlife, and established wildlife sanctuaries where some or all species of wildlife could not be harvested. The Crown regulated hunting techniques and equipment. Territorial laws regulated trapping as a commercial activity and restricted, and then eventually virtually eliminated, other commercial harvesting of wildlife. Dangerous hunting provisions and prohibitions against the abandonment or wasting of meat fit for human consumption have also had some effect on Indigenous hunting methods and activities.

An approach to the allocation of harvestable surpluses based on equal opportunities for all users may be appropriate for a government-owned common property resource, but it can also result in resistance to special entitlements, such as those held by Indigenous persons. Tension, if not conflict, between sportsmen hunters and Indigenous hunters over access to game and to hunting areas has been one unfortunate result.[23]

Wildlife Conservation and Management Regimes in the Territories

In the territories, Indigenous peoples are a significant proportion of the total population. Approximately 86 percent of the total population of Nunavut,[24] 52 percent of the total population of the NWT,[25] and 23 percent of the total population of the Yukon Territory[26] is Indigenous. These populations are widely distributed in small communities and they continue to depend on wildlife harvesting for food, cultural, and spiritual uses. In many of these remote communities, access to wildlife is also a food security issue of significant importance.

Since 1984, a series of comprehensive land claim agreements have been negotiated between Indigenous peoples and Canada, and the territorial governments. The relevant agreements include:

- The *Inuvialuit Final Agreement* (*IFA*) (1984);
- The *Gwich'in Comprehensive Land Claim Agreement* (1992);
- The *Nunavut Agreement* (1993);
- The *Umbrella Final Agreement* (*UFA*) (Yukon 1993);
- The *Sahtu Dene and Metis Comprehensive Land Claim Agreement* (1994); and
- *The Tlicho Agreement* (2005).[27]

While these agreements vary considerably in specific content, they share important common elements in their approach to, and effect on, the state's wildlife management.

Wildlife rights were of central importance in the negotiations for these land claims. Wildlife negotiations were initiated early and detailed provisions addressing beneficiaries' rights to wildlife are included in all these land claims. One of the fundamental principles of the *IFA* for example is "to protect and preserve the Arctic wildlife, environment and biological diversity."[28] A review of the wildlife rights chapters of these land claims indicates that they systematically roll back the effects of the state paradigm. Aboriginal harvesters' rights to harvest without a licence, without restrictions as to age, sex, or size of wildlife and using any means available are confirmed. No seasons or times of day are applicable to Aboriginal harvesting. The only harvesting limits are the requirements of conservation, public safety, and humane trapping and killing. The right to barter, trade, and sell wildlife amongst beneficiaries, and sometimes to others, is protected. Exclusive or preferential rights to harvest some species of wildlife are included within the claims' settlement areas and on Aboriginal private lands.

The land claims establish Aboriginal institutions—community hunters and trappers' organizations or renewable resource committees as well as regional organizations. These bodies make decisions about the exercise of Aboriginal rights, quota allocations, and harvesting activities, which are a common feature of many land claims, thus bringing important harvesting decision-making home to the community level.

In addition, the land claims establish wildlife co-management bodies that are institutions of public government. In all cases, these co-managers are indicated to be the primary authority for wildlife management within the land claim settlement area.[29] All significant government wildlife management decisions in the territories take place in the context of these comanagement processes. The membership of these tribunals is made up of at least half nominees or appointees from the land claims organizations. No major decision on wildlife management takes place in an area with a settled land claim without the advice—or in some cases decision—of the co-management body. In many areas[30] the co-management tribunal works in concert with community-based institutions representing beneficiaries. Wildlife management in the territories has become decidedly more local since the advent of land claims.

The rights granted through land claims are protected by section 35 of the *Constitution Act, 1982*. Co-management regimes in the land claims must be honoured by the Crown. In *First Nation of Nacho Nyak Dun v. Yukon*,[31] the Supreme Court of Canada held, "[a]lthough not exhaustively so, reconciliation is found in the respectful fulfillment of a modern treaty's *terms*."[32]

The Supreme Court made clear the application of the *Nacho Nyak Dun* decision to the overall resource management framework established in the Yukon by the *UFA*.

In this decision, the court identified and emphasized the fundamental importance of the comanagement regimes that characterize comprehensive land claim agreements across northern Canada. The *Nacho Nyak Dun* decision underscores the constitutional underpinning of these arrangements and their importance in the quest for reconciliation on northern landscapes. The court signalled that governments are required to consult First Nations with land claim agreements and may only make changes under these co-management regimes in a manner consistent with the land claims and with the honour of the Crown. In *Nacho Nyak Dun*, the court also strongly emphasized the importance of good faith participation in the co-management process set out in the *UFA* for land-use planning.

This reasoning is equally applicable to the Crown's role and participation in wildlife comanagement regimes established under land claims. Constitutionally protected comprehensive land claims have fundamentally altered the relationship between the state and community-based wildlife paradigms in a way that, absent agreement, cannot be reversed. Moreover, as will be set out below, land claims and co-management have had a forcing effect on wildlife statutes in the territories in a way that also advances the interests of reconciliation. The approach taken recently by the territorial governments to developing new wildlife legislation reflects the requirements of accommodation and reconciliation as set out in Supreme Court jurisprudence and could serve as a model for similar initiatives in other jurisdictions.

YUKON

In 2002, the Yukon government amended the *Wildlife Act*[33] to include Part 13 which addresses the *IFA* and its application on the Yukon North Slope. Overall, the Part 13 development process and its contents give clear indication that collaborative development of wildlife legislation is the optimal approach in an area to which land claims rights and harvesting privileges apply. Part 13 was developed with direct involvement by representatives from the Inuvialuit Game Council (IGC)[34] and the Wildlife Management Advisory Council (North Slope) (WMAC[NS]).[35] The development of the legislation was collaborative and Inuvialuit representatives and co-managers had direct access to legislative drafters and the opportunity to comment directly on drafts of Part 13 as the legislation was developed. Section 198 of the Act makes it clear that Part 13 prevails over any other provision of the Act in a case of conflict or inconsistency and that the *IFA* prevails over the Act in any similar situation. Part 13 only applies to the North Slope.

This part of the Act reflects Inuvialuit rights to harvest, to methods of harvesting, to exchange or barter wildlife products, and to move harvested wildlife anywhere in the Inuvialuit Settlement Region without a permit, including export from the Yukon. The exemption from licensing requirements and special harvesting entitlements of Inuvialuit are reflected in Part 13. The process for establishing subsistence quotas and total allowable harvests, in a case where conservation needs require it, is set out in a manner consistent with the *IFA*. Harvest allocation processes are also set out consistent with the land claim, including arrangements for respecting Hunters and Trappers Committees' harvesting bylaws.

NUNAVUT

The Nunavut government (GN) rewrote its wildlife legislation as a priority after the territory was established in 1999. In Nunavut, there is a single land claim covering the whole territory. GN invited Nunavut Tunngavik Incorporated (the Nunavut Inuit rights-bearing organization) and the Nunavut Wildlife Management Board (NWMB)[36] to join a working group that systematically analyzed the impact of the Nunavut Agreement on the *Wildlife Act*.[37] All parties had counsel and the legislative drafting process was centred on the working group process with all parties receiving and commenting directly on draft provisions. This process was novel and took several years to complete. A new *Wildlife Act*[38] was enacted in 2003.

The *Wildlife Act* includes species at risk provisions and was written to specifically accommodate Inuit wildlife rights and the roles of both Inuit wildlife organizations (community and regional), and the NWMB. Section 1 of the statute asserts:

> Purpose of this Act
>
> (1) The purpose of this Act is to establish a comprehensive regime for the management of wildlife and habitat in Nunavut, including the conservation, protection and recovery of species at risk, in a manner that implements provision of the Nunavut Land Claims Agreement respecting wildlife, habitat and the rights of Inuit in relation to wildlife and habitat.

This part of the Act explicitly incorporates Inuit traditional knowledge into the interpretation of the legislation using Inuit concepts set out in Inuktitut. Part 2 explicitly acknowledges the rights to harvest confirmed for Inuit by the Nunavut Agreement.

Overall, the statute respects and reflects the wildlife rights set out in the Nunavut Agreement and provides an excellent example of the integration of these rights into a modern wildlife statute.

NORTHWEST TERRITORIES

The government of the NWT (GNWT) faced an even more complex task. At the time wildlife legislation reform was initiated there were four settled land claims and at least three others in the negotiation process, including Metis Claim negotiations. There are differences in both the specific rights granted to land claim beneficiaries and in the roles and authorities of the co-management tribunals established by the claims. In addition, Treaties 8 and 11 apply in the NWT.

The GNWT invited all interested Aboriginal governments to join a Wildlife Act Working Group (WAWG) and began an exploration of the changes required to wildlife legislation to accommodate and reflect Aboriginal rights.

GNWT chose to use the WAWG to develop both a *Species at Risk Act*[39] and a *Wildlife Act*.[40] The legislation is framed around collaborative wildlife management. Land claim, Treaty, and Aboriginal rights are reflected in the text as are the institutions established by land claims. GNWT's approach was to treat all Aboriginal organizations as "governments" and to build direct engagement and consultation with these governments into these statutes.

Land claim and common law harvesting rights based on section 35 of the *Constitution Act, 1982* are reflected in the text of the Acts. Decisions made by co-management bodies are a required precursor to ministerial decision-making. GNWT has continued its use of the WAWG for the development of wildlife regulations and ongoing Aboriginal consultation. Despite the complexity of the Aboriginal rights framework in the NWT, it is important to note that all the leadership of members represented on the WAWG agreed to the final bill that went into the legislature.

GNWT's success in this initiative should put to rest any argument that incorporating Aboriginal rights into legislation is too complicated and that the best approach is a non-derogation clause and to let the courts sort out disputes. The non-derogation clause approach falls short of the effort required to achieve reconciliation.

Reconciliation and the Future of Northern Wildlife

In early cases such as *R v. Sparrow* and *R v. Horseman*, where Canadian courts first considered the infringement of section 35 rights, judicial discussion of reconciliation was limited.[41] In more recent jurisprudence, however, the Supreme Court has clearly articulated that the purposes of section 35 include the reconciliation of Indigenous interests with those of non-Indigenous peoples[42] and the protection of Indigenous rights.[43]

According to the Federal Court of Appeal, reconciliation is a process that requires Indigenous and non-Indigenous peoples to make "good faith efforts to understand each other's concerns and move to address them."[44] In *R v. Van der Peet*, the Supreme Court explained that "true reconciliation" accounts for both the Indigenous and Euro-Canadian perspectives.[45] The goal of reconciliation is to foster a "mutually respectful long-term relationship" between and to bridge the cultures of Indigenous and non-Indigenous peoples.[46]

The Supreme Court's characterization of reconciliation demands more than the limited recognition of Indigenous hunting rights found in most provincial hunting and wildlife laws. Reconciliation demands that those drafting wildlife and hunting legislation reconcile Indigenous rights to wildlife with other interests, including the competing interests of recreational hunters and conservationists. An appropriate reconciliation of these interests must account for Indigenous community perspectives on wildlife management and involve good faith efforts to understand and address Indigenous people's rights and interests in wildlife.

Arguably, in the context of wildlife rights, reconciliation has been successfully effected through the negotiation of modern treaties in the North.

Modern treaties, as "expressions of partnership between nations," are "critical in fostering reconciliation."[47] In *First Nation of Nacho Nyak Dun v. Yukon*, the Supreme Court held up the Yukon *UFA* as a "model for reconciliation" because "[a]greements falling under the *UFA* are intended to foster a positive and mutually respectful long-term relationship between the signatories."[48] The *UFA*, in particular, "establishes institutions for self-government and management of lands and resources"[49] and "set[s] out in precise terms a co-operative governance relationship."[50]

Negotiated approaches to wildlife management, such as those found in the North, are consistent with the theme of reconciliation adopted by the Supreme Court of Canada in recent section 35 cases. In the context of the management of resources such as wildlife, "land claim negotiations provide the best opportunity to overcome long-standing rules or policies that fail to reflect the interconnectedness of all resources, and fail to link a diverse range of strategies and techniques in managing resources."[51]

Territorial governments have taken the lead in responding to this guidance from the courts. Their wildlife statutes have been adapted to incorporate Aboriginal rights and the new institutions established by land claims. The collaborative approach taken to the drafting of this legislation has resulted in an inclusive statutory framework and processes for ensuring that wildlife and habitats are protected in the interests of all Northern residents. Collaborative wildlife management has led to instances like the call by the Tlicho Government for a total allowable harvest of zero for Bathurst herd barren ground caribou in a 2016 proceeding before the Wek'èezhìi Renewable Resources Board.[52]

Co-management gives a voice to Aboriginal harvesters and a direct role in decision-making. Wildlife management challenges and the need to protect habitats are more likely to be addressed successfully in a collaborative wildlife management framework.

Conclusion

Land claims and the Supreme Court's reconciliation jurisprudence have converged in the legislation and approach to wildlife management in the territories. The result is a collaborative decision-making regime that promises better wildlife management outcomes for all. The northern approach to the development of these wildlife laws could be useful in other jurisdictions where legislation does not fully reflect Indigenous rights and interests. If we hope to ensure the continued presence of wildlife and habitats on our landscapes, we must do better. Ensuring that our wildlife laws better accommodate Aboriginal rights and interests would be a good place to start.

NOTES

1 Counsel at Wilms & Shier Environmental Lawyers LLP, Toronto. The research assistance of Nicole Petersen, Erin Garbett, and Raeya Jackiw is gratefully acknowledged.

2 This paper is focused on the general history and management of wildlife in the Yukon, Northwest Territories, and Nunavut, collectively the "territories."

3 See e.g., Dr Peter J Usher, *The Devolution of Wildlife Management and Prospects for Wildlife Conservation in the Northwest Territories, Policy Paper 3* (Ottawa: Canadian Arctic Resources Committee, 1986) [Usher]; Fikret Berkes, *Sacred Ecology: Traditional Ecological Knowledge and Resource Management* (Philadelphia: Taylor & Francis, 1999) [Berkes]; Fikret Berkes, *Common Property Resources: Ecology and Community-Based Sustainable Development* (London: Belhaven Press, 1975).

4 The term "Aboriginal rights" is used inclusively. It is intended to include Treaty rights, inherent Indigenous rights recognized or asserted through the common law system, and rights derived from modern land claim agreements, unless the context suggests a narrower usage.

5 Collectively referred to as "wildlife rights" below.

6 This dynamic tension was played out as a subplot in the litigation surrounding *Baker Lake (Hamlet) v Canada (Minister of Indian Affairs and Northern Development)* (1979), 107 DLR (3d) 513, 3 CNLR 17 (FCTD). Inuit in the Kivalliq region of Nunavut were of the view that uranium exploration was driving the Beverly and Kaminuriaq caribou herds away. Government biologists testified that the problem was Inuit over-harvesting of these herds. Later, caribou surveys indicated that government census techniques were significantly under-counting the caribou. The views of the biologists supporting the dominant paradigm held sway and the community of Baker Lake's request for an injunction to prevent further mineral exploration was unsuccessful.

7 The first comprehensive land claim settled north of 60 was the *Inuvialuit Final Agreement* (*IFA*) brought into force by the *Western Arctic (Inuvialuit) Claims Settlement Act*. *Inuvialuit Final Agreement as Amended* (April 2005; accessed 27 November 2021), online (pdf): *Inuvialuit Regional Corporation* <irc.inuvialuit.com/sites/default/files/Inuvialuit%20Final%20Agreement%202005.pdf> [*IFA*]; *Western Arctic (Inuvialuit) Claims Settlement Act*, SC 1984, c 24 [Inuvialuit Settlement Act].

8 *Constitution Act, 1982*, s 35, being Schedule B to the Canada Act 1982 (UK), 1982, c 11.

9 The first of the important section 35 wildlife cases was *R v Sparrow*, [1990] 1 SCR 1075, 1990 CanLII 104.

10 The term "wildlife" requires definition for purposes of this paper. I have focused on laws related to birds and terrestrial mammals under the jurisdiction of the territorial legislatures unless the context requires otherwise.

11 For a description of this evolution, see John Donihee, *The Evolution of Wildlife Law in Canada*, Occasional Paper #9 (Calgary: Canadian Institute of Resources Law, 2000).

12 For an analysis set in the northern context, see RG McCandless, *Yukon Wildlife: A Social History* (Edmonton: University of Alberta Press, 1981).

13 I do not suggest that all Indigenous systems are the same. In fact, the opposite is probably true, but common elements emerge from even a brief review of the literature in this area. Likewise, I do not suggest that only Indigenous populations developed locally based systems. For some examples, see Evelyn Pinkerton, *Cooperative Management of Local Fisheries* (Vancouver: U BC Press, 1989).

14 FG Speck, "The Family Hunting Band as the Basis of Algonkian Social Organization" (1915) 17:2 American Anthropologist 289.

15 Arlene Stairs & George Wenzel, "'I Am I and the Environment': Inuit Hunting, Community and Identity" (1992) 3:1 Journal of Indigenous Studies 1 at 4.

16 Usher, *supra* note 3.

17 Berkes, *supra* note 3 at 48.

18 See e.g., Inuvialuit Settlement Act, *supra* note 7, s 3(3).

19 *Migratory Birds Convention Act, 1994*, SC 1994, c 22.

20 See e.g., *Northwest Territories Act*, RSC 1985, c N-27 (repealed), s 18, and Game Ordinance, RSNWT, c G-1. See Donihee, *supra* note 11 at 35–37.

21 Ordinances were laws promulgated by the Commissioner in Council until 1999 when the present Northwest Territories was created: now see the *Northwest Territories Act*, SC 2014, c 2.

22 The populations are once again seriously reduced. Total allowable harvests established by co-management tribunals under land claims are now in place for most NWT and Nunavut populations.

23 Brian Louis Calliou, *Losing the Game: Wildlife Conservation and the Regulation of First Nations Hunting in Alberta, 1880–1930* (LL.M. thesis, University of Alberta, Spring 2000) [unpublished] at 149. For another good overview of the effect of the application of federal and provincial game laws on Indigenous hunting activities, see Bennett McArdle, *The Rules of the Game: The Development of Government Controls over Indian Hunting and Trapping in Treaty Eight (Alberta) to 1930* (May 1976), Treaty and Aboriginal Rights Research, Indian Association of Alberta [unpublished].

24 Statistics Canada, *Inuit: Fact Sheet for Nunavut* (Ottawa: Statistics Canada, 2016), online: <www150.statcan.gc.ca/n1/pub/89-656-x/89-656-x2016017-eng.htm>.

25 Statistics Canada, *Aboriginal Peoples: Fact Sheet for Northwest Territories* (Ottawa: Statistics Canada, 2016), online: <www150.statcan.gc.ca/n1/pub/89-656-x/89-656-x2016013-eng.htm>.

26 Statistics Canada, *Aboriginal Peoples: Fact Sheet for Yukon* (Ottawa: Statistics Canada, 2016), online: <www150.statcan.gc.ca/n1/pub/89-656-x/89-656-x2016012-eng.htm>.

27 *IFA*, *supra* note 7; *Gwich'in Comprehensive Land Claim Agreement Between Her Majesty the Queen in Right of Canada and the Gwich'in as Represented by the Gwich'in Tribal Council* (1992), online (pdf): *The Government of Canada* <rcaanc-cirnac.gc.ca/DAM/DAM-INTER-HQ-LDC/STAGING/texte-text/gwichin_Land_Claim_Agreement_PDF_1427372111130_eng.pdf> [Gwich'in Land Claim]; *Agreement between the Inuit of the Nunavut Settlement Area and Her Majesty the Queen in Right of Canada*" (1993), online (pdf): *Government of Nunavut* <gov.nu.ca/sites/default/files/Nunavut_Land_Claims_Agreement.pdf> [Nunavut Agreement]; *Umbrella Final Agreement Between the Government of Canada, the Council for Yukon Indians and the Government of the Yukon* (1993), online (pdf): *Government of Canada* <www.rcaanc-cirnac.gc.ca/DAM/

DAM-CIRNAC-RCAANC/DAM-TAG/STAGING/texte-text/al_ldc_ccl_fagr_ykn_umb_1318604279080_eng.pdf>; *Sahtu Dene and Metis Comprehensive Land Claim Agreement* (1994), online (pdf): *Government of Canada* <rcaanc-cirnac.gc.ca/DAM/DAM-CIRNAC-RCAANC/DAM-TAG/STAGING/texte-text/sahtu_dene-metis-CLCA-2010_2015__1547582651983_eng.pdf>; *Land Claims and Self-Government Agreement among the Tłįchǫ and the Government of the Northwest Territories and the Government of Canada* (2005), online (pdf): *Government of Canada* <rcaanc-cirnac.gc.ca/DAM/DAM-CIRNAC-RCAANC/DAM-TAG/STAGING/texte-text/ccl_fagr_nwts_tliagr_tliagr_1302089608774_eng.pdf>.

28 *IFA*, *supra* note 7, s l(c).

29 For example, s 12.8.1 of the Gwich'in Comprehensive Claim establishes a Renewable Resources Board that is the "main instrument for wildlife management in the settlement area" and is required to act "in the public interest." Gwich'in Land Claim, *supra* note 27, s 12.8.1.

30 The Sahtu Settlement Area and Nunavut are two examples.

31 *First Nation of Nacho Nyak Dun v Yukon*, 2017 SCC 58 [*Nacho Nyak Dun*].

32 *Ibid* at para 38.

33 *Wildlife Act*, RSY 2002, c 229.

34 The IGC is the rights-bearing organization established by s 14(73) of the *IFA* to represent Inuvialuit in wildlife management in the Inuvialuit Settlement Region, which includes the North Slope. See *IFA*, *supra* note 7, s 14(73).

35 WMAC(NS) is a co-management tribunal established by s 12(46) of the *IFA* to oversee wildlife management in the North Slope area of Yukon. See *ibid*, s 12(46).

36 An institution of public government established by s 5.2.1 of the Nunavut Agreement. See Nunavut Agreement, *supra* note 27, s 5.2.1.

37 *Wildlife Act*, RSNWT 1988, c W-4. This was NWT legislation enacted before division and remained in place until replaced by Nunavut's new *Wildlife Act*.

38 *Wildlife Act*, SNu 2003, c 26.

39 *Species at Risk Act*, SNWT 2009, c 16.

40 *Wildlife Act*, SNWT 2013, c 30.

41 See e.g., *R v Sparrow*, [1990] 1 SCR 1075, 1990 CarswellBC 105; and *R v Horseman*, [1990] 1 SCR 901,1990 CarswellAlta 47.

42 *Delgamuukw v British Columbia*, [1997] 3 SCR 1010, 1997 CanLII 302 at para 186 [*Delgamuukw*]; *Beckman v Little Salmon Carmacks First Nation*, 2010 SCC 53 at para 10 [*Beckman*].

43 *Tsilhqot'in Nation v British Columbia*, 2014 SCC 44 at para 118.

44 *Prophet River First Nation v Canada (Attorney General)*, 2017 FCA 15, 408 DLR (4th) 165 at para 49 [*Prophet River*].

45 *R v Van der Peet*, [1996] 2 SCR 507, 1996 CanLII 216 at para 50.

46 *Beckman*, *supra* note 42 at para 10; *Delgamuukw*, *supra* note 42 at para 81.

47 *Nacho Nyak Dun*, *supra* note 31 at para 1.

48 *Ibid* at para 10.

49 *Ibid*.

50 *Ibid* at para 33.

51 Barry Stuart, "The Potential of Land Claims Negotiations for Resolving Resource Use Conflicts" in Monique Ross & J Owen Saunders, eds, *Growing Demands on a Shrinking*

Heritage: Managing Resource Use Conflicts (Calgary: Canadian Institute of Resources Law, 1992) at 131.

52 Wek'èezhìi Renewable Resources Board, *Reasons for Decision Related to a Joint Proposal for the Management of the Bathurst (Barren-Ground Caribou) Herd, Part A* (Yellowknife, NT: Wek'èezhìi Renewable Resources Board, May 2016), online (pdf): <wrrb.ca/sites/default/files/Bathurst%20Reasons%20for%20Decision%20Part%20A%20FINAL%20REPORT%20-%2026may16.pdf>.

13

Buffalo in Banff National Park: Framework for Reconciliation in Wildlife Management

Robert Hamilton[1]

Introduction

In June 2017, sixteen buffalo were transported to Banff National Park. The plan was that by 2020, a nascent herd would be roaming largely free of constraint, over a hundred years since the last wild buffalo had been seen in the park. The re-introduction is an example of shared wildlife management, where Canadian and Indigenous legal systems work together toward the achievement of shared goals. This chapter explores how the re-introduction of buffalo to key sites in Canada and the United States represents a framework for reconciliation in wildlife management.

Buffalo Return to Banff: Canadian Legal Perspectives

A number of civil society groups and Indigenous nations advocated for the return of buffalo to Banff. Before the re-introduction could move forward, however, several requirements of Canadian law had to be met. As a national park, Banff is subject to regulation by federal statute. The park was created under, and is managed by authority derived from, the *Canada National Parks Act*[2] (the Act). A national park is in many ways "full" of Canadian state law. Regulations under the Act govern the identification of wilderness areas,[3] traffic regulations,[4] garbage disposal,[5] wildlife,[6] aircraft access,[7] fishing,[8] and more. In Banff National Park specifically, there are also extensive regulations governing the town itself[9] and commercial ski areas.[10] National parks are highly regulated spaces, and this concentration of state law has historically worked to exclude Indigenous peoples and their laws from these areas.[11]

In respect of the re-introduction of buffalo in Banff, the prevalence of state law meant that the project could not move forward until certain Canadian legal requirements were met. An environmental impact analysis (EIA), for example, had to be carried out.[12] At the time, Parks Canada had authority to carry out EIAs for projects on "federal lands" under section 67 of the *Canadian Environmental Assessment Act*.[13] This requires an assessment of whether the project is likely to "cause significant adverse environmental effects" and, if so, if such effects can be justified.[14] Parks Canada performed a detailed EIA, assessing the impact on "soil, vegetation and fire; wildlife resources; aquatic resources; cultural resources; species at risk; visitor experience; and the socio-economic dynamics of surrounding human communities."[15] The assessment determined that the impact would be "insignificant."[16]

In the pilot phase of the project (2017–2022), the buffalo were limited to an area designated as a "Wilderness Zone" under the Act. As such, the "wilderness character" of the area is a priority, and it is not accessible by trail with a motorized vehicle.[17] The "re-introduction zone" is further subdivided into three "bison management zones" in accordance with the "Bison Excursion Prevention and Response Plan."[18] Until June 2018, the animals were kept in an enclosed "soft-release" pasture, at which point they were released into a broader 1,892-km^2 "re-introduction zone." The animals were monitored closely throughout this period and, if they ventured into a peripheral "hazing zone," would be herded, hazed, or baited back into the re-introduction zone. At the end of the five-year pilot period, the project will be evaluated in light of project targets and a decision will be made about whether the project should continue.[19] As can be seen from this cursory overview, re-introducing a species to a national park requires considerable movement from Canadian state law.

Buffalo Return to Banff: Indigenous Legal Perspectives

In September 2014, ten Indigenous nations from both sides of the Canada-US border came together in Montana to sign the *Buffalo Treaty*.[20] The aim of the treaty is cooperation regarding "the restoration of bison on reserves or co-managed lands within the U.S. and Canada."[21] The treaty was the outgrowth of the Iinnii Initiative, conceived by leaders of the Blackfoot Confederacy in 2009 to re-introduce buffalo to their nations.[22] Two years after the treaty signing, 87 plains buffalo were transferred from Elk Island National Park to the Blackfeet Nation.[23] Since the initial signing, a dozen more First Nations in Canada have signed the treaty.[24]

The signatory nations drafted the *Buffalo Treaty* in recognition of the historical importance of buffalo to Indigenous peoples of the region. It is an initiative aimed not only at strengthening buffalo populations by re-introducing them into traditional habitats, but at reinvigorating and recovering Indigenous cultural, spiritual, and legal practices associated with the buffalo. As Professor Leroy Little Bear said, "the treaty speaks to issues such as culture, health, research, and conservation."[25] This is reflected in the full name of the treaty: *The Buffalo: A Treaty of Co-operation, Renewal and Restoration.* The purpose of the treaty as stated in the text:

> To honor, recognize, and revitalize the time immemorial relationship we have with BUFFALO, it is the collective intention of WE, the undersigned NATIONS, to welcome BUFFALO to once again live among us as CREATOR intended by doing everything within our means so WE and BUFFALO will once again live together to nurture each other culturally and spiritually. It is our collective intention to recognize BUFFALO as a wild free-ranging animal and as an important part of the ecological system; to provide a safe space and environment across our historic homelands, on both sides of the United States and the Canadian border, so together WE can have our brother, the BUFFALO, lead us in nurturing our land, plants and other animals to once again realize THE BUFFALO WAYS for our future generations.[26]

The *Buffalo Treaty* is an example of Indigenous law at work. Indigenous peoples had, and continue to have, systems and practices of law internal to their nations and communities.[27] They also have traditions of transnational law—that is, law between Indigenous nations.[28] When Europeans began entering into treaties with Indigenous peoples, they carried on not only European traditions of treaty-making, but Indigenous ones.[29] Treaty-making has historically been an important aspect of inter-Indigenous transnational law. The *Buffalo Treaty* is a contemporary example of this.

The treaty acts as an assertion of Indigenous law by articulating standards and norms derived from Indigenous legal traditions and world views.

For example, the treaty states: "We, collectively, agree to perpetuate all aspects of our respective cultures related to BUFFALO including customs, practices, harvesting, beliefs, songs, and ceremonies."[30] This is notable, as many customs, songs, and ceremonies have important legal dimensions, often acting as sources of legal principles and legal reasoning.[31] The re-introduction of the buffalo reinvigorates a "lifeworld" in which Indigenous legal regimes exist.[32] The treaty also speaks to land and resource use on both sides of the Canada-US border.[33] The territorial scope of the jurisdiction claimed under the treaty tracks Indigenous geographies, not state borders. Among the initiatives supported by the treaty signatories was the re-introduction of buffalo to Banff National Park.

Overlapping Law, Shared Jurisdiction, and Reconciliation

In the Canadian context, there are geographic regions where multiple legal orders are working, at times in relation to the same subject matters. Where multiple legal orders exist in this way, they always sit in relationships of tension and accommodation. Achieving reconciliation between state and Indigenous legal orders requires taking the fact of legal pluralism as a starting point.[34] In a practical sense, this means clearly identifying the legal barriers to the recognition of Indigenous legal orders and drawing on examples of where those barriers have been overcome.

The Truth and Reconciliation Commission (TRC), in its 94 *Calls to Action*, called on Canada to "repudiate harmful principles such as the Doctrine of Discovery and *Terra Nullius*."[35] An analysis of why it may have done so sheds light on the question of how to move toward meaningful reconciliation. A first step in this regard is identifying where the doctrine of discovery is still alive in Canadian law. In its simplest form, this doctrine expresses the view that European powers gained territorial sovereignty and legal authority over lands in North America upon "discovering" them. A full accounting of the doctrine, however, requires a broader lens. As Tracey Lindberg writes, the doctrine of discovery is "a dogmatic body of shared theories (informing theory, law, and understanding) pertaining to the rightfulness and righteousness of settler belief systems and the supremacy of institutions (legal, economic, governmental) that are based upon those belief systems."[36] *Terra nullius* is a complementary doctrine through which lands were categorized as legally vacant, a crucial prerequisite to "discovery" and the answer to the question, "how can a continent full of people be 'discovered?'" Though *terra nullius* was official policy in Australia, in Canada it was not.[37] Yet, as a corollary to the doctrine of discovery, it was relied on in important ways nonetheless. Though the doctrine of discovery in its simplest form may seem like an antiquated idea, it animates much judicial reasoning on Indigenous rights and continues to shape the relationship between Indigenous peoples and the state in important ways.[38]

The doctrine became an explicit part of Indigenous rights law in the common law world in the 1823 American case of *Johnson v. M'Intosh*.[39] There, Marshall CJ held that the "principle was that discovery gave title to the government by whose subjects or by whose authority it was made against all other European governments."[40] Though the title gained through discovery was good "against all other European governments,"[41] discovery also affected Indigenous peoples. As Marshall CJ held, "the rights of the original inhabitants were in no instance entirely disregarded, but were necessarily to a considerable extent impaired. They were admitted to be the rightful occupants of the soil, with a legal as well as just claim to retain possession of it, and to use it according to their own discretion; but their rights to complete sovereignty as independent nations were necessarily diminished."[42] This decision shaped the Canadian approach. Discussing the nature of Indigenous land rights and Crown authority in *Guerin v. The Queen*, the Supreme Court cited *Johnson v. M'Intosh* in stating that: "The principle of discovery . . . justified these claims and gave the ultimate title in the land in a particular area to the nation which had discovered and claimed it."[43]

Following the constitutional recognition of Aboriginal and Treaty Rights in 1982, the doctrine of discovery animated the court's approach to interpreting section 35 rights in two ways. First, in *R v. Sparrow*, the court held that section 35 rights can be unilaterally infringed by the Crown subject to a justification analysis.[44] The court cited the 1823 decision of the US Supreme Court, *Johnson v. M'Intosh*, as authority for the proposition that "there was from the outset never any doubt that sovereignty and legislative power, and indeed the underlying title, to such lands vested in the Crown.[45] While the court made a move to question this by citing, with seeming approval, Professor Noel Lyon's argument that section 35 opens the door for courts to question Crown sovereign authority, it nonetheless held onto that unilateral authority as the basis for the power to infringe section 35 rights.[46] The doctrine is also still present in the doctrine of Aboriginal title. The Supreme Court has established a framework that takes the assertion of sovereignty as the key date for establishing Aboriginal title.[47] Employing what is known as the "crystallization thesis," the court has held that Aboriginal title crystalized upon the assertion of Crown sovereignty.[48] The Crown's ability to gain sovereignty by assertion is rooted in the doctrine of discovery.

These principles then shaped the development of the duty to consult. The court has repeatedly emphasized that the duty to consult does not include a veto power.[49] What this framing means is that the Crown retains the power to act unilaterally in the face of Indigenous opposition, subject only to the procedural requirements elaborated under the duty. Further, under the consultation framework, the courts insist they hold power to unilaterally determine the relative rights and obligations of the parties. Indigenous rights are, therefore, *asserted* until such point as they are proven in court, while Crown entitlements are assumed. The legitimacy of such unilateralism is based on a hierarchical organization of legal systems. While the courts have undoubtedly pushed Aboriginal rights forward in important respects, often in the face of intransigent state actors,[50] the doctrines of discovery and *terra nullius* are engrained in section 35 jurisprudence. How, then, can the unilateralism and engrained hierarchy of the constitutional rights framework be challenged?

Increasingly, the *United Nations Declaration on the Rights of Indigenous Peoples* (UNDRIP) is cited as a source of foundational substantive norms that can guide Crown-Indigenous relations.[51] Self-determination and free, prior, and informed consent, in particular, provide legal language through which Indigenous people are now voicing their claims to control affairs in their traditional territories. With British Columbia[52] and most recently the federal government, having passed implementation legislation,[53] questions about what this implementation will look like are now top of mind. There is considerable debate about what implementation might look like and how UNDRIP interacts with section 35.[54] While there is considerable uncertainty regarding the definition of "consent" in UNDRIP and the extent to which UNDRIP pushes past current section 35 jurisprudence, it seems clear that UNDRIP envisages states as legally pluralistic spheres.[55] The unilateralism that grounds section 35, therefore, seems inimical to UNDRIP. When the TRC calls for a repudiation of the doctrine of discovery, it is calling for a repudiation of the hierarchical ordering of legal systems and the unilateralism of Crown sovereign authority that has historically shaped Crown approaches to Indigenous decision-making authority. This, in turn, requires that legal authority be negotiated rather than dictated by the state and the state's courts.[56] How, then, does this relate to wildlife management projects of the type described here?

Reconciliation Frameworks and Wildlife Management

The re-introduction of buffalo into Banff National Park included elements of both Canadian state law and Indigenous law. The *Buffalo Treaty* is aimed at the re-introduction of buffalo in sites across the region and the care of existing populations. This is being undertaken to reinvigorate Indigenous cultural, spiritual, and legal orders. In specific locales, such as Banff, the re-introduction requires significant movement from state law. Parks Canada has recognized the importance of Indigenous involvement. As Parks Canada explains: "Making sure that bison received proper blessings before they returned to the Banff landscape was a key part of the project. Parks Canada hosted a blessing ceremony on the shore of Lake Minnewanka with *Buffalo Treaty* signatories and celebrated at a second ceremony at Elk Island to mark the departure of the herd to Banff."[57] Both state and Indigenous protocols had a role to play. The *Buffalo Treaty* signatories have consciously sought out this form of collaboration. When the Mistawasis First Nation signed, for example, "[o]ther groups were on hand to sign as supporters of the treaty. Those groups included Saskatchewan Polytechnic, the Canadian Parks and Wilderness Society, and the City of Prince Albert, which was represented by Mayor Greg Dionne."[58] While co-management regimes under modern treaty and land claims agreements are reasonably well known, such agreements are impractical or undesirable for many Indigenous nations. Yet, as the *Buffalo Treaty* example shows, there are other ways to move forward.

There are several other examples taking place in National Parks under Parks Canada initiatives to "connect with Indigenous partners."[59] In Jasper National Park, a section of the park "is closed to the general public for a week to allow members of a B.C. First Nation to hunt on their traditionally used lands, which fall within the park boundary."[60] Similarly, in 1993, the Champagne and Aishihik First Nations, and in 2003 for the Kluane First Nation, negotiated the resumption of traditional harvesting in Kluane National Park.[61] The "Healing Broken Connections" project has since attempted to build on these legal gains by encouraging Indigenous participation in a range of activities in the park, strengthening the connection between the people and the place.[62] In these examples, Indigenous peoples work within the existing National Parks framework to create space for the exercise of Indigenous law.

In other examples, Indigenous peoples have asserted their law as the primary source of authority and pushed the state to work within Indigenous legal frameworks. One example of this is the creation of "tribal parks." The Tla-o-qui-aht, Tsilhqot'in, Haida, and Doig River First Nations have established tribal parks. Tribal parks are areas of Indigenous jurisdiction, subject to Indigenous law. They are, with one exception, not yet formally recognized under Canadian law. The park with the most well-known origins is likely the first park established by the Tla-o-qui-aht in 1984.[63] The provincial government in British Columbia had provided a licence to harvest old growth forest on Meares Island, a small island on the west coast of Vancouver Island. As part of their opposition to the project, the Tla-o-qui-aht declared the island to be a tribal park under their jurisdiction. While the Tla-o-qui-aht ultimately secured an injunction to stop the logging (which has stood to this day), the courts did not acknowledge or speak to the existence of the tribal park.[64] Yet, the Tla-o-qui-aht continue to manage the island as a tribal park. They have since declared three more parks in their territory.[65]

The Haida Nation also asserted a tribal park, with somewhat different results. In 1982, the Council of the Haida Nation passed a resolution aimed at prohibiting logging on over 227,000 hectares of Haida Gwaii, declaring the area a tribal park under Haida jurisdiction. In 2008, the government of British Columbia ultimately recognized the claim by making the area a park under provincial law.[66] The Haida retain ongoing "traditional use" rights, including "monumental cedar and cedar bark harvesting, seaweed harvesting, medicinal plant harvesting, hunting, fishing, trapping and food gathering" in Duu Guusd.[67] The area is now a park under two legal regimes, a fact explicitly noted in the park's co-management outline. More recently, the Tsilhqot'in have declared a tribal park—Dasiqox Tribal Park—encompassing some 90,000 hectares of their traditional territory adjacent to the lands over which the Supreme Court recognized their Aboriginal title in 2014.[68] It is yet to be seen how this will interact with federal and provincial laws.

Conclusion

Whether created under federal, provincial, or Indigenous authority, what the approaches discussed above have in common is that they move beyond a unilateral approach, allowing for the terms of engagement between Indigenous peoples and Canadian governments to be subject to negotiation. That is, negotiation is not constrained to the exercise of particular "rights." Jurisdiction, and along with it the terms of coexistence, are being negotiated on a small scale in these illustrative examples. These examples also illustrate that developing notions of self-determination and free, prior, and informed consent need not disrupt wildlife management in Canada. Frameworks for reconciliation in wildlife management can be developed on the basis of negotiation and in relation to specific locales and issues.

NOTES

1 Assistant Professor, Faculty of Law, University of Calgary.

2 *Canada National Parks Act*, SC 2000, c 32.

3 *National Parks Wilderness Area Declaration Regulations*, SOR/2000-387.

4 *National Parks Highway Traffic Regulations*, CRC, c 1126.

5 *National Parks Garbage Regulations*, SOR/80-217.

6 *National Parks Wildlife Regulations*, SOR/81-401.

7 *National Parks of Canada Aircraft Access Regulations*, SOR/97-150.

8 *National Parks of Canada Fishing Regulations*, CRC, c 1120.

9 See *Order Fixing the Boundaries of the Town of Banff in Banff National Park and Adding a Description of the Boundaries as Schedule IV to the Act*, SOR/90-45; *National Parks Town, Visitor Centre and Resort Subdivision Designation Regulations*, SOR/91-8.

10 *Canada National Parks Act*, *supra* note 2, Schedule 5.

11 See Stan Stevens, ed, *Indigenous Peoples, National Parks, and Protected Areas: A New Paradigm Linking Conservation, Culture, and Rights* (Tucson: University of Arizona Press, 2014).

12 Parks Canada, "Detailed Environmental Impact Analysis, Plains Bison Reintroduction in Banff National Park: Pilot Project 2017–2022, Executive Summary" (Calgary: Parks Canada), online (pdf): <files.constantcontact.com/9d75bccb401/885014cb-6471-4011-9616-19f51766eaaf.pdf> [perma.cc/9QVH-727X] [*EIA*].

13 *Canadian Environmental Assessment Act*, 2012, SC 2012, c 19, s 52. The process detailed here took place under the 2012 regime. Under the *Impact Assessment Act*, SC 2019, c 28, s 1 the relevant section is 82.

14 *Ibid* at s 67.

15 *EIA*, *supra* note 12.

16 *Ibid* at 7.

17 *Ibid* at 2.

18 *Ibid.*

19 *Ibid.*

20 "Historic Treaty Signed among 10 First Nations and Tribes in Banff", *CBC News* (14 August 2015, accessed 10 July 2021), online: <cbc.ca/news/canada/calgary/historic-treaty-signed-among-10-first-nations-and-tribes-in-banff-1.3190715>. See James Sakej Youngblood Henderson, "Wild Buffalo Recovery and Ecological Restoration of the Grasslands" in Oonagh E Fitzgerald & Kathleen Mahoney, eds, *Environmental Challenges on Indigenous Lands: A CIGI Essay Series* (Special Report: Centre for

International Governance Innovation, 2019), online: <cigionline.org/environmental-challenges-indigenous-lands>.

21 Collette Derworiz, "Historic Buffalo Treaty Signed by First Nations to Bring Back Bison", *Calgary Herald* (23 September 2014, accessed 15 July 2021), online: <calgaryherald.com/news/local-news/historic-buffalo-treaty-signed-by-first-nations-to-bring-back-bison>.

22 Blackfeet Nation, "Iinnii Buffalo Spirit Center" (accessed 15 July 201), online: <blackfeetnation.com/iinnii-buffalo-spirit-center/> [Blackfeet Nation].

23 *Ibid.*

24 Shari Narine, "Gains in Bison Conservation Recognized at Annual Conference: Aboriginal Multi-Media Society of Alberta", *Windspeaker* (15 October 2016, accessed 15 July 2021), online: <mail.windspeaker.com/news/gains-in-bison-conservation-recognized-at-annual-conference>; Jason Kerr, "Bringing Back the Buffalo", *Prince Albert Daily Herald* (20 September 2017, accessed 15 July 2021), online: <paherald.sk.ca/2017/09/20/bringing-back-buffalo/> [Kerr].

25 As cited in Amy Spark, "Portals for Collaboration" (18 July 2017, accessed 15 July 2021), online (blog): <albertaecotrust.com/portals-for-collaboration/>.

26 "The Buffalo: A Treaty of Co-operation, Renewal and Restoration" (accessed 25 November 2021), online: *Buffalo Treaty* <buffalotreaty.com/treaty> [the *Buffalo Treaty*].

27 See e.g., John Borrows, *Canada's Indigenous Constitution* (Toronto: University of Toronto Press, 2010) [Borrows].

28 For an application of the term "transnational law" in the Indigenous context, see e.g., James (Sakéj) Youngblood Henderson, "First Nations' Legal Inheritances in Canada: The Mi'kmaq Model" (1996) 23 Manitoba LJ 1; Robert Hamilton, "Indigenous Legal Traditions, Inter-Societal Law, and the Colonization of Marine Spaces" in Stephen Allen, Nigel Bankes, & Oyvind Ravna, eds, *The Rights of Indigenous Peoples in Marine Areas* (Oxford: Hart Publishing, 2019).

29 See Robert A. Williams Jr, *Linking Arms Together: American Indian Treaty Visions of Law and Peace, 1600–1800* (Oxford: Oxford University Press, 1997).

30 The *Buffalo Treaty*, *supra* note 26.

31 Borrows, *supra* note 27; Hadley Friedland & Val Napoleon, "Gathering the Threads: Developing a Methodology for Researching and Rebuilding Indigenous Legal Traditions" (2015–2016) 1:1 Lakehead LJ 16; James (Sákéj) Youngblood Henderson, "Postcolonial Indigenous Legal Consciousness" (2002) 1 Indigenous LJ 1.

32 See Aaron Mills, "The Lifeworlds of Law: On Revitalizing Indigenous Legal Orders Today" (2016) 61 McGill LJ 847 at 853.

33 See Blackfeet Nation, *supra* note 22.

34 Paul Berman refers to "the fact of legal pluralism" in international and federal state contexts: Paul Schiff Berman, *Global Legal Pluralism: A Jurisprudence of Law Beyond Borders* (Cambridge: Cambridge University Press, 2012). Gordon Christie uses the phrase "fact of strong legal pluralism" in the domestic Canadian context with specific reference to state and Indigenous legal orders. Gordon Christie, "Indigenous Legal Orders, Canadian Law and UNDRIP" in Oonagh Fitzgerald & Risa Schwatz, eds, *UNDRIP Implementation: Braiding International, Domestic and Indigenous Laws* (Waterloo: Centre for International Governance Innovation, 2017) at 49 [Christie].

35 Truth and Reconciliation Commission of Canada, "Truth and Reconciliation Commission of Canada: Calls to Action" (2015, accessed 15 July 2021), online (pdf):

<ehprnh2mwo3.exactdn.com/wp-content/uploads/2021/01/Calls_to_Action_English2.pdf> (specifically calls 39, 46, 47).

36 Tracey Lindberg, "The Doctrine of Discovery in Canada" in Robert J Miller et al, eds, *Discovering Indigenous Lands: The Doctrine of Discovery in the English Colonies* (Oxford: Oxford University Press, 2010) at 94.

37 On the use of *terra nullius*, see Stuart Banner, "Why *Terra Nullius*? Anthropology and Property Law in Early Australia" (2005) 23:1 LHR 95. For a comparison between Canada and Australia, see Arthur J Ray, *Aboriginal Rights Claims and the Making and Remaking of History* (Montreal-Kingston: McGill-Queen's University Press, 2016) at 3–16 [Ray].

38 John Borrows, "The Durability of *Terra Nullius*: Tsilhqot'in Nation v. British Columbia" (2015) 48:3 UBC L Rev 701. For how the doctrine and related presuppositions have shaped the doctrine of Aboriginal rights, see Robert Hamilton & Joshua Nichols, "The Tin Ear of the Court: *Ktunaxa Nation* and the Foundation of the Duty to Consult" (2019) 56:3 Alta L Rev 729.

39 *Johnson v M'Intosh*, 21 US (8 Wheat) 543 (1823).

40 *Ibid* at 573.

41 *Ibid.*

42 *Ibid* at 574.

43 *Guerin v The Queen*, [1984] 2 SCR 335, 1984 CanLII 25 at 378.

44 *R v Sparrow*, [1990] 1 SCR 1075, 1990 CanLII 104.

45 *Ibid.*

46 *Ibid* at 1105–1106. See also Mark Walters, "'Looking for a Knot in the Bulrush': Reflections on Law, Sovereignty, and Aboriginal Rights" in Patrick Macklem & Douglas Sanderson, eds, *From Recognition to Reconciliation: Essays on the Constitutional Entrenchment of Aboriginal and Treaty Rights* (Toronto: University of Toronto Press, 2016) at 35–62; Joshua Nichols, *A Reconciliation without Recollection? An Investigation of the Foundations of Aboriginal Law* (Toronto: University of Toronto Press, 2020).

47 *Delgamuukw v British Columbia*, [1997] 3 SCR 1010, 1997 CanLII 302 at para 143; *Tsilhqot'in Nation v British Columbia*, 2014 SCC 44 at paras 25–26.

48 For a critique of this approach, see John Borrows, "Sovereignty's Alchemy: An Analysis of *Delgamuukw v British Columbia*" [1999] 37 Osgoode Hall LJ 537.

49 *Chippewas of the Thames First Nation v Enbridge Pipelines Inc*, 2017 SCC 41 at para 59; *Ktunaxa Nation v British Columbia (Forests, Lands and Natural Resource Operations)*, 2017 SCC 54 at paras 80, 89, 119.

50 See e.g., Ray, *supra* note 37 at 67–104.

51 *United Nations Declaration on the Rights of Indigenous Peoples*, A/Res 61/295, UNGAOR (2007), online: <un-documents.net/a61r295.htm> [perma.cc/98HC-JQPP] [UNDRIP].

52 *Declaration on the Rights of Indigenous Peoples Act*, SBC 2019 c 44.

53 Department of Justice, "Legislation to Implement the United Nations Declaration on the Rights of Indigenous Peoples Becomes Law" (22 June 2021), online: *Government of Canada* <canada.ca/en/department-justice/news/2021/06/legislation-to-implement-the-united-nations-declaration-on-the-rights-of-indigenous-peoples-becomes-law.html> [perma.cc/KKV7-DWZF].

54 See generally John Borrows et al, eds, *Braiding Legal Orders: Implementing the United Nations Declaration on the Rights of Indigenous Peoples* (Waterloo: Centre for International Governance Innovation Press, 2019).

55 See Christie, *supra* note 34.

56 *Ibid.*

57 Parks Canada, "Banff National Park Plains Bison Reintroduction: Frequently Asked Questions" (accessed 15 July 2021), online: *Government of Canada* <pc.gc.ca/en/pn-np/ab/banff/info/gestion-management/bison/faq>.

58 Kerr, *supra* note 24.

59 Parks Canada, "Indigenous Relations at Parks Canada: Connecting with Indigenous Partners" (30 March 2017, accessed 15 July 2021), online: <pc.gc.ca/en/agence-agency/aa-ia/te-wt/chap01> [Indigenous Relations at Parks Canada].

60 Karen Bartko, "Part of Jasper National Park Closed for Traditional Hunt", *Global News* (6 October 2017, accessed 15 July 2021), online: <globalnews.ca/news/3789694/part-of-jasper-national-park-closed-for-traditional-hunt/>.

61 Indigenous Relations at Parks Canada, *supra* note 59.

62 *Ibid.*

63 Grant Murray & Leslie King, "First Nations Values in Protected Area Governance: Tla-o-qui-aht Tribal Parks and Pacific Rim National Park Reserve" (2012) 40:3 Human Ecology 385 at 389.

64 *MacMillan Bloedel Ltd v Mullin*, [1985] 2 CNLR 58, 1985 CanLII 696 (BCSC).

65 Tla-o-qui-aht Tribal Parks & Wilderness Committee, "Free Report: Welcome to Tla-o-qui-aht Tribal Parks" (2013), online (pdf): *Wilderness Committee* <wildernesscommittee.org/sites/all/files/publications/2013_tla-o-qui-aht_Paper-Web-2.pdf>.

66 On 29 May 2008, the Duu Guusd Conservancy was established by Bill 38. See Bill 59, *Protected Areas of British Columbia (Conservancies and Parks) Amendment Act, 2008*, 4th Sess, 38th Parl, British Columbia, 2008 (assented to 29 May 2008).

67 British Columbia Parks, "Duu Guusd Heritage Site/Conservancy" (accessed 15 July 2021), online: <env.gov.bc.ca/bcparks/explore/cnsrvncy/duu_guusd/>.

68 Dasiqox Tribal Park, "Draft Position Paper Nexwagwez?an Dasiqox Tribal Park: Nexwagwez?an 'There for us'" (June 2016, accessed 15 July 2021), online (pdf): <dasiqox.org/wp-content/uploads/2018/03/DasiqoxPositionPaper-March2016.pdf>.

14

An Overview of Wildlife Legislation in Alberta

Sara Jaremko[1]

Wildlife in Alberta is subject to federal, provincial, and international laws and policies, and in the case of urban areas, municipal law, and policy. Municipal law falls primarily under provincial jurisdiction with limits and exceptions. Wildlife laws have traditionally been based around hunting, but increasingly involve habitat protection and protection of species at risk. In Alberta, a developing commitment to regional and land-use planning along with biodiversity may affect wildlife and habitat management. This paper provides an overview of the jurisdictional landscape of laws on wildlife, and traditional tools for wildlife management with an emphasis on the provincial perspective.[2]

Jurisdiction

Wildlife in Canada is not expressly contemplated in the *Constitution Act, 1867*,[3] but has been considered to fall under provincial legislative authority under section 92(13) (property and civil rights in the province) and section 92(16) (generally all matters of a merely local or private nature in the province), and section 109 (all lands, mines, minerals, and royalties [belong to the provinces]).[4] Wildlife is generally considered to be property owned by the Crown as a result of the legal tradition considering wildlife to be part of the land, and associating land ownership with a "right to harvest wildlife."[5] An individual may gain an ownership interest, for example, under the *Wildlife Act*.[6]

Areas including the environment and natural resources fall under concurrent federal and provincial legislative competence.[7] In 2006, Kennedy and Donihee noted that the federal government has jurisdiction over migratory birds,[8] matters of international trade and commerce,[9] interjurisdictional wildlife, and fisheries.[10] Wildlife management on federal lands within provinces also remains under federal jurisdiction.[11] The federal government jurisdiction also has legislative authority over federal species at risk,[12] and Indian reserves.[13] Kennedy and Donihee stress the importance of cooperation between both levels of government:

> Both levels of government have essential roles to play in our national framework for the protection of and management of wildlife. In order to ensure a coordinated framework for wildlife management, cooperative federalism is essential. Our constitution sets out a division of powers which includes limits on both federal and provincial jurisdiction over wildlife. Only a cooperative effort will ensure the long-term presence of wildlife on our landscapes.[14]

Traditional Wildlife Management

John Donihee has discussed the following three stages in the evolution of Canadian wildlife law:

> Stage 1: the "game management era" (Confederation to the 1960s);
>
> Stage 2: the "wildlife management era" (1960s to mid-1980s); and
>
> Stage 3: the "sustainable wildlife management era" (mid-1980s to the time of writing [2000]).[15]

In a 2006 comparative overview of wildlife laws across the country, Monique Passelac-Ross noted:

> The wildlife management paradigm embodied in wildlife acts is characterized by the following features identified by Valerius Geist: public ownership of the wildlife, strict controls on killing of wildlife, elimination or strict management of market hunting, allocation of harvestable surpluses based on equal opportunities for all users, and interjurisdictional cooperation.[16]

Traditional Mechanisms

Passelac-Ross completed a functional analysis across Canadian jurisdictions, on the "typical contents of wildlife statutes and regulations and their traditional wildlife management mechanisms,"[17] as follows:

- **Administration**: empowering a minister, as well as wildlife officers and often advisory boards or committees, often provisions for interjurisdictional agreements among governments or with First Nations groups;[18]
- **Property rights in wildlife**: generally, the Crown owns live wildlife, but ownership may be transferred by permit or licence when lawfully killed;[19]
- **Licensing provisions**: "The legislation usually contains a general prohibition against hunting without a licence."[20] "Central to the wildlife management paradigm," the licensing system is extensive.[21] Licenses are issued and cancelled at the discretion of the minister, by fee, and with conditions and limitations;
- **Rules for hunting**: relating to animals, season, time, territory, and manner of hunting;[22]
- **Possession, use, and sale of wildlife**: Generally, prohibiting possession, use and sale, without a licence, as well as regulating transportation and import/export;[23]
- **Prohibitions**: "The most important general prohibition concerns hunting without a licence or contrary to the terms and conditions of a licence, and hunting outside an open season."[24] Also, against harassing, disturbing, feeding wildlife, or disturbing habitat or abode, and not respecting traplines;[25]
- **Enforcement**: extensive—wildlife officers "have and may exercise the powers and authority of peace officers. . . . The enforcement powers granted to wildlife officers and to other persons appointed by the Minister are very similar across jurisdictions";[26]
- **Offences and penalties**: similar across Canada—"Offences created by provincial wildlife laws are summary conviction offences and are often continuing offences, that is they constitute

separate offences for each day on which the offence is committed or continues."[27] Penalties include fines, imprisonment, seizure, forfeiture, creative sentencing, administrative penalties, licence/ permit amendment, suspension or cancellation, or prohibition;

- **Regulations**: often extensive, may include "licensing system, the designation of areas, places or territories where hunting is allowed or prohibited, the rules relating to hunting, fishing and trapping, guide-outfitting, the rules relating to the possession, use and commerce of wildlife, the protection of wildlife and its habitat, the protection of species at risk, etc."[28]

Land-based Management: Monique Passelac-Ross then analyzes land-based wildlife management in habitat protection provisions in the wildlife statutes.[29] As Kumpf and Hughes write, "[h]abitat protection is ultimately deemed to be the most effective tool for conservation since a species' survival is ultimately dependent on its habitat. Types of habitat protection include legally protected areas, land stewardship, prohibitions against harming a nest or dwelling, and through the minister acquiring land or designating private or public land as protected."[30] Passelac-Ross noted:

> There are two ways in which wildlife habitat may be protected. First, the legislation establishes general protection mechanisms for the abode or residence of wildlife species, as well as their habitat. Second, the legislation enables the Lieutenant Governor in Council or the Minister to set aside or acquire lands necessary for habitat protection. The designation of protected areas may occur on both public and private lands. Once designated, the lands are subject to various use restrictions.[31]

In addition, habitat conservation funds are created by legislation in several jurisdictions, sometimes within wildlife acts, to conserve, enhance, acquire and/or manage land.[32]

Species at Risk

Passelac-Ross analyzes species at risk legislation across Canada and identifies the importance of federal and provincial cooperation. She notes that "the protection of endangered species is accomplished in large part by means of habitat protection measures."[33] A brief history on species at risk follows the 1992 *United Nations Convention on Biological Diversity* (*CBD*), ratified by Canada in December 1992,[34] the 1999 interjurisdictional *Accord for the Protection of Species at Risk*,[35] the creation of the Canadian Endangered Species Conservation Council (CESCC) and recognition of the Committee on the Status of Endangered Species in Canada (COSEWIC), and the federal *Species at Risk Act* (*SARA*)[36] in force in 2004. Provinces have species-at-risk provisions in stand-alone legislation or within their wildlife legislation.[37] Provincial statutes on species at risk share the following components, as discussed by Passelac-Ross:[38]

- Establishment of a **committee** or commission to facilitate the protection of species at risk
- **Designation** process for species at risk
- **Species protection measures**, often with prescribed exceptions or defences, such as prohibitions regarding hunting/taking/injuring/killing of endangered or threatened species, often including possession, disturbance, harassment, interference, as well as selling, exporting, and trafficking.[39]
- **Habitat protection measures** in two ways: "First, the legislation establishes prohibitions against destroying, disturbing or interfering with the habitat of the protected species, as well as with their abode or residence. . . . The second, more proactive way in which legislation achieves habitat protection is by allowing the acquisition or setting aside of land necessary for species protection."[40]
- **Penal provisions** vary among jurisdictions, but include fines and/or imprisonment and/or alternatives (e.g. re licences).
- **Recovery plans**: "Some provinces have enacted legislative provisions concerning the preparation and implementation of recovery plans for designated species."[41]
- **Conformity** with the *Accord for the Protection of Species at Risk* and with *SARA* varies between jurisdictions. Passelac-Ross notes "the fact that the 'safety net' provisions of SARA allow the fed-

eral Minister of the Environment to recommend to Cabinet that regulations to protect the critical habitat of listed species should be enacted and applied to provincial or private land, where the Minister is of the opinion that provincial laws and policies are inadequate."[42]

International

Returning to Alberta's interjurisdictional framework, Canada has a variety of formal and informal international commitments with respect to wildlife.[43] Additional international instruments may be applicable to endangered species and migratory birds.[44] One such instrument is the *Convention on the International Trade in Endangered Species of Wild Fauna and Flora*[45] (*CITES*).

Canada is a signatory to the *CBD*.[46] The *CBD* requires signatories to "translate this overarching international framework into revised and updated national biodiversity strategies and action plans."[47] The *CBD*'s objective is "the conservation of biological diversity, the sustainable use of its components and the fair and equitable sharing of the benefits."[48] The *CBD Strategic Plan for Biodiversity 2011–2020* was created in 2010.

Federal

Canada first ratified the *CBD* in 1992, prompting development of the *Canadian Biodiversity Strategy*.[49] The purpose of this strategy "is to conserve biodiversity, use biological resources sustainably, and contribute internationally to biodiversity efforts."[50] Canada's revised national biodiversity strategy and action plan is reflected in the *2020 Biodiversity Goals and Targets for Canada*,[51] the *Biodiversity Outcomes Framework*, and the *Canadian Biodiversity Strategy*.[52] Canada's *Wild Animal and Plant Protection and Regulation of International and Interprovincial Trade Act*[53] (*WAPPRIITA*) is based on *CITES*.

As discussed above, Canada has federal jurisdiction over the environment and natural resources (concurrent with the provinces), and authority regarding migratory birds[54] and interjurisdictional wildlife, as well as species at risk, fisheries, and federal lands, including national parks and Indian reserves. Kumpf and Hughes have noted that "[g]enerally, the federal legislation applies to federal land and federal species (migratory birds, fisheries), while provincial legislation applies to provincial land. If the province has inadequate coverage, the federal legislation will step in."[55]

Provincial

Alberta's wildlife legislation relates primarily to issues associated with hunting, in the traditional paradigm discussed above. Wildlife legislation in the province is not habitat-based but includes designation of protected areas including habitat conservation areas, wildlife sanctuaries, migratory bird lure sites, and wildlife control areas.[56] Considerations for land-based wildlife management support regional and land-based approaches to biodiversity, such as regional land-use planning and use of municipal regional planning.

The relevant provincial statutes include the *Wildlife Act*, and the *Environmental Protection and Enhancement Act*,[57] which governs environmental matters generally. The government has included provisions in the *Wildlife Act* that addresses endangered species[58] and habitat protection.[59] The province has adopted a policy concerning species at risk called *Alberta's Strategy for the Management of Species at Risk 2009–2014*.[60] The provincial government had commenced creating a provincial biodiversity policy[61] in 2015, but the policy has not yet been completed.

Land-use Planning

The provincial government instituted an innovative, comprehensive provincial land-use planning framework starting in 2008 through the *Land Use Framework* (*LUF*)[62] and its enacting legislation; the *Alberta Land Stewardship Act*[63] (*ALSA*). By its nature, this framework covers wildlife habitat generally and has potential for more direct regulation and management. *ALSA* categorizes the province into seven land-use regions based on river basins and directs that comprehensive regional land-use plans be created for each region.[64] Alberta's *LUF* is both provincial law and policy. Notably, *ALSA* has superordinate authority over other provincial laws: *ALSA* provides that *ALSA* will prevail over other enactments in the event of a conflict,[65] and regional plans, considered to be regulations,[66] will prevail over other regulatory instruments or regulations but not over acts in the event of a conflict.[67] To date, the Lower Athabasca Regional Plan[68] (LARP) which incorporates the city of Fort McMurray and oil sands mines, and the South Saskatchewan Regional Plan[69] (SSRP) which includes the Calgary area, have been completed and are effective. The North Saskatchewan Regional Plan[70] (NSRP), which includes the Edmonton area, is under development.

The *LUF* and its regional plans contemplate biodiversity extensively. As well, each regional plan is intended to include a biodiversity management framework (BMF) as a sub-regional plan. No BMFs have been finalized to date. Linear management frameworks that will affect habitat are also underway. In addition, the SSRP was amended on May 31, 2018, to implement the Porcupine Hills—Livingstone Land Footprint Management Plan (LFMP).[71] Alberta's 2017 *Draft Provincial Woodland Caribou Range Plan* is a "form of land-use planning covering 23 percent of the province, and incorporates social and economic considerations. Thus, it will be a sub-regional plan under regional plans [and will] form the main component of the LARP landscape management plan."[72] Woodland caribou are listed as threatened species under federal and provincial legislation and are the subject of recovery plans at both levels. This illustrates the potential implications for broader and future wildlife management through the *LUF*.

The draft SSRP BMF's objectives include

- maintaining terrestrial and aquatic biodiversity;
- continuing to provide a range of benefits to communities, Albertans, and First Nations, including the continued ability to exercise constitutionally protected rights to hunt, fish, and trap for food, and other First Nations' cultural practices, through biodiversity and healthy, functioning ecosystems;
- sustaining long-term regional ecosystem health and resiliency;
- recovering species at risk and not designating new species at risk; and
- sustaining intact grasslands habitat.[73]

New tools: The *LUF* and *ALSA* provide for "stewardship of private lands in Alberta through the development of incentives and market-based instruments."[74] These novel tools include the transfer of development credits (TDCs), land trusts, charitable easements, land conservation offsets, lease-swapping, and dealing with existing tenure rights in ecologically sensitive areas.[75]

Municipal

Provincial wildlife legislation prevails in municipal jurisdictions. Municipalities restrict hunting within their boundaries.[76] In the urban context, wildlife is also affected by municipal biodiversity measures and pest control.[77] Biodiversity in municipalities, with impacts on habitat and wildlife, is governed by law and, mostly, policy: including components of Calgary and Edmonton's municipal development plans[78] and biodiversity policies.[79]

The cities of Calgary and Edmonton are signatory[80] to the Durban Commitment: Local Governments for Biodiversity,[81] thereby acknowledging "accountability and responsibility for the health and wellbeing of our communities through protecting, sustainably utilizing and managing biodiversity and recognizing its role as the foundation of our existence."[82]

Changes made in 2017 to the *Municipal Government Act*[83] support metropolitan and municipal regional planning and potentially other environmental considerations[84] that are likely to affect habitat protection in and around urban areas. Amendments include changes to mandates for municipal development plans and growth plans for the Calgary and Edmonton metropolitan regions.[85] The contents of a growth plan should address density, infrastructure, "corridors for recreation, transportation, energy transmission, utilities and inter-municipal transit,"[86] and "policies regarding environmentally sensitive areas."[87]

Conclusion

As discussed above, wildlife in Alberta falls primarily under provincial jurisdiction, within the context of federal, international, and provincial laws, and in the case of urban areas, municipal law and policy. Historically, wildlife laws have been created to address hunting activities, but more recently have focused on habitat protection and protection of species at risk. In the province, an emerging commitment to regional and land-use planning along with biodiversity, may have implications for wildlife and habitat management in the future.

NOTES

1 Research Fellow, Canadian Institute of Resources Law.

2 This chapter will not provide extensive or comprehensive discussion of wildlife law in relation to First Nations.

3 *Constitution Act, 1867* (UK), 30 & 31 Vict, c 3, reprinted in RSC 1985, Appendix II, No 5. Section 109 was extended to the prairie provinces by operation of the *Natural Resources Transfer Agreement* and the *Constitution Act, 1930*. See *Constitution Act, 1930* (UK), 20 & 21 Geo V, c 26, reprinted in RSC 1985, Appendix II, No 26.

4 See Priscilla Kennedy & John Donihee, *Wildlife and the Canadian Constitution, Canadian Wildlife Law Project Paper #4* (Calgary: Canadian Institute of Resources Law, August 2006), (accessed 15 July 2021), online (pdf): <live-cirl.ucalgary.ca/sites/default/files/Wildlife%20Law%20Papers/Wildlife%20Law%20Paper%20%234.pdf> [Kennedy & Donihee].

5 *Ibid* at 7.

6 Laura D Kumpf & Elaine L Hughes, "Wildlife Sector Overview" in Elaine L Hughes, Arlene J Kwasniak & Alastair R Lucas, *Public Lands and Resources Law in Canada* (Toronto: Irwin Law Inc, 2016) at 293–307 [Kumpf & Hughes].

7 Kennedy & Donihee, *supra* note 4 at 4.

8 *The Migratory Birds Convention*, 16 August 1916, UKTS 1917, No 17, via the *Migratory Birds Convention Act*, SC 1994, c 22.

9 *Wild Animal and Plant Protection and Regulation of International and Interprovincial Trade Act* (*WAPPRIITA*), SC 1992, c 52—incorporates the *Convention on International Trade in Endangered Species of Wild Fauna and Flora* (1973, ratified by Canada 1975) [*CITES*].

10 Kennedy & Donihee, *supra* note 4.

11 See *Canada National Parks Act*, SC 2000, c 32. See also Kennedy & Donihee, *supra* note 4.

12 *Species at Risk Act*, SC 2002, c C-5.

13 Indian lands fall under federal jurisdiction under s 91(24) of the *Constitution Act, 1867*, *supra* note 3.

14 Kennedy & Donihee, *supra* note 4 at 14.

15 John Donihee, *The Evolution of Wildlife Law in Canada*, CIRL Occasional Paper #9 (Calgary, Canada: Canadian Institute of Resources Law, May 2000), online (pdf): <live-cirl.ucalgary.ca/sites/default/files/Occasional%20Papers/Occasional%20Paper%20%239.pdf> at vii.

16 Monique Passelac-Ross, *Overview of Provincial Wildlife Laws*, Canadian Wildlife Law Project Paper #3 (Calgary: Canadian Institute of Resources Law, July 2006), online (pdf): <live-cirl.ucalgary.ca/sites/default/files/Wildlife%20Law%20Papers/Wildlife%20Law%20Paper%20%233.pdf> [Passelac-Ross], citing Valerius Geist, "North American Policies of Wildlife Conservation" in Valerius Geist, *Wildlife Conservation Policy* (Calgary: Detselig Enterprises Ltd., 1995) at 77–127.

17 *Ibid* at 2.

18 *Ibid* at 3–5.

19 *Ibid* at 6.

20 *Ibid* at 7.

21 *Ibid* at 7.

22 *Ibid* at 10.

23 *Ibid* at 12–13.

24 *Ibid* at 14.

25 *Ibid* at 14–15.

26 *Ibid* at 16.

27 *Ibid* at 17. See also Arlene J Kwasniak, *Enforcing Wildlife Law*, Canadian Wildlife Law Project Paper #2 (Canada: Canadian Institute of Resources Law, March 2006), online (pdf): <live-cirl.ucalgary.ca/sites/default/files/Wildlife%20Law%20Papers/Wildlife%20Law%20Paper%20%232.pdf>.

28 Passelac-Ross, *supra* note 16 at 18.

29 *Ibid*.

30 Kumpf & Hughes, *supra* note 6 at 295, citing Passelac-Ross, *supra* note 16 at 18.

31 Passelac-Ross, *supra* note 16 at 18.

32 *Ibid* at 23.

33 *Ibid* at 24.

34 The *Convention on Biological Diversity of 5 June 1992*, 1760 UNTS 69. Article 8 pertains to protection and recovery of threatened species and government commitments to their protection through legislation and/or regulation (*ibid*, art 8).

35 Environment and Natural Resources Canada, "Protection of Species at Risk: Federal, Provincial and Territorial Accord: Accord for the Protection of Species at Risk" (September 1999, accessed 15 July 2021), online: <registrelep-sararegistry.gc.ca/default.asp?lang=En&n=92D90833-1>.

36 *Species at Risk Act*, SC 2002, c 29 [*SARA*].

37 *Wildlife Act*, RSA 2000, c W-10 (Alberta's species at risk provisions fall within the *Wildlife Act*).

38 Passelac-Ross, *supra* note 16 at 25ff.

39 *Ibid* at 29.

40 *Ibid* at 30–31.

41 *Ibid* at 32.

42 *Ibid* at 33.

43 See Nigel Bankes, *International Wildlife Law*, Canadian Wildlife Law Project Paper #1 (Canada: Canadian Institute of Resources Law, February 2006), online (pdf): <live-cirl.ucalgary.ca/sites/default/files/Wildlife%20Law%20Papers/Wildlife%20Law%20Paper%20%231.pdf>.

44 See Kumpf & Hughes, *supra* note 6 at 307.

45 *Convention on the International Trade in Endangered Species of Wild Fauna and Flora* (3 March 1973), 993 UNTS 243, 27 UST 1087, 12 ILM 1085 [*CITES*].

46 *United Nations Convention on Biological Diversity*, entered into force 29 December 1993, 1760 UNTS 79 11 June 1992, 31 ILM 818 (1992) [*CBD*].

47 City of Calgary, *Our BiodiverCity: Calgary's 10-Year Biodiversity Strategic Plan* (approved by Council in March 2015 along with the accompanying Biodiversity Policy), (accessed 15 July 2021), online (pdf): <calgary.ca/content/dam/www/csps/parks/documents/planning-and-operations/biodivercity-strategic-plan.pdf> at 42.

48 Canadian Wildlife Federation & Hinterland Who's Who, *Benefits of Wildlife*, (accessed 15 July 2021), online: *Hinterland Who's Who*, <hww.ca/en/issues-and-topics/benefits-of-wildlife.html>.

49 Biodivcanada, *Canadian Biodiversity Strategy*, (1995, accessed 15 July 2021), online: <biodivcanada.chm-cbd.net/documents/canadian-biodiversity-strategy#:~:text=The%20Canadian%20Biodiversity%20Strategy%20is%20a%20response%20to,Strategy%20may%20not%20be%20relevant%20in%20some%20jurisdictions>.

50 Kumpf & Hughes, *supra* note 6 at 303–304, citing the Species at Risk Public Registry, "Species at Risk Conservation: National Framework", online: *Government of Canada* <www.registrelep-sararegistry.gc.ca/default.asp?lang=En&n=236A2A34-1>.

51 Biodivcanada, "2020 Biodiversity Goals and Targets for Canada" (2020, accessed 15 July 2021), online: <biodivcanada.chm-cbd.net/2020-biodiversity-goals-and-targets-canada>.

52 Government of Canada, "Backgrounder: 2020 Biodiversity Goals and Targets for Canada" (last modified 23 December 2016), online: <canada.ca/en/parks-canada/news/2016/12/2020-biodiversity-goals-targets-canada.html>. See also "Pathway to Canada Target 1" (accessed 15 July 2021), online: *Conservation 2020* <conservation2020canada.ca>.

53 *Wild Animal and Plant Protection and Regulation of International and Interprovincial Trade Act*, SC 1992, c 52 [*WAPPRIITA*].

54 See the *Migratory Birds Convention Act*,1994, SC 1994, c 22.

55 Kumpf & Hughes, *supra* note 6 at 303.

56 See *Wildlife Act*, *supra* note 37, ss 103(1)(b), (p); *Wildlife Regulation*, Alta Reg 143/1997, Schedules 11–12. See also Passelac-Ross, *supra* note 16.

57 *Environmental Protection and Enhancement Act*, RSA 2000, c E-12.

58 See e.g., *Wildlife Act*, *supra* note 37, s 6; *Wildlife Regulation*, *supra* note 56, s 7.

59 See e.g., *Wildlife Act*, *supra* note 37, ss 36, 103(1)(b).

60 Alberta Government, *Alberta's Strategy for the Management of Species at Risk (2009–2014)* (2008, accessed 15 July 2021), online: *Alberta.ca* <open.alberta.ca/dataset/5d53e131-0608-431c-8827-5e25d5e4c278/resource/29be46df-88fa-4de1-9e70-ebca53b19a32/download/albertas-strategy-management-species-risk-2009-2014.pdf#:~:text=In%201996%20Alberta%20signed%20the%20national%20Accord%20for,Risk%20Act%20%28SARA%29%20was%20passed%20by%20Canada%E2%80%99s%20parliament>.

61 Alberta Environmental Network, *Alberta's Biodiversity Policy DRAFT* (Alberta: 2015) Draft [unpublished], (accessed 15 July 2021) online: <aenweb.ca/sites/default/files/draft_albertas_biodiversity_policy_december_2014.pdf#:~:text=%EE%80%80Alberta%E2%80%99s%20Biodiversity%20Policy%EE%80%81%20outlines%20the%20province%E2%80%99%EE%80%80s%EE%80%81%20commitment%20to,on%20%EE%80%80Alberta%EE%80%81%E2%80%99%EE%80%80s%EE%80%81%20landscape%20and%20aims%20to%20respond%20to>.

62 Alberta Environment and Parks, *Land Use Framework* (December 2008, accessed 15 July 2021), online (pdf): <landuse.alberta.ca/LandUse%20Documents/Land-use%20Framework%20-%202008-12.pdf> [*LUF*].

63 *Alberta Land Stewardship Act*, SA 2009, c A-26.8 [*ALSA*].

64 See Sara L Jaremko, *A Critical Exploration of the South Saskatchewan Regional Plan in Alberta*, CIRL Occasional Paper #54 (Calgary, Canada: Canadian Institute of Resources Law, March 2016), online (pdf): <live-cirl.ucalgary.ca/sites/default/files/Occasional%20Papers/Occasional%20Paper%20%2354.pdf>.

65 *ALSA*, *supra* note 63, s 17(4).

66 *Ibid*, s 13(2). The regional plans themselves include policy as well as regulatory components.

67 *Ibid*, ss 17(1), (3).

68 Alberta Government, *Lower Athabasca Regional Plan 2012–2011* (Edmonton: Alberta Government, 2012), (accessed 15 July 2021), online (pdf): *Alberta Environment and Parks* <landuse.alberta.ca/LandUse%20Documents/Lower%20Athabasca%20Regional%20Plan%202012-2022%20Approved%202012-08.pdf>.

69 Alberta Government, *South Saskatchewan Regional Plan 2014–2024: An Alberta Land-use Framework Integrated Plan*, amended February 2017 (Edmonton: Alberta Government, 2014), online (pdf): *Alberta Environment and Parks* <landuse.alberta.ca/LandUse%20Documents/South%20Saskatchewan%20Regional%20Plan%202014-2024%20-%20February%202017.pdf>.

70 See Alberta Environment and Parks, "Land-use Framework: North Saskatchewan Region" (accessed 15 July 2021), online: <landuse.alberta.ca/RegionalPlans/NorthSaskatchewanRegion/Pages/default.aspx>.

71 Alberta Government, "South Saskatchewan Regional Planning: South Saskatchewan Regional Plan amended" (accessed 15 July 2021), online: *Alberta Environment and Parks* <landuse.alberta.ca/RegionalPlans/SouthSaskatchewanRegion/SSRPPlanning/Pages/default.aspx>.

72 Alberta Government, "DRAFT Provincial Woodland Caribou Range Plan" (Alberta: December 2017) (accessed 15 July 2021) at 61–62, online (pdf): <open.alberta.ca/dataset/932d6c22-a32a-4b4e-a3f5-cb2703c53280/resource/3fc3f63a-0924-44d0-b178-82da34db1f37/download/draft-caribourangeplanandappendices-dec2017.pdf>.

73 Alberta Government, *South Saskatchewan Region Biodiversity Management Framework* (March 2015, accessed 15 July 2021), online: *Canadian Parks and Wilderness, Southern Alberta Chapter* <cpaws-southernalberta.org/wp-content/uploads/2018/06/SSR_Phase2_BMF_Preworkshop_Package_March_11_2015.pdf#:~:text=The%20South%20Saskatchewan%20region%20BMF%20supports%20the%20achievement,for%20biodiversity%20included%20in%20the%20regional%20plan%20are%3A> at 1.

74 *LUF*, *supra* note 62 at 33.

75 *Ibid.*

76 See City of Calgary, bylaw 20M88, *A Bylaw of the City of Calgary to Control and Regulate the Use of Streets in the City and to Restrict and Regulate Activities on, Adjacent, or Near to Streets* (17 October 1988), ss 8–11.1. "Dangerous and Unlawful Practices," which prohibit and restrict discharge of weapons and projectiles within the city. See also Criminal Code, RSC 1985, c C-46, s 175(1)(d). More research would be needed to clarify the authorities around restrictions of the *Wildlife Act* within municipalities.

77 For example, Calgary's *Integrated Pest Management Plan* includes provisions regarding beavers and ground squirrels. *Integrated Pest Management Plan* (accessed 6 December 2021), online: *City of Calgary* <calgary.ca/csps/parks/planning-and-operations/pest-management/managing-pests.html>.

78 City of Calgary, *Municipal Development Plan* (Calgary: Office Consolidation, 2017 August) (accessed 15 July 2021), online: *City of Calgary* <calgary.ca/MDP>; City of Edmonton, *The Way We Grow: Municipal Development Plan, Bylaw 15100* (26 May 2010, accessed 16 July 2021), online (pdf): <edmonton.ca/sites/default/files/public-files/

documents/PDF/MDP_Bylaw_15100.pdf>. The City of Calgary's MDP was adopted by council on September 2009. The City of Calgary's MDP went through an update that was approved by the council on 8 February 2021.

79 City of Calgary, *Our BiodiverCity: Calgary's 10-year Biodiversity Strategic Plan* (approved by council in March 2015 along with the accompanying biodiversity policy), (accessed 16 July 2021), online (pdf): <calgary.ca/CSPS/Parks/Documents/Planning-and-Operations/BiodiverCity-strategic-plan.pdf>; and City of Edmonton, *Natural Connections: City of Edmonton Integrated Natural Areas Conservation Plan* (Edmonton: 2007), (accessed 16 July 2021), online (pdf): <edmonton.ca/public-files/assets/document?path=PDF/Natural_Connections_-_Strategic_Plan_JUNE_09.pdf>.

80 Edmonton signed in 2008; Calgary signed in 2016. Montreal is also a signatory to the Durban Commitment.

81 ICLEI & LAB, *The Durban Commitment: Local Governments for Biodiversity, ICLEI: Local Governments for Sustainability*, (accessed 16 July 2021), online (pdf): *Weaselhead* <theweaselhead.com/wp-wh/assets/DurbanCommitment_rotated_document.pdf>. The Durban Commitment is an acknowledgment within a program coordinated by a non-profit group, Local Action for Biodiversity [LAB], coordinated by ICLEI—Local Governments for Sustainability, and does not carry the legal authority of signing a United Nations convention.

82 Calgary Parks, *Calgary's Biodiversity* (accessed 16 July 2021), online: <calgary.ca/csps/parks/planning-and-operations/biodiversity.html?redirect=/biodiversity>.

83 *Municipal Government Act*, RSA 2000, c M-26 [*MGA*].

84 See Dr Judy Stewart, *Do Recent Amendments to Alberta's Municipal Government Act Enable Management of Surface Water Resources and Air Quality?* CIRL Occasional paper #62 (Canada: Canadian Institute of Resources Law, December 2017), (accessed 16 July 2021), online (pdf): <live-cirl.ucalgary.ca/sites/default/files/Occasional%20Papers/Occasional%20Paper%20%2362.pdf>.

85 See *MGA*, *supra* note 83, Parts 17, 17.1; *Capital Region Board Regulation*, Alta Reg 38/2012 (now *Edmonton Metropolitan Region Board Regulation*, Alta Reg 189/2017); *Calgary Metropolitan Region Board Regulation*, Alta Reg 190/2017.

86 *Capital Region Board Regulation*, *supra* note 85, s 9(1)(c).

87 *Ibid*, s 9(1)(e).

15

Wildlife and Habitat Protection/ Management Other Than by Wildlife Laws: Roles for Courts

Arlene Kwasniak[1]

Introduction

Wildlife laws *per se*, such as wildlife or species at risk legislation, only go part of the way, and a relatively minor part of the way, towards protecting or managing wildlife or habitat (wildlife/habitat). A myriad of other laws, both common and legislative, are relevant to wildlife/habitat impacts, for better or worse. This chapter looks at the limitations of wildlife laws, and then discusses other law-based protection or management of wildlife/habitat approaches falling under the broad category of "other than wildlife laws" (OTWLs). The chapter takes a broad-brush approach. The aim is not to inspect details; it is rather to demonstrate how wildlife/habitat issues permeate an immense assortment of laws and to show how courts can play significant roles regarding the outcomes for wildlife/ habitat.

About Wildlife Laws[2]

Law commentator, John Donihee, identifies three eras of wildlife management: game management (Confederation to 1960s), transitional wildlife management (1960s to mid-1980s), and sustainable wildlife management (mid-1980s to present).[3] Game management legislation regulates wildlife as resources, e.g. by regulating hunting, trapping, predation, and marketing. Although such laws may contain limited immediate habitat protection provisions (e.g. nests, dens), they aim to preserve the game for utilization. Transitional wildlife management "is characterized by the ongoing refinement and detail of hunting control mechanisms, using a combination of geographic areas, seasons and harvest restrictions."[4] Typical regulatory mechanisms include "habitat protection and management, and artificial replenishment, including restocking, [and] game farming. . . ."[5] Sustainable wildlife management reflects evolving values regarding wildlife in recognizing its intrinsic and resource values. It is typified by legislation with a strong environmental or ecological focus, legislated endangered species, and habitat protection. Indigenous rights and entitlements also may be recognized in this era, as well as strengthened controls on trade in wildlife.[6]

If one only considered wildlife laws *per se*, it would be difficult to make the argument that legislation better protects wildlife/habitat in the "sustainable wildlife management era" than before it, with few exceptions. One is the Nunavut *Wildlife Act*[7] with its incorporation of the *Nunavut Land Claims Agreement* respecting wildlife, habitat, and the rights of Inuit.[8] Another is that few wildlife laws (outside of species at risk laws) provide habitat protection beyond immediate habitat. Even then, such provisions are limited: for example, powers to designate habitat protection areas on Crown land, or to regulate unique interferences with habitat.[9] Other exceptions are the many provincial, territorial, and federal species at risk laws. As important as these are to wildlife/habitat protection/management, they are limited and reactive and may trigger too late. Generally, species members must be gasping for breath, and their natural habitat be primarily developed for these acts to kick in.

Wildlife laws *per se* are not enough to effectively protect or manage wildlife/habitat. Wildlife laws, except for species at risk laws, have little to do with wildlife/habitat impacts from development, or wildlife/habitat protection. In our complex society, we must look beyond wildlife laws to better comprehend the law-based sources that permit impacts on or provide protection for wildlife/habitat.

Wildlife and Habitat Protection/Management Other Than by Wildlife Laws

OTWLs may fall under common law, legislation, or other categories such as private and public stewardship and economic instruments. OTWLs are ubiquitous, and it is a safe wager that more wildlife/habitat is protected or impacted through the application of OTWLs than wildlife laws. Below are some examples of OTWLS and the courts' involvement with them.

COMMON LAW

OTWLs based in common law offer a number of approaches to protect/manage wildlife/habitat.[10] Here are a few:

Contracts

Contracts that could be used to assist in wildlife/ habitat protection include contracts between conservation organizations and landowners to monitor habits, to restore habitat, or to refrain from land-use practices that could adversely affect habitat. However, contracts are limited by a term of time, and apply only to the parties to the contract, unless the obligations are assigned. Also, a contract, unaccompanied by an interest in land, does not "run with the land" and bind future landowners who are not a party to it.

A case in point is *Willman v. Ducks Unlimited (Canada)*.[11] The defendant, Ducks Unlimited Canada (DUC), filed a caveat against the plaintiff's land to give notice of DUC's interest in a landowner agreement that enabled DUC to access the land and carry out waterfowl management activities. The Manitoba Court of Appeal struck down the caveat on the basis that caveats give notice of *interests in land* by their nature. The landowner's agreement did not, the court found, confer an interest in land, and did not bind future owners. It was instead a personal contract that permitted DUC to enter the land to carry out certain activities.

Easements and Restrictive Covenants

Unless modified by statute, easements and restrictive covenants require two separate parcels of land: a dominant and servient tenement. The dominant tenement must benefit from restrictions on (restrictive covenants) or permissions or rights in relation to (easements) the servient tenement. Properly constituted easements and restrictive covenants run with the land and bind future owners.

Easements and restrictive covenants could have many uses for wildlife/habitat protection. For example, a conservation organization could enter into a restrictive covenant with a landowner to restrict the owner's utilization of the land to benefit connected wildlife habitat on the organization's lands in the same area. The organization might negotiate an access easement to monitor compliance.

An example of a statutory modification is section 219 of the British Columbia *Land Title Act*,[12] which authorizes the environment minister, a municipality, and certain others to enter into a covenant with a landowner to secure certain amenities. The covenant that runs with the land may impose negative or positive obligations and does not require a dominant tenement. "Amenity" under the Act includes environmental, wildlife, and plants, and the government has used such covenants to protect wildlife habitat.[13]

Windset Greenhouses (Ladner) Ltd v. The Corporation of Delta[14] considered the validity of a section 219 covenant. The municipality of Delta required Windset to enter into covenants to, among other things, enhance wildlife habitat, and restrict heat sources and light emissions, as a pre-condition to Windset being granted a development permit. Windset executed the covenant on its understanding that they were temporary and would be replaced by a municipal bylaw governing these matters. Delta did not get to pass the bylaw as officials reasoned that they could rely on the covenants. The British Columbia Supreme Court agreed with Windset that the covenants were intended to be temporary and that Windset executed them because a bylaw would replace them within a reasonable time. The court issued an order under the *Property Law Act*[15] to cancel portions of them. The court was careful to draw a distinction between bylaws, which can be changed, and section 219 covenants, which might be perpetual.

Leases

Leases—time-limited interests in land that give a right to occupy—can protect wildlife/ habitat in a variety of ways. A conservation organization, for example, could lease land to restore and protect habitat. A lease, such as a Crown grazing lease, or Crown oil and gas lease, could include habitat protection conditions.

Hansen Drilling Ventures Ltd v. Alberta Conservation Association (ACA), an Alberta Surface Rights Board decision, provides an example relating to an oil and gas lease.[16] The ACA, with the Alberta Fish and Game Association, owned land for the purpose of restoring it to native vegetation to provide habitat for endangered species, in particular sage grouse. Hansen's industrial activities would interfere with the restoration and re-vegetation. The panel was asked to set the compensation that Hansen must pay for its use of the land. The ACA presented twelve comparable loss of use agreements. In the end, the panel raised annual compensation from $2,000 to $4,261, which was more in line with the comparable agreements. It is interesting that instead of questioning whether restoration to native habitat for listed species was a use of land or trying to quantify the actual value of the loss of use, the panel stated that "the marketplace is usually the best determinant of fair and reasonable rates of compensation."[17]

Licence

A person may give a licence to another to do something on a land. Regarding wildlife/habitat, a licence could include, for example, a right to enter the land to restore, maintain, and monitor habitat conditions. A licence, on its own, does not bestow a property interest. This can be important as a property interest typically includes rights to enforce the interest against third parties that interfere with the interest.

A case in point is *Chingee v. British Columbia*.[18] Harry Chingee held a guiding territory certificate and two registered traplines, both issued by the province under the *Wildlife Act*.[19] Chingee claimed that the Crown authorized logging activities on the Crown land, interfering with his interests. He claimed damages on the basis of nuisance and trespass, among others. British Columbia asked the British Columbia Supreme Court to strike out Chingee's statement of claim.

Chingee claimed his interests were profits á prendre. A profit á prendre gives the right to enter another's land and take some profit, such as wildlife, hay, trees, etc. It is a property interest but does not confer exclusive possession of the land. It is limited to the exclusive right of entering the land to remove the profit.[20]

The court found that the interests would not support a trespass action. Trespass is a wrongful interference with land in the plaintiff's possession. Chingee was not in possession in the required sense, and the Crown expressly authorized the defendants' logging activities, so any interference was not "wrongful."[21] Although the court entertained the claim that the trapline interest could be a profit á prendre, the court found that the elements of a nuisance—unreasonable interference with the use and enjoyment of land—were not met against the Crown or other defendants.[22] The court relied on British Columbia's public lands legislation that prescribed a multiple-use approach to public land management. The court stated that the "realization of wildlife values is one of many considerations among the purposes and functions of the Ministry described in its legislation. Other objectives relate to maximizing forest productivity, timber harvesting, and recognizing the financial interests of the government."[23] The legislated resource management multiple-use scheme shaped and limited what would constitute "unreasonable interference."[24]

Statutory

Countless statutes are OTWLs, in that their application can protect or impact wildlife/habitat. In this paper, only a few are discussed. However, it would be remiss not to at least mention other types of OTWLs below and provide examples in the endnotes:

- legislated plans that authorize or guide government decision-making regarding land use;[25]
- legislation that designates land for environmental/ecological protection;[26]
- municipal planning legislation that authorizes zoning that excludes areas from development;[27]
- although not usually legislated, international conventions and commitments concerning wildlife/habitat;[28]
- government wildlife/habitat policies;[29]
- legislation and policies creating or sanctioning economic instruments like offsets regarding impacted wildlife/habitat.[30]

Conservation Easements

Most provinces/territories have conservation easement/covenant statutes. These statutes create a property interest in land. To constitute the interest, a landowner enters into a voluntary agreement with a person authorized by statute to protect the natural or other authorized values of all or a part of his/her land by restricting development, for a term of time or in perpetuity. When registered at the appropriate land registry, a conservation easement/covenant runs with the land and development restrictions are enforceable in accordance with its terms and the legislation.[31]

Transfer of Development Credits

Transfer of development credit (TDC) programs provide a legal process to preserve natural, agricultural, or heritage values of rural or urban land by permitting the transfer of development potential from one area and conferring it on another area that is more appropriate for development.[32] Unlike traditional zoning, TDC programs enable compensation to a landowner for the loss of development potential in order to carry out public conservation policies. Such programs have been hailed as "an innovative way to accommodate both preservation interests and development interests."[33]

Environmental/Sustainability Impact Assessment

All provinces/territories and the federal government have impact assessment legislation.[34] Impact assessment processes can also be carried out pursuant to Indigenous communities/government co-management agreements and legislation.[35] Government decision-makers need information to decide whether to issue a statutory authorization (e.g. a mining permit). This is especially so if a proposed project could have significant adverse environmental effects or other social costs. Impact assessment offers governments a planning and decision tool to prevent or mitigate environmental or other sustainability-related problems that will likely result from a project, including impacts on wildlife/habitat.

Traditionally, impact assessment has focused on environmental impacts and has been called "environmental assessment." But impact assessment can also focus on a broader range of sustainability impacts, such as impacts on economy, health, society, and culture. In the latter case, the assessment may be referred to as a sustainability impact assessment. In this chapter, both focuses are referred to simply as "impact assessment" or "IA."

Through IA processes, governments may become aware of a development project's overall impact on the environment/sustainability. Armed with this awareness, decision-makers determine whether to issue the required statutory authorization so that the project may go ahead, to issue the authorization with conditions, or to not issue the authorization at all.

Project IA (assessment that focuses on a single project, such as a dam or a mine) may relate to wildlife and habitat protection or management in many ways. For example, a project that could impact wildlife/habitat that is being assessed will likely require a wildlife baseline analysis. As summarized by a consultant/biologist, data requirements might include[36]

- Lists of expected species present on site, emphasizing species of conservation concern

- Site-specific features (e.g., bear dens, mineral licks, raptor nests)
- Identified habitats of importance (e.g., ungulate winter range, areas of known concentration)
- Documented seasonal habitat use
- Estimates of animal abundance (listed by habitat and season)
- Historical distributions and habitat use
- Behavioural responses to development activities.

Project IA may bring to light the presence of

- species at risk, and the application of the federal *Species at Risk Act*,[37] or provincial/territorial species at risk legislation that could lead to wildlife/habitat protection;
- Indigenous rights related to wildlife and habitat and potential protection of rights; and
- public and stakeholder concerns that could lead to protection, project rejection or abandonment, or stricter development conditions to better protect wildlife and habitat.

In contrast to project IA, a regional IA (RIA) plan covers a geographic area and can involve

- a comprehensive ecological baseline study;
- identification of areas or categories of life or culture particularly susceptible to development, or otherwise meriting preservation and protection; and
- a risk analysis regarding impacts of existing and planned project developments, including cumulative impacts studies, and a mapping out of where development to specified degrees may occur and where it is off-limits.

Accordingly, RIA takes into account wildlife/habitat and provides degrees of insulation from development.[38]

A strategic impact assessment (SIA) focuses on the environmental/sustainability effects of a government's policies, plans, and programs. For example, if a province considered adopting the Yellowstone to Yukon Conservation Initiative (Y2Y) program, which strives to secure connective wildlife habitat from Yellowstone to the Yukon, then assessing the environmental and other impacts of adopting the program and developing policy concerning Y2Y would constitute an SIA.

Both SIA and RIA may be operative in project IA, including potential wildlife/habitat impacts of a proposed project.

Project Impact Assessment—The Proof Is in the Permit and What Follows

Assessing environmental and sustainability effects alone will not protect or manage wildlife or habitat. It is what is done with the information that matters. Following an IA, a project could be turned down, approved with conditions, or approved without conditions. Conditions may include mitigation to lessen adverse effects, including on wildlife/habitat. Conditions need to be monitored and followed up on to ascertain their effectiveness. Where unforeseen impacts result irrespective of conditions, adaptive management requirements on approval (if any) can oblige a proponent to alter environmental management to alleviate issues and impacts. As a final comment in this section, the research disclosed very few instances where an impact assessment clearly resulted in a lack of harm or destruction of wildlife/habitat coupled with the actual protection of existing wildlife/habitat. If a project has positive results for wildlife/habitat, it is more likely that it is because the assessment led to avoiding, minimizing, or mitigating wildlife/habitat impacts. Even then, such positive results depend on IA recommendations being followed through in apt permit conditions, monitoring, follow-up, adaptive management, and wildlife/habitat-nurturing reclamation conditions, which does not always occur.[39]

IMPACT ASSESSMENT AND COURTS

There is no shortage of court enforcement/interpretation of IA matters in relation to wildlife/habitat in Canada. A CanLII search on May 5, 2020, disclosed 78 cases involving the *Canadian Environmental Assessment Act* (2012 and 1992) (predecessors of the federal *Impact Assessment Act* (2019)) alone. A case demonstrating some positive results for wildlife/habitat is the 1998

British Columbia Supreme Court decision *George v. Marczyk*.[40] This was the first British Columbia decision on the then-new provincial IA law.

The case concerned the proposed open-pit Huckleberry Copper Mine. In 1995, Huckleberry applied for a certificate under the provincial *Mine Development Assessment Act*.[41] The assessment process began under that Act but then transitioned to the new *Environmental Assessment Act*.[42] The certificate was granted, subject to certain conditions. The validity of the certificate was challenged on numerous grounds, including that "[t]he issue of the impacts of the project on wildlife and the consequent potential adverse effect on First Nations was not addressed prior to certification. In particular, the mapping presented to the committee was unacceptable and that until such mapping is completed [,] work on the compensation for impacts and wildlife could not take place [,] and in fact [,] it was never done."[43] These wildlife impacts and mitigation, the petitioners argued, should have been identified in the IA process and would have been available as a basis for constitutionally required First Nations consultation. The court agreed and added that the proponent should have provided such data under the provincial *Environmental Assessment Act*.[44] The court ordered that such data be produced within a given timeframe, that First Nation consultation resume with this new information, and that the certificate subsequently be amended as appropriate.[45] Ultimately, the provincial and federal approvals were finalized but subject to the proponent's developing reclamation plans to restore or enhance fish and wildlife habitat after mine closure.[46] Interestingly, in 2015 Huckleberry Mines won an award in the metal mine reclamation category from the British Columbia Technical and Research Committee on Reclamation (TRCR). The award was for its "habitat compensation work in a successful remediation of fishways (using fish ladders) in a local creek in the vicinity of the Huckleberry copper mine."[47] The creek contained no fish until 1996, a year after the start of the reclamation work.

The Moral of the Story

Impacts on wildlife/habitat, for good or bad, may result from the application of a myriad of laws. Individuals and organizations wanting to preserve and protect wildlife/habitat must work with the larger law-based puzzle pieces and connect these pieces to realize their aims. In addition to law-based pieces, such individuals and groups can pursue other avenues, not discussed here, such as grants, land acquisition, lobbying, education, and stewardship programs. The

Y2Y initiative, already mentioned, is a good example. Its website describes it as "a joint Canada-U.S. not-for-profit organization that connects and protects habitat from Yellowstone to Yukon so people and nature can thrive."[48] Y2Y uses a variety of methods and relies on legislative provisions of statutes from a number of jurisdictions, and the collaboration of hundreds of people and groups, to accomplish its work. If the validity of a piece of Y2Y's puzzle of connective habitat were to be challenged and put before a court, the court, of course, would have to examine the relevant legislation and the particulars of the circumstances. The author hopes that when doing its job, courts include among these particulars, the intricate legislative and non-statutory overlay of elements of protection/management of wildlife/habitat and consider how using court interpretation and enforcement powers could sometimes reinforce or topple it. Courts have tools to take this perspective, and when appropriate, find for wildlife/habitat protection rather than destruction, such as relying on purpose clauses (where applicable), incorporating principles of international law, considering the public interest, public trust, and principles of equity. Though these, and other court tools, cannot be spelled out here, the author hopes that further research will explore how courts can improve and advance wildlife/habitat protection and sustainable management in its considerations and decisions.

NOTES

1 Professor Emeritus, Faculty of Law, University of Calgary.

2 See also Arlene Kwasniak, *Alberta Wetlands: A Law and Policy Guide*, 2nd ed (Calgary: Canadian Institute of Resources Law, 2016) [Arlene Kwasniak (2016)].

3 John Donihee, *The Evolution of Wildlife Law in Canada* (Calgary: Canadian Institute of Resources Law, 2000) at 12–17 [John Donihee].

4 *Ibid.*

5 *Ibid.*

6 *Ibid* at 16–17.

7 *Wildlife Act*, SNu 2003, c 26 [*Wildlife Act*, SNu]. For more examples of "sustainable management" legislation, see e.g., *Wildlife Conservation Act*, RSPEI 1988, c W-4.1; Quebec's *An Act Respecting the Conservation and Development of Wildlife*, CQLR s C-61.1; Nova Scotia's *Wildlife Act*, RSNS 1989, c 504. For more information, see Monique Passelac-Ross, *Overview of Provincial Wildlife Laws* (Calgary: Canadian Institute of Resources Law, 2006).

8 *Wildlife Act*, SNu, *supra* note 7, s 1.

9 See e.g., British Columbia's *Wildlife Act*, RSBC 1996, c 488, ss 5–6 (authorizes critical habitat designations in wildlife management areas on Crown land). Section 77 makes releasing livestock in wildlife habitat an offence (*ibid*, s 77).

10 For a more comprehensive discussion, see Arlene Kwasniak (2016), supra note 2 at c 16; Arlene Kwasniak, *Legal and Economic Tools and Other Incentives to Achieve Wildlife Goals* (Calgary: Canadian Institute of Resources Law, 2006).

11 *Willman v Ducks Unlimited (Canada)*, 2004 MBCA 153.

12 *Land Title Act*, RSBC 1996, c 250, s 219.

13 See e.g., "Ecosystems: Restrictive Covenants" (accessed 29 November 2021), online: *Government of British Columbia* <env.gov.bc.ca/lower-mainland/ecosystems/restrictive_covenants/>.

14 *Windset Greenhouses (Ladner) Ltd v The Corporation of Delta*, 2001 BCSC 462.

15 *Property Law Act*, RSBC 1996, c 377. Section 35(1)(e) enables a court to change or cancel such covenants (*ibid*, s 35(1)(e)).

16 *Hansen Drilling Ventures Ltd v Alberta Conservation Association*, 2013 ABSRB 856.

17 *Ibid* at para 3.

18 *Chingee v British Columbia*, 2016 BCSC 760 [*Chingee*]. Chingee appealed to the British Columbia Court of Appeal. The Court of Appeal dismissed the actions on summary judgment on the basis that "[n]one of the pleaded causes of action has any reasonable prospect of success. The pleadings do not state material facts with sufficient specificity to ground the various causes of action." See Summary *Chingee v British Columbia*, 2017 BCCA 250.

19 *Ibid* at para 2.

20 "Profit á prendre" in *Halsbury's Laws of England*, 2nd ed, vol 27, (London: Butterworth & Co, 1934) at 607.

21 *Chingee*, *supra* note 18 at para 68.

22 *Ibid* at paras 72–73.

23 *Ibid* at para 53.

24 *Ibid* at para 72.

25 An example is Newfoundland and Labrador's sustainable forest management plans made pursuant to the *Sustainable Forest Management Planning Regulation*, NL 61/13, under the *Forestry Act*, RSNL 1990, c F-23. Such plans can exclude from harvesting areas of environmental or ecological importance, such as connective wildlife habitat.

26 The multitude of federal, provincial, and territorial park and wildlands protection legislation includes the *Wilderness Areas Protection Act*, SNS 1998, c 27.

27 For example, s 10.2.1 of the land use bylaw (6-2015) for Alberta's Strathcona County explains that its purpose is "[t]o provide for the preservation of environmentally sensitive lands which have significant natural capability for conservation, passive recreation and education." There are no permitted uses, and only a couple of passive outdoor-based discretionary uses, online (pdf): <strathcona.ca/files/files/at-pds-draftlub-part10-0304.pdf>.

28 See e.g., John Donihee, *supra* note 3, c 15. One example is the Ramsar Convention on Wetlands of National Importance, (11 ILM 969 (1972, in force 1975)) under which wetlands can be designated, and the jurisdiction of the designation agrees to protect and manage sites for their ecological values.

29 See e.g., "Canadian Biodiversity Strategy" (accessed 10 December 2021), online: <biodivcanada.chm-cbd.net/documents/canadian-biodiversity-strategy>.

30 The 2013 Alberta Wetland Policy is an off-set example. Although not legislated (cabinet approved only), compliance with it can be required by approvals under the *Water Act*, RSA 2000, c W-3.

31 In Alberta, conservation easements fall under the *Alberta Land Stewardship Act*, SA 2009, c A-26.8, ss 28–35.

32 For an overview of TDCs previous to their statutory status in Alberta, see Arlene Kwasniak, "The Potential for Municipal Transfer of Development Credits Programs in Canada" (2004) 15:2 JELP at 47.

33 Deborah Bowers & Tom Daniels, *Holding Our Ground: Protecting America's Farms and Farmland* (Washington: Island Press, 1997) at 171.

34 In Alberta, for example, environmental assessment of a project may be required by the provincial government, under the *Environmental Protection and Enhancement Act*, RSA 2000, c E-12, or by the federal government under the *Impact Assessment Act*, SC 2019, c 28, s 1, or by both in a single harmonized assessment. The *Impact Assessment Act* was preceded by the *Canadian Environmental Assessment Act*, 2012, SC 2012, c 19, s 52, and the *Canadian Environmental Assessment Act* of 1992, SC 1992, c 37.

35 For example, the *Nunavut Land Claims Agreement* (1993) established the Nunavut Impact Review Board (NIRB), which is responsible for assessing all projects in Nunavut, and the *Inuvialuit Final Agreement* (1987) established the Environmental Impact Screening Committee.

36 EDI Environmental Dynamics Inc., *Wildlife Baseline and Monitoring Overview of Wildlife Information Requirements in Environmental Assessment*, online (pdf): <edynamics.com/uploads/documents/factsheets/Wildlife%20Baseline_Studies_27May2010_cm.pdf>.

37 *Species at Risk Act*, SC 2002, c 29.

38 See e.g., "Class EA for Forest Management on Crown Lands in Ontario" (20 March 2014, last updated 8 July 2021), online: <ontario.ca/page/class-ea-forest-management-crown-lands-ontario-mnr-71> which was developed to inform regulating timber management and harvesting on Crown lands. A disputed issue was the EA's adequacy in protecting wildlife and habitat.

39 The point is well illustrated in Meinhard Doelle, "The Disconnect between EA & Implementation: A Look at the Methylmercury Issue in the Lower Churchill Project" (20 November 2015), online: *Dalhousie University Environmental Law News* <blogs.dal.ca/melaw/2015/11/20/the-disconnect-between-ea-implementation-a-look-at-the-methylmercury-issue-in-the-lower-churchill-project/>.

40 *George v Marczyk*, 1998 CanLII 6737 (BCSC).

41 *Mine Development Assessment Act*, SBC 1990, c 55.

42 *Environmental Assessment Act*, SBC 1994, c 35, s 41.

43 *George v Marczyk*, *supra* note 40 at para 4.

44 *Ibid* at paras 69–70.

45 Ibid at para 75.

46 Canadian Environmental Assessment Agency, *Cumulative Effects Assessment Practitioners' Guide Huckleberry Copper Mine: Case Study Highlights* (Calgary: Axys Environmental Consulting Ltd, 1999), online: <canada.ca/en/impact-assessment-agency/services/policy-guidance/cumulative-effects-assessment-practitioners-guide.html#appb>.

47 Peter Caulfield, "Huckleberry Mines Wins Award for Mine Reclamation", *Canadian Mining and Energy* (5 May 2016), online: <miningandenergy.ca/sustainability/article/huckleberry_mines_wins_award_for_mine_reclamation/>.

48 Yellowstone to Yukon Conservation Initiative, online: <y2y.net/vision/about-us>.

16

A Role for the Courts in Market-Based Conservation

David W. Poulton[1]

There is an irony in seeking to address economic instruments for environmental protection in a book entitled *Environment in the Courtroom* and which is focused upon issues of enforcement. The irony lies in the fact that such instruments are conceived of as an alternative to our focus on enforcement and on the courtroom.

Rather than rely on legal sanctions, market-based instruments seek to alter human behaviour by appealing to economic self-interest. They aim to internalize more environmental costs into resource decisions, changing the economic drivers of development and exploitation. In various and diverse forms, they create new liabilities for environmental bad, and new rights, sometimes including property rights, in environmental goods. Like the laws of contract and property, when they operate properly, their biggest effect comes through broad acceptance and voluntary compliance, with the courts and legal sanctions positioned in the background in a supporting role.

In the conventional legal framework, laws for the protection of wildlife and the environment fit awkwardly into the broader legal system. Our doctrines of property and commerce are abundantly focused upon making resources available for human use. Those doctrines underlie an economic system that has enabled social growth for hundreds of years and that forms people's expectations respecting the opportunity to create prosperous and useful lives. The more recent development of laws of environmental protection runs counter to this overall trend. It presents environmental protection as a barrier to the pursuit of economic self-interest. This contrary nature of environmental protection sets up the dichotomy of economy versus environment that dominates so much of our public discourse, including environmental litigation.

In contrast to that conflictual paradigm, the development of market-based instruments for environmental protection seeks to travel upstream in the flow of economic forces and alter price signals, and other economic factors in order to assure that interests of the environment are taken into account in the formation of life and business plans, that economics and environment become harmonized, both held to be necessary and beneficial for human life.

Much of the thinking on economic instruments has originated in academia and then been adopted into policy discussions. This is happening at an increasing rate. A 2017 report found that almost one hundred jurisdictions worldwide use some form of market-based policy instrument for the protection of biodiversity.[2]

But while policy discussions have been dynamic, there has not been the same level of attention paid to such instruments in the promulgation of our statutory law. Individual components and building blocks of market-based programs, such as conservation easements or land use planning authority, may be found in some statutes, but it may not be clear on the face of a statute how they are intended to fit into the larger policy picture. As well, many market-based environmental policies are being promoted through regulatory structures and jurisdictions that were originally conceived of when such intention was unknown. Courts may become fora for consideration of how traditional statutory jurisdictions will mesh with innovative environmental-economic policy initiatives. In considering these matters, the courts may contribute to the harmonization of economic and environmental incentives or may frustrate that policy direction. Because the entirety of a policy framework, including its non-legal aspects, may not be brought before a court, a court might take either direction inadvertently.

This chapter reviews some cases where the courts have added their voice, even if inadvertently, to the policy debate in this area, and touches on some situations where they have—benignly in my view—left the field to policymakers and regulator decision-makers. The paper touches on four market-based instruments of environmental policy.

Conservation Offsetting

As a tool of environmental protection, conservation offsetting demonstrates the range of approaches that might be taken to combining law and policy.

Offsetting links the right to develop or use a resource, and to thereby create some environmental loss, to the obligation to create an environmental enhancement equivalent to the loss, with the objective of leaving no net loss of the environmental values in question. Offsetting uses a price mechanism to encourage environmental stewardship. By requiring a development proponent to bear the replacement cost of the environmental components and values it proposes to degrade or destroy, offsetting creates an incentive to minimize that loss.

Long a tool for carbon emissions, offsetting for habitat and biodiversity is now found in programs in ninety-nine countries worldwide[3] and getting increasing attention from policy makers across Canada. Here I shall focus on offsetting for biodiversity, leaving aside the elaborate field of carbon offsetting.

In Canada, we see various avenues by which conservation offsetting is enabled by statutory provisions. The first is by the measure being explicitly authorized by statute and regulation. This is very rare in Canadian law. One of the very few such provisions is found in British Columbia's *Water Sustainability Act*.[4] The following section sets out the authority of a regulator when faced with impacts to a stream or aquifer that cannot be mitigated:

> 16(2) If the decision maker considers that the [adverse effects] cannot be addressed, or cannot fully be addressed, by mitigation measures proposed by the applicant but can be compensated for by other mitigation measures taken on a different part of the stream or aquifer than the part to which the proposal relates, the decision maker may impose . . . terms and conditions requiring the applicant to take compensatory mitigation measures that meet the prescribed criteria, in place of or supplemental to any mitigation measures proposed by the applicant, on a different part of the stream or aquifer to which the application relates.
>
> (3) With the consent of the applicant, the terms or conditions of an authorization . . . may require that the applicant take compensatory mitigation measures on a different stream or aquifer in respect of which the application is made.[5]

More detailed rules for the terms of compensatory mitigation measures on designated "sensitive streams" are found in regulation.[6] We see, then, that this decision maker has a clear authority to order offsetting (i.e. compensatory mitigation measures), as well as some guidance in regulation as to how that authority is to be applied.

The *Alberta Land Stewardship Act* (*ALSA*)[7] contains a general statement of interest in exploring market-based instruments to support land stewardship.[8] Part 3 of the statute enables a series of such tools. Conservation offsetting is to be enabled by the promulgation of a series of regulations including the relationship of offsetting to impactful development activity,[9] the establishment of "stewardship units" as a medium of exchange for comparing development and offset impacts,[10] and the establishment of an exchange in stewardship units.[11] These provisions are extremely broadly drafted, so much so that they enable a wide variety of potential regulatory directions. To date, however, no regulations have been put in place, so this avenue remains undeveloped.

Despite these two examples, the explicit provision for conservation offsetting in statutory law is rare in Canada. It is much more common that offsetting requirements are based on the general jurisdiction of a regulator to impose environmental conditions on development or use permitting. Thus, for example, the federal fish habitat compensation has been based upon section 35 of the *Fisheries Act*, which reads in part:

> 35 (1) No person shall carry on any work, undertaking or activity that results in the harmful, alteration, disruption or destruction of fish habitat.
>
> (2) A person may carry on a work, undertaking or activity without contravening subsection (1) if
>
> . . .
>
> (b) the carrying on of the work, undertaking or activity is authorized by the Minister and the work, undertaking or activity is carried on in accordance with the conditions established by the Minister;[12]

No mention is made of offsetting or compensation in this section. Rather it is implicitly seen as within the scope of the discretion of the regulator to impose conditions. In the case of the fisheries regime this has supported an offset program since the late 1980s (though the wording of Section 35 has been amended in ways unrelated to this point). The real substance of that program, however, has been found in policy guidance without legal force.[13]

In a similar vein, Alberta offset policy for wetland conservation[14] relies upon the following sections of the province's *Water Act*:[15]

> 36 (1) . . . no person may commence or continue an activity (i.e., altering a water body, including a wetland) except pursuant to an approval . . .
>
> 38 (3) The Director may issue an approval subject to any terms and conditions that the Director considers appropriate.

Again, the discretion to impose conditions is the legal foundation for offset requirements, but the details of the expected conditions are determined by reference to policy guidance lacking the force of law.[16]

Similar jurisdiction to impose conditions is found in dozens of resource statutes across Canada and depending on the particular wording of each, might form a foundation for many different offset programs. The precise nature of those programs, however, is not found in the statutes that enable them. This means that any judicial ruling on the nature of the foundation may reverberate through offset systems, rendering them more or less functional, though the nature of the policy edifice and the significance of the ruling may not be brought before the court in any particular case.

While jurisprudence ought not to be distilled out of the absence of litigation, the fact that such jurisdiction to impose offsetting has been so little challenged despite years of the operation of some offset programs may be taken as an indication of the mainstream acceptability of such programs. Accordingly, the courts ought not to be hasty in seeking to limit them.

Conservation Easements

A contrast to the distance between statutory provisions and implementation details in conservation offsetting may be found with another conservation policy tool, conservation easements. A conservation easement is an interest in land created by statute. It provides a means by which a private landowner may covenant to undertake or forgo certain activities or developments in order to preserve the natural features and ecosystem functions of his or her land. When registered, the covenant runs with the land and is binding on subsequent owners. This is, therefore, an important way of securing environmental benefits for the future, and those secure benefits, while important in themselves, may also underpin other market-based environmental policy tools and programs. One significant point of distinction from a common law easement is that a conservation easement does not require a dominant tenement, though it does require a qualified second party to receive the easement and hold the power to enforce it.

Almost all jurisdictions in Canada have legislation providing for conservation easements, though in some cases they may be referred to by different names such as conservation covenants.[17] In Alberta, the legislation is the *ALSA*, specifically sections 28 through 35. Section 29 reads, in part:

> 29(1) A registered owner of land may, by agreement, grant to a qualified organization a conservation easement in respect of all or part of the land for one or more of the following purposes:
>
> (a) The protection, conservation and enhancement of the environment;
>
> (b) The protection, conservation and enhancement of natural scenic or esthetic values;
>
> (c) The protection, conservation and enhancement of agricultural land or land for agricultural purposes.[18]

The Alberta Court of Queen's Bench had occasion to consider this provision in the case of *Nature Conservancy of Canada v. Waterton Land Trust Ltd.*[19] The defendant operated a bison ranch on land which it owned near Waterton Lakes National Park. It purported to give a conservation easement to the Nature Conservancy of Canada (NCC) to the effect that the landowner would not use "wildlife-proof fences" on the land, as well as some other restrictions. Presumably, the purpose of this was to maintain wildlife movement across the land. Unfortunately, the form and execution of the easement document was beset by a myriad of errors and points of confusion. The landowner employed fencing that the NCC objected to and the NCC brought suit to enforce the terms of the easement. The defendant brought a countersuit seeking a declaration that the easement was invalid.

A good deal of the case dealt with contractual issues of mutual mistake and rectification, but one argument of the defendant landowner was that the easement was ultra vires the Alberta statute, based upon the above-quoted wording. It claimed that the plaintiff was required to prove the validity of the easement by calling expert evidence to establish its conservation purpose, and that its failure to do so placed the easement outside the statute. To its credit, the court dispensed with this argument succinctly:

> I disagree with what amounts to a presumption of invalidity. I disagree that *a priori* a conservation easement is unenforceable unless the grantee demonstrates with scientific evidence that the conservation easement, or the specified term of it to be enforced, *accomplishes* at least one of the statutory purposes for the legislators creating conservation easements, now set out in *ALSA*. Section 29 permits conservation easements to exist where the grantor had at least one of the stated purposes for the conservation easement. Proof of accomplishing one of those purposes, or proof of the probability of accomplishing one of those purposes, or proof of potentially or even possibly accomplishing one of those purposes is not required. The prerequisite is that the grantor had one of the purposes in mind. There will be many ways to prove such intent, most notably by inference from the wording of the conservation easement. On the face of a conservation easement it will usually be apparent whether the grantor's purposes fell within at least one of the statutory purposes. [Italics in original.][20]

In another part of its judgment the court noted the public interest served by conservation easements:

> By relinquishing such rights of ownership in support of conservation-minded restrictions the landowner is in effect donating them in favour of a conservation purpose. Thus, conservation easements enable private capital from charitable benefactors to be deployed for public interest purposes, such as environmental protection, enhancement, and sustainability.[21]

While the particular conservation easement in question, in this case, was ruled unenforceable on other grounds—the vagueness of the term "wildlife-proof fence"—the liberal and purposive interpretation of the statutory provision for conservation easements will help create confidence in that important conservation policy tool.

Trade of Development Credits

Trade of development credits (TDC) schemes are a municipal planning tool that allows for development pressures to be shifted from an area of higher conservation interest to an area of lower conservation interest. Under such a scheme, a municipality is called upon to designate areas preferred for development (the "receiving parcel") and those preferred for lower impact and lower density uses, compatible with conservation objectives broadly understood (the "sending parcel"). Development rights are allocated to both parcels, but those wishing to develop in the receiving parcel may increase the density of development there by buying development rights from the sending parcel. Accordingly, landowners in the sending parcel who wish to conserve their land may receive some compensation for their forsaken development rights. Proponents of such schemes claim that they enable better municipal planning, incent conservation, and fairly distribute the economic benefits of development among the whole community.

In *Keller v. Municipal District of Bighorn No. 8*[22] a landowner challenged the jurisdiction of the municipality to implement a TDC scheme. At the time the municipal district of Bighorn adopted the TDC scheme at issue, there was no specific provision allowing such schemes in Alberta legislation, including the *Municipal Government Act.*

However, Madam Justice Hunt Macdonald of the Alberta Court of Queen's Bench had no difficulty reading the jurisdiction into the *Act* using a "broad and purposive approach," saying:

> Under s. 632(a)(ii), an MDP [municipal development plan] must address the manner of future development within the municipality. Under s. 632(b)(iii) and s. 632(3)(b)(vi), it may address environmental matters and the physical, social and economic development of the municipality. Though the legislation does not refer specifically to a TDC scheme, in my view such a scheme clearly falls within the broad powers of regulation and control provided to the municipality under

> these sections of the *MGA*. Similarly, s. 640(4)(o) very clearly provides authority to the municipality to provide for density in its LUB [land-use bylaw], and s. 633(2)(a) requires a municipality to address issues of land use and population density in any ASP [area structure plan].[23]

The applicant put forward a second argument against the scheme that was based on *ALSA*, which was passed subsequent to the municipal bylaws in question in *Keller*. *ALSA* did explicitly provide for municipalities to adopt TDC schemes (section 48) but required that any such scheme be approved by the lieutenant governor in council. The applicant argued that that provision should negate the Bighorn bylaws, which had no such cabinet approval. The court, however, found that *ALSA* had no retroactive impact on the validity of the bylaws passed before it was adopted.[24]

Again, in this case the court adopted a broad and purposive approach and, in the process, reinforced the validity and viability of an important municipal tool for market-based conservation. Unfortunately, however, we must turn to quite a contrary situation.

Rights in Environmental Goods

One of the tools in the market-based toolbox is the creation of property rights in environmental goods and services. This is one way of avoiding the "tragedy of the commons" where the benefits of a person's environmentally responsible behaviour are dissipated throughout a larger community. Instead, it allows a person to have a means of retaining the benefit for their own use, and thereby incents more responsible actions in the future. The property right might attach to the actual resource conserved, or it may attach to the credit for the beneficial action. For example, in the United States, one may earn a valuable credit for creating a wetland and retain and then use that credit even after passing on the title to the wetland itself.[25]

One case that touched on this question was *Water Conservation Trust of Canada v. Alberta (Environmental Appeals Boards) et al.*[26] The Water Conservation Trust of Canada (WCTC) was a non-profit organization formed for the purpose, among other things, of holding water licences to maintain aquatic ecosystem health.[27] A water licence is the right to use a given amount of water (owned by the Crown) in a given location. ConocoPhillips Canada held a water licence for the stated purpose of industrial use on a particular reach of the Red Deer River in southern Alberta. Through its own water conservation efforts, the company came to the conclusion that it no longer needed the water licence and attempted to donate and transfer it to the WCTC for conservation purposes. The WCTC intended to hold the licence, securing the water instream for the benefit of the aquatic environment. The transfer required a change both in the name of the holder of the licence and also the stated purpose, from "industrial" to "habitat enhancement, recreation, fish and wildlife management and water management," both of which required the approval of Alberta Environment and Sustainable Resource Development (AESRD), as the department was then known. The director of AESRD refused the transfer. The WCTC appealed the refusal to the Environmental Appeals Board (EAB), which recommended that the refusal stand. That decision was then appealed to the Alberta Court of Queen's Bench, which ruled that the EAB decision was reasonable and should stand.

The case involved several issues, most of which are not addressed here. My focus is on the position taken by AESRD on whether the WCTC, as a private party, had the right to hold a water licence for a conservation purpose, and how that position was seen both by the EAB and the Court of Queen's Bench. That turned on the interpretation of the relationship between two parts of section 51 of Alberta's *Water Act.*[28]

Section 51(1) empowers the director of AESRD to issue or refuse to issue a water licence to any person who may apply:

> 51(1) On application for a license by a person in accordance with this Act, the Director may, subject to subsection (2) . . . [and other provisions not relevant here]
>
> (b) a license to that person for
>
> (i) the diversion of water, or
>
> (ii) the operation of a works, for any purpose specified in the regulations.

The applicable regulation is the *Water (Ministerial) Regulation*.[29] Section 11 lists the permissible purposes for which a water licence may be issued, including several apparent conservation purposes:

> 11 A license may be issued for any or all of the following purposes:
>
> . . .
>
> (h) management of fish;
> (i) management of wildlife;
> (j) implementing a water conservation objective;
> (k) habitat enhancement;
> (l) recreation;
> (m) water management;
> (n) any other purpose specified by the Director.

Recall, however, that the authority to grant a person a licence for any of the listed purposes is subject to the *Water Act* subsection 51(2), which reads:

> 51(2) On application by the Government in accordance with this Act, the Director may issue a License to the Government but no other person, or may refuse to issue a license, for
>
> (a) the diversion of water,
> (b) the operation of a works, or
> (c) providing or maintaining a rate of flow of water or water level requirements for the purpose of implementing a water conservation objective.

Implementing a water conservation objective (WCO) is therefore a purpose that can underlie the issue of a water licence to any person under subsection 51(1) but is reserved only to the Government by subsection 51(2), which takes priority. "Water conservation objective" is a defined term in the legislation:

> 1(hhh) "water conservation objective" means the amount of quality water established by the Director under Part 2, based on information available to the Director, to be necessary for the

(i) protection of a natural water body or its aquatic environment, or any part of them,
(ii) protection of tourism, recreational, transportation or waste assimilation uses of water, or
(iii) management of fish or wildlife, and may include water necessary for the rate of flow or water level requirements.[30]

A WCO was in fact in place at the time that ConocoPhillips sought to transfer its licence to the WCTC. One of the key questions before AESRD, the EAB, and the Court of Queen's Bench, was to what extent the reserving of licences to the government for a WCO under subsection 51(2) occupied the entire field of holding water instream for environmental purposes? Conversely, to what extent could the private parties—ConocoPhillips and the WCTC—retain the right to the environmental benefit created by ConocoPhillips' efforts to conserve water? The answer which all three levels of authority gave was disappointing.

The position of AESRD was summarized in the EAB decision:

> The Director stated that if water is held instream as a rate of flow for a water conservation objective, then the water is not available for other purposes which are generally economic purposes. The Director stated the Government is in the best position to consult with the public and weigh the opportunity costs and broader implications of keeping water instream as opposed to allocating it for other uses. The Director explained creating a water conservation objective requires: (1) balancing social, economic, and environmental factors; (2) looking at changing values of water use and addressing water scarcity; and (3) balancing protection of the aquatic environment with water allocation for consumptive purposes.[31]

In short, conserving water in stream for environmental reasons is a matter for the government alone and cannot be entrusted to private parties. This position was accepted more or less uncritically by both the EAB and the Court of Queen's Bench. The strong suggestion was that the savings generated by ConocoPhillips water conservation measures, motivated by environmental responsibility, were to be reallocated for other industrial uses. Both their interest and the interest of their donee, the WCTC was to be negated, the direct opposite of the market-based trend to establish enforceable rights in environmental goods and services.

Further, this conclusion could have been avoided. The WCTC argued that the other purposes listed for private water licences—management of fish and wildlife, habitat enhancement, recreation, etc.—could characterize the holding of the licence by the WCTC. It also drew attention to the threshold wording at the beginning of subsection 51(2), "Upon the application by the Government." No application had been brought by the government, so arguably subsection 51(2) had not been triggered, leaving the full range of subsection 51(1) in play. Both of these arguments were summarily dismissed by both the AEAB and the Court of Queen's Bench.

The WCTC's position, in this case, is not without its challenges. It is unfortunate, however, that its opportunity to steward the water in question was lost because of a policy position that denied that private parties could be proper stewards and accordingly have enforceable rights. An opportunity to advance thinking in line with market-based conservation was thus lost.

Conclusion

Increasingly, market-based policy instruments are playing a prominent role in environmental and resource planning and protection. These programs may never come before a court for consideration in their entirety, for that is not in the nature of the instruments. Nevertheless, individual building blocks or components may become the objects of litigation and may come before a court without a clear signal of their significance to larger environmental programs.

This paper has very briefly touched on just a few of the array of market-based environmental instruments. It has reviewed two cases where important conservation components were impugned, and where the courts upheld their validity by taking a broad and purposive approach to interpretation. It has also looked at one case where an unfortunately narrow approach to resource stewardship was accepted. Finally, it touched on the broad scope of jurisdiction of many resource regulators to place conditions on permitting and how that process has provided a window for a whole realm of environmental programs and done so with little involvement of the courts.

NOTES

1 Principal at David W Poulton Environmental Strategies, Calgary.

2 Genevieve Bennett, Melissa Gallant, & Kerry ten Kate, *State of Biodiversity Mitigation 2017: Markets and Compensation for Global Infrastructure Development* (Washington DC: Forest Trends, 2017), online: <forest-trends.org/releases/p/sobm2017>.

3 *Ibid.*

4 SBC 2014, c 15.

5 *Ibid*, s 16(2)–(3).

6 *Water Sustainability Regulation*, BC Reg 36/2016.

7 SA 2009, c A-26.8 [*ALSA*].

8 *Ibid*, s 23.

9 *Ibid*, s 47.

10 *Ibid*, s 46.

11 *Ibid*, s 45.

12 RSC 1985, c F-14, s 35.

13 The most recent version of this policy guidance is "Policy for Applying Measures to Offset Adverse Effects in Fish and Fish Habitat under the Fisheries Act" (December 2019), online: *DFO* <dfo-mpo.gc.ca/pnw-ppe/reviews-revues/policies-politiques-eng.html>.

14 Alberta Government, *Alberta Wetland Policy* (1 September 2013, accessed 19 July 2021), online: *Open Alberta* <open.alberta.ca/publications/9781460112878>.

15 RSA 2000, c W-3.

16 "Alberta Wetland Policy Implementation" (accessed 19 July 2021), online: *Alberta Government* <alberta.ca/alberta-wetland-policy-implementation.aspx>.

17 *Conservation Easements Act*, RSNB 2011, c 130 (New Brunswick); *The Conservation Easements Amendment Act*, 2010, SS 2010, c 6 (Saskatchewan); *Conservation Easements Act*, SNS 2001, c 28 (Nova Scotia).

18 *ALSA*, *supra* note 7, s 29.

19 2014 ABQB 303.

20 *Ibid* at para 388.

21 *Ibid* at para 20.

22 2010 ABQB 362.

23 *Ibid* at para 26.

24 *Ibid* at para 54–58.

25 For a fuller discussion of this point in the Alberta context see: David W Poulton et al, "The Application of Property Rights to Ecosystem Service Markets" (2019) Alberta Land Institute, online: *ALI* <albertalandinstitute.ca/public/download/files/103299>.

26 2015 ABQB 686.

27 On the nature and role of water trusts generally, see: Arlene J Kwasniak, "Quenching Instream Thirst: A Role for Water Trusts in the Prairie Provinces" (2006) 16:3 JELP.

28 *Water Act*, *supra* note 15.

29 Alta Reg 205/1998.

30 *Water Act*, *supra* note 15, s 1(hhh).

31 *Water Conservation Trust of Canada v Director, Central Region, Operations Division, Alberta Environment and Sustainable Resource Development* (8 March 2013), Appeal No. 10-056-R (AEAB) at para 58.

17

Management and Enforcement Challenges for Highly Migratory Species: The Case of Atlantic Bluefin Tuna

Phillip Saunders[1]

Introduction

THE ATLANTIC BLUEFIN TUNA[2]

Atlantic bluefin tuna (ABFT) (*Thunnus thynnus*) is both an iconic sport fish, with a history of competitive fishing in the Atlantic region (including the largest individual ever caught, in Auld's Cove, Nova Scotia),[3] and the target of a significant commercial fishery throughout much of its range. The latter is partly driven by the fact that the species is "highly valued in the sushi and sashimi markets,"[4] but it also has wider markets. The combination of a "recreational" and large-scale industrial fishery is an unusual, if not unique, challenge with respect to the choice of management approaches.

ABFT is a highly migratory species, ranging throughout temperate and tropical areas in the Atlantic Ocean and in the Mediterranean and Black Seas, which in itself presents serious obstacles to effective management. The major spawning grounds have been identified as the Gulf of Mexico (western Atlantic) and the Mediterranean (eastern Atlantic). However, in recent years it has been determined that there is intermixing of these stocks in the mid-Atlantic, and other potential spawning grounds have been identified in the western Atlantic.[5] Both of these factors further complicate the development of management measures. The focus of this chapter is on the management of the western Atlantic stocks, and in particular the measures in place for the Canadian ABFT fishery.

HISTORICAL DEVELOPMENT OF THE FISHERY

ABFT have been fished for millennia in the Mediterranean and the eastern Atlantic, and in the modern period there have been cycles of growth and collapse; while catches of the eastern ABFT were relatively stable (at around 30,000 tonnes) in the 1950s and early 1960s, there was a decline later in the 1960s (to 10,000–15,000 tonnes), followed by overall increases until a peak of about 50,000 tonnes in 1996.[6] From that point, the eastern Atlantic fishery was subjected to management measures (including establishment of a total allowable catch [TAC]) by the International Commission for the Conservation of Atlantic Tunas (ICCAT) (see the summary of ICCAT's origin and management record, below), including implementation of a fifteen-year recovery program adopted in 2006 and implemented beginning in 2007.[7]

The fishery in the western Atlantic was historically much smaller, but in the late 1960s to 1970s, a Japanese longliner fleet (which had previously fished off Brazil) moved into areas in the Gulf of Mexico and off the northeastern United States, with catches climbing until the imposition of the first ICCAT TACs effective in 1982. Despite the management efforts, by 1998 the western Atlantic stocks were in such a state of decline that a recovery and rebuilding program was adopted by ICCAT effective in 1999, including closure to fishing in the Gulf of Mexico spawning grounds, closed seasons, and multi-year allocations of TAC by country.[8]

International Governance Regime

UNITED NATIONS CONVENTION ON THE LAW OF THE SEA 1982 (UNCLOS)[9] AND THE *UNITED NATIONS FISH STOCKS AGREEMENT 1995 (UNFA)*[10]

The management of ABFT, both at the international level via ICCAT and inside national jurisdictional zones, takes place within the overall structure provided by the *United Nations Convention on the Law of the Sea* (*UNCLOS*) and the *United Nations Fish Stocks Agreement* (*UNFA*). The *UNCLOS* established the rights and responsibilities of coastal states to manage and control the living resources within the exclusive economic zones (EEZs) out to 200 nautical miles from shore, and the preservation of fishing as a "high seas freedom" (with some limited responsibilities), outside the areas of national jurisdiction. This structure, however, left significant ambiguities as to the management of highly migratory species (HMS) such as tuna, which range widely through coastal state EEZs and high seas areas, and thus are not subject to any one overarching jurisdictional authority.[11]

With respect to HMS, the "sovereign rights" of the coastal state over fisheries in the EEZ were conditioned by a duty to "cooperate directly or through appropriate international organizations with a view to ensuring conservation and promoting the objective of optimum utilization" of the species.[12] The lack of precision in this obligation to cooperate, coupled with the significant economic interests in HMS stocks, led to a period of inevitable conflict between coastal states and the distant water fishing nations (DWFNs), which exploited these stocks, and the ultimate negotiation of *UNFA*, signed in 1995, as an "implementing agreement" for the relevant elements of the *UNCLOS*.

A full consideration of the impact and management innovations of *UNFA* is beyond the scope of this chapter, but a central aspect is the confirmation that regional fisheries management organizations (RFMOs) would be the primary mechanisms by which the *UNCLOS* obligation to cooperate is to be given effect. For example, if such an organization has "competence" over a defined fishery or fisheries, then coastal and fishing states are to "give effect to their duty to cooperate by becoming members of such organization[s] or participants in such arrangement."[13] ICCAT, although established in the 1970s (pursuant to a convention signed in 1966, well before the *UNCLOS*), is the RFMO with international management responsibility for the ABFT (one of approximately thirty species under its purview).

INTERNATIONAL COMMISSION FOR THE CONSERVATION OF ATLANTIC TUNAS—MANDATE, STRUCTURE, AND RECORD

ICCAT was established and in operation by the early 1970s, in response to widespread concerns about overexploitation and lack of management of tuna and other migratory species.[14] Its governing body is the commission (comprised of the contracting parties to the convention), and its work is conducted through a number of constituent bodies, including a Standing Committee on Statistics and Research (SCRS) and a Conservation and Management Measures Compliance Committee (COC).[15] ABFT management measures are based on western and eastern stocks, divided geographically (despite concerns about the scope of inter-mixing of stocks as referred to above).

The first TACs for ABFT were established in 1981 (again based on western and eastern stocks). In the following decades, a number of management measures were recommended to contracting parties, including, *inter alia*, size limits; area and time closures; bycatch restrictions; and enforcement and compliance measures, including monitoring and surveillance, a vessel registry, and port state inspection.[16] Following years of decline in stocks, long-term recovery and rebuilding programs were put in place following 2006, including long-term TAC allocations and additional measures.[17] The management of ABFT over the years since the establishment of ICCAT, despite some successes and limited recoveries, was regarded as a large-scale failure, as stated by ICCAT's own independent review in 2008:

> ICCAT [*contracting parties*'] performance in managing fisheries on bluefin tuna particularly in the eastern Atlantic and Mediterranean Sea is widely regarded as an international disgrace and the international community which has entrusted the management of this iconic species to ICCAT deserve better performance from ICCAT than it has received to date.[18]

The reasons for this record are common to many RFMOs and include rejection of optimistic TAC recommendations in favour of even higher levels; failure of parties to comply with agreed management obligations, including data collection and enforcement measures against their own nationals; and the use of a consensus approach to decision-making (to avoid possible objection procedures). In recent years, reform efforts have focused on amendment of the convention to better incorporate sustainability principles, development of improved harvest control rules (HCR), and implementation of a management strategy evaluation (MSE) methodology.[19] There are signs of improvement, but political will and effective enforcement are still absolute requirements for eventual success. In this regard, it should be noted that at its 2017 meeting, the commission (based on some initial favourable results from rebuilding efforts), agreed on increases in the TAC for the eastern ABFT from 28,200 tonnes in 2018 to 36,000 tonnes in 2020.

Management at the National Level—Canada

FISHERIES ACT AND RELATED MEASURES

The Canadian ABFT allocation, within the overall western Atlantic TAC set by ICCAT, is relatively small when compared to the eastern Atlantic and Mediterranean quotas discussed above. For 2018, Canada was allocated 515.9 tonnes (including scientific catches and bycatch from other fisheries), or about 22 percent of the western Atlantic total of 2,350,020 tonnes.[20]

There are approximately 775 individual licences issued in Atlantic Canada and Quebec, for the Gulf of St. Lawrence, the Scotian Shelf, Bay of Fundy, and Newfoundland and Labrador.[21] These are divided among seven geographically defined inshore fleets, and an offshore licence, with additional allocations for Aboriginal fisheries, scientific research (catch and release), and "other fleets" (i.e. bycatch from directed fisheries for swordfish and other tuna). In addition, a catch-and-release charter boat fishery is licenced in some areas, with an allowance made for mortality from this activity.[22]

Management of the ABFT fishery is the responsibility of the Department of Fisheries and Oceans (DFO), acting under the authority of the federal *Fisheries Act*.[23] The department allocates the available TAC to the various fleets, and in cooperation with the industry defines an integrated fisheries management plan (IFMP) for ABFT.[24] While IFMPs are not directly enforceable,[25] the measures set out can be subject to further regulations (see below) and incorporated as binding conditions of licences. This allows for a range of enforcement actions, including suspensions/terminations of licences for violations of their terms,[26] or prosecution, whether for fishing without a permit, or violating the regulations or the terms of a permit.[27]

The applicable IFMP sets out a number of significant management measures that are given effect in this manner, including the following:

- Strict log-book requirements on all fishing activity, including "the provision of information on all discards, dead or alive"; these reporting requirements form the basis of Canada's fulfillment of its reporting obligations to ICCAT.[28]
- Individual reporting of each fish caught, which must be "tagged and tracked to market so that the end product is traceable."[29]

- Closed seasons and areas, including special protected areas (such as the Gully Marine Protected Area) limits.
- Size limits.
- Gear restrictions (rod and reel and tended line fisheries in inshore fleets). Extensive catch reporting in ports, with dockside monitoring required for all catch.
- Prohibition of transshipment at sea.
- On-board observers where required, with a target of 5 percent coverage.[30]

As noted above, some of these measures have been given regulatory effect, in particular through the *Atlantic Fishery Regulations 1985*.[31] These include, *inter alia*, close times,[32] weight limits,[33] gear restrictions,[34] bycatch reporting,[35] and tagging procedures and requirements.[36]

Prosecutions for violation of the regulations and licence terms and conditions related to ABFT fishing can result in significant penalties, and in recent years there has been some indication that courts are willing to take seriously the deterrent purposes of both fines and other penalties,[37] in the light of the high profits available in the industry. In *R v. Henneberry*[38] in 2009, the Nova Scotia Court of Appeal considered penalties imposed at trial for various offences committed by a fishing company and several individuals. During a three-month period, five vessels fishing under two companies and three individual licences, had caught 176 ABFT, of which 135 were taken in contravention of the Act and regulations; the illegally caught fish had been sold for a total of $1,196,412.23.[39] The offences included a litany of violations:

> [T]he eight appellants were convicted on March 1, 2006 on a host of charges . . . failing to immediately enter confirmation numbers; failing to return incidental catch; the use of a tuna license concurrently with a shark license; failing to hail immediately; permitting an unauthorized person to fish a licence; fishing while a temporary replacement permit was in place; fishing without authorization; fishing without a fisher's registration card; and selling illegally caught fish.[40]

The penalties imposed by the trial judge included individual fines and penalties applicable under section 78 of the *Fisheries Act*, ranging from $500.00 to $25,000.00 for the corporate defendant (coupled with a one-year licence suspension under section 79.1). The more significant penalty, however, was the levying of an amount of $643,234.00 under section 79 of the Act, which provides as follows:

> 79. Where a person is convicted of an offence under this Act and the court is satisfied that as a result of committing the offence the person acquired monetary benefits or monetary benefits accrued to the person, the court may, notwithstanding the maximum amount of any fine that may otherwise be imposed under this Act, order the person to pay an additional fine in an amount equal to the court's finding of the amount of those monetary benefits.

The trial judge interpreted this provision as allowing her to impose a penalty based on the gross sale proceeds from the seventy fish caught as a result of the most serious violations. On appeal, both the Nova Scotia Supreme Court and the Nova Scotia Court of Appeal found this approach to be within the parameters of section 79, which is not restricted to a narrow definition of net profits.[41]

ALTERNATIVE APPROACHES UNDER THE *SPECIES AT RISK ACT*

Given the serious decline in ABFT stocks in past decades, measures related to endangered species protection have been proposed at both the international and national levels. In 2010 an effort to have ABFT listed for a ban on trade under the *Convention on International Trade in Endangered Species of Wild Fauna and Flora* (*CITES*) failed,[42] with Canada being an opposing state. Similarly, a move to have ABFT listed as endangered under the United States' *Endangered Species Act of 1973*[43] was rejected in 2011, although it was listed as a "species of concern."[44]

In May 2011, the Committee on the Status of Endangered Wildlife in Canada (COSEWIC), the independent committee of experts that designates species as within "at-risk" categories under the *Species at Risk Act* (*SARA*),[45] proposed that ABFT be listed as "endangered"[46]—a status which, if ultimately accepted and implemented by the government, could have led to extensive recovery measures, including widespread prohibitions on taking and killing of the species.[47] A negative preliminary response was prepared for DFO in 2011,[48] and in May 2017 the government formally decided not to designate ABFT under *SARA*.[49] The reasons focused on the socio-economic impact of a small, but valuable fishery, including impact on the Aboriginal fishery, and pointed to more recent ICCAT assessments that indicated improved stock status.[50] By way of response to concerns raised, the government promised to update the ABFT IFMP, including consideration of increased observer coverage.

While *SARA* designation may have been an attractive option for those who see the species as under continuing threat from exploitation throughout its range, the possibility appears to be off the table for the foreseeable future. Moreover, it has not really been demonstrated that designation in Canada, with no equivalent measures taken throughout the range of the ABFT, could have a significant impact on the overall prospects of the species.

Conclusions

The fundamental challenges facing the sustainability of ABFT stocks, including enforcement of management measures, remains at the international level, as the development of truly sustainable policies and associated commitment to national compliance actions (despite some progress in recent years) continue to face resistance. At the national level in Canada, enforcement of the internationally agreed policies is feasible, given the relatively small size of the industry, the ability to track catches from origin to market, and the relatively benign fishing methods that are mandated in the regulations. The major impact on stocks, however, comes from the much larger fisheries in the eastern Atlantic, and it would be difficult for unilateral steps in Canada, such as *SARA* designation, to significantly affect that broader outlook.

It should also be noted that the adequacy of scientific information on ABFT stocks remains a concern, and both ICCAT and the Canadian government are in fact making significant efforts in this regard, including tagging programs and improving information on spawning grounds. Added to the current management difficulties is the foreseen, but yet unquantified, impact of climate change on the range, productivity, and health of these stocks.

NOTES

1 QC, Associate Professor, Schulich School of Law, Dalhousie University.

2 This section summarizes a longer discussion in J Phyne et al, "Sustainability and the Atlantic Bluefin Tuna: Science, Socioeconomic Forces, and Governance" (2013) 16:2 J Int'l Wildlife L & Pol'y at 198–204 [Phyne et al].

3 *Ibid* at 198. See also Canadian Science Advisory Secretariat (DFO), "Recovery Potential Assessment for Western Atlantic Bluefin Tuna (*Thunnus thynnus*) in Canadian Waters" Science Advisory Report 2011/056 (Ottawa: DFO, September 2011) at 3 [Science Advisory Report].

4 Phyne et al, *supra* note 2 at 198.

5 David E Richardson et al, "Discovery of a Spawning Ground Reveals Diverse Migration Strategies in Atlantic Bluefin Tuna (*Thunnus thynnus*)" (22 March 2016) 113:12 P NA S 3299, online (pdf): <pnas.org/content/113/12/3299.full.pdf>.

6 For a fuller discussion, see P Saunders & M Haward, "Politics, Science and Species Protection Law: A Comparative Consideration of Southern and Atlantic Bluefin Tuna" (2016) 47:4 Ocean Devel & Int'l L at 349–350 [Saunders & Haward]. See also Phyne et al, *supra* note 2 at 205–210, 348.

7 Saunders & Haward, *supra* note 6 at 350.

8 *Ibid.*

9 *United Nations Convention on the Law of the Sea*, 10 December 1982, 1833 UNTS 396 (entered into force 16 November 1994) [*UNCLOS*].

10 *Agreement for the Implementation of the Provisions of the United Nations Convention on the Law of the Sea of 10 December 1982 Relating to the Conservation and Management of Straddling Fish Stocks and Highly Migratory Fish Stocks* (4 August 1995, entered into force 11 November 2001), UN Doc A/CONF164/37, online: <un.org/ga/search/view_doc.asp?symbol=A/CONF.164/37&Lang=E> [*UNFA*].

11 Similar problems of transboundary management were encountered with straddling stocks, which exist at the limits of the EEZ and adjacent high seas areas. These stocks are also dealt with in *UNFA*, but are not addressed in this paper.

12 *UNCLOS*, *supra* note 9, art 4(1).

13 *UNFA*, *supra* note 10, art 8(3). This obligation can be satisfied by agreeing to apply the conservation and management measures established by the organization.

14 Saunders & Haward, *supra* note 6 at 350.

15 For a more complete review of the organs of ICCAT, their functions, and decision-making procedures, see Phyne et al, *supra* note 2 at 219–221.

16 See *ibid* at 221–223 for a discussion of management measures put in place by ICCAT from the 1980s onward.

17 See the discussion of the "rebuilding" efforts in Saunders & Haward, *supra* note 6 at 351.

18 International Commission for the Conservation of Atlantic Tunas, "Report of the Independent Performance Review of International Commission for the Conservation of Atlantic Tunas (ICCAT)" (2008) at 22, online (pdf): <iccat.int/Documents/Other/PERFORM_%20REV_TRI_LINGUAL.pdf>.

19 See the discussion of recent reform efforts in Saunders & Haward, *supra* note 6 at 351–353.

20 ICCAT, "Recommendation by ICCAT for an Interim Conservation and Management Plan for Western Atlantic Bluefin Tuna", PLE 17-06 (November 2018), online (pdf): <iccat.int/Documents/Recs/compendiopdf-e/2017-06-e.pdf>.

21 For fleet allocations by percentage share, see e.g., DFO, "Bluefin Tuna—Atlantic Canada" (2012), online: <dfo-mpo.gc.ca/fisheries-peches/ifmp-gmp/bluefin-tuna-thon-rouge/bluefin-thonrougeatl-eng.html>. PEI and Southwest Nova have had the highest allocations, for a combined share of over 50 percent of the inshore allocations.

22 *Ibid.*

23 *Fisheries Act*, RSC 1985, c F-14.

24 See *ABFT Integrated Fisheries Management Plan (IFMP) 2007*, online: <dfo-mpo.gc.ca/fisheries-peches/ifmp-gmp/bluefin-tuna-thon-rouge/bluefin-thonrouge2007-eng.html>. Annex I sets out the terms of reference for the Atlantic Large Pelagic Advisory Committee (ALPAC). The IFMP was updated in 2017, online: <dfo-mpo.gc.ca/fisheries-peches/ifmp-gmp/bluefin-tuna-thon-rouge/bluefin-tuna-thonrouge2017-eng.html>.

25 The following provision is required in all IFMPs:

This IFMP is not a legally binding instrument which can form the basis of a legal challenge. The IFMP can be modified at any time and does not fetter the Minister's discretionary powers set out in the Fisheries Act. DFO, "IFMP Template—Appendix A" (2018), online: <dfo-mpo.gc.ca/fisheries-peches/ifmp-gmp/guidance-guide/preparing-ifmp-pgip-elaboration-eng.html#app-a>.

26 The ability of DFO to administratively suspend or refuse renewal of licenses can, in many circumstances, provide a more serious effective penalty than a fine or similar measure, and can be done more expeditiously, without the time and cost of a prosecution.

27 For the prosecution powers and penalties under the *Fisheries Act*, see s 78, ss 78.1–78.6, s 79, and ss 79.1–79.7. Ticketable offences are dealt with in s 79.7.

28 For a summary of current measures at DFO, see "Atlantic Bluefin Tuna—Monitoring and Enforcement" (2010), online: *DFO* <dfo-mpo.gc.ca/international/tuna-thon/Enforcement-eng.htm>.

29 *Ibid.*

30 *Ibid.*

31 *Atlantic Fishery Regulations 1985*, SOR/1986-21.

32 *Ibid*, s 99, Schedule XXV.

33 *Ibid*, s 102.

34 *Ibid*, s 100.

35 *Ibid*, s 103.

36 *Ibid*, s 104.

37 As noted earlier, suspensions of licences can also have a significant impact. In a 2016 case involving violations arising from a charter boat trip (intended to be catch-and-release), three fishers were fined a total of $ 65,000 and had their licenses suspended for five years. See "Zappa 1 Tuna Fishermen Handed Five-year Suspension after Guilty Pleas", *CBC News* (29 February 2016), online: <cbc.ca/news/canada/nova-scotia/zappa-1-tuna-fishery-licencesuspension-antigonish-nova-scotia-1.3469650>.

38 *R v Henneberry*, 2009 NSCA 112 (CanLII).

39 *Ibid* at para 4.

40 *Ibid* at para 5.

41 *Ibid*. In *Henneberry*, the Court of Appeal left open the possibility that a "net proceeds" approach could be applied, depending on the facts, but that this decision was best left to the trial judge for a full assessment of the evidence. It was further noted that in some cases, the additional fish will in fact provide a monetary benefit to the "bottom line" beyond a simple net profit calculation. *Ibid* at para 65.

42 See "CITES Press Release: Governments Not Ready for Trade Ban on Bluefin Tuna" (18 March 2010), online: *CITES* <cites.org/eng/news/pr/2010/20100318_tuna.shtml>.

43 *Endangered Species Act of 1973*, 16 USC c 35 § 1531–1534.

44 See National Oceanic and Atmospheric Administration, "NOAA Issues Atlantic Tuna Management Measures", online: <noaa.gov/media-release/noaa-issues-atlantic-tuna-management-measures>. See also National Oceanic and Atmospheric Administration, "Status Review Report of Atlantic Bluefin Tuna" (20 May 2011), which lists the Bluefin as a "species of concern", online: <repository.library.noaa.gov/view/noaa/17716>.

45 *Species at Risk Act*, SC 2002, c 29. See the discussion of the COSEWIC action in Saunders & Haward, *supra* note 6 at 354. For a summary of the process and responsible agencies, see Environment and Climate Change Canada, "About the Species at Risk Act", online: <canada.ca/en/environment-climate-change/services/environmental-enforcement/acts-regulations/about-species-at-risk-act.html>. For a critique of *SARA* in the marine context, see J Hutchings, T Stephens & DL VanderZwaag, "Marine Species at Risk Protection in Australia and Canada: Paper Promises, Paltry Progressions" (2016) 47:4 Ocean Devel & Int'l L at 238–246.

46 COSEWIC, "COSEWIC Assessment and Status Report on the Atlantic Bluefin Tuna (*Thunnus thynnus*) in Canada" (May 2011), online: <registrelep.gc.ca/default.asp?lang=En&n=BDA1F68B-1>. The status report focused on the severe decline of stocks in the face of over-fishing throughout its range, effects of seismic and other activities and the possible impact of the Deepwater Horizon spill on spawning areas.

47 See the discussion at Saunders & Haward, *supra* note 6 at 354.

48 Science Advisory Report, *supra* note 3.

49 *List of Wildlife Species at Risk (Decisions Not to Add Certain Species) Order*, SI/2017-24.

50 *Ibid*.

18

Challenges in Receiving *Species at Risk Act* Protections: A Killer (Whale) Case Study

Dyna Tuytel and Margot Venton[1]

The *Species at Risk Act*[2] (*SARA*), enacted in 2002 and which came into force fully in 2004, includes important tools to protect species at risk but has been plagued by poor implementation. Since it was enacted, listed species have thus far continued to decline, on average by 2.7 percent annually.[3]

This chapter uses a *SARA*-listed endangered aquatic species, the Southern Resident Killer Whale (SRKW) population, to illustrate the challenges that listed species face in actually receiving the protections promised by *SARA*. These challenges can occur even when a species is listed as endangered, is an iconic charismatic megafauna species, and is entirely under federal jurisdiction.

The plight of SRKW illustrates two fundamental problems with *SARA* implementation: first, reluctance on the part of the responsible federal ministers to implement its protections at all, whether they are discretionary or mandatory, sometimes necessitating litigation by civil society groups; and second, failure to implement *SARA* in a timely manner that is commensurate with halting and reversing the decline of species and degradation of their habitat before it is too late. These problems undermine the purpose of *SARA*.

Overview of Purposes and Selected Provisions of the *Species at Risk Act*

The purposes of *SARA* are to prevent species from being extirpated or becoming extinct and to provide for the recovery of species that are endangered or threatened due to human activity.[4]

SARA sets out a listing process to identify species at risk. Once listed, species and their habitat receive certain legal protections:

- It is an offence to kill, harm, harass, capture, or take an individual member of a species (s 32(1));
- The competent minister must, within a specified timeline, prepare a recovery strategy that identifies the species' critical habitat and threats to the species and its critical habitat, describes the broad strategy to be taken to address those threats, and indicates when an action plan will be completed (ss 37, 41(1), 42 & 43);
- The competent minister must prepare one or more action plans based on the recovery strategy, which must include: identification of critical habitat, including any portions not yet protected; examples of activities likely to result in destruction of critical habitat; as well as a statement of the measures proposed to protect critical habitat and implement the recovery strategy, including when these measures will take place (ss 47–50);
- Once critical habitat is identified for a species under federal jurisdiction (aquatic species, migratory birds and species with critical habitat on federal lands), the competent minister must ensure that critical habitat is legally protected from destruction within 180 days, at which point it becomes an offence to destroy critical habitat (ss 57–58);
- Activities affecting listed species, or any part of their critical habitat require permits, which the competent minister may only issue if he or she is of the opinion that all reasonable alternatives have been considered and the best solution adopted, measures have been taken to minimize the activity's impact, and the activity will not jeopardize survival or recovery (ss 73–74); and
- Listed species and their critical habitat are protected from the potentially adverse effects of proposed projects or activities (ss 79 and 77(1)).

Key Facts about Southern Resident Killer Whales

SRKW were listed under Schedule I of *SARA* in 2001.[5] They are listed as "endangered," defined as "facing imminent extirpation or extinction."[6] The SRKW recovery strategy was finalized in 2008. The recovery strategy has been amended twice since 2008. It was first amended in 2011 following litigation and subsequently amended again in 2018 to include identification of additional critical habitat for these populations and to provide minor updates to background and species information.[7] The action plan was finalized in 2017. Since they were listed, the population has decreased from approximately 85 to 72 as of April 2020.

The competent ministers responsible for protection of the SRKW and their critical habitat are the minister of the environment, who, as the minister responsible for Parks Canada, is charged with protecting the small portions of critical habitat that are on federal lands administered by Parks Canada, and the minister of fisheries and oceans.

There are three types of killer whales in Canadian Pacific waters: offshore, Bigg's (or transient), and resident. They each have distinct diets, genetics, morphology, and behaviour. They do not interbreed and avoid each other rather than interact. The two resident populations off the British Columbia coast—the threatened northern residents and the endangered SRKW—have overlapping but distinct ranges, are linguistically distinct and genetically isolated, and do not interact.[8]

SRKW are among the world's best-studied marine mammals. They have been closely monitored, including with an annual census, since 1976. The census accounts for the SRKW population as of July 1 and December 31 each year. As of the last census, the population of SRKW is 74.[9] SRKW have a unique social structure and language. They feed almost exclusively on salmon, and particularly large, fatty Chinook salmon. They have evolved in an important migratory corridor for Chinook salmon, and their location and movements are dictated largely by their diet.[10]

SRKW critical habitat is located in the transboundary waters of the Salish Sea, off the south coast of British Columbia and the north coast of Washington state. Critical habitat includes not only this area itself but also its important attributes for SRKW: acoustic quality, marine environmental quality, and the availability of Chinook salmon.[11]

SRKW are considered endangered due to their small population size and low reproductive rate, as well as exposure to three main threats: lack of availability of their primary prey, Chinook salmon; acoustic and physical disturbance from vessels; and contamination of their environment.[12]

Unfortunately, this already endangered population is experiencing an ongoing decline. The threat that appears most urgent and most directly correlated with their current decline is the lack of availability of Chinook salmon—a threat that is exacerbated by physical and acoustic disturbance from boats.[13]

History of Efforts to Achieve *Species at Risk Act* Protections for Southern Resident Killer Whale

CRITICAL HABITAT: LITIGATION TO ACHIEVE IDENTIFICATION AND LEGAL PROTECTION

To recover species to healthy population levels, *SARA* prescribes a process for species at risk to be listed and given legal protections, which process includes the development of a recovery strategy.[14] Subsection 41(1)(c) of *SARA* requires the recovery strategy for a species to identify critical habitat, including biological features, and threats to it.

The first SRKW recovery strategy was finalized in 2011, approximately eighteen months behind the mandatory timelines in section 42 of *SARA* (the 2011 *Recovery Strategy*).[15] Delay resulted from disagreements between the recovery team preparing the recovery strategy and DFO, and to a lesser extent, the Department of National Defence, over whether to include information identifying critical habitat and, in particular, references to the acoustic degradation and prey availability threats.[16] Ultimately, the 2011 *Recovery Strategy* did identify the presence and availability of prey as a component of critical habitat, and included diminished prey availability, chemical and biological contamination, and acoustic degradation as threats to critical habitat.[17]

Sections 57–58 of *SARA* require that the critical habitat identified in a recovery strategy be legally protected from destruction within 180 days of the recovery strategy being finalized in one of two ways. It can be protected indirectly under another Act of Parliament, if this is confirmed through a protection statement under section 58(5)(b) of *SARA* that describes how critical habitat is already protected through the other Act. If it is not already protected by another Act, the minister must issue a protection order under section

58(4) of *SARA*, which applies the prohibition against destruction of critical habitat under section 58(1) to the habitat described in the protection order.[18]

In the case of SRKW, the minister of fisheries and oceans initially took the approach of issuing a protection statement that relied on habitat protection through non-binding policy and guidelines, and on discretionary provisions of the *Fisheries Act*. Further, the minister took the position that *SARA* only required protection of the geophysical attributes of critical habitat, and not the biological attributes, such as prey availability.[19]

Nine conservation organizations filed an application for judicial review in October 2008, alleging that the minister erred by relying on non-binding policy, prospective legislation and ministerial discretion, none of which legally protect critical habitat for the purposes of section 58 of *SARA*, and further erred by including only geophysical elements of critical habitat, not biological attributes.[20]

In February of 2009, DFO reversed itself and the minister replaced the protection statement with a protection order. DFO refused to confirm that the protection order protected biological features of critical habitat when the applicants sought confirmation. The applicants filed a second application for judicial review, this time of the protection order, on the basis that it was limited to geospatial areas or geophysical elements of critical habitat and excluded biological attributes.[21]

The two applications were consolidated and heard by Justice Russell of the Federal Court. Russell J. held that a protection statement can only be used in place of a protection order where the legal protection under other Acts of Parliament is equal to that provided under a protection order; ministerial discretion under another Act of Parliament is not adequate legal protection of critical habitat under section 58 of *SARA*, nor are prospective laws or regulations. He further held, as the Federal Court had decided previously[22] and as the minister conceded during the proceeding, that critical habitat includes not only a location but also ecosystem features, and therefore, it was unlawful to limit the protection order to geophysical aspects alone.[23]

The minister appealed the Federal Court's declaration that ministerial discretion under the *Fisheries Act* cannot legally protect critical habitat for the purposes of section 58. The Federal Court of Appeal dismissed the appeal and confirmed that "Ministerial discretion does not legally protect habitat within the meaning of section 58," which instead requires non-discretionary, compulsory protection. The court also re-iterated that critical habitat includes both a geographic location and the attributes that make it important for the species.[24]

The Federal Court of Appeal further clarified the importance of critical habitat protection, and the mandatory nature of *SARA* protections.[25] The court held that Parliament's intent "was to provide for compulsory and non-discretionary legal protection for the identified critical habitat of listed endangered or threatened aquatic species," and that section 58 should be interpreted accordingly.[26] The court further held that

> A textual, contextual and purposive analysis of section 58 shows that Parliament is precisely seeking to avoid the destruction of identified critical habitat of listed endangered and threatened aquatic species through any means, including through activities authorized under discretionary permits or licences.[27]

Under section 58(1) and an order made under section 58(4), the critical habitat of SRKW is now protected against destruction of "any part" of it, including the biological "parts" or attributes such as acoustic quality.[28]

This example illustrates two challenges that endangered species have experienced in receiving *SARA* protections. First, ensuring implementation of the protections promised by *SARA* too often requires extraordinary efforts by civil society. Second, delay in meeting mandatory timelines under *SARA* is a perennial problem, even for aquatic species that are unambiguously within federal jurisdiction.[29] The recovery strategy for SRKW was delayed for eighteen months because DFO did not want to fully identify critical habitat and threats to it. The action plan for SRKW was delayed by four years; this is discussed further in the next section.

THE SOUTHERN RESIDENT KILLER WHALE ACTION PLAN: DELAYS AND A LACK OF ACTION

Action plans are one of the key practical instruments in *SARA* for achieving its purposes of preventing extinction and providing for recovery. As described above, they must identify critical habitat, including any portions that have not yet been protected; include a "statement of the measures that are to be taken to protect the species' critical habitat"; and include a statement of the measures that will be taken "to implement the recovery strategy, including those that address the threats to the species and those that help to achieve the population and distribution objectives," and when those measures will take place.[30] The minister must make any regulations that in his or her opinion are necessary to implement the measures, or recommend them to the Governor in Council if they concern protection of critical habitat.[31] The minister may do so using powers under any other Act of Parliament.[32]

The SRKW Action Plan was published four years behind schedule. The 2011 *Recovery Strategy* established a deadline of March 31, 2013, for the action plan. DFO made a draft action plan available for public comment in March 2014 and made a proposed action plan available for public comment in June 2016. The final action plan was published in March 2017.

There is a troubling lack of action in the action plan. Instead of setting out measures to protect critical habitat and implement the recovery strategy, with timelines for each measure, it is primarily a plan for further research and monitoring, replete with words such as "examine," "investigate," "identify," "assess," and "monitor"; the action plan itself states that "the majority of activities in the plan focus on research."[33] Where it refers to actually implementing measures, it most often does so using the non-committal formulation of "investigate . . . and implement where appropriate." Where it does refer to some more concrete-sounding outcomes, those outcomes are characterized as "guidelines and/or regulations," leaving open the question of whether measures will be enforceable. The timelines given for several items are "Unknown" or "Uncertain."

The action plan does not comply with either the broad purposes or the specific requirements of *SARA*. It should contain concrete actions that help recover SRKW. Instead, it fails to mitigate or prevent threats to SRKW or their critical habitat or prevent extinction and provide for recovery. By focusing on research to the exclusion of action, it maintains status quo conditions. The action plan does not "implement" the recovery strategy, as required by section 49(1)(d) of *SARA*. It does not describe how the minister will use his or her powers under *SARA* or other Acts of Parliament to make regulations to implement the action plan.

This example illustrates challenges to species receiving *SARA* protections in two ways: first, the chronic problem of delay in *SARA* implementation, and second, the fact that formal implementation of *SARA* provisions does not necessarily translate into protection on the ground.

THE TRANS MOUNTAIN EXPANSION PROJECT ENVIRONMENTAL ASSESSMENT: LITIGATION OVERTURNS AN UNLAWFUL FIRST APPROVAL UNDER THE *SPECIES AT RISK ACT*, AND A SECOND APPROVAL WITHOUT CONCRETE MITIGATION FOR SOUTHERN RESIDENT KILLER WHALES EVADES JUDICIAL REVIEW

The Trans Mountain Expansion Project is set to triple the capacity of the existing Trans Mountain oil pipeline from Alberta to British Columbia. The number of oil tankers departing the Westridge Marine Terminal in Burnaby and travelling through SRKW critical habitat to the open ocean will increase from approximately five to approximately thirty-four Aframax class tankers per month. The increased oil tanker traffic will adversely affect SRKW by exacerbating physical and acoustic disturbance in critical habitats and by increasing the risk of an oil spill or vessel strike of a whale in critical habitat.

The National Energy Board (the NEB) (now the Canada Energy Regulator [CER]) conducted the review and environmental assessment of the project. It concluded that project-related marine shipping "is likely to result in significant adverse effects to the southern resident killer whale," will "further contribute to cumulative effects that are already jeopardizing the survival and recovery of [SRKW]," will "impact numerous individuals of the [SRKW] population in a habitat identified as critical to [their] recovery," and will result in vessel noise that is "a threat to the acoustic integrity of . . . critical habitat."[34] It found that the project-related death of an individual SRKW could "result in population-level impacts and could jeopardize recovery."[35] It cited the recovery strategy statement that "while the probability of [SRKW] being exposed to an oil spill is low, the impact of such an event is potentially catastrophic."[36]

Nevertheless, the NEB recommended approval of the project without conditions to mitigate these effects, and the Governor in Council followed this recommendation. Two conservation organizations represented by Ecojustice sought and were granted leave for a judicial review of the Governor in Council's approval, arguing that it had failed to comply with sections 79(2) and 77(1) of *SARA*.

As stated above, the express purposes of *SARA* include preventing wildlife species from becoming extinct and providing for the recovery of species that are endangered due to human activity.[37] In support of these purposes, *SARA*'s protective provisions, including sections 77 and 79, work together to protect endangered species from existing threats and ensure that the effects of new activities are addressed before they begin to prevent extinction and allow for recovery. To give effect to sections 79 and 77 of *SARA*, the NEB and the Governor in Council had to consider the project in a way that fulfilled these broad statutory purposes.

Section 77 of *SARA* is intended to protect critical habitat from potential harm that may result from activities authorized under other Acts of Parliament. Subsection 77(1) applies to any person or body other than a competent minister who is authorized under any other Act to "issue or approve . . . any . . . authorization that authorizes an activity that may result in the destruction of any part of the critical habitat" of a *SARA*-listed species. Before issuing any authorization, this person must consider the impact on critical habitat and be of the opinion that "all feasible measures will be taken to minimize the impact of the activity on the species' critical habitat."

The applicants argued that the Governor in Council erred in authorizing the project because, when faced with the NEB's factual findings indicating that project-related shipping may destroy critical habitat, the Governor in Council either failed to form an opinion that all feasible measures would be taken, or, if it did, that opinion was unreasonable in the absence of any conditions to mitigate the effects of marine shipping on SRKW critical habitat identified by the NEB.

Section 79 of *SARA* is intended to protect endangered species and their critical habitat from the effects of new projects. It ensures that the effects of new activities that might further imperil species at risk are addressed as part of the review and approval process before those new activities occur. Section 79(2) of *SARA* was triggered by the *Canadian Environmental Assessment Act, 2012*[38] (*CEAA 2012*) and applies when a proposed project that is subject to an environmental assessment is likely to affect a listed species or its critical habitat.[39] Subsection 79(1) requires the person conducting the environmental assessment or making the determination to notify the competent minister(s) if the project is likely to affect a *SARA*-listed species or its critical habitat. Subsection 79(2) further requires that person to identify the project's effects on the listed species and its critical habitat and to "ensure that measures are taken to avoid or lessen" them. The measures must be taken in a way that is consistent with any applicable recovery strategy or action plan.

The applicants argued that section 79(2) should have applied because shipping is part of the "designated project" as defined in section 2(1) of *CEAA 2012* (being "incidental" to it). Despite its factual conclusions about the effects of marine shipping on SRKW, the NEB took the position that section 79(2) of

SARA did not apply to its assessment of shipping, on the basis that the project for the purposes of *CEAA 2012* included only the pipeline and facilities, up to the Westridge Marine Terminal. The NEB conceded that it had not ensured any measures to avoid or lessen the effects of shipping on SRKW on its recommended conditions.[40] The Governor in Council approved the NEB's recommendations and adopted its recommended conditions without changes.[41]

The application for judicial review on *SARA* grounds was consolidated with other applications brought by First Nations and municipalities and heard by the Federal Court of Appeal. The court decided in *Tsleil-Waututh Nation v. Canada (Attorney General)*[42] that the NEB had unreasonably excluded project-related shipping from the scope of the project in its environmental assessment, and as a result failed to comply with mandatory requirements of *CEAA 2012* and *SARA*, such that the Governor in Council was not able to assess the project's effects and make its decision. The court emphasized that section 79(2) of *SARA* required the NEB to identify all feasible measures to avoid or lessen the project's effects on SRKW so that "the Governor in Council would be in a position to see that, if approved, the Project was not approved until all technically and economically feasible mitigation measures within the authority of the federal government were in place."[43] The court further held that section 77(1) did not apply to the order in council because that decision itself did not authorize marine shipping.[44] The court quashed the approval and remitted the matter back to the Governor in Council for redetermination.[45]

In response to the court's decision, the Governor in Council ordered the NEB to conduct a reconsideration process to assess the effects of project-related shipping. Following the reconsideration, the NEB released a revised report.[46] It found that project-related shipping will have significant adverse environmental effects on the SRKW and their critical habitat by increasing underwater noise and the risk of ship strikes.

Nevertheless, the NEB did not recommend any conditions to lessen or avoid effects on SRKW; instead, it made "recommendations" of actions the Governor in Council could take, some of which were directly or indirectly relevant to SRKW. The recommendations are distinct from conditions on the project: they lack timelines or any guarantee that they will be in place before operations begin or remain in place for the duration of operations, they are not enforceable, and they are not known to be feasible or to be effective in reducing effects. The NEB decided that these recommendations satisfied section 79(2) of *SARA* despite, in its words, not being immediate mitigation measures.

The Governor in Council approved the project for a second time based on the NEB's reconsideration report, relying on the recommendations to satisfy section 79(2) of *SARA*, and concluding that the significant adverse environmental effects were justified in the circumstances.[47]

The two conservation organizations represented by Ecojustice sought leave for an application for judicial review of this second approval. They sought leave to argue that the recommendations did not satisfy section 79(2), and that the Governor in Council had no jurisdiction to issue the order in council until the requirements of section 79(2) were met, and no jurisdiction to decide under *CEAA 2012* that significant adverse environmental effects are justified when those effects are contrary to the purposes and provisions of *SARA*. They were denied leave in a decision by a single judge of the Federal Court of Appeal, on the basis that the applications did not raise a "fairly arguable case," which is the leave test for judicial review of a federal pipeline approval.[48]

The leave decision took an arguably novel approach to the "arguable case" test and appeared to reflect a misunderstanding of the basis for the proposed application.[49] The applicants had taken the position that section 79(2) of *SARA* creates independent, mandatory requirements when a project undergoes a federal environmental assessment that are a condition precedent to approval by the Governor in Council, and therefore that an approval relying on recommendations rather than on immediate mitigation measures was unlawful. This was based on the court's confirmation in *Tsleil-Waututh* that section 79(2) requires measures to be in place before a project is approved.[50] The leave decision seemed to contradict *Tsleil-Waututh*, treating this proposition as not even fairly arguable.

The applicants unsuccessfully sought leave to appeal this leave decision to the Supreme Court, to address two questions: what the duty in section 79(2) of *SARA* requires, and whether the Governor in Council has jurisdiction under *CEAA 2012* to justify significant adverse effects on a federally protected species that would not be permissible under *SARA*. Because they did not get leave at the Federal Court of Appeal or the Supreme Court, these questions remain unanswered.

This example illustrates four challenges with *SARA* protection: the need for civil society to resort to litigation due to government inaction (in this case, for *SARA* to be applied in the first place, and in an unsuccessful attempt to have it applied consistently with its purposes and provisions), the fact that litigation is an imperfect tool for ensuring *SARA* protections are applied, the ongoing uncertainty concerning what *SARA* requires that result in a lack of protection, and the inability of a critical habitat protection order to protect critical habitat in and of itself.

With respect to the second challenge, litigation is an imperfect tool due to its inherent unpredictability and procedural hurdles. The leave requirement hurdle that prevented the challenge to the second approval from being heard only applies to approvals of pipeline projects assessed by the NEB; if the case had concerned the approval of a different category of project, the applicants' arguments would have been heard and decided. Furthermore, the decision to deny leave was not expected by the parties.[51] As a result of the leave test and unexpected leave decision, litigation could not resolve the question of how *SARA* applied in this case.

With respect to the third challenge, uncertainty in the law, the Federal Court has held that legal uncertainty around *SARA* has "environmental costs" and may result in "serious collateral consequences for other species in need of protection but lacking champions to bring their cause before the Court."[52] In this case, the uncertainty has broad implications. A total of 578 species are listed under *SARA*. Any federal environmental assessment of a project likely to affect one or more of them will require compliance with *SARA* and trigger section 79. As of September 24, 2019, 64 of 68 projects undergoing federal environmental assessments by the Impact Assessment Agency, Canadian Nuclear Safety Commission, or CER may affect one or more *SARA*-listed species and therefore could trigger section 79. The legal uncertainty around section 79(2) resulting from the leave decision could be exploited in future.

Finally, this example illustrates that a critical habitat protection order does not, in and of itself, protect critical habitat. This project was approved twice despite involving activities identified in the recovery strategy as likely to result in destruction of SRKW critical habitat.

EMERGENCY ORDER: A LAST RESORT

Subsection 80(1) of *SARA* enables the Governor in Council to make an emergency order to provide for the protection of a listed species on the recommendation of the competent minister. Pursuant to section 80(2), "[t]he competent minister must make the recommendation if he or she is of the opinion that the species faces imminent threats to its survival or recovery." An emergency order may include, in the case of an aquatic species, identification of habitat that is necessary for survival or recovery, and provisions requiring actions that protect the species and that habitat and prohibiting activities that may adversely affect the species and habitat (section 80(4)).

This tool has only been used twice, for the greater sage-grouse and the western chorus frog. In both cases it was only used after conservation organizations initiated litigation.[53]

Despite the legal protections afforded to SRKW and their critical habitat under *SARA*, and the existence of the 2011 *Recovery Strategy* and the *Action Plan*, as of January 2018, measures had not been taken to reduce the threats identified in the 2011 *Recovery Strategy*. DFO conducted a "science-based review of recovery actions"—a step not required by *SARA*—in 2017.[54] It revealed that only research-based, information-gathering, and monitoring measures are underway, and that DFO was unable to report at all on the status of several action plan measures.[55]

On January 30, 2018, five conservation organizations with a long-standing interest in SRKW wrote to the minister of fisheries and oceans and minister of environment to demand that they recommend an emergency order for SRKW by March 1, 2018.[56] At that time, the species' current decline had become apparent, with the population dropping to 76. Individual whales were showing signs of malnutrition, the majority of pregnancies were failing, and, troublingly, some reproductive-aged females were dying instead of living into their post-reproductive years as would normally be expected. The ongoing decline, and the size and demographics of the population, put the population in a precarious position. When DFO convened a symposium to discuss SRKW in October 2017, two of the leading experts on the population—Dr. John Ford, emeritus DFO scientist and SRKW specialist, and Dr. Lance Barrett-Lennard, a long-time SRKW researcher and a co-author of the recovery strategy—both stressed the need for urgent actions to support SRKW.

The petition to the ministers summarized the best available information on the status of SRKW and threats to them and conveyed the petitioners' position that the only reasonable conclusion to draw was that there are imminent threats to the survival and recovery of SRKW, such that the ministers must recommend an emergency order. The petition included measures that should be included in an emergency order.

Following the petition, the ministers introduced measures in the June 2018 summer season designed to help SRKW that summer, including fisheries measures and voluntary measures related to noise, and permanently, through an amendment to the allowed approach distance for SRKW in the *Marine Mammal Regulations*.[57] The petitioners considered these to be positive but inadequate steps.

The ministers also issued a summary imminent threat assessment on May 25, 2018,[58] and a complete version on July 30, 2018,[59] in which they concluded that the SRKW face imminent threats to their survival and recovery. However, the ministers did not recommend that cabinet issue an emergency order and would not confirm whether they would do so or when.

The conservation organizations then filed an application for judicial review at the Federal Court in September 2018, seeking a mandamus order compelling the ministers to comply with their duty under section 80(2) of *SARA* to recommend that the cabinet issue an emergency order, in light of their imminent threat opinion, and an order that their ongoing delay in making a recommendation was unlawful.[60] The litigation concluded when, on the eve of the deadline to file the ministers' evidence, cabinet issued an order in council stating that the ministers had recommended an emergency order but declining to make an emergency order, citing other measures that had been or would be taken.[61]

Following the conclusion of the litigation, the current recovery strategy was finalized, and the current critical habitat protection order was made in December 2018, to incorporate a new area of critical habitat, the legal protection of which was one of the petition's requests.

This petition and litigation should not have been necessary. SRKW have a recovery strategy, protected critical habitat, and an action plan—more than many listed species have—and the species and its critical habitat are entirely within federal jurisdiction. Yet, until 2018, their emergency situation was not treated as one.

Furthermore, while the federal government has taken steps with the expanded area of critical habitat and with yearly measures concerning protection of the SRKW, which are important progress, SRKW continue to decline in numbers, and new projects that will adversely affect them continue to be approved, indicating that significantly more effort is needed to reduce existing threats and to prevent new ones from emerging.

On April 14, 2021, the government of Canada announced measures to protect SRKW, including fisheries closure protocol to increase the availability of Chinook salmon and reduce vessel disturbance and contamination, interim sanctuary zones in three places, pilot closure protocol for recreational and commercial salmon fishing.[62] There is also Canada's Oceans Protection Plan, Whales Initiative, and an additional federal investment of $61.5 million for the protection of SRKW.[63] It is hoped that the plague of poor and slow implementation would not affect these measures.

Conclusions: Difficulties in Receiving *Species at Risk Act Protections*

The case of the SRKW shows that, even a species that is charismatic and an icon of the west coast, critically endangered, and entirely within federal jurisdiction—and has received, on paper, the full suite of *SARA* protections—has been granted protections belatedly, or only due to litigation forcing the government's hand, or not at all. Further, effective protection is still lacking, with the result that the species is declining. This supports two broad conclusions.

First, *SARA* and the ministers responsible for *SARA*-listed species are not doing their job if *SARA* is only implemented when civil society groups resort to litigation, and sometimes not even then. This is not a sustainable or effective way for *SARA* to be applied.

Second, *SARA* is only as good as its implementation. Research and scientific information are essential but cannot be pursued indefinitely to the exclusion of concrete action. Persistent reluctance to act, chronic foot-dragging, and the failure to make endangered species' survival and recovery a priority, undermine *SARA*'s effectiveness.

NOTES

1 Dyna Tuytel is a staff lawyer at Ecojustice Canada in Vancouver; Margot Venton is the director of the nature program at Ecojustice Canada in Vancouver.

2 SC 2002, c 29 [*SARA*].

3 World Wildlife Fund Canada, "Living Planet Report Canada: A National Look at Wildlife Loss" (Toronto: World Wildlife Fund-Canada, October 2017) at 9–10.

4 *SARA*, *supra* note 2, s 6.

5 Species at Risk Registry, "Species Profile: Killer Whale Northeast Pacific Southern Resident Population" (accessed 23 July 2021) *Government of Canada*, online: <wildlife-species.canada.ca/species-risk-registry/species/speciesDetails_e.cfm?sid=699>.

6 *SARA*, *supra* note 2, s 2(1).

7 Fisheries and Oceans Canada, *Recovery Strategy for the Northern and Southern Resident Killer Whales (*Orcinus orca*) in Canada: Species at Risk Act Recovery Strategy Series* (Ottawa: Fisheries & Oceans Canada, 2018), (accessed 26 July 2021) online (pdf): <wildlife-species.canada.ca/species-risk-registry/virtual_sara/files/plans/Rs-ResidentKillerWhale-v00-2018dec-Eng.pdf> [*Recovery Strategy*].

8 *Ibid* at 2–3.

9 Center for Whale Research, "Orcas Population" (accessed 26 July 2021), online: *Center for Whale Research* <www.whaleresearch.com/orca-population>.

10 *Recovery Strategy*, *supra* note 7 at 5, 7.

11 *Ibid* at 5, 45, 47–52.

12 *Ibid* at 17; *Canada (Fisheries and Oceans) v David Suzuki Foundation*, 2012 FCA 40 at para 27 [*Canada v David Suzuki Foundation*].

13 See Ecojustice Canada, "Petition for an Emergency Order for the Southern Resident Killer Whales under s 80 of the Species at Risk Act: To the Honourable Dominic LeBlanc, Minister of Fisheries and Oceans Canada, and the Honourable Catherine McKenna, Minister Responsible for Parks Canada Agency; on Behalf of David Suzuki Foundation, Georgia Strait Alliance, Natural Resources Defense Council, Raincoast Conservation Foundation and World Wildlife Fund Canada Prepared by Ecojustice" (2018, accessed on 26 July 2021), online (pdf): <ecojustice.ca/wp-content/uploads/2018/01/Petition-for-SRKW-Emergency-Order.pdf> at 4–9 [Emergency Order Petition].

14 *David Suzuki Foundation v Canada (Fisheries and Oceans)*, 2010 FC 1233 at para 13 [*David Suzuki Foundation v Canada*].

15 Fisheries and Oceans Canada, *Recovery Strategy for the Northern and Southern Resident Killer Whales (Orcinus orca) in Canada, Species at Risk Act Recovery Strategy Series* (Ottawa: Fisheries & Oceans Canada, 2011) [*2011 Recovery Strategy*]. A revised recovery strategy was published in 2018 to include updated critical habitat identification and threat information.

16 *David Suzuki Foundation v Canada*, *supra* note 14 at paras 13–26.

17 *2011 Recovery Strategy*, *supra* note 15 at 41.

18 *David Suzuki Foundation v Canada*, *supra* note 14 at paras 31–22.

19 *Ibid* at paras 31–36.

20 *Ibid* at para 37.

21 *Ibid* at paras 38–45.

22 See *Environmental Defence Canada v Canada (Fisheries and Oceans)*, 2009 FC 878.

23 *David Suzuki Foundation v Canada*, *supra* note 14 at para 340.

24 *Canada v David Suzuki Foundation*, *supra* note 12 at paras 150, 150.

25 *Ibid* at paras 8, 9, 115, 117, 124, 125.

26 *Ibid* at para 8.

27 *Ibid* at para 125.

28 *Critical Habitats of the Northeast Pacific Northern and Southern Resident Populations of the Killer Whale (*Orcinus orca*) Order*, SOR/2009-68. In 2018 the minister replaced this with a new order that protects the expanded area of critical habitat described in the revised 2018 recovery strategy: *Critical Habitat of the Killer Whale (*Orcinus orca*) Northeast Pacific Southern Resident Population Order* SOR/2018-278.

29 In 2014, the Federal Court heard an application for judicial review by five conservation organizations of the minister of fisheries and oceans and minister of environment's failure to comply with statutory timelines for the preparation and publication of recovery strategies, using four *SARA*-listed species (a terrestrial mammal and migratory bird for whom the minister of environment is responsible, and an aquatic mammal and a fish for whom the minister of fisheries and oceans is responsible) to represent this endemic, systemic problem: *Western Canada Wilderness Committee v Canada (Fisheries and Oceans)*, 2014 FC 148.

30 *SARA*, *supra* note 2, ss 47–50.

31 *Ibid*, ss 53, 59.

32 *Ibid*, s 54.

33 Fisheries and Oceans Canada, *Action Plan for the Northern and Southern Resident Killer Whale (*Orcinus orca*) in Canada, Species at Risk Act Action Plan Series* (Ottawa: Fisheries and Oceans Canada, 2017) at 26 (accessed 26 July 2021), online: <wildlife-species.canada.ca/species-risk-registry/document/default_e.cfm?documentID=2944> [*Action Plan*].

34 National Energy Board, *National Energy Board Report: Trans Mountain Expansion Project OH-001-2014* (Calgary: National Energy Board, May 2016) at xii, 351, 350 [NEB Report].

35 *Ibid* at 398.

36 *Ibid.*

37 *SARA*, *supra* note 2, s 6.

38 SC 2012, c 19, s 52.

39 In light of new federal environmental assessment legislation, s 79(2) of *SARA* has been amended and is now triggered by determinations under s 82(a) of (b) of the *Impact Assessment Act*, SC 2019, c 28, s 1.

40 NEB Report, *supra* note 34 at 332, 349, 350.

41 *Order in Council*, PC 2016-1069 (29 November 2016).

42 *Tsleil-Waututh Nation v Canada (Attorney General)*, 2018 FCA 153 at paras 456, 764–766 [*Tsleil-Waututh*].

43 *Ibid* at para 456.

44 *Ibid* at para 463.

45 *Ibid* at para 774.

46 National Energy Board, *Application for the Trans Mountain Expansion Project: National Energy Board Reconsideration of Aspects of Its OH-001-2014 Report as Directed by Order in Council PC 2018-1177, MH-052-2018* (Calgary: National Energy Board, February 2019) [Reconsideration Report].

47 Order in Council PC 2019-820 (18 June 2019).

48 *Raincoast Conservation Foundation v Canada (Attorney General)*, 2019 FCA 224.

49 See Nigel Bankes, Martin Olszynski & David Wright, "Federal Court of Appeal Provides Reasons in TMX Leave Applications" (September 11, 2019), online (pdf): *ABlawg* <ablawg.ca/wp-content/uploads/2019/09/Blog_NB_MO_DW_Raincoast.pdf> [Nigel Bankes et al].

50 *Tsleil-Waututh*, *supra* note 42 at para 456.

51 The respondents took no position on the leave applications. See Nigel Bankes et al, *supra* note 49 at 4.

52 *David Suzuki Foundation v Canada*, *supra* note 14 at paras 66, 245.

53 Regarding the greater sage-grouse, the Alberta Wilderness Association, Western Canada Wilderness Committee, Nature Saskatchewan, and Grasslands Naturalists brought an application for judicial review of the minister of environment's refusal to recommend an emergency order on 14 February 2012 (Federal Court File T-341-12). Cabinet ultimately issued an emergency order and the application was discontinued. Regarding the western chorus frog, see *Centre québécois de droit et de l'environnement v Canada (Environment)*, 2015 FC 773.

54 Department of Fisheries and Oceans Canada, *Southern Resident Killer Whale: A Science-based Review of Recovery Actions for Three At-risk Whale Populations* (2017 accessed 27 July 2021), online: <dfo-mpo.gc.ca/species-especes/whalereview-revuebaleine/review-revue/killerwhale-epaulard/page01-eng.html>.

55 *Ibid* at 12, 17–28.

56 Emergency Order Petition, *supra* note 13.

57 SOR/93-56; Transport Canada, "The Government of Canada Takes Immediate Action to Protect Endangered Whales through the Oceans Protection Plan" (22 June 2018, accessed 26 July 2021), online: *Newswire.ca* <newswire.ca/news-releases/the-government-of-canada-takes-immediate-action-to-protect-endangered-whales-through-the-oceans-protection-plan-686272471.html>.

58 Government of Canada, "Summary of the Imminent Threat Assessment for the Southern Resident Killer Whale" (24 May 2018, accessed 26 July 2021), online: <canada.ca/en/environment-climate-change/services/species-risk-public-registry/related-information/summary-ita-sr-killerwhale.html>.

59 Government of Canada, "Southern Resident Killer Whale Imminent Threat Assessment" (30 July 2018, accessed 26 July 2021), online: <species-registry.canada.ca/index-en.html#/consultations/3327>.

60 Federal Court file T-1618-18.

61 *Order Declining to Make an Emergency Order for the Protection of the Killer Whale Northeast Pacific Southern Resident Population*, SI/2018-102, (2018) C Gaz II, 152:23.

62 Government of Canada, "2021 Management Measures to Protect Southern Resident Killer Whales" (14 April 2021, accessed 26 July 2021), online: <pac.dfo-mpo.gc.ca/fm-gp/mammals-mammiferes/whales-baleines/srkw-measures-mesures-ers-eng.html>.

63 "Ottawa Strengthening Measures to Protect Southern Resident Killer Whales", *weeklyvoice.com* (4 May 2021, accessed 26 July 2021), online: <weeklyvoice.com/ottawa-strengthening-measures-to-protect-southern-resident-killer-whales/>.

19

Administrative Penalties in Alberta: Overview and Latest Trends

Gilbert Van Nes[1]

Scope of This Chapter

Unfortunately, while administrative penalties are used in Alberta's environmental regulatory scheme, they are not used directly to address wildlife protection. Administrative penalties can be used incidentally to protect wildlife under legislation such as the *Environmental Protection and Enhancement Act*[2] (*EPEA*), the *Water Act*,[3] and the *Public Lands Act*[4] (*PLA*).

This chapter provides an overview of the administrative penalty regime in Alberta and will examine a recent case before the Alberta Environmental Appeals Board (EAB), *Alberta Reclaim and Recycling Company Inc v. Alberta Environment and Parks* (*Alberta Reclaim*).[5] It will conclude with a brief overview of some of the economic models used by the US Environmental Protection Agency (EPA) with respect to administrative penalties.

Environmental Protection and Enhancement Act

EPEA was the first Alberta environmental statute to include administrative penalties. *EPEA* provides:

> **237(1)** Where the Director is of the opinion that a person has contravened a provision of this Act that is specified for the purposes of this section in the regulations, the Director may, subject to the regulations, by notice in writing given to that person require that person to pay to the Government an administrative penalty in the amount set out in the notice for each contravention.

(2) A notice of administrative penalty may require the person to whom it is directed to pay either or both of the following:

> (a) a daily amount for each day or part of a day on which the contravention occurs and continues;
> (b) a one-time amount to address economic benefit where the Director is of the opinion that the person has derived an economic benefit directly or indirectly as a result of the contravention.

(3) A person who pays an administrative penalty in respect of a contravention may not be charged under this Act with an offence in respect of that contravention.

(4) Subject to the right to appeal a notice of administrative penalty to the Environmental Appeals Board, where a person fails to pay an administrative penalty in accordance with the notice of administrative penalty and the regulations, the Minister may file a copy of the notice of administrative penalty with the clerk of the Court of Queen's Bench and, on being filed, the notice has the same force and effect and may be enforced as if it were a judgment of the Court.

The original provisions for administrative penalties were brought into force on September 1, 1993. However, the ability to assess "a one-time amount to address economic benefit" was enacted in 2002.

The *Administrative Penalty Regulation*[6] (the Regulation) details what is required to be included in the administrative penalty and provides for a two-year limitation period.

Notice of administrative penalty
2(1) The provisions set out in the Schedule are the provisions in respect of which a notice of administrative penalty may be given under section 237 of the Act.

(2) A notice of administrative penalty must be given in writing and must contain the following information:

(a) the name of the person required to pay the administrative penalty;
(b) particulars of the contravention;
(c) the amount of the administrative penalty and the date by which it must be paid;
(d) a statement of the right to appeal to the Environmental Appeals Board given under section 91(1)(n) of the Act.

(3) A notice of administrative penalty may not be issued more than 2 years after the later of

(a) the date on which the contravention to which the notice relates occurred, or
(b) the date on which evidence of the contravention first came to the notice of the Director.

The Regulation also details how the penalty is to be assessed, including the determination of the base penalty and the factors to be considered in adjusting the base penalty. The Regulation prescribes a maximum of $5000 per day.

Penalty assessment
3(1) Subject to subsections (2) and (3), the amount of an administrative penalty for each contravention that occurs or continues is the amount set out in the Base Penalty Table but that amount may be increased or decreased by the Director in accordance with subsection (2).

BASE PENALTY TABLE
Type of Contravention

		Major	Moderate	Minor
Potential for Adverse Effect	Major	$5000	$3500	$2500
	Moderate	3500	2500	1500
	Minor to None	2500	1500	1000

(2) In a particular case, the Director may increase or decrease the amount of the administrative penalty from the amount set out in the Base Penalty Table on considering the following factors:

(a) the importance to the regulatory scheme of compliance with the provision;
(b) the degree of wilfulness or negligence in the contravention;
(c) whether or not there was any mitigation relating to the contravention;
(d) whether or not steps have been taken to prevent reoccurrence of the contravention;
(e) whether or not the person who receives the notice of administrative penalty has a history of non-compliance;
(f) whether or not the person who receives the notice of administrative penalty has derived any economic benefit from the contravention;
(g) any other factors that, in the opinion of the Director, are relevant.

(3) The maximum administrative penalty that may be imposed for the purposes of section 237(2)(a) of the Act is $5000 for each contravention or for each day or part of a day on which the contravention occurs and continues, as the case may be.

The structure of the administrative penalty regime under the *Water Act* and the *PLA*, and other environmental legislation, is substantially similar. However, the key detail that is missing from all of this legislation is how to deal with "a one-time amount to address economic benefit." No guidance is provided in either the Acts or the regulations as to how to determine this amount.

Appealing Administrative Penalties

One of the key pieces in any administrative penalty scheme is provision for an appeal mechanism as follows:

> **91(1)** A notice of appeal may be submitted to the Board by the following persons in the following circumstances:
>
> > (n) where the Director requires a person to pay an administrative penalty under section 237, the person to whom the notice is directed may submit a notice of appeal;[7]

With an appeal mechanism in place, the administrative penalty can be registered as an order of the court and enforced without the need to prove the administrative penalty in court.

Alberta Reclaim and Recycling

The first time an economic benefit case came before the EAB was in *Alberta Reclaim*[8] as follows:

> Alberta Environment and Parks (AEP) issued an Administrative Penalty for $844,778.00 to Alberta Reclaim and Recycling Company Inc., Mr. Johnny Ha, and Mr. Shawn Diep (the Appellants) for contraventions of the Beverage Container Recycling Regulation under the Environmental Protection and Enhancement Act. AEP determined the Appellants transported beverage containers into the Province of Alberta to operate a non-permitted bottle depot in Edmonton, obtained refunds for these beverage containers, and failed to comply with the terms and conditions of the Permit for the operation of the Andrew Bottle Depot. The Administrative Penalty included a penalty assessment of $75,000.00 and an economic benefit assessment of $769,778.00 for a total of $844,778.00.

The key issue, in this case, was what should the economic benefit calculation be based upon, total revenue or total profit? The director (the statutory decision maker for Alberta Environment and Parks) based the assessment on total revenue.

In the *Alberta Reclaim* case, the board discussed the following four possible approaches to determine the basis for the economic benefit calculation:[9]

> [95] . . . [The] Director discussed four different approaches to determining how economic benefit should be assessed. The Director suggests that different approaches should be used depending on the "type" of contravention that occurred.
>
> [96] Under the first approach, the activity is described as "always unlawful," meaning there was no lawful way to carry out the activity. An activity that is "always unlawful" cannot be made lawful by way of an authorization (i.e., an approval, licence, or permit) under the regulatory scheme. According to the Director, in such a situation the economic benefit should be assessed as the total revenue generated by the activity without any deduction for costs.
>
> [97] Under the second approach, the activity was unlawful at the time the revenue was generated, but it could be made lawful by meeting certain requirements. This type of activity is one that was carried out without the appropriate regulatory authorizations but is one for which the proper authorizations could have been obtained. If the proper authorization had been obtained, the activity would have been lawful. According to the Director, in such a situation the economic benefit should be assessed as the total revenue generated by the activity less the reasonable costs associated with the activity.
>
> [98] The Director did not review the third and fourth approaches in significant detail in his evidence because, in his view, the first approach was appropriate for dealing with this case. The third and fourth approaches both relate to contraventions resulting from the failure to expend funds to be in compliance with the regulatory scheme. The third approach was described as applying where actions were taken to avoid incurring costs, where subsequent expenditures

> cannot correct the non-compliance. The fourth approach was described as applying where actions were taken to delay incurring costs, where subsequent expenditures in the present can correct the non-compliance. The Director did not state how the economic benefit should be assessed in these cases; but presumably, it would be the total revenue earned as a result of the avoidance or delay in incurring the costs of compliance, adjusted for the reasonable costs associated with carrying out the activity. However, in these cases, the time value of money would play a more significant role in determining the economic benefit.

The board agreed with the director that the appropriate basis upon which to assess the economic benefit amount was the total revenue. As stated, this was a case where the actions of the appellants would always be unlawful.

There are other cases before the EAB and the Public Lands Appeal Board that will continue to expand the analysis of economic benefit in administrative penalties.

United States of America's Environmental Protection Agency

The best resources to understand how administrative penalties work can be found at the EPA.[10] Among the resources to be considered is the *Resource Conservation and Recovery Act—Civil Penalty Policy.*[11]

In addition to this policy, the EPA has developed a number of penalty and financial models to assist in the determination of the appropriate economic benefit amount. These models have yet to be used in Alberta but are likely the next step in the development of economic benefit analysis.

These models[12] include:

> BEN—Calculates a violator's economic benefit of noncompliance from delaying or avoiding pollution control expenditures.
>
> . . .
>
> ABEL—Evaluates a corporation's ability to afford compliance costs, cleanup costs or civil penalties.

. . .

INDIPAY—Evaluates an individual's ability to afford compliance costs, cleanup costs or civil penalties.

. . .

MUNIPAY—Evaluates a municipality's or regional utility's ability to afford compliance costs, cleanup costs or civil penalties.

. . .

PROJECT (6.7.0)—Calculates the real cost to a defendant of a proposed supplemental environmental project.

. . .

Conclusion

The use of administrative penalties has many benefits over quasi-criminal penalty schemes. For example, administrative penalties are usually quicker, have few defences, and require a lower level of proof. However, until the introduction of economic benefit, the limitation on the penalty amount could be viewed as "just the cost of doing business." With the ability to take away the economic benefit that is gained from a violation, administrative penalties have become a very effective tool in deterring non-compliance with a legislative scheme.

In Alberta, this area of law is still emerging, with the foundation for determining the amount of the economic benefit just being established. The next development will likely be the use of the EPA penalty and financial models to adjust the economic benefit amount.

Addendum: April 15, 2020

On April 15, 2020, use of the economic benefit component of administrative penalties was extended to the *PLA*.[13] The *PLA* provides:

59.3 The director may, in accordance with the regulations, require a person to pay an administrative penalty in an amount determined by the director if the person

(a) contravenes a provision of an ALSA regional plan, this Act or the regulations that is prescribed in the regulations for the purposes of this section,

(b) without legal authority makes use of public land,

(c) as a holder of a disposition or of an authorization under section 20, without the consent of the director, or a person authorized by the Minister to provide consent, makes use of the public land that is the subject of the disposition or authorization for any purpose other than the purpose for which the disposition or authorization is granted,

(d) contravenes a term or condition of a disposition or of an authorization under section 20,

(e) contravenes a decision or order made under regulations made under section 9(b.1) or (b.2),

(f) contravenes section 62.1 or a regulation made under that section, or

(g) fails to notify the Minister of a transfer, redemption or allotment of shares to which section 114.1(4) applies.

59.4(1) If the director requires a person to pay an administrative penalty under this Act or the regulations, the director shall serve by personal service or registered mail a notice of administrative penalty demanding payment of the penalty.

(2) A notice of administrative penalty must state the grounds on which the penalty was assessed.

(3) An administrative penalty to which a notice under subsection (1) relates must be paid within 30 days of the date of service of the notice.

(4) A notice of administrative penalty under this section may require one or more of the following:

(a) payment of the penalty determined by the director under section 59.3;

(b) any person who in the director's opinion is in receipt of proceeds derived directly or indirectly from any use of public land in contravention of this Act or the regulations to provide an accounting of the proceeds believed by the director to have been received by that person;

(c) payment by a person referred to in clause (b) of any proceeds referred to in that clause, or an amount equivalent to the value of the proceeds if the person has converted the proceeds. [Emphasis added.]

59.5 A person is liable for an administrative penalty for each day or part of a day on which the contravention occurs or continues, and where this Act or the regulations prescribe the maximum amount of an administrative penalty, the maximum is the maximum for each day or part of a day on which the contravention occurs or continues.

59.6 A person who pays an administrative penalty in respect of a contravention by the person shall not be prosecuted under this Act for an offence in respect of the same contravention.

59.7 A notice of administrative penalty may not be issued more than 2 years after

(a) the date on which the contravention to which the notice relates occurred, or

(b) the date on which evidence of the contravention first came to the notice of the director,

whichever is later.

59.8(1) Subject to any right to appeal the notice of administrative penalty, the director may file a copy of the notice of administrative penalty with the clerk of the Court of Queen's Bench and, on filing, the notice may be enforced as a judgment of the Court.

(2) On application by the director, the Court may make any order necessary to compel the person receiving a notice under section 59.4 to carry out the terms of the notice.

These provisions were enacted in 2009. However, it is only recently that cases have started to come before the Public Lands Appeal Board. The following cases were heard and decided in 2020. The board quoted the administrative penalties imposed by the director in the cases as follows:

Colette Benson v. Director, Regional Compliance, Alberta Environment and Parks[14] (*Colette Benson*). The administrative penalty provides:

[t]he Parties contravened [a Department Licence of Occupation] . . . by subletting the land without written consent of the Director; received money or other consideration, as monthly payments for the purpose of allowing access to and use of the public lands without authority; and did receive money in the form of proceeds from the public auction sale of the [Department of Licence Occupation] or other consideration for the purpose of gaining access to the Public Land. . . . I am assessing an administrative penalty of $1,415,572.50 pursuant to [section] 59.3(b) of the Public Lands Act (for unauthorized use) and 59.3(d) of the Public Lands Act (for contravention of conditions) which has be calculated in accordance with section 171 of the Public Lands Administration Regulation.

Jason King and Kingdom Properties Ltd v. Director, Regional Compliance, Lower Athabasca Region, Alberta Environment and Parks[15] (*King and Kingdom Properties*). The administrative penalty provides:

The Parties contravened [two Department of Licence Occupations] . . . by subletting the land without written consent of the Director, [and] received monies for the purpose of allowing access to and use of the public lands without authority. I am assessing an administrative penalty of $734,500.00 pursuant to [sections] 59.3 and 59.4(4) of the Public Lands Act which has been calculated in accordance with section 171 of the Public Lands Administration Regulation. . . .

Normand Menard and Normko Resources Inc. v. Director, Regional Compliance, Lower Athabasca Region, Alberta Environment and Parks[16] (*Normand Menard*). The administrative penalty provides:

[T]he Parties, being a holder of [a Department Licence of Occupation], sublet the land to three separate card lock fuel vendors and additional companies without written consent of the Director and received monies for the purpose of allowing access to and use of public lands without authorization. I am assessing an administrative penalty of $45,000.00 pursuant to [section] 59.3 of the Public Lands Act. I am also assessing payment of $538,448.21 for total proceeds received pursuant to [s]ection 59.4(4) of the Public Lands Act.

The three cases above have now been heard and determined. The *Colette Benson* case was decided on September 14, 2020. The board held that the amount of the administrative penalty should be calculated based on net proceeds instead of gross proceeds, and as the evidence was unclear, the board determined that it would be reasonable to deduct $144,615.32 to determine the net proceeds amount. The board also found in its decision that the director failed to follow the board's order to give the appellant additional disclosure that constituted a breach of procedural fairness, which cannot be remedied by the board's hearing process. The board, therefore, advised the minister to reverse the administrative penalty. The administrative penalty was reversed by the minister of environment and parks.[17]

As for the *King and Kingdom Properties Ltd.* and *Normand Menard* cases, which are both decisions on applications to stay administrative penalties imposed on the applicants, both applications were granted by the board.

It is important to note, whereas the *EPEA*[18] and the *Water Act*[19] speak in terms of "economic benefits," the *PLA* speaks in terms of the "proceeds" of the unauthorized activity. The scope and differences between economic benefits and proceeds will be an interesting issue to follow.

NOTES

1 General Counsel and Settlement Officer for the Alberta Environmental Appeals Board and the Alberta Public Lands Appeal Board.

2 *Environmental Protection and Enhancement Act*, RSA 2000, c E-12 [*EPEA*].

3 *Water Act*, RSA 2000, c W-3.

4 *Public Lands Act*, RSA 2000, c P-40 [*PLA*].

5 *Alberta Reclaim and Recycling Company Inc et al v Director, Red Deer–North Saskatchewan Region, Alberta Environment and Parks* (18 August 2016), Appeal Nos. 14-025-027-D (AEAB) [*Alberta Reclaim*].

6 *Administrative Penalty Regulation*, AR 23/2003.

7 *Environmental Protection and Enhancement Act*, RSA 2000, c E-12, s 91(1)(n).

8 *Alberta Reclaim*, *supra* note 5, Executive Summary.

9 *Ibid* at paras 95–98.

10 United States Environmental Protection Agency, online: <epa.gov>.

11 United States Environmental Protection Agency et al, *Resource Conservation and Recovery Act—Civil Penalty Policy* (Washington, DC: Environmental Protection Agency, June 2003), online (pdf): <epa.gov/sites/default/files/2020-05/documents/june2003rcracivilpenaltypolicyamended050620.pdf>.

12 See: "Penalty and Financial Models", Environmental Protection Agency (accessed August 30, 2021), online: <www.epa.gov/enforcement/penalty-and-financial-models>.

13 *PLA*, *supra* note 4.

14 *Colette Benson and CRC Open Camp and Catering Ltd v Director, Regional Compliance, Lower Athabasca Region, Alberta Environment and Parks* (14 September 2020), Appeal Nos. 18-0015-R (APLAB), 2020 ABPLAB 14.

15 *Jason King and Kingdom Properties Ltd v Director, Regional Compliance, Lower Athabasca Region, Alberta Environment and Parks* (31 July 2020), Appeal Nos. 19-0005-0006-R (APLAB), 2020 ABPLAB 12.

16 *Normand Menard and Normko Resources Inc v Director, Regional Compliance, Lower Athabasca Region, Alberta Environment and Parks* (10 November 2020), Appeal Nos. 19-0245-0246 (APLAB), 2020 ABPLAB 20.

17 Alberta Environment and Parks, Ministerial Order 61/2020, online: <open.alberta.ca/publications/ep-61-2021>.

18 *EPEA*, *supra* note 2.

19 *Water Act*, *supra* note 3.

SECTION 3

Enforcement of Canadian Greenhouse Gas Emissions Laws

20

Canada's International Climate Obligations and Provincial Diversity in Greenhouse Gas Emissions: A Fertile Ground for Multifaceted Litigation

Sophie Lavallée[1]

Introduction

There is little to say about Canada's international climate commitments, except that, under the *Paris Agreement*, each country presents its nationally determined contribution (NDC) as it sees fit, and that the Canadian NDC, like that of all parties to this Agreement, contains only voluntary commitments. After recalling the Canadian NDC and the pillars of the *Pan-Canadian Framework on Clean Growth and Climate Change*, we will review provincial diversity in energy and greenhouse gas (GHG) emissions. We will then see that this context explains the existence of climate-related legal litigation in the country, which takes several forms that, although not presenting the same debate, often raise complex constitutional law issues.

Canadian Context

To assess Canada's contribution to the global climate effort under the *Paris Agreement*, it is necessary to assess Canada's share of global GHG emissions, as well as the distribution of emissions within the federation. This then provides an informed look at the *Pan-Canadian Framework on Clean Growth and Climate Change*, which proposes six pillars to guide Canada's climate change effort announced at the Conference of the Parties (COP) 21.

CANADIAN EMISSIONS

In 2018, Canada's total GHG emissions amounted to 725 megatonnes of carbon (CO_2 equivalent), or 21 percent (126 megatonnes CO_2 equivalent) above 1990 emissions (603 megatonnes CO_2 equivalent). Canada, which accounts for 0.5 percent of the world's population, accounts for about 1.5 percent of global CO_2 emissions. Oil sands account for 11.5 percent of Canada's GHG emissions and about 0.2 percent of global GHG emissions.[2] At first glance, Canada appears to be a country with relatively small global emissions, but in terms of per capita emissions, it is becoming a major player.[3] Amongst G-20 countries in 2018, only the United States and Australia are doing worse.[4]

By carefully examining the emissions for each Canadian province, it is clear that a great disparity exists between the emissions of the ten Canadian provinces, due to the disparate use of fossil fuels and hydroelectricity across the country. The provinces of Quebec and British Columbia have the best record, given their hydroelectric resources. The provinces of Alberta and Saskatchewan, on the other hand, have the worst record, with GHG emissions much higher than the worst ranked comparator, Australia. Canada's emissions have been largely flat since 2005, while Alberta's emissions increased 18 percent between 2005 and 2018, mainly due to increased oil and gas operations.[5] Overall, in Canada, emissions have increased by 21 percent since 1990, the base year of the *Kyoto Protocol*. The energy sectors (stationary combustion, transportation, and fugitive sources) account for 82 percent of Canadian emissions, with remaining emissions being attributable to agriculture (8 percent), industrial processes and product use (8 percent), and waste (2 percent).[6]

In this context, it is not surprising that the repudiation of the *Kyoto Protocol* was not supported across the country, that it was the subject of a legal challenge, and that litigation has existed for many years in Canada, concerning, on the one hand, the imposition of a carbon tax by the federal government, and on the other hand, the pipeline projects allowing increased exploitation of our non-renewable petroleum resources, including the oil sands.

THE CANADIAN NATIONALLY DETERMINED CONTRIBUTION IN THE *PARIS AGREEMENT* AND THE *PAN-CANADIAN FRAMEWORK ON CLEAN GROWTH AND CLIMATE CHANGE*

Breaking with the Conservative government of Stephen Harper, Justin Trudeau's new Liberal government did well at COP 21, announcing significant support for the *Paris Agreement*, through expressed support for the text of the Agreement, which stresses that states should strive not to exceed, if possible, 1.5 degrees Celsius. Canadian cooperation was also demonstrated by the announcement of $2.65 billion Canadian in financial support to the Green Climate Fund for 2015–2020.[7] However, the country's NDC was the one presented by the Canadian Conservative government in Copenhagen, which was in line with that of its neighbour and trading partner, the United States.

The Canadian Nationally Determined Contribution in the Paris Agreement

In its NDC under the *Paris Agreement*, Canada plans to reduce its GHG emissions by 30 percent from its 2015 emissions by 2030.[8] From 730 megatonnes of carbon dioxide equivalent (referred to as megatonnes of CO_2) to 511 megatonnes will result in a reduction of 219 megatonnes. This target represents a decrease of only 15 percent from 1990, which was the base year for the *Kyoto Protocol*, which Canada ratified in 2005. Canada adopted 2005 as the reference year because the United States, who were not bound by the *Kyoto Protocol*, had adopted, at the Copenhagen Conference, this reference year at the Copenhagen Conference under the Obama presidency.[9] Canada has an actual emission reduction target of only 15 percent with respect to 1990; instead of applying a reduction of 30 percent with respect to 1990 (603 megatonnes), it established it at a much higher level (730 megatonnes).[10]

What happens if Canada does not meet its 2030 target? Although the *Paris Agreement* does not define its legal status, it makes "NDCs supplements to its provisions and a condition of its ratification."[11] Article 4.2 states that "[e]ach Party shall prepare, communicate and maintain successive nationally determined contributions that it intends to achieve."[12] It further states that "Parties shall pursue domestic mitigation measures, with the aim of achieving the objectives of such contributions."[13] However, these NDCs are not found in an annex to the Agreement, but in a separate register, depriving their contents of [translation] "an implied or explicit conventional value."[14] The NDC is therefore described by doctrine as a unilateral state act. Hugues Hellio explains the legal status as follows:

> [Translation] Formally, a unilateral state act is a legal act attributable to a single state which, acting in the name of its sovereignty and within its capacity, ensures sufficient publicity of its state will. In doing so, "the State has discretion and is determined essentially on the

basis of its own interests." This is the case with NDCs. Attributable to a single Party, the NDC is the unilateral and sovereign act of that Party, which has discreetly and in accordance with its own interests, determined its climate objectives and actions.

While NDCs are unilateral acts, they are linked to the *Paris Agreement*. Such acts are sometimes referred to as acts conditioned by conventional norms. They are frequently used to enhance conventional engagement without enshrining in the treaty differences in treatment between its Parties as revealed by the analysis of conditioned unilateral acts. This duality between the common conventional framework and the differentiated treatment of the Parties reinforces the qualification of unilateral acts conditioned by the NDCs, both of which, specific to each Party, remain governed by the common obligations of the *Paris Agreement*.[15]

For example, the common NDC obligations set out in the *Paris Agreement* mean that a transparency framework[16] requires disclosure and that the communicated NDC must represent progress against the previously communicated NDC by the state.[17] This enhanced transparency framework must provide a "clear understanding of climate change actions . . . including clarity and tracking of progress towards achieving Parties' individual nationally determined contributions"[18]. Thus, "[e]ach Party shall regularly provide . . . b) Information necessary to track progress made in implementing and achieving its nationally determined contribution"[19]. These mechanisms are conventional in that they fall under the *Paris Agreement*, a multilateral international treaty.

Finally, if the State fails to comply with its NDC, Article 15 of the *Paris Agreement* establishes a "mechanism to facilitate implementation of and promote compliance with the provisions of this Agreement." It is not a sanction mechanism but a compliance mechanism, frequent in international environmental law and focused on facilitation and transparency, while also being non-adversarial and non-punitive.[20]

Pan-Canadian Framework on Clean Growth and Climate Change

To implement and respect its NDC, the federal government adopted the *Pan-Canadian Framework on Clean Growth and Climate Change* in 2016.[21] The key pillars of this *Pan-Canadian Framework*, a cornerstone of Canada's climate plan, are:

1. Putting a price on carbon: provinces must adopt a cap-and-trade system or a carbon tax;.
2. Eliminate coal-fired power in the few remaining provinces, and other complementary measures to further reduce emissions in Canada;.
3. Accommodation measures;.
4. Make significant investments in green infrastructure and public transit.

This *Pan-Canadian Framework* was adopted in concert with the provinces, because constitutionally, the federal government did not have a solid legal basis for adopting a carbon tax and imposing it on the provinces. The provinces of Alberta, Ontario, Manitoba, and Saskatchewan challenged the constitutional basis of this tax in the courts, as we will now see.[22]

Canadian Constitutional Debates on Energy and Climate

The Canadian constitution does not provide for the environment as a legislative head of power. The *Constitution Act* of 1867 provides for the division of powers between the federal and provincial legislatures in this country, and the environment is obviously not there. The result is that the environment is a shared jurisdiction between provincial and federal authorities. To determine which legislature, federal or provincial, has jurisdiction over a given environmental matter, the "*pith and substance*" must be determined.[23]

This has led to numerous challenges, the most recent of which are the federal carbon price (see section 2.3) and the approval of Kinder Morgan's Trans Mountain pipeline expansion, the only crude and refined oil pipeline from Alberta to the British Columbia coast through the Rocky Mountains (see section 2.4).

Two other cases also involve the application of Canadian constitutional law, but under two other heads. These are constitutional law professor Daniel Turp's challenge to Canada's withdrawal from the *Kyoto Protocol* (see section

2.1) and the challenge to the approval of a pipeline, Northern Gateway, also in western Canada (see section 2.2).

REPUDIATION OF THE *KYOTO PROTOCOL*

In 2008, Canadian emissions were 31 percent above Canada's *Kyoto Protocol* target to reduce its 1990 emissions by 6 percent by the end of the first *Kyoto Protocol* commitment period, which was the end of 2012.[24] This was not a surprise for anybody since the federal government and the Alberta government had always supported carbon intensity reductions only, while the reduction that Canada had to meet according to the *Kyoto Protocol* could not be attained without strong legislative measures, such as severe regulations aimed at major emitters of GHGs, measures on the fuel efficiency of all vehicles sold in Canada, and the imposition of carbon pricing through the implementation of a carbon tax or a cap-and-trade system. On December 15, 2011, the Canadian Conservative government of the day sent out the required notice of withdrawal to repudiate the *Kyoto Protocol*. This repudiation was legal under international law, with Canada following the procedure set out in Article 27 of the Protocol:

> **Art. 27 Kyoto Protocol:**
>
> (1) At any time after three years from the date on which this Protocol has entered into force for a Party, that Party may withdraw from this Protocol by giving written notification to the Depositary.
> (2) Any such withdrawal shall take effect upon expiry of one year (. . .)

However, this repudiation has been challenged in the courts. Being of the opinion that it was not legal under Canadian constitutional law, international law professor Daniel Turp requested that it be struck down through a judicial review process before the Federal Court. He argued that this repudiation was contrary to the *Kyoto Protocol Implementation Act* (SC 2007, c 30), a private member's bill passed by the House of Commons on June 22, 2007, at the initiative of the opposition in the House of Commons, since this act, in his opinion, required the government to put measures in place to meet Canada's commitment under the *Kyoto Protocol*.

The Federal Court held that this was a decision of the political sphere ("high policy") and that it was not for the courts to rule on the exercise of this discretionary power of the government.[25] It followed the precedents of two cases, *Turp v. Chrétien* and *Friends of the Earth*.[26] In *Turp v. Chrétien*, the court concluded that "except for a violation of the Canadian Charter of Rights and Freedoms . . . matters of high policy are not subject to review by the courts"[27]. In *Friends of the Earth*, the court ruled that section 7 of the *Kyoto Protocol Implementation Act* did not appear to contain an obligation for the government to make the regulatory changes required to comply with the *Kyoto Protocol*: "[a]ll of the above measures are directed at ensuring compliance with Canada's substantive Kyoto commitments . . . the subject matter of which is mostly not amenable or suited to judicial scrutiny".[28]

CARBON TAXATION

In Canada, the federal government has the exclusive monopoly to enter into international treaties under the Royal Prerogative,[29] but the implementation of these treaties in the domestic legal order requires respect for the constitutional division of legislative powers between the federal government and provincial legislatures.[30] On the issue of climate change and GHG emissions control, the provinces have the bulk of the legislative authority to implement Canada's commitments in the *Paris Agreement* and their inaction or lack of ambition can seriously compromise the achievement of the reduction targets announced by the central government in the Canadian NDC.

Ottawa had initially adopted this framework one year after COP 21, after tense discussions with the provinces. It was originally adopted without the provinces of Manitoba and Saskatchewan. Manitoba briefly rallied, but the province of Saskatchewan did not. Premier Brad Wall, during his term, maintained his categorical refusal to have Ottawa impose a price on carbon on its businesses, fearing a negative economic impact on his province. In January 2018, Premier Wall reiterated that his government would not hesitate to take the case to court if the federal government "tried to impose a carbon tax on Saskatchewan families and businesses."[31] Premier Scott Moe, his successor, decided to take legal action to determine whether the federal government's legislation[32] to impose the carbon tax complied with the Constitution.[33] As well, Premier Rachel Notley of Alberta, a province rich in oil sands, announced in early October 2016 that she would not support the federal government's carbon pricing plan until the federal government approved the construction of new pipelines to open up the province. In November 2016, the Trans Mountain pipeline project was approved by the federal government.

On November 29, 2016, Alberta Premier Rachel Notley welcomed the announcement of the federal approval of this pipeline; it would allow the province to see "light at the end of the tunnel," because the oil produced could open up new markets in Asia, among others.[34] It was nevertheless surprising that Alberta opposed the federal government's carbon tax as it was the first province to impose a carbon tax in 2007. The province also, in 2016, amended its legislation to raise the tax to about $20 per tonne in January 2017 and to $30 in 2018 and to expand the scope of the tax to apply to all areas of its economy.[35]

The efforts on the part of the federal government to convince the provinces to show themselves team players and implement a carbon pricing system through a tax or a cap-and-trade system must be understood not only within the framework of cooperative federalism,[36] but also within a context where the imposition of carbon pricing by the federal government is complicated by the search for a solid constitutional basis on which the federal Parliament can establish its authority.[37] The difficulty of constitutionally incorporating the federal carbon tax into Canadian law undoubtedly explains why the federal government has announced that the proceeds of the federal carbon tax, for the provinces that do not adopt it, will revert entirely to the provinces.[38] Politically, it is true, it is difficult to make the Canadian oil-producing provinces accept this tax, as Professor Jean-Maurice Arbor explains:

> According to a report written for the Canadian government, it is recognized that carbon pricing can have significant negative repercussions for companies exposed very strongly to competition on national or international markets and push some of them to transfer their production and their investments abroad, where there is no such carbon pricing (a phenomenon called carbon leakage; according to the same working group, "establishing a price . . ."). The question is important in the Canada-US reports. This is the reason, it seems, for the federal government to impose performance or intensity standards on these companies for their various production activities, instead of a carbon tax.[39]

Parliament claimed its constitutional jurisdiction as the foundation for the *Greenhouse Gas Pollution Pricing Act*,[40] which came into force on January 1, 2019. This law, which imposes a price on polluting emissions from several business sectors in provinces that do not have carbon pricing measures, was challenged in Canadian courts by the governments of the provinces of Alberta, Manitoba, Ontario, and Saskatchewan.[41]

The central government could have adopted its carbon tax through its constitutional jurisdiction over criminal matters, by providing for prohibitions with penalties. The Supreme Court had already ruled, in *R v. Hydro-Québec*, that this head of jurisdiction was less dangerous than the theory of national interest, that the responsibility of the human being towards the environment was a fundamental value of our society, that Parliament can use its criminal law power to highlight this value, "and that criminal law must be able to adapt to and protect our new values."[42]

Indeed, the other three constitutional options of federal taxation, national urgency, and national concern[43] do not seem to be able to establish the legality of the federal tax. In fact, the federal government can tax only to create revenues;[44] in the case of an emergency, it can only legislate provisionally, and as far as the national interest is concerned, the Supreme Court had already recognized that this is a theory which is dangerous for federal balance.[45] However, the federal government successfully argued the national interest before the courts of Ontario and Saskatchewan. The Saskatchewan Court of Appeal, majority (two-judges-to-one), held that the imposition of minimum national price standards for GHG emissions provides the flexibility necessary so that the carbon tax respects the contours of the national interest theory. It held that there was no constitutional requirement that federal laws should apply uniformly across the country and that the levies imposed by federal law were not taxes, rather they were many regulatory measures at the heart of the federal environmental regulations.[46] The majority of the Ontario Court of Appeal held that the environment is "an area of shared jurisdiction," that the "essence" of the federal regulations on the federal carbon tax was "the establishment of minimum national GHG pricing standards to reduce GHG emissions," and that following the criteria set out in *Crown Zellerbach*, the establishment of such minimum standards was a single, distinct, and indivisible matter of power under national interest based on "peace, order and good government." According to the Court, "no single province or group of provinces acting together can establish minimum national standards to reduce GHG emissions. Their efforts may be undermined by the action or inaction of other provinces. Therefore, the reduction of GHG emissions cannot be managed in a fragmentary fashion. It must be addressed as a single issue to ensure its effectiveness. This is exactly what the establishment of minimum national standards do."[47]

The two judgments contain dissents. That of Justices Ottenbreit and Caldwell of the Saskatchewan Court of Appeal relied on the lack of distinctiveness of the Federal Act to find its constitutional validity in the national interest, and on the fact that GHG emissions are a sub-category of air pollutants previously considered to be a local issue under provincial jurisdiction. As for Justice Huscroft, the sole dissenter from the Ontario Court of Appeal, she concluded that the federal minimum standards were "floating" and left the question too vague to be circumscribed appropriately in order to be classified as a question of national interest. Regarding the majority decision that a national standard was necessary to regulate GHGs, she instead believed that the inaction of a single province was indicative not of a provincial inability to regulate GHG emissions but rather of a political disagreement.[48]

These two dissents, along with the decision of the Alberta Court of Appeal, which, in a four-to-one majority decision, did not find that the national interest was a valid constitutional basis for the federal tax, were brought before the Supreme Court, which decided this delicate constitutional question on March 25, 2021. The Supreme Court majority decided that, "global warming causes harm beyond provincial boundaries and that it is a matter of national concern under the '*peace, order and good government*' clause of the Constitution."[49]

We must remember that as soon as a subject is qualified as being of national interest, Parliament has exclusive and absolute jurisdiction to legislate on this matter, including its provincial aspects.[50] If the federal government only prescribes a minimum standard allowing the provinces to act themselves through legislative initiatives, the balance of federalism can be preserved. The issue of the legal debate here is obviously the preservation of the constitutional division of powers in the fight against climate change.

APPROVAL OF NEW OR EXPANDED PIPELINES

As global conventional oil reserves eventually reach their peak, Alberta's oil sands resources become increasingly important globally. Alberta's oil sands contain more than 1.65 trillion barrels of bitumen, an oil substance mixed with sand.[51]

The US economy is heavily dependent on oil imports and the US is clearly the largest consumer of Canadian oil. Demand in other major countries, such as China and India, is growing even faster. The demand for fuel from Canada's oil sands will therefore exist for an indeterminate period of time; and, as analyses predict, the value of the resource will only increase over time as global oil supply becomes scarce. Many countries are indeed concerned about the security of their energy supplies. This is not the case for Canada, which will be able to meet its domestic needs for a long period of time. However, the picture is more complex when you consider the Canadian NDC and the necessary energy transition to achieve it.

As we know, the main problem with the oil sands is their energy-intensive extraction process, since extraction techniques result in significant GHG emissions. For every litre of gasoline produced, oil sands extraction emits three times more GHG emissions than conventional crude oil extraction. How should Canada's oil sands be developed? The answer to this question divides the powerful political forces that confront each other, some encouraging their rapid development to encourage foreign investment in Canada and ensure global energy security, others advocating a more gradual and limited development of this important resource in the name of combating climate change.

Canada's pipeline system can move about 4.6 million barrels per day, which was the average production for 2015.[52] However, the Canadian Association of Petroleum Producers (CAPP) expects oil production to increase by 28 percent over the next fifteen years, from 4.6 million barrels per day in 2015 to 5.9 million barrels per day by 2035.[53] These increases will exceed the capacity of the existing pipeline system. "The need to build new energy infrastructure within Canada is clearly urgent," said Tim McMillan of CAPP, adding that this would allow Canada to prosper economically and better meet the world's energy needs.[54]

The federal government—under both Conservatives and Liberal leaderships—has approved pipeline projects in recent years. As noted above, in November 2016, the Canadian government authorized the expansion of the US Kinder Morgan Trans Mountain pipeline and approved the replacement of Alberta's Enbridge Line 3 pipeline. It also approved the Pacific NorthWest LNG project in northern British Columbia, which has an estimated climate impact of between 8.8 and 9.3 million tonnes of GHG emissions per year.[55]

Northern Gateway Pipeline Project

The Northern Gateway project was a 1,177 kilometre twin pipeline from Bruderheim, Alberta to Kitimat, British Columbia, that would have transported an average of 525,000 barrels of oil per day to supply international markets. In June 2014, the government of Stephen Harper approved this $7.9 billion project, subject to 209 conditions. These conditions were necessary as the pipeline would have crossed the Great Bear Rainforest and 1000 water bodies in Indigenous territories.

The Federal Court of Appeal overturned the Canadian government's approval of the Northern Gateway project in June 2016, noting the lack of government consultation with West Coast First Nations. The Court ruled that consultation with First Nations, who had been denouncing the project for several years, was simply "inadequate." The constitutional obligation of the federal and provincial Crown to consult Indigenous peoples stems from section 35 of the *Constitution Act, 1982*, which is part of the Canadian Constitution and which confirms the existing rights of the Indigenous peoples of Canada, be they land claims or claims of Aboriginal rights to fish or hunt.

In 2004, the Supreme Court clarified the content and scope of this consultation based on the Canadian Constitution, stating that

- The purpose of these consultations is to preserve the honour of the Crown and to reconcile Aboriginal and Crown interests;
- These consultations must be held even when only "claims" of Aboriginal rights and title are involved; and
- The consultation process should not be conducted by a third party (e.g. proponent, although they are often actively involved).

This obligation may also involve, "where appropriate," accommodating the concerns of Aboriginal peoples, such as changing a route to minimize its impact on traditional activities or imposing strict environmental conditions. The Supreme Court of Canada has clarified that the scope of the duty to consult and accommodate Indigenous peoples varies depending on the circumstances of each case, the merits of the claim, and the seriousness of the potential or apprehended harm. For example, where the claim is "based on sound prima facie evidence, where the right and potential harm are of high importance to Aboriginal people and where the risk of uncompensated harm is high," it may be incumbent upon the Crown to conduct extensive consultations with the parties involved.[56]

With respect to the Northern Gateway Pipeline Project, the Federal Court of Appeal applied these principles and concluded that the federal government's decision to allow this pipeline was illegal because it had not been made following proper consultation with their nations:

> [8] When considering whether that duty has been fulfilled—i.e., the adequacy of consultation—we are not to insist on a standard of perfection; rather, only reasonable satisfaction is required.
>
> [325] We have applied the Supreme Court's authorities on the duty to consult to the uncontested evidence before us. We conclude that Canada offered only a brief, hurried and inadequate opportunity in Phase IV—a critical part of Canada's consultation framework—to exchange and discuss information and to dialogue.
>
> The inadequacies—more than just a handful and more than mere imperfections—left entire subjects of central interest to the affected First Nations, sometimes subjects affecting their subsistence and well-being, entirely ignored. It would have taken Canada little time and little organizational effort to engage in meaningful dialogue on these and other subjects of prime importance to Aboriginal peoples. But this did not happen.
>
> [332] Overall, bearing in mind that only reasonable fulfilment of the duty to consult is required, we conclude that in Phase IV of the consultation process—including the execution of the Governor in Council's role at the end of Phase IV—Canada fell short of the mark.[57]

Subsequently, the TransCanada Energy East pipeline, which was to proceed and was also challenged by Indigenous groups in eastern Canada, was also abandoned by TransCanada.[58] Energy East was a 4,500-kilometre pipeline project that would have transported about 1.1 million barrels of oil per day from Alberta and Saskatchewan to refineries in eastern Canada. Some have said that the abandonment of this pipeline was a business decision by

TransCanada because it had already secured enough new pipelines in western Canada to reach international markets, especially in Asia.[59] Nevertheless, this corporate decision has certainly also been influenced by potential Aboriginal challenges, and by the fact that the new pipeline approval process must take into account the GHG emissions generated by oil sands extraction from the outset, and not just emissions caused by pipeline transportation itself.[60]

Authorization for Trans Mountain Pipeline Expansion

The Trans Mountain expansion has divided Canada, particularly western Canada, for several years now. British Columbia is opposed to this project, which runs through its territory, and launched a court case in the province to determine its right to refuse such a project under its constitutional jurisdiction.

This pipeline was built in 1952 and is still operating today. The current route, which runs from Strathcona County (near Edmonton) in Alberta to Burnaby, British Columbia, a distance of 1,150 kilometres, is the subject of the expansion. On November 29, 2016, the government of Canada approved the expansion project following a review that concluded on May 19, 2016, when the National Energy Board (NEB) concluded that the project was in the Canadian public interest and recommended to the Governor in Council that it approve the expansion, subject to 157 conditions. The expansion aims to build a combined pipeline that will increase its capacity from 300,000 barrels a day to 890,000 barrels a day toward international markets.

To put an end to the controversy surrounding this project, and in the face of the risk that it might end up as it eventually did in the action recently brought by British Columbia, Ottawa announced on May 29, 2018, that the project was in the national interest and that the federal government would purchase the pipeline expansion project from the Texas firm Kinder Morgan by August 2018. Canada decided to provide a loan to Kinder Morgan to begin work immediately.[61]

However, on August 30, 2018, the Federal Court of Appeal ruled that the government representatives had not conducted reasonable consultations based on a genuine dialogue with the Indigenous applicants and that the Governor in Council's authorization rested upon a flawed consultation framework, notably because the NEB's report did not address all the issues requiring consultations.[62] For example, the NEB had not reached a conclusion on the nature and scope of the established or asserted Aboriginal rights (including title),[63] that neither Trans Mountain nor the NEB had assessed the effects of the project on each affected Aboriginal group,[64] nor had the assessment of the potential effects of the project on freshwater fisheries been considered. The paragraphs following in the judgment are relevant in this regard:

> [559] On the whole, the record does not disclose responsive, considered and meaningful dialogue coming back from Canada in response to the concerns expressed by the Indigenous applicants. While there are some examples of responsiveness to concerns, these limited examples are not sufficient to overcome the overall lack of response. The Supreme Court's jurisprudence repeatedly emphasizes that dialogue must take place and must be a two-way exchange. The Crown is required to do more than to receive and document concerns and complaints.
>
> Further, Phase III was to focus on two questions: outstanding concerns about Project-related impacts and any required incremental accommodation measures. Canada's ability to consult and dialogue on these issues was constrained by two further limitations: first, Canada's unwillingness to depart from the Board's findings and recommended conditions so as to genuinely understand the concerns of the Indigenous applicants and then consider and respond to those concerns in a genuine and adequate way; second, Canada's erroneous view that it was unable to impose additional conditions on Trans Mountain.
>
> [562] I begin the analysis by underscoring the need for meaningful two-way dialogue in the context of this Project and then move to describe in more detail the three significant impediments to meaningful consultation: the Crown consultation team's implementation of their mandate essentially as note takers, Canada's reluctance to consider any departure from the Board's findings and recommended conditions, and Canada's erroneous view that it lacked the ability to impose additional conditions on Trans Mountain. I then discuss Canada's late disclosure of its assessment of the Project's impact on the Indigenous applicants. Finally, I review instances that show that

as a result of these impediments the opportunity for meaningful dialogue was frustrated.

The jurisprudence of the Supreme Court on the duty to consult is clear. The Indigenous applicants were entitled to a dialogue that demonstrated that Canada not only heard but also gave serious consideration to the specific and real concerns the Indigenous applicants put to Canada, gave serious consideration to proposed accommodation measures, and explained how the concerns of the Indigenous applicants impacted Canada's decision to approve the Project.

The following examples show how Canada fell short of its obligations.

(i) The need for meaningful two-way dialogue

[564] As a matter of well-established law, meaningful dialogue is a prerequisite for reasonable consultation. As explained above at paragraphs 499 to 501, meaningful consultation is not simply a process of exchanging information. Where, as in this case, deep consultation is required, a dialogue must ensue and the dialogue should lead to a demonstrably serious consideration of accommodation. The Crown must be prepared to make changes to its proposed actions based on information and insight obtained through consultation.[65]

Following this ruling, the premier of Alberta announced that the province was withdrawing from its commitment to impose an increase in its Alberta carbon tax to meet the price of the federal carbon tax.[66] The central government's decision to purchase the project aimed to end the jurisdictional wrangling between the different levels of government on this issue. Having not decided to appeal the judgment to the Supreme Court of Canada, the federal government complied with the requirements of this judgment by resuming the process to respect the framework for consultations, so as to meet, this time, the constitutional requirements for Indigenous consultation interpreted by the Court in this judgment. This bet was won if we believe the Federal Court of Appeal, which decided that the additional consultations surrounding the Trans Mountain project had been adequate, conducted in good faith, and conducted following discussions to try to understand and take into account the main concerns of the First Nations and to consider and consent to accommodation measures in certain cases. The Federal Court of Appeal recalled that case law stated that although Indigenous peoples can express their opposition to a project, they cannot use the consultation process as a tactic to try to veto it.[67] The Supreme Court of Canada refused to hear the First Nations' appeal. This legal debate is therefore over. In a unanimous decision, the Supreme Court also dismissed British Columbia's claim to have recognition that it had the right to limit the transportation of petroleum on its territory, ruling that the federal government has sole jurisdiction to regulate interprovincial transportation of petroleum.[68]

Conclusion

The parameters of Canada's energy policy cannot be ignored in order to fully understand Canada's international and domestic climate change policy. When you read the data on where the country is in global energy production, you can see that nothing is less easy than being the minister of the environment and climate change in this country:

> Internationally, Canada is a small economy. Its GDP represents just 1.76% of world output. Nevertheless, it ranks among the world's leading energy producers, sixth with 3.1% of global production, behind China, the United States, Russia, Saudi Arabia and India.
>
> Thanks to the diversity of its natural resources, Canada is able to position itself as a leader in the production of many forms of energy:
>
> Oil: In 2011, Canada was the sixth-largest black-gold producer in the world, producing 169 megatonnes (Mt) of crude oil or 4.2% of world production. It was overtaken by Saudi Arabia, Russia, the United States, Iran and China. In the same year, it was also the 8th largest producer of petroleum products with 2.6% of world production.[69]

In this context, it is not surprising that in March 2017, a report from the Canadian Senate shows that Canada's NDC cannot be reached without a gradual decline in oil production and a consequent change in the way energy is produced and consumed in Canada.[70] An energy transition master plan would be required to meet Canada's 2030 emission reduction target under its

NDC. Our political leaders know this, but the economic forces and the limited role of non-renewable resource development in the Canadian economy hold them back. This energy transition is nevertheless necessary, even if it must be done gradually. Some energy policy experts use Germany and Denmark as examples, whose energy consumption has declined significantly since 1990, but without hindering their economic growth.[71] Canada uses twice as much energy to produce the same growth.[72] Germany's emissions fell in all sectors, and globally they fell by 28 percent between 1990 and 2014. In Canada, over the same period, emissions increased by 20 percent in all sectors, except in the energy-producing industries, and our emissions increased by 37 percent in the transportation sector.[73]

Achieving this energy transition requires realizing the full "technical-economic potential of Canada,"[74] by investing public funds in renewable energy and public transit, by "developing Canada on existing railways"[75] and by increasing the insulation and renovation of buildings in an energy-efficient manner as quickly as possible. Without government decisions in the direction of this energy and ecological transition, climate trials such as those brought by young people in *Environnement Jeunesse*[76] or *La Rose*[77] will multiply, thereby imitating the climate trials around the world,[78] hundreds of which are taking place among our neighbours, the Americans, who have become the world champions of shale oil, in an attempt to influence federal and provincial policies in the country.

NOTES

1 Court of Appeal of Quebec.

2 Government of Canada, "Global Greenhouse Gas Emissions" (15 April 2021), online: *Government of Canada* <www.canada.ca/en/environment-climate-change/services/environmental-indicators/global-greenhouse-gas-emissions.html>; Government of Canada, "National Inventory Report: Greenhouse Gas Sources and Sinks in Canada" (accessed 28 June 2021) 1990–2018, online: *Government of Canada* <publications.gc.ca/site/eng/9.506002/publication.html>.

3 *Ibid.*

4 World Bank, "CO_2 Emissions (Metric Tons per Capita)" (accessed 28 June 2021), online: *World Bank* <data.worldbank.org/indicator/EN.ATM.CO2E.PC>.

5 *Supra* note 2 at 11. For an enlightening comment, see: Jean-Maurice Arbour, "L'impossible défi canadien : lutter efficacement contre les changements climatiques, exporter davantage de pétrole, respecter les compétences constitutionnelles des provinces [The Impossible Canadian Challenge: to effectively fight climate change, to

export more oil, to respect the constitutional jurisdictions of the provinces]" (2017) Special no. HS17 Revue juridique de l'environnement 73.

6 *Supra* note 2 at 7.

7 "Le Canada consacrera 2,65 milliards pour lutter contre les changements climatiques [Canada will dedicate $2.65 billion to fight climate change]", *Radio Canada* (27 November 2015), online: <ici.radio-canada.ca/nouvelle/752192/changement-climatique-canada-aide-pays-ges-environnement-trudeau-dion>.

8 In 2021 the Prime Minister announced a new target of 40–45 percent below 2005 emissions. Prime Minister of Canada, "Prime Minister Trudeau Announces Increased Climate Ambition" (22 April 2021, accessed 28 June 2021), online: <pm.gc.ca/en/news/news-releases/2021/04/22/prime-minister-trudeau-announces-increased-climate-ambition>.

9 2009 decision to reduce GHGs by 17 percent from 2005 to 2020. "Emissions Target Set Ahead of Copenhagen Climate Summit", *The Hill* (11 November 2009), online: <thehill.com/homenews/administration/69417-obama-to-go-to-copenhagen-for-climate-summit>. For the Canadian government, it is always a matter of levelling the playing field with the Americans, given the integration of the two economies. Environment Canada, "Emissions Trends in Canada 2014" (accessed 28 June 2021), online: <www.canada.ca/en/environment-climate-change/services/climate-change/publications/emission-trends-2014/executive-summary.html> at n 1.

10 Environment Canada, *ibid.*

11 Hugues Hellio, "Les 'contributions déterminées au niveau national,' instruments au statut juridique en devenir ["Nationally determined contributions," instruments with a legal status in the making]" (2017) HS17 RJE 33 at para 8.

12 *Paris Agreement, being an Annex to the Report of the Conference of the Parties on Its Twenty-first Session, Held in Parties from 30 November to 13 December 2015—Addendum Part Two: Action Taken by the Conference of the Parties at Its Twenty-first Session, 12 December 2015*, UN Doc FCCC/CP/2015/10/Add.1, 55 ILM 740 (entered into force 4 November 2016) art 4.2.

13 *Ibid.*

14 Hellio, *supra* note 11 at para 8.

15 *Ibid* at paras 21–22.

16 *Paris Agreement*, being an Annex to the *Report of the Conference of the Parties on Its Twenty-first Session, Held in Parties from 30 November to 13 December 2015—Addendum Part Two: Action Taken by the Conference of the Parties at Its Twenty-first Session*, 12 December 2015, UN Doc FCCC/CP/2015/10/Add.1, 55 ILM 740 (entered into force 4 November 2016) [*Paris Agreement*] art 13.

17 *Ibid* art 4(3).

18 *Ibid* art 13(5).

19 *Ibid* art 13(7).

20 *Ibid* art 15(2).

21 Government of Canada, "Pan-Canadian Framework on Clean Growth and Climate Change Canadian Plan for Climate Change and Economic Growth" (2016, accessed 28 June 2021), online: <www.canada.ca/en/services/environment/weather/climatechange/pan-canadian-framework/climate-change-plan.html>.

22 *References re Greenhouse Gas Pollution Pricing Act*, 2021 SCC 11 [*GGPPA*].

23 *Ward v Canada (AG)*, [2002] 1 SCR 569 at para 17; *Reference re Firearms Act (Can)*, [2000] 1 SCR 783 at para 16; *R v Morgentaler*, [1993] 1 SCR 462.

24 Office of the Auditor General of Canada, "2009 Spring Report of the Commissioner of the Environment and Sustainable Development" (2009, accessed 28 June 2021) ch 2, online: <publications.gc.ca/collections/collection_2009/bvg-oag/FA1-2-2009-1-0E.pdfl>.

25 *Turp v Canada (Justice)*, [2012] 1 FCR 439. Abandoned on appeal.

26 *Turp v Chrétien*, 2003 FCT 301; *Friends of the Earth v Canada*, 2008 FC 1183, [2009] 3 FCR 201 [*Friends of the Earth*].

27 *Friends of the Earth*, *supra* note 26 at para 13.

28 *Ibid* at para 43.

29 *The Constitution Act, 1867*, s 9 para 132.

30 *Canada (AG) v Ontario (AG)*, [1937] AC 326; Henri Brun, Guy Tremblay & Eugénie Brouillet, *Droit constitutionnel*, 6th ed (Cowansville, QC: Yvon Blais, 2014) at 496–499; Hugo Cyr, *Canadian Federalism and Treaty Power* (Brussels: Peter Lang, 2009).

31 Andréanne Apablaza, "La Saskatchewan entend mener une bataille judiciaire contre la taxe carbone fédérale [Saskatchewan intends to fight the federal carbon tax]," *Radio Canada* (18 May 2017), online: <ici.radio-canada.ca/nouvelle/1034579/saskatchewan-bataille-judiciaire-ottawa-taxe-carbone>.

32 Bill C-74, *An Act to Implement Certain Provisions of the Budget Tabled in Parliament on February 27, 2018 and Other Measures*, 1st Sess, 42nd Parl, 2018, (as passed by the House of Commons 21 June 2018) at part 5.

33 "La Saskatchewan conteste la taxe carbone d'Ottawa devant les tribunaux [Saskatchewan intends to fight the federal carbon tax]", *Radio Canada* (25 April 2018), online: <ici.radio-canada.ca/nouvelle/1097253/contestation-cour-cadre-pancanadien-climatique>.

34 "Décision du fédéral sur les pipelines : l'Alberta est satisfaite [Federal decision on pipelines: Alberta is satisfied]", *Radio Canada* (29 November 2016), online: <ici.radio-canada.ca/nouvelle/1002930/rachel-notley--satisfaite-decision-ottawa-projets-enbridge-pipelines-northern-gateway-transmountain>.

35 Government of Alberta, *Climate Leadership Plan: Progress Report 2016–2017* (1 December 2017) at table PL 1.2, online: <open.alberta.ca/publications/climate-leadership-plan-progress-report-2016-17]>. For a review on this subject, see: Jean-Maurice Arbour, *supra* note 5.

36 *Québec (AG) v Canada (AG)*, 2015 SCC 14, [2015] 1 RCS 693 at para 154: "the principle of cooperative federalism—which permits a government at one level to pass laws that have an impact on the powers of the other level"; Brooke Jeffrey, "Les relations intergouvernementales: une ére nouvelle?" BP-111F (Ottawa: Library of Parliament, December 1984).

37 Nathalie Chalifour, "The Constitutional Authority to Levy Carbon Taxes" in Thomas J Courchene & John Allan, eds, *The State of the Federation, Institute of Intergovernmental Relations* (Montreal: McGill-Queen's University Press, 2009).

38 Government of Canada, "Carbon Pollution Pricing Systems across Canada" (2021), online <www.canada.ca/en/environment-climate-change/services/climate-change/pricing-pollution-how-it-will-work.html>.

39 Jean-Maurice Arbour, *supra* note 5 at 79.

40 SC 2018, c 12, s 186.

41 *GGPPA*, *supra* note 22.

42 *R v Hydro-Québec*, [1997] 3 SCR 213; *Ibid.* The federal legislative authority over criminal matters, which is based on section 91(27) of the *Constitution Act, 1867*, would likely allow it the constitutional foundation to adopt its carbon tax, had the legislator done so as to regulate GHGs by means of criminal sanctions. Indeed, the Supreme Court of Canada has already ruled, by interpreting the federal jurisdiction in criminal matters in a broad manner, that a prohibition with a penal sanction is criminal law and that Part II of the *Canadian Environmental Protection Act* is valid under this federal head of power. Part II applies to the control of toxic substances released into the environment.

43 *R v Crown Zellerbach Canada Ltd.*, [1988] 1 SCR 401; Nathalie Chalifour, *supra* note 37.

44 *Re: Exported Natural Gas Tax*, [1982] 1 SCR 1004.

45 *R v Hydro Québec*, [1997] 3 SCR 213: "Determining that a particular subject matter is a matter of national concern involves the consequence that the matter falls within the exclusive and paramount power of Parliament and has obvious impact on the balance of Canadian federalism. In Crown Zellerbach, the minority (at 453) expressed the view that the subject of environmental protection was all-pervasive, and if accepted as falling within the general legislative domain of Parliament under the national concern doctrine, could radically alter the division of legislative power in Canada."

46 *In the Matter of Reference re Greenhouse Gas Pollution Pricing Act, 2019*, SKCA 40.

47 *Reference re Greenhouse Gas Pollution Pricing Act*, 2019 ONCA 54 at paras 233–237, 241.

48 *Ibid.*

49 Supreme Court of Canada, "References re Greenhouse Gas Pollution Pricing Act" (25 March 2021), online: <www.scc-csc.ca/case-dossier/cb/2021/38663-38781-39116-eng.aspx>; *GGPPA*, *supra* note 22.

50 *GGPPA*, *supra* note 22 at 433.

51 Alberta Energy Regulator, "Oil Sands" 2021, online: <www.aer.ca/providing-information/by-topic/oil-sands>.

52 "Estimated Production of Canadian Crude Oil and Equivalent" 2015, online: *Canada Energy Regulator* <www.cer-rec.gc.ca/en/data-analysis/energy-commodities/crude-oil-petroleum-products/statistics/estimated-production-canadian-crude-oil-equivalent.html>.

53 Canadian Association of Petroleum Producers, "2019 Crude Oil Forecast, Markets and Transportation" (2019) 2019-008, online (pdf): <www.capp.ca/wp-content/uploads/2019/11/2019_Crude_Oil_Forecast_Markets_and_Transportation-338794.pdf> at 5.

54 "Il faut de nouveaux pipelines, dit l'Association canadienne des producteurs pétroliers [New pipelines are needed, says the Canadian Association of Petroleum Producers]," *Radio Canada* (23 June 2016), online: <ici.radio-canada.ca/nouvelle/789101/petrole-pipeline-oleoduc-sables-bitumineux-production-economie>.

55 Canadian Environmental Assessment Agency, "Pacific NorthWest LNG Project Environmental Assessment Report" 2016, s 6.2.2.

56 *Haida Nation v British Columbia (Minister of Forests)*, [2004] 3 SCR 511; *Mikisew Cree First Nation v Canada (Minister of Canadian Heritage)*, [2005] 3 SCR 388.

57 *Gitxaala Nation et al v Canada (AG) et al*, 2016 FCA 187.

58 Alexandre Shields, "TransCanada annonce la fin du projet Énergie Est [TransCanada Announces End of Energy East Project]", *Le Devoir* (5 October 2017).

59 Joël-Denis Bellavance, "Abandon d'Énergie Est: une décision d'affaires, dit le ministre Carr [Abandon Energy East: A Business Decision, says Minister Carr]", *La Presse* (5 October 2017).

60 *An Act to Enact the Impact Assessment Act and the Canadian Energy Regulator Act, to Amend the Navigation Protection Act and to Make Consequential Amendments to Other Acts*, SC 2019, c 28. This Act, better known as "Bill C-69," established the new *Impact Assessment Act* that replaced the *Canadian Environmental Assessment Act, 2012*, SC 2012, c 19, s 52 [*CEAA 2012*], thereby modifying the federal environmental assessment system and adding various measures to take climate change into account in impact assessments. These measures are a return to the pendulum, inasmuch as Parliament had incorporated in its 2012 budget implementation bill provisions (C-38), providing for the replacement of the federal environmental assessment process by the new process assessment set out in *CEAA 2012*. See *Jobs, Growth and Long-term Prosperity Act*, SC 2012, c 19; Bill C-38, *An Act to Implement Certain Provisions of the Budget Tabled in Parliament on March 29, 2012 and Other Measures*, 1st Sess, 41st Parl, 2012, (as passed by the House of Commons 29 June 2012) at s 52 that promulgated *CEAA 2012*. Considering that the shortcomings of the environmental assessment process constituted an obstacle to economic development, the government successfully passed Bill C-38 in June 2012. For a full discussion on this, see: Penny Becklumb & Tim Williams, *The New Federal Environmental Assessment Process in Canada*, 2012-36-F (Ottawa: Library of Parliament, 28 December 2012).

61 Peter Dietsch, "Un vrai compromis est possible au sujet du pipeline Trans Mountain [True compromise is possible on the Trans Mountain Pipeline]", *Le Devoir* (31 May 2018), online: <www.ledevoir.com/opinion/idees/529107/un-vrai-compromis-est-possible-au-sujet-du-pipeline-trans-mountain>.

62 *Tseil-Waututh Nation v Canada (Attorney General)*, 2018 FCA 153.

63 *Ibid*, para 567.

64 *Ibid*, para 568.

65 *Ibid*, paras 559–564.

66 "Notley se retire du plan sur le climat après la décision sur Trans Mountain [Notley withdraws from climate plan after Trans Mountain decision]", *La Presse* (30 August 2018), online: <www.lapresse.ca/affaires/economie/energie-et-ressources/201808/30/01-5194799-notley-se-retire-du-plan-sur-le-climat-apres-la-decision-sur-trans-mountain.php>.

67 *Coldwater et al v Canada (AG) et al*, 2020 CAF 34.

68 *Reference re Environmental Management Act, 2020*, SCC 1.

69 International Energy Agency, *Key World Energy Statistics* (2012), online: <www.oecd-ilibrary.org/>; Montreal Economic Institute, "Canada's Energy Profile in 40 Questions" (2012).

70 Senate Canada, "Positioning Canada's Electricity Sector in a Constrained Carbon Future. Report of the Standing Senate Committee on Energy, the Environment and Natural Resources" (March 2017), online (pdf): <gardn.org/wp-content/uploads/2017/03/2017-02-24-ENEV-Interim-Electricity-Report_FINAL_e.pdf>.

71 J Whitmore & Pierre-Olivier Pineau, État de *l'énergie au Québec 2018* [*State of Energy in Quebec 2018*] Energy Sector Management Chair, HEC (Montréal: December 2017); Pierre-Olivier Pineau, "Transition énergétique au Québec : prospérer dans la sobriété [Energy Transition in Quebec: Growing in Sobriety]," Conference by Pierre-Olivier

Pineau, Université Laval (Quebec City: 13 February 2017), online: <www.drne.ulaval.ca/fr/pierre-olivier-pineau-transition-energetique-au-quebec-prosperer-dans-la-sobriete>.

72 *Ibid.*

73 *Ibid.*

74 Pierre-Olivier Pineau, "Transition énergétique", *supra* note 71.

75 *Ibid.*

76 *Environnement Jeunesse v Attorney General of Canada*, 2019 QCSC 2885. Decision appealed to the Québec Court of Appeal: declaration of appeal 2019-08-19 (CA), 500-09-028523-199.

77 *La Rose v Her Majesty the Queen, Federal Court of Canada*, No. T-1750-19 FC, 2019 (25 October 2019).

78 Columbia University's Sabin Center maintains a database of more than 1,300 climate actions worldwide, more than eight hundred of which take place in the United States: Sabin Center, Climate Change Litigation Databases, online: <climatecasechart.com>; see on the subject: D Markell & J-B Ruhl, "An Empirical Assessment of Climate Change in the Courts: A New Jurisprudence or Business as Usual?" (2012) 64:1 Fla L Rev 27; Christel Cournil, "The Convergence of Climate Action against the State: Comparative Study of National Litigation" (2017) EJN 246; Mathilde Hautereau-Boutonnet, "Le procès climatique par la doctrine du procès climatique [Climate Trials by the Doctrine on Climate Trials]" in C Cournil and L Varison, eds, *Les procès climatique, Entre la national et l'international* [Climate Trials between the International and the National] (Paris: Pedone, 2018) at 31–32.

21

National Carbon Pricing in Canada

Fenner L. Stewart[1] *and Scott A. Carrière*[2]

Introduction

The need for decarbonization mechanisms in Canada, like the *Greenhouse Gas Pollution Pricing Act* (*GGPPA*),[3] is unquestionable. On October 8, 2018, the United Nation's Intergovernmental Panel on Climate Change released an urgent plea, warning that the world had less than twelve years to radically alter its consumption of carbon-intensive fuels or suffer catastrophic consequences.[4] Sound science, reading more like science fiction, backs this warning.[5]

This chapter provides an overview of *GGPPA* and its enforcement mechanisms. Part II sketches out the rationale for greenhouse gas (GHG) pricing. Part III locates *GGPPA* on the GHG governance landscape. Part IV outlines how *GGPPA* works. Part V considers *GGPPA*'s enforcement mechanisms. Part VI is the conclusion.

A Rationale for Greenhouse Gas Pricing

Arthur Pigou first articulated the rationale for imposing price as a corrective measure for air pollution.[6] In *The Economics of Welfare*, he explores the theory of cost externalization (i.e. when the total cost of a product's production and consumption are not reflected fully in its price). He explains the idea in the following example:

> One person, A, in the course of rendering some service, for which payment is made, to a second person, R, incidentally also disservices to others (not producers of like services), of such a sort that payment

> cannot be exacted from the benefited parties or compensation enforced on behalf of the injured parties.[7]

As Pigou's example highlights, the central problem of such an externalization arises when a third party is forced to pay for some or all of the excluded cost.

Another example provides additional clarity. Tupou is a company that manufactures and sells widgets. A production technology exists for making widgets that prevent the contamination of groundwater, but it is expensive. Tupou elects not to use it. As a result, Tupou manufactures its products at a lower cost compared to some of its competitors.

Tupou manufactures high-quality widgets at low cost due to its inexpensive production process. Moreover, it passes this reduced cost on to its customers, helping to ensure their loyalty. This strategy has led Tupou to achieve strong annual profits for years. Many people find good value in their widgets.

However, not everyone is happy with this arrangement. Scientists have established that the effluent from Tupou's factory is poisoning the groundwater. Plants, animals, and people living close to the factory are increasingly sick. Farmers' crops are failing, and their animals are dying. Strange forms of cancer are on the rise. People who try to sell their property and leave the community find that their property value has decreased sharply—if they can sell it at all.[8]

In a world without tort law and government intervention, neither Tupou nor its customers will pay for these costs. Tupou's choice not to adopt the technology has benefited many, but only at the expense of others. From the Pigouvian perspective, the cost of polluting has been externalized upon those who have been made worse off.[9]

In *The Problem of Social Cost*, Ronald Coase both refutes and refines Pigou's theory by shifting focus from preventing externalities to optimizing harm reduction. He asserts:

> The problem which we face in dealing with actions which have harmful effects is not simply one of restraining those responsible for them. What has to be decided is whether the gain from preventing the harm is greater than the loss which would be suffered elsewhere as a result of stopping the action which produces the harm.[10]

Coase uses the example of when one farmer's cattle stray into another farmer's field and destroy crops to illustrate his point:

> In the case of the cattle and the crops, it is true that there would be no crop damage without the cattle. It is equally true that there would be no crop damage without the crops . . . If we are to discuss the problem in terms of causation, both parties cause the damage. If we are to attain an optimum allocation of resources, it is therefore desirable that both parties should take the harmful effect (the nuisance) into account in deciding on their course of action. It is one of the beauties of a smoothly operating pricing system that, as has already been explained, the fall in the value of production due to the harmful effect would be a cost for both parties.[11]

What Coase is alluding to in the last sentence is his theorem (which employs a form of market modelling), whose calculus identifies the optimal outcome of such hypotheticals.[12] Gareth Bryant provides succinct elaboration:

> Coase's framework universalises responsibility for fixing environmental problems to all parties—polluters and non-polluters alike . . . impacts that are viewed as external to the market are to be internalised by expanding the sphere of market until everything is covered by property rights, enrolling all actors into the market solution. Popularised as the "Coase theorem," the argument is that given clearly defined property rights and no transaction costs, trade between private actors will produce an efficient allocation of resources and maximize the total value of production.[13]

Applying the Coase theorem to the example of the two farmers requires working out the ideal combination of transactions involving cattle, crops, and compensation to achieve the optimal economic outcome. One must assume "a smoothly operating pricing system" exists (i.e. limited regulation other than contract and property law, zero transaction costs, full information, and rational actors).[14]

Today, Coase's work helps to establish a fundamental and common understanding between most economists, which supports the agreement that GHG pricing is an essential regulatory device amongst the suite of policy options.[15]

Accordingly, prominent environmental economists have advanced the calculus of costs and benefits, working out market solutions to climate change.[16] For instance, William Nordhaus takes two variables into consideration: one is the costs and benefits of adopting the mitigation measures that maximize the reduction of climate change damage regardless of the total cost, and the other is the costs and benefits of doing nothing and letting climate change take its course.[17] He then explains how balancing these endpoints achieves a midground, which optimizes the *social cost of carbon*.[18] William Nordhaus, and others, see GHG pricing mechanisms as a tool for helping steer policy toward such results.[19]

Others question the marketization of climate change, pointing to how the "dominant narratives in existing research do not sit well with the practical experience of marketized climate policy."[20] Today, the need for climate policy action is acute as the world's response to climate change continues to fall well short of the *Paris Agreement*'s targets for 2040.[21] This shortfall is alarming since the Secretariat of the United Nations Framework Convention on Climate Change freely admits that the "plan to meet the 2°C target" of the *Paris Agreement* will only "offer a 50:50 chance of avoiding the worst effects of climate change."[22]

Locating the *Greenhouse Gas Pollution Pricing Act* on the Greenhouse Gas Governance Landscape

GHG governance is not limited to government action.[23] Canadian governments at both the national and subnational levels operate within a more layered, or "multi-scalar, regulatory environment."[24] The decentering of regulation has led governments to share their rule-making authority and, more importantly, their responsibility for doing so with both industry (e.g. self-regulation) and civil society (e.g. corporate social responsibility mechanisms).[25] As a result, these non-state actors are not only rule-takers in a narrowly conceived economic sense, but also private rule-makers (e.g. banks as controllers of lending practices and non-governmental organizations as certifiers of corporate responsibility).[26] Conversely, governments are becoming rule-takers (e.g. through participatory and collaborative mechanisms for decision-making).[27] The resulting regulatory intricacy is easy to underestimate, hinting at some of the potential opportunities and challenges that multi-scalar governance presents today.[28]

The *GGPPA* also exists within a broad policy portfolio with other GHG emission reduction tools. Such tools take three basic forms at the state level: (1) command and control instruments, (2) market-based instruments, and (3) financial instruments.[29] Command and control instruments usually take one of two types. The first type mandates technology-based standards (i.e. dictating equipment or processes to be adopted, such as the rate of electric car adoption or the use of carbon-capture mechanisms). The second mandates a performance-based standard (i.e. dictating the emission ends but not the means, such as an emissions ceiling for a new power station).[30] Although the *GGPPA* possesses penalties for non-compliance,[31] it more closely resembles market-based regulation.

Market-based instruments can also be subcategorized. Such instruments create a price for emitting through either a levy on emissions (i.e. setting a regulatory charge per unit of emission) or an emissions market (i.e. producing a supply of, and demand for, allowances or permits for emissions that can be traded between emitters).[32]

Finally, financial instruments can be a fiscal measure (i.e. using the processes of collecting and spending government revenue to incentivize lower emissions, such as tax credits or subsidies), a price-support mechanism (i.e. creating advantages for the purchase of low-emission goods or services, such as minimum price guarantees for, or mandated use of, available renewable energy), or an investment incentive (i.e. granting funds for or low-cost financing to the research, development, and/or marketing of lower emission products).[33] Like other governments,[34] Canada does not rely on employing only one option; it adopts a mix of command and control, market-based, and financial instruments.[35]

Of these potential forms of state action, economists largely agree that market-based strategies are superior.[36] In particular, they tend to favour trading markets, since they reward those who can reduce emissions at the lowest cost, which in turn can optimize the cost of reducing GHG emissions.[37] That said, these market-based strategies are not without detractors. Some environmentalists challenge the suggestion that the climate change crisis can be framed as a "market failure" whose optimal solution is a price on GHG emissions.[38] They caution that this framing results in—whether intentional or not—a narrowing of "political pathways,"[39] which limits the potential for more meaningful "climate justice."[40] Both the *Kyoto Protocol* and the *Paris Agreement* sided with the former, endorsing market-based strategies as the central means to reducing GHG emissions.[41] Following this lead, Canada has made the *GGPPA* a "core element" of its emissions reduction strategy.[42]

Greenhouse Gas Pricing in Canada

The *GGPPA* sets a floor for GHG pricing throughout Canada,[43] called the benchmark.[44] On October 23, 2018, Prime Minister Justin Trudeau issued a press release confirming that starting in 2019, the benchmark would be $20 per tonne of emissions (CO_2 equivalence), which will increase $10 each year to $50 per tonne in 2022.[45]

The *GGPPA*'s operation is detailed in two parts. Part 1 provides for a fuel charge levied formally on distributors, importers, and producers,[46] but in practice, these costs are expected to be passed on to consumers, either fully or partially. Part 2 sets out a regime for industrial facilities with emissions above a specified per tonne threshold.

If a province fails to meet the benchmark, the federal government will impose it through an enforcement mechanism called the backstop.[47] The backstop is triggered when a province becomes listed.[48] A "listed province" is defined as "a province or area listed in Part 1 of Schedule 1."[49] When a province fails to meet the benchmark, the Governor in Council (i.e. the federal cabinet) lists the province, making it subject to the application of the *GGPPA*.[50]

As of 2021, Ontario, Manitoba, Saskatchewan, Yukon, and Nunavut are listed with respect to both Parts 1 and 2 of *GGPPA*; Alberta is listed under Part 1; and Prince Edward Island is listed for Part 2.[51] The *GGPPA* was not initially applied to Alberta due to its *Climate Leadership Act*,[52] legislation substantially similar to the federal backstop; however, the province became listed after its legislation was repealed in 2019.[53] Alberta later introduced the *Technology Innovation and Emissions Reduction Implementation Act*,[54] which was accepted as an equivalent for the purposes of *GGPPA* Part 2,[55] but has not moved to (re)introduce an equivalent fuel charge or similar instrument. Prince Edward Island adopted its own *Climate Leadership Act* in 2019, which included a fuel levy but not a regime for large emitters;[56] the province has elected to rely on the backstop for the latter rather than craft its own policy.[57]

Enforcement of Greenhouse Gas Pricing in Canada

GHG pricing does not create an absolute prohibition, and the penalty for consumption is price. The benchmark will increase the price for emitting GHGs over time.[58] In this way, *GGPPA* allows Canadians and firms to transition to a low-carbon lifestyle by offering financial incentives for making low-carbon choices (e.g. buying an electric car or smart energy technologies).[59]

In theory, when the cost of emitting is high enough, market actors will avoid emitting by decreasing emissions-producing activities or seeking efficiencies.[60] This shift will create demand for less emissions-intensive inputs into production and consumer goods, which in turn will create opportunities for profit.[61] Entrepreneurs will attempt to seize these opportunities, which will incentivize innovation.[62] Accordingly, they will invest in new technologies that provide both enhanced energy efficiency and alternative energy sources because it is profitable to do so.[63] Thus, the *GGPPA* leverages markets to drive decarbonization through price signals, optimizing polluter compliance and decarbonization innovation.[64]

From a different vantage point on enforcement, the *GGPPA* would never be imposed upon provinces in an ideal world. The federal government would set the benchmark, and all provinces would comply. To do so, each province would tailor a flexible, decentralized pricing mechanism, which would be calibrated for its local economic circumstances.[65] Thus, the federal government would set the benchmark, and tailored provincial regulation would enforce it. The architecture of GHG pricing would be politically negotiated, allowing for broad diversity at the subnational level—a model of cooperative federalism.[66] An uncontested *GGPPA* has the capacity to accomplish this end.

The *GGPPA* is generous to provinces with smaller economies. It acknowledges that creating, implementing, and enforcing regulation is not costless. Each province has the discretion to be added voluntarily to the register of listed provinces, allowing the federal government to administer GHG pricing on its behalf.[67] In this way, such a province could avoid the administrative costs associated with a GHG pricing mechanism, while still receiving the benefit of the "net amount" of revenue, if it exists.[68] For instance, Prince Edward Island has adopted this approach in part, deciding to administer its own fuel charge, while teaming up with the federal government to administer *GGPPA*'s regime for industrial emitters.[69]

However, Canadian federalism is not as cooperative as it would be in an ideal world, and the *GGPPA* acknowledges this fact, granting the federal government enough power so that it does not have to negotiate GHG pricing with provinces.[70] The federal government can seize total jurisdiction over the entire field of regulation, removing the listed province from exercising any discretion over the matter.[71] After a province is listed, the federal government will impose the *GGPPA* in the jurisdiction of the listed province, and retain the discretion to grant, or not, any of the net amount of revenues to a province directly.[72] It enjoys the privilege of spending said revenues in the province as it sees fit, funding the climate change or revenue recycling initiatives that it prefers, removing the province completely from the GHG pricing initiative.[73]

Concluding Thoughts

Canada adopted the *GGPPA* as a national response to the global call to reduce GHG emissions. This pricing mechanism allows GHG emitters to adjust their economic choices, increasing incentives to decarbonize over time.

If a province or territory refuses to cooperate, the *GGPPA* utilizes some of the tremendous authority that the Constitution bestows on Parliament. This assertion of authority triggered a constitutional challenge. Constitutional analysis suggested GHG pricing can be valid under the criminal law power, but the drafters of *GGPPA* elected a different route, testing the boundaries of the federal government's residual power.

The Supreme Court of Canada had to decide whether to approve the *GGPPA* in its current form (which introduces unknowns for the future balance of federalism) or deem the *GGPPA* invalid in whole or in part. The court elected the former. It is foreseeable that all provinces will eventually appreciate that cooperating with the federal government's administration of the benchmark is the best option (i.e. if the primary goal is to maximize jurisdictional autonomy).[74]

Whatever form the *GGPPA* eventually settles into, the basic policy mechanism will not change. The federal government will use the benchmark to set the standard for pricing, and the provinces will pursue plans that account for their unique economies and geographies within its rubric. When the dust settles, a coordinated network of subnational regulatory laboratories for GHG pricing will emerge. Each will be customized in its means; all will be coordinated in their ends. In this way, the *GGPPA* allows for tremendous freedom and discretion to achieve a targeted result; the only thing a province or territory cannot do is fail to meet the benchmark. In fact, the backstop's form is of little matter so long as each subnational jurisdiction customizes its own pricing mechanism and assumes that benchmark compliance is always the best option.

NOTES

1 Associate Professor at the University of Calgary, Faculty of Law.

2 Articling Student at Osler, Hoskin & Harcourt LLP in Calgary.

3 *Greenhouse Gas Pollution Pricing Act*, SC 2018, c 12, s 186 [*GGPPA*].

4 United Nations Intergovernmental Panel on Climate Change, "Summary for Policymakers of IPCC Special Report on Global Warming of 1.5°C approved by governments" (8 October 2018), online: <www.ipcc.ch/2018/10/08/summary-for-policymakers-of-ipcc-special-report-on-global-warming-of-1-5c-approved-by-governments/>.

5 See e.g., Solomon Hsiang et al, "Estimating Economic Damage from Climate Change in the United States" (2017) 356:6345 Science 1362.

6 Stefan Speck, "The Design of Carbon and Broad-Based Energy Taxes in European Countries" (2008) 10 VJEL 31 at 36.

7 Arthur Cecil Pigou, *The Economics of Welfare*, 4th ed (London: Macmillan, 1932) at 183.

8 For those who believe such a scenario is farfetched, consider the alleged facts of residences from Parkersburg, West Virginia. See e.g., Nathaniel Rich, "The Lawyer Who Became DuPont's Worst Nightmare", *New York Times* (6 January 2016), online: <www.nytimes.com/2016/01/10/magazine/the-lawyer-who-became-duponts-worst-nightmare.html>; Roy Shapira & Luigi Zingales, "Is Pollution Value-Maximizing? The DuPont Case" (2017) National Bureau of Economic Research Working Paper No 23866, online (pdf): <www.nber.org/papers/w23866.pdf>.

9 Pigou, *supra* note 7 at 183.

10 RH Coase, "The Problem of Social Cost" (1960) 3 JL & Econ 1 at 27.

11 *Ibid* at 13.

12 *Ibid* at 6–8.

13 Gareth Bryant, *Carbon Markets in a Climate-Changing Capitalism* (Cambridge, UK: Cambridge University Press, 2019) at 22.

14 Economists have struggled to find theoretical solutions to similar problems before Coase, which have become axioms of his theorem. See e.g., Jonathan Law, ed, *A Dictionary of Law*, 8th ed (Oxford: Oxford University Press, 2015): "Kaldor-Hicks efficiency . . . A Pareto efficiency arises when at least one person is made better off and no one is made worse off. In practice, however, it is extremely difficult to make any change without making at least one person worse off. Under the Kaldor-Hicks efficiency test, an outcome is efficient if those who are made better off could *in theory* compensate those who are made worse off and so produce a Pareto efficient outcome." For origins of the theory, see JR Hicks, "The Foundations of Welfare Economics" (1939) 49:196 Economic J 696; Nicholas Kaldor, "Welfare Propositions in Economics and Interpersonal Comparisons of Utility" (1939) 49:195 Economic J 549.

15 Bryant, *supra* note 13. "The external conception of nature views nature as external from society, often as 'pristine, God-given, autonomous' . . . Smith, along with Harvey, links the externalisation of nature with projects aimed at the 'subjugation' or 'domination' of nature. This is also evident in the Pigouvian faith that society can perfect its use of nature (i.e., carbon pollution) with appropriate market-based solutions. The universal conception of nature, in contrast, views society as nature, and therefore, governed by natural laws. Coase's notion of the reciprocity of costs is presented in a similarly universal manner, where the efficiency of markets becomes a ubiquitous

natural law. The political implications of the universal conception of nature is not its subjugation or domination, but rather submission to nature (i.e., the market), because 'capitalism is natural; to fight it is to fight human nature'. Coasian market solutions universalise responsibility for climate change by implicating all actors in the pursuit of economic optimality" at 23–24. See e.g., Andrea Baranzini et al, "Carbon Pricing in Climate Policy: Seven Reasons, Complementary Instruments, and Political Economy Considerations" (2017) 8 WIREs Climate Change 1 at 4–5; Ross McKitrick, "A Practical Guide to the Economics of Carbon Pricing" (2016) 9:28 SPP Research Papers at 5; and Canada's Ecofiscal Commission, *Bridging the Gap: Real Options for Meeting Canada's 2030 GHG Target* (Montreal, QC: McGill University, 2019), online (pdf): <ecofiscal.ca/wp-content/uploads/2019/11/Ecofiscal-Commission-Bridging-the-Gap-November-27-2019-FINAL.pdf>. "Several factors will offset the effects of gradually rising carbon prices, including behavioural change, technological change, and rebates that will rise over time alongside the carbon price. Our modelling finds that a carbon price that rises from $30 per tonne in 2020 to $210 per tonne in 2030 can meet Canada's Paris target. This translates into a 3.8 cents per year average annual increase in the price of gas. This gradual increase gives businesses and households time to respond and prepare, which helps reduce the overall costs of the policy" at 18.

16 See e.g., William D Nordhaus, *A Question of Balance: Weighing the Options on Global Warming Policies* (New Haven, CT: Yale University Press, 2008) at 1–29 [Nordhaus, *A Question of Balance*]. "In practice, an economic analysis of climate change weighs the costs of slowing climate change against the damages of more rapid climate change. On the side of the costs of slowing climate change, countries must consider whether, and by how much, to reduce their GHG emissions. Reducing GHGs, particularly if the reductions are to be deep, will primarily require taking costly steps to reduce CO_2 emissions. Some steps involve reducing the use of fossil fuels; others involve using different production techniques or alternative fuels and energy sources. Societies have considerable experience in employing different approaches to changing energy production and use patterns. Economic history and analysis indicate that it will be most effective to use the market mechanism, primarily higher prices on carbon fuels, to give signals and provide incentives for consumers and firms to change their energy use and reduce their carbon emissions. In the longer run, higher carbon prices will provide incentives for firms to develop new technologies to ease the transition to a low carbon future" at 5. See also William D Nordhaus, "Revisiting the Social Cost of Carbon" (2017) 114:7 PNAS 1518 [Nordhaus, "Revisiting the Social Cost of Carbon"].

17 For a plain language understanding of his thought, see William D Nordhaus, "Climate Change: The Ultimate Challenge for Economics" (Nobel Prize Lecture in Economic Sciences delivered at the Aula Magna, Stockholm University, 8 December 2018), online: <www.nobelprize.org/prizes/economic-sciences/2018/nordhaus/lecture/>.

18 *Ibid.*

19 Nordhaus, *A Question of Balance*, *supra* note 17 at 148.

20 Bryant, *supra* note 13 at 2.

21 International Energy Agency, *World Energy Outlook* (Paris: OECD/IEA, 2017) at 327 [World Energy Outlook 2017]. See also *Paris Agreement, being an Annex to the Report of the Conference of the Parties on Its Twenty-first Session, Held in Parties from 30 November to 13 December 2015—Addendum Part Two: Action Taken by the Conference of the Parties at Its Twenty-first Session*, 12 December 2015, UN Doc FCCC/CP/2015/10/Add.1, 55 ILM 740 (entered into force 4 November 2016) [*Paris Agreement*].

22 Clive L Spash, "This Changes Nothing: The Paris Agreement to Ignore Reality" (2016) 13:6 Globalizations 928 at 929.

23 Michael P Vandenbergh & Jonathan M Gilligan, "Forks in the Road," 31 Duke Envtl L & Pol'y F [forthcoming in 2020]. Noting the layers of GHG governance in the US context to include "public policymakers (e.g., international, federal, state, and local government officials) and private policymakers (e.g., managers of philanthropies, corporations, civic and cultural groups, colleges and universities, and advocacy groups)" at 2. For a broader commentary on the shift from government to governance, see David Levi-Faur, "From 'Big Government' to 'Big Governance'?" in David Levi-Faur, ed, *The Oxford Handbook of Governance* (Oxford: Oxford University Press, 2012) 3 at 8; and RAW Rhodes, "Waves of Governance" in David Levi-Faur, ed, *The Oxford Handbook of Governance* (Oxford: Oxford University Press, 2012) 33. "Governance signifies a change in the meaning of government, referring to new processes of governing; or changed conditions of ordered rule; or new methods by which society is governed" at 33.

24 Cristie Ford, Innovation and the State: Finance, Regulation, and Justice (Cambridge, UK: Cambridge University Press, 2017) at 3.

25 Rhodes, *supra* note 23 at 35; *ibid* "Many aspects of modern societies are far too complex, diverse, and dynamic to be regulated in a centralized, command-and-control fashion" at 19 and "The subtlety of [such governance's] crucial distinction from neoconservative strategies could be all too easy to ignore, in favor of a superficial and ultimately false consensus around decentralization, self-regulation, and knocking down rigid pre-existing regulatory apparatuses" at 128. Fenner L Stewart, "Dominium and the Empire of Laws" (2019) 36 Windsor YB Access Just 36 at 43 [Stewart, "Dominium"]: "This regulatory architecture provides a prime example of how [civil society movements have] supported the shift from government to governance and, in doing so, [have] also reconstituted today's understanding of public-private governance (that is, how 'states, markets, civil society groups, and individuals interact'), challenging long-held notions about the essential elements of law" at 44–45; Fenner L Stewart & Anthony Cioni, "Holistic Security Risk Management Strategies for E&Ps: Optimizing Performance by Reducing Surface Risk" (2018) 11 J World Energy L & Bus 49: "[T]he combinations of market mechanisms and corporate social responsibility architectures are gaining traction, representing some of the best examples of intelligent institutional design today. And yet the mapping of such governance reveals there is much work to be done, considering the 'multitude of overlapping and sometimes inconsistent' combinations of 'network-design' in the global ether" at 71.

26 Stewart, "Dominium", *supra* note 25: "[The shift away from government] also marks a collective acknowledgement in policy circles that government—in particular, the welfare state—failed to be effective, leading to the conclusion that governments needed help from civil society and regulated actors (for example, business). Put differently, modern society was not going to run smoothly if government acted as the parent and regulated actors acted as the semi-cooperative children. From this perspective, the goal of dismantling the welfare state was not to create a deregulated free-for-all but, rather, to trigger a period of regulatory experimentalism, where new regulatory tools (for example, the CSR's non-state regulatory tools) could be introduced and then calibrated to improve or replace antiquated governance processes" at 41–42.

27 *Ibid.*

28 Rhodes, *supra* note 23: "The intrinsic rationality of markets, the path dependency of institutions, and the state's new toolkit for managing both the mix of governing structures and networks do not explain patterns of governance and how they change

. . . Governance arises out of the diverse actions and practices inspired by varied beliefs and traditions. It is the contingent product of diverse actions and political struggles informed by the beliefs of agents rooted in traditions" at 44.

29 Paul Haynes & Yongfu Huang, "Policies and Measures for Mitigating Climate Change" in Terry Barker & Douglas Crawford-Brown, eds, *Decarbonising the World's Economy: Assessing the Feasibility of Policies to Reduce Greenhouse Gas Emissions* (London: Imperial College Press, 2015) 29 at 33–43.

30 *Ibid* at 33–35.

31 *GGPPA*, *supra* note 3, ss 133–40.

32 Haynes & Huang, *supra* note 29 at 36–38.

33 Haynes & Huang, *supra* note 29 at 39–42.

34 Carolyn Fischer, Louis Preonas, & Richard G Newell, "Environmental and Technology Policy Options in the Electricity Sector: Are We Deploying Too Many?" (2017) 4:4 J Assoc Environmental & Resource Economists 959: "concerns about global warming, local air quality, and energy security have led to a plethora of actual and proposed initiatives aiming to reduce emissions from the power sector, promote electricity generation from renewable sources, and encourage energy conservation. Examples include portfolio standards and market share mandates, such as those requiring production shares for renewable or 'clean' energy sources; subsidies and tax relief for renewable sources like wind power and solar, geothermal, and biomass generation; policies to price greenhouse gas (GHG) emissions through cap and trade or a carbon tax; and performance standards, such as maximum emission rates per kilowatt-hour (kWh) of electricity and energy efficiency standards for household appliances. Those policies frequently coexist within the same jurisdiction, yet little attention has been paid to whether they work together or at cross purposes" at 959–960.

35 See e.g., Environment and Climate Change Canada, *Final Report of the Expert Panel on Sustainable Finance: Mobilizing Finance for Sustainable Growth* (Gatineau, QC: Environment and Climate Change Canada, 2019) [Final Report on Sustainable Finance]; and Environment and Climate Change Canada, *Pan-Canadian Framework on Clean Growth and Climate Change: Canada's Plan to Address Climate Change and Grow the Economy* (Gatineau, QC: Environment and Climate Change Canada, 2016) [*Pan-Canadian Framework*].

36 See e.g., Baranzini et al, *supra* note 15 at 4–5; and Nordhaus, "Revisiting the Social Cost of Carbon", *supra* note 16.

37 Bryant, *supra* note 13 at 9: "Carbon markets are preferred over carbon taxation because different actors have different marginal abatement costs. In this context, the ability to trade is said to offer the most efficient way to find 'least cost' emission reductions" at 9; and Organisation for Economic Co-operation and Development, *Effective Carbon Prices* (Paris: OECD, 2013): "The challenge facing the world community in relation to climate change is so enormous that it is unlikely that it can be met unless countries apply policy instruments that are as cost-effective as possible" at 13.

38 Bryant, *supra* note 13 at 9.

39 *Ibid* at 146.

40 See e.g., Brandon B Derman, *Struggles for Climate Justice: Uneven Geographies and the Politics of Connection* (London: Palgrave Macmillan, 2020): "Understanding climate change and climate injustice in wider, systemic perspective—as a biogeochemical phenomenon tightly linked with the social relations and material practices of

dispossession, privilege, and profit—enables linking them with a wide variety of already-meaningful objects of political force and opportunity. Successful articulation of this kind politicizes climate change, deepening and broadening self-identification by individuals and groups as 'stakeholders' in struggles for just and effective responses, and opening avenues for those struggles to unfold" at 185; and Paul Chatterton, David Featherstone, & Paul Routledge, "Articulating Climate Justice in Copenhagen: Antagonism, the Commons, and Solidarity" (2013) 45:3 Antipode 602: "Briefly defined, climate justice refers to principles of democratic accountability and participation, ecological sustainability and social justice and their combined ability to provide solutions to climate change. Such a notion focuses on the interrelationships between, and addresses the roots causes of, the social injustice, ecological destruction and economic domination perpetrated by the underlying logics of pro-growth capitalism. In particular, climate justice articulates a rejection of capitalist solutions to climate change (e.g. carbon markets) and foregrounds the uneven and persistent patterns of eco-imperialism and 'ecological debt' as a result of the historical legacy of uneven use of fossil fuels and exploitation of raw materials, offshoring, and export of waste" at 606.

41 *Kyoto Protocol to the United Nations Framework Convention on Climate Change*, 10 December 1997, 37 ILM 22 (1998), 2303 UNTS 148, UN Doc FCCC/CP/1997/7/Add.1 (entered into force 16 February 1997); and *Paris Agreement*, *supra* note 21.

42 Final Report on Sustainable Finance, *supra* note 35; and *Pan-Canadian Framework*, *supra* note 35.

43 Office of the Prime Minister of Canada, "Prime Minister Justin Trudeau Delivers a Speech on Pricing Carbon Pollution" (3 October 2016), online: <pm.gc.ca/eng/news/2016/10/03/prime-minister-trudeau-delivers-speech-pricing-carbon-pollution>.

44 *Pan-Canadian Framework*, *supra* note 35 at 49.

45 John Paul Tasker, "Trudeau Promises Rebates as Ottawa Moves to Levy Carbon Tax on Provinces Outside the Climate Plan", *CBC News* (23 October 2018), online: <www.cbc.ca/news/politics/tasker-carbon-tax-plan-trudeau-1.4874258>.

46 *GGPPA*, *supra* note 3, ss 17, 20, 21.

47 *Pan-Canadian Framework*, *supra* note 35 at 49.

48 *GGPPA*, *supra* note 3, ss 10, 16–17, 38, 40.

49 *Ibid*, s 3.

50 *Ibid*, ss 3, 166(2).

51 *Ibid*, schedule 1.

52 SA 2016, c C-16.9.

53 *An Act to Repeal the Carbon Tax*, SA 2019, c 1.

54 2019, SA 2019, c 16.

55 See *Part 1 of the Greenhouse Gas Pollution Pricing Act Regulations* (Alberta), SOR/2019-294.

56 RSPEI 1988, c C-9.1 [*Climate Leadership Act*].

57 See Government of Prince Edward Island, "Carbon Levy" (7 March 2019), online: <www.princeedwardisland.ca/en/information/finance/carbon-levy>.

58 *GGPPA*, *supra* note 3, preamble. See also Environment and Climate Change Canada, *Technical Paper on the Federal Carbon Pricing Backstop* (Gatineau, QC: Environment and Climate Change Canada, 2017) at 4, online (pdf): <www.canada.ca/content/dam/eccc/documents/pdf/20170518-2-en.pdf>; *Pan-Canadian Framework*, *supra* note 35 at 49; Government of Canada, "Supplemental Benchmark Guidance", online: <www.canada.ca/

en/services/environment/weather/climatechange/pan-canadian-framework/guidance-carbon-pollution-pricing-benchmark/supplemental-benchmark-guidance.html>.

59 *GGPPA*, *supra* note 3, preamble.

60 For projection as to how high carbon prices must be to affect change, see World Energy Outlook 2017, *supra* note 21 at 47–48.

61 Anita Rønne, "Smart Cities and Smart Regulation: Accelerating Innovative Renewable Technologies in Energy Systems to Mitigate Climate Change" in Donald Zillman et al, eds, *Innovation in Energy Law and Technology: Dynamic Solutions for Energy Transitions* (Oxford: Oxford University Press, 2018) at 55–8.

62 *Ibid.*

63 Consider the discussion of the connected demand for both energy efficiency and low-carbon fuels, World Energy Outlook 2017, *supra* note 21 at 309–329.

64 For more of the model and theories of modern environmental regulation, see Cary Coglianese & Jennifer Nash, "The Law of the Test: Performance-Based Regulation and Diesel Emissions Control" (2017) 34 Yale J Reg 33; Dayna Nadine Scott & Adrian A Smith, "Sacrifice Zones in the Green Energy Economy: Toward an Environmental Justice Framework" (2016) 62:3 McGill LJ 861; Steven Cohen, *Understanding Environmental Policy* (New York: Columbia University Press, 2014); Lori S Bennear & Cary Coglianese, "Flexible Approaches to Environmental Regulation" in Michael Kraft & Sheldon Kamieniecki, eds, *The Oxford Handbook of U.S. Environmental Policy* (Oxford: Oxford University Press, 2012); Neil Gunningham, Peter Grabosky, & Darren Sinclair, *Smart Regulation: Designing Environmental Policy* (Oxford: Oxford University Press, 1998); and Eric W Orts, "Reflexive Environmental Law" (1995) 89 Nw UL Rev 1227.

65 *GGPPA*, *supra* note 3, ss 17–35, 40, 48, 165.

66 See David Cameron & Richard Simeon, "Intergovernmental Relations in Canada: The Emergence of Collaborative Federalism" (2002) 32:2 Publius (The Journal of Federalism) 49.

67 *GGPPA*, *supra* note 3, s 3.

68 *Ibid*, s 165(2).

69 See *Climate Leadership Act*, *supra* note 56; and Government of Prince Edward Island, *supra* note 57.

70 *GGPPA*, *supra* note 3, ss 10, 16–17, 38, 40.

71 Some will be mindful of the occupants of the Supreme Court of Canada being reluctant to assume that the federal government intended to seize the entire field of jurisdiction overlap with a province, however, that this must be different as to whether or not the federal government can do so with clear intention, see Peter W Hogg, *Constitutional Law of Canada*, 5th ed (Toronto: Carswell, 2007) (loose-leaf updated 2013, release 1) at 16–15.

72 *GGPPA*, *supra* note 3, ss 17–35, 40, 48, 165. See also *Pan-Canadian Framework*, *supra* note 35 at 49.

73 *Pan-Canadian Framework*, *supra* note 35 at 49.

74 For more on rational choice theory, consider Gary S Becker, "Nobel Lecture: The Economic Way of Looking at Behavior" (1993) 101:3 J Political Economy 385.

22

Municipalities and Greenhouse Gas Regulation and Management

Arlene Kwasniak[1]

Introduction

Municipalities, urban and rural, traverse landscapes in Canada, each with its own regulatory regime. Depending on authorizing legislation, they may have powers to regulate and manage activities, projects, and infrastructure that mitigate or contribute to climate change.[2] The powers include local development, businesses, transportation, and roads; zoning and land use planning; waste management and garbage control; collection, disposal, recycling, and landfills; and, over their own infrastructure, energy use and demands. In fact, the Federation of Canadian Municipalities (FCM) points out that up to half of greenhouse gas (GHG) emissions "are under the direct or indirect control or influence of municipal governments."[3] Municipalities also bear the brunt of climate change impacts including emergency response, floods, droughts, transportation interruptions, resident health and so on. Yet municipalities generally are not seen as front-line players as climate change regulators and managers.[4] This role is left to the federal and provincial governments.

This chapter considers the role of municipalities in the regulation and management of GHGs in relation to climate change.[5] Section B looks at municipal jurisdiction to make laws that directly limit GHG emissions. Section C presents a case study that tests the validity of a hypothetical municipal bylaw that limits GHGs from landfills. Section D describes municipal-related initiatives, other than direct regulation of GHG emissions, that result in reduced GHG emissions.

This paper focuses on climate change mitigation, meaning measures that lessen human contributions to climate change, primarily through limiting or alleviating GHG emissions. Mitigation may be contrasted with adaptation, which involves conducting risk management scenarios, anticipating the adverse impacts of climate change, and taking actions to prevent, minimize, or alleviate adverse impacts.[6]

Municipal Authority in Canada

THE CONSTITUTION AND MUNICIPAL AUTHORITY

The Canadian Constitution divides legislative powers between the federal and provincial governments. There is no constitutional head of power for municipalities. Municipal powers are derived from provincial legislation since provinces have legislative jurisdiction over municipal institutions.[7] Judicial decisions firmly establish that municipalities, like all statutory creations, have no authority beyond the powers expressly or implicitly conferred by legislation. If a municipality acts beyond conferred powers, a court may determine an action to be *ultra vires* (beyond authority) and accordingly without legal effect.

Court Interpretation of Municipal Authority: Dillon's Rule, Spraytech, and Rothmans

In the past, courts strictly limited municipal powers in accordance with what is known as "Dillon's Rule." The rule derives from a 1907 case that states:

> It is a general and undisputed proposition of law that a municipal corporation possesses and can exercise the following powers and no others, first, those granted in express words; second, those necessarily or fairly implied in or incident to the powers expressly granted; third, those essential to the declared objects and purposes of the corporation, not simply convenient, but indispensable. Any fair, reasonable doubt concerning the existence of power is resolved by the courts against the corporation, and the power is denied.[8]

Through the years, the courts more liberally construed Dillon's Rule. A significant evolution occurred in the Supreme Court of Canada (SCC) decision, *Spraytech v. Town of Hudson*.[9] The plaintiff, Spraytech, challenged the validity of a town bylaw that restricted the cosmetic use of pesticides (e.g. to kill dandelions). The town passed the bylaw under its general and omnibus power to make bylaws for the health of its residents under *The Cities and Towns Act*.[10] Spraytech argued that under Dillon's Rule, the bylaw was invalid because as the Act contained no express power authorizing it, and argued that the town could not rely on its general/omnibus bylaw-making power since the bylaw conflicted with federal and provincial legislation, and paramountcy rendered the municipal bylaw invalid. The Court disagreed and held that as long as the bylaw is within municipal authority, even if there is, or could be, federal or provincial legislation in the same area, there is no conflict as long as it is possible to comply with the municipal bylaw and the federal or provincial law. In this case, there was no conflict. The Court stated that a municipal bylaw being more restrictive than federal or provincial legislation does not constitute a conflict. A conflict arises only when both the municipal bylaw and provincial or federal legislation cannot be complied with at the same time, resulting in the impossibility of dual compliance.

Rothmans, Benson & Hedges Inc v. Saskatchewan[11] concerned a federal law and a provincial law, though its principles may be applied to test the validity of a municipal bylaw. The issue was whether a section of the Saskatchewan *Tobacco Control Act*[12] was inoperative because of a conflict with a section of the federal *Tobacco Act*.[13] The Saskatchewan law regulated the retail display of tobacco products; for example, it prohibited displaying tobacco products where young persons may be present. The federal *Tobacco Act* expressly permitted tobacco products to be displayed for retail. The applicant argued that the federal and provincial laws conflicted, and federal paramountcy required the Court to declare the provincial law inoperative to the extent of the conflict. The Court found no conflict as there was no impossibility of dual compliance. Both laws could be complied with through compliance with the provincial law. The federal law was permissive, not mandatory. However, the Court added a test to determine whether a provincial legislative provision is inoperative in light of a federal law. The test is that if the provincial provision frustrates the purpose of a federal law, the federal law will prevail. On the facts, the court ruled that there was no frustration.[14]

EXPRESS LEGISLATIVE TEST

The express legislative test overrides the impossibility of the dual compliance test. The express legislative test applies where legislation prescribes when a legal provision or acting on a legal provision will be invalid or inoperative. To illustrate, in *Peacock v. Norfolk County*,[15] an Ontario municipal bylaw prohibited siting intensive livestock operations within certain land use zones. However, the province had approved the plaintiff's operations within the zones under provincial legislation.[16] Section 61 of the *Nutrient Management Act* stated that "[a] regulation supersedes a bylaw of a municipality or a provision in that bylaw if the bylaw or provision addresses the same subject matter as the regulation." The Court found that the provincial regulation under which the Peacocks received their approval addressed the same subject as the municipal bylaw, and that the express legislative test applied and not the impossibility of dual compliance. The bylaw prohibition under the bylaw was thus inoperative.

Direct Municipal Regulation of Greenhouse Gases—Landfill Gas Case Study

As stated by the US Environmental Protection Agency (EPA):

> Landfill gas (LFG) is a natural byproduct of the decomposition of organic material in landfills. LFG is composed of roughly 50 percent methane (the primary component of natural gas), 50 percent carbon dioxide (CO_2) and a small amount of non-methane organic compounds. Methane is a potent greenhouse gas 28 to 36 times more effective than CO_2 at trapping heat in the atmosphere over a 100-year period . . .[17]

Environment and Climate Change Canada notes that "[e]missions from Canadian landfills account for 20% of national methane emissions."[18]

Clearly, effective climate change mitigation requires reducing and managing LFG.[19] This case study considers municipal jurisdiction in such mitigation.

The case study concerns a municipality, "Greensboro," that passes a bylaw prohibiting LFG emissions over specified quantities (the LFG Bylaw). A developer of a proposed private landfill contests the validity of the bylaw, claiming it is beyond municipal jurisdiction. Is the LFG Bylaw valid?

As not all provinces can be dealt with here, the case study assumes that Greensboro is in Alberta. A comparable exercise could be undertaken for the rest of the Canadian provinces.

CHARTER CITIES VERSUS OTHER MUNICIPALITIES

The term "municipality" in this chapter includes the range of local governments that provincial legislation may establish. For example, the *Municipal Government Act*[20] (*MGA*) defines "municipality" to include a city, village, town, summer village, and municipal district (section 1(1)(s)). Provincial laws that create and regulate municipalities typically apply to the entire range though some authorities may vary given a municipality's size and type.[21] However, a few large urban Canadian municipalities enjoy special status under city charters. A charter city is governed by stand-alone legislation that modifies the general municipal legislation and provides charter cities with greater autonomy and additional jurisdiction and powers.

In Canada, Saint John's, Montreal, Winnipeg, Lloydminster, and Vancouver are charter cities. Calgary and Edmonton joined this group in 2018. To ascertain a charter city's regulatory authority regarding GHGs, in addition to reviewing the general municipal legislation, one must also examine the city's charter legislation. This part of the chapter first considers the case study in relation to the jurisdiction of Alberta municipalities under the general municipal legislation, the *MGA*, and then considers it with respect to special authorities given under charters.

MUNICIPAL PURPOSES

A primary question is whether the LFG Bylaw falls within municipal purposes. If not, a court could declare it to be *ultra vires* and of no effect.[22]

The purposes of the *MGA* (section 3) include:

> (a) to provide good government,
> (a.1) to foster the well-being of the environment, . . . [added in 2017]
> (c) to develop and maintain safe and viable communities . . .

Spraytech requires purposes to be interpreted flexibly and broadly. As mitigating climate change fosters the well-being of the environment (a.1) and safe and vibrant communities (c), the LFG Bylaw should fall within municipal purposes, provided it is intended to benefit the municipality.

Another question is, does the provincial legislation authorize a municipal bylaw that limits LFG emissions, such as the LFG Bylaw? The *MGA* contains general and specific grants of bylaw-making power. General grants are to be interpreted broadly, specific grants more narrowly, and limitations on specific grants cannot be enhanced through general grants (sections 9 and 10). General grants (section 7) that arguably could authorize the LFG Bylaw include:

> 7. A council may pass bylaws for municipal purposes respecting the following matters:
>
> > (a) the safety, health and welfare of people and the protection of people and property; . . .[23] [and]
> > (e) businesses, business activities and persons engaged in business . . .

The most relevant specific grants are in Part 17, which sets out municipal authority to regulate planning, subdivision, and development. Did Greensboro have the authority to pass the LFG Bylaw under Part 17? A landfill would be a development, as "development" includes any changes of use of land or intensity of use.[24] Accordingly, an Alberta municipality likely could require a development permit for a landfill that included limitations on LFG emissions.

LEGISLATIVE RESTRICTIONS ON MUNICIPAL AUTHORITY

The *MGA* limits what a municipality may do in exercising its bylaw and other authorities, even if the exercise is within municipal purposes and otherwise falls within jurisdiction. In a given situation, one or more of the following *MGA* provisions could limit municipal jurisdiction in regard to the LFG Bylaw.

- Section 13 states that "[i]f there is an inconsistency between a bylaw and this or another enactment, the bylaw is of no effect to the extent of the inconsistency." "Enactment" means a provincial or federal statute and subordinate legislation (section 1(1)(j)).

"Inconsistency" here presumably means impossibility of dual compliance, as per *Spraytech*. Currently, to the writer's knowledge, no provincial law directly limits all landfill GHGs. Neither Alberta's *Waste Control Regulation*[25] under the *Environmental Protection and Enhancement Act* (*EPEA*)[26] nor the Code of Practice for Landfills speaks to GHG emissions. The *Emissions Management and Climate Resilience Act*[27] regulates emissions under the *Technology Innovation and Emissions Reduction Regulation*[28] (*TIERR*). *TIERR* does not apply to biomass CO_2 emissions,[29] which includes some elements of LFG. Although biomass methane emissions could be regulated under the *TIERR*, that regulation aims at large emitters (100,000 tonnes+ of regulated emissions per year), thus leaving room for municipal regulation of LFG under that threshold. Recall that a bylaw, more strict than provincial regulation, may be valid under *Spraytech* provided that an operator can abide by both the provincial and municipal regulation, and the bylaw does not frustrate the purposes of the provincial legislation.

Under section 619 of the *MGA*, an authorization "granted by the [Natural Resources Conservation Board (NRCB), Energy Resources Conservation Board, Alberta Energy Regulator, Alberta Utilities Commission] . . . prevails . . . over any statutory plan, land use bylaw, subdivision decision or development decision . . . or any other authorization under . . . Part [17]." The section directs a municipality to approve an application before it to the extent that it complies with such provincial authorization. Thus, section 619 contains an express legislative test, overriding *Spraytech*.

To illustrate, suppose an operator obtained an *EPEA* authorization for a landfill on the condition that it would emit no more than X tonnes of LFG per year. The operator also required a development permit under Greensboro's LFG Bylaw, which, say, permitted no more than X–Y tonnes emissions per year, an amount less than X. Does section 619 impact the application of the bylaw? No, simply because section 619 does not apply to *EPEA* authorizations.[30] The situation would be different if, say, the NRCB issued the provincial authorization, in which case the higher maximum would prevail.[31]

Under section 620 of the *MGA*, a condition of an authorization "granted pursuant to an enactment . . . prevails over any condition of a development permit that conflicts with it."

Consider the scenario discussed under section 619. Under section 620, an *EPEA* authorization would prevail over Greensboro's development permit condition. Assuming that "prevails over" means overrides or supersedes,[32] then the permit's lower emission limit would not be operative.

Section 620, however, does not deprive municipalities of development permit authority when a provincial authorization is required.[33] Municipalities retain that authority and may include conditions that do not conflict with the provincial authorization. Indeed, there is case authority that a municipality may even reject an application for a permit for a provincially authorized development without violating section 620, since a refusal does not involve conditions.[34]

Under section 618, "Every statutory plan, land use bylaw and action undertaken pursuant to . . . Part [17] by a municipality . . . must be consistent with the land use policies" established by cabinet. Where there is an *Alberta Land Stewardship Act*[35] regional plan applicable to an area, then all municipal bylaws, policies, plans etc. must be consistent with the plan.

Currently, provincial land-use policies and regional plans do not seem to restrict municipal authorities with respect to managing GHG emissions, so the Greensboro LFG Bylaw would pass this test.

CHARTER CITIES

How do Alberta's charter cities, Edmonton and Calgary (E&C), fare with respect to the case study? Recall that charter cities' legislation may modify general municipal legislation as it otherwise applies to municipalities and provide additional authorities.

They fare very well when it comes to regulation and management of GHGs, including those in LFG, because the E&C charters add to the general jurisdiction to pass bylaws (section 7 *MGA*):

> (h.1) the well-being of the environment, including bylaws providing for the creation, implementation, and management of programs respecting any or all of the following: . . .
> (ii) climate change adaptation and greenhouse gas emission reduction . . .[36]

The E&C charters require the cities to establish climate change mitigation and adaptation plans.[37]

The express bylaw-making power to implement and manage GHG reduction programs makes it clear that an LFG Bylaw is within bylaw making authority. However, a charter city is still subject to the limitations in sections 13, 618, 619, or 620 of the *MGA*.

Other Municipal Contributions to Greenhouse Gas Reduction

Sections A to C set out a method to determine whether a municipality may directly regulate GHG emissions by, for example, setting emission limits on developments. The sections show that in Alberta, at least, municipalities likely have the power to regulate GHGs provided that provincial (or federal) legislation or authorizations do not limit, prevail over, or conflict with municipal regulation and that municipal regulation does not frustrate the purpose of the other jurisdiction's laws. But municipalities can contribute to climate change mitigation otherwise than by direct regulation of emissions. This section describes just a few of such GHG reduction approaches:

- The FCM reports that "159 GHG reduction municipal initiatives "have been approved for funding [totalling over 12 million dollars] through three infrastructure programs funded by the Government of Canada."[38]
- Municipalities can use land use planning, subdivision, and development powers to manage and reduce GHG emissions. For example, in 2016, the Vancouver city council approved a Zero Emissions Building Plan, "a phased approach to aggressively combat and reduce carbon pollution in Vancouver by transitioning to zero emissions for most new building types by 2025."[39]
- Municipalities can develop and carry out climate change mitigation and adaptation plans. The Region of Waterloo (Waterloo, Kitchener, and Cambridge) is a good example. As a result of its plans, together with other initiatives,
    - Residential growth has largely converted from urban sprawl to growth in already built-up areas, reducing the need for additional infrastructure and associated upstream and downstream GHG emissions.
    - Annual water consumption has decreased by 5 billion litres (over 10 years) and reduced GHG emissions by 535 tonnes through the implementation of their Water Master Plan.

- GHG reduction targets have been successfully met and increased (from a 10 percent reduction below 2009 levels to 25 percent).
- Both costs and GHG emissions have been reduced by switching to LED traffic signals.[40]

- Municipal energy incentive programs for residents and businesses encourage the use of solar or wind to reduce GHGs.[41] Provincial and/or federal programs can do this in respect of municipalities.[42]

Through increased public transit[43] and bike lanes,[44] municipalities contribute to GHG emissions reductions. Although these initiatives are mainly driven at the municipal level, other levels of government have a role in encouraging and even requiring them. For example, provinces can legislatively mandate that municipalities develop and carry out GHG reduction plans, as evidenced by the E&C charters discussed earlier.

NOTES

1 Professor Emerita of Law, Canadian Institute of Resources Law.

2 E.g., Cynthia Rosenzweig, "All Climate Is Local" (2011) 305(2) Scientific American 70–73.

3 Federation of Canadian Municipalities (FCM), Partners for Climate Protection, online: <fcm.ca/home/programs/partners-for-climate-protection/about-climate-change.htm>.

4 For a US review of this issue, see Katherine A. Trisolini, "All Hands on Deck: Local Governments and the Potential for Bidirectional Climate Change Regulation" (2010) 62(3) Stanford Law Review 669–746.

5 Many thanks to the University of Calgary Law Student David Hillier for his research relating to this paper.

6 I discuss adaptation and municipalities in Arlene Kwasniak, *Climate Change and Water: Law and Policy Options for Alberta*, CIRL Occasional Paper #57 (Calgary: CIRL, 2017), online (pdf): <cirl.ca/files/cirl/water-and-climate- change_kwasniak.pdf>.

7 S 91(8), *Constitution Act, 1867*, formerly the British North America Act, 1867, 30 & 31 Victoria, c 3.

8 *Hunter v City of Pittsburgh*, [1907] 207 US 161.

9 *114957 Canada Ltée (Spraytech Société d'arrosage) v Hudson (Town)*, [2001] 2 SCR 241, [2001] SCJ No 42, 200 DLR (4th) 419, 171 NR 201, 19 MPLR (3d) 1, 2001 SCC 40, *Spraytech v The Town of Hudson*, [2001] SCJ No 42 [*Spraytech*].

10 CQLR c C-19.

11 *Rothmans, Benson & Hedges Inc v Saskatchewan*, [2005] 1 SCR 188.

12 *The Tobacco Control Act*, SS 2001, c T-14.1.

13 *The Tobacco Act*, SC 1997, c 13.

14 *Rothmans, Benson & Hedges Inc v Saskatchewan, supra* note 11 at para 25.

15 *Peacock et al v The Corporation of Norfolk County, and The Ontario Pork Producers' Marketing Board, Intervenor*, [2006] 81 OR (3d) 530, 269 DLR (4th) 45; leave to appeal to the SCC refused in [2006] SCCA No. 371.

16 *Nutrient Management Act, 2002*, SA 2002, c 4, s 61, and AR 267/03.

17 EPA, "Landfill Methane Outreach Program (LMOP)", online: <www.epa.gov/lmop/basic-information-about-landfill-gas>.

18 ECC, "Solid Waste and Greenhouse Gases", online: <www.ec.gc.ca/gdd-mw/default.asp?lang=En&n=6f92e701-1&wbdisable=true>.

19 Management approaches include capture and combustion or utilizing LFG for "various energy purposes", *ibid.*

20 *Municipal Government Act*, RSA 2000, c M-26 [*MGA*].

21 E.g., under s 16 of the *MGA* cities own roads, but the Crown owns the road in other types of municipalities.

22 In *Shell Canada Products Ltd v Vancouver (City)*, [1994] 1 SCR 231, the SCC held that a Vancouver resolution to "not do business with Shell Canada 'until Royal Dutch/Shell completely withdraws from South Africa'" was not within municipal purposes as it constituted boycotting on matters external to the interests of the citizenry (232).

23 The City of Calgary, for example, bases its authority to pass a waste management and recycling bylaw on this power. See online (pdf): <www.calgary.ca/CA/city-clerks/Documents/Legislative-services/Bylaws/20M2001-WasteAndRecycling.pdf>.

24 *MGA*, s 616 (b)(iii) and (iv).

25 AR 192/96.

26 *EPEA*, RSA 2000, c E-12.

27 SA 2003, c E-7.8.

28 AR 133/2019.

29 *Ibid*, ss 1(1)(g) and (n).

30 *Northland Material Handling Inc. v Parkland (County)*, 2012 ABQB 407 at para 47.

31 The Court, *ibid*, states "The Legislature clearly intended to make a distinction between environmental legislation on the one hand, and certain other types of regulation on the other."

32 As suggested in *ibid*, and in the SDAB decisions cited in the following note.

33 *SDAB2015-0007 (Re)*, 2015 CGYSDAB 7 and SDAB 2015-0007 (Re), 2015 CGYSDAB 007.

34 *Northland Material Handling Inc. v Parkland (County), supra* note 30.

35 *Alberta Land Stewardship Act*, SA 2009, c A-26.8.

36 *City of Edmonton Charter, 2018*, AR 39/2018, s 4(2)(ii), and *City of Calgary Charter, 2018*, AR 40/2018, s 4(2)(ii).

37 *Ibid*, Part 16.1, both regulations.

38 FCM at <fcm.ca/en/news-media/backgrounder/fcmp/communities-across-canada-receive-support-159-initiatives-07082018>.

39 FCM, "National Measures Report 2018", online (pdf): <icleicanada.org/wp-content/uploads/2019/07/pcp-national-measures-report-2018-en.pdf> at 14. The FCM is an

organization of more than 2000 Canadian municipalities representing more than 90 percent of the Canadian population, online: <fcm.ca/en/about-fcm>.

40 FCM, "FCM Green Champions Awards" (November 15, 2016), online: <web.archive.org/web/20161224112022/https://fcm.ca/home/awards/fcm-green-champions-awards.htm>.

41 E.g., the Medicine Hat, Alberta "Solar Electric Incentive Program offers rebates to residential utility customers to purchase and install solar PV systems on their home", online: <www.medicinehat.ca/government/departments/hat-smart/solar-electric>.

42 E.g., the Alberta Municipal Solar Program provides "financial incentives to Alberta municipalities who install grid-connected solar photovoltaics (PV) on municipal facilities or land", online: <www.mccac.ca/programs/AMSP>. Taking advantage of this, Calgary added more "than 2.3 megawatts of energy capacity to six public buildings using solar power, . . . offsetting more than 47,500 tonnes of greenhouse gas emissions", online: <www.alberta.ca/release.cfm?xID=48860B36563C9-D0DA-D755-D61464CFBDCDBC2A>.

43 See the Canadian Urban Transit Association, "The GHG Reduction Impact of Public Transit" (July 2019), Issue Paper 52, online (pdf): <cutaactu.ca/wp-content/uploads/2021/01/issue_paper_52_-_the_ghg_reduction_impact_of_public_transit_.pdf>.

44 Hilary Angus, "Building Bike Lanes Could Slow Climate Change", *News Advocacy* (5 July 2016), online: <momentummag.com/building-bike-lanes-slow-climate-change-new-study-finds/> quotes a McGill study that notes a reduction "of close to 2% in GHG emissions . . . for an increase of 7% in the length of the [Montreal] bicycle network."

23

The Cap-and-Trade System for Greenhouse Gas Emission Allowances: The Quebec Experience

Hélène Trudeau[1]

The possibility of "offshoring" greenhouse gas (GHG) emission reductions is central to the choice of using a carbon market to achieve a given GHG reduction target. Thus, the obligation imposed on reporting emitters located in a territory can be facilitated by allowing those emitters to obtain emission "quotas" or "reduction units" corresponding to reductions made in a territory under another jurisdiction. Carbon markets authorize the trading of reduction units between reporting emitters within a single jurisdiction or even between jurisdictions, based on the economists' belief that achieving an overall emission reduction objective can prove less costly than imposing uniform emission standards on every emitter.[2] As set out in the *United Nations Framework Convention on Climate Change*, the "policies and measures to deal with climate change should be cost-effective so as to ensure global benefits at the lowest possible cost."[3] Carbon markets would, therefore, meet this objective of economic efficiency.

A carbon market can be established in various ways, but in general, it requires that the nation choosing to resort to it set an overall cap for GHG emissions that will be authorized during a given period for its reporting emitters. That cap will be lowered over the years until eventually allowing only emissions that reflect compliance with the previously established reduction target. The nation will have to create tradeable units, each one representing a fraction of the allocated emissions, within the initial overall cap set, and distribute them among the reporting emitters. Then the carbon market established by the nation will be able to allow, in various ways, the purchasing and trading of emission units that will be needed for the continued operation of the emitters. They will have obligations to report their emissions and to "cover" their emissions through tradeable units, based on successive compliance periods provided for by the applicable legislation.

In its 2006–2012 climate change action plan entitled "Quebec and Climate Change: A Challenge for the Future," the Quebec government was already announcing its intention to turn to a carbon emissions trading scheme.[4] The Quebec government then decided to give the province an ambitious GHG emissions reduction target by the year 2020.[5] The government has passed the necessary legislation and regulations needed for achieving that goal. The *Environment Quality Act*[6] was amended in 2009 to add sections 46.1 to 46.18, which empower the government to implement via regulations a cap-and-trade system (CATS) to help meet the targets set by the government and mitigate the costs associated with GHG reduction and limitation efforts. The *Regulation Respecting the Mandatory Reporting of Certain Emissions of Contaminants into the Atmosphere*[7] stipulates the thresholds at which companies, facilities, or institutions become subject to the obligation to report their GHG emissions and states the information they must provide.[8] On December 14, 2011, the government of Quebec passed the *Regulation Respecting a Cap-and-Trade System for Greenhouse Gas Emission Allowances*,[9] which sets out the rules for the operation of the CATS by determining which emitters are required to "cover" their emissions;[10] the terms and conditions for registering the system to have the accounts needed for purchasing and trading emission allowances; and the terms and conditions for the issue, use, and trading of GHG emission allowances.

The Quebec system was created in the context of Quebec's participation in the Western Climate Initiative (WCI) Inc., an organization made up of US states and Canadian provinces with the objective of providing a structure to enable partner entities to "expand" their own CATS by also having access to that of other entities. The government of Quebec linked the CATS with the system established by the government of California, and the two sub-state entities have developed, through the WCI, a common carbon market. Such a market enables Quebec's reporting emitters to have access not only to the emission allowances representing the reductions achieved in Quebec, but also to those representing reductions achieved under the California CATS, thereby potentially reducing those reporting emitters' overall cost of meeting the targets set by the Quebec government.

The genesis of this joint market seems quite complex and began in the mid-2000s. The State of California passed Assembly Bill 32 (AB 32), entitled the *California Global Warming Solutions Act of 2006*,[11] committing to reduce its GHG emissions in 2020 to the state's 1990 level and to consult with other governments to facilitate the development of integrated and cost-effective regional, national, and international GHG reduction programs. On February 28, 2007, the WCI was created by the signing of an agreement among the governors of five US states:[12] Arizona, California, New Mexico, Oregon, and Washington.[13] The objective of this initiative was to develop regional GHG emission reduction targets, establish an inter-state register to inventory GHG emissions in the region, and develop a market-based program to achieve the targets set.[14] In 2008, British Columbia, Manitoba, Ontario, and Quebec became members of the WCI.[15] The objective is to create a common market for emission allowances based on harmonized state and provincial legislation starting January 1, 2012.[16] Moving forward in the global climate struggle in the United States, a number of US states would eventually withdraw from the WCI in 2011,[17] and Canadian provinces then would develop the desired links with California. In winter 2018, only representatives from the governments of Quebec, Ontario, British Columbia,[18] and California were on the WCI board of directors.[19]

However, between 2007 and 2010, the state and provincial governments that were WCI members agreed to develop a model that included the main elements of each jurisdiction's need for a CATS to be harmonized under a regional program. As such, the *Modèle recommandé pour le programme régional de plafonds-échanges de la Western Climate Initiative*, as well as the *Cadre de mise en oeuvre du programme régional de la Western Climate Initiative*, led to the establishment of the common structures needed for the carbon market to operate.[20] Quebec and California first developed their own CATS through legislation and regulation, and in 2013 linked their efforts in a joint carbon market. That was done through an administrative agreement between the two governments: the *Agreement Between the Gouvernement du Québec and the California Air Resources Board Concerning the Harmonization and Integration of Cap-and-Trade Programs for Reducing Greenhouse Gas Emissions*,[21] which was signed in Sacramento on September 25, 2013, and in

Montreal on September 27, 2013.[22] That agreement came into effect on January 1, 2014.

By the spring of 2020, the joint carbon market had been operating for six years. The first joint auction of emission units by the governments of Quebec and California was held on November 25, 2014; the units of the 2014 vintage sold at a median price of C$13.74 (US$12.15).[23] On August 14, 2018, the sixteenth joint auction of emission units was held, at a median selling price of C$20.03 (US$15.25) for units of the current 2016 and 2018 vintage and C$19.65 (US$14.96) for units of the subsequent 2020 vintage, applying a gradual price increase provided for in the legislation of both sub-state entities.[24] In May 2020, the twenty-third joint auction was held, with a minimal selling price of C$23.17 (US$16.68) for both current vintage units and units of the future 2023 vintage. As previously discussed, it has always been agreed between the first two partners in this carbon market that other interested partners could join in the future. Ontario implemented a CATS in 2017 within Ontario[25] and joined the Quebec-California carbon market in 2018. As a result of this development, a new tripartite agreement was signed on September 22, 2017, namely the *Agreement Respecting the Harmonization and Integration of Cap-and-Trade Programs for Greenhouse Gas Emissions between the Government of Quebec, the Government of California and the Government of Ontario*.[26] This agreement replaced the one between Quebec and California.[27] However, the new Conservative government elected in Ontario in the summer of 2018 announced its intention to abolish its carbon market and did so. But the 2017 agreement still governs the CATS between the two remaining parties, Quebec and California.

So it was on the basis of an initial administrative agreement negotiated between the executive authorities of two sub-state entities, then a second one replacing the first and officially uniting three sub-state entities, and then back to two entities that the main North American carbon market evolved in 2018. The agreement provides for mutual recognition of emission allowances between parties,[28] while providing the emitting party with the option of withdrawing from the contract or cancelling emission allowances held by registered participants, if they were not issued in accordance with its regulations.[29] This method, therefore, establishes an emissions trading and fungibility tool in partner jurisdictions, and a market that covers a significant (and potentially growing) number of emitters from key industrial sectors.

The agreement between California and Quebec thus initiated the necessary cooperation between the partners to ensure that the carbon market operates. It provided for the harmonization of the regulatory provisions, the establishment of the required administrative services, and the sharing of the costs for those services. In 2011, the WCI was created, a not-for-profit corporation that provides administrative and technical support to the partners to facilitate implementation and linking of their respective CATS.[30] It is therefore the entity responsible for the carbon market infrastructure. The WCI subcontracts managing several of its responsibilities to private entities, including the administration of a central registry that lists transactions,[31] the holding of joint auctions by the parties,[32] and verification of emission allowances trading in the secondary market.

Although some aspects of the structure and operation of the carbon market have been pooled by the parties to these agreements, they remain autonomously responsible for deciding the main parameters in their fight against global warming[33] and their CATS for GHG emission allowances. Each of the partners has set out in their legislation emissions reduction targets, the emitters subject to reduction obligations, the applicable caps, and what constitutes "emission allowances" accepted for the purpose of meeting the emission coverage obligations.[34]

NOTES

1 Professor, Faculty of Law, Université de Montréal.

2 This idea had already been put forward in the context of the negotiations around the *Kyoto Protocol to the United Nations Framework Convention on Climate Change*, 11 December 1997, 2302 UNTS 148, 37 ILM 32, and in the subsequent implementation of instruments to combat global warming. See in general: Jacques Papy, "Le rôle de la propriété et du marché dans le régime québécois de plafonnement et d'échange de droits d'émissions de carbone" (2010) 89 Can Bar Rev 315; Jacques Papy, "L'échange de droits d'émission de gaz à effet de serre sous la loupe de l'analyse économique du droit" (2013) 54 C de D 851; Jacques Papy, "L'encadrement de l'échange de droits d'émission dans le marché réglementé du carbone au Québec sera-t-il efficace? Enjeux, constats et prédictions" (2014) 44 RGD 7; Érick LaChapelle et al, "Enquête sur les entreprises touchées par le Système de plafonnement et d'échange de droits d'émission de gaz à effet de serre du Québec" (CATS), Rapport Bourgogne, CIRANO, 2017; Auditor General of Quebec, "Marché du carbone : portrait et enjeux", in Rapport du Vérificateur général du Québec à l'Assemblée nationale pour l'année 2016–2017. Rapport du commissaire au développement durable, Quebec, Spring 2016, c 4.

3 *United Nations Framework Convention on Climate Change*, 9 May 1992, 1771 UNTS 107 s 3 (3).

4 Quebec Ministry of Sustainable Development, Environment and Parks, *2006–2012 Action Plan—Quebec and Climate Change, A Challenge for the Future* (2008) at 26.

5 The commitment announced in 2009 by the Government of Quebec is, by 2020, to reduce GHG emissions in Quebec 20 percent below emissions in 1990: *Décret du 18 novembre 2009 concernant l'adoption de la cible de réduction des émissions de gaz à effet de serre du Québec à l'horizon 2020*, D1187-2009 (2009) GOQ II, 5871. A new target for 2030 was set in 2015: *Décret du 18 novembre 2015 concernant l'adoption de la cible de réduction des émissions de gaz à effet de serre du Québec pour 2030*, D1018-2015 (2015) GOQ II, 4687. Thus, [translation] "Quebec aims to reduce its GHG emissions 20% below the 1990 level by 2020 and to reduce them 37.5% by 2030, while committing, as part of the Under2 MOU, to an 80% to 95% reduction by 2050. This level of reduction is further to the recommendations of the Intergovernmental Panel on Climate Change for Industrialized Countries," see Quebec Ministry of Sustainable Development, Environment and the Fight against Climate Change, "Quebec's Commitments, Our GHG Emission Reduction Targets" (accessed 21 May 2020), online: <http://www.mddelcc.gouv.qc.ca/changementsclimatiques/engagement-quebec.asp>.

6 *Environment Quality Act*, CQLR, c Q-2.

7 *Regulation Respecting Mandatory Reporting of Certain Emissions of Contaminants into the Atmosphere*, CQLR, c Q-2, r 15.

8 *Ibid*, s 2.

9 *Regulation Respecting a Cap-and-Trade System for Greenhouse Gas Emission Allowances*, CQLR, c Q-2, r 46.1.

10 The categories of reporting emitters are specified in section 2 of the regulation, *ibid*, and the coverage obligations for each one are set out in section 19 of the regulation. The original regulation essentially created two categories of emitters. They were "industrial emitters" ([translation] "2013–2014 period: people or municipalities that operate an establishment whose annual GHG emissions, excluding CO_2 emissions pertaining to biomass burning, are equal to or greater than 25,000 metric tonnes CO_2 equivalent, and that distribute electricity produced outside Quebec and whose emissions associated with producing it are equal to or greater than 25,000 metric tonnes CO_2 equivalent" [*Environment, supra* note 6, s 2, original version]) and "fuel distributors." ([translation] "2015–2020 period: In addition is the distribution of fuels and fossil fuels with emissions equal to or greater than 25 $ktCO_2eq$" (*ibid*, s 19, original version). Subsequent amendments to the regulation have, among other things, broadened the definition of reporting emitters to include fuel distributors starting at 200 litres and to incorporate persons or municipalities "reporting for an establishment, in keeping with subsection 1 of section 6.1 of the Regulation respecting mandatory reporting of certain emissions of contaminants into the atmosphere (chapter Q-2, r 15), annual greenhouse gas emissions in a quantity equal to or greater than 10,000 metric tonnes CO_2 equivalent and that registers for the system for one of its establishments covered by the reporting without being required to do so" (*Regulation Respecting a Cap-and-Trade System, supra* note 9, s 2.1).

11 *California Global Warming Solutions Act of 2006*, AB 32 (2006) § 1, Division 25.5, Health and Safety Code [*California Global Warming Solutions Act of 2006*].

12 Western Climate Initiative, "History" (accessed 22 June 2021), online: <westernclimateinitiative.org/index.php?option=com_content&view=article&id=29&Itemid=44>.

13 The WCI was originally based on the individual efforts of these states in addition to those of two regional initiatives: the West Coast Global Warming Initiative created by California, Oregon, and Washington, and the Southwest Climate Change Initiative created by Arizona and New Mexico: see *ibid.* Two other US states joined the following year: Montana and Utah.

14 *Ibid.*

15 *Ibid.*

16 Western Climate Initiative, "Program Design" (accessed 22 June 2021), online: <westernclimateinitiative.org/index.php?option=com_content&view=article&id=1&Itemid=4>.

17 Sustainable Business, "6 States Pull Out of Western Climate Initiative" (22 November 2011, accessed 21 May 2020), online: <www.sustainablebusiness.com/6-states-pull-out-of-western-climate-initiative-49859/>.

18 Although it remained active in the WCI's work, British Columbia decided to introduce a carbon tax in 2008 and therefore did not develop a CATS.

19 Manitoba has been a WCI partner, but has not developed an effective plan for joining the CATS.

20 Government of Quebec, Ministry of Sustainable Development, Environment and the Fight against Climate Change, "Le marché du carbone, Western Climate Initiative" (accessed 21 May 2020), online: <www.mddelcc.gouv.qc.ca/changements/carbone/WCI.htm>.

21 *Agreement Between the Gouvernement du Québec and the California Air Resources Board Concerning the Harmonization and Integration of Cap-and-Trade Programs for Reducing Greenhouse Gas Emissions* (2013), online: (pdf): <www.energy.ca.gov/sites/default/files/2019-12/CA_Quebec_linking_agreement_ada.pdf>.

22 This agreement was ratified by Order in Council of the Government of Quebec: *Agreement between the Government of Quebec and the California Air Resources Board Concerning the Harmonization and Integration of Cap-and-Trade Programs for Greenhouse Gas Emissions—Ratification*, OC 1181-2013, (2013) GOQ II 5275.

23 Government of Quebec, Ministry of Sustainable Development, Environment and the Fight against Climate Change, "California's Cap-and-Trade Program and Quebec's Cap-and-Trade System, November 2014 Joint Auction #1: Summary Report of Results" (3 December 2014, accessed 22 June 2021), online (pdf): <www.environnement.gouv.qc.ca/changements/carbone/ventes-encheres/2014-11-25/Summary-report.pdf>.

24 Government of Quebec, Ministry of Sustainable Development, Environment and the Fight against Climate Change, "California's Cap- and-Trade Program and Quebec's Cap-and-Trade System, August 2018 Joint Auction #16: Summary Report of Results" (21 August 2018, accessed 21 May 2020), online (pdf): <www.environnement.gouv.qc.ca/changements/carbone/ventes-encheres/2018-08-14/resultats20180814-en.pdf>.

25 *Climate Change Mitigation and Low-carbon Economy Act*, 2016, SO 2016, C 7 and *The Cap and Trade Program*, O Reg 144/16.

26 "Agreement on the Harmonization and Integration of Cap-and-Trade Programs for Reducing Greenhouse Gas Emissions" (22 September 2017, accessed 22 June 2021), online (pdf): <www.ieta.org/resources/News/California/Agreement%20on%20the%20Harmonization%20and%20Integration%20of%20CapTrade-22Sept.pdf> [Tripartite Agreement].

27 See the *Décret concernant l'entérinement de l'Avenant à l'Entente entre le Gouvernement du Québec et le California Air Resources Board concernant l'harmonisation et l'intégration des programmes de plafonnement et d'échange de droits d'émission de gaz à effet de serre*, D 1135-2017, (2017) GOQ II 5534.

28 Thus, s 6, para 1 of the Tripartite Agreement sets out the following: "In order to achieve harmonization and integration of the Parties' cap-and-trade programs, mutual recognition of the Parties' compliance instruments shall occur as provided for under their respective cap-and-trade program regulations." See: Tripartite Agreement, *supra* note 26, s 6 para 1.

29 "If a Party determines that a compliance instrument that it has issued should not have been issued or must be voided, it shall notify the other Parties. Each Party recognizes and respects the authority of the other Parties to take actions to recover or void compliance instruments that have been surrendered or that are held by registered participants": *ibid*, s 6 para 2.

30 The WCI Inc. website therefore reports on the three components of the organization's mandate: "Develop a compliance tracking system that tracks both allowances and offsets certificates; Administer allowance auctions; and Conduct market monitoring of allowance auctions and allowance and offset certificate trading" Western Climate Initiative, (accessed 21 May 2020), online: <westernclimateinitiative.org/index.php?option=com_content&view=category&layout=blog&id=6&Itemid=6>.

31 This is the Compliance Instrument Tracking System Service (CITSS).

32 Emission allowances are issued electronically and are identified so as to differentiate them, mainly based on their type, source, and "vintage."

33 Thus, in Quebec, the *2013–2020 Climate Change Action Plan* sets out the Government of Quebec's actions to help transition to a low-carbon economy. It is mainly through the use of the Green Fund, the revenues of which are generated mainly by the carbon market, that additional reduction measures, as well as adaptation measures, will be put in place. The Green Fund is expected to generate approximately $3 billion by 2020; see Quebec, Ministry of Sustainable Development, Environment and the Fight against Climate Change, *2013–2020 Climate Change Action Plan* (2012, accessed 22 June 2021), online (pdf): <www.environnement.gouv.qc.ca/changements/plan_action/pacc2020.pdf>.

34 An emission allowance is defined in the Quebec legislation as follows: ". . . a greenhouse gas emission unit, offset credit or early reduction credit, and any emission allowance issued by a partner entity, each allowance having a value corresponding to one metric ton of greenhouse gas CO_2 equivalent": *Regulation Respecting a Cap-and-Trade System*, *supra* note 9, at s 3 para 5.

24

Enforcement and Withdrawal under the California-Quebec (and Not Ontario) Cap-and-Trade Linkage Agreement

David V. Wright[1]

Introduction

Federal governments in Canada and the United States continue to face challenges in developing and implementing nation-wide carbon pricing mechanisms. While the Canadian context has changed with the introduction of the *Greenhouse Gas Pollution Pricing Act*,[2] there continues to be no comprehensive nation-wide regime in the United States. In this context, sub-national initiatives continue to define much of climate law and policy in North America, with the California-Quebec-Ontario linkage breaking transnational ground in recent years.[3] Such an approach, however, remains highly experimental in nature.[4]

Two dimensions of critical importance to the efficacy of any emissions trading regime are enforcement and withdrawal. The California-Quebec-Ontario linkage provides an opportunity to observe these dimensions in action. Ontario's withdrawal, for better or worse, marks a timely opportunity to consider the formal withdrawal process under the linkage, as well as collateral legal implications.

The first part of this chapter provides a short overview of the California-Quebec-Ontario linkage, including its origins in the Western Climate Initiative (WCI) and evolution into a functioning multi-jurisdiction emissions trading regime. Next, the chapter focuses on enforcement under the linkage, discussing the reciprocal nature of the arrangement and the enforcement regime in each jurisdiction. For completeness, Ontario is included in that discussion, notwithstanding its withdrawal in June 2018. The chapter then provides a short overview of the linkage withdrawal mechanism before then moving on to identify some of the legal implications flowing from Ontario's withdrawal. Finally, the conclusion provides reflections on this sub-national-led North American regime and future directions.

Overview of the California-Quebec-Ontario Linkage Agreement

Cooperation between Canadian provinces and US states on GHG emissions reductions has been taking place for more than a decade.[5] For example, at its peak, the Regional Greenhouse Gas Initiative included nine states as participants and six provinces as observers in anticipation of eventually linking cap-and-trade markets.[6] Meanwhile, in 2008 the US west coast states and the province of British Columbia entered into the Pacific Coast Collaborative Agreement (PCCA),[7] and adopted the Pacific Coast Action Plan on Climate and Energy in 2013.[8] The latter included stated intentions of linking programs,[9] though no carbon markets have linked under this umbrella to date.

The longest-running state-province collaboration, and most relevant for the purposes of this paper, is the WCI. The WCI began in 2007 as an agreement across several western US states but expanded in subsequent years to include the Canadian provinces of British Columbia, Manitoba, Ontario, and Quebec.[10] These eleven jurisdictions collectively produced the 2008 "Design Recommendations for the WCI Regional Cap and Trade Program"[11] and the 2010 "Design for the WCI Regional Program."[12] The objective was to then put in place an inter-jurisdictional market-based program to reach agreed-upon emission reduction targets.[13] As was observable in June 2018, most WCI members did not follow through to the point of implementing linked cap-and-trade systems under the agreed-upon timeline.[14] The exceptions, of course, are Quebec and California, and for a brief period, Ontario. With much fanfare,[15] these jurisdictions carried the collaboration through to a fully operational multi-jurisdiction, cross-border cap-and-trade system. California and Quebec signed a linkage agreement in September 2013, with the linkage becoming formally operational on January 1, 2014. In September 2017, Ontario entered into the linkage agreement, and on January 1, 2018, Ontario formally joined the market (though the provincial cap-and-trade market had been functioning since January 2017), only to withdraw in June 2018, soon after a change of government following the provincial election.[16] In May 2018, the three parties held the fifteenth joint cap-and-trade auction,[17] and in August 2018, Quebec and California held the sixteenth joint auction, that one without Ontario.[18] In May 2020, Quebec and California held the twenty-third joint auction.[19]

At the core of the linkage is the formal agreement: *Agreement between the California Air Resources Board and the Gouvernement du Québec Concerning the Harmonization and Integration of Cap-and-Trade Programs for Reducing Greenhouse Gas Emissions* (Linkage Agreement or Agreement).[20] The Linkage Agreement was updated when Ontario joined.[21] The Agreement codifies the collaborative arrangements between the parties through 23 Articles spread across three chapters: General Provisions, Harmonization and Integration Process, and Operation of the Agreement.[22] The Agreement sets the rules in areas such as consultation, regulatory harmonization, recognition and trade of compliance instruments, joint auctions, supervision and enforcement, administrative and technical support, confidentiality, withdrawal, amendments, resolution of differences, and coming into force.[23]

However, while the Agreement is the centrepiece of the integrated cap-and-trade markets, it represents just one piece in a broader framework. This system is reciprocal in nature and is comprised of statutes, regulations, and guidance put in place by each jurisdiction. For example, California's legal context is underpinned by the 2006 *Global Warming Solutions Act* (typically and hereinafter referred to as AB 32), which empowered the California Air Resources Board (CARB) to "adopt a regulation that establishes a system of market-based declining annual aggregate emission limits for sources or categories of sources that emit greenhouse gas emissions" and to "consult with other governments to facilitate the development of integrated and cost-effective regional, national and international greenhouse gas reduction programs."[24] The California regime is fleshed out further through the *Air Resources Board Regulation for the Mandatory Reporting of Greenhouse Gas Emissions*[25] and the *Air Resources Board Cap-and-Trade Regulation*.[26] Notably, for the present discussion regarding enforcement, the California context is also shaped by SB 1018,[27] which, as discussed in Part II below, required the governor to make specific findings (including in relation to enforcement) prior to CARB taking action to approve the linkage.[28] In 2017, the California legislature passed AB 398, extending the state's cap-and-trade program to 2030 (there was an initial horizon of 2020).[29] AB 398 also includes measures, such as a price ceiling, to protect against extreme market fluctuations.[30]

For Quebec's part, in 2009, the province passed Bill 42, *An Act to Amend the Environment Quality Act and Other Legislative Provisions in Relation to Climate*,[31] which, similar to California, granted the Quebec government powers to enact regulations that create a cap-and-trade system and to enter into an agreement with another government for the harmonization and integration of cap-and-trade systems.[32] The regime is structured and implemented through regulations, namely: the *Regulation Respecting Mandatory Reporting of Certain Emissions of Contaminants into the Atmosphere*,[33] and the *Regulation Respecting a Cap-and-Trade System for Greenhouse Gas Emission Allowances*.[34] As well, GHG emissions caps in line with Quebec's 2020 GHG emissions reduction goal are set through *Order in Council 1185-2012 Determination of Annual Caps on Greenhouse Gas Emission Units Relating to the Cap-and-Trade System for Greenhouse Gas Emission Allowances for the 2013–2020 Period*.[35]

Legislative steps toward linking Ontario began in 2009 with the passing of the *Environmental Protection Amendment Act (Greenhouse Gas Emissions Trading), 2009*.[36] That Act provided the government with broad authority to implement a cap-and-trade system and to establish associated rules.[37] Similar to the California and Quebec enabling statutes, the Act contemplated integration with other cap-and-trade regimes. This statutory basis was eventually updated with more detail and explicit authorities through the *Climate Change Mitigation and Low Carbon Economy Act* (*CCMLCEA*),[38] which was passed in February 2016. The regime was further fleshed out by the *Cap-and-Trade Program Regulation*[39] and the *Quantification, Reporting and Verification of Greenhouse Gas Emissions*,[40] both of which took effect on January 1, 2017. Ontario also put in place the *Guideline for the Quantification, Reporting and Verification of Greenhouse Gas Emissions*.[41] As will be discussed in the final part of this chapter, following the June 2018 provincial election, the new Ontario government cancelled the cap-and-trade program, including the revocation of these regulations and repeal of the *CCMLCEA*.

Enforcement Under the Linkage Agreement

The linkage is premised on an approach of reciprocity and harmonization within a context that acknowledges each jurisdiction's sovereignty in the administration of each respective program.[42] Such architecture began through cooperation under the WCI. For example, the WCI *Design Recommendations for the WCI Regional Cap-and-Trade Program*[43] recommended that "each WCI Partner jurisdiction will retain and/or enhance its regulatory and enforcement authority and responsibilities to enforce compliance with the cap-and-trade program within its own jurisdiction."[44] Similarly, the *Design for the WCI Regional Program* document, which provided a roadmap for WCI partner jurisdictions developing respective implementing regulations, stated that each jurisdiction "will use its authority to enforce compliance with the WCI Cap-and-Trade program within its own jurisdiction."[45] It went on to explain that harmonization and compliance verification are essential to ensure consistent outcomes and a level playing field, but acknowledged that "the degree of harmonization is subject to each WCI partner jurisdiction's legislative and administrative processes and acknowledges that each jurisdiction maintains sovereignty in the administration of its program."[46]

This approach was explicitly included in the 2014 Quebec-California Linkage Agreement,[47] and was carried into the updated 2017 Ontario-Quebec-California Linkage Agreement[48] (the latter included some slightly updated language but did not substantively alter enforcement and withdrawal aspects).

Article 11 sets out the supervision and enforcement regime:

> The Parties shall work cooperatively to maintain market integrity, including preventing fraud, abuse and market manipulation and to ensure the reliability of the joint auction and their respective programs. The Parties shall work cooperatively in applying their respective program requirements governing the supervision of all transactions carried out among registered participants of each of the Parties and of any auction or reserve sale.
>
> The Parties shall facilitate, in accordance with the privacy, and other statutes and regulations applicable in each of their jurisdictions and the provisions of article 15 hereunder, the sharing of information to support the effective administration and enforcement of each party's statutes and regulations.

This exists within the broader context of harmonization required under Article 4:

> The Parties shall continue to examine their respective regulations for the reporting of greenhouse gas emissions and for the cap-and-trade program in order to promote continued harmonization and integration of the Parties' programs.
>
> In the case where a difference between certain elements of the Parties' programs is identified, the Parties shall determine if such elements need to be harmonized for the proper functioning and integration of the programs . . .
>
> A Party may consider making changes to its respective programs, including changes or additions to its emissions reporting regulation, cap-and-trade program regulations, and program related operating procedures. To support the objective of harmonization and integration of the programs, any proposed changes or additions to those programs shall be discussed between the Parties . . .[49]

These rules for harmonization and cooperation in enforcement under the linkage are supported by further requirements with respect to robust offset protocols,[50] compliance instruments,[51] trade,[52] and accounting mechanisms.[53] In practice, compliance and enforcement—and trading—depend on the Compliance Instrument Tracking System Service (CITSS), which is the registry of compliance instruments for the entire cap-and-trade program. It acts as a management and tracking system for accounts and compliance instruments issued through the cap-and-trade linkage, allowing market participants to hold and retire compliance instruments and to trade compliance instruments with other account holders. In short, CITSS is the market hub that facilitates the flow of tradable allowances.

Under this approach of reciprocity and respect for sovereignty, which may be the product of constitutional constraints on cross-border activities of sub-national governments,[54] the respective state or provincial enforcement regimes of each party are of primary importance. California legislators recognized this in the lead-up to entering into the initial linkage with Quebec. As a safeguard, they passed SB 1018, which required the governor to confirm that the program to be linked had environmental and enforcement requirements that were "equivalent to or stricter than" the California program, that the state was able to enforce its laws to constitutional limits, and that there would be no "significant liability" imposed on California for any "failure associated with linking to the Quebec program or related participation in WCI, Inc."[55] Such a review and confirmation by the governor's office was indeed completed ahead of California's linking with Quebec,[56] and then again prior to Ontario joining.[57]

CALIFORNIA

California's enforcement regime flows from the statute and regulations referenced above. Specifically, the regulation expressly includes prohibitions on any trading involving a manipulative device, a cornering of or an attempt to corner the market, fraud, attempted fraud, or false or inaccurate reports.[58] Under the regulations, violations of the regulations can result in civil or criminal penalties,[59] and perjury statutes apply.[60] Administratively, the California program includes mechanisms to monitor and prevent market manipulation.[61]

Institutionally, it is CARB that leads enforcement. CARB has the authority to issue orders to covered entities and to set and issue penalties for violations. For example, under the cap-and-trade regulations, if a covered entity misses an annual or triennial obligation deadline, then it must submit emission allowances equal to four times the entity's excess emissions.[62]

Beyond that, if the entity does not submit allowances of excess emission after thirty days, then CARB may issue a $25,000 fine per missing allowance per forty-five days.[63] Additionally, CARB has the authority to suspend, revoke, or restrict holding accounts for covered entities.[64]

QUEBEC

Quebec's enforcement regime flows from the statute and regulations referenced above. Several enforcement tools exist, including administrative monetary penalties (AMPs), quasi-criminal offences (and associated penalties), and several other specific measures such as suspension, withdrawal, or cancellation of an emissions allowance. These powers are administered by the Ministère de l'Environnement et de la Lutte contre les changements climatiques (MELCC).

With respect to AMPs and regulatory offences, the *Environment Quality Act* provides a general framework for applying administrative sanctions in connection with penal proceedings. Specific penalties and applicable AMPs are set out in the cap-and-trade regulation, which contains several financial and legal penalties of varying degrees depending on the infraction and severity of transgressions at issue.[65] The regulation provides for penalties of $500–$500,000 and up to eighteen months of imprisonment for an individual, or $10,000–$3 million in the case of non-compliance for a corporation.[66] Additionally, financial penalties double in the case of a second offence.

In some circumstances the minister may suspend, withdraw, or cancel any allowance for certain violations.[67] The minister may also refuse to register an emitter for an auction or sale if the emitter provides false or misleading information, omits required information, or contravenes a rule of procedure.[68] In some cases, such as providing false or misleading information, transgressors risk being guilty of an offence as well as being barred from the market.[69]

With respect to meeting emission reduction requirements under the cap, if an emitter does not have sufficient allowances by November 1 of the year following the end of a compliance period (i.e. in 2015, 2018, and 2021), then the entity's account will be suspended along with a requirement to pay a penalty of three emissions allowances for each missing allowance.[70] If after thirty days the emitter cannot produce required allowances, the minister will subtract the owed allowances from the emitter's next free allowance allocation.[71]

ONTARIO

Enforcement under Ontario's regime was primarily set out in the legislation referenced above, though, compared to Quebec and California, Ontario had more specifics at the statute level. Similar to Quebec, enforcement in Ontario featured financial and legal penalties of varying degrees depending on the infraction and severity of transgression at issue. Under the *CCMLCEA*, individuals convicted of an offence could be liable for fines of $5,000 to $6 million and imprisonment for up to a year.[72] Corporations could be liable for fines of $25,000 to $10 million.[73] Once again, such penalties enforced specific prohibitions in relation to trade such as fraud and market manipulation or providing misleading or untrue information.[74] These also applied with respect to prohibitions on disclosure[75] and obstructing administration of the Act.[76]

In terms of non-compliance with emission reductions obligations under the cap, the *CCMLCEA* imposed a penalty similar to Quebec. If a market participant failed to submit all required allowances by the deadline, the Act required additional emission allowances in an amount equal to three times the shortfall[77] and provided authority to issue fines and impose other consequences.[78]

Ontario's enforcement regime also included AMPs by way of the *Administrative Penalties Regulation*,[79] which provides a list of contraventions to which the penalties apply, including failure to follow provisions regarding the trading of emission allowances or credits, coordinating bidding, or perpetuating fraud contrary to the Act; failure to quantify and report the amount of greenhouse gas emitted, or to use the appropriate quantification methodology, contrary to the *Quantification, Reporting and Verification of Greenhouse Gas Regulation*; failure to register as a mandatory participant within the time prescribed under the *Cap-and-Trade Program Regulation*; and failure to provide a reversal report, or the failure of an accredited verification body to provide a verification report, as required pursuant to the *Ontario Offset Credits Regulation*. The AMP regime was underpinned by s 57 of the *CCMLCEA*, which provided general authority for AMPs to be imposed for the purposes of ensuring compliance with the Act and to prevent any participant from deriving an economic benefit from contravening the Act.[80]

These respective enforcement regimes function in parallel across the entire linkage to ensure that market actors comply with all applicable rules and face significant penalties for failing to do so. Regular compliance reports are made publicly available by CARB and the MELCC.[81]

Ontario Withdrawal from the Linkage

As a "first order of business" following the June 2018 provincial election,[82] the newly elected premier pulled Ontario out of the linkage by revoking the cap-and-trade regulations and suspending all trading on July 3, 2018. Such a withdrawal is explicitly contemplated under the Linkage Agreement. Article 17 states:

> A Party may withdraw from this Agreement by giving written notice of intent to withdraw to the other Parties. A Party that intends to withdraw from this Agreement shall endeavour to give 12 months notice of intent to withdraw to the other Parties. A Party that intends to withdraw from this Agreement shall endeavor to match the effective date of withdrawal with the end of a compliance period.

Notably, Article 17 provides some clarity to California and Quebec as the parties remaining in the linkage:

> If a Party withdraws, the Agreement shall remain in force for the remaining Parties.

While this process of withdrawal is prescribed in relatively clear terms in the Linkage Agreement, it was not clear in 2018 that Ontario followed the process because the government of Ontario had not published documentation of its "written notice of intent to withdraw" pursuant to Article 17. It is possible that such was provided to California and Quebec; however, no such documentation has surfaced in the public domain. Further, it is abundantly clear that Ontario did not "endeavour to give 12 months notice of intent to withdraw to the other Parties," nor did it "endeavor to match the effective date of withdrawal with the end of a compliance period." Rather, the withdrawal was made without formal notice at all, other than statements made by the new premier soon after the provincial election and an apparent refusal by Ontario to participate in the sixteenth joint auction.

The clearest discussion of Ontario's withdrawal was from California when CARB issued the following update in September 2018:

> On July 3, 2018, the Ontario government published a regulation (386/18) revoking Ontario's cap-and-trade regulation (144/16), and suspended all Ontario entity CITSS accounts. With Ontario's departure from the linked carbon market, California and Québec are working together to ensure that the environmental integrity and stringency of our cap-and-trade program and market is maintained. Our goals are to make certain that the program continues to reduce emissions of climate-changing gases as a crucial part of our efforts to combat the existential threat of climate change, while also continuing the smooth operation and integrity of our joint carbon market.
>
> Please note that all compliance instruments in accounts registered in California or Québec are valid for compliance purposes and for trading or selling between participants of the two jurisdictions.[83]

This suggests that California acknowledged Ontario's formal withdrawal under the Linkage Agreement, notwithstanding the seeming lack of formal notice under Article 17. It may well be the case that California's interest in the success of the linkage and efficacy of the Linkage Agreement has resulted in it not wanting to draw attention to the fact that Ontario did not follow the terms of the Agreement.

Meanwhile, Ontario's withdrawal included legal steps beyond the process set out in the Linkage Agreement. On July 3, 2018, the new Ontario government filed Ontario Regulation 386/18 (Regulation), which prohibits participants in the cap-and-trade scheme from purchasing, selling, trading, or otherwise dealing with emission allowances and credits.[84] On July 25, 2018, the Ontario government introduced *Bill 4: The Cap and Trade Cancellation Act* to formally wind down the Ontario cap-and-trade program. The Act repealed Ontario's cap-and-trade legislation[85] and provided for the "retiring" or "cancelling" of cap-and-trade instruments (including those created under the Quebec or California systems), the payment of compensation by the government to a select few types of market participants (approximately 250 capped participants total), and the barring of any legal recourse against the government.[86] The Act does require Ontario to establish GHG reduction targets and to prepare a climate change plan,[87] which was released in November 2018 as part of "Preserving and Protecting our Environment for Future Generations: A Made-in-Ontario Environment Plan."[88]

In the wake of the relatively sudden and fundamental change in Ontario policy and law, it was unclear what value emission credits would hold. Ontario's move generated more legal questions than answers for market participants.[89] As summarized by a commentary from the private bar, "businesses holding some $2.8 billion in allowances have no market to offload their purchases, and it is unclear what legal remedies are available to these parties or whether refunds are forthcoming."[90] Litigation seemed inevitable. One of the first suits out of the gate was a case brought by Ecojustice on behalf of several environmental groups. It alleged that the Ford government unlawfully failed to provide for public consultation on both the Regulation and on the *Bill 4: Cap and Trade Cancellation Act*, as required by the Ontario *Environmental Bill of Rights* (*EBR*).[91] In an October 2019 decision, the Ontario Superior Court agreed, ruling that the new Ontario government contravened the *EBR*.[92] More recently, at least one market participant has brought suit against WCI Inc., claiming damages flowing from a trading freeze imposed following Ontario's departure.[93] That litigation is ongoing at the time of publication. Overall, it appears market participants have limited legal recourse, particularly given the limits placed on compensation by the *Cap and Trade Cancellation Act*. Meanwhile, the remaining market between Quebec and California continues to function.[94] The May 2020 auction was heralded as a success,[95] though in the lead up to that auction, prices dipped below the cap-and-trade program's minimum 2020 price due to the effects of the Covid-19 pandemic.[96]

Conclusion

While this sub-national linkage across the Canada-US border demonstrates that much can be accomplished in the absence of federal leadership, it also reveals fundamental weaknesses. The respective enforcement regimes of California, Quebec and, formerly, Ontario are comprehensive, robust, and, with various tools and penalties available, relatively nuanced. High compliance rates (and, therefore, significant emission reductions) suggest that the respective and harmonized enforcement regimes have been effective at encouraging good market behaviour and deterring delinquency. However, the recent experience with Ontario's withdrawal reveals a fundamental weakness in the system: easy withdrawal with minimal consequences. Notwithstanding the carefully designed and implemented architecture of the linkage in most regards, this readily available low-resistance path to leaving the market undermines overall market integrity and subverts the otherwise strong enforcement regime.

As the design and implementation of multi-jurisdictional carbon markets evolve, parties and regulated entities would be wise to build in stronger withdrawal mechanisms that augment the enforcement regimes by increasing the difficulty of a jurisdiction departing, thus providing more market certainty and reliability for all actors involved. Unfortunately, there may be political barriers to doing so, given that a stronger locking in of a jurisdiction's commitment to link may deter linking in the first place. Additionally, legal barriers such as constitutional dimensions continue to constrain how far states and provinces can go with entering international agreements that contain binding obligations.[97]

Ultimately, the foregoing examination of the linkage's enforcement and withdrawal dimensions demonstrates the limitations of a sub-national led approach. While state-province collaboration has provided important momentum and action leading to GHG emission reductions, thanks in part to effective enforcement regimes, there is no substitute for federal leadership and coordination in both Canada and the US. This does not mean that linkages between nation-states would not also be susceptible to parties withdrawing, but the ability for nation-states to enter into binding agreements would better safeguard against sudden, disruptive withdrawal, and would also lend itself to strong enforcement regimes. In the meantime, however, carbon markets worldwide will continue to benefit from lessons learned through the ambitious and laudable actions of sub-national actors.

NOTES

1 Assistant Professor, Faculty of Law, University of Calgary.

2 SC 2018, c 12.

3 See Ministère du Développement durable, de l'Environnement et de la Lutte contre les changements climatiques, "Québec-California-Ontario Carbon Market: A Strong Example of North American Collaboration", *Newswire* (28 February 2018), online: <www.newswire.ca/news-releases/quebec-california-ontario-carbon-market-a-strong-example-of-north-american-collaboration-675459933.html>.

4 Note that many consider sub-national efforts to be a "second-best" option, believing a comprehensive federal regime—either cap-and-trade or carbon tax—to be preferable. See e.g., Cary Coglianese & Jocelyn D'Ambrosio, "Policymaking Under Pressure: The Perils of Incremental Responses to Climate Change" (2008) 40 Conn L Rev 1413; Valentina Bosetti & David G Victor, "Politics and Economics of Second-Best Regulation of Greenhouse Gases: The Importance of Regulatory Credibility" (2011) 32:1 Energy J 1; Matthew Ranson & Robert Stavins, "Linkage of Greenhouse Gas Emissions Trading Systems: Learning from Experience" (2013) Harvard Kennedy School Faculty Research Working Paper Series ES 13-2; Ann Carlson, "Designing Effective Climate Policy: Cap-and-Trade and Complementary Policies" (2012) 49:2 Harv J on Legis 207. Note also that Canada's federal *Greenhouse Gas Pollution Pricing Act* is premised on a cooperative federalism approach that allows provinces and territories to implement their own regime so long as it satisfies federal minimum requirements. The Quebec and now-abandoned Ontario regimes discussed in the present article are instances of this. See *Reference Re Greenhouse Gas Pollution Pricing Act*, 2019 ONCA 554 at 135 [*GHGPPA Reference*] (explaining that the *GGPPA* makes room "for the operation of provincial carbon pricing legislation of sufficient stringency"). See also *Reference re Greenhouse Gas Pollution Pricing Act*, 2019 SKCA 40 at 122.

5 For example, Council of Atlantic Premiers, "Conference of New England Governors and Eastern Canadian Premiers Highlights Importance of Cross-Border Relationship" (17 May 2021), online: <cap-cpma.ca/conference-of-new-england-governors-and-eastern-canadian-premiers-highlights-importance-of-cross-border-relationship/> (mentions the 2001 climate change commitments).

6 See Regional Greenhouse Gas Initiative, "Program Design Archive" (2020), online: <www.rggi.org>. Once RGGI became fully operational, it stopped using observer status as a term or designation. Instead, today any interested person, state, or other

stakeholder is able to attend a meeting or provide comment, without need for a designated status. There are currently no provinces formally participating in RGGI.

7 Pacific Coast Collaborative, "Memorandum to Establish the Pacific Coast Collaborative" (30 June 2008), online (pdf): <pacificcoastcollaborative.org/wp-content/uploads/2018/09/Memorandum-PCC_2008.pdf>.

8 Pacific Coast Collaborative, "Pacific Coast Action Plan on Climate and Energy" (28 October 2013), online (pdf): <pacificcoastcollaborative.org/wp-content/uploads/2018/09/Pacific-Coast-Climate-Action-Plan.pdf>.

9 *Ibid.*

10 See Western Climate Initiative, "History" (2013) online: <westernclimateinitiative.org/index.php?option=com_content&view=article&id=29&Itemid=44>.

11 Western Climate Initiative, "Design Recommendations for the WCI Regional Cap-and-Trade Program" (23 September 2008), online (pdf): <www.mddelcc.gouv.qc.ca/changements/carbone/documents-WCI/modele-recommande-WCI-en.pdf> [WCI Design Recommendations].

12 Western Climate Initiative, "Design for the WCI Regional Program" (27 July 2010), online: <www.westernclimateinitiative.org/the-wci-cap-and-trade-program/program-design> [WCI Regional Program Design].

13 See *ibid.*

14 *Ibid.*

15 *Supra* note 2.

16 The Linkage Agreement was updated to include Ontario in September 2017; however, it is now back to a two-party agreement.

17 Government of Quebec, Ministry of Sustainable Development, Environment and the Fight against Climate Change, "California Cap-and-Trade Program and Québec Cap-and-Trade System, May 2018 Joint Auction #15: Summary Results Report" (23 May 2018), online (pdf): <www.mddelcc.gouv.qc.ca/changements/carbone/ventes-encheres/2018-05-15/resultats-vente20180515-en.pdf>.

18 Government of Quebec, Ministry of Sustainable Development, Environment and the Fight against Climate Change, "California Cap-and-Trade Program and Québec Cap-and-Trade System, August 2018 Joint Auction #16: Summary Results Report" (21 August 2018), online (pdf): <www.mddelcc.gouv.qc.ca/changements/carbone/ventes-encheres/2018-08-14/resultats20180814-en.pdf>.

19 Government of Quebec, Ministry of Sustainable Development, Environment and the Fight against Climate Change, "California Cap-and-Trade Program and Québec Cap-and Trade System, Joint Auction of Greenhouse Gas Allowances On May 20, 2020" (20 March 2020), online (pdf): <www.environnement.gouv.qc.ca/changements/carbone/ventes-encheres/2020-03-20/avis-vente-20200320-en.pdf>.

20 *Agreement between the California Air Resources Board and the Gouvernement du Québec Concerning the Harmonization and Integration of Cap-and-Trade Programs for Reducing Greenhouse Gas Emissions* (27 September 2013), online (pdf): <www.arb.ca.gov/cc/capandtrade/linkage/ca_quebec_linking_agreement_english.pdf> [Linkage Agreement 2013].

21 *Agreement on the Harmonization and Integration of Cap-and-Trade Programs for Reducing Greenhouse Gas Emissions between the Gouvernement du Québec, the Government of California and the Government of Ontario*, (22 September 2017), online: <news.ontario.ca/en/backgrounder/46294/agreement-on-the-harmonization-and-

integration-of-cap-and-trade-programs-for-reducing-greenhouse-gas-emissions> [Linkage Agreement 2017] (All references throughout are to this updated Agreement unless otherwise specified).

22 *Ibid.*

23 *Ibid.*

24 *Global Warming Solutions Act of 2006*, AB 32 (2006) at § 38564.

25 CCR tit 17, §§ 95100-95158 (2015).

26 CCR tit 17, §§ 95800 to 96023 (2013).

27 CGC § 12894(f) (West 2013) [SB 1018].

28 *Ibid.*

29 *California Global Warming Solutions Act of 2006*, as amended 2017-18, AB 398, Reg Sess, Cal, 2017.

30 See Rahul Rana et al, "An Impact Analysis of AB398 on California's Cap-and-Trade Market" (2017), online (pdf): <californiacarbon.info/wp-content/uploads/2017/07/AB398-_Impact_Analysis.pdf>.

31 Bill 42, *Act to Amend the Environment Quality Act and Other Legislative Provisions in Relation to Climate*, 1st Sess, 39th Leg, Quebec, 2009.

32 *Environment Quality Act*, RSQ 2015, c Q-2, s 46.14 (it was pursuant to this provision that the Linkage Agreement was entered into) [*EQA*].

33 CQLR, c Q-2, r 15.

34 CQLR, c Q-2, r 46.1 [Cap-and-Trade Regulation].

35 OC 1185-2012, (2012) GOQ II 3612.

36 Bill 185, *An Act to Amend the Environmental Protection Act with Respect to Greenhouse Gas Emissions Trading and Other Economic and Financial Instruments and Market-Based Approaches*, 1st Sess, 39th Leg, Ontario, 2009.

37 *Ibid* at s 176.1.

38 SO 2016, c 7 [*CCMLCEA*].

39 O Reg 144/16.

40 O Reg 143/16.

41 Ontario, Ministry of the Environment and Climate Change, *Guideline for Quantification, Reporting and Verification of Greenhouse Gas Emissions* (November 2017), online (pdf): <www.downloads.ene.gov.on.ca/envision/env_reg/er/documents/2017/013-1457_d_Guide.pdf>.

42 WCI Regional Program Design, *supra* note 12.

43 WCI Design Recommendations, *supra* note 11.

44 *Ibid* at art 12.1.

45 WCI Regional Program Design, *supra* note 12 at 24.

46 *Ibid.*

47 Linkage Agreement 2013, *supra* note 20.

48 Linkage Agreement 2017, *supra* note 21.

49 *Ibid* art 4.

50 *Ibid* art 5.

51 *Ibid* art 6.

52 *Ibid* art 7.

53 *Ibid* art 8.

54 See David Wright, "Cross-Border Constraints on Climate Change Agreements: Legal Risks in the California-Quebec Cap-and-Trade Linkage" (2016) 46:10478 ELR. See also Jennifer Hijazi, "Cap-and-Trade Feud May Chill Cross-Border Pacts", *E&E News* (11 March 2020), online: <www.eenews.net/stories/1062570265>. See also *United States v California et al* (12 March 2020) Cal Dist Ct 2:19-cv-02142 WBS EFB (memorandum and order re. cross-motions for summary judgment).

55 See United States, California, Department of Justice, *Memorandum of Attorney General's Advice to the Governor Concerning Linkage of California and Quebec Cap-and-Trade Programs* (5 March 2015), online (pdf): <web.archive.org/web/20171219080703/https://www.gov.ca.gov/docs/AG_Letter_SB_1018.pdf>.

56 United States, California, Office of the Governor, Governor Brown letter of April 8, 2013, online (pdf): <www.ca.gov/archive/gov39/wp-content/uploads/2017/09/Request_for_SB_1018_Findings.pdf>. See also United States, California, Office of the Governor, *SB 1018 Request for Cap-and-Trade Program Equivalency Findings* (26 February 2013), online: <www.ca.gov/archive/gov39/2013/02/26/news17933/index.html>.

57 Letter from Edmund G Brown Jr (Governor of California) to Mary D Nichols (16 March 2017), online (pdf): <www.arb.ca.gov/cc/capandtrade/linkage/response_to_sb_1018_request.pdf>.

58 SB 1018, *supra* note 27, § 95921(f)(2).

59 *Ibid*, § 96013.

60 See e.g., *ibid* § 95832 (Designation of Representatives and Agents) and § 95914 (c)(3) (Auction Participation and Limitations).

61 See California Air Resources Board, *Regulatory Guidance Document* (6 November 2017), online: <www.arb.ca.gov/cc/capandtrade/guidance/guidance.htm>.

62 SB 1018, *supra* note 27, § 95857(b).

63 *Ibid* at § 96014.

64 *Ibid* at § 95921(g)(3).

65 Cap-and-Trade Regulation, *supra* note 34, at ss 71–75.5.

66 *Ibid*.

67 See e.g., *ibid* s 47 (suspension of emissions allowance allocation); See also s 46.2.

68 See e.g., *ibid* ss 47 (auction), 60 (sale); see also *EQA*, *supra* note 32 at s 46.12.

69 See e.g., Cap-and-Trade Regulation, *supra* note 34, ss 75.2, 60 (operating in tandem).

70 *Ibid*, s 22.

71 *Ibid*.

72 *CCMLCEA*, *supra* note 38, ss 51(1), 51(5).

73 *Ibid*, s 51(2), 51(4).

74 *Ibid*, s 29.

75 *Ibid*, s 32(6), 32(7).

76 *Ibid*, s 64.

77 *Ibid*, s 14(7).

78 *Ibid*, s 14(8).

79 O Reg 540/17.

80 *CCMLCEA*, *supra* note 38, s 57.

81 See e.g., MDDELCC, "Linked California and Québec Cap-and-Trade Programs Carbon Market Compliance Instrument Report—Aggregated by Type and Account" (5 October 2018), online (pdf): <www.mddelcc.gouv.qc.ca/changements/carbone/ventes-encheres/Rapport_soldes/20181005-rapport-soldes-en.pdf>.

82 Amara McLaughlin, "Doug Ford Vows to Scrap Ontario's Cap-and-Trade Program as His 1st Act as Premier", *CBC News* (15 June 2018), online: <www.cbc.ca/news/canada/toronto/doug-ford-cap-and-trade-1.4707728>.

83 California Air Resources Board, "Program Linkage" (7 September 2018), online: <www.arb.ca.gov/cc/capandtrade/linkage/linkage.htm>.

84 O Reg 386/16.

85 Specifically, it repeals the *CCMLCEA*, SO 2016, c7.

86 See Richard Corley et al, "Ontario Introduces Bill to Cancel Cap and Trade and Launches Carbon Tax Case" (2018), online (pdf): <www.goodmans.ca/files/file/08_07_2018%20-%20Cleantech%20and%20Environmental%20Law%20Update.pdf> (for a summary).

87 Bill 4, *An Act Respecting the Preparation of a Climate Change Plan, Providing for the Wind Down of the Cap and Trade Program and Repealing the Climate Change Mitigation and Low-carbon Economy Act*, 2016, 1st Sess, 42nd Leg, Ontario, s 4(1).

88 Ontario, Ministry of the Environment, Conservation and Parks, "Preserving and Protecting our Environment for Future Generations: A Made-in-Ontario Environment Plan" (2018) at 18, online (pdf): <prod-environmental-registry.s3.amazonaws.com/2018-11/EnvironmentPlan.pdf>.

89 See generally, Chios Carmody, "A Guide to Emissions Trading under the Western Climate Initiative" (2019) at 30–31, online (pdf): <www.cigionline.org/sites/default/files/documents/Guide%20to%20Emissions_Carmody_Special%20Report_lowres_0.pdf>.

90 Thomas Timmins et al, "From Cap-and-Trade to White Pines: What Lies Ahead in Ontario's Energy Sector" (2018), online: <gowlingwlg.com/en/insights-resources/articles/2018/from-cap-and-trade-to-white-pines/>.

91 See Ecojustice, "Challenging Ontario's Gutting of Cap and Trade Program", online: <www.ecojustice.ca/case/challenging-ontarios-gutting-of-cap-and-trade-program/> (accessed 1 June 2020). See also *GreenPeace Canada v Ontario (Minister of the Environment, Conservation and Parks)* (11 September 2018) Toronto, ONSC 575/18 (notice of application for judicial review), online (pdf): <www.ecojustice.ca/wp-content/uploads/2018/09/Notice-of-Application-issued.pdf>.

92 *Greenpeace Canada v Minister of the Environment (Ontario)*, 2019 ONSC 5629.

93 *WO Stinson & Son Ltd v Western Climate Initiative* (10 February 2020) Ottawa, ONSC CV20-82778 (statement of claim).

94 See Quebec, Ministère du Développement durable, de l'Environnement et de la Lutte contre les changements climatiques, "California Cap-and-Trade Program and Québec Cap-and-Trade System Joint Auction of Greenhouse Gas Allowances" (20 March 2020), online (pdf): <www.environnement.gouv.qc.ca/changements/carbone/ventes-encheres/2020-03-20/avis-vente-20200320-en.pdf>. See also Michael Mastrandrea et al, "Assessing California's Progress Toward Its 2020 Greenhouse Gas Emissions Limit" (2020) 138 Energy Policy, DOI:<10.1016/j.enpol.2019.111219>.

95 See Katelyn Roedner Sutter, "California-Quebec Carbon Auction Kicks Off 2020 with Record Allowance Price" (26 February 2020), online: <blogs.edf.org/

climate411/2020/02/26/california-quebec-carbon-auction-kicks-off-2020-with-record-allowance-price/>.

96 International Carbon Action Partnership, "Update: ETSs Around the World Respond to Coronavirus" (7 May 2020), online: <icapcarbonaction.com/en/news-archive/703-etss-around-the-world-respond-to-coronavirus>.

97 See Wright, *supra* note 54.

25

Enforcing Canada's Federal Methane Regulations for the Upstream Oil and Gas Industry

Allan Ingelson[1]

Introduction

Methane (CH_4), a potent greenhouse gas (GHG), has a global warming potential of more than seventy times that of carbon dioxide (CO_2) over a twenty-year period.[2] Methane is a significant component of natural gas.[3] Environment and Climate Change Canada (ECCC) monitors national GHG emissions and has reported that the Canadian oil and gas sector was responsible for releasing 25 percent of the nation's GHG emissions during the period 1990 to 2012, with trends indicating a continuous increase in the volume of methane emissions. In 2017, ECCC reported that 44 percent of Canada's methane emissions were from the same industry.[4]

In light of Canada's commitments under the *Paris Agreement*,[5] on June 29, 2016, Prime Minister Justin Trudeau announced that by 2025 the federal government would reduce national methane emissions from the oil and gas industry to 40–45 percent below the 2012 levels.[6] The federal government has promoted the *Pan-Canadian Framework on Clean Growth and Climate Change*, which is a national plan directed toward reducing the effects of climate change, under which more stringent methane emission standards have been recommended.[7] In April 2018, pursuant to section 332(1) of the *Canadian Environmental Protection Act*,[8] ECCC published "Regulations Respecting Reduction in the Release of Methane and Certain Volatile Organic Compounds (Upstream Oil and Gas Sector)," in Part II of the *Canada Gazette*.[9] These regulations apply to methane emissions from a variety of upstream facilities, such as gathering and transmission pipelines; natural gas gathering, boosting, and transmission compression stations; and natural gas processing plants. The regulations largely focus on the extraction, primary processing, transportation, and storage of hydrocarbons.[10] The 2018 federal methane regulations that are currently being phased in are designed to establish uniform national requirements to further significantly reduce methane emissions from upstream offshore and onshore operations.

The Federal Methane Regulations

The federal methane regulations are designed to reduce the immediate or long-term harmful effects of methane emissions and the associated volatile organic compounds (VOCs).[11] Some of the negative health effects of methane emissions are cardiovascular and respiratory morbidity, heart and asthma attacks, and premature adult mortality.[12] In 2020, it was reported that the upstream oil and gas industry emitted 34 percent of the nation's VOCs.[13] The regulations focus on reducing methane emissions from the largest and emerging sources in Canada's upstream oil and gas industry: equipment leaks, venting, and new oil and gas wells.[14] ECCC estimates that the regulatory requirements to further reduce the volume of emissions by prompting the installation of new equipment should, by 2025, result in an emissions reduction equivalent to 232 million tonnes of CO_2 by 2035.[15]

EQUIPMENT LEAKS

According to ECCC, oil and gas facility equipment leaks account for 34 percent of the industry's emissions.[16] In section 2 of the regulations, the term "fugitive emissions" refers to natural gas leaks from equipment defined as "the emission of hydrocarbon gas from an upstream oil and gas facility in an unintentional manner."[17] The regulations focus on reducing these emissions from larger facilities—those that receive more than 60,000 standard m^3 of hydrocarbon gas during a 12-month period.[18] These larger facilities are responsible for approximately 75 percent of Canada's vented emissions.[19] Addressing a smaller number of larger sources of emissions (facilities) reflects a high leverage approach. To reduce emissions, section 29 of the regulations require operators to carry out leak detection and repair programs as follows:

> Operators of a facility must . . . establish and carry out at the facility a) a regulatory leak detection and repair program [LDAR] that

satisfies sections 30–33; or b) an alternative leak detection and repair program referred to in subsection 35(1) that results in at most the same quantity of those fugitive emissions as would result from a regulatory program referred to in paragraph a).[20]

As far as the types of LDAR options that are available to facility operators, subsection 35(1) of the regulations provide flexibility in regard to the types of leak repair programs employed on the condition that the repair provides the same required reduction in emissions.

Section 32 of the regulations provides that, in most cases, a leak must be repaired within thirty days of it being detected:

> A leak from an equipment component that is detected, whether as a result of an inspection or otherwise, must be repaired a) if the repair can be carried out while the equipment component is operating, within 30 days after the day on which it was detected; and b) in any other case, the equipment component must be repaired within the period before the end of the next planned shutdown unless that period is extended under Section 33.[21]

In regard to facility inspections, the regulations provide that:

> An equipment component at an upstream oil and gas facility must be inspected . . . on or before the later of May 1, 2020, and the day that occurs 60 days after the day on which production at the facility first began; and . . . at least 3 times/year and at least 60 days after a previous inspection.[22]

The regulations mandate three annual inspections.[23] The types of technologies that will be used during inspections, such as infrared cameras, sniffers, drones, and satellite systems, are specified in the regulations to avoid arguments and disputes that could arise regarding whether there have been emissions that exceed the level permitted under the regulations.

The federal requirements convey the increased emphasis that ECCC is placing on operators to take action to prevent, detect, and repair equipment methane leaks in a timely manner to further significantly reduce the volume of emissions from larger oil and gas facilities. The fact that time periods are specified in the regulations by which operators must complete equipment repairs should prompt facility operators to pay closer attention to the current volume of emissions from equipment leaks. In addition to the general provisions in the regulations that govern equipment leaks, there are specific provisions that apply to different types of equipment.

It is estimated that 20 percent of methane emissions from the Canadian oil and gas industry are from pneumatic device leaks.[24] A variety of automated instruments called pneumatic devices are employed throughout the industry that utilize natural gas to pump liquids and for other purposes. Some of these devices release methane into the atmosphere. As with other types of oil industry equipment, the regulations prescribe operating efficiency standards for pneumatic controllers and pumps.[25] The methane regulations require operators to replace certain types of high-bleed pneumatic controllers that produce a larger volume of emissions with low bleed or no-bleed controllers that will release a smaller volume of emissions than in the past. As with the other types of equipment, the repairs and/or equipment replacements must be completed within the time period specified in the regulations. As with other types of equipment, to provide facility operators with reasonable notice to budget for equipment upgrades or purchase new equipment to replace existing equipment, the provisions that apply to pneumatic devices are scheduled to come into force in 2023.[26]

VENTING

Venting is a common industry practice that releases methane directly into the atmosphere, which accounts for 23 percent of oil and gas industry methane emissions.[27] As natural gas is used to control pressurized equipment, including pumps in multiple industry operations, methane is intentionally released from equipment in processing facilities through vents. The regulations are designed to reduce by 95 percent the volume of methane that is intentionally vented from larger oil and gas facilities. To achieve this objective, section 26 of the regulations creates an annual venting limit for an upstream oil and gas facility to no more than 15,000 m^3 of hydrocarbon gas during a year. One exception to the maximum emissions limit in the regulations provides flexibility to facility operators and allows them to apply for approval to vent methane for safety reasons in exceptional cases, such as to avoid an explosion, an emergency depressurization, or a plant maintenance upset at a larger gas processing facility.[28]

In non-emergency situations, as an alternative to venting gas, the regulations require operators to capture and use at least 95 percent of the methane in facilities for a beneficial purpose rather than releasing and wasting the gas. The regulations stipulate that, at a minimum, 95 percent of the gas must be captured and used for one of three beneficial purposes stipulated in the regulations. Section 5 of the regulations require a minimum equipment operating efficiency as follows: "[h]ydrocarbon gas conservation equipment that is used at an upstream oil and gas facility must be operated in such a manner that at least 95% of the hydrocarbon gas is captured and conserved."[29] Section 7 of the regulations stipulates that gas must be captured and conserved in one of the three following methods:

> (a) used at the facility as fuel in combustion device that releases at most 5 percent of the combusted hydrocarbon gas to the atmosphere as hydrocarbon gas;
> (b) delivered; or
> (c) injected into an underground geological deposit for a purpose other than to dispose of the gas as waste.[30]

In regard to the first option, the regulations specify that no more than 5 percent of the gas can be released. The second option, "delivered," refers to piping the gas to be sold and used. The third option, subsurface injection (also referred to as enhanced recovery), requires natural gas to be reinjected into an oil and gas reservoir to avoid the release of methane into the atmosphere.

Another type of equipment is compressors, which account for approximately 9 percent of Canada's methane emissions. These are mechanical devices used to increase the pressure in pipelines to move natural gas from production sites to consumers.[31] Different types of compressors emit different levels of methane, and the regulations contain special provisions that limit the volume of emissions that can be vented from different types of compressors.[32] To reduce the volume of emissions from each type of compressor, there is a federal requirement that industry operators complete annual measurements to ensure that the emission limits stipulated in the regulations are satisfied. Section 14(a) requires measurement of gas flow volumes as the first step toward further reducing the volume of methane emissions. Section 16(3) requires operators to take initial and subsequent gas flow measurements during specific time periods, as follows:

The flow rate must be initially measured on January 1, 2021, if the compressor is installed at the facility before January 1, 2020, and the 365th day after the day on which the compressor was installed at the facility in any other case; and subsequently, the period that ends on the 365th day after the day on which a previous measurement was taken.

Section 14 provides for optimal equipment performance that takes into account the different types of compressors used at different sites, and the regulations focus on regular equipment maintenance and efficiency to minimize the level of emissions.[33] As with other types of equipment, compressor operators are required to conserve or destroy methane to reduce the volume of methane in the atmosphere and meet the relevant gas release limits tailored to the type of compressor. Corrective action is required if emissions exceed the limit applicable to the compressor, which depends on the installation date, the type of compressor, and its rated brake power.[34] Timelines of thirty days and ninety days are specified in the regulations to complete the required work on compressors to reduce methane emissions.[35]

Another potential source of methane emissions addressed in the regulations is hydraulic fracturing (HF) operations and well completions at newly drilled oil and gas wells.

HYDRAULIC FRACTURING AND COMPLETION OF OIL AND GAS WELLS

HF refers to the process used to create cracks or fractures in a rock that allows oil and gas to move more freely to the well surface. It is an essential process at most shale oil and gas wells today in order for there to be economic hydrocarbon production.[36] However, fluids that contain methane in solution flow back to the wellsite surface and can release the gas into the atmosphere if not properly managed. Recently, technology has been refined to detect and monitor methane releases from oil and gas wells. Employing satellite data, atmospheric methane emission trends in North America have been analyzed and compared before and after unconventional shale gas development. It has been reported that the concentration of fugitive emissions has increased in areas with shale oil and gas development.[37] Compared to conventional wells, it is estimated that in some areas HF of shale oil and gas wells can release 40 to 60 percent more methane into the atmosphere, where more than 8 to 12 percent of the methane escapes through equipment leaks and venting.[38]

To prevent methane emissions from new oil and gas wells drilled throughout Canada, section 11(2) of the regulations entitled "No Venting," prohibits venting at new well sites and requires combustion/destruction of the gas or the capture and use of natural gas for a beneficial purpose. The section provides that "hydrocarbon gas associated with flowback at a well . . . must not be vented during flowback but must instead be captured and routed to hydrocarbon gas conservation equipment or hydrocarbon gas destruction equipment." The prohibition on venting gas at new oil and gas wells will prevent an increase in methane emissions from these wells.

In light of pre-existing provincial standards at the time the federal regulations were adopted in 2018 in British Columbia and Alberta that limit emissions from HF of oil and gas wells, section 13 of the federal regulations entitled "Non-application—British Columbia and Alberta" provides:

> Sections 11 and 12 do not apply in respect of an upstream oil and gas facility that is located in
> **(a)** British Columbia, if the facility is subject to the requirements with respect to well completion involving hydraulic fracturing that are set out in the guideline entitled *Flaring and Venting Reduction Guideline*, published by the Oil and Gas Commission of British Columbia in June 2016; and
> **(b)** Alberta, if the facility is subject to the requirements with respect to well completion involving hydraulic fracturing that are set out in the directive entitled *Directive 060: Upstream Petroleum Industry Flaring, Incinerating, and Venting*, published by the Alberta Energy Regulator on March 22, 2016.[39]

Section 13 of the regulations provides that operators which satisfy the existing provincial requirements in British Columbia[40] and Alberta,[41] do not have to comply with the new federal standards in the regulations as well, as the federal government concluded that the 2016 provincial requirements that apply to emissions from HF and completion of new wells were adequate.[42]

In 2018 and 2019, the Alberta Energy Regulator revised *Directive 060: Upstream Petroleum Industry Flaring, Incinerating, and Venting*[43] and created *Directives 084*[44] and *017*,[45] which further contribute to the province's ongoing efforts to create provincial emissions reduction requirements that better align with the 2018 federal regulations.

Since then, the federal government has provided broader equivalency agreements for the regulations in Alberta, British Columbia, and Saskatchewan.[46]

Enforcement

There is no reported decision on a completed enforcement action under the federal regulations adopted in 2018.[47] In the United States, in 2012, the first emissions reduction rules were released and then in 2016, "Oil and Natural Gas Sector—New Source Performance Standards" were developed by the US Environmental Protection Agency (EPA) and adopted to reduce oil and gas industry emissions further.[48] However, in responding to the former President Donald Trump's goals to reduce the number of federal regulations and regulatory actions that may burden domestic energy production and development, in 2017 the US Bureau of Land Management rescinded its rule "Oil and Gas: Hydraulic Fracturing on Federal and Indian Lands,"[49] and in 2018 the EPA changed its emissions reduction requirements.[50]

The first enforcement action initiated during the Obama administration was taken against a natural gas gathering, transportation, and processing company for venting excess emissions. The action was settled in April 2018.[51] Pursuant to section 113(b) of the *Clean Air Act (CAA)*[52] and *Pennsylvania Air Pollution Control Act*,[53] the US Department of Justice, EPA, and the Pennsylvania Department of Environmental Protection filed a complaint against MarkWest Liberty Midstream & Resources, LLC, and Ohio Gathering Company, LLC (collectively MarkWest), for contravening the "Prevention of Significant Deterioration" provisions,[54] and the "Non-Attainment New Source Review" provisions,[55] due to venting excess emissions in Pennsylvania and Ohio.[56] In addition to being charged for releasing excess emissions from its facilities, the MarkWest was charged for failing to secure the required permits and the failure to maintain records for its stand-alone facilities and compressor stations. The defendant expressly denied any liability for contravening the emissions limits.[57] Federal and state regulators sought injunctive relief and civil penalties.[58]

According to Christopher Rimkus, managing counsel for MarkWest, workers had arrived at a site to carry out routine pipeline maintenance.[59] The maintenance activities were performed daily, weekly, or monthly to avoid the buildup of condensate in gas gathering and transmission pipelines. The operations required venting gas to reduce any pressure in the pipeline before site maintenance activities could proceed. The federal government agents arrived at the site for inspection at approximately 8 a.m.; they halted routine maintenance activities, began questioning the workers, and collected samples. The agents finished the site inspection and made requests for production of documents. However, no additional action was taken by the federal agents at that time.[60] The managing counsel noted that after the execution of the federal search warrant, it became clear to him that "the search warrant was based in large part on a number of misconceptions." Specifically, the operations "were not occurring in secret" as they "were routinely scheduled," and the activities in question "did not vent the larger volume of the entire pipeline segment to the atmosphere—but a much smaller amount when inserting or retrieving a tool."[61] The managing counsel also noted that:

> Employees capture any natural gas liquids (NGLs) or other liquids that may be in the barrel in a storage vessel and do not release them to the ground. The public was categorically not at risk from the operations and no evidence has ever been presented to substantiate any claim to the contrary. Worker safety is protected during the operations as the studies conducted pre-search warrant attest to.[62]

The action taken by the federal and state regulators was framed as an "Air Pollution Emergency Claim" pursuant to section 303 of the *CAA*. Counsel for the defendant reported that the basis for the search warrant and preliminary discussions with both the Department of Justice and the EPA focused on protecting industry workers and public health. He notes that "previous and subsequent scientific studies demonstrate there was no imminent and substantial danger to workers or public,"[63] and that the "EPA, state regulators and industry have traditionally been under the impression that emissions from the operations in question were de minimis."[64]

After the site inspection and the review of its operations, the corporate defendant "identified a small subset of its sites (less than 10%) where emissions might have been above Pennsylvania state de minimis permitting thresholds."[65] The managing counsel also noted that there was no motivation or benefit for the company not to acquire the relevant permits, as they were easily obtainable either for minor sources of emissions or under other criteria.

Furthermore, operational design changes are easy and inexpensive to make so that the emissions fall below "de minimis" levels.[66] In addition, the defendant operator had previously investigated and evaluated new technologies for sampling and estimating the level of VOCs in emissions from its operations and had previously undertaken design enhancements that substantially reduced methane, VOCs, and methane emissions from its compressor stations and stand-alone facilities in Pennsylvania and Ohio.[67]

Notwithstanding the above practices and a denial of liability, the company settled the enforcement action before trial.[68] In the US Consent Decree, both the defendant operator and governments acknowledged that "the settlement agreement was negotiated in good faith to avoid further litigation and that it is fair, reasonable, and in the public interest."[69] The settlement provides for payment of a US $610,000 civil penalty and completion of three supplemental community environmental improvement projects costing the operator a minimum of US$2 million, designed to reduce emissions from oil and gas facilities.[70]

As part of what we refer to as a creative sentence in Canada, the 2018 settlement agreement required the operator to install air pollution control equipment at more than three hundred facilities to reduce emissions further and improve air quality in Pennsylvania and Ohio.[71] The EPA estimates that the new emissions controls will result in a reduction of 706 tons per year of VOCs and decrease annual emissions by 91.5 percent from the company's natural gas gathering system.[72] Under the settlement agreement, the operator must also install and operate ambient air monitoring stations near two compressor stations. The information collected from the monitoring stations about the nature and volume of emissions from the company's operations must be shared with the general public. Furthermore, the operator must make available and share with other industry operators its innovative technologies developed to reduce emissions and allow other operators to use through licences on a royalty-free basis, these technologies to further reduce emissions.[73]

In light of the federal methane reduction regulations, could an enforcement action that poses similar issues arise in Canada? I submit yes, as section 1 of the Canadian regulations indicate that, as in the United States, they are designed to prevent environmental deterioration from methane emissions and the associated VOCs and to protect the health and safety of Canadians. The Consent Decree/settlement agreement in the MarkWest enforcement action is 104 pages long.[74] Canadian counsel may find it is useful to consider the issues that arose in the US enforcement action and how they were resolved. The following fourteen actions provide some examples of those that the US corporate defendant agreed to take to reduce the possibility that it and other industry operators would contravene the US methane emissions regulations:

1. To ensure the defendant's managers, employees, and contractors are aware of the enforcement action to reduce the potential for releasing excess emissions in the future, the defendant must provide a copy of the settlement agreement to all of its officers and managers to ensure that employees and contractors whose responsibilities may include compliance with the agreement are made aware of the terms of the agreement and the defendant company must place an electronic version of the agreement in a section of its internal website related to environmental matters. The company is clearly responsible for ensuring that all employees and contractors that perform any future work carry out that work in compliance with the terms of the agreement;[75]

2. The agreement specifies the type of emissions reduction technology that must be used at compressor stations and the minimum efficiency (98 percent) that must be achieved to destroy and reduce emissions;[76]

3. A date is specified in the settlement agreement by which the defendant operator must implement the specified emissions reduction program;[77]

4. For the purpose of complying with the agreement, the defendant company is obligated to calculate the mass of the VOC emissions;[78]

5. In regard to improving the containment of liquids at compressor stations and facilities to prevent emissions, new facilities that are built must incorporate liquid containers with grounded steel receptacles that are covered at all times when not in use;[79]

6. The financial penalty is shared between the federal and state governments with 80 percent to the federal government and 20 percent to the state government, with interest payable on any amount that is past due at a rate specified in the agreement;[80]

7. The financial penalty is not tax-deductible;[81]

8. The settlement agreement prohibits the defendant from using the reduced emissions from projects completed under the creative sentence, for clean development emissions reductions that include emissions offsets and obtaining, trading, or selling any emission reduction credits;[82]

9. In regard to the sale or transfer of its facilities, the agreement provides that the obligations are binding on the successors or assignees of the

company,[83] and that the company must provide written notification to a successor or assignee and the government(s) of the existence of the agreement before the closing of the sale or transfer;[84]

10. The defendant must condition any sale or transfer of ownership or operation "of any Covered Facilities upon the execution by the Third Party of a modification" to the agreement "to make the terms and conditions of [the agreement] related to the ownership or operation of the transferred Covered Facilities applicable to the Third Party";[85]

11. The defendant must spend a minimum of US$2 million to implement the projects to reduce emissions under the creative sentence,[86] and the projects must not be the ones that the defendant was planning or intending to build, carry out, or implement other than for the purpose of settling the enforcement action;[87]

12. The company must share with other industry operators the lessons learned from the enforcement action by posting information on its website and offering educational presentations that include hosting four demonstration or training sessions per year during a three-year period;

13. In regard to transferring the proven innovative emissions control technology that the defendant developed, it must provide, on a royalty-free basis, licences to other operators to use its proprietary design proven to decrease liquid accumulation and emissions. To promote rapid adoption and use of the innovative technology by other operators, the defendant must make available on a website that is publicly accessible no later than six months after the effective date of the agreement, a royalty-free licence and information on the design of the technology. The defendant must make its technical staff available in person at every educational session to demonstrate the installation and adoption of the VOC emissions reduction technology. The defendant must create comprehensive educational materials on the installation and maintenance of the technology to reduce emissions;[88]

14. Regarding ambient air quality monitoring of emissions from compressors, the defendant must install and operate, for a minimum of 720 days, one meteorological station and two air sampling stations to sample and analyze the level of total VOCs and reduced sulphur compounds. The defendant must submit, by 120 days from the effective date of the agreement, an ambient air monitoring plan to the EPA for approval. The defendant must follow the approved monitoring plan and submit quarterly information reports and annual reports to the EPA.[89]

In addition to the actions required under the settlement agreement, three specific practices that could be taken to protect workers from emissions include:

1. Incorporating standard operating procedures into training materials that include protocols for response to alarms;
2. Laminated job safety checklists for each site; and
3. Respiratory protection for changing filters at compressor stations.[90]

Conclusion

The Canadian federal methane regulations should further reduce the volume of methane that is released from equipment leaks and venting at facilities and new oil and gas wells. Starting on January 1, 2020, facility operators have implemented LDAR programs. The regulations require the implementation of LDAR programs within a specified time period at facilities along with three annual equipment inspections. Some provisions in the regulations were to be phased in during the five years following the regulations coming into effect in order to allow facility operators to budget for equipment upgrades and replacement. The regulations create a cap on the volume of emissions that can be vented from facilities. There is a maximum venting limit from larger oil and gas facilities of 250 m^3 of methane per month or a cumulative annual total of 3,000 m^3. ECCC now has the technical capability to detect and measure the volume of emissions from facilities to enforce new venting limits. To comply with the venting limits, operators have two basic options. The preferred option is to capture and use otherwise wasted methane for beneficial purposes, such as facility heating or generating electricity. A second, less desirable option, is a more efficient combustion (flaring) of natural gas, which results in a smaller volume of emissions than venting. The regulations prohibit venting at new oil and gas wells and require gas capture.[91] The regulations indicate that the current Alberta, British Columbia, and Saskatchewan provincial requirements are equivalent. Therefore, operators that satisfy the provincial standards in those provinces do not have to satisfy the federal emissions reduction standards as well. However, in other provinces such as Manitoba, where new oil and gas wells are being drilled and hydraulically fractured, operators must satisfy the federal requirements. As there are no reported Canadian prosecutions to date under the federal methane regulations that have gone to trial and been settled, the MarkWest enforcement action provides examples of the types of issues that arose in an earlier methane emissions enforcement action and the significant financial consequences for the US pipeline operator that failed to comply with similar US federal regulations. Should a similar enforcement action be taken in Canada in the future, the US MarkWest case provides examples of the conditions agreed to by the corporate defendant and prosecutors in the United States that could also arise in Canada.

NOTES

1 Professor, University of Calgary and Executive Director, Canadian Institute of Resources Law.

2 Environment and Climate Change Canada, "Canada's Methane Regulations for Upstream Oil and Gas" (April 2018), online: <www.canada.ca/en/environment-climate-change/services/canadian-environmental-protection-act-registry/proposed-methane-regulations-additional-information.html>; see also ECCC, "Canada Finalizes Major Commitment to Reduce Carbon Pollution" (26 April 2018), online: <www.canada.ca/en/environment-climate-change/news/2018/04/canada-finalizes-major-commitment-to-reduce-carbon-pollution.htm>.

3 American Geosciences Institute, "Methane Emissions in the Oil and Gas Industry" (1 June 2018), online: <www.americangeosciences.org/critical-issues/factsheet/pe/methane-emissions-oil-gas-industry>.

4 ECCC, "General Factsheet Regarding the Release of Methane and Certain Volatile Organic Compounds" (January 2020), online: <www.canada.ca/en/environment-climate-change/services/canadian-environmental-protection-act-registry/factsheet-general-information-regulations-reduction-methane.html>.

5 United Nations, "Climate Change" entered into force November 4, 2016, online: <unfccc.int/process/the-paris-agreement/status-of-ratification>.

6 Drew Nelson, "The Power of Three: Mexico Aligns with U.S and Canada on Oil and Gas Methane Pollution" (29 June 2016), online: <blogs.edf.org/energyexchange/2016/06/29/the-power-of-three-mexico-aligns-with-u-s-and-canada-on-oil-and-gas-methane-pollution/>; Global Methane, "Proposed Methane Regulations—A Significant Step in Addressing Climate Change in Canada" (June 2017), online (pdf): <www.globalmethane.org/documents/1_Canada_James%20Diamond_post_508.pdf>.

7 Government of Canada, Environment and Climate Change Canada, *Pan-Canadian Framework on Clean Growth and Climate Change: Canada's Plan to Address Climate Change and Grow the Economy* (Gatineau, Quebec: Environment and Climate Change Canada, 2016).

8 *Canadian Environmental Protection Act*, SC 1999, c 33.

9 *Regulations Respecting Reduction in the Release of Methane and Certain Volatile Organic Compounds (Upstream Oil and Gas Sector)*, SOR 2018-66, PC 2018-3296 2018-04-03, online: <laws-lois.justice.gc.ca/eng/regulations/SOR-2018-66/FullText.html>.

10 *Ibid* at s 1.

11 *Supra* note 9.

12 EPA, "Overview of Final Amendment to Air Regulations for the Oil and Natural Gas Industry" (accessed 22 June 2021), online (pdf): <www.epa.gov/sites/production/files/2016-09/documents/natural_gas_transmission_fact_sheet_2012.pdf>.

13 Environment and Climate Change Canada, "Canada's Air Pollutant Emissions Inventory Reports 2020: chapter 2.4" (13 March 2020), online (pdf): <publications.gc.ca/collections/collection_2020/eccc/En81-30-2018-eng.pdf>.

14 *Supra* note 2.

15 *Regulations Respecting reduction in the Release of Methane and Certain Volatile Organic Compounds (Upstream oil and Gas Sector)* (2018) 152 (1) C Gaz 11 62 (Regulatory Impact Analysis Statement), (accessed 22 June 2021), online: <gazette.gc.ca/rp-pr/p2/2018/2018-04-26-x1/html/sor-dors66-eng.html>.

16 *Supra* note 4.

17 *Supra* note 9.

18 *Ibid* at ss 26–45.

19 Government of Canada, "Technical Backgrounder: Proposed Federal Methane Regulations for the Oil and Gas Sector" (23 August 2018), online: <www.canada.ca/en/services/environment/weather/climatechange/climate-action/technical-backgrounder-proposed-federal-methane-regulations-oil-gas-sector.html>.

20 *Ibid* at s 29.

21 *Ibid* at s 32.

22 *Ibid* at ss 30(1)–(3).

23 *Ibid.*

24 *Supra* note 15.

25 *Ibid* at ss 37(1), 37(2), 39(1).

26 *Ibid.*

27 *Supra* note 15.

28 *Ibid.*

29 *Supra* note 9.

30 *Ibid.*

31 *Supra* note 2.

32 *Supra* note 9, ss 14(b), 16(3).

33 *Ibid*, ss 18(2), 18(3).

34 *Ibid*, s 14.

35 *Supra* note 9.

36 Canadian Centre for Energy Information, "Our Petroleum Challenge" 8th ed at 140.

37 Oliver Schneising et al, "Remote Sensing of Fugitive Methane Emissions from Oil and Gas Production in North American Tight Geologic Formations" (2014) 2:10 Earth's Future 548.

38 Robert Howarth et al, "Natural Gas: Should Fracking Stop?" (2011) 477:7364 271 Nature; Robert Howarth et al, "Methane and the Greenhouse-Gas Footprint of Natural Gas from Shale Formations" (2011) 106 Climatic Change 679.

39 *Supra* note 9.

40 BC Oil and Gas Commission, "Flaring and Venting Reduction Guideline" (May 2018), online: <www.bcogc.ca/node/5916/download>.

41 Alberta Energy Regulator, "Upstream Petroleum Industry Flaring, Incinerating and Venting, AER Directive 060" (12 May 2020), online (pdf): <www.aer.ca/documents/directives/Directive060.pdf>.

42 *Supra* note 9, ss 11, 12.

43 *Supra* note 41.

44 Alberta Energy Regulator, "Requirements for Hydrocarbon Emission Controls and Gas Conservation in the Peace River Area, AER Directive 084" (11 September 2018), online (pdf): <www.aer.ca/documents/directives/Directive084.pdf>.

45 Alberta Energy Regulator, "Measurement Requirements for Oil and Gas Operations, AER Directive 017" (12 May 2020), online (pdf): <www.aer.ca/documents/directives/Directive017.pdf>.

46 SOR 2020-233, SOR 2020-60, and SOR 2020-234, respectively.

47 *Supra* note 9.

48 US Environmental Protection Agency, "Actions and Notices about Oil and Natural Gas Pollution Standards", online: <www.epa.gov/controlling-air-pollution-oil-and-natural-gas-industry/actions-and-notices-about-oil-and-natural-gas>; "EPA Releases First-Ever Standards to Cut Methane Emissions from the Oil and Gas Sector" (12 May 2016), online: <archive.epa.gov/epa/newsreleases/epa-releases-first-ever-standards-cut-methane-emissions-oil-and-gas-sector.html>.

49 Hydraulic Fracturing on Federal and Indian Lands, Rescission of a 2015 Rule, 82 Fed Reg 61,924, 29 December 2017; codified at 43 CFR, pt 3160.

50 US Environmental Protection Agency, "EPA Amends Narrow Portions of Fugitive Emissions Requirements in the 2016 New Source Performance Standards for the Oil and Natural Gas Industry", online (pdf): <www.epa.gov/sites/production/files/2018-03/documents/epa_amends_certain_aspects_of_nsps.fact_sheet.2.23.18.pdf>.

51 US Environmental Protection Agency, "MarkWest Clean Air Act Settlement Information Sheet" (13 April 2020), online: <www.epa.gov/enforcement/markwest-clean-air-act-settlement-information-sheet>.

52 42 USC § 7413(b).

53 PL 2119, No. 787, 1959, as amended.

54 42 USC §§ 7490-7492.

55 42 USC §§ 7501-7515.

56 Civil Action No. 2:18-cv-00520-LPL (US Dist Ct Western Penn).

57 *Ibid.*

58 US Environmental Protection Agency, Consent Decree, online: <www.epa.gov/sites/production/files/2018-04/documents/markwest-cd.pdf> at 1.

59 Christopher Rimkus, "Launcher and Receiver Operational Enhancement: A Case Study" (14 March 2018), online (pdf): *Rocky Mountain States Section of the Air and Waste Management Association* <awma-rmss.org/wp-content/uploads/2018.3.8-LR-Slides-for-AWMA-Mtg2.pdf>.

60 *Ibid.*

61 *Ibid.*

62 *Ibid.*

63 *Ibid.*

64 *Ibid.*

65 *Ibid.*

66 *Ibid.*
67 *Ibid.*
68 *Supra* note 51.
69 *Supra* note 56.
70 *Ibid.*
71 *Ibid.*
72 *Ibid.*
73 *Ibid.*
74 *Ibid.*
75 *Ibid* at para 8.
76 *Ibid* at para 13.
77 *Ibid* at para 14.
78 *Ibid* at para 11.
79 *Ibid* at para 23.
80 *Ibid* at para 24.
81 *Ibid* at para 27.
82 *Ibid* at para 47.
83 *Ibid* at para 3.
84 *Ibid* at para 4.
85 *Ibid* at para 5.
86 *Ibid* at para 28.
87 *Ibid* at para 29.
88 *Ibid* at para 28.
89 *Ibid* at para 28.
90 *Supra* note 9.
91 *Ibid* at s 11(2).

26

Regulation and Enforcement of Oil Sands Emissions

Alastair R. Lucas[1] *and Diego Almeida*[2]

The Oil Sands

Oil sands activity is a major source of Canadian greenhouse gas (GHG) emissions, accounting for 12 percent of Canadian emissions.[3] These emissions have increased from 15 Mt in 1990 to 84 in 2018,[4] and remain significant.[5] Though the oil sands sector is centred in Alberta, it has national significance, comprising 97 percent of Canadian oil reserves that overall rank third globally.[6] There is little doubt that hydrocarbons, particularly oil, are a key element of the Canadian national economy.[7]

A Provincial Field

Though the 2018 federal climate change initiatives reviewed below are significant for oil sands GHG emissions reduction, it is the provinces, particularly Alberta, that will continue to be key oil sands emissions regulators. This is a consequence of provincial constitutional jurisdiction over property and civil rights,[8] management and sale of public lands,[9] and conservation and management of non-renewable natural resources[10] within a province. A significant part of the oil sands picture extends beyond Alberta, including the sale of oil sands raw and upgraded bitumen in national and international markets.[11] This is a matter primarily within federal trade and commerce jurisdiction. Pipelines to marine terminals that permit oil sands crude to reach international markets beyond North America are primarily within federal jurisdiction.[12] Impacts of these pipelines on First Nations is also a federal responsibility.[13] There is federal jurisdiction over marine tanker traffic under the Sea Coast and Inland Fisheries power.[14] In 2018, several provinces judicially challenged federal jurisdiction to enact a national carbon tax, arguing that the federal taxation power is insufficient support and that this cannot be characterized as a matter of national concern within the "peace, order and good government" power.[15] The Ontario and Saskatchewan reference case challenges of the federal *Greenhouse Gas Pollution Pricing Act* (*GGPPA*) rejected by divided provincial appeal courts, was heard by the Supreme Court of Canada (SCC) on August 2020.[16] A similar challenge by Alberta was upheld by the Alberta Court of Appeal.[17] An SCC majority decided that the *GGPPA* can be characterized as addressing a national concern.[18]

Alberta Regulation and Enforcement

Alberta has a full suite of climate change legislation. This began almost two decades ago with the *Climate Change and Emissions Management Act*[19] and the *Specified Gas Emitters Regulation*.[20] The system was one of intensity-based emissions targets for large industrial emitters. Compliance alternatives were 1) investment to achieve compliance, 2) tendering purchased emissions credits, or 3) paying $15 per ton into a climate fund. The latter was overwhelmingly the preferred option. Though this was general legislation, the major impact was felt by the oil and gas sector—particularly the oil sands. As overall emissions increased, fuelled by oil sands expansion, the lack of a hard emissions cap was heavily criticized.[21]

CARBON CAPTURE AND STORAGE

This led to provincial government review with a focus on mitigation, particularly carbon capture and storage. The showcase was an industry-government pilot carbon-capture-and-storage (CCS) program, including the Shell-led Quest Project designed to sequester approximately 35 percent of CO_2 emissions from the Scotford upgrader.[22] Provincial grant funding for CCS is authorized under the *Carbon Capture and Storage Funding Act*.[23] There has also been considerable industry-government work to reduce emissions in oil sands mining and processing, including management of tailings, an important GHG emission source.[24]

Under the Notley government in 2015, a panel review recommended an emissions management approach that centred on carbon pricing.[25] Concerning oil sands emissions, the panel said:

As a panel, we developed the following defining principles for the application of our proposed carbon pricing model to oil sands:

> 1. Greenhouse gas policy for oil sands must enable and reward innovation.
> 2. Greenhouse gas policy must recognize the trade exposure of the oil sands sector and design must prevent emissions leakage.
> 3. Greenhouse gas policy for oil sands must consider the current state of the industry and the long-run implications of policy choices today on economic activity within the province.
> 4. Greenhouse gas policy for oil sands must reward best-in-class emissions-intensity performance, regardless of the underlying factors which contribute to that performance.
> 5. Complementary policies should promote innovation and new technology development and deployment in Alberta to both lower emissions and lower production costs to maintain a globally carbon competitive oil sector in Alberta.[26]

The result was a carbon tax; along with a 100 Mt cap on overall oil sands GHG emissions, which in 2017 were 70 Mt.[27]

There has also been an attempt to address concerns of First Nations in the oil sands area, in part through the creation of the provincial Aboriginal Consultation Office.[28] Much of the focus here has been not on emissions reduction but on direct environmental and social impacts of oil sands projects. An example is the Fort Mackay First Nation's challenge to the Dover oil sands project located adjacent to the First Nation's Moose Lake Reserve. After obtaining Alberta Court of Appeal leave for its appeal of the Alberta Energy Regulator (AER)'s approval,[29] the First Nation reached an agreement with the proponent Brion Energy,[30] resulting in a community benefits package that included training, employment opportunities, and community services.

REGULATION OF GREENHOUSE GAS EMISSIONS BY THE ALBERTA ENERGY REGULATOR AND ALBERTA ENVIRONMENT AND PARKS

Alberta Energy Regulator Oil Sands Facility Approvals

As noted, most of the oil sands operators complied with the *Climate Change and Emissions Management Act* by paying $15 per ton of emissions. The AER and its predecessors, the Alberta Energy and Utilities Board (AEUB) and the Energy Resources Conservation Board (ERCB), resisted arguments by intervenors in facility approval proceedings that GHG emissions limits should be imposed as conditions of regulatory approvals. Its reasons for the decision provided no basis for approval conditions and did not address enforcement. In the 2004 TrueNorth Oil Sands Plant and Cogeneration application, for example, the applicant simply submitted that it was "committed to using leading technologies to minimize GHG emissions, including a low temperature extraction process, thickened tailings, heat recovery from process water, and cogeneration of electricity."[31] The complete AEUB reasons section on GHGs was:

> The Board endorses TrueNorth's commitment to using leading technologies to minimize GHG emissions. The Board believes that the issue of GHGs is best dealt with through initiatives and policies at the federal and provincial levels. The Board recommends that Alberta continue to implement measures that would achieve continuous improvement in emissions per unit of product.[32]

The board was even more laconic in its reason for approving a Petro-Canada upgrader application in 2009:

> The Board is satisfied that [the applicant] will design the facility to be carbon capture ready and will implement measures to reduce GHGs and maximize energy efficiency. The Board notes that [Alberta Environment] is the responsible authority for GHG emissions management through the Climate Change and Emissions Management Act.[33]

The Joint AEUB/Canadian Environmental Assessment Agency Panel reviewing the Imperial Oil Kearl oil sands project application addressed GHG emissions by "support[ing] Alberta developing appropriate [*Environmental*

Protection and Enhancement Act] approval requirements to address [various air emissions control and monitoring matters including], GHG emission intensity targets."[34] In a judicial review of the decision brought by the Pembina Institute, the Federal Court set the decision aside and sent the matter back to the Joint Panel.[35] A major reason for the court's decision was the panel's failure to provide any rationale for its conclusion that GHG emissions from the project would be insignificant. Subsequently, the panel re-reviewed the GHG issue and reached the same conclusion, stating that it had to give Alberta's per-barrel intensity target approach "considerable weight."[36] It concluded that "there was very little evidence [that project GHG emissions] will result in significant environmental effects."[37] On this basis, the federal government fast tracked re-approval, issuing a new Fisheries Act authorization.[38]

Alberta Energy Regulator Methane Initiative

When the government of Alberta announced its Climate Leadership Plan in 2015, the AER was directed to develop requirements to reduce methane emissions from upstream oil and gas operations by 45 percent below 2014 levels by 2025. The AER constituted multi-stakeholder groups in collaboration with the Clean Air Strategic Alliance (CASA)[39] which included representatives from industry, non-governmental organizations (NGOs), and research bodies that provided input in this process. Specific requirements were developed and implemented through amendments to Directive 060: Upstream Petroleum Industry Flaring, Incinerating, and Venting,[40] and Directive 017: Measurement Requirements for Oil and Gas Operations.[41]

Directive 060 was originally based on CASA recommendations developed following AER stakeholder consultations. Subsequently, a CASA-coordinated study produced a revision of Directive 060 in 2006. The 2018 directive update that created more stringent standards is based on the review, public consultation, and extension of these earlier initiatives, including adoption of the previously developed methodology.[42] In May 2020, the federal and Alberta governments announced a methane emissions equivalency agreement[43] under which the Alberta methane regulations will operate in place of federal regulations.[44]

Alberta Energy Regulator Oil Sands Tailings Requirements

The AER has established requirements for tailings management that include progressive reclamation, environmental effects assessment, and regular inspections and audits.[45] This will limit the extent of liquid tailings ponds that produce greater quantities of GHG emissions than dry tailings.

THE ALBERTA CLIMATE LEADERSHIP PLAN AND IMPLEMENTING LEGISLATION: ALBERTA ENVIRONMENT AND PARKS

Alberta's 2015 Climate Leadership Plan[46] was the blueprint for a new system of GHG emission regulation that emphasizes carbon pricing. In part, it builds on the original *Climate Change and Emissions Management Act/Specified Gas Emitters Regulation* emissions intensity regime, replacing this with the *Carbon Competitiveness Incentive Regulation* (*CCIR*).[47] However, it moved beyond the emissions intensity approach by establishing a carbon price for GHG emissions,[48] specifying an overall oil sands GHG emissions cap, and reducing methane emissions by 45 percent by 2025. Broader objectives include phasing out coal generated emissions by 2030 and developing more renewable energy.[49]

Implementation is through replacement of the *Specified Gas Emitters Regulation*, which created emissions intensity limits for particular facilities, including oil sands facilities, and a compliance system involving emissions credits, offsets, and fund payments. The *CCIR*[50] is described as an output-based allocation. According to the Alberta government,

> An oil sands specific output-based allocation approach will replace the current approach. A $30/tonne carbon price will be applied to oil sands facilities based on results already achieved by high performing facilities—to drive towards reduced emissions and carbon competitiveness, rather than rewarding past intensity levels.
>
> A legislated emissions limit on the oil sands of a maximum of 100 MT in any year with provisions for cogeneration and new upgrading capacity. This limit will help drive technological progress and ensures Alberta's operators have the necessary time to develop and implement new technology. . . ."[51]

As noted in the *2016–2017 Climate Leadership Plan Progress Report*,[52] the oil sands sector accounted for approximately one-quarter of Alberta's annual emissions, emitting 68.6 Mt in 2015. To put this into perspective, the amount of emissions from oil sands activities is higher than the total amount of emissions produced by British Columbia.[53]

The Climate Leadership Plan was abandoned by the Kenney government in 2019. This included repeal of the general provincial carbon tax statute, the *Climate Leadership Act*. A new Technology Innovation and Emissions Reduction (TIER) System replaced the *Carbon Competitive Incentive Regulation*.[54] These requirements apply to oil sands (and other) facilities that emitted 100,000 tonnes or more of GHGs in 2016 or any subsequent year. Benchmarking is facility specific, based on past performance not on best-in-class factors. Emissions must be reduced by 10 percent below benchmarks in 2020, with 1 percent reductions in subsequent years. Compliance options include direct emissions reduction, excess credits from compliant facilities, and payments into a TIER fund.

OIL SANDS EMISSIONS LIMIT ACT

The *Oil Sands Emissions Limit Act*[55] caps oil sands GHG emissions at a combined 100 Mt in any year. In 2017, combined emissions were approximately 70 Mt.

Oil sands emissions under the 100 Mt cap will be monitored. The methodology and formula for allocation of this cap space will be developed and presumably promulgated as regulations under the *Oil Sands Emissions Limit Act*. Meanwhile, GHG emissions from oil sands have been increasing at a consistent rate. Questions remain about the specific implications of the cap.[56] These include: how will emitters share the cap? Will these shares be assignable? How will the cap share of new emitters be determined? Will the 100 Mt limit be adjusted over time?

ALBERTA ENFORCEMENT AND COMPLIANCE

Enforcement of oil sands GHG emissions requirements and limits is carried out by the Alberta Environment and Parks under the TIER System[57] under a generic enforcement and compliance approach. The AER, which regulates methane emissions, relies on reporting requirements and on administrative monetary penalties under the *Administrative Penalty Regulation*.[58]

The AER has an *Integrated Compliance Assurance Framework*[59] that outlines a principled approach with an operational focus on investigation, verifying compliance, and enforcement. A list of relevant factors includes complaints, emergencies, operational history, potential adverse effects, and unique circumstances. Tools include notices of noncompliance, warnings, administrative orders, fees, administrative penalties, and prosecution. A Compliance Dashboard provides updated information on enforcement activities.

On the industry side, Canada's Oil Sands Innovation Alliance (COSIA)[60] includes GHG programs to improve measurement, monitoring, and verification, and development and improvement of various technologies to reduce GHG emissions.

Federal Role

The federal *GGPPA*[61] sets baseline carbon prices and provides that it will apply in default to provinces that fail to enact equivalent carbon-pricing legislation. Saskatchewan and Ontario refused to comply and advocated for other provinces to refuse the application of this carbon tax.[62] In August 2018, Alberta also announced that it was "pulling out of the federal scheme," citing alleged federal failure to take environmental and First Nations consultation action sufficient to support federal approval of the Trans Mountain oil sands pipeline expansion project from Alberta to the British Columbia coast.[63] Another federal regulatory measure to limit emissions is the 2018 methane reduction regulations under the *Canadian Environmental Protection Act*.[64]

On another front, the North American Commission for Environmental Cooperation (CEC) accepted a citizen complaint concerning oil sands tailings ponds under the *North American Agreement on Environmental Cooperation*.[65] The allegation is that Canada "failed to effectively enforce"[66] provisions of the federal *Fisheries Act*[67] concerning hydrocarbon leaching into fish habitat from oil sands tailings ponds.[68] An investigation was carried out and a factual record prepared by the CEC secretariat.[69] The factual record itself states that it "draws no conclusions regarding Canada's alleged failures to effectively enforce its environmental law, nor does it draw conclusions regarding the effectiveness of Canada's enforcement efforts."[70]

FEDERAL–PROVINCIAL NEGOTIATIONS TO 2020

Federal–provincial negotiations concerning "equivalency agreements" under section 10 of the *Canadian Environmental Protection Act* to provide for equivalent provincial laws to operate in place of federal *GGPPA* carbon levy requirements continued from 2018 into 2020.[71] Meanwhile, the provincial constitutional challenges to the *GGPPA* eventually led to the SCC issuing a reference decision of their own.[72] In this decision, the SCC Majority found that the *GGPPA* is constitutional and *intra vires* Parliament on the basis of the national concern doctrine.

Conclusion

Oil sands activity remains a significant and increasing source of Canadian and global GHG emissions. Though these emissions are subject to both federal and provincial regulation, Alberta continues to be the dominant regulator. Provincial requirements include a $30 per tonne carbon price and an overall oil sands emissions cap administered by Alberta Environment and Parks. These measures raise questions and uncertainties as implementation continues. There have also been initiatives by the AER to tighten oil sands methane release requirements and to shift toward the deposit of dry tailings. Though the AER considers the impacts of GHG emissions in assessing new oil sands project applications, it has essentially relied on emissions limits under the general Alberta GHG emissions legislation that is now centred on the TIER system and the oil sands emissions cap.

Federal authority is exercised in oil sands project assessment through the *Fisheries Act*. More recently, the *GGPPA* aims at driving down GHG emissions from large emitters. This Act was conceived as a national backstop on carbon pricing, with provinces acting as primary regulators under equivalent legislation. After years of court challenges, in 2021, the SCC confirmed the validity of this approach.

NOTES

1 Professor Emeritus, Faculty of Law, University of Calgary.

2 Corporate Law Clerk, Lundin Mining Corp, Toronto.

3 Environment and Climate Change Canada, *National Inventory Report 1990–2018: Greenhouse Gas Sources and Sinks in Canada, Part I* (2020), online (pdf): <publications.gc.ca/collections/collection_2020/eccc/En81-4-2018-1-eng.pdf> at 56.

4 *Ibid.*

5 Pembina Institute, "The Real GHG Trend" (4 October 2017), online: <www.pembina.org/blog/real-ghg-trend-oilsands>.

6 Natural Resources Canada, "What Are the Oil Sands?" (28 July 2020), online: <www.nrcan.gc.ca/energy/oil-sands/18089>.

7 See Philip Cross, "A National Project: How Oil Sands Investment and Production Benefit Canada's Economy" (April 2021), online: *Macdonald-Laurier Institute* <www.macdonaldlaurier.ca/not-enough-canadians-know-how-important-the-oilsands-are-philip-cross-in-the-financial-post/>; Alberta Energy, "Oil Sands, Facts and Statistics", online: <www.alberta.ca/oil-sands-facts-and-statistics.aspx>.

8 *Constitution Act, 1867*, s 92 (13).

9 *Ibid*, s 92(5).

10 *Ibid*, s 92A.

11 *Ibid*, s 91(2).

12 *Ibid*, s 92(10)(a).

13 *Ibid*, s 91(24).

14 *Ibid*, s 91(10).

15 Stuart Thomson and Tyler Dawson, "Anti-carbon Tax Provinces Team Up to Argue for 'the Right Not to Cooperate' with Federal Climate Plan", *National Post* (2 August 2018), online: <nationalpost.com/news/politics/anti-carbon-tax-provinces-team-up-to-argue-for-the-right-not-to-cooperate-with-federal-climate-plan>.

16 *Reference re Greenhouse Gas Pollution Pricing Act*, 2019 SKCA 40; *Reference Greenhouse Gas Pollution Pricing Act*, 2019 ONCA 544.

17 *Reference re Greenhouse Gas Pollution Pricing Act*, 2020 ABCA 74.

18 *References re Greenhouse Gas Pollution Pricing Act*, 2021 SCC 11.

19 *Climate Change and Emissions Management Act*, SA 2003, c C-16.7, now *Emissions Management and Climate Resilience Act*, SA 2003 c E-7.8.

20 *Specified Gas Emitters Regulation*, Alta Reg 139/2007. Replaced on January 1, 2020 by the *Technology Innovation and Emissions Reduction Regulation*, Alta Reg 133/2019.

21 Taylor Gray E, "Canada: Alberta's GHG Emissions Control System: A Model for Others?" *Mondaq* (18 October 2012), online: <www.mondaq.com/canada/clean-air-pollution/202178/albertas-ghg-emissions-control-system-a-model-for-others>.

22 According to Alberta Energy, "The Alberta Government has committed $1.24 billion over 15 years to two commercial-scale carbon capture and storage projects. The two projects are moving forward to help reduce the CO2 emissions from the oil sands and fertilizer sectors. When both projects are completed, they will reduce Alberta's greenhouse gas emissions by 2.76 million tonnes each year" (accessed 29 June 2021), online: <www.alberta.ca/carbon-capture-and-storage.aspx#:~:text=Alberta%20has%20committed%20%241.24%20billion,2.76%20million%20tonnes%20each%20year>.

23 *Carbon Capture and Storage Funding Act*, SA 2009 c C-2.5.

24 Commission for Environmental Cooperation, "Submission: Alberta Tailings Ponds II", SEM-17-001 (26 June 2017), online: <www.cec.org/sem-submissions/alberta-tailings-ponds-ii>; CEC, "Alberta Tailings Ponds II: Factual Record regarding Submission SEM-17-001" (4 September 2020), online (pdf): Commission for Environmental Cooperation <www.cec.org/wp-content/uploads/wpallimport/files/17-1-ffr_en.pdf>.

25 Climate Leadership, *Report to the Minister* (November 2015).

26 *Ibid* at 60.

27 *Oil Sands Emissions Limit Act*, SA 2016, c O-7.57 at 2(1).

28 Ministers of Energy and Environment and Sustainable Resource Development, Ministerial Order 105/2014 under the *Responsible Energy Development Act*, 31 October, 2014.

29 *Fort McKay First Nation v Alberta Energy Regulator*, 2013 ABCA 355.

30 Brion Energy, "Brion Energy Corporation and the community of Fort McKay reach agreement on Dover Commercial Project" (21 February 2014), online: <www.newswire.ca/news-releases/brion-energy-corporation-and-the-community-of-fort-mckay-reach-agreement-on-dover-commercial-project-513791671.html>.

31 *TrueNorth Energy Corporation Application to Construct and Operate an Oil Sands Mine and Cogeneration Plant in the Fort McMurray Area*, 2002 AEUB 089 at 46.

32 *Ibid* at 47.

33 *Petro-Canada Oil Sands Inc. Application to Construct and Operate an Oil Sands Upgrader in Sturgeon County*, 2009 ABERCB 002 at 41.

34 *Imperial Oil Resources Ventures Limited, Application for an Oil Sands Mine and Bitumen Processing Facility (Kearl Oil Sands Project) in the Fort McMurray Area*, 2007 AEUB 013 [*Kearl Report*]. This was a decision of the Canadian Environmental Assessment Agency and Alberta Energy and Utilities Board (now AER), Kearl Oil Sands Project Joint Review Panel.

35 *Pembina Institute for Appropriate Development v Canada (Attorney General)*, 2008 FC 302.

36 Impact Assessment Agency of Canada, "Archived—Joint Panel Report Kearl Oil Sands Project Addendum to EUB Decision 2007-013 Additional rationale for the joint review panel's conclusion on air emissions" (6 May 2008).

37 *Ibid.*

38 Sean Nixon & Melissa Gorrie, "Nothing (Significant) to See Here: The Kearl Cases and the Growing Mess in the Alberta Oil Sands" in William Tilleman and Alastair Lucas, *Litigating Canada's Environment: Leading Canadian Environmental Cases by the Lawyers Involved* (Toronto: Thomson Reuters, 2017) 283 at 302.

39 Alberta Energy Regulator, "Directive 060: Upstream Petroleum Industry Flaring, Incinerating, and Venting" (12 March 2018) at 103, Appendix Background to Directive 060.

40 *Ibid* at 10–13.

41 Alberta Energy Regulator (31 March 2016). Under review in August 2018, current version is May 2020.

42 Alberta Energy Regulator, "Directive 060: Directive 060: Upstream Petroleum Industry Flaring, Incinerating, and Venting" (21 April 2021), online (pdf): <static.aer.ca/prd/documents/directives/Directive060.pdf>.

43 Under s 10 of the *Canadian Environmental Protection Act*.

44 Janet French, "Alberta, Ottawa Reach Preliminary Deal on Methane Emissions Regulation", *CBC* (13 May 2020), online: <www.cbc.ca/news/canada/edmonton/alberta-ottawa-reach-preliminary-deal-on-methane-emissions-regulation-1.5568924>.

45 Alberta Energy Regulator, "Directive 085: Fluid Tailings Management for Oil Sands Mining Projects" (12 October 2017).

46 Osler, "Alberta's New Climate Change Leadership Plan" (23 November 2015), online: <www.osler.com/en/resources/regulations/2015/alberta-s-new-climate-change-leadership-plan>.

47 Alta Reg 255/2017.

48 Ministerial Order 58/2017 under the *Climate Change and Emissions Management Act*, RSA 2003C-16.7, establishing a $30 per tonne price for 2018.

49 *Supra* note 46.

50 Alta Reg 255/2017.

51 Government of Alberta, "Capping Oil Sands Emissions" (accessed 12 July 2021), online: <www.alberta.ca/climate-oilsands-emissions.aspx>.

52 Alberta Government, *Climate Leadership Plan Progress Report 2016–2017* (December 2017).

53 Government of Canada, "Greenhouse Gas Emissions" (15 April 2021), online: <www.canada.ca/en/environment-climate-change/services/environmental-indicators/greenhouse-gas-emissions.html>.

54 Alta Reg 255/2017.

55 SA 2016 c O-7.5.

56 Nigel Bankes, "Oil Sands Limit Legislation: A Real Commitment or Kicking It Down The Road?" *ABlawg* (3 November 2016), online: <ablawg.ca/2016/11/03/oil-sands-emission-limit-legislation-a-real-commitment-or-kicking-it-down-the-road/>; Brenda Heelan Powell, "Climate Change Legal Roadmap: Oil Sands Emission Limit Under the Climate Change Leadership Plan" (Edmonton: Environmental Law Centre, 2017).

57 Alta Reg 133/2019.

58 Alta Reg 140/2007; *Methane Emission Reduction Regulations* Alta Reg 244/2018.

59 Alberta Energy Regulator, February 2016.

60 COSIA, "We Aspire to Produce Oil with Lower Greenhouse Gas Emissions than Other Sources of Oil" (accessed 12 July 2021), online: <www.cosia.ca/initiatives/greenhouse-gases>.

61 *Greenhouse Gas Pollution Pricing Act*, SC 2018, c 12, s 186.

62 Janyce McGregor, "Alberta Joins Saskatchewan in Opposing Federal Carbon Tax Plan", *CBC News* (20 July 2018).

63 "Premier Rachel Notley Pulls Alberta Out of Federal Climate Plan over Trans Mountain Ruling", *CBC News* (30 August 2018).

64 *Canadian Environmental Protection Act 1999*, SC 1999 c 33; *Regulations Respecting Reduction in the Release of Methane and Certain Volatile Organic Compounds (Upstream Oil and Gas Sector)* SOR/2018-66.

65 *Agreement between the United States, Canada and Mexico*, 14–15 September 1993, Can TS No 3, 32 ILM 1480 [*NAAEC*].

66 *Ibid* art 14.

67 RSC 1985, c F-14, s 36(3).

68 *NAAEC* s 15(2).

69 CEC, *supra* note 24.

70 *Ibid* at 65.

71 E.g., Government of Canada, "Canada-Saskatchewan Equivalency Agreement Regarding Greenhouse Gas Emissions from Electricity Producers" (5 October 2019), online: <www.canada.ca/en/environment-climate-change/services/canadian-environmental-protection-act-registry/agreements/equivalency/canada-saskatchewan-greenhouse-gas-electricity-producers.html>.

72 *References re Greenhouse Gas Pollution Pricing Act*, 2021 SCC 11.

27

Reducing Greenhouse Gas Emissions from Canadian Agriculture

Jamie Benidickson[1]

Introduction: Agriculture and Global Climate Law

"To ensure that food production is not threatened" would not be widely recognized as one of three explicit considerations applicable to the *United Nations Framework Convention on Climate Change* (*UNFCCC*)'s over-arching climate objective of "stabilization of greenhouse gas concentrations . . ."[2] Equally noteworthy is recognition in the 2015 *Paris Agreement* of "the fundamental priority of safeguarding food security and ending hunger, and the particular vulnerabilities of food production systems to . . . climate change." Combining concerns for mitigation and adaptation, the *Paris Agreement* refers specifically to "[i]ncreasing the ability to adapt to the adverse impacts of climate change and foster climate resilience and low greenhouse gas emissions development, in a manner that does not threaten food production."[3]

More generally, policymakers have been advised of three global limits: "the quantity of food that can be produced under a given climate; the quantity needed by a growing and changing population; and the effect of food production on the climate."[4] While we can, therefore, assume that global climate law encompasses agriculture, it is noteworthy that the activity mentioned is food production rather than agriculture. Noting the tendency to focus on adaptation and resilience, this chapter seeks to highlight opportunities and challenges associated with mitigation.[5]

Delineating the Scope of the Agriculture Sector for Climate Change

On the assumption that you cannot confidently regulate what you cannot define, it is worth asking about the relative scope of food production and agriculture. A recent analysis explains that greenhouse gas (GHG) emissions attributed to agriculture for purposes of the *UNFCCC* instruments originate from a range of sources—some but not all involving land-use, and some involving CO_2 as well as other gases, notably methane and nitrous oxide. These sources were not being treated in "an integrated, sector-specific way," with the consequence that the Intergovernmental Panel on Climate Change (IPCC) eventually formulated the AFOLU (agriculture, forestry and other land uses) category to address inconsistencies and double counting.[6]

Challenges of categorization also arise within domestic frameworks. Agriculture and Agri-Food Canada (AAFC), for example, notes that its agricultural GHG indicator: "does not attempt to capture carbon dioxide emissions from fossil fuel consumption by farm machinery, as these emissions are typically reported by the manufacturing and transportation sectors."[7] For its part, the House of Commons Standing Committee on Environment and Sustainable Development advances a wide-ranging recommendation for the reduction of GHG emissions from "Canada's forestry, agricultural, and waste sectors."[8] For the purposes of the federal *Greenhouse Gas Pollution Pricing Act* (*GGPPA*), agriculture is equated with "farming," the latter defined to include "tillage of the soil, livestock raising or exhibiting, maintaining of horses for racing, raising of poultry, fur farming, dairy farming, fruit growing and the keeping of bees, but does not include an office or employment under a person engaged in the business of farming."[9]

A description of agricultural processes, to inventory highlights, may involve land preparation, seed planting, nutrient application, pest management, irrigation, harvesting or collection, storage and delivery. If delivered for processing or as an ingredient, agricultural produce will then be processed, packaged, and distributed to retail, commercial, or industrial consumers. The continuing storyline at the household level includes purchase, transport, preparation, consumption, and waste. Appropriate modifications would produce a livestock narrative.

This approach to agriculture extends its scope significantly beyond activities on the farm. The Food and Agricultural Organization (FAO) adopted this broader approach in its formulation of climate smart agriculture. Climate smart agriculture might involve on-farm activity, including land-management practices, food-processing arrangements, retail distribution processes, and consumption.[10] The agriculture and agri-food system, as understood by AAFC is also multi-dimensional: "a complex and integrated supply chain that includes input and service suppliers, primary producers, food and beverage processors, food retailers and wholesalers, and foodservice providers."[11]

Climate smart agriculture has gained some traction in Canada and is of interest in achieving "agriculture that sustainably increases productivity, resilience (adaptation), reduces/ removes GHGs (mitigation), and enhances achievement of national food security and development goals."[12]

The extent to which mitigation initiatives in agriculture merit attention depends ultimately on their potential to make a difference. With 36 million hectares of active cropland, Canada was ranked seventh by arable land surface in the years 1961–2019 after the USSR, the United States, India, Russia, Mainland China, and Brazil.[13] The size of Canadian farming operations varies, but if a successful initiative to reduce GHG emissions on one not-necessarily-large farm might be replicated across 200,000 other Canadian farms of similar size, a difference could be made. Regrettably, it is not quite so straightforward.

Scale and its relation to adaptation was addressed in the Working Group II (WGII) contribution to the Fifth IPCC Assessment Report: "adaptations can occur at a range of scales from field to policy."[14] WGII further observed: "effective adaptation will often require changes in institutional arrangements and policies to strengthen the conditions favorable for effective adaptation including investment in new technologies, infrastructure, information and engagement processes."[15] Also noteworthy is a reference to "the sector-specific nature of many adaptations." Similar considerations apply to mitigation.

Greenhouse Gas Emissions from Agriculture

As much as 29 percent of global GHG emissions can be attributed to "food systems."[16] Setting aside divergent understandings of food systems and agricultural sectors, let alone the challenge of orderly reconciliation, it is possible to report Canadian data. Prominent conventional assessments have attributed as much as 10 percent of Canadian GHG emissions to agriculture with 8.1 percent as a current assessment.[17] Viewed provincially, however, agriculture is recognized as a far more significant contributor, with, for example, Manitoba's agricultural sector producing 30 percent.[18]

As communicated by AAFC, Environment Canada's *National Inventory Report for 1990–2011* elaborates the process of calculation:

> In 2011, the net GHG emissions (emissions minus absorption by soils) from Canadian agricultural activities, excluding fossil fuel use, amounted to 42 million tonnes of CO_2 equivalents (Mt CO_2e), which is equal to about 6% of Canada's overall GHG emissions. Total agricultural GHG emissions (not factoring in carbon sequestration by agricultural soils) comes to 8% of Canada's total emissions.[19]

In addressing trends, the AAFC noted that the contribution of methane (largely attributable to livestock operations) had increased by 2 percent with nitrous oxide emissions (associated with fertilizer use and manure) up by 31 percent.[20] These GHGs are highlighted for their dramatically greater greenhouse effect in comparison with the benchmark CO_2. Noting a long-term decline in net agricultural GHG emissions, the AAFC summarized long-term findings:

> The index illustrates a relatively constant trend since 1981, with emissions caused by increased production being largely countered by improvements in production efficiency and by enhanced carbon storage in soils due to tillage reductions.[21]

The accompanying analysis identified several relevant trends. Firstly, prairie farmland is functioning more effectively as a carbon sink, a change attributed to the adoption of improved land management practices. Reduced GHG emissions were also associated with declining animal populations, notably beef and dairy cattle. Countering the declines were increased emissions associated with increased volumes of nitrogen fertilizer[22] and eastern Canadian farm activity.[23]

Mitigation in Agriculture

NATIONAL FRAMEWORK

The *Pan-Canadian Framework on Clean Growth and Climate Change* combines agriculture with forestry and waste in a highly generalized statement noting opportunities for carbon storage through land management practices and bioenergy. The framework was elaborated on through the 2017 Canadian Agricultural Partnership, including a projected investment of $3 billion. Pursuant to this arrangement, provinces "will make investments to enhance carbon storage in agricultural soils, generate bioproducts and biofuels, and advance research and innovation to support GHG emission reductions in the agriculture sector."[24]

Several national research initiatives are seeking supportive insights, including a 2013 report by the Council of Canadian Academies. The project surveyed research oriented, in part, around climate change impacts and irrigation efficiencies using less energy to meet water requirements in the primary agricultural sector.[25] That invitation for research around the intersection of climate, water, energy, and agriculture[26] was echoed and elaborated in the 2016 call for Strategic Partnership Grant Applications from the Natural Sciences and Engineering Research Council (NSERC). In connection with the theme of "adapting agricultural production systems to climate change," NSERC invited researchers to identify adaptation options and risk management tools while encouraging attention to synergies and trade-offs between adaptation and mitigation.[27]

AAFC's Agricultural Greenhouse Gases Program has sponsored GHG reduction or removal projects on livestock systems and cropping practices. Among the former are studies of cattle grazing systems, beef cattle diets, and hog manure application. One of the cropping studies seeks to increase soil carbon sequestration and reduce nitrous oxide emissions by comparing perennial cereal crop systems with annual cropping.[28]

PROVINCIAL MITIGATION INITIATIVES

The implementation of specific operational initiatives is most apparent provincially. Alberta, for example, echoing FAO's climate smart agriculture framework, anticipates improved productivity, strengthened resilience, and reduced GHG emissions. With a specific focus on GHGs, Alberta seeks to:

1. Reduce emissions from livestock, fertilizer, manure and fuel
2. Replace fossil fuels with bio-based renewable energy
3. Remove atmospheric carbon and store it in soils.[29]

Most other jurisdictions are pursuing a comparable suite of measures directed at croplands, livestock, and energy, with the latter divisible into energy efficiency initiatives and renewable production.[30] Renewable biofuel programs, in turn, have on-farm and off-farm dimensions.

CROPLANDS

The emphasis in relation to croplands and GHG emissions/carbon retention is on farm practices, especially tillage, nutrient management, and irrigation.[31] Conservation or "one-pass" tillage reduces soil disruption and lowers energy use. Agronomic improvements, particularly in relation to fallowing and cover crops, offer opportunities to reduce nitrous oxide emissions. The timing and monitoring of fertilizer applications via precision agriculture similarly offer benefits associated with lower fuel consumption and avoidance of unnecessary distribution of fertilizer.

Turning to irrigation, the individual farmer's search for water efficiencies may initially be driven by the prospect of adapting to shortages, but the resulting innovations typically involve reduced energy use. This is a farm-level cost saving that contributes to substantial emission reductions.

Statistics Canada distinguishes several types of irrigation (sprinklers, micro-irrigation, and surface) and analyses their use in relation to separate categories of crops (field crops, e.g. canola and soybeans; forage crops such as hay and alfalfa; fruit operations where irrigation is also used as protection against frost and heat; and vegetable crops).[32]

In addition to conventional water-conservation practices such as night/morning watering; water/energy-saving nozzles; pressure reduction; and soil enhancement and monitoring innovations are being introduced with a view to refining information on irrigation needs for particular crops in precise soil conditions with reference to current weather forecasting.[33]

LIVESTOCK

Ruminants and their diets are the second centre of innovation.[34] This activity, in Alberta's Ministry of Agriculture and Forestry assessment, has the potential to increase feed utilization, lower costs, and reduce methane emissions. This represents the Canadian domestic equivalent of the Clean Development Mechanism projects that TransAlta Utilities initiated with Indian and Ugandan farmers nearly two decades ago in the *Kyoto Protocol* context.[35]

Manure is a further focus of attention. Legislation designed to reduce nutrient flows into waterways and thereby prevent pollution has hugely expanded the use of manure management systems, including storage tanks.[36] Many of these are now being viewed as viable sources of methane-based biogas.

ENERGY EFFICIENCY AND BIOFUELS

In addition to the energy savings noted in connection with cropland management, a number of highly particularized energy efficiency programs and proposals are being developed, as illustrated by the guidance provided by the Ontario Ministry of Agriculture, Food and Rural Affairs that is specifically relevant to corn, grains, and hay.[37] On the livestock side, some advice is targeted at dairy producers, or exclusively designed for poultry operations, or aimed uniquely at hog farms. A similar approach is evident in British Columbia, where energy-saving guidance is directed to dairy, field crop, grain, greenhouse, nursery, orchard, poultry, and vineyard operations.[38] Even more, general guidance documents promoting energy savings within the climate response agenda underscore the complexity of agricultural operations. Instructional materials include efficiency guidance for lighting, fuel, ventilation, irrigation, crop drying and storage, and for standby emergency power systems.[39]

As noted above, improved manure management facilitates methane capture for on-farm use or allows transfer off-site to centralized facilities. Threshold-based requirements along these lines have been introduced in some US states, or projects may be encouraged where offset arrangements operate to support the necessary capital investment.[40] In Canada, agricultural biogas is promoted alongside other green energy opportunities in Ontario,[41] while in Alberta—with financing from major GHG emitters in the province—Lethbridge BioGas draws on an abundance of local manure (dairy, hog, and poultry) in combination with other organic materials to produce power for the energy marketplace.[42]

Agricultural Related Non-Farm Mitigation

Additional mitigation opportunities involving the agricultural sector as producer, supplier, and shipper may also be noted.

The Canola Council of Canada emphasizes new market opportunities in biodiesel, including the European Union renewable fuels market.[43] More generally, in terms of market enhancement, the constitutionality of Canada's *Renewable Fuels Regulations*[44] was upheld with specific reference to the strategic inter-relationship between energy, environment, and agriculture.[45]

A California company, Apeel Sciences, is developing fruit and vegetable coatings from natural materials. This innovation offers the possibility of lower energy requirements for shipping and refrigeration accompanied by reduced wastage.[46]

Continued improvements to rail transportation—involving substantial food shipments—offer a significant opportunity for emissions reduction.[47]

The Legal Framework

Through nutrient management legislation, or regulations calling for emissions reporting[48] or requiring the use of renewable fuels in specified circumstances,[49] for example, certain supports for mitigation initiatives in agriculture have been firmly established. Pricing of methane emissions federally is now addressed, together with specified exemptions for "farming" in the *GGPPA*. At the provincial level, British Columbia exempted agriculture from the carbon tax regime, while Manitoba has expressed concern that exempting agriculture from GHG reduction initiatives would place a disproportionate burden on other sectors.[50] Other observers point to differential impacts on a large agricultural sector as an argument for cap-and-trade over carbon taxes.[51] Other mitigation support measures with firm legal foundations include the availability of favourable tax treatment (accelerated capital cost allowances) on investments in renewable energy equipment.[52]

Generally, however, GHG mitigation measures in agriculture (more narrowly defined) have been encouraged or facilitated through policy rather than formally required. A software program made available through AAFC at no charge allows users at the farm level to estimate their current GHG emissions and then, by making an online substitution of a current practice for an alternative (adopting a new cropping rotation, for example) to obtain information estimating new GHG emission levels accompanied by a cost-benefit analysis.[53] A farm practice alteration offering GHG mitigation in a cost advantageous manner would presumably be adoptable on a voluntary win-win basis.

Conclusion

While agriculture has not been overlooked from the mitigation perspective, its potential significance may not be fully appreciated. Given the internal diversity and complexity of the sector—with food production systems as a still more challenging consideration—it is easy to underestimate the extent of the agricultural or agri-food sector and its intersection with energy, water, transportation, and waste—on-site and off.

At least partially, in consequence, governmental measures have tended towards facilitation rather than prescriptive regulation.[54] Large-scale agricultural and food processing operations obviously have industrial attributes that invite appropriate regulatory interventions. But aspects of the overall agri-food landscape may be culturally distinctive because of the number of individual and smaller-scale operations involved.

To the extent that beneficial management practices offer both environmental and economic benefits, research to identify these and measures to enhance awareness and encourage adoption are highly attractive. In the same way that agricultural sustainability might benefit from a comprehensive, high-level national vision,[55] wider efforts to advance climate mitigation may be attractive alongside adaptation measures that have thus far tended to receive more attention.

NOTES

1 Professor of Environmental Law, University of Ottawa.

2 *The United Nations Framework Convention on Climate Change*, 12 June 1992, 1771 UNTS 107 arts 2 and 2.1(b) (entered into force 21 March 1994) [*UNFCCC*]. See also *Kyoto Protocol to the United Nations Framework Convention on Climate Change*, 11 December 1997, 2303 UNTS 162 art 10(b)(i) (entered into force 16 February 2005).

3 *Paris Agreement*, 22 April 2016, Preamble and 2.1(b) (entered into force 4 November 2016).

4 J Beddington et al, "Achieving Food Security in the Face of Climate Change: Final Report from the Commission on Sustainable Agriculture and Climate Change" (March 2012) at 7, online: CGIAR Research Program on Climate Change, Agriculture and Food Security <ccafs.cgiar.org/publications/achieving-food-security-face-climate-change-final-report-commission-sustainable#.XqmZqWhKiUk>.

5 On adaptation in Canadian agriculture, see Ellen Wall, Barry Smit & Johanna Wandel, eds, *Farming in a Changing Climate: Agricultural Adaptation in Canada* (Vancouver: UBC Press, 2007).

6 Jonathan Verschuuren, "Climate Change and Agriculture under the United Nations Framework Convention on Climate Change and Related Documents" in Mary Jane Angelo & Anél Du Plesis, eds, *Research Handbook on Climate Change and Agricultural Law* (Massachusetts: Edward Elgar Publishing, 2017) 21 at 22–23.

7 Agriculture and Agri-Food Canada, "Agricultural Greenhouse Gas Indicator" (25 June 2021), online: <agriculture.canada.ca/en/agriculture-and-environment/climate-change-and-air-quality/agricultural-greenhouse-gas-indicator>.

8 House of Commons, Standing Committee on Environment and Sustainable Development, *Clean Growth and Climate Change in Canada: Forestry, Agriculture and Waste*, 42nd Parl, 1st Sess, No 18 (April 2019) (Chair: John Aldag).

9 *Greenhouse Gas Pollution Pricing Act*, SC 2018 c 12, s 186, s 3. For applicable exemptions see ss 17(2)(a)(iii) and 36(1)(b)(vii).

10 Joseph Macharia & Hope Johnson, "Co-producing Climate Smart Agriculture Knowledge through Social Networks: Future Direction for Climate Governance" in Tim Cadman, Rowena Maguire & Charles Sampford, eds, *Governing the Climate Change Regime: Institutional Integrity and Integrity Systems* (Abingdon, UK: Routledge, 2017) 212 at 215. The second edition of the FAO's CSA Sourcebook is online at: <www.fao.org/climate-smart-agriculture-sourcebook/en>.

11 Agriculture and Agri-Food Canada, "An Overview of the Canadian Agriculture and Agri-Food System 2016" (April 2016), online (pdf): <publications.gc.ca/collections/collection_2016/aac-aafc/A38-1-1-2016-eng.pdf>.

12 FAO 2010 as quoted in Macharia & Johnson, *supra* note 10 at 214.

13 "FAOSTAT: Land Use" (accessed 12 July 2021), online: *FAO* <www.fao.org/faostat/en/#data/RL/visualize>.

14 John R Porter et al, "Food Security and Food Production Systems" in CB Field et al, eds, *Climate Change 2014: Impacts, Adaptation, and Vulnerability. Part A: Global Security and Sectoral Aspects. Contribution of Working Group II to the Fifth Assessment Report of the Intergovernmental Panel on Climate Change* (Cambridge: Cambridge University Press, 2014) at 513, online (pdf): <www.ipcc.ch/site/assets/uploads/2018/02/WGIIAR5-Chap7_FINAL.pdf> [perma.cc/6S72-NW49].

15 Ibid at 514.

16 Olivier De Schutter & Emilie Frison, "Modern Agriculture Cultivates Climate Change—We Must Nurture Biodiversity", *The Guardian* (9 January 2017), online: <www.theguardian.com/global-development/2017/jan/09/modern-agriculture-cultivates-climate-change-nurture-biodiversity-olivier-de-schutter-emile-frison> [perma.cc/7MC3-PN56]. IPCC WG II in the Fifth Assessment Report attributes roughly 25 percent of anthropogenic GHG emissions to the AFOLU category: IPCC, "Summary for Policymakers" in V Masson-Delmotte et al, eds, *Global Warming of 1.5°C* (Geneva: World Meteorological Organization: 2018) 32. See also, Green Budget Coalition, "Recommendations for Budget 2019" (accessed 30 June 2021), online (pdf): <greenbudget.ca/wp-content/uploads/sites/4/2020/04/Green-Budget-Coalitions-final-Recommendations-for-Budget-2019-September-5-2018b.pdf>.

17 Government of Canada, "Greenhouse Gas Sources and Sinks: Executive Summary 2021" (12 April 2021), online: *Government of Canada* <www.canada.ca/en/environment-

climate-change/services/climate-change/greenhouse-gas-emissions/sources-sinks-executive-summary-2021.html>.

18 Todd MacKay & Robin Speer, "Farmers Worry about Climate Change, But a Prius Can't Pull an Air Seeder", *The Globe and Mail* (17 May 2018), online: <www.theglobeandmail.com/report-on-business/rob-commentary/farmers-worry-about-climate-change-but-a-prius-cant-pull-an-air-seeder/article31820673/> [perma.cc/ECA9-Y6E2].

19 Agriculture & Agri-Food Canada, *supra* note 7.

20 *Ibid.*

21 *Ibid.*

22 "The application of nitrogen fertilisers increased more than twice as fast as agricultural production since the early 2000s, and faster than in any other OECD member country": OECD, *OECD Environmental Performance Reviews: Canada* (Paris: OECD Publishing, 2017) at 23.

23 Environment Canada, generally distinguishing on-farm fuel use, crop production, and animal production, presents a somewhat different historical narrative accompanied by projections to 2030. For discussion of agricultural pollution measurement methodology, including fuels, see Environment and Climate Change Canada, *Canada's Air Pollutant Emissions Inventory Report 1990–2019* (Ottawa: Environment and Climate Change Canada, 2021), online (pdf): <publications.gc.ca/collections/collection_2021/eccc/En81-30-2019-eng.pdf> at Annex 2.4.

24 *Pan-Canadian Framework on Clean Growth and Climate Change: First Annual Synthesis Report on the Status of Implementation* (December 2017) at 12, online (pdf): <www.canada.ca/content/dam/themes/environment/weather/climatechange/PCF-FirstSynthesis_ENG.pdf>.

25 The Expert Panel on Sustainable Management of Water in the Agricultural Landscapes of Canada, "Water and Agriculture in Canada: Towards Sustainable Management of Water Resources" (26 February 2013), online: <www.scienceadvice.ca> [perma.cc/9M3Q-46P8].

26 Tony Allan, Martin Keulertz & Eckart Woertz, "The Water-Food-Energy Nexus: An Introduction to Nexus Concepts and some Conceptual and Operational Problems" (2015) 31:3 Intl J Water Resources Development 301.

27 Natural Sciences and Engineering Research Council of Canada, "Strategic Partnership Grants Target Area Descriptions" (13 December 2016), online: <www.nserc-crsng.gc.ca/Search-Recherche/Search-Recherche_eng.asp?q=Strategic+Partnership+Grants+Target+Area+Descriptions&site=english&ns=1> [perma.cc/WMU2-74HD].

28 Results and Delivery Management Committee, "Evaluation of the Agricultural Greenhouse Gases Program (2016–17 to 2020–21)" (12 December 2019), online: Agriculture and Agri-Food Canada <agriculture.canada.ca/en/about-our-department/transparency-and-corporate-reporting/audits-and-evaluations/evaluation-agricultural-greenhouse-gases-program-2016-17-2020-21>. See also the Global Research Alliance on Agricultural Greenhouse Gases, online: <globalresearchalliance.org/>.

29 Government of Alberta, "Climate Smart Agriculture in Alberta" (accessed 12 July 2021), online (pdf): <www1.agric.gov.ab.ca/$Department/deptdocs.nsf/all/cl9706/$FILE/CSA-Intro-July-4-2018.pdf>.

30 Government of Quebec, *Le Québec en action vert 2020: Plan d'action 2013–2020 sur les changements climatiques* (2012) at 31, online (pdf): <www.environnement.gouv.

qc.ca/changements/plan_action/pacc2020.pdf>; Government of Manitoba, "Soil Management Guide: Greenhouse Gases in Agriculture" (accessed 12 July 2021), online: <www.gov.mb.ca/agriculture/environment/soil-management/soil-management-guide/greenhouse-gases-in-agriculture.html>.

31 Other more specific challenges are also getting attention. See, for example, Braden Hursh, "Grain Bag Recycling in Western Canada", *Grainews* (25 February 2019), online: <www.grainews.ca/features/grain-bag-recycling-in-western-canada/>.

32 Statistics Canada, "Environment Fact Sheets: Irrigation Methods and Conservation Practices on Canadian Farms, 2014" (8 July 2016), online: <www150.statcan.gc.ca/n1/pub/16-508-x/16-508-x2016001-eng.htm>.

33 "The Internet of Farming" (May 2017) 15:01 *CyberTrend* 38.

34 Adam Satariano, "The Business of Burps: Scientists Smell Profit in Cow Emissions", *New York Times* (1 May 2020), online: <www.nytimes.com/2020/05/01/business/cow-methane-climate-change.html?smid=em-share>.

35 Andrew Pape-Salmon, "Canada's Potential Role in the Clean Development Mechanism" *Pembina Institute* (November 2000) at 10, online (pdf): <www.pembina.org/reports/cdm-canada-role.pdf>.

36 For example, *Nutrient Management Act, 2002*, SO 2002, c4.

37 Ontario Ministry of Agriculture, Food and Rural Affairs, "Energy Efficiency, Conservation and Management" (accessed 12 July 2021), online: <www.omafra.gov.on.ca/english/engineer/con_energy.htm>.

38 Climate and Agriculture Initiative BC, "Tools & Resources Library" (accessed 12 July 2021), online: <www.climateagriculturebc.ca/library/>.

39 The Canadian Federation of Independent Business (CFIB) reported that 63 percent of farmers "are investing in equipment, machinery, or vehicles that are more energy-efficient or environmentally friendly": Carly Barefoot & Mandy D'Autremont, "Realities of Agriculture in Canada: A Sector of Innovation and Growth" (8 October 2014), online (pdf): CFIB <www.cfib-fcei.ca/sites/default/files/article/documents/5590_0.pdf>.

40 For a survey of US law and policy, see Michelle Nowlin & Emily Spiegel, "Much Ado about Methane: Intensive Animal Agriculture and Greenhouse Gas Emissions" in Mary Jane Angelo & Anél Du Plesis, eds, *Research Handbook on Climate Change and Agricultural Law* (Massachusetts: Edward Elgar Publishing, 2017) 228. For further examples, see Manure Manager's publications on anaerobic digestion, online: <www.manuremanager.com/energy/anaerobic-digestion>.

41 Ontario Ministry of Agriculture, Food and Rural Affairs, "Green Energy Generation" (accessed 12 July 2021), online: <www.omafra.gov.on.ca/english/engineer/energy.html>.

42 Lethbridge Biogas, "Welcome to Lethbridge BioGas" (2020), online: <www.lethbridgebiogas.ca/>. See also Tony Kryzanowski, "Canada's Largest Biogas Plant", *Manure Manager* (18 March 2014), online: <www.manuremanager.com/canadas-largest-biogas-plant-15093/>.

43 Geoffrey Morgan, "Shell Canada Focuses on Green Energy", *Edmonton Journal* (7 June 2017), online: <www.pressreader.com/canada/edmonton-journal/20170607/282063391938533>.

44 SOR/2010-189.

45 *Syncrude Canada v Canada* (AG), 2016 FCA 160 at paras 64–70.

46 Stephanie Strom, "An (Edible) Solution to Extend Produce's Shelf Life", *The New York Times* (13 December 2016), online: <www.nytimes.com/2016/12/13/business/an-edible-

solution-to-extend-produces-shelf-life.html>. See also Paul Hawken, ed, *Drawdown: The Most Comprehensive Plan Ever Proposed to Reverse Global Warming* (New York: Penguin Books, 2017).

47 Government of Canada, *Canada Transportation Act Review, Pathways: Connecting Canada's Transportation System to the World*, vol 1 (2015) c 6 at 88, online (pdf): <tc.canada.ca/sites/default/files/migrated/ctar_vol1_en.pdf>.

48 *Regulation Respecting Mandatory Reporting of Certain Emissions of Contaminants into the Atmosphere*, CQLR, c Q-2, r 15.

49 *Renewable Fuels Regulations*, SOR/2010-189.

50 MacKay & Speer, *supra* note 18.

51 Sylvain Charlebois, "Carbon Tax Could Compromise Canadian Food Sovereignty", *The Globe and Mail* (19 December 2016), online: <www.theglobeandmail.com/report-on-business/rob-commentary/carbon-tax-could-compromise-canadian-food-sovereignty/article33359914/> [perma.cc/52HK-M9A6].

52 Miller Thomson, "Canadian Renewable & Conservation Expense 'Green' Energy Tax Incentives" (17 April 2013), online: <www.millerthomson.com/en/publications/communiques-and-updates/tax-notes/april-2013/canadian-renewable-conservation-expense-2/>.

53 Agriculture & Agri-Food Canada, "Holos Software Program" (accessed 12 July 2021), online: <agriculture.canada.ca/en/scientific-collaboration-and-research-agriculture/agricultural-research-results/holos-software-program>.

54 Agricultural exemptions from otherwise applicable mitigation requirements are not uncommon elsewhere.

55 Nathalie Chalifour & Heather C McLeod-Kilmurray, "The Carrots and Sticks of Sustainable Farming in Canada" (2016) 17 VJEL 303 at 338. However, for caution about the effectiveness of environmental stewardship programs in Canadian agriculture, see Peter C Boxall, "Evaluation of Agri-Environmental Programs: Can We Determine if We Grew Forward in An Environmentally-Friendly Way?" (14 April 2018) 66:2 *Canadian Journal of Agricultural Economics* 171.

28

Regulating Greenhouse Gas Emissions from International Shipping

Peter L'Esperance[1]

Introduction

THE INTERNATIONAL SHIPPING SECTOR, SUSTAINABLE DEVELOPMENT, AND CLIMATE CHANGE

The international shipping industry has been described as the "lifeblood" of the global economy, responsible for connecting distant markets, creating linkages in international supply chains, facilitating the exploitation of economies of scale and comparative advantages in production, and ultimately moving a wide range of goods between countries, both developing and developed.[2]

International shipping is the most cost-efficient mode for transporting goods, with estimates suggesting that international shipping carries as much as 90 percent of the volume of world trade.[3] Further, international shipping is the most energy-efficient and least emissions-intensive method of transporting goods between countries, generating an estimated 3–8 grams of greenhouse gases (GHGs) per tonne-kilometre; significantly less than ground and air transportation, which respectively generate 80 and 435 grams of GHGs per tonne-kilometre.[4]

The international shipping industry's superior cost and energy efficiencies coupled with its integral role in facilitating trade and economic development more broadly suggest the industry's continuing importance in facilitating sustainable development, defined as "development which meets the needs of current generations without compromising the ability of future generations to meet their own needs," having regard to social, economic, and environmental criteria.[5]

Yet, the international shipping industry does not operate without environmental impacts. The industry generates a wide variety of pollutants: marine and atmospheric, operational and accidental. With regard to climate change, combustion of the heavy fuel oil, marine diesel oil, and liquefied natural gas relied on by the international shipping sector for propulsion generates significant quantities of potent GHG, including carbon dioxide (CO_2), methane (CH_4), and nitrous oxide (N_2O).[6] These emissions join those from other anthropogenic sources to increase overall concentrations in the atmosphere, contributing directly to climate change.

Accordingly, despite international shipping's characterization as an industry playing an integral role in facilitating global trade and economic growth, it is also an industry that contributes directly to climate change. This contribution has the real potential to compromise sustainable global development.

OVERVIEW

To deconstruct this tension, this paper explores the topic of regulating GHGs generated by the international shipping industry through:

1. quantifying GHG emissions generated by the international shipping sector;
2. exploring the history of and challenges encountered in regulating GHG emissions from international shipping under the *United Nations Framework Convention on Climate Change (UNFCCC)*, the *Kyoto Protocol*, and the *Paris Agreement*;
3. exploring the history and evolution of International Maritime Organization (IMO) efforts to regulate GHG emissions from international shipping;
4. constructing a framework to compare the relative effectiveness of current and proposed IMO policies to regulate GHGs from international shipping; and
5. applying the comparative framework to proposed IMO market-based measures regulating emissions from international

shipping with a view to identifying which IMO policy is best positioned to reduce emissions from international shipping to levels consistent with international targets.

Quantifying Emissions Generated by the International Shipping Sector

AGGREGATE EMISSIONS FROM THE INTERNATIONAL SHIPPING SECTOR AS A SHARE OF GLOBAL ANTHROPOGENIC GREENHOUSE GAS EMISSIONS

International shipping is the least emissions-intensive method of transporting goods internationally. Yet, in absolute terms and as a percentage of global emissions, emissions from international shipping remain significant. The *Fourth IMO GHG Emissions Study*, completed in 2020, estimated 2018 emissions for international shipping to equal 1,076 million tonnes of CO_2 equivalent (CO_2e) for GHGs combining CO_2, CH_4, and nitrous oxide N_2O.[7] As a proportion of global anthropogenic emissions, shipping represented 2.9 percent of CO_2e emissions in 2018.[8] To provide some context on the international shipping industry's absolute contributions to anthropogenic GHG emissions with reference to those of other states, Canada generated approximately 728 million tonnes of CO_2e in 2018; Germany generated approximately 856 million tonnes of CO_2e in 2018; France generated approximately 452 million tonnes of CO_2e in 2018; and the Russian Federation generated approximately 2,134 million tonnes of CO_2e in 2018.[9] Note that among Annex I state parties to the *UNFCCC*, only the United States, Russia, and Japan generate a higher volume of CO_2e emissions than the international shipping industry.

PROJECTED INCREASES IN EMISSIONS FROM THE INTERNATIONAL SHIPPING SECTOR FROM 2018–2050

The *Fourth IMO GHG Emissions Study* (the study) projected pathways for shipping emissions from 2018–2050. The IMO based the future pathways on projected increases in demand for maritime transport services, projected improvements in fleet fuel consumption, and projected improvements in operational efficiency. The pathways predict emissions from international shipping to increase between 0–50 percent in the period up to 2050.[10] The range in the projected increases flows from different assumptions regarding demand, improvements in operational efficiency, and projections regarding fuel type.[11] The study reveals that as an emissions source, the international shipping industry is a significant contributor in absolute terms, with absolute emissions that are higher than most *UNFCCC* Annex I countries.[12] Projected increases in shipping emissions from 2018–2050 suggest that the industry's contribution to anthropogenic GHG emissions—and climate change—will continue to increase. These points provide an important perspective in contextualizing later discussion on the effectiveness of regulatory responses to GHG emissions generated by the international shipping sector.

History of Regulating International Shipping Emissions

In 1992, the United Nations adopted the *UNFCCC* to provide the architecture in which subsequent international negotiations would take place to achieve the *UNFCCC*'s ultimate objective: the "stabilization of greenhouse gas concentrations in the atmosphere at a level that would prevent dangerous anthropogenic interference with the climate system."[13] Although the *UNFCCC* did not directly address shipping emissions, it established the Subsidiary Body for Scientific and Technological Advice (SBSTA) tasked with conducting preliminary investigations into regulating GHG emissions from international shipping in concert with the IMO.[14] The SBSTA and the IMO identified five primary options for assigning responsibility for emissions from international shipping, specifically:

1. No allocation;
2. Allocation to the country where the bunker fuel is sold;
3. Allocation to the nationality of the transporting company, or to the country where the vessel is registered, or to the country of the operator;
4. Allocation to the country of departure or destination of a vessel. Alternatively, the emissions could be shared between the country of departure and country of arrival; or
5. Allocation to the country of departure or destination of passenger or cargo. Alternatively, the emissions related to the journey of a passenger or cargo could be shared by the country of departure and the country of arrival.[15]

The five proposed options generated debate but did not produce any agreement on a preferred allocation option. This early failure to adopt a method for allocating GHG emissions from international shipping among *UNFCCC* parties foreshadowed the exclusion of GHG emissions from international shipping from later protocols developed under the *UNFCCC*, including the *Kyoto Protocol* and the more recent *Paris Agreement*.

In 1997, *UNFCCC* parties established legally binding GHG emission reduction targets through the adoption of the *Kyoto Protocol*.[16] The *Kyoto Protocol* reflected the "common but differentiated responsibilities" (CBDR) principle animating the *UNFCCC*: the concept that all countries have an obligation to undertake action to address climate change but that developed countries should assume greater obligations given their historical responsibility for the bulk of anthropogenic GHG emissions currently effecting climate change.[17] Consistent with the CBDR principle, developed countries committed to reducing GHG emissions to an average of 5 percent relative to 1990 levels over the five-year period between 2008 and 2012.[18] Although international shipping was not included in these targets, Article 2.2 of the *Kyoto Protocol* expresses that the task of regulating emissions and developing emissions reductions targets would fall to the parties working through the IMO.[19]

In 2015, 195 members of the *UNFCCC* adopted the *Paris Agreement*: a global, legally binding agreement designed to stabilize increases in global average temperature below 2°C above pre-industrial levels and to pursue efforts to limit the temperature increase to 1.5°C above pre-industrial levels.[20] The *Paris Agreement*, like the *Kyoto Protocol*, reflects the CBDR in Article 2(2), which provides that, "[t]his Agreement will be implemented to reflect equity and the principle of common but differentiated responsibilities and respective capabilities, in the light of different national circumstances."[21] However, unlike the *Kyoto Protocol*, the *Paris Agreement* makes no explicit reference to emissions from marine bunker fuels or from international shipping.[22] Accordingly, the IMO continues to serve as the primary forum through which *UNFCCC* parties and non-parties negotiate emissions reductions targets for the international shipping sector.

International Maritime Organization Regulation of Greenhouse Gas Emissions from Shipping

INTRODUCTION TO THE INTERNATIONAL MARITIME ORGANIZATION

The IMO is the United Nations body responsible for the safety and security of shipping and the prevention of marine pollution by ships.[23] The IMO's membership structure is unique, and accommodates flag states, coastal states, intergovernmental organizations, and non-governmental organizations representing industry and environmental interests.[24] Since its establishment in 1958, the IMO has facilitated the development, adoption, and implementation of an impressive constellation of international instruments regulating all facets of shipping, international and domestic. As the international community began to appreciate the relationship between emissions from international shipping and climate change, its focus shifted to regulating GHG emissions generated by the industry. The decision to exempt emissions from international shipping from the *UNFCCC* meant that the IMO would be responsible for fulfilling this task.

In September 1997, parties to the *1973 International Convention for the Prevention of Pollution by Ships* as amended by the *1978 Protocol* (*MARPOL*)—the primary treaty addressing operational and accidental marine environmental pollution from shipping—adopted the *1997 Protocol to MARPOL*.[25] The *1997 Protocol* added Annex VI to *MARPOL: Regulations for the Prevention of Air Pollution from Ships*.[26] Annex VI did not address GHG emissions from shipping. Specifically, during negotiations preceding the instrument's adoption, parties agreed that CO_2 was not an air pollutant as such and, therefore, would not be covered by the regulations.[27] However, the parties did agree on a separate resolution to address "CO_2 emissions from ships." The resolution invited the IMO to:

(a) collaborate with the executive secretary of the *UNFCCC* in exchanging information on the issue;

(b) commission a study of GHG emissions from ships to establish the amounts and percentage share of GHG emissions from shipping as part of a global inventory of GHG emissions; and

(c) consider through its Marine Environmental Protection Committee potential emissions reductions measures.[28]

This resolution formally initiated the IMO's work in developing a regulatory strategy to reduce GHG emissions from ships. Following the resolution, the IMO commissioned its first *IMO Study on GHG Emissions from Ships* in June 2000 to evaluate the shipping sector's absolute and relative contributions to global anthropogenic GHG emissions.[29] Since that time, the IMO has commissioned three additional GHG studies in 2009, 2014, more recently in 2020.[30] The studies measure the shipping sector's absolute and relative contributions to global GHG emissions, project future increases in the shipping sector's emissions through to 2050, evaluate the potential of technical and operational measures to reduce emissions, evaluate the potential of proposed market based measures to reduce emissions, and, more generally, inform the IMO and its members about the task of developing a GHG reduction regime for the international shipping sector.

Significantly, the CBDR principle, which animates the *UNFCCC* and the *Paris Agreement*, is in tension with foundational principles that have traditionally informed IMO regulatory approaches. Specifically, the CBDR principle conflicts with the IMO principle of equal treatment of ships (also known as "no more favourable treatment" or NMFT).[31] The ostensible conflict between the two principles is especially evident when one considers that three-quarters of all merchant vessels by deadweight tonnage engaged in international trade are registered in countries traditionally categorized as "developing"; countries that are not subject to binding emissions reduction targets under the earlier *Kyoto Protocol* adopted under the *UNFCCC*.[32] This pattern of ship registration automatically makes the traditional approach to IMO regulation via the flag state unsuitable for regulating GHG emissions in a manner sensitive to the CBDR principle.

CURRENT INTERNATIONAL MARITIME ORGANIZATION MEASURES TO REGULATE EMISSIONS FROM INTERNATIONAL SHIPPING

The tables below introduce the GHG reductions options currently developed and proposed by the IMO. The succeeding sections will critically evaluate each option in its ability to achieve the purpose underlying the *Paris Agreement*—regulating emission reductions to stabilize temperature increases below 2°C by the end of this century. The sections will employ a structured analysis to evaluate the effectiveness of proposed regulatory options based on criteria developed in the *Second IMO GHG Study* and informed by legal regulatory theory. The objective of this analysis will be to attempt to identify the option or collection of options offering the most promise in achieving the stated objective of reducing GHG emissions from the international shipping sector and anticipating those issues which the IMO must address in implementing the particular options identified.

GHG control or reduction measures developed or proposed by the IMO fall into two distinct categories, each of which will be examined in turn:

1. energy efficiency measures (efficiency-based measures), and
2. market-based measures.

Due to space constraints, this chapter applies a comparative analysis that focuses on those measures which IMO GHG studies have identified as the most effective in reducing sector-wide emissions (see Table 28.1 and Table 28.2).

Table 28.1 Efficiency-based Measures

Measure	*Description*	*Status*	*Base Documents*
Energy Efficiency Design Index (EEDI)	Mandatory regulatory mechanism requiring all new ships of prescribed classes to meet a minimum threshold for energy efficient design.	Entered into force January 1, 2013	MEPC.203(62), *Amendments to the Annex of the Protocol of 1997: To Amend the International Convention for the Prevention of Pollution from Ships, 1973, as Modified by the Protocol of 1978 Relating Thereto,* adopted 17 July 2011 (entered into force 1 January 2013)
Ship's Efficiency Management Plan (SEEMP)	Mandatory regulatory mechanism applicable to all ships within prescribed classes designed to improve the operational energy efficiency of a ship in a cost-effective manner. The SEEMP includes a mechanism to enable ship owners and operators to track ship or fleet efficiency performance over time, the Energy Efficiency Operational Indicator (EEOI).	Entered into force January 1, 2013	MEPC.203(62), *Amendments to the Annex of the Protocol of 1997: To Amend the International Convention for the Prevention of Pollution from Ships, 1973, as Modified by the Protocol of 1978 Relating Thereto,* adopted 17 July 2011 (entered into force 1 January 2013);

Table 28.2 Market-based Measures

Measure	*Description*	*Proponents*	*Base Documents*
Global Emissions Trading System (ETS) for International Shipping	Establish a sector-wide cap on emissions from international shipping. Auction a number of emissions allowances to the international shipping sector annually, sufficient to meet the pre-set cap. Shipowners/operators can trade emissions allowances to the extent their emissions fall above or below the sector cap.	Norway	MEPC 60/4/22; MEPC 60/4/26; MEPC 60/4/41; MEPC 60/4/54; GHG-WG 3/3/5; GHG-WG 3/3/6; GHG-WG 3/3/8
International Fund for GHG Emissions from Ships	Establish a system requiring shipowners/operators to pay a fee per unit of bunker fuel purchased. Fees collected would be allocated to a separate International Fund for GHG Emissions from Ships, which would further allocate funds to GHG mitigation and adaptation projects in developing countries, and research and development into technical measures for more energy-efficient ship design and propulsion methods.		MEPC 60/4/8

Evaluative Framework

To measure the comparative effectiveness of current and proposed IMO efficiency and market-based policies to reduce GHG emissions from international shipping, this chapter will apply the below framework to each of the policy options identified earlier in the paper (see Figure 28.1).[33]

1. Environmental Effectiveness
- i. Total amount of emissions under the policy's scope
- ii. Impacts on shipping in other sectors
- iii. Range of and depth of emissions reductions measures rewarded
- iv. Policy applicability

2. Cost Effectiveness
- i. Cost effectiveness of emissions reductions measures
- ii. Administrative costs to implement schemes

3. Incentives for Positive Technological Change
- i. Goal-based and non-prescriptive
- ii. Conducive to technological innovation and improvements in energy efficiency

4. Practical Feasibility of Implementation
- i. Administrative complexity and ease of implementation
- ii. Transparent and Fraud Free

5. Legal Enforcement
- i. Legal enforceability of policy measures
- ii. Practical effectiveness of enforcement mechanisms
- iii. Availability and effectiveness of the legal penalties for non-compliance

6. Impacts on Developing Countries

Figure 28.1 Evaluative Framework

Applying the Evaluative Framework to Efficiency and Market-Based Measures

The tables below (see Table 28.3 and Table 28.4) apply these factors to the two primary efficiency-based measures and the two primary market-based measures identified above.

Table 28.3 Evaluative Framework Applied to Efficiency-based Measures

Criteria	*EEDI*	*SEEMP/EEOI*
1. Environmental Effectiveness	***Strengths*** - Ensures *new ships* meet efficiency performance targets and defined emissions intensity reduction targets - Significant long-term emissions reductions potential—*regulates incremental improvements in energy efficiency performance* - Low predicted impacts on other sectors - Low risks of policy evasion	***Strengths*** - Mandatory obligation to possess a valid SEEMP applies to *new and old ships of prescribed types 400 gross tonnage and above* - *Increased short term emissions reduction potential* relative to the EEDI - Obligation to prepare a SEEMP makes it more likely for ship owners/ operators to adopt the measures articulated in the management plans - Low predicted impacts on other sectors
	Weaknesses - Only applies to *new ships of prescribed types 400 gross tonnage and above* *- Limited ability to impose an absolute cap on emissions* - Potential rebound effects	***Weaknesses*** *- No obligation to implement SEEMP measures nor to use EEOI to track energy efficiency performance* *- Substantive implementation of the policy entirely dependent on ship owner/operator uptake, something which in turn depends on multiple market factors* - Cost-effectiveness appears to be the limit on adoption *- Limited ability to impose an absolute cap on emissions*

Criteria	*EEDI*	*SEEMP/EEOI*
2. Cost-effectiveness	***Strengths*** *- Straightforward/lowest cost to implement and enforce* *- Many measures feature negative emissions abatement costs*	***Strengths*** *- Cost-effective with potential for negative emissions abatement costs—many operational measures have low/non-existent capital costs* *- Straightforward/low cost to implement and enforce*
	Weaknesses - Limits ship owners/ operators to adopting prescribed technical measures	***Weaknesses*** - Limits ship owners/ operators to adopting prescribed operational measures
3. Incentives for Positive Technological Change	***Strengths*** - Goal-based/non-prescriptive within the range of prescribed technologies - Ensures international shipping fleet adopts and implements leading technology over time	***Strengths*** - Goal-based and non-prescriptive - Rewards a broader set of measures than does the EEDI - Although conditional on ship owner/operator uptake, potential to reward an increased range of measures and volume of emissions reductions on an ongoing basis
	Weaknesses *- Does not appear to reward compliance over and above the prescribed threshold* - Effectiveness will depend on the degree to which EEDI targets fall below EEDI reference level	***Weaknesses*** - No incentive for ship owners/operators to implement measures contained in the SEEMP

Table 28.3 (*continued*)

Criteria	*EEDI*	*SEEMP/EEOI*
4. Practical Feasibility of Implementation	***Strengths*** - Most straightforward and low cost to implement	***Strengths*** - Straightforward and low cost for ship owners/operators to develop and implement
5. Legal Enforcement	***Strengths*** - Mandatory - Monitoring compliance and enforcement straightforward and low cost - Compliance and enforcement provisions dovetail with those already required under *MARPOL*	***Strengths*** - Straightforward and low cost for both flag and port states to enforce possession of a valid SEEMP through registration and inspection
6. Impacts on Developing Countries	***Strengths*** - 4-year waiver provision for states seeking to delay implementation	***Strengths*** - 4-year waiver provision for states seeking to delay implementation
	Weaknesses - No explicit provision for CBDR	***Weaknesses*** - No explicit provision for CBDR - No penalties for non-compliance appear to be developed

Table 28.4 Evaluative Framework Applied to Market-based Measures

Criteria	*GHG Fund*	*ETS*
1. Environmental Effectiveness	***Strengths*** - Potential to reduce emissions by 13–40% by 2030 relative to business-as-usual emissions measured in 2007—*highest estimated emissions reductions potential* - Potential to impose an *industry cap* on emissions through reliance on external emissions reductions credits - Potential to apply to *all ships*, regardless of size, type, function, or build date - *Potential to reward all emissions reductions measures*—both operational and technical on an ongoing basis - *Dual effect of incentivizing decreased duel consumption and mobilizing funding for mitigation and adaptation activities*, including in- and out-of-sector mitigation and adaptation activities, and research and development for in-sector energy efficiency improvements - Policy may be applied to non-party states purchasing at bunker fuel suppliers located in the territories of state parties	***Strengths*** - Potential to reduce emissions by 13–40% by 2030 relative to business-as-usual emissions measured in 2007—*highest estimated emissions reductions potential* - Potential to impose an *industry cap* on emissions through reliance on external emissions reductions credits - Potential to apply to *all ships*, regardless of size, type, function, or build date - *Potential to reward all emissions reductions measures*—both operational and technical on an ongoing basis - *Dual effect of incentivizing decreased duel consumption and mobilizing funding for mitigation and adaptation activities*, including in- and out-of-sector mitigation and adaptation activities, and research and development for in-sector energy efficiency improvements
	Weaknesses - Potential to cause a price increase, modal shift, and carbon leakage for short sea marine shipping services provided that prices for air- and land-based modes of transportation do not increase simultaneously - Risks of evasion medium unless policy universally adopted	***Weaknesses*** - Potential to cause a price increase, modal shift and carbon leakage for short sea marine shipping services provided that prices for air- and land-based modes of transportation do not increase simultaneously - Risks of evasion high unless policy universally adopted

Table 28.4 (*continued*)

Criteria	*GHG Fund*	*ETS*
2. Cost-effectiveness	***Strengths*** - Provides ship owners/operators with maximum latitude to develop and implement all technical and operational measures to reduce fuel consumption and GHG emissions for ships of varying size, type, function, and operational route - Enables the industry to access external emissions reductions and mitigation opportunities, which may have smaller or negative emissions abatement costs - Many ship owner/operator obligations dovetail with those already required under *MARPOL*, Annex VI - Administrative costs low relative to other market-based measures	***Strengths*** - Provides shipowners/operators with maximum latitude to develop and implement all technical and operational measures to reduce fuel consumption and GHG emissions for ships of varying size, type, function, and operational route - Enables the industry to access external emissions reductions and mitigation opportunities, which may have smaller or negative emissions abatement costs - Many ship owner/operator obligations dovetail with those already required under *MARPOL*, Annex VI
	Weaknesses - Administrative costs higher than under EEDI/SEEMP	***Weaknesses*** - Administrative costs significantly higher than under the GHG Fund or EEDI/SEEMP
3. Incentives for Positive Technological Change	***Strengths*** - *Goal-based non-prescriptive*—significant and ongoing incentive for technological change	***Strengths*** - *Goal-based non-prescriptive*—significant and ongoing incentive for technological change
	Weaknesses - Access to out-of-sector emissions mitigation/adaptation activities may limit in-sector investment	***Weaknesses*** - Access to out-of-sector emissions mitigation/adaptation activities may limit in-sector investment - *Volatility in emissions allowance/carbon price may impede investment in efficiency improvement or emissions reductions technology*

Criteria	*GHG Fund*	*ETS*
4. Practical Feasibility of Implementation	***Strengths*** - Relatively low cost/ straightforward compared with other market-based measures - Precedent in IOPF Administrator	***Strengths*** - Precedent in European Union ETS
	Weaknesses - Relatively more administratively complex than EEDI/SEEMP	***Weaknesses*** - Administratively complex *- Estimated to be significantly more expensive to establish and maintain than GHG Fund* *- Industry opposition*
5. Legal Enforcement	***Strengths*** - Flag/coastal state compliance and enforcement obligations dovetail with those already applicable under *MARPOL*	***Strengths*** - Flag/coastal state compliance and enforcement obligations dovetail with those already applicable under *MARPOL*
	Weaknesses - Requirement to develop a legal structure to establish and govern international GHG Fund administrator operations	***Weaknesses*** - Requirement to develop a legal structure to establish and govern ETS system

Table 28.4 (*continued*)

Criteria	*GHG Fund*	*ETS*
6. Impacts on Developing Countries	***Strengths*** - GHG Fund may direct funding to mitigation/adaptation activities, research and development in least developed countries, landlocked developing countries, and small island developing states - Provision for involvement of least developed countries, landlocked developing countries, and small island developing states in fund allocation process	***Strengths*** - Proceeds of potential auction of emissions allowances may be directed to mitigation/adaptation activities, research and development in least developed countries, landlocked developing countries, and small island developing states - Exemptions for approved voyages to developing countries
	Weaknesses - Increased cost of shipping may negatively impact the export capacity of developing countries—may be mitigated through inclusion of rebate mechanism	***Weaknesses*** - Increased cost of shipping may negatively impact export capacity of developing countries—may be mitigated through inclusion of rebate mechanism

The efficiency-based EEDI and SEEMP measures perform complementary roles in regulating the technical and operational aspects of ship design, construction, and operations with a view to maximizing energy efficiency and minimizing emissions.

The EEDI's application to new ships means that it will target a small albeit increasing share of emissions generated by the global fleet. This means that the measure's potential to achieve emissions reductions through regulation in the short term is low, while its potential to do so in the long term is high. Moreover, the EEDI's administrative simplicity suggests that it is a cost-effective measure well suited to ensuring fleet-wide improvements in energy efficiency and corresponding reductions in emissions intensities. The critical ingredients to the measure's success will be the degree to which the EEDI reference level mandates improvements in energy efficiency over and above those which would apply at business-as-usual levels of investment.

The mandatory requirement to prepare EEOI and SEEMP measures for both *old* and *new* ships suggests that the policy's potential to achieve emissions reductions across the global fleet is high. However, the fact that implementing the measures contained in a ship's SEEMP or implementing the EEOI is purely *voluntary* significantly diminishes the policy's effectiveness in regulating emissions reductions. Moreover, cost-effectiveness appears to impose a ceiling on shipowner/operator investment in operational measures to improve energy efficiency.

As efficiency-based measures, the policy's ability to impose a cap or restrict industry emissions is limited. For these reasons, IMO members recognize that reliance on efficiency-based measures alone will not be adequate to restrict emissions from international shipping to a level consistent with that required under the *UNFCCC*.[34]

On the basis of the comparative evaluations above, the GHG Fund appears to be better positioned to regulate emissions generated by international shipping to levels consistent with the *UNFCCC* objective to stabilize global increases in temperature below 2°C relative to pre-industrial levels.

The IMO estimates both the GHG Fund and ETS policies to have an equal ability to reduce sector-wide emissions by between 13 percent and 40 percent by 2030 relative to business-as-usual emissions measured from a 2008 base year.[35] Both policies have the practical effect of incentivizing decreased fuel consumption and decreased emissions, while simultaneously mobilizing funding for mitigation and adaptation activities. However, the GHG Fund appears to be positioned to achieve these emissions reductions through a simpler mechanism at a reduced cost. With regards to administrative costs borne by ship owners/operators, the IMO estimates potential additional onboard workload costs for the GHG Fund policy to be $0.1 billion compared with $0.7 billion for the maritime ETS policy. The IMO estimates gross administrative costs for the GHG Fund policy to range from US$8–11 billion in 2020 to US$15–25 billion in 2030.[36] Contrast this with gross administrative costs for the ETS estimated to range from US$24–27 billion in 2020 to US$40–49 billion in 2030.[37] These estimates suggest that the GHG Fund is positioned to deliver equal emissions reduction potential for approximately half the costs of a maritime ETS—supporting that measure's superior cost-effectiveness.

Admittedly, the ETS is better positioned to impose a cap on absolute levels of GHG emissions from the international shipping industry. However, in theory, the GHG Fund also has the ability to control absolute levels of emissions through a combination of adjusting the contribution price or relying on approved out-of-sector emissions reductions credits.

Under both the GHG Fund and the ETS policies, linkages to external carbon markets and the relationship between the contribution or allowance price and external carbon prices will play an important role in determining the level of investment in the in-sector efficiency improvement and emissions reductions technologies. Access to external emissions reductions opportunities are positive in the sense that it may enable industry to access a broader, more cost-effective range of emissions reductions opportunities. Further, purchasing out-of-sector emission reductions credits may enable the industry to meet a sector-wide cap on emissions without compromising growth after the potential for reasonably cost-effective in-sector emissions reductions measures have been exhausted. Arguably, however, financing in-sector energy-efficiency improvements is the most effective way of reducing the international shipping industry's actual and ongoing contributions to reductions in anthropogenic GHG emissions.

Both policies provide ship owners/operators with maximum latitude to develop and implement *all* technical and operational measures to reduce fuel consumption and GHG emissions for ships of varying size, type, function, and operational route. Both policies are positioned to incentivize ship owners/operators to develop and implement ongoing emissions reductions measures. However, the fixed levy price under the GHG Fund proposal is positioned to provide ship owners/operators with greater certainty surrounding returns on investment in efficiency improvement and emissions reductions measures. Uncertainty or volatility in the emissions allowance or emissions reductions prices within the ETS may impede investment in efficiency improvement/ emissions reductions technology.

Both policies are of some administrative complexity. However, the GHG Fund's significantly lower administrative costs relative to the ETS suggest it will face fewer barriers to practical implementation. Moreover, the international shipping industry has expressed a preference for a levy-based rather than a cap-and-trade-based GHG regulation policy suggests the GHG Fund will face fewer *political* barriers to implementation.

Both policies appear positioned to reconcile both the CBDR principle as well as the IMO NMFT principle. However, the ability of the ETS policy to do so will be contingent on emissions allowances being allocated by means of auctioning, a policy feature that remains uncertain.

Recent Developments

In October 2016, the seventieth session of the IMO's Marine Environment Protection Committee (MEPC 70) approved a roadmap for the development of a "comprehensive IMO Strategy on the reduction of GHG emissions from ships" for application within the international shipping industry.[38] The roadmap adopted a three-phase approach to ship energy efficiency towards the development of a revised IMO GHG strategy for implementation in 2023. The key phases for the adoption of the revised strategy are set out as follows:[39]

Spring 2018 (MEPC 72)	Adoption of the *Initial IMO Strategy on Reduction of GHG Emissions from Ships* (the Initial Strategy),[40] including, inter alia, a list of candidate short-, mid-, and long-term further measures with possible timelines, to be revised as appropriate as additional information becomes available
January 2019	Start of phase 1: data collection (ships to collect data)
Spring 2019 (MEPC 74)	Initiation of *Fourth IMO GHG Study* using data from 2012–2018
Summer 2020	Data from 2019 to be reported to IMO
Autumn 2020 (MEPC 76)	Start of phase 2: data analysis (no later than autumn 2020) Publication of *Fourth IMO GHG Study* for consideration by MEPC 76

Spring 2021 (MEPC 77)	Secretariat report summarizing the 2019 data pursuant to regulation 22A.10 Initiation of work on adjustments on initial IMO strategy, based on data collection system data
Summer 2021	Data for 2020 to be reported to IMO
Spring 2022 (MEPC 78)	Phase 3: decision step Secretariat report summarizing the 2020 data pursuant to regulation 22A.10
Summer 2022	Data for 2021 to be reported to IMO
Spring 2023 (MEPC 80)	Secretariat report summarizing the 2021 data pursuant to regulation 22A.10 Adoption of revised IMO strategy, including short-, mid- and long-term further measure(s), as required, with implementation schedules

The adoption of the Initial Strategy in 2018 was aimed at enhancing IMO's contribution to global emissions reductions measures consistent with the *Paris Agreement* and identifying actions and measures to be implemented by the international shipping sector in achieving these objectives.[41] The strategy prescribes a first-time reduction in total GHG emissions by at least 50 percent by 2050 compared to 2008 levels, while at the same time, working to phase out the use of carbon fuel sources in the industry.[42] In achieving these goals, the Initial Strategy is structured around commitments or "levels of ambition" for the international shipping sector, which, once implemented, will allow the IMO to achieve emissions targets consistent with the *Paris Agreement*.[43] The levels of ambition are listed as follows:

1. Carbon intensity of the ship to decline through implementation of further phases of the EEDI for new ships—to review with the aim to strengthen the energy efficiency design requirements for ships with the percentage improvement for each phase to be determined for each ship type, as appropriate;
2. Carbon intensity of international shipping to decline—to reduce CO_2 emissions per transport work, as an average across international shipping, by at least 40 percent by 2030, pursuing efforts towards 70 percent by 2050, compared to 2008; and
3. GHG emissions from international shipping to peak and decline—to peak GHG emissions from international shipping as

soon as possible and to reduce the total annual GHG emissions by at least 50 percent by 2050 compared to 2008 whilst pursuing efforts towards phasing them out as called for in the vision as a point on a pathway of CO_2 emissions reduction consistent with the *Paris Agreement* temperature goals.[44]

Phases 1 and 2 of the roadmap, which involved data collection and the creation of the *Fourth IMO GHG Study 2020*[45] and its executive summary[46] by the secretariat, have since been executed. The IMO website summarized the results of this study as follows:

> The Fourth IMO GHG Study 2020 estimated that total shipping emitted 1,056 million tonnes of CO2 in 2018, accounting for about 2.89% of the total global anthropogenic CO2 emissions for that year, and that under a voyage-based allocation method, the share of international shipping represented 740 million tonnes of CO2 in 2018. According to a range of plausible long-term economic and energy business-as-usual scenarios, emissions could represent 90–130% of 2008 emissions by 2050.[47]

In achieving these levels of ambition, the Initial Strategy identifies a number of short-, medium-, and long-term candidate measures to be implemented and agreed upon by the member states. The candidate short-term measures focus on improving existing emissions reductions mechanisms, including EEDI and SEEMP, encouraging states to adopt national action plans to address GHG emissions, and developing an "Existing Fleet Improvement Program."[48] The medium-term measures include measures intended to directly reduce emissions from ships and support action to reduce GHG emissions, including encouraging the use of alternative low-carbon fuels, developing operational energy-efficiency measures for new and existing ships, and developing market-based measures to incentivize GHG emissions reduction.[49] For the long-term measures, the Initial Strategy invites IMO members to pursue the development of zero-carbon or fossil-fuel-free fuels to assist in the decarbonization of the global shipping industry and encourage and facilitate new and innovative reductions measures.[50]

The Initial Strategy identifies that in adopting GHG emissions reductions measures, specific attention should be paid to the needs of developing counties and small island developing states. The Initial Strategy recognizes that certain emissions reductions approaches may have a disproportionally negative impact on developing counties, which must be addressed in considering the implementation of each measure. In an application of the CBDR principle, the Initial Strategy calls for member states to consider potential impacts, such as geographic remoteness, connectivity to main markets, cargo value and type, transport dependency, transport cost, food security, disaster response, cost-effectiveness, and socio-economic progress and development.[51] The recognition of the presence of potential disproportionate impacts differs from the measures previously adopted by the IMO, which favoured the equal application of measures over the CBDR principle.[52]

In furtherance of the objectives of the Initial Strategy, member states also approved a four-step procedure for identifying and assessing the potential disproportionate impacts of proposed candidate measures on developing countries, small island development states, and particularly, the world's least developed nations.[53] Initially adopted at MEPC 73 and formally approved in May 2019 (MEPC 74), the procedure allows for the submission of commentary by member states and, if necessary, a comprehensive response or evidence-based impact assessment process. The steps of the approved procedure can be summarized as follows:

> Step 1: initial impact assessment, to be submitted as part of the initial proposal to the MEPC for candidate measures;
>
> Step 2: submission of commenting document(s), if any;
>
> Step 3: comprehensive response, if requested by commenting document(s); and
>
> Step 4: comprehensive impact assessment, if required by the MEPC.[54]

Since the adoption of the Initial Strategy, the IMO and member states have taken a number of steps towards its final implementation. In October 2018, member states approved a follow-up program to the Initial Strategy (the Program) to be used as a planning tool to meet the short-, medium-, and long-term deadlines identified within the Initial Strategy.[55] The Program sets out a timeline of necessary actions up to 2023 for each category of measure and sets out the draft terms of reference for a *Fourth IMO GHG Study*.[56]

The IMO has also taken steps to adopt and implement the energy-efficiency measures outlined within the Initial Strategy. Most notably, member states adopted amendments to *MARPOL* Annex VI to accelerate the commencement of phase 3 of the EEDI from 2022 to 2025 and strengthen the energy efficiency requirements for new ships.[57] These measures include enhanced energy efficiency standards for a number of different ship types. For container ships, for example, the EEDI reduction rate is enhanced, significantly for larger ship sizes, as follows:

- For a containership of 200,000 deadweight tonnage and above, the EEDI reduction rate is set at 50 percent from 2022
- For a containership of 120,000 deadweight tonnage and above but less than 200,000, 45 percent from 2022
- For a containership of 80,000 deadweight tonnage and above but less than 120,000, 40 percent from 2022
- For a containership of 40,000 deadweight tonnage and above but less than 80,000, 35 percent from 2022
- For a containership of 15,000 deadweight tonnage and above but less than 40,000, 30 percent from 2022.[58]

In May 2019, member states took additional steps to encourage emissions reduction throughout the shipping sector. Resolution MEPC.323(74) invites member states to encourage ports within their jurisdiction to adopt regulatory, technical, operational, and economic procedures to facilitate the reduction of GHG emissions from ships.[59] The resolution provides that such measures could include working with ports in their jurisdiction to enhance onshore power supplies, safe and efficient bunkering of alternative low-carbon and zero-carbon fuels and support the optimization of port calls.[60] Although these measures are voluntary, it demonstrates the forward progression on some of the measures identified within the Initial Strategy.

The Initial Strategy was intended to be a framework for further action, identifying and envisioning approaches that could be implemented to curb GHG emissions within the industry. The Initial Strategy represents an important step forward in the development of a comprehensive emissions reductions regime within the international shipping industry. The developments outlined above are encouraging, and have, in some cases, led to concrete emissions reductions measures, but only time will tell as to whether the Initial Strategy will lead to the adoption of meaningful and comprehensive reduction measures in the international shipping sector. This success will be subject to further negotiation and approval.

Conclusion

For the international community to avoid the most devastating effects of climate change, the Intergovernmental Panel on Climate Change predicts that it must reduce anthropogenic CO_2 emissions by 41–72 percent by 2050 relative to 2010 levels and by 78–118 percent by 2100 relative to 2010.[61] Recognizing this, *UNFCCC* parties convened in Paris in December 2015 to negotiate the *Paris Agreement*: a global, legally binding agreement designed to stabilize increases in a global average temperature below 2°C above pre-industrial levels and to pursue efforts to limit the temperature increase to 1.5°C above pre-industrial levels.[62]

Yet, the *Paris Agreement* excluded emissions from the international shipping industry, which produces an estimated 1,076 million tonnes of GHGs annually, accounts for 2.9 percent of global anthropogenic GHG emissions, and whose GHG emissions are projected to increase by 0–50 percent between the present and 2050.[63] Consequently, the IMO remained the international organization responsible for regulating international shipping's significant and growing share of global anthropogenic GHG emissions.

Atmospheric GHG concentrations are cumulative. If the international community aspires to achieve the emissions reductions required to stabilize atmospheric GHG concentrations and global temperatures, the shipping industry must be part of that solution. The IMO must develop and implement emissions reductions measures in coordination with *UNFCCC* parties. To do otherwise risks compromising the achievement of the *UNFCCC*'s ultimate objective: the "stabilization of greenhouse gas concentrations in the atmosphere at a level that would prevent dangerous anthropogenic interference with the climate system."[64]

This chapter employed a structured analysis to evaluate the comparative effectiveness of current and proposed IMO measures in reducing emissions in a manner sensitive to the industry's international character and role as an instrument of sustainable global development. The efficiency-based EEDI and SEEMP/EEOI measures are a good start in approaching the task of regulating GHG emissions from international shipping. However, reliance on efficiency-based measures alone will not be adequate to restrict emissions from international shipping to a level consistent with those required under the *UNFCCC*.[65] This chapter concludes that the GHG Fund policy is the market-based measure best situated to regulate emissions from the international shipping industry, based on the proposed policy's: (1) environmental effectiveness; (2) cost-effectiveness; (3) incentives for positive technological change; (4) practical feasibility of implementation; (5) legal enforcement; and (6) impacts on developing countries. This conclusion is consistent with that of two similar studies,[66] as well as others comparing the relative effectiveness of a levy rather than a cap-and-trade scheme.[67]

The author suggests that in approaching the task of regulating GHG emissions from international shipping, the IMO should focus its efforts on the GHG Fund policy. Because uncertainty in a policy's application can detract from the consensus required to implement that policy, the IMO should undertake a comprehensive evaluation of the design, implementation, and anticipated effects of the GHG Fund policy, that provides for special consideration of the policy's effects on developing countries. Experience from the *UNFCCC* context suggests that ensuring that the policy is designed and implemented in a manner conforming to the CBDR principle will be critical to the policy's success, both practical and political.

NOTES

1 Associate at McInnes Cooper Halifax, with assistance from Dan Vanclieaf.

2 International Chamber of Shipping (ICS), "ICS Film—International Shipping: Lifeblood of World Trade" (25 September 2009), online: YouTube <www.youtube.com/watch?v=x_G_kfcR_QQ from https://www.ics-shipping.org/>.

3 ICS, "Shipping and World Trade: Driving Prosperity" (accessed 12 July 2021), online: <www.ics-shipping.org/shipping-facts/shipping-and-world-trade>.

4 ICS, "Shipping, World Trade and the Reduction of CO2 Emissions: United Nations Framework Convention on Climate Change" (London: ICS, 2014).

5 World Commission on Environment and Development, *Our Common Future* (Oxford: Oxford University Press, 1987), online (pdf): <sustainabledevelopment.un.org/content/documents/5987our-common-future.pdf> [*Brundtland Report*].

6 In 2018, 79 percent of the international shipping fleet fuel used was heavy fuel oil (marine bunkers). More specifically, in 2018 international shipping consumed an estimated 221.8 million tonnes of heavy fuel oil, 61.5 million tonnes of marine diesel oil,

and 11.3 million tonnes of liquefied natural gas, all expressed in heavy fuel oil equivalent tonnes: *Fourth IMO Greenhouse Gas Study 2020* (London: IMO, 2020), online (pdf): *IMO* <wwwcdn.imo.org/localresources/en/OurWork/Environment/Documents/Fourth%20IMO%20GHG%20Study%202020%20-%20Full%20report%20and%20annexes.pdf> at 1 and 97 [*Fourth IMO GHG Study*].

7 *Ibid* at 1.

8 *Ibid.*

9 United Nations Framework Convention on Climate Change, "Greenhouse Gas Inventory Data—Flexible Queries Annex I Parties" (accessed 14 June 2021), online: <di.unfccc.int/flex_annex1>. The figures exclude emissions from land use, land-use change, and forestry [*UNFCCC, National Greenhouse Gas Inventory Data*].

10 *Fourth IMO GHG Study, supra* note 6 at 236.

11 *Ibid.*

12 *UNFCCC, National Greenhouse Gas Inventory Data, supra* note 9.

13 *United Nations Framework Convention on Climate Change*, 9 May 1992, 1771 UNTS 107, art 16 (entered into force 21 March 1994) [*UNFCCC*].

14 *Ibid*, art 9.

15 Iulian Florin Vladu & Bernd Hackmann, "International Maritime Transport under the *UNFCCC* Process" in Regina Asariotis & Hassiba Benamara, eds, *Maritime Transport and the Climate Change Challenge* (New York: Routledge, 2012), 61 at 67.

16 *Kyoto Protocol to the United Nations Framework Convention on Climate Change*, 11 December 1997, 2303 UNTS 148 (entered into force 16 February 2005) [*Kyoto Protocol*].

17 *Ibid.*

18 Vladu & Hackmann, *supra* note 15 at 67.

19 *Kyoto Protocol, supra* note 16, art 2(2).

20 *Adoption of the Paris Agreement*, FCCC/CP/2015/L.9/Rev.1 art 2(1)(a) (12 December 2015) [*Paris Agreement*].

21 *1978 Protocol Relating to the 1973 International Convention for the Prevention of Pollution from Ships*, 17 February 1978, 1340 UNTS 61 (entered into force 2 October 1983); *1997 Protocol to Amend the 1973 International Convention for the Prevention of Pollution from Ships*, as modified by the 1978 Protocol, 26 September 1997, [2007] ATS 37 (entered into force 19 May 2005) [*MARPOL*].

22 See "COP21: Paris Remains Silent on Shipping and Aviation" (14 December 2015), online: *Offshore Energy* <worldmaritimenews.com/archives/178732/cop21-paris-remains-silent-on-shipping-and-aviation/>; and "Shipping Dropped from Paris Climate Deal" (10 December 2015), online: *Offshore Energy* <worldmaritimenews.com/archives/178438/shipping-dropped-from-paris-climate-deal/>.

23 IMO, "Introduction to IMO", online: <www.imo.org/en/About/Pages/Default.aspx>.

24 IMO, "Membership", online: <www.imo.org/en/About/Membership/Pages/Default.aspx>.

25 *1997 Protocol to Amend the International Convention for the Prevention of Pollution by Ships, as Modified by the 1978 Protocol*, 26 September 1997, [2007] ATS 37 (entered into force 19 May 2005) [*1997 Protocol to MARPOL*].

26 *Ibid.*

27 Andreas Chrysostomou & Eivind S Vågslid, "Climate Change for IMO Too" in Regina Asariotis & Hassiba Benamara, eds, *Maritime Transport and the Climate Change Challenge* (New York: Earthscan, 2012) 75 at 78.

28 Conference of Parties to *MARPOL*, "Resolution to Address CO_2 Emissions from Ships", 22 October 1997, MP/CONF.3/35, 1997 [Conference of Parties]; IMO, *Second IMO GHG Study 2009* (London: IMO, 2009) at 1.2 [*Second IMO GHG Study 2009*]; Chrysostomou & Vågslid, *supra* note 27 at 78.

29 *Study of Greenhouse Gas Emissions from Ships: Final Report of the International Maritime Organization* (London: IMO, 2000).

30 Conference of Parties, *supra* note 28; *Second IMO GHG Study 2009*, *supra* note 28 at 1.2; IMO, *Third IMO GHG Study 2014* (London: IMO, 2014); *Fourth IMO GHG Study*, *supra* note 6.

31 Nadine Heitmann & Seterah Khalilian, "Accounting for Carbon Dioxide Emissions from International Shipping: Burden Sharing under Different UNFCCC Allocation Options and Regime Scenarios" (2011) 35 Marine Policy 682 at 684. See also Article 1(b) of the *International Convention on the International Maritime Organization*, adopted 6 March 1948, 289 UNTS 48 which articulates the organization's purpose as "[t]o encourage the removal of discriminatory action and unnecessary restrictions by Governments affecting shipping engaged in international trade so as to promote the availability of shipping services to the commerce of the world without discrimination."

32 For information on global fleet ownership and registration, see UNCTAD, *Review of Maritime Transport 2015* (New York: United Nations, 2015) at 36 and 42; Heitmann & Khalilian, *supra* note 31 at 684.

33 The authors selected the evaluative criteria based on the work of the IMO, "Report of the Marine Environment Protection Committee on Its Fifty-Seventh Session" (7 April 2008) MEPC 57/21 at 4.107.

34 IMO, "Report of the Marine Environment Protection Committee on Its Fifty-Ninth Session" (27 July 2009) MEPC 59/24 para 4.106 [MEPC, 59/24].

35 IMO, "Reduction of GHG Emissions from Ships: Full Report of the Work Undertaken by the Expert Group on Feasibility Study and Impact Assessment of Possible Market-Based Measures" (13 August 2010) MEPC 61/INF.2] at para 14.37 [*MBM Feasibility Study and Impact Assessment*].

36 *Ibid* at table 9-3.

37 *Ibid* at table 14-3.

38 IMO, "Initial IMO Strategy on Reduction of GHG Emissions from Ships" (13 April 2018) Resolution MEPC.304(72), online (pdf): <unfccc.int/sites/default/files/resource/250_IMO%20submission_Talanoa%20Dialogue_April%202018.pdf> [Initial Strategy] at Annex 2, para 36. Note that the full text of the IMO Initial Strategy was included within the IMO's submission to the Talanoa Dialogue established by the UN Climate Change secretariat for countries and stakeholders to contribute information regarding climate action.

39 *Ibid* at art 6.2.

40 *Supra* note 38.

41 *Ibid* at art 1.7.

42 *Ibid* at art 3.3.

43 *Ibid* at art 3.1.

44 *Ibid*.

45 *Fourth IMO GHG Study 2020*, supra note 6.

46 Ibid at 5.

47 IMO, "Greenhouse Gas Emissions" (accessed 22 September 2021), online: <www.imo.org/en/OurWork/Environment/Pages/GHG-Emissions.aspx>.

48 *Ibid* at art 4.7.

49 *Ibid* at art 4.8.

50 *Ibid* at art 4.9.

51 IMO, *Reducing Greenhouse Gas Emissions from Ships* (2019), online: <www.imo.org/en/MediaCentre/HotTopics/Pages/Reducing-greenhouse-gas-emissions-from-ships.aspx>.

52 *Ibid* at art 4.10–4.12.

53 *Supra* note 38.

54 *Ibid.*

55 IMO, *Next Steps to Deliver IMO GHG Strategy* (2018), online: <www.imo.org/en/MediaCentre/PressBriefings/Pages/18-MEPCGHGprogramme.aspx>.

56 *Ibid.*

57 IMO, "UN Agency Pushes Forward on Shipping Emissions Reduction" (20 May 2019), online: <www.imo.org/en/MediaCentre/PressBriefings/Pages/11-MEPC-74-GHG.aspx>.

58 *Ibid*; see also IMO, "2018 Guidelines on the Method of Calculation of the Attained Energy Efficiency Design Index (EEDI) for New Ships" (26 October 2018) Resolution MEPC.308(73), online (pdf): <wwwcdn.imo.org/localresources/en/OurWork/Environment/Documents/Air%20pollution/MEPC.308(73).pdf>.

59 IMO, "Invitation to Member States to Encourage Voluntary Cooperation between the Port and Shipping Sectors to Contribute to Reducing GHG Emissions from Ships" (17 May 2019) Resolution MEPC.323 (74), online (pdf): <wwwcdn.imo.org/localresources/en/KnowledgeCentre/IndexofIMOResolutions/MEPCDocuments/MEPC.323%2874%29.pdf>.

60 *Ibid.*

61 International Panel on Climate Change, *Climate Change 2014 Synthesis Report Summary for Policymakers Chapter* (Geneva, Switzerland: IPCC, 2014), online (pdf): <www.ipcc.ch/pdf/assessment-report/ar5/syr/AR5_SYR_FINAL_SPM.pdf> at 22 [IPCC Report 2014].

62 *Paris Agreement*, *supra* note 20 art 2(1)(a).

63 *Fourth IMO GHG Study*, *supra* note 6.

64 *United Nations Framework Convention on Climate Change*, 9 May 1992, 1771 UNTS 107, art 2 (entered into force 21 March 1994) [*UNFCCC*].

65 IMO, "Report of the Marine Environment Protection Committee on its Fifty-Ninth Session" (27 July 2009) MEPC 59/24 para 4.106 [MEPC, 59/24].

66 Yubing Shi, "Reducing Greenhouse Gas Emissions from International Shipping: Is It Time to Consider Market-based Measures?" (2016) 64 Marine Policy 123 at 128 at 129; see also Harliaos N Psaraftis, "Market-based Measures for Greenhouse Gas Emissions from Ships: A Review" (2012) 11 World Maritime University Journal of Maritime Affairs 212 at 222.

67 See Congressional Budget Office, *Policy Options for Reducing CO_2 Emissions* (February 2008), online (pdf): <www.cbo.gov/sites/default/files/110th-congress-2007-2008/reports/02-12-carbon.pdf>; see also Friends of the Earth, "Clearing the Air: Moving on from Carbon Trading to Real Climate Solutions" (November 2010), online (pdf): <web.archive.org/web/20131024075840/http://www.foe.co.uk/resource/reports/clearing_air.pdf>.

List of Contributors

Peter J. Cullen, Partner, Stikeman Elliott LLP, Montréal

Shanti Dogra, General Counsel—Canada-Nova Scotia Offshore Petroleum Board, Halifax

Suzanne Lalonde, PhD (Cantab), Faculty of Law, Université de Montréal

A. William Moreira, QC, FCIArb, Partner, Stewart McKelvey, Halifax

Magdalena AK Muir, Research Associate of the Arctic Institute of North America, University of Calgary

Linda Nowlan, Senior Director, University of British Columbia Sustainability Initiative, Vancouver

Alexander Kirby, Associate, Arvay Finlay LLP, Vancouver

Georgia Lloyd-Smith, Staff Lawyer, West Coast Environmental Law Association, Vancouver

Doug Neasloss, Chief Councillor, Kitasoo/Xai'xais First Nation

Peter Pamel, Justice, Federal Court of Canada

Robert C. Wilkins, Retired Advocate and Honorary Life Member, Canadian Maritime Law Association, Montreal

Catherine A. LeBlanc, Associate, Stewart McKelvey, Moncton

Christopher J. Stewart, Partner, Stewart McKelvey, Moncton

Douglas Wallace, Canada Excellence Research Chair in Ocean Science and Technology, Department of Oceanography, Dalhousie University, Halifax

Daniel Watt, Partner, McInnes Cooper LLP, Halifax

Nigel Bankes, Professor Emeritus, Faculty of Law, University of Calgary

John Donihee, Counsel Wilms & Shier Environmental Lawyers LLP, Toronto

Robert Hamilton, Assistant Professor, Faculty of Law, University of Calgary

Sara Jaremko, Research Fellow, Canadian Institute of Resources Law, Calgary

Arlene Kwasniak, Professor Emeritus, Faculty of Law, University of Calgary

David W. Poulton, Principal, David W. Poulton Environmental Strategies Inc., Calgary

Phillip Saunders, QC, Associate Professor, Schulich School of Law, Dalhousie University, Halifax

Dyna Tuytel, Staff Lawyer, Ecojustice Canada, Vancouver

Margot Venton, Program Director—Nature, Ecojustice Canada, Vancouver

Gilbert Van Nes, General Counsel and Settlement Officer for the Alberta Environmental Appeals Board and the Alberta Public Lands Appeal Board, Edmonton

Sophie Lavallée, Justice, Court of Appeal of Quebec

Fenner L. Stewart, Associate Professor, Faculty of Law, University of Calgary

Scott A. Carrière, Articling Student at Osler, Hoskin & Harcourt LLP, Calgary

Hélène Trudeau, Associate Professor, Faculty of Law, Université de Montréal

David V. Wright, Assistant Professor, Faculty of Law, University of Calgary

Allan Ingelson, Professor of Law, University of Calgary and Executive Director, Canadian Institute of Resources Law, Calgary

Alastair R. Lucas, Professor Emeritus, Faculty of Law, University of Calgary

Diego Almeida, Corporate Law Clerk, Lundin Mining Corp, Toronto

Jamie Benidickson, Professor of Law, University of Ottawa

Peter L'Esperance, Associate, McInnes Cooper, Halifax

Index

SECTION 1

SECTION 2

SECTION 3